The Complete KETO DIET Cookbook

1000 Recipes For Quick & Easy Low-Carb Homemade Cooking

Gerald Hubbell

CONTENTS

POULTRY 39

PORK 62

BEEF & LAMB 79

SMOOTHIES & BEVERAGES 142

SWEETS & DESSERTS 145

OTHER KETO FAVORITES **166**

KETO SMALL APPLIANCE RECIPES **170**

INDEX 186

MEASUREMENTS & CONVERSIONS 190

INTRODUCTION

It's widely-spread knowledge that our bodies are designed to run primarily on carbs. We use them to provide our bodies with the energy required to boost our state, exercise, or just normal body functioning. However, most people are clueless about the fact that carbs are not the only source of fuel our bodies can use. Just like they can run on carbs, our bodies can also use fat sources. When we ditch the carbs and focus on providing our bodies with more fat, we are embarking on the ketogenic train.

The ketogenic diet is not just another fad diet. It has been around since 1920 and has resulted in outstanding results and amazingly successful stories. If you are new to the keto world and have no idea what I am talking about, let me simplify this for you.

For you to truly understand what the keto diet is all about and why you should start it as soon as you can, let me first explain what happens to your body after consuming a carb-loaded meal.

Imagine you have just swallowed a giant bowl of spaghetti. Your tummy is full, your taste buds are satisfied, and your body is provided with more carbs than necessary. After consumption, your body immediately starts the process of digestion, during which your body will break down the consumed carbs into glucose, which is a source of energy your body depends on. So one might ask, "What is wrong with carbs?" For starters, there are some things: they raise the blood sugar, make your body work excessively to offset the effects of that sugar, and kindly storing it as another layer of fat, usually around the belly, but many times around the organs too. That's extremely dangerous. Sounds scary? I know.

By now, you've undoubtedly heard of the keto diet and the many people who have had success losing weight and keeping it off. But just what is a ketogenic diet, and how does it work to reach your weight loss goal.

The keto diet is a food plan that is high in fat and low in carbs. The human body uses carbohydrates as its primary fuel source; however, when fats replace carbs, the body enters a metabolic state known as "ketosis." During ketosis, because of the lack of carbs, the body will burn stored fat as fuel, which can help you lose weight.

Not only can the keto diet promote weight loss, but it also comes with numerous health benefits:

- Management of diabetes
- Lower cholesterol
- Improved mental clarity
- Reduces the risk and symptoms of polycystic ovary syndrome (POS)
- Lower risk of some cancers
- Lower risk of cardiovascular disease

The keto diet requires a change in your wearing habits. It's easier to make these changes when you have your partner or other family members' active support. As a couple, you'll be able to encourage each other on those days that are more difficult than others for sticking to your food plan.

THE KETOSIS

Switching to high fat moderate protein cycle, your liver now has a new "fuel boss" - the fat. Once your liver begins preparing your body for the fuel change, the fat from the liver will start producing ketones – hence the name Ketogenic. What glucose is for the carbs, the ketones are for the fat, meaning they are the tiny molecules created once the fat is broken down to be used as energy. The switch from glucose to ketones is something that has pushed many people away from this diet. Some people consider this to be a dangerous process, but the truth is, your body will run just as efficiently on ketones as it does on glucose.

Once your body shifts to using ketones as fuel, you are in the state of ketosis. Ketosis is a metabolic process that may be interpreted as a little 'shock' to your body. However, this is far from dangerous. Every change in life requires adaptation, and so does this. This adaptation process is not set in stone, and every person goes through ketosis differently. However, for most people, it takes around 2 weeks to adapt to the new lifestyle fully.

Note! This is all biological and completely healthy. You have spent your whole life packing your body with glucose; naturally, you need time to adapt to the new dietary change.

FOODS ALLOWED ON THE KETO DIET

Plan your meals and snacks around the following foods:
- Eggs
- Meats, including beef, pork, chicken, and veal
- Fish, including fish high in fat such as mackerel, trout, and salmon
- Cheeses
- Nuts and seeds, including nut and seed butter
- Cream and butter
- Avocadoes
- Healthy oils, such as olive, avocado, and coconut oils
- Low-carb vegetables, such as peppers, onions, tomatoes, and green vegetables
- Herbs and spices, including salt and pepper

To be sure you're getting enough of the right nutrients, eat a wide variety of meats, vegetables, seeds, and nuts on the allowed food list.

FOODS RESTRICTED ON THE KETO DIET

These are the foods that are restricted on a ketogenic food plan:
- Grains and starches, such as bread, pasta, cereal, and rice
- Carrots, potatoes, yams, sweet potatoes, and parsnips
- Beans and legumes, including chickpeas, lentils, and peas
- Fruit, except for small quantities of berries
- Sugar in any form, including foods that contain fructose
- Processed diet foods and Alcohol
- Condiments that contain sugar
- Unhealthy fats, such as processed vegetable oils and mayonnaise
- Alcohol

GETTING STARTED WITH YOUR KETO DIET

Before starting the keto diet, take some time researching the foods on the allowed list and those restricted foods. Plan your meals ahead of time and shop accordingly, filling your kitchen with keto-friendly foods.

Healthy snacks

To make it easier to stick to the keto diet, it's important to have healthy snacks. If you're on the keto diet with your partner, have keto-approved snacks on hand that you both enjoy. Approved snacks include:

- Hard-boiled eggs, cheese, and olives
- A handful of nuts and seeds
- Celery and red pepper sticks with guacamole and salsa
- No-sugar plain yogurt mixed with berries

Intermittent Fasting and the Keto Diet

Intermittent fasting is all about restricting the number of calories you consume within a period so that you put your body into a "fasted" state. When this happens, the body's insulin levels will start to lower, which increases the fat burning process.

THE BENEFITS OF INTERMITTENT FASTING INCLUDE:

- Weight loss
- Improved mental clarity
- Management and reducing the risk of type 2 diabetes
- Lower risk of cardiovascular disease
- Lower risk of some cancers

The most common fasting method is to fast each day for 14 to 16 hours, restricting the time you eat to a "window" of 8 to 10 hours. During the eating window, you should be eating at least 2 to 3 healthy keto meals. An excellent way to approach intermittent fasting is eating your last meal by 8 pm on any day and not eating your first meal until midnight the next day.

Another intermittent fasting method includes the 5:2 rule, where you only eat 500 to 600 calories per day on two days of the week, eating a healthy keto diet for the other five days. Another fasting method is the eat-stop-eat plan, where you fast for 24 hours twice a week.

Both intermittent fasting and the keto diet put the body into a ketosis state to use up stored fat for energy. When you combine intermittent fasting with the keto diet, you may be able to put your body into ketosis faster than dieting alone. This can lead to faster and more efficient weight loss.

WHAT TO EXPECT ON THE KETO DIET & KETO "FLU"

During the first few days of starting the Keto, you may experience an increase in hunger, lack of energy, and problems sleeping. Some people may also experience nausea and digestive issues. These flu-like symptoms are known as the "keto flu." To alleviate these symptoms, consider doing a low-carb diet for a week, slowly transitioning into the full keto diet. During the first month, always eat until you feel full without focusing on restricting calories. Ease into the food plan, so you're less likely to stop eating a ketogenic diet.

The keto diet changes the mineral and water balance of your body. Make sure that you're drinking more water each day. As well, taking a mineral supplement and adding a bit of extra salt to your diet can keep help maintain a healthy balance of minerals and water, helping to relieve any of the flu-like symptoms. For a mineral supplement, take 300 mg of magnesium and 1,000 mg of potassium.

DIET – THE NEW LIFESTYLE

THE BENEFITS OF KETO DIET

Even though it is still considered 'controversial,' the keto diet is the best dietary choice one can make. From weight loss to longevity, here are the benefits that following a ketogenic diet can bring to your life:

Loss of Appetite

You can't tame your cravings? Don't worry. While on ketosis, you won't feel exhausted or with a rumbling gut. The keto diet will help you say no to that second piece of cake. Once you train your body to run on fat and not on carbs, you will experience a drop in appetite that will work magic for your figure.

Weight Loss

Since the body is forced to produce only a small amount of glucose, it will lower insulin production. When that happens, your kidneys will start getting rid of the extra sodium, which will lead to weight loss.

HDL Cholesterol Increase and Drop in Blood Pressure

While consuming a diet high in fat and staying clear of harmful glucose, your body will experience a rise in good HDL cholesterol levels, which will, in turn, reduce the risk for many cardiovascular problems. Cutting back on carbs will also drop your blood pressure. The drop in blood pressure can prevent many health problems such as strokes or heart diseases.

Lower Risk of Diabetes

Although this probably goes without saying, it is essential to mention this one. When you ditch the carbs, your body is forced to lower the glucose productivity significantly, which leads to a lower risk of diabetes, including a reverse in the condition if you already have it.

Improved Brain Function

Many studies have shown that replacing carbohydrates with fat as an energy source leads to mental clarity and improved brain function. This is yet another reason why you should go Keto.

Should You Try the Keto Diet?

The keto diet can help you lose weight and keep it off. When you're eating nutritiously, exercising, and following a ketogenic food plan, you'll be joining the many other people around the world who have successfully lost weight.

Whether you're starting the keto diet on your own or as a couple, begin with the keto food plan basics to become familiar with the foods you can and can't eat. As you start to lose weight and learn how to customize your meals, the keto diet plan will become a natural part of your lifestyle, allowing you to maintain your health and weight loss.

BASIC & SIMPLE RECIPES

Power Green Smoothie

Ingredients for 2 servings

1 cup collard greens, chopped
3 stalks celery, chopped
1 ripe avocado, pitted, sliced
1 cup ice cubes
2 cups spinach, chopped
1 cucumber, peeled and diced
Chia seeds to garnish

Directions and Total Time: approx. 5 minutes

Add the collard greens, celery, avocado, and ice cubes in a blender, and blend for 50 seconds. Add the spinach and cucumber, and process for another 40 seconds or until smooth. Transfer the smoothie into glasses, sprinkle with chia seeds and serve.

Per serving: Cal 187; Fat 12g; Net Carbs 7.6g; Protein 3.2g

Green Cheesy Bowls

Ingredients for 4 servings

½ cup baby kale
2 zucchinis, spiralized
1/3 cup crumbled goat cheese
1/3 cup crumbled feta cheese
½ lemon, juiced
1 tbsp olive oil
¼ tsp Dijon mustard
1 tbsp dill, chopped
2 tbsp toasted pine nuts
Salt and black pepper to taste

Directions and Total Time: approx. 10 minutes

Place the zucchinis in a bowl and season with salt and pepper. In a small bowl, mix the lemon juice, olive oil, and mustard. Pour the mixture over the zucchini and toss evenly. Add the dill, kale, goat cheese, feta cheese, and pine nuts. Toss to combine and serve.

Per serving: Cal 323; Net Carbs 8.1g; Fat 26g; Protein 15g

Homemade Guacamole

Ingredients for 4 servings

2 avocados, peeled, pitted
½ yellow onion, minced
½ lime, juiced
1 tomato, peeled, chopped
2 tbsp fresh cilantro, chopped
Salt and chili powder to taste

Directions and Total Time: approx. 10 minutes

Mash the avocado with a fork in a bowl. Mix in the onion, lime juice, tomato, chili powder, and salt. Sprinkle with cilantro and serve immediately.

Per serving: Cal 173; Net Carbs 1.4g; Fat 15.8g; Protein 2g

Bacon & Cheese Fat Bomb

Ingredients for 3 servings (6 fat bombs)

¼ cup Chèvre cheese, grated
¼ cup cream cheese, softened
2 tbsp butter, softened
4 bacon slices, chopped

Directions and Total Time: approx. 45 minutes

Fry the bacon in a skillet over medium heat for 5 minutes. Grease a baking sheet with the bacon fat and set aside. In a bowl, stir together the Chèvre cheese, cream cheese, butter, and stir-fried bacon until well blended. Roll the mixture into 8 "balls" and place them on the sheet. Freeze for 30 minutes.

Per serving: Cal 282; Net Carbs 0.1g; Fat 26g; Protein 11g

Avocado Boats with Bacon & Eggs

Ingredients for 4 servings

4 eggs
2 avocados, halved and pitted
2 bacon slices, chopped
2 tbsp chives, chopped
1 tsp smoked paprika
Salt and black pepper to taste

Directions and Total Time: approx. 25 minutes

Preheat the oven to 360 F. Scoop out some of the avocado flesh into a bowl. Place the avocado halves in a greased baking dish and crack an egg into each half. Season with paprika, salt, and black pepper and sprinkle with bacon. Bake for 14-16 minutes or until set. Top with fresh chives and serve.

Per serving: Cal 319; Fat 28g; Net Carbs 0.8g; Protein 11g

Avocado Fries with Chipotle Mayo Sauce

Ingredients for 4 servings

2 avocados, sliced
1 cup almond flour
¼ cup olive oil
2 tbsp lemon juice
2 large eggs, beaten
2 chipotle sauce
½ cup mayonnaise
Salt and black pepper to taste

Directions and Total Time: approx. 20 minutes

Mix the almond flour with salt and black pepper. Toss avocado slices in the eggs and then dredge in the flour mixture. Heat olive oil in a deep pan and fry the avocado slices until golden brown, 2-3 minutes per side. In a bowl, mix the mayonnaise, chipotle sauce, lemon juice, and salt. Serve the fries with the sauce.

Per serving: Cal 633; Net Carbs 2.7g; Fat 58g; Protein 11g

Classic Pigs In Blankets

Ingredients for 4 servings

8 Vienna sausages
8 thin bacon slices

Directions and Total Time: approx. 30 minutes

Preheat oven to 360 F. Wrap each sausage tightly with a slice of bacon. Lay the bacon-wrapped sausages on a greased baking sheet and roast for 18-20 minutes until the bacon is crisp and golden. Serve and enjoy!

Per serving: Cal 620; Net Carbs 0g; Fat 56g; Protein 28g

Avocado Mousse with Bacon "Croutons"

Ingredients for 4 servings

2 ripe avocados, pitted, halved
4 oz bacon, sliced
1 cup sour cream
2 tbsp cilantro, chopped
½ lime, juiced and zested
Salt and black pepper to taste

Directions and Total Time: approx. 15 minutes

Set a skillet over medium heat and stir-fry the bacon until crispy, about 5 minutes. Transfer to a paper towel to soak up the excess fat. In a bowl, mix the avocado flesh, sour cream, lime juice, lime zest, salt, and pepper. Stir until everything is well mixed and smooth. Spoon the mousse into glass cups and top with bacon and fresh cilantro. Serve warm or chilled.

Per serving: Cal 481; Net Carbs 0.6g; Fat 43g; Protein 14g

Scrambled Eggs with Smoked Salmon

Ingredients for 4 servings

4 oz smoked salmon, chopped   2 tbsp fresh dill, chopped
8 eggs   2 tbsp butter
½ cup sour cream   Salt and black pepper to taste

Directions and Total Time: approx. 15 minutes

Whisk the eggs into a medium bowl along with sour cream, salt, and pepper. Melt the butter in a skillet over medium heat and add the eggs, stirring quickly. Lower the heat and gently mix them with a spatula; cook until the eggs are barely set, 2-3 minutes. Remove from heat and stir in the salmon. Top with dill and serve.

Per serving: Cal 275; Net Carbs 0.7g; Fat 22g; Protein 17g

Bacon & Cheddar Egg Muffins

Ingredients for 4 servings

1 green onion, chopped   2 tbsp sour cream
4 bacon slices   4 eggs
2 oz cheddar cheese, grated   1 tsp red chili flakes

Directions and Total Time: approx. 15 minutes

Place the bacon on a preheated skillet over medium heat and cook for 2 minutes per side; set aside. Grease 4 ovenproof cups with the bacon fat. Line the bottom and the sides of the cups with the bacon slices. Spread half of the cheese over, and cover with sour cream. Carefully crack an egg into each cup and finish with the remaining cheese. Place the cups in the microwave for 1-2 minutes until the cheese melts. Sprinkle with green onion and red chili flakes and serve.

Per serving: Cal 121; Net Carbs 0.3g; Fat 10g; Protein 8g

Avocado a la Carbonara

Ingredients for 4 servings

2 eggs, beaten   1 teaspoon onion powder
1 ½ cups cream cheese   ½ teaspoon garlic powder
5 ½ tbsp psyllium husk   ¼ cup olive oil
1 avocado, peeled and pitted   Salt and black pepper to taste
1 ¾ cups coconut cream   ¼ cup grated Parmesan
Juice of ½ lemon   4 tbsp toasted pecans

Directions and Total Time: approx. 30 minutes

Preheat oven to 300 F. In a bowl, add the eggs, cream cheese, psyllium husk, and salt to taste. Whisk until smooth batter forms. Line a baking sheet with wax paper, pour in the batter, and cover with another wax paper. Use a rolling pin to flatten the dough into the sheet. Bake for 12 minutes, then take off the wax papers and slice the "pasta" into thin strips lengthwise.

Cut each piece into halves, pour into a bowl, and set aside. In a blender, combine avocado, coconut cream, lemon juice, onion and garlic powders and puree until smooth. Pour olive oil over the "pasta" and stir to coat. Pour the avocado sauce on top and mix well. Sprinkle with salt, pepper, and freshly grated Parmesan cheese. Garnish with toasted pecans and serve.

Per serving: Cal 769; Net Carbs 8g; Fat 56g; Protein 35g

Golden Saffron Cauli Rice

Ingredients for 4 servings

A pinch of saffron soaked in ¼-cup almond milk
1 tbsp butter   2 cups cauli rice
2 tbsp olive oil   ¼ cup vegetable broth
6 garlic cloves, sliced   2 tbsp chopped parsley
1 yellow onion, thinly sliced   Salt and black pepper to taste

Directions and Total Time: approx. 15 minutes

Warm olive oil in a saucepan over medium heat and fry garlic until golden brown but not burned; set aside. Sauté butter and onion in the saucepan for 3 minutes. Stir in cauli rice. Remove the saffron from the milk and pour the milk and stock into the saucepan. Mix, cover, and cook for 5 minutes. Season with salt, black pepper, and parsley. Fluff the cauli rice and dish into serving plates. Garnish with the fried garlic and serve.

Per serving: Cal 89; Net Carbs 5.9g; Fat 6g; Protein 2g

Zucchini Pasta Puttanesca

Ingredients for 4 servings

4 anchovies in olive oil, drained   1 tbsp capers, chopped
2 lb zucchinis, spiralized   ¼ cup black pitted olives, halved
2 tbsp olive oil   2 (14-oz) cans diced tomatoes
2 garlic cloves, sliced   ¼ cup Parmesan cheese, grated
½ tsp cayenne pepper   2 tbsp fresh basil, chopped
½ tsp dried oregano   Salt and black pepper to taste

Directions and Total Time: approx. 30 minutes

Warm the olive oil in a saucepan and toss in zucchini; stir quickly for about 1 minute. Season to taste and set aside.

To the saucepan, add garlic, cayenne pepper, oregano, capers, and anchovies; cook for 2-4 minutes until the anchovies melt into the oil. Pour in tomatoes and simmer for 10-12 minutes, stirring often, until the sauce thickens slightly; season. Pour the sauce over zucchini pasta and top with olives, Parmesan cheese, and basil to serve.

Per serving: Cal 186; Net Carbs 6.9g; Fat 11g; Protein 11g

Five Seed Crackers

Ingredients for 4 servings (30 crackers)

2 tbsp coconut oil, melted   ¼ cup sunflower seeds
1 tsp flax seeds   ¼ cup sesame seeds
¼ cup chia seeds   1 tsp psyllium husk powder
¼ cup almond flour   1 tsp salt
¼ cup pumpkin seeds   ¾ cup boiling water

Directions and Total Time: approx. 30 minutes

Preheat oven to 350 F. Combine almond flour with the seeds, psyllium husk, and salt. Pour in coconut oil and boiling water and mix until a dough forms with a gel-like consistency. Line a baking sheet with parchment paper and place the dough on the sheet. Cover with another parchment paper and with a rolling pin to flatten into the baking sheet. Remove the parchment paper from the top. Use a pizza cutter to cut the dough into 1-inch squares. Bake for 15-20 minutes, or until golden. Serve cooled.

Per serving: Cal 71; Net Carbs 2g; Fat 5g; Protein 2.8g

Keto Mac & Cheese

Ingredients for 4 servings

4 zucchinis, spiralized	1 cup heavy cream
2 tbsp butter, melted	1 cup cream cheese
Salt and black pepper, to taste	1 tsp garlic paste

Directions and Total Time: approx. 20 minutes

Top the zucchinis with melted butter, salt, and pepper and toss to coat. Cook in a saucepan over medium heat for 5-6 minutes. Remove to a serving plate.

In the same pan, pour the heavy cream, garlic paste, and cream cheese and heat through, stirring frequently. Reduce heat to low and simmer for 2-3 minutes or until the sauce thickens. Adjust the seasoning. Coat the zucchinis in the cheese sauce and serve immediately.

Per serving: Cal 686; Fat 72g; Net Carbs 3.9g; Protein 10g

Mediterranean Salmon with Asparagus

Ingredients for 2 servings

2 tbsp olive oil	½ lemon, juiced
½ tsp dried dill	½ lb asparagus, trimmed
½ tsp garlic powder	½ lemon, sliced thinly
2 salmon fillets	Salt and black pepper to taste

Directions and Total Time: approx. 30 minutes

Preheat the oven to 390 F. In a bowl, mix 1 tbsp of olive oil, dill, garlic powder, salt, and pepper. Rub the mixture onto the salmon. Place the fish on a lined baking sheet. Drizzle with lemon juice. Brush the asparagus with the remaining olive oil and season with salt and pepper. Arrange asparagus around the salmon. Roast for 12-16 minutes, until the salmon fillets flake easily with a fork. Serve topped with lemon slices.

Per serving: Cal 381; Fat 25g; Net Carbs 2.3g; Protein 37g

Speedy Salmon in Creamy Parsley Sauce

Ingredients for 2 servings

1 tbsp Parmesan cheese, grated	
2 salmon fillets	1 tbsp parsley, chopped
1 cup heavy cream	½ lemon, zested and juiced
1 tbsp mayonnaise	Salt and black pepper to taste

Directions and Total Time: approx. 25 minutes

In a bowl, mix the heavy cream, parsley, mayonnaise, lemon zest, lemon juice, salt, and pepper; set aside. Season the fish with salt and black pepper, drizzle lemon juice on both sides of the fish, and arrange the fillets on a parchment paper-lined baking sheet. Spread the mayo-parsley mixture and sprinkle with Parmesan cheese. Bake in the oven for 15 minutes at 380 F. Great served with steamed broccoli.

Per serving: Cal 554; Fat 30g; Net Carbs 2.2g; Protein 56g

Simple Pork Tenderloin

Ingredients for 2 servings:

4 tbsp butter	1 zucchini, sliced
½ lb pork tenderloin, sliced	Salt and black pepper to taste

Directions and Total Time: approx. 30 minutes

Warm the butter in a large skillet over medium heat. Season the pork with salt and pepper and place it in the skillet. Cook for 8-10 minutes per side until just browned. Remove and tent with a foil to keep warm. Season the zucchini slices with salt and pepper and cook in the skillet for 2 minutes per side. Serve with the pork.

Per serving: Cal 381; Fat 27g; Net Carbs 1.7g; Protein 31g

Shimp & Vegetable Stir-Fry

Ingredients for 2 servings:

½ lb peeled shrimp	¼ tsp paprika
1 zucchini, cut into half-moons	2 tsp butter
1 shallot, sliced	1 tbsp parsley, chopped
½ green bell pepper, chopped	2 lemon wedges
2 garlic cloves, minced	

Directions and Total Time: approx. 20 minutes

Melt butter in a skillet over medium heat. Place in the zucchini, shallot, and bell pepper and sprinkle with garlic and paprika. Sauté for 5-6 minutes until tender. Add in the shrimp and parsley and cook for 5 additional minutes, until the shrimp are pink. Spoon the shrimp and vegetables into a bowl, garnish with lemon wedges, and serve.

Per serving: Cal 176; Fat 5.5g; Net Carbs 3.3g; Protein 26g

Avocado-Chicken Lettuce Wraps

Ingredients for 4 servings:

1 tbsp avocado oil	2 tsp fresh cilantro, chopped
½ avocado, pitted, peeled	1 chicken breast, sliced
⅓ cup mayonnaise	Salt and black pepper to taste
1 tsp lime juice	1 head lettuce, leaves separated

Directions and Total Time: approx. 25 minutes

Preheat a grill pan over medium heat. Season the chicken with salt and pepper and brush with avocado oil. Place the chicken slices on the grill and cook for 5-6 minutes. Remove to a plate and allow to cool, then chop into cubes or strips. In a medium bowl, mash the avocado with mayonnaise, lime juice, and cilantro until well blended. Stir in the chopped chicken and adjust the seasoning. Add spoonfuls of the chicken mixture to the lettuce leaves, wrap them and serve.

Per serving: Cal 220; Fat 17g; Net Carbs 2.2g; Protein 8g

Beef Steak Carnitas

Ingredients for 4 servings:

2 tbsp olive oil	1 avocado, pitted, peeled
1 yellow onion, thinly sliced	1 tomato, chopped
1 green bell pepper, thinly sliced	1 tsp fresh cilantro, chopped
1 lb skirt steak, cut into strips	½ tsp onion powder
1 tbsp taco seasoning	Salt and black pepper to taste

Directions and Total Time: approx. 25 minutes

Warm the olive oil in a large skillet over medium heat. Sauté the onion and bell pepper until they soften. Add the steak and cook until the steak is cooked through, about 8-10 minutes. Sprinkle with taco seasoning.

In a bowl, mash the avocado with a fork. Add the tomato, onion powder, salt, pepper, and cilantro and mix to combine. Top the beef and vegetables with the avocado mixture and serve.

Per serving: Cal 545; Fat 41g; Net Carbs 7.2g; Protein 34g

Beef & Broccoli

Ingredients for 4 servings:

3 tbsp olive oil	1 tsp red pepper flakes
1 lb skirt steak, sliced	Salt and black pepper to taste
1 lb broccoli florets	

Directions and Total Time: approx. 25 minutes

Steam the broccoli for 5-7 minutes, until crisp-tender but still vibrant green. Season with salt and drizzle with some olive oil; set aside. Warm the remaining olive oil in a large skillet over medium heat. Sauté the steak for 6-8 minutes. Remove to a plate and sprinkle with red pepper flakes, salt, and pepper. Add the broccoli to the plate and serve.

Per serving: Cal 361; Fat 22g; Net Carbs 1.9g; Protein 34g

Raspberry Yogurt Parfait

Ingredients for 2 servings:

1 cup Greek yogurt	3 mint sprigs, chopped
1 cup fresh raspberries	2 tbsp chia seeds
½ lemon, zested	2 drops liquid stevia

Directions and Total Time: approx. 10 minutes

In a small bowl, whisk the Greek yogurt with stevia. Divide half of the yogurt, raspberries, lemon zest, mint, and chia seeds between medium serving glasses. Repeat with another layer. Serve cold.

Per serving: Cal 183; Fat 10g; Net Carbs 8.9g; Protein 7.8g

Keto Chocolate Fat Bombs

Ingredients for 4 servings

½ cup almond butter	4 tbsp cocoa powder
½ cup almond oil	½ cup xylitol

Directions and Total Time: approx. 5 min + cooling time

In the microwave, melt butter and almond oil for 45 seconds, stirring twice until thoroughly combined. Stir in cocoa powder and xylitol until completely combined. Transfer to muffin molds and refrigerate for 4 hours to firm up. Serve and enjoy!

Per serving: Cal 445; Fat 43g; Net Carbs 3.8g; Protein 8.4g

Oven-Baked Crispy Bacon

Ingredients for 4 servings

8 bacon slices

Directions and Total Time: approx. 25 minutes

On a parchment-lined baking sheet, arrange the bacon slices, spacing them ¼ inch apart. Bake in the preheated to 400 F oven for 18-20 or until crispy. Place the bacon on a paper towel–lined plate to soak up any excess grease.

Per serving: Cal 206; Fat 16g; Net Carbs 0g; Protein 14

Chia & Blackberry Pudding

Ingredients for 4 servings

½ cup Greek yogurt	1 tsp vanilla extract
1 cup fresh blackberries	7 tbsp chia seeds
1 ½ cups coconut milk	3 tbsp chopped almonds
4 tsp sugar-free maple syrup	Mint leaves to garnish

Directions and Total Time: approx. 45 minutes

Place the coconut milk, Greek yogurt, maple syrup, and vanilla extract in a bowl and stir until evenly combined. Mix in the chia seeds. Mash half of the blackberries in a bowl using a fork and fold in the yogurt mixture. Share the mixture into mason jars, cover the lids and refrigerate for 30 minutes to thicken the pudding. Remove the jars, take off the lid, and stir the mixture. Garnish with the remaining blackberries, almonds, and mint leaves. Serve.

Per serving: Cal 299; Fat 23g; Net Carbs 6.3g; Protein 7g

Cauliflower Rice

Ingredients for 4 servings

1 head cauliflower, cut into florets	
2 tbsp olive oil	Salt and black pepper to taste
1 shallot, chopped	2 tbsp fresh cilantro, chopped

Directions and Total Time: approx. 15 minutes

Blend the cauliflower florets in a food processor until they become small rice-like granules. Warm the olive oil in a skillet over medium heat and sauté the shallot for 3 minutes until softened. Add the cauliflower rice and cook for 5-6 minutes, stirring occasionally. Season with salt and pepper. Serve topped with cilantro, and enjoy!

Per serving: Cal 114; Fat 14g; Net Carbs 5g; Protein 3.9g

Simple Shirataki Noodles

Ingredients for 4 servings

2 (8 oz) packs shirataki noodles
Salt and black pepper to taste   2 tbsp soy sauce

Directions and Total Time: approx. 3 minutes

In a pot, bring 2 cups of water to a boil. Strain the shirataki pasta and rinse well under hot running water. Drain and transfer to the boiling water. Cook for 3 minutes and strain again. Place a dry skillet and stir-fry the shirataki pasta until visibly dry, 1-2 minutes. Season with salt and pepper. Serve topped with soy sauce.

Per serving: Cal 4; Net Fat 0.1g; Carbs 0g; Protein 0.5g

Coconut Butter Coffee

Ingredients for 2 servings

2 cups freshly brewed coffee	2 tbsp coconut oil
3 tbsp unsalted butter	½ tsp ground cinnamon

Directions and Total Time: approx. 3 minutes

Transfer the brewed coffee to a blender and add the coconut oil and butter. Blend the mixture until frothy and smooth. Serve topped with cinnamon.

Per serving: Cal 329; Fat 34g; Net Carbs 0g; Protein 2g

BREAKFAST & EGGS

Coconut Crêpes with Vanilla Cream

Ingredients for 4 servings

2 tbsp unsweetened cocoa powder

2 cups coconut flour	2 cups flax milk
6 eggs	1 tbsp coconut oil, melted

Vanilla cream

¼ cup butter	½ tsp vanilla extract
2 tbsp erythritol	½ cup coconut cream

Directions and Total Time: approx. 35 minutes

Beat the eggs with a whisk in a bowl. Add the coconut flour, cocoa powder, flax milk, and coconut oil and mix until well combined. Set a skillet over medium heat, grease with cooking spray, and pour in a ladleful of the batter. Swirl the pan quickly to spread the dough around the skillet and cook the crepe for 2-3 minutes. Slide the crepe into a flat plate. Continue cooking until the remaining batter has finished.

Melt the butter in a saucepan over medium heat. Pour in the coconut cream and erythritol, reduce the heat to low, and let the sauce simmer for 6-8 minutes while stirring continually. Turn the heat off and stir in the vanilla extract. Drizzle the sauce over the crepes and serve.

Per serving: Cal 326; Fat 22g; Net Carbs 5.1g; Protein 10g

Turkey Bacon & Spinach Crepes

Ingredients for 4 servings

3 eggs	4 oz mozzarella, shredded
½ cup cottage cheese	1 garlic clove, minced
1 tbsp coconut flour	½ onion, chopped
⅓ cup Parmesan, grated	2 tbsp butter
A pinch of xanthan gum	½ cup heavy cream
1 cup spinach	Fresh parsley, chopped
4 oz turkey bacon, cubed	Salt and black pepper, to taste

Directions and Total Time: approx. 35 minutes

In a bowl, combine cottage cheese, eggs, coconut flour, xanthan gum, and Parmesan cheese to obtain a crepe batter. Grease a pan with cooking spray over medium heat, pour some of the batter, spread well into the pan, cook for 2 minutes, flip, and cook for 40 seconds more or until golden. Do the same with the rest of the batter. Stack all the crepes on a serving plate.

In the same pan, melt the butter and stir in the onion and garlic; sauté for 3 minutes until tender. Stir in the spinach for 5 minutes. Add in the turkey bacon, heavy cream, mozzarella cheese, salt, and pepper and stir. Cook for 2-3 minutes. Fill each crepe with the mixture, roll up each one, and arrange on a serving plate. Top with parsley.

Per serving: Cal 321; Fat 21g; Net Carbs 5.2g; Protein 26g

Lemon Crepes

Ingredients for 2 servings

1 cup almond milk	½ tbsp granulated Swerve
3 large eggs	1 cup almond flour
A pinch of salt	1 tsp butter
1 tbsp lemon juice	¾ cup powdered Swerve

Directions and Total Time: approx. 25 minutes

In a bowl, mix almond milk, eggs, granulated Swerve, salt, and almond flour until well incorporated. Grease a frying pan with cooking spray and set over medium heat. Cook the crepes until the edges start to brown, about 2 minutes. Flip and cook the other side for a further 2 minutes; repeat the process with the remaining batter. Put the crepes on a plate. In the same pan, mix powdered Swerve, butter and ½ cup of water; simmer for 6 minutes as you stir. Add in lemon juice and allow to sit until the syrup is thick. Pour the syrup over the crepes and serve.

Per serving: Cal 251; Fat 20g; Net Carbs 5.3g; Protein 7g

Crespelle al Mascarpone

Ingredients for 2 servings

½ cup almond flour	1 large egg
2 tsp liquid stevia	¼ cup olive oil
1 tsp baking powder	Whole raspberries to garnish
½ cup almond milk	1 cup mascarpone cheese
1 tsp vanilla extract	1 tsp mint, chopped

Directions and Total Time: approx. 35 minutes

Beat the egg in a bowl. Add in the almond milk, vanilla extract, and half of the stevia and stir to combine. In another bowl, whisk the almond flour and baking powder together. Then, pour the egg mixture into the almond flour mixture and continue whisking until smooth.

Heat olive oil in a pan over medium heat and pour in 1 soup spoon of batter. Cook on one side for 2 minutes, flip the pancake, and cook the other side for 2 minutes.

Transfer the pancake to a plate and repeat the cooking process until the batter is exhausted. Mix the mascarpone with the remaining stevia and mint in a small bowl. Spread each mini pancake with mascarpone and scatter raspberry over to serve.

Per serving: Cal 687; Fat 61g; Net Carbs 5.2g; Protein 23g

Perfect Buttermilk Pancakes

Ingredients for 4 servings

3 eggs	1 vanilla pod
½ cup buttermilk	2 tbsp unsalted butter
½ cup almond flour	2 tbsp olive oil
½ tsp baking powder	3 tbsp sugar-free maple syrup
1 tbsp Swerve	Blueberries to serve
1 lemon, juiced	Greek yogurt to serve

Directions and Total Time: approx. 25 minutes

In a small bowl, whisk the buttermilk, lemon juice, and eggs. In another bowl, mix almond flour, baking powder, and Swerve. Fold in the egg mixture and whisk until smooth. Cut the vanilla pod open and scrape the beans into the flour mixture. Stir to incorporate evenly.

In a skillet, melt a quarter of the butter and olive oil and spoon in 2 tablespoons of the pancake mixture into the pan. Cook for 4 minutes or until small bubbles appear.

Flip and cook for 2 minutes or until set and golden. Repeat the cooking until the batter finishes using the remaining butter and olive oil in the same proportions. Plate the pancakes, drizzle with maple syrup, top with a generous dollop of yogurt, and scatter some blueberries on top.

Per serving: Cal 172; Net Carbs 1.6g; Fat 12g; Protein 7g

Ginger Pancakes

Ingredients for 2 servings

1 cup almond flour	1 tsp ginger powder
1 tsp cinnamon powder	1 egg
2 tbsp Swerve	1 cup almond milk
¼ tsp baking soda	2 tbsp olive oil

Lime sauce

¼ cup liquid stevia	½ lime, juiced and zested
½ tsp arrowroot starch	2 tbsp butter

Directions and Total Time: approx. 20 minutes

Combine together the almond flour, cinnamon powder, Swerve, baking soda, ginger powder, egg, almond milk, and olive oil in a mixing bowl. Heat oil in a skillet over medium heat and spoon 2-3 tablespoons of the mixture into the skillet. Cook the batter for 1 minute, flip it and cook the other side for another minute.

Remove the pancake onto a plate and repeat the cooking process until the batter is exhausted. Mix the stevia and arrowroot starch in a saucepan. Set the pan over medium heat and gradually stir 1 cup water until it thickens, about 1 minute. Turn the heat off and add the butter, lime juice, and lime zest. Stir the mixture until the butter melts. Drizzle the sauce over the pancakes and serve warm.

Per serving: Cal 343; Fat 25g; Net Carbs 6.1g; Protein 8g

Belgium Waffles with Cheese Spread

Ingredients for 2 servings

½ cup cream cheese, softened	½ cup almond milk
1 lemon, zested and juiced	3 eggs
2 tbsp liquid stevia	½ cup almond flour
2 tbsp olive oil	

Directions and Total Time: approx. 25 minutes

In a bowl, combine the cream cheese, lemon juice, lemon zest, and stevia. In a separate bowl, whisk the olive oil, almond milk, and eggs. Stir in almond flour and combine until no lumps exist. Let the batter sit for 5 minutes to thicken. Spritz a waffle iron with a cooking spray.

Ladle a ¼ cup of the batter into the waffle iron and cook for about 5 minutes. Repeat with the remaining batter. Slice the waffles into quarters; apply the lemon spread in between each of two waffles, snap, and serve.

Per serving: Cal 322; Fat 26g; Net Carbs 7.7g; Protein 11g

Spinach & Feta Cheese Pancakes

Ingredients for 2 servings

½ cup almond flour	½ cup spinach, chopped
½ tsp baking powder	2 tbsp coconut milk
½ cup feta cheese, crumbled	1 egg, beaten

Directions and Total Time: approx. 20 minutes

In a medium bowl, put the egg, almond flour, baking powder, feta, coconut milk, and spinach and whisk to combine. Set a skillet over medium heat for a minute. Fetch a soup spoonful of the mixture and cook for 2 minutes. Flip the pancake and cook further for 1 minute. Remove onto a plate and repeat the cooking process until the batter is exhausted. Serve with your favorite topping.

Per serving: Cal 412; Fat 32g; Net Carbs 5.9g; Protein 12g

Jalapeno Waffles with Bacon & Avocado

Ingredients for 2 servings

2 tbsp butter, melted	½ jalapeño pepper, minced
¼ cup almond milk	4 eggs
2 tbsp almond flour	½ cup cheddar, crumbled
Salt and black pepper to taste	4 slices bacon, chopped
½ tsp parsley, chopped	1 avocado, sliced

Directions and Total Time: approx. 20 minutes

In a skillet over medium heat, fry the bacon until crispy, about 5 minutes. Remove to a plate. In a bowl, combine the remaining ingredients, except for the avocado. Preheat waffle iron and grease with cooking spray. Pour in the batter and close the lid. Cook for 5 minutes or until the desired consistency is reached. Do the same with the rest of the batter. Top with avocado and bacon.

Per serving: Cal 771; Fat 67g; Net Carbs 6.9g; Protein 27g

Peanut Butter & Pastrami Gofres

Ingredients for 2 servings

4 eggs	¼ tsp salt
½ tsp baking soda	½ tsp dried rosemary
2 tbsp peanut butter, melted	3 tbsp tomato puree
4 tbsp coconut flour	4 oz pastrami, chopped

Directions and Total Time: approx. 20 minutes

Preheat your waffle iron to high. In a mixing bowl, thoroughly whisk the eggs, rosemary, and salt. Stir in the coconut flour, baking soda, and peanut butter. Continue whisking until everything is well incorporated. Add a third of the batter to the waffle iron and cook for 3 minutes until golden. Repeat with the remaining batter. Spread the tomato puree over each gofre and top with pastrami. Serve.

Per serving: Cal 411; Fat 27g; Net Carbs 4.2g; Protein 25g

Savory Waffles with Cheese & Tomato

Ingredients for 2 servings

2 eggs, beaten	Salt and black pepper, to taste
2 tbsp sour cream	1/3 cup Gouda cheese, grated
¼ tsp allspice	1 tomato, sliced

Directions and Total Time: approx. 20 minutes

Mix the eggs, allspice, black pepper, salt, and sour cream in a shallow bowl. Add in the shredded cheese. Spritz a waffle iron with a cooking spray. Pour in half of the batter. Cook for 5 minutes until golden. Repeat with the remaining batter. Serve with tomato slices.

Per serving: Cal 254; Fat 18g; Net Carbs 1.7g; Protein 17g

Zesty Zucchini Bread with Nuts

Ingredients for 4 servings

4 eggs	2/3 cup ground almonds
2/3 cup coconut flour	1 lemon, zested and juiced
2 tsp baking powder	1 cup finely grated zucchini
1 cup butter, softened	1 cup whipped cream
1 cup erythritol	1 tbsp chopped hazelnuts

Directions and Total Time: approx. 50 min + cooling time

Preheat oven to 380 F. Grease a springform pan with and line with parchment paper. Set aside. In a bowl, beat the butter and erythritol until creamy and pale. Add eggs one after another while whisking. Add in coconut flour and baking powder and stir along with ground almonds, lemon zest, juice, and zucchini. Spoon the mixture into the pan. Bake for 40 minutes or until risen and a toothpick inserted into the cake comes out clean. Let cool inside the pan for 10 minutes. Transfer to a wire rack. Spread whipped cream on top and sprinkle with hazelnuts. Serve and enjoy!.

Per serving: Cal 781; Net Carbs 3.7g; Fat 69g; Protein 32g

Bacon, Cheese & Avocado Mug Cakes

Ingredients for 2 servings

2 eggs	Salt and black pepper, to taste
¼ cup flax meal	2 tbsp ricotta cheese
2 tbsp buttermilk	2 oz bacon, sliced
2 tbsp pesto	1 avocado, sliced
¼ cup almond flour	

Directions and Total Time: approx. 15 minutes

Whisk eggs, buttermilk, and pesto in a bowl. Season with salt and pepper. Gently add in flax meal and almond flour and divide the mixture between two greased ramekins. Place in the microwave and cook for 1-2 minutes. Leave to cool slightly before filling.

In a nonstick skillet over medium heat, cook the bacon until crispy, about 5 minutes; set aside. Invert the ramekins onto a plate and cut in half, crosswise. Assemble the sandwiches by spreading ricotta cheese and topping with bacon and avocado slices.

Per serving: Cal 488; Fat 37g; Net Carbs 3.9g; Protein 17g

Pumpkin & Zucchini Bread

Ingredients for 4 servings

1 cup pumpkin, shredded	¾ tsp baking soda
1 cup zucchini, shredded	1 tbsp cinnamon powder
1/3 cup coconut flour	½ tsp salt
6 eggs	½ cup buttermilk
1 tbsp olive oil	1 tsp apple cider vinegar

Directions and Total Time: approx. 60 minutes

Preheat oven to 360 F. In a bowl, mix all the ingredients and stir to form a dough. Pour the batter into a greased loaf pan and bake for 45 minutes or until a toothpick comes out clean. Let cool for 5 minutes. Serve sliced.

Per serving: Cal 202; Fat 12g; Net Carbs 4.5g; Protein 12g

Ham & Cheese Keto Sandwiches

Ingredients for 2 servings

4 eggs	2 tbsp psyllium husk powder
½ tsp baking powder	2 slices mozzarella cheese
5 tbsp butter, softened	2 slices smoked ham
4 tbsp almond flour	

Directions and Total Time: approx. 20 minutes

To make the buns, whisk together almond flour, baking powder, 4 tbsp of butter, husk powder, and eggs in a bowl; mix until a dough forms. Place the batter in two oven-proof mugs and microwave for 2 minutes or until firm. Remove, flip the buns over, cool, and cut in half.

Put a slice of mozzarella cheese and a slice of ham on one bun half and top with the other. Warm the remaining butter in a skillet. Add sandwiches and grill until the cheese is melted. Serve and enjoy!

Per serving: Cal 516; Fat 45g; Net Carbs 2.3g; Protein 23g

Almond & Raspberries Cakes

Ingredients for 4 servings

2 cups almond flour	8 oz cream cheese, softened
2 tsp baking soda	¼ cup butter, melted
1 tsp vanilla extract	1 egg
2 tbsp almond flakes	10 raspberries
½ tsp salt	1 cup almond milk
2 tbsp liquid stevia	

Directions and Total Time: approx. 35 minutes

Mash the raspberries with a fork and set aside. Mix the almond flour, baking soda, vanilla, and salt in a large bowl. In a separate bowl, whisk the egg and almond milk. Add in the cream cheese, stevia, and butter and beat until well incorporated. Fold in the flour and mashed raspberries and spoon the batter into greased muffin cups two-thirds way up. Top with almond flakes. Bake for 20 minutes at 400 F until golden brown, remove to a wire rack to cool slightly for 5 minutes before serving.

Per serving: Cal 353; Fat 33g; Net Carbs 8.6g; Protein 9.4g

Bacon & Blue Cheese Cups

Ingredients for 4 servings

2 tbsp olive oil	½ cup blue cheese, crumbled
6 eggs	4 oz bacon, chopped
2 tbsp coconut milk	2 tbsp chives, chopped
Salt and black pepper to taste	1 serrano pepper, minced

Directions and Total Time: approx. 30 minutes

Preheat oven to 390 F. Beat the eggs in a bowl and whisk in coconut milk until combined. Season with salt and pepper; fold in the blue cheese.

Grease muffin cups with olive oil and spread the bottom of each one with bacon. Fill each with the egg mixture two-thirds way up. Top with serrano pepper and bake in the oven for 18 minutes or until golden. Remove and allow cooling for a few minutes. Serve topped with chives.

Per serving: Cal 354; Fat 28g; Net Carbs 1.5g; Protein 24g

Sesame & Poppy Seed Bagels

Ingredients for 4 servings

½ cup coconut flour	½ tsp garlic powder
6 eggs	1 tsp dried oregano
½ cup flaxseed meal	1 tsp sesame seeds
½ tsp onion powder	1 tsp poppy seeds

Directions and Total Time: approx. 30 minutes

Mix the coconut flour, eggs, ½ cup of water, flaxseed meal, onion powder, garlic powder, and oregano. Spoon the mixture into a greased donut tray. Sprinkle with poppy seeds and sesame seeds. Bake the bagels for 20 minutes at 360 F. Let cool for 5 minutes before serving.

Per serving: Cal 431; Fat 20g; Net Carbs 1.3g; Protein 29g

Nut Porridge with Strawberries

Ingredients for 2 servings

6 fresh strawberries, halved	6 tbsp heavy whipping cream
4 tbsp chopped walnuts	2 oz butter
2 tbsp chopped pecans	2 eggs
2 tbsp coconut flour	2 tbsp lemon juice
1 tsp psyllium husk powder	1 tsp cinnamon powder

Directions and Total Time: approx. 20 minutes

Place a saucepan over low heat. Combine the flour, psyllium husk, whipping cream, butter, egg, lemon juice, and cinnamon in a bowl. Mix to combine. Pour in the saucepan and cook for 10 minutes, stirring constantly but do not boil until thickened. Top with the strawberries, walnuts, and pecans.

Per serving: Cal 590; Net Carbs 5.9g; Fat 60g; Protein 11g

Cheesy Coconut Cookies

Ingredients for 4 servings

½ cup grated Gruyere cheese	¼ cup butter, melted
1/3 cup coconut flour	¼ tsp salt
¼ tsp baking powder	½ tsp xanthan gum
¼ cup coconut flakes	2 tsp garlic powder
4 eggs	¼ tsp onion powder

Directions and Total Time: approx. 35 minutes

Preheat oven to 350 F. Line a baking sheet with parchment paper. In a food processor, mix eggs, butter, and salt until smooth. Add coconut flour, coconut flakes, xanthan gum, baking powder, garlic and onion powders, and Gruyere cheese and stir to combine. Mold 12 balls out of the mixture and arrange them on the baking sheet at 2-inch intervals. Bake for 25 minutes or until the cookies are golden brown. Let cool and serve. Enjoy!

Per serving: Cal 269; Net Carbs 5g, Fat 26g, Protein 11g

Spiced Biscuits

Ingredients for 4 servings

2 tbsp butter, melted	¼ tsp black pepper
½ tsp baking soda	¼ tsp garlic powder
1 cup almond flour	½ tsp paprika powder
1 egg	½ tbsp plain vinegar
½ tsp salt	½ cup mixed dried herbs

Directions and Total Time: approx. 35 minutes

Preheat oven to 350 F. Line a baking sheet with wax paper. In a bowl, mix flour, butter, egg, salt, pepper, garlic powder, baking soda, paprika, vinegar, and dried herbs and stir until smoothly combined. Mold 12 balls out of the mixture and arrange on the baking sheet at 2-inch intervals. Bake for 25 minutes until golden brown.

Per serving: Cal 69; Net Carbs 0.6g, Fat 7g, Protein 1.5g

Berry Hemp Seed Breakfast

Ingredients for 2 servings

1 cup berry medley	2 tbsp hemp seeds
2 cups coconut milk	4 tsp liquid stevia
¼ tsp vanilla extract	2 tbsp chopped pitted dates
4 oz heavy cream	

Directions and Total Time: approx. 10 min + cooling time

Mash the berries with a fork until pureed in a medium bowl. Pour in the coconut milk, heavy cream, hemp seeds, vanilla, and liquid stevia. Mix and refrigerate the pudding overnight. Spoon the pudding into serving glasses, top with dates, and serve.

Per serving: Cal 532; Fat 42g; Net Carbs 5.3g; Protein 14g

Morning Chia Pudding

Ingredients for 2 servings

2 tbsp chia seeds	½ tsp vanilla extract
¾ cup coconut milk	½ cup blueberries
1 tbsp chopped walnuts	

Directions and Total Time: approx. 10 min + chilling time

Pour the coconut milk, vanilla, and half of the blueberries into a blender. Process the ingredients until the blueberries are incorporated into the liquid. Mix in the chia seeds. Share the mixture into 2 jars, cover, and refrigerate for 4 hours to allow it to gel. Garnish with the remaining blueberries and walnuts. Serve.

Per serving: Cal 299; Net Carbs 6g; Fat 19g; Protein 9g

Broccoli, Egg & Pancetta Gratin

Ingredients for 2 servings

10 oz broccoli florets	1 tsp dried oregano
1 red bell pepper, chopped	Salt and black pepper to taste
4 slices pancetta, chopped	4 fresh eggs
2 tsp olive oil	4 tbsp Parmesan cheese

Directions and Total Time: approx. 30 minutes

Preheat oven to 420 F. Line a baking sheet with wax paper. Warm the olive oil in a pan over medium heat and stir-fry the pancetta for 3 minutes. Place the broccoli, bell pepper, and pancetta on the baking sheet and toss to combine. Season with salt, oregano, and pepper. Bake for 10 minutes until the vegetables have softened. Remove, create 4 indentations, and crack an egg into each one. Sprinkle with Parmesan cheese. Return to the oven and bake for 5-7 minutes or until the egg whites are firm and the cheese melts. Remove from the oven and serve.

Per serving: Cal 464; Fat 38g; Net Carbs 4.2g; Protein 24g

Keto French Toast with Berry Yogurt

Ingredients for 2 servings

½ cup strawberries, halved
½ cup blueberries
½ cup raspberries
2 eggs
2 cups Greek yogurt
2 tbsp sugar-free maple syrup
¼ tsp cinnamon powder
¼ tsp nutmeg powder
2 tbsp almond milk
4 slices zero carb bread
1 ½ tbsp butter
1 tbsp olive oil

Directions and Total Time: approx. 20 min + chilling time

In a bowl, mix yogurt, maple syrup, and berries. Chill for 1 hour. In another bowl, whisk eggs, cinnamon, nutmeg, and almond milk. Set aside. Cut each bread slice into four strips. Heat butter and olive oil in a skillet over medium heat. Dip each strip into the egg mixture and fry until golden brown on both sides, about 5-6 minutes. Serve warm with berry yogurt.

Per serving: Cal 211; Net Carbs 7.3g; Fat 12g; Protein 7.7g

Seeded Morning Loaf

Ingredients for 6 servings

4 tbsp sesame oil
6 eggs
1 cup cream cheese, softened
¾ cup heavy cream
¾ cup coconut flour
1 cup almond flour
3 tbsp baking powder
2 tbsp psyllium husk powder
2 tbsp desiccated coconut
5 tbsp sesame seeds
¼ cup flaxseed meal
¼ cup hemp seeds
1 tsp ground caraway seeds
1 tbsp poppy seeds
1 tsp salt
1 tsp allspice

Directions and Total Time: approx. 55 minutes

Preheat oven to 350 F. In a bowl, mix coconut and almond flours, baking powder, psyllium husk, desiccated coconut, sesame seeds, flaxseed meal, hemp seeds, ground caraway seeds, poppy seeds, salt, and allspice. In another bowl, whisk eggs, cream cheese, heavy cream, and sesame oil. Pour the mixture into the dry ingredients and combine both into a smooth dough. Pour the dough into a greased loaf pan. Bake for 45 minutes. Remove onto a rack and let cool.

Per serving: Cal 591; Net Carbs 7.4g; Fat 48g; Protein 21g

Rolled Smoked Salmon with Avocado

Ingredients for 2 servings

2 tbsp cream cheese, softened
1 lime, zested and juiced
½ avocado, pitted, peeled
1 tbsp mint, chopped
Salt to taste
2 slices smoked salmon

Directions and Total Time: approx. 10 min + cooling time

Mash the avocado with a fork in a bowl. Add in the cream cheese, lime juice, zest, mint, and salt and mix to combine. Lay each salmon slice on a plastic wrap, spread with cream cheese mixture. Roll the salmon up and secure both ends by twisting. Refrigerate for 2 hours, then remove plastic, cut off both ends of each wrap, and cut wraps into half-inch wheels. Serve.

Per serving: Cal 410; Fat 26g; Net Carbs 2.7g; Protein 38g

Cauliflower Bake with Dilled Mayo

Ingredients for 4 servings

10 oz cauliflower florets
2 tbsp butter, melted
Salt and black pepper to taste
1 pinch red pepper flakes
½ cup mayonnaise
¼ tsp Dijon mustard
3 tbsp Pecorino cheese, grated
1 tbsp dill, chopped
1 tsp garlic powder

Directions and Total Time: approx. 40 minutes

Preheat oven to 400 F. Mix the mayonnaise, garlic powder, mustard, dill, and salt in a bowl. Keep in the fridge. Combine the cauli florets, butter, salt, pepper, and flakes in a bowl until mixed. Arrange cauliflower florets on a greased baking dish. Sprinkle with Pecorino cheese and bake for 25 minutes until the cheese has melted and golden brown on the top. Remove, let sit for 3 minutes, and serve with the dilled sauce.

Per serving: Cal 233; Fat 19g; Net Carbs 4.2g; Protein 6.3g

Mini Raspberry Tarts

Ingredients for 4 servings
For the crust

2 cups almond flour
1 tsp cinnamon powder
6 tbsp butter, melted
1/3 cup xylitol

For the filling

¼ cup butter, melted
3 cups raspberries, mashed
½ tsp fresh lemon juice
½ tsp cinnamon powder
¼ cup xylitol sweetener

Directions and Total Time: approx. 25 min + chilling time

Preheat oven to 350 F. Lightly grease 4 mini tart tins with cooking spray. In a bowl, blend butter, almond flour, xylitol, and cinnamon. Divide the dough between the tart tins and bake for 15 minutes.

In another bowl, mix the filling ingredients and stir to combine. Pour filling into the crust, gently tap on a flat surface to release air bubbles, and refrigerate for 1 hour.

Per serving: Cal 437; Net Carbs 4.6g, Fat 27g, Protein 2g

Spinach Nests with Eggs & Cheese

Ingredients for 2 servings

1 tbsp olive oil
1 tbsp dried dill
1 lb spinach, chopped
1 tbsp pine nuts
Salt and black pepper to taste
¼ cup feta cheese, crumbled
2 eggs

Directions and Total Time: approx. 30 minutes

Sauté spinach in the olive oil over medium heat for 5 minutes. Season with salt and pepper and set aside.

Grease a baking sheet with cooking spray, mold 2 (firm and separate) spinach nests on the sheet, and crack an egg into each nest. Top with feta and scatter with dill. Bake for 15 minutes at 350 F just until the egg whites have set and the yolks are still runny. Plate the nests and serve sprinkled with pine nuts.

Per serving: Cal 218; Fat 16g; Net Carbs 4.4g; Protein 12g

Bacon & Mushroom "Tacos"

Ingredients for 2 servings

1 egg, hard-boiled and chopped
1 cup mushrooms, sliced
3 oz mozzarella cheese, grated
3 oz bacon, chopped
1 shallot, sliced
1 avocado, sliced
1 tbsp salsa
1 tbsp sour cream

Directions and Total Time: approx. 30 minutes

Preheat the oven to 350°F. Place 2 piles of mozzarella cheese on a parchment-lined baking dish, flatten gently with hands to form taco shells (circle tortillas). Bake in the oven for 10-12 minutes until the edges start to brown; remove and let them cool slightly.

Fry the bacon in a skillet over medium heat for 4 minutes until crispy; transfer to a bowl. Sauté the shallot and mushrooms in the same grease for 5 minutes. Remove to the bacon bowl. Mix in the egg. Divide the mixture between the taco shells, top with avocado, salsa, and sour cream, and serve.

Per serving: Cal 613; Fat 48g; Net Carbs 1.5g; Protein 34g

Roasted Stuffed Avocados

Ingredients for 2 servings

2 large avocados, halved
3 eggs
1 tbsp Parmesan, grated
Salt and black pepper to taste
1 tbsp parsley, chopped

Directions and Total Time: approx. 20 minutes

Scoop out some of the flesh of the avocados into a bowl. Mash with a fork and whisk in the eggs; season with salt and pepper. Fill the avocado halves with the mixture and arrange them on a greased baking dish. Top with Parmesan cheese and bake in the preheated to 380 F oven for 8-10 minutes or until eggs are cooked and cheese is melted. Garnish with fresh parsley and serve.

Per serving: Cal 284; Fat 23g; Net Carbs 0.8g; Protein 15g

Mushroom & Cheese Lettuce Cups

Ingredients for 2 servings

1 tbsp olive oil
½ onion, chopped
Salt and black pepper, to taste
½ cup mushrooms, chopped
¼ tsp cayenne pepper
2 fresh lettuce leaves
2 slices Gruyere cheese
1 tomato, sliced

Directions and Total Time: approx. 20 minutes

Warm the olive oil in a pan over medium heat. Sauté the onion for 3 minutes, until soft. Stir in the mushrooms and cayenne and cook for 4-5 minutes until tender. Season with salt and pepper. Spoon the mushroom mixture into the lettuce leaves, top with tomato and cheese slices to serve.

Per serving: Cal 481; Fat 42g; Net Carbs 5.7g; Protein 20g

Zucchini & Pepper Caprese Gratin

Ingredients for 4 servings

2 zucchinis, sliced
1 red bell pepper, sliced
Salt and black pepper to taste
1 cup ricotta cheese, crumbled
4 oz fresh mozzarella, sliced
2 tomatoes, sliced
2 tbsp butter
¼ tsp xanthan gum
½ cup heavy whipping cream

Directions and Total Time: approx. 50 minutes

Preheat oven to 370 F. Make a layer of zucchinis and bell peppers into a greased baking dish overlapping. Season with salt and pepper, and sprinkle with some ricotta cheese and repeat the layering process a second time. Combine butter, xanthan gum, and whipping cream in a microwave dish for 2 minutes, stir to mix completely, and pour over the vegetables. Top with the remaining ricotta. Bake the gratin for 30 minutes or until golden brown on top. Remove from the oven and cover with tomato and fresh mozzarella slices. Bake for 5-10 more minutes. Cut into slices and serve warm.

Per serving: Cal 283; Fat 22g; Net Carbs 5.6g; Protein 16g

Arabic Poached Eggs in Tomato Sauce

Ingredients for 2 servings

4 large eggs
¼ cup yogurt
1 tsp olive oil
1 garlic clove, minced
1 small white onion, chopped
1 red bell pepper, chopped
1 small green chili, minced
1 cup diced tomatoes
½ cup tomato sauce
1 tsp cumin powder
1/3 cup baby kale, chopped
½ tsp dried basil
½ lemon, juiced
Salt and black pepper to taste

Directions and Total Time: approx. 40 minutes

Warm olive oil in a deep skillet and sauté garlic, onion, bell pepper, and green chili until softened, 5 minutes. Stir in tomatoes, tomato sauce, salt, pepper, and cumin. Cover and cook for 10 minutes. Add in the kale and cook until wilted. Stir in basil. Create four holes in the sauce with a wooden spoon and crack an egg into each hole. Cover with a lid and cook until the eggs are firm, 8-10 minutes. In a bowl, mix yogurt with lemon juice. Top the meal with the yogurt mixture and serve.

Per serving: Cal 319; Net Carbs 8g; Fat 17g; Protein 16g

Tuna & Egg Salad with Chili Mayo

Ingredients for 4 servings

4 eggs
14 oz tuna in brine, drained
½ small head lettuce, torn
2 spring onions, chopped
¼ cup ricotta, crumbled
2 tbsp sour cream
½ tbsp mustard powder
½ cup mayonnaise
½ tbsp lemon juice
½ tbsp chili powder
2 dill pickles, sliced
Salt and black pepper, to taste

Directions and Total Time: approx. 20 minutes

Boil the eggs in salted water over medium heat for 8 minutes. Place in an ice bath, let cool, and chop into small pieces. Transfer them to a bowl. Place in tuna, onion, mustard powder, ricotta cheese, lettuce, and sour cream. In a separate bowl, mix in mayonnaise, lemon juice, and chili powder; season to taste. Add in the tuna mixture and stir to combine well. Serve topped with pickle slices.

Per serving: Cal 311; Fat 19g; Net Carbs 1.5g; Protein 31g

Avocado Shakshuka

Ingredients for 2 servings

4 eggs	1 red bell pepper, sliced
1 avocado, chopped	1 yellow bell pepper, sliced
1 tbsp olive oil	1 medium tomato, diced
1 medium red onion, sliced	1 cup vegetable broth
1 zucchini, sliced	1 tbsp chopped parsley

Directions and Total Time: approx. 25 minutes

Warm olive oil in a skillet and sauté the zucchini, onion, and bell peppers for 10 minutes. Pour in the tomato and broth. Bring to a boil and simmer until the sauce thickens slightly. Create 4 holes in the sauce and break an egg into each hole. Allow the eggs to cook through and turn the heat off. Top with avocado and parsley and serve warm.

Per serving: Cal 448; Net Carbs 5.6g; Fat 29g; Protein 18g

Microwave Bacon Frittata

Ingredients for 2 servings

4 eggs	½ tsp oregano
4 tbsp coconut milk	Salt and black pepper, to taste
½ cup bacon, cubed	1 spring onion, sliced

Directions and Total Time: approx. 5 minutes

In a bowl, crack the eggs and beat until combined; season with salt and black pepper. Add coconut milk, bacon, spring onion, and oregano. Pour the mixture into two microwave-safe cups. Microwave for 1 minute. Serve.

Per serving: Cal 370; Fat 17g; Net Carbs 1.9g; Protein 23g

Lazy Eggs with Feta Cheese

Ingredients for 2 servings

4 eggs	1 garlic clove, minced
¼ cup coconut milk	¼ tsp dried dill
¼ cup feta cheese, grated	¼ tsp red pepper flakes

Directions and Total Time: approx. 10 minutes

Beat the eggs lightly with a fork in a bowl. Mix in the feta, flakes, garlic, and coconut milk. Divide the mixture between greased microwave-safe mugs. Microwave the mugs for 40 seconds. Stir well and microwave for another 70 seconds. Sprinkle with dill and serve.

Per serving: Cal 234; Fat 16g; Net Carbs 2.7g; Protein 17g

Deli Ham Eggs

Ingredients for 2 servings

2 tbsp butter	4 eggs
1 shallot, chopped	1 thyme sprig, chopped
Salt and black pepper to taste	½ cup olives, pitted and sliced
2 slices deli ham, chopped	

Directions and Total Time: approx. 20 minutes

Beat the eggs lightly with a fork. Over medium heat, set a skillet and warm butter. Sauté the shallot for 4 minutes until tender. Stir in the ham, pepper, and salt; cook for 5-6 more minutes. Add in the eggs and sprinkle with thyme. Cook for 4 minutes. Garnish with olives and serve.

Per serving: Cal 321; Fat 26g; Net Carbs 3.1g; Protein 16g

Serrano Ham Frittata with Salad

Ingredients for 2 servings

2 tbsp olive oil	1 tbsp balsamic vinegar
3 slices serrano ham, chopped	4 eggs, beaten
1 tomato, cut into chunks	1 cup Swiss chard, chopped
1 cucumber, sliced	Salt and black pepper to taste
1 small red onion, sliced	1 green onion, sliced

Directions and Total Time: approx. 25 minutes

Whisk vinegar, 1 tbsp of olive oil, salt, and pepper in a salad bowl. Add in the tomato, red onion, and cucumber and toss to coat. Sprinkle with serrano ham.

Heat the remaining olive oil in a pan over medium heat. Sauté the onion and Swiss chard for 3 minutes. Season with salt and pepper, and cook for 2 minutes. Pour the eggs over, reduce the heat to low, cover, and cook for 4 minutes. Transfer the pan to the oven. Bake to brown on top for 5 minutes at 390 F. Serve sliced with the salad.

Per serving: Cal 364; Fat 26g; Net Carbs 4.7g; Protein 20g

Goat Cheese Frittata with Asparagus

Ingredients for 2 servings

1 tbsp olive oil	½ habanero pepper, minced
½ onion, chopped	Salt and red pepper, to taste
1 cup asparagus, chopped	¾ cup goat cheese, crumbled
4 eggs, beaten	1 tbsp parsley, chopped

Directions and Total Time: approx. 35 minutes

Preheat oven to 370 F. Sauté the onion in warm olive oil over medium heat until caramelized, 6-8 minutes. Place in the asparagus and cook until tender, about 5 minutes. Add in habanero pepper and eggs; season with red pepper and salt. Cook until the eggs are set. Scatter goat cheese and parsley over the frittata, transfer to the oven and cook for approximately 20 minutes, until the frittata is set in the middle. Slice into wedges before serving.

Per serving: Cal 345; Fat 27g; Net Carbs 5.3g; Protein 22g

Chorizo & Cheese Frittata

Ingredients for 2 servings

4 eggs	½ red bell pepper, crumbled
Salt and black pepper, to taste	1 tsp chipotle paste
1 chorizo sausage, sliced	½ cup kale
1 tbsp butter	¼ cup cotija cheese, shredded
1 green onion, chopped	

Directions and Total Time: approx. 30 minutes

Whisk the eggs in a bowl, and season with black pepper and salt. Warm butter in a skillet over medium heat. Sauté the onion until soft. Add in chorizo sausage, chipotle paste, and bell pepper, and cook for 5-7 minutes. Place in the kale and cook for 2 minutes. Add in the eggs. Spread the mixture evenly over the skillet and set into the oven. Bake for 8 minutes at 370 F or until the top is set and golden. Scatter crumbled cotija cheese over and bake for 3 more minutes or until the cheese melts completely. Slice and serve while still warm.

Per serving: Cal 288; Fat 21g; Net Carbs 5.3g; Protein 17g

Bell Pepper & Cheese Frittata

Ingredients for 2 servings

½ green bell pepper, diced
½ cup feta cheese, crumbled
1 tomato, sliced
4 eggs
1 tbsp olive oil
2 scallions, diced
1 tsp dill, chopped
Salt and black pepper, to taste

Directions and Total Time: approx. 30 minutes

Preheat oven to 360 F. In a bowl, whisk the eggs along with the pepper and salt, until combined. Stir in the bell pepper, feta cheese, and scallions. Pour the mixture into a greased casserole, top with the tomato slices, and bake for 20 minutes until the frittata is set in the middle. Sprinkle with dill and serve immediately.

Per serving: Cal 311; Fat 25g; Net Carbs 3.6g; Protein 16g

Crabmeat Frittata with Onion

Ingredients for 2 servings

1 tbsp olive oil
½ onion, chopped
Salt and black pepper to taste
3 oz crabmeat, chopped
4 large eggs, slightly beaten
½ cup sour cream

Directions and Total Time: approx. 30 minutes

Put a skillet over medium heat and warm the oil. Sweat the onion until soft; place in the crabmeat and cook for 2 minutes. Season with salt and pepper. Distribute the ingredients at the bottom of the skillet. Whisk the eggs with sour cream. Transfer the mixture to the skillet. Set the skillet in the oven and bake for 17 minutes at 350 F or until eggs are cooked through. Slice into wedges and serve.

Per serving: Cal 265; Fat 16g; Net Carbs 6.5g; Protein 23g

Italian-Style Croque Madame

Ingredients for 4 servings

2 cups ricotta cheese
12 eggs
2 tbsp ground psyllium husk
½ cup coconut oil
8 oz Parma ham
2 cups sliced mozzarella
1 red onion, chopped
½ cup basil leaves
⅓ cup toasted pine nuts
¼ cup grated Parmesan
1 garlic clove, peeled
¼ cup + 2 tbsp olive oil

Directions and Total Time: approx. 30 minutes

In a food processor, puree basil, pine nuts, Parmesan cheese, garlic, and ¼ cup of olive oil until desired consistency is reached; set aside the resulting pesto. In a bowl, beat 8 eggs, ricotta cheese, and psyllium husk until smooth and no more lumps. Leave to thicken for about 5 minutes.

Warm the coconut oil in a skillet over medium heat. Fetch a soup spoonful of mixture into the skillet and cook for 2 minutes per side. Repeat the cooking process until the batter is exhausted. Spread half of the pancakes with pesto and top with ham, cheese, and onion. Cover with the remaining pancakes. Warm the remaining olive oil in a skillet over medium heat and crack in the remaining 4 eggs. Cook until the whites set but the yolks are still soft and runny. Place the eggs on the pancakes and serve.

Per serving: Cal 928; Net Carbs 3g; Fat 116g; Protein 47g

Arugula Pesto Egg Scramble

Ingredients for 2 servings

1 tbsp butter
4 eggs
1 tbsp almond milk
Salt and black pepper, to taste

Arugula pesto

1 cup arugula
1 cup Parmesan cheese, grated
1 tbsp pine nuts
1 garlic clove, minced
¼ cup olive oil
1 tbsp lime juice

Directions and Total Time: approx. 20 minutes

Beat the eggs in a bowl along with almond milk, salt, and pepper. Set a skillet over medium heat and warm the butter. Pour in the egg mixture and stir-fry until the eggs are set but still tender and moist. Set aside.

In a blender, place all the ingredients for the pesto, excluding the olive oil. Pulse until smooth. While the machine is still running, slowly add in the olive oil until your desired consistency is obtained. Serve with the scrambled eggs and enjoy!

Per serving: Cal 512; Fat 44g; Net Carbs 6.7g; Protein 21g

Sausage Cakes with Poached Eggs

Ingredients for 2 servings

½ lb sausage patties
1 tbsp olive oil
2 tbsp guacamole
½ tsp vinegar
Salt and black pepper to taste
2 eggs
1 tbsp cilantro, chopped

Directions and Total Time: approx. 20 minutes

Fry the sausage patties in warm olive oil over medium heat until lightly browned, 6-8 minutes. Remove the patties to a plate. Spread the guacamole on top.

Boil the vinegar with 2 cups of water in a pot over high heat, and reduce to simmer, without boiling. Crack each egg into a bowl and gently put the egg into the simmering water; poach for 2-3 minutes. Remove from the water on a paper towel to dry. Top each cake with a poached egg, sprinkle with cilantro, salt, and pepper and serve.

Per serving: Cal 523; Fat 43g; Net Carbs 2.5g; Protein 28g

Morning Herbed Eggs

Ingredients for 2 servings

1 spring onion, finely chopped
2 tbsp butter
1 tsp fresh thyme
4 eggs
½ tsp sesame seeds
2 garlic cloves, minced
½ cup parsley, chopped
½ cup sage, chopped
¼ tsp cayenne pepper
Salt and black pepper, to taste

Directions and Total Time: approx. 15 minutes

Melt butter in a skillet over medium heat. Add garlic, parsley, sage, and thyme and stir-fry for 30 seconds. Carefully crack the eggs into the skillet. Lower the heat and cook for 4-6 minutes. Adjust the seasoning. When the eggs are just set, turn the heat off and transfer to a serving plate. Drizzle the cayenne pepper and sesame seeds. Top with spring onion to serve.

Per serving: Cal 283; Fat 23g; Net Carbs 5.3g; Protein 13g

Yummy Blue Cheese & Mushroom Omelet

Ingredients for 2 servings

4 eggs, beaten
4 button mushrooms, sliced
Salt to taste
1 tbsp olive oil
½ cup blue cheese, crumbled
1 tomato, thinly sliced
1 tbsp parsley, chopped

Directions and Total Time: approx. 15 minutes

Set a pan over medium heat and warm the olive oil. Sauté the mushrooms for 5 minutes until tender; season with salt. Add in the eggs and cook as you swirl them around the pan using a spatula, until partially set. Top with blue cheese, fold the omelet in half to enclose filling. Decorate with tomato and parsley and serve.

Per serving: Cal 310; Fat 25g; Net Carbs 1.5g; Protein 18g

Scrambled Eggs with Tofu & Mushrooms

Ingredients for 4 servings

5 fresh eggs
1 tbsp butter
1 cup mushrooms, sliced
2 cloves garlic, minced
16 oz firm tofu, crumbled
Salt and black pepper to taste
1 tomato, chopped
2 tbsp sesame seeds

Directions and Total Time: approx. 30 minutes

Melt the butter in a skillet over medium heat, and sauté the mushrooms for 5 minutes until tender. Add the garlic and cook for 1 minute. Crumble the tofu in, and season with salt and pepper. Stir-fry for 6 minutes. Add the tomato and cook until soft, for 5 minutes. Whisk the eggs in a bowl and pour all over the tomato. Use a spatula to immediately stir the eggs while cooking until scrambled and no more runny, 5 minutes. Sprinkle with sesame seeds, and serve.

Per serving: Cal 315; Fat 27g; Net Carbs 4.5g; Protein 25g

Bacon & Artichoke Omelet

Ingredients for 2 servings

¼ cup canned artichoke hearts, drained and chopped
4 eggs, beaten
1 tbsp heavy cream
4 bacon slices, chopped
1 tbsp olive oil
1 green onion, chopped
Salt and black pepper to taste

Directions and Total Time: approx. 20 minutes

Warm the olive oil in a skillet over medium heat. Cook the bacon for 3 minutes. Add in the green onion, heavy cream, and artichokes and stir-fry for 2 minutes. Pour the eggs over. Cook for 5-6 minutes, flipping once the omelet until the egss are set. Season with salt and pepper. Serve.

Per serving: Cal 427; Fat 35g; Net Carbs 1g; Protein 26g

Chili Omelet with Avocado

Ingredients for 2 servings

2 tsp olive oil
1 ripe avocado, chopped
2 spring onions, chopped
2 spring garlic, chopped
4 eggs
1 cup buttermilk
2 tomatoes, sliced
1 green chili pepper, minced
2 tbsp fresh cilantro, chopped
Salt and black pepper, to taste

Directions and Total Time: approx. 15 minutes

Crack the eggs into a bowl and whisk buttermilk, salt, and black pepper. Set a pan over high heat and warm the olive oil. Sauté garlic and onions until tender and translucent. Pour into the pan and use a spatula to smooth the surface; cook until the eggs become puffy and brown at the bottom. Add cilantro, chili pepper, avocado, and tomatoes, to one side of the omelet. Fold in half and slice into wedges. Serve immediately.

Per serving: Cal 392; Fat 28g; Net Carbs 3.6g; Protein 19g

Bacon & Cheese Cloud Eggs

Ingredients for 2 servings

4 eggs, whites and yolks separated
Salt and black pepper to taste
2 bacon slices
1 tbsp chives, finely chopped,
3 tbsp grated Pecorino cheese

Directions and Total Time: approx. 15 minutes

Heat a skillet over medium heat. Fry the bacon until crispy on both sides, about 5 minutes. Let it cool, then crumble it. Using an electric mixer, beat the egg whites and salt until stiff peaks form. Fold in the Pecorino cheese and bacon. Spoon the mixture into 4 mounds on a parchment-lined baking sheet. Create an indention in each pile. Carefully spoon an egg yolk into each indention; season with salt and pepper. Bake in the preheated to 450 F oven for 3 minutes until the yolks are set. Sprinkle with chives and serve.

Per serving: Cal 237; Fat 19g; Net Carbs 0.7g; Protein 21g

Canadian Bacon Eggs Benedict

Ingredients for 2 servings

1 tsp white wine vinegar
2 large eggs
4 Canadian bacon slices
1 tbsp fresh parsley, chopped

Directions and Total Time: approx. 20 minutes

Heat a skillet over medium heat and fry the bacon for 3-4 minutes per side. Remove to a paper towel to soak up the excess fat. Boil water with the vinegar in a pot over high heat and reduce to simmer. Crack each egg into a bowl and gently put the egg into the simmering water; poach for 2-3 minutes. Use a perforated spoon to remove from the water on a paper towel to dry. Place the bacon on 2 plates. Top each with an egg. Sprinkle with parsley.

Per serving: Cal 161; Fat 9g; Net Carbs 0.4g; Protein 18g

Chorizo Egg Cups

Ingredients for 2 servings

1 tsp butter, melted
4 eggs, beaten
Salt and black pepper, to taste
1 cup mozzarella, grated
2 chorizo sausages, chopped
1 tbsp parsley, chopped

Directions and Total Time: approx. 20 minutes

In a bowl, stir the eggs, sausages, and cheese; season with salt and pepper. Add to greased with butter muffin cups, and bake in the oven for 8-10 minutes at 400 F. Sprinkle with parsley to serve.

Per serving: Cal 512; Fat 35g; Net Carbs 5.4g; Protein 41g

SALADS & SOUPS

Feta & Sun-Dried Tomato Salad

Ingredients for 2 servings

5 sun-dried tomatoes in oil, sliced
3 oz bacon slices, chopped
4 basil leaves
1 cup feta cheese, crumbled

2 tsp extra virgin olive oil
1 tsp balsamic vinegar
Salt to taste

Directions and Total Time: approx. 10 minutes

Fry the bacon in a pan over medium heat, until golden and crisp, about 5 minutes. Remove with a perforated spoon and set aside. Arrange the sun-dried tomatoes on a serving plate. Scatter feta cheese over and top with basil leaves. Add the crispy bacon on top, drizzle with olive oil and sprinkle with vinegar and salt.

Per serving: Cal 411; Fat 36g; Net Carbs 2.5g; Protein 16g

Cobb Salad with Roquefort Dressing

Ingredients for 4 servings

½ cup Roquefort cheese, crumbled
½ cup whipping cream
¼ cup buttermilk
½ cup mayonnaise
1 tbsp Worcestershire sauce
1 tbsp chives, chopped
3 eggs, hard-boiled, chopped
1 chicken breast
4 oz bacon, cooked, crumbled

1 cup endive, chopped
½ romaine lettuce, chopped
1 cup watercress
1 avocado, pitted and diced
1 large tomato, chopped
½ cup feta cheese, crumbled
Salt and black pepper to taste

Directions and Total Time: approx. 20 minutes

In a bowl, whisk the whipping cream, buttermilk, mayonnaise, and Worcestershire sauce. Stir in the Roquefort cheese, salt, pepper, and chives. Keep in the fridge.

Preheat the grill pan over high heat. Season the chicken with salt and pepper. Grill for 3 minutes on each side. Remove to a plate to cool for 3 minutes, and cut into bite-size chunks. Place the lettuce, endive, and watercress on a salad bowl and add the avocado, tomato, eggs, bacon, and chicken. Sprinkle the feta cheese over the salad and drizzle with the cheese dressing.

Per serving: Cal 527; Fat 43g; Net Carbs 7.2g; Protein 28g

Pesto Caprese Salad with Tuna

Ingredients for 2 servings

4 oz canned tuna chunks in water, drained
1 tomato, sliced
1 ball fresh mozzarella, sliced
4 basil leaves
½ cup pine nuts

½ cup Parmesan, grated
½ cup extra virgin olive oil
½ lemon, juiced

Directions and Total Time: approx. 10 minutes

Put in a food processor the basil leaves, pine nuts, Parmesan cheese, and extra virgin olive oil, and blend until smooth. Stir in the lemon juice. Arrange the cheese and tomato slices on a serving plate. Scatter the tuna chunks and pesto over the top and serve.

Per serving: Cal 364; Fat 31g; Net Carbs 1g; Protein 21g

Sausage & Pesto Salad with Cheese

Ingredients for 2 servings

½ cup mixed cherry tomatoes, cut in half
½ lb pork sausage links, sliced
1 cups mixed lettuce greens
¼ cup radicchio, sliced
1 tbsp olive oil
¼ lb feta cheese, cubed

½ tbsp lemon juice
¼ cup basil pesto
6 black olives, pitted, halved
Salt and black pepper, to taste
1 tbsp Parmesan shavings

Directions and Total Time: approx. 10 minutes

Cook the sausages in warm olive oil over medium heat for 5-6 minutes, stirring often. In a salad bowl, combine the mixed lettuce greens, radicchio, feta cheese, pesto, cherry tomatoes, black olives, and lemon juice and toss well to coat. Season with salt and black pepper and add the sausages. Sprinkle with Parmesan shavings and serve.

Per serving: Cal 611; Fat 48g; Net Carbs 7.5g; Protein 31g

Smoked Salmon, Bacon & Egg Salad

Ingredients for 4 servings

2 eggs
1 head romaine lettuce, torn
4 oz smoked salmon, chopped

3 slices bacon
4 cherry tomatoes, halved
Salt and black pepper to taste

Dressing:

½ cup mayonnaise
½ tsp garlic puree

1 tbsp lemon juice
1 tsp tabasco sauce

Directions and Total Time: approx. 20 minutes

In a bowl, mix well the dressing ingredients and set aside. Bring a pot of salted water to a boil. Crack each egg into a small bowl and gently slide into the water. Poach for 2-3 minutes. Remove with a perforated spoon, transfer to a paper towel to dry, and plate. Put the bacon in a skillet over medium heat and fry until browned and crispy, about 6 minutes, turning once. Remove, allow cooling, and chop into small pieces. Toss the lettuce, smoked salmon, bacon, and dressing in a salad bowl. Divide the salad between plates, top with the eggs each, and serve immediately or chilled.

Per serving: Cal 291; Fat 19g; Net Carbs 6.4g; Protein 15g

Classic Egg Salad with Olives

Ingredients for 2 servings

4 eggs
¼ cup mayonnaise
½ tsp sriracha sauce
½ tbsp mustard
¼ cup scallions

¼ stalk celery, minced
Salt and black pepper, to taste
1 head romaine lettuce, torn
¼ tsp fresh lime juice
10 black olives

Directions and Total Time: approx. 15 minutes

Boil the eggs in salted water over medium heat for 10 minutes. When cooled, peel and chop them into bite-size pieces. Place in a salad bowl. Stir in the remaining ingredients, except for the scallions, until everything is well combined. Scatter the scallions all over and decorate with black olives to serve.

Per serving: Cal 312; Fat 22g; Net Carbs 6.3g; Protein 17g

Spinach & Brussels Sprout Salad

Ingredients for 2 servings

1 lb Brussels sprouts, halved
2 tbsp olive oil
Salt and black pepper to taste
1 tbsp balsamic vinegar

2 tbsp extra virgin olive oil
1 cup baby spinach
1 tbsp Dijon mustard
½ cup hazelnuts

Directions and Total Time: approx. 35 minutes

Preheat oven to 400 F. Drizzle the Brussels sprouts with olive oil, sprinkle with salt and pepper, and spread on a baking sheet. Bake until tender, 20 minutes, tossing often.

In a dry pan over medium heat, toast the hazelnuts for 2 minutes, cool, and then chop into small pieces. Transfer the Brussels sprouts to a salad bowl and add the baby spinach. Mix until well combined. In a small bowl, combine vinegar, mustard, and olive oil. Drizzle the dressing over the salad and top with hazelnuts to serve.

Per serving: Cal 511; Fat 43g; Net Carbs 9.6g; Protein 14g

Chicken Salad with Parmesan

Ingredients for 2 servings

½ lb chicken breasts, sliced
¼ cup lemon juice
2 garlic cloves, minced
2 tbsp olive oil

1 romaine lettuce, shredded
3 Parmesan crisps
2 tbsp Parmesan, grated

Dressing

2 tbsp extra virgin olive oil
1 tbsp lemon juice

Salt and black pepper to taste

Directions and Total Time: approx. 30 min + chilling time

In a Ziploc bag, put the chicken, lemon juice, oil, and garlic. Seal the bag, shake to combine, and refrigerate for 1 hour. Preheat the grill to medium heat and grill the chicken for about 2-3 minutes per side. Combine the dressing ingredients in a small bowl and mix well. On a serving platter, arrange the lettuce and Parmesan crisps. Scatter the dressing over and toss to coat. Top with the chicken and Parmesan cheese to serve.

Per serving: Cal 529; Fat 36g; Net Carbs 4.3g; Protein 34g

Smoked Mackerel Lettuce Cups

Ingredients for 2 servings

½ head Iceberg lettuce, firm leaves removed for cups
4 oz smoked mackerel, flaked
Salt and black pepper to taste
2 eggs
1 tomato, seeded, chopped

2 tbsp mayonnaise
¼ red onion, sliced
1 tsp lemon juice
1 tbsp chives, chopped

Directions and Total Time: approx. 20 minutes

Boil the eggs in a small pot with salted water for 10 minutes. Then, run the eggs in cold water, peel, and chop into small pieces. Transfer them to a salad bowl. Add in the smoked mackerel, red onion, and tomato and mix evenly with a spoon. Mix the mayonnaise, lemon juice, salt, and pepper in a small bowl and stir to combine. Lay two lettuce leaves each as cups and divide the salad mixture between them. Sprinkle with chives and serve.

Per serving: Cal 314; Fat 25g; Net Carbs 3g; Protein 16g

Kale & Broccoli Slaw with Bacon & Parmesan

Ingredients for 2 servings

2 tbsp olive oil
1 cup broccoli slaw
1 cup kale slaw
2 slices bacon, chopped

2 tbsp Parmesan, grated
1 tsp celery seeds
1 ½ tbsp apple cider vinegar
Salt and black pepper, to taste

Directions and Total Time: approx. 10 minutes

Fry the bacon in a skillet over medium heat until crispy, about 5 minutes. Set aside to cool. In a salad bowl, whisk the olive oil, vinegar, salt, and pepper. Add in the broccoli, kale, and celery seeds and mix to combine well. Sprinkle with bacon and Parmesan and serve.

Per serving: Cal 305; Fat 29g; Net Carbs 3.7g; Protein 7.3g

Turkey Bacon & Turnip Salad

Ingredients for 4 servings

2 turnips, cut into wedges
2 tsp olive oil
1/3 cup black olives, sliced
1 cup baby spinach
6 radishes, sliced
3 oz turkey bacon, sliced

4 tbsp buttermilk
2 tsp mustard seeds
1 tsp Dijon mustard
1 tbsp red wine vinegar
Salt and black pepper to taste
1 tbsp chives, chopped

Directions and Total Time: approx. 40 minutes

Fry the turkey bacon in a skillet over medium heat until crispy, about 5 minutes. Set aside, then crumble it.

Line a baking sheet with parchment paper, toss the turnips with black pepper, drizzle with the olive oil, and bake in the oven for 25 minutes at 390 F, turning halfway through. Let cool. Spread the baby spinach at the bottom of a salad platter and top with the radishes, bacon, and turnips. Mix the buttermilk, mustard seeds, mustard, vinegar, and salt. Pour the dressing over the salad, stir well and scatter with the chives and olives to serve.

Per serving: Cal 95; Fat 5g; Net Carbs 3.4g; Protein 6g

Fiery Shrimp Cocktail Salad

Ingredients for 4 servings

2 tbsp olive oil
½ head Romaine lettuce, torn
1 cucumber, cut into ribbons
½ lb shrimp, deveined
1 cup arugula
½ cup mayonnaise

2 tbsp Cholula hot sauce
½ tsp Worcestershire sauce
Salt and chili pepper to season
1 tbsp lemon juice
1 lemon, cut into wedges
4 dill weed

Directions and Total Time: approx. 15 min + cooling time

Season the shrimp with salt and chili pepper. Warm the olive oil over medium heat and fry the shrimp for 3 minutes on each side until pink and opaque. Set aside to cool. Place the mayonnaise, lemon juice, hot sauce, and Worcestershire sauce and mix until smooth and creamy in a bowl. Divide the lettuce and cucumber between 4 glass bowls. Top with shrimp and drizzle the hot dressing over. Scatter arugula on top and decorate with lemon wedges and dill to serve.

Per serving: Cal 201; Fat 11g; Net Carbs 3.9g; Protein 14g

Chicken, Avocado & Egg Bowls

Ingredients for 2 servings

1 chicken breast, cubed	2 tbsp olive oil
1 tbsp avocado oil	2 tbsp lemon juice
2 eggs	1 tsp Dijon mustard
2 cups green beans	1 tbsp mint, chopped
1 avocado, sliced	Salt and black pepper to taste

Directions and Total Time: approx. 25 minutes

Blanch the green beans in salted water over medium heat for 4-5 minutes until the beans are bright green and crisp-tender. Refresh in cold water and drain. In the same boiling water, place the eggs and cook for 10 minutes. Remove to an ice bath to cool. Then, peel and slice them.

Warm the avocado oil in a pan over medium heat. Cook the chicken for about 4 minutes. Divide the green beans between two salad bowls. Top with chicken, eggs, and avocado slices. In another bowl, whisk together the lemon juice, olive oil, mustard, salt, and pepper, and drizzle over the salad. Top with fresh mint and serve.

Per serving: Cal 612; Fat 48g; Net Carbs 6.9g; Protein 27g

Spinach Salad with Pancetta & Mustard

Ingredients for 2 servings

1 cup spinach	2 pancetta slices
1 large avocado, sliced	½ lettuce head, shredded
1 spring onion, sliced	1 hard-boiled egg, chopped

Vinaigrette

Salt to taste	1 tsp Dijon mustard
¼ tsp garlic powder	1 tbsp white wine vinegar
3 tbsp olive oil	

Directions and Total Time: approx. 20 minutes

Chop the pancetta and fry in a skillet over medium heat for 5 minutes until crispy. Set aside to cool. Mix spinach, lettuce, egg, and spring onion in a bowl. Whisk the vinaigrette ingredients in another bowl. Pour the dressing over, toss to combine. Top with avocado and pancetta. Serve immediately

Per serving: Cal 547; Fat 51g; Net Carbs 4g; Protein 12g

Mediterranean Artichoke Salad

Ingredients for 2 servings

6 baby artichoke hearts, halved	¼ tsp lemon zest
½ lemon, juiced	2 tsp balsamic vinegar
½ red onion, sliced	1 tbsp chopped dill
¼ cup cherry peppers, halved	Salt and black pepper to taste
¼ cup pitted olives, sliced	1 tbsp capers
¼ cup olive oil	

Directions and Total Time: approx. 30 minutes

Bring a pot of salted water to a boil. Add in the artichokes. Lower the heat and let simmer for 20 minutes until tender. Drain and place the artichokes in a bowl to cool. Add in the rest of the ingredients, except for the olives; toss to combine well. Top with the olives and serve.

Per serving: Cal 464; Fat 32g; Net Carbs 9.5g; Protein 13g

Arugula & Watercress Turkey Salad

Ingredients for 4 servings

1 tbsp xylitol	Salt and black pepper, to taste
1 red onion, chopped	1 cup arugula
2 tbsp lime juice	1 cup watercress
3 tbsp olive oil	½ lb turkey breasts, boneless
1 ¾ cups raspberries	4 oz goat cheese, crumbled
1 tbsp Dijon mustard	½ cup walnut halves

Directions and Total Time: approx. 25 minutes

Start with the dressing: In a blender, combine xylitol, lime juice, 1 cup raspberries, pepper, mustard, ¼ cup water, onion, olive oil, and salt and pulse until smooth. Strain this into a bowl and set aside.

Heat a pan over medium heat and grease lightly with cooking spray. Coat the turkey with salt and black pepper and cut in half. Place skin side down into the pan. Cook for 8 minutes, flipping to the other side and cooking for 5 minutes. Place arugula and watercress in a salad platter, scatter with the remaining raspberries, walnut halves, and goat cheese. Slice the turkey, put over the salad, and top with raspberries dressing to serve.

Per serving: Cal 511; Fat 35g; Net Carbs 7.5g; Protein 37g

Spinach Salad with Goat Cheese & Nuts

Ingredients for 2 servings

2 cups spinach	2 tbsp white wine vinegar
½ cup pine nuts	2 tbsp extra virgin olive oil
1 cup hard goat cheese, grated	Salt and black pepper, to taste

Directions and Total Time: approx. 20 min + cooling time

Preheat oven to 390 F. Place the grated goat cheese in two circles on two parchment paper pieces. Place in the oven and bake for 10 minutes. Find two same bowls, place them upside down, and carefully put the parchment paper on top to give the cheese a bowl-like shape. Let cool that way for 15 minutes. Divide spinach among the bowls, sprinkle with salt and pepper, and drizzle with vinegar and olive oil. Top with pine nuts to serve.

Per serving: Cal 410; Fat 32g; Net Carbs 3.4g; Protein 27g

Thai-Style Prawn Salad

Ingredients for 2 servings

2 cups watercress	1 tbsp cilantro, chopped
1 green onion, sliced	¼ tsp sesame seeds
½ lb prawns, cooked	1 tbsp lemon juice
1 avocado, sliced	2 tsp liquid stevia
1 Thai chili pepper, sliced	½ tsp fish sauce
1 tomato, sliced	1 tbsp sesame oil

Directions and Total Time: approx. 20 minutes

In a bowl, whisk the stevia, sesame oil, fish sauce, and lemon juice. Add the prawns and toss to coat. Refrigerate covered for 10 minutes. Combine watercress, avocado, tomato, Thai chili pepper, and green onion on a serving platter. Top with prawns and drizzle the marinade over. Sprinkle with sesame seeds and cilantro and serve.

Per serving: Cal 420; Fat 29g; Net Carbs 1.8g; Protein 29g

Modern Greek Salad with Avocado

Ingredients for 2 servings

1 red bell pepper, roasted and sliced
2 tomatoes, sliced   1 tbsp vinegar
1 avocado, sliced   1 tbsp olive oil
6 kalamata olives   1 tbsp parsley, chopped
¼ lb feta cheese, sliced

Directions and Total Time: approx. 10 minutes

Arrange the tomato slices on a serving platter and place the avocado slices in the middle. Place the olives and bell pepper around the avocado slices and drop pieces of feta on the platter. Drizzle with olive oil and vinegar and sprinkle with parsley to serve.

Per serving: Cal 411; Fat 35g; Net Carbs 5.2g; Protein 13g

Seared Rump Steak Salad

Ingredients for 2 servings

1 cup green beans, steamed and sliced
½ lb rump steak   2 tsp yellow mustard
3 green onions, sliced   Salt and black pepper to taste
3 tomatoes, sliced   3 tbsp extra virgin olive oil
1 avocado, sliced   1 tbsp balsamic vinegar
2 cups Romaine lettuce, torn

Directions and Total Time: approx. 20 minutes

In a bowl, mix the mustard, salt, black pepper, balsamic vinegar, and extra virgin olive oil. Set aside.

Preheat a grill pan over high heat while you season the meat with salt and pepper. Place the steak in the pan and brown for 4 minutes per side. Remove to a chopping board and let it sit for 4 minutes before slicing.

In a salad bowl, add the green onions, tomatoes, green beans, lettuce, and steak slices. Drizzle the dressing over and toss to coat. Top with avocado slices and serve.

Per serving: Cal 611; Fat 45g; Net Carbs 6.4g; Protein 33g

Cheesy Beef Salad

Ingredients for 4 servings

½ lb beef rump steak, cut into strips
1 tsp cumin   ½ cup ricotta, crumbled
3 tbsp olive oil   ½ cup pecans, toasted
Salt and black pepper to taste   2 cups baby spinach
1 tbsp thyme   1 ½ tbsp lemon juice
1 garlic clove, minced   ¼ cup fresh mint, chopped

Directions and Total Time: approx. 15 minutes

Preheat the grill to medium heat. Rub the beef with salt, 1 tbsp of olive oil, garlic, thyme, black pepper, and cumin. Place on the preheated grill and cook for 10 minutes, flipping once.

Sprinkle the pecans on a dry pan over medium heat and cook for 2-3 minutes, shaking frequently. Remove the grilled beef to a cutting board, leave to cool, and slice into strips. In a salad bowl, combine baby spinach with mint, remaining olive oil, salt, lemon juice, ricotta, and pecans, and toss well to coat. Top with the beef slices.

Per serving: Cal 437; Fat 42g; Net Carbs 4.2g; Protein 16g

Pickled Pepper Salad with Grilled Steak

Ingredients for 2 servings

½ cup feta cheese, crumbled   1 cup lettuce salad
1 lb skirt steak, sliced   1 cup arugula
Salt and black pepper to taste   3 pickled peppers, chopped
1 tsp olive oil   2 tbsp red wine vinegar

Directions and Total Time: approx. 15 minutes

Preheat grill to high heat. Season the steak slices with salt and black pepper and drizzle with olive oil. Grill the steaks on each side to the desired doneness, about 5-6 minutes. Remove to a bowl, cover, and leave to rest while you make the salad. Mix the lettuce salad and arugula, pickled peppers, and vinegar in a salad bowl. Add the beef and sprinkle with feta cheese.

Per serving: Cal 633; Fat 34g; Net Carbs 4.7g; Protein 72g

Parma Ham & Egg Salad

Ingredients for 4 servings

8 eggs   1 ½ tsp lime juice
1/3 cup mayonnaise   Salt and black pepper, to taste
1 tbsp minced onion   10 lettuce leaves
½ tsp mustard   4 Parma ham slices

Directions and Total Time: approx. 20 minutes

Boil the eggs for 10 minutes in a pot filled with salted water. Remove and run under cold water. Then peel and chop. Transfer to a mixing bowl together with the mayonnaise, mustard, black pepper, lime juice, onion, and salt. Top with lettuce leaves and ham slices to serve.

Per serving: Cal 723; Fat 53g; Net Carbs 5.6g; Protein 47g

Chicken Salad with Gorgonzola Cheese

Ingredients for 2 servings

½ cup gorgonzola cheese, crumbled
1 chicken breast, boneless, skinless, flattened
Salt and black pepper to taste   1 cup arugula
1 tbsp garlic powder   1 tbsp red wine vinegar
2 tsp olive oil

Directions and Total Time: approx. 15 minutes

Rub the chicken with salt, black pepper, and garlic powder. Heat half of the olive oil in a pan over medium heat and fry the chicken for 4 minutes on both sides or until golden brown. Remove to a cutting board and let cool before slicing.

Toss the arugula with vinegar and the remaining olive oil; share the salads onto plates. Arrange the chicken slices on top and sprinkle with gorgonzola cheese.

Per serving: Cal 291; Fat 24g; Net Carbs 3.5g; Protein 12g

Cheddar & Turkey Meatball Salad

Ingredients for 4 servings

3 tbsp olive oil   1 head romaine lettuce, torn
1 tbsp lemon juice   2 tomatoes, sliced
1 lb ground turkey   ¼ red onion, sliced
Salt and black pepper to taste   3 oz yellow cheddar, shredded

Directions and Total Time: approx. 30 minutes

Mix the ground turkey with salt and black pepper and shape into meatballs. Refrigerate for 10 minutes.

Heat half of the olive oil in a pan over medium heat. Fry the meatballs on all sides for 10 minutes until browned and cooked within. Transfer to a wire rack to drain oil. Mix the lettuce, tomatoes, and red onion in a salad bowl, season with the remaining olive oil, salt, lemon juice, and pepper. Toss and add the meatballs on top. Scatter the cheese over the salad and serve.

Per serving: Cal 312; Fat 22g; Net Carbs 1.9g; Protein 19g

Warm Cauliflower Salad

Ingredients for 4 servings

1 cup roasted bell peppers, chopped
2 tbsp celery leaves, chopped
10 oz cauliflower florets
1 red onion, sliced
¼ cup extra-virgin olive oil
1 tbsp wine vinegar

1 tsp yellow mustard
Salt and black pepper, to taste
½ cup black olives, chopped
½ cup cashew nuts

Directions and Total Time: approx. 15 minutes

Steam cauliflower in salted water in a pot over medium heat for 5 minutes; drain and transfer to a salad bowl. Add in roasted peppers, olives, and red onion.

In a small dish, combine salt, olive oil, mustard, black pepper, and vinegar. Sprinkle the mixture over the veggies. Top with cashew nuts and celery and serve.

Per serving: Cal 213; Fat 16g; Net Carbs 7.4g; Protein 5.2g

Arugula & Roasted Pepper Salad

Ingredients for 4 servings

2 lb red bell peppers, deseeded and cut into wedges
1/3 cup arugula
½ cup Kalamata olives, pitted
3 tbsp chopped walnuts
½ tsp Swerve sugar
2 tbsp olive oil

1 tbsp mint leaves
½ tbsp balsamic vinegar
¼ cup crumbled goat cheese
Toasted pine nuts for topping
Salt and black pepper to taste

Directions and Total Time: approx. 30 minutes

Preheat oven to 400 F. Pour bell peppers on a roasting pan; season with Swerve sugar and drizzle with half of the olive oil. Roast for 20 minutes or until slightly charred; set aside to cool.

Put arugula in a salad bowl and scatter with roasted bell peppers, olives, mint, walnuts, and drizzle with vinegar and olive oil. Season with salt and pepper. Toss and top with goat cheese and pine nuts.

Per serving: Cal 159; Net Carbs 4.3g; Fat 13g; Protein 3.3g

Smoked Salmon Salad

Ingredients for 2 servings

2 slices smoked salmon, chopped
1 tsp onion flakes
3 tbsp mayonnaise
½ Romaine lettuce, shredded
1 tbsp lime juice

1 tbsp extra virgin olive oil
Sea salt to taste
½ avocado, sliced

Directions and Total Time: approx. 10 minutes

Combine the salmon, mayonnaise, lime juice, olive oil, and salt in a bowl; mix to combine. On a salad platter, arrange the shredded lettuce and onion flakes. Spread the salmon mixture over and top with avocado slices.

Per serving: Cal 231; Fat 20g; Net Carbs 2.2g; Protein 8.5g

Greek Beef Meatball Salad

Ingredients for 4 servings

2 tbsp almond milk
1 lb ground beef
1 onion, grated
¼ cup pork rinds, crushed
1 egg, whisked
1 tbsp fresh parsley, chopped
Salt and black pepper, to taste
1 garlic clove, minced

1 tbsp fresh mint, chopped
½ tsp dried oregano
4 tbsp olive oil
1 cup cherry tomatoes, halved
1 Lebanese cucumber, sliced
1 cup butterhead lettuce, torn
1½ tbsp lemon juice
1 cup Greek yogurt

Directions and Total Time: approx. 20 minutes

In a bowl, mix the almond milk, ground beef, salt, onion, parsley, black pepper, egg, pork rinds, oregano, and garlic. Roll the mixture into balls. Warm half of the oil in a pan over medium heat and fry the meatballs for 8-10 minutes. Remove to a paper towel–lined plate to drain.

In a salad plate, combine lettuce, cherry tomatoes, and cucumber. Mix in the remaining oil, lemon juice, black pepper, and salt. Whisk the yogurt with mint and spread it over the salad; top with meatballs to serve.

Per serving: Cal 488; Fat 31g; Net Carbs 6.3g; Protein 42g

Caprese Salad Stacks with Anchovies

Ingredients for 4 servings

4 anchovy fillets in oil
12 fresh mozzarella slices
4 red tomato slices

4 yellow tomato slices
1 cup basil pesto

Directions and Total Time: approx. 10 minutes

Take a serving platter and alternately stack a tomato slice, a mozzarella slice, a yellow tomato slice, another mozzarella slice, a red tomato slice, and then a mozzarella slice on it. Repeat making 3 more stacks in the same way. Spoon pesto all over. Arrange anchovies on top and serve.

Per serving: Cal 182; Net Carbs 3.5g; Fat 6g; Protein 17g

Classic Greek Salad

Ingredients for 2 servings

3 tbsp extra virgin olive oil
½ lemon, juiced
2 tomatoes, sliced
2 Persian cucumbers, diced
1 red bell pepper, sliced

1 small red onion, chopped
10 Kalamata olives
4 oz feta cheese, cubed
1 tsp parsley, chopped
Salt to taste

Directions and Total Time: approx. 10 minutes

Mix olive oil with lemon juice and salt in a bowl. In a salad bowl, combine tomatoes, cucumber, red onion, bell pepper, and parsley; toss with the dressing. Top with feta and olives. Serve.

Per serving: Cal 288; Fat 28g; Net Carbs 6.8g; Protein 10g

Warm Mushroom & Pepper Salad

Ingredients for 4 servings

1 cup mixed mushrooms, chopped

2 tbsp sesame oil

2 yellow bell peppers, sliced

1 garlic clove, minced

2 tbsp tamarind sauce

½ tsp hot sauce

1 tsp sugar-free maple syrup

½ tsp ginger paste

Chopped toasted pecans

Sesame seeds to garnish

Salt and black pepper to taste

Directions and Total Time: approx. 20 minutes

Warm half of the sesame oil in a skillet over medium heat and sauté bell peppers and mushrooms for 8-10 minutes. Season with salt and pepper. In a bowl, mix garlic, tamarind sauce, hot sauce, maple syrup, and ginger paste. Stir the mix into the vegetables and stir-fry for 2-3 minutes. Drizzle the salad with the remaining sesame oil and garnish with pecans and sesame seeds. Serve.

Per serving: Cal 291; Net Carbs 5.2g; Fat 27g; Protein 4.2g

Cauliflower-Watercress Salad

Ingredients for 4 servings

2 tbsp sesame oil

1 lemon, zested and juiced

10 oz cauliflower florets

12 green olives, chopped

8 sun-dried tomatoes, drained

3 tbsp chopped scallions

A handful of toasted peanuts

3 tbsp chopped parsley

½ cup watercress

Salt and black pepper to taste

Directions and Total Time: approx. 15 minutes

In a pot over medium heat, bring water to a boil. Insert a steamer basket and pour in the cauliflower. Soften for 8 minutes. Transfer cauliflower to a salad bowl. Add in olives, tomatoes, scallions, lemon zest and juice, sesame oil, peanuts, parsley, and watercress. Season with salt and pepper and mix using a spoon. Serve.

Per serving: Cal 198; Net Carbs 6.4g; Fat 15g; Protein 6.6g

Shrimp Salad with Avocado

Ingredients for 4 servings

2 tomatoes, chopped

½ lb medium shrimp

3 tbsp olive oil

1 avocado, chopped

1 tbsp cilantro, chopped

1 lime, zested and juiced

1 head Iceberg lettuce, torn

Salt and black pepper to taste

Directions and Total Time: approx. 20 minutes

Heat 1 tbsp olive oil in a skillet over medium heat and cook the shrimp until opaque, 8-10 minutes. Place the lettuce on a serving plate and top with shrimp, tomatoes, and avocado. Whisk together the remaining olive oil, lime zest, juice, salt, and pepper in a bowl. Pour the dressing over the salad and sprinkle with cilantro to serve.

Per serving: Cal 229; Fat 18g; Net Carbs 4.2g; Protein 10g

Green Salad with Feta & Blueberries

Ingredients for 4 servings

2 cups broccoli slaw

2 cups baby spinach

2 tbsp poppy seeds

1/3 cup sunflower seeds

1/3 cup blueberries

2/3 cup chopped feta cheese

1/3 cup chopped walnuts

2 tbsp olive oil

1 tbsp white wine vinegar

Salt and black pepper to taste

Directions and Total Time: approx. 10 minutes

In a bowl, whisk olive oil, vinegar, poppy seeds, salt, and pepper; set aside. In a salad bowl, combine the broccoli slaw, spinach, walnuts, sunflower seeds, blueberries, and feta cheese. Drizzle the dressing on top, toss, and serve.

Per serving: Cal 401; Net Carbs 4.9g; Fat 4g; Protein 9g

Bacon & Gorgonzola Salad

Ingredients for 4 servings

1 ½ cups gorgonzola cheese, crumbled

1 head lettuce, separated into leaves

4 oz bacon

1 tbsp white wine vinegar

3 tbsp extra virgin olive oil

Salt and black pepper to taste

2 tbsp pumpkin seeds

Directions and Total Time: approx. 15 minutes

Chop the bacon into small pieces and fry in a skillet over medium heat for 6 minutes, until browned and crispy. In a small bowl, whisk the white wine vinegar, olive oil, salt, and black pepper until dressing is well combined.

To assemble the salad, arrange the lettuce on a serving platter, top with the bacon and gorgonzola cheese. Drizzle the dressing over the salad, lightly toss, and top with pumpkin seeds to serve.

Per serving: Cal 339; Fat 32g; Net Carbs 2.9g; Protein 16g

Green Squash Salad

Ingredients for 4 servings

2 tbsp butter

2 lb green squash, cubed

1 fennel bulb, sliced

2 oz chopped green onions

1 cup mayonnaise

2 tbsp chives, finely chopped

2 tbsp chopped dill

A pinch of mustard powder

Directions and Total Time: approx. 15 minutes

Place a pan over medium heat and melt butter. Fry squash until slightly softened, about 7 minutes; let cool. In a bowl, mix squash, fennel, green onions, mayonnaise, chives, and mustard powder. Garnish with dill.

Per serving: Cal 321; Net Carbs 3g; Fat 31g; Protein 4g

Chorizo & Tomato Salad with Olives

Ingredients for 4 servings

2 tbsp olive oil

4 chorizo sausages, chopped

2 ½ cups cherry tomatoes

2 tsp red wine vinegar

1 small red onion, chopped

2 tbsp chopped cilantro

8 sliced Kalamata olives

1 head Boston lettuce, shredded

Salt and black pepper to taste

Directions and Total Time: approx. 10 minutes

Warm 1 tbsp of olive oil in a skillet and fry chorizo until golden. Cut in half cherry tomatoes. In a salad bowl, whisk the remaining olive oil with vinegar, salt, and pepper. Add the lettuce, onion, tomatoes, cilantro, and chorizo and toss to coat. Garnish with olives to serve.

Per serving: Cal 141; Net Carbs 5.2g; Fat 9g; Protein 7g

Tomato & Colby Cheese Salad

Ingredients for 2 servings

½ cucumber, sliced
2 tomatoes, sliced
½ yellow bell pepper, sliced
½ red onion, sliced thinly
½ cup colby cheese, cubed

10 green olives, pitted
½ tbsp red wine vinegar
4 tbsp olive oil
½ tsp dried oregano
Salt and black pepper to serve

Directions and Total Time: approx. 10 minutes

Place the bell pepper, tomatoes, cucumber, red onion, and colby cheese in a bowl. Drizzle red wine vinegar and olive oil all over and season with salt, pepper, and oregano; toss to coat. Top with olives and serve.

Per serving: Cal 578; Net Carbs 13g; Fat 51g; Protein 15g

Cranberry & Tempeh Broccoli Salad

Ingredients for 4 servings

1 lb broccoli florets
¾ lb tempeh, cubed
2 tbsp butter

2 tbsp almonds
½ cup frozen cranberries
Salt and black pepper to taste

Directions and Total Time: approx. 15 minutes

In a deep skillet, melt butter over medium heat and fry tempeh cubes until brown on all sides. Add in broccoli and stir-fry for 6 minutes. Season with salt and pepper. Turn the heat off. Stir in almonds and cranberries to warm through. Share the salad into bowls and serve.

Per serving: Cal 738; Net Carbs 7g; Fat 68g; Protein 12g

Lettuce, Beet & Tofu Salad

Ingredients for 4 servings

2 tbsp butter
2 oz tofu, cubed
8 oz red beets, washed
½ red onion, sliced

1 cup mayonnaise
1 small romaine lettuce, torn
2 tbsp freshly chopped chives
Salt and black pepper to taste

Directions and Total Time: approx. 55 minutes

Place the beets in a pot over medium heat, cover with salted water and bring to a boil for 40 minutes or until soft. Drain and allow cooling. Slip the skin off and slice the beets. Melt butter in a pan over medium heat and fry tofu until browned, 3-4 minutes. Remove to a plate.

In a salad bowl, mix beets, tofu, red onion, lettuce, salt, pepper, and mayonnaise. Garnish with chives and serve.

Per serving: Cal 415; Net Carbs 2g; Fat 40g; Protein 7g

Cream Soup with Avocado & Zucchini

Ingredients for 4 servings

3 tsp vegetable oil
1 leek, chopped
1 rutabaga, sliced
3 cups zucchinis, chopped

1 avocado, chopped
Salt and black pepper to taste
4 cups vegetable broth
2 tbsp fresh mint, chopped

Directions and Total Time: approx. 40 minutes

Warm the vegetable oil in a pot over medium heat. Sauté the leek, zucchini, and rutabaga for 7-10 minutes. Season with pepper and salt. Pour in broth and bring to a boil.

Lower the heat and simmer for 20 minutes. Lift from the heat. In batches, add the soup and avocado to a blender. Blend until creamy and smooth. Top with mint and serve.

Per serving: Cal 378; Fat 24.5g; Net Carbs 9.3g; Protein 8g

Chinese Tofu Soup

Ingredients for 2 servings

2 cups chicken stock
1 tbsp soy sauce, sugar-free
2 spring onions, sliced
1 tsp sesame oil, softened
2 eggs, beaten

1-inch piece ginger, grated
Salt and black pepper to taste
½ lb extra-firm tofu, cubed
1 tbsp fresh cilantro, chopped

Directions and Total Time: approx. 15 minutes

Boil in a pan over medium heat, soy sauce, chicken stock and sesame oil. Place in eggs as you whisk to incorporate thoroughly. Change heat to low and add salt, spring onions, black pepper and ginger; cook for 5 minutes. Place in tofu and simmer for 1 to 2 minutes. Divide into soup bowls and serve sprinkled with fresh cilantro.

Per serving: Cal 163; Fat 10g; Net Carbs 2.4g; Protein 14g

Summer Gazpacho with Cottage Cheese

Ingredients for 4 servings

1 green pepper, roasted
1 red pepper, roasted
1 avocado, flesh scoped out
1 garlic clove
1 spring onion, chopped
1 cucumber, chopped
½ cup olive oil

1 tbsp lemon juice
2 tomatoes, chopped
4 oz cottage cheese, crumbled
1 small red onion, chopped
1 tbsp apple cider vinegar
Salt to taste

Directions and Total Time: approx. 15 min + cooling time

In a blender, put the peppers, tomatoes, avocado, red onion, garlic, lemon juice, olive oil, vinegar, half of the cucumber, 1 cup of water, and cottage cheese. Blitz until your desired consistency is reached; adjust the seasoning. Transfer the mixture to a pot. Cover and chill in the fridge for at least 2 hours. Serve the soup topped with the remaining cucumber, spring onion, and an extra drizzle of olive oil.

Per serving: Cal 373; Fat 34g; Net Carbs 7.1g; Protein 5.8g

Fresh Avocado-Cucumber Soup

Ingredients for 4 servings

3 tbsp olive oil
1 small onion, chopped
4 large cucumbers, chopped
1 avocado, peeled and pitted
Salt and black pepper to taste
1 ½ cups water

½ cup Greek yogurt
1 tbsp cilantro, chopped
2 limes, juiced
1 garlic clove, minced
2 tomatoes, chopped
1 chopped avocado

Directions and Total Time: approx. 10 min + cooling time

Pour all the ingredients, except for the tomatoes and avocado, into the food processor. Puree for 2 minutes or until smooth. Pour the mixture into a bowl. Cover and refrigerate for 2 hours. Top with avocado and tomatoes.

Per serving: Cal 343; Fat 26g; Net Carbs 5.3g; Protein 10g

Zuppa Toscana with Kale

Ingredients for 4 servings

2 cups chicken broth
1 tbsp olive oil
¼ cup heavy cream
1 cup kale
3 oz pancetta, chopped
1 parsnip, chopped

1 garlic clove, minced
Salt and black pepper, to taste
¼ tsp red pepper flakes
½ onion, chopped
1 lb hot Italian sausage, sliced
2 tbsp Parmesan, grated

Directions and Total Time: approx. 40 minutes

Warm the olive oil in a pan over medium heat. Stir-fry the garlic, onion, pancetta, and sausage for 5 minutes. Pour in chicken broth and parsnip and simmer for 15-20 minutes. Stir in the remaining ingredients, except for the Parmesan cheese, and cook for about 5 minutes. Serve topped with Parmesan cheese.

Per serving: Cal 543; Fat 45g; Net Carbs 5.6g; Protein 24g

Awesome Chicken Enchilada Soup

Ingredients for 4 servings

½ lb boneless, skinless chicken thighs
2 tbsp coconut oil
¾ cup red enchilada sauce
1 onion, chopped
3 oz canned diced green chilis
1 avocado, sliced

1 cup cheddar, shredded
1 pickled jalapeño, chopped
½ cup sour cream
1 tomato, diced

Directions and Total Time: approx. 35 minutes

Put a large pan over medium heat. Add coconut oil and warm. Place in the chicken and cook until browned on the outside. Stir in onion, jalapeño, and green chilis and cook for 2 minutes. Pour in 4 cups of water and enchilada sauce. Allow simmering for 20 minutes until the chicken is cooked through. Spoon the soup on a serving bowl and top with the cheese, sour cream, tomato, and avocado.

Per serving: Cal 643; Fat 44g; Net Carbs 9.7g; Protein 48g

Cauliflower Soup with Crispy Bacon

Ingredients for 4 servings

2 tbsp olive oil
1 onion, chopped
¼ celery root, grated
10 oz cauliflower florets

Salt and black pepper to taste
1 cup almond milk
1 cup white cheddar, shredded
2 oz bacon, cut into strips

Directions and Total Time: approx. 25 minutes

Heat a skillet over medium heat and fry the bacon for 5 minutes until crispy; set aside on a paper towel–lined plate. In the same skillet, add warm the olive oil and sauté the onion for 3 minutes until fragrant. Include the cauliflower florets and celery root and sauté for 3 minutes until slightly softened. Add 3 cups of water and season with salt and pepper. Bring to a boil, and then reduce the heat to low. Cover and cook for 10 minutes. Puree the soup with an immersion blender until the ingredients are evenly combined and stir in the almond milk and cheese until it melts. Adjust taste with salt and black pepper. Top with crispy bacon and serve hot.

Per serving: Cal 323; Fat 27g; Net Carbs 7.6g; Protein 23g

Reuben Soup

Ingredients for 4 servings

1 parsnip, chopped
1 onion, diced
3 cups beef stock
1 celery stalk, diced
1 garlic clove, minced
1 cup heavy cream

½ cup sauerkraut, shredded
½ lb corned beef, chopped
2 tbsp lard
½ cup mozzarella, shredded
Salt and black pepper, to taste
Chopped chives for garnish

Directions and Total Time: approx. 30 minutes

Melt the lard in a large pot. Add parsnip, onion, garlic, and celery and fry for 3 minutes until tender.

Pour the beef stock over and stir in sauerkraut, salt, and black pepper. Bring to a boil. Reduce the heat to low, and add the corned beef. Cook for about 15 minutes, adjust the seasoning. Stir in heavy cream and cheese and cook for 1 minute. Garnish with chives to serve.

Per serving: Cal 463; Fat 41g; Net Carbs 5.8g; Protein 21g

Mushroom Cream Soup with Herbs

Ingredients for 4 servings

12 oz white mushrooms, chopped
1 onion, chopped
½ cup heavy cream
¼ cup butter
1 tsp thyme leaves, chopped
1 tsp parsley leaves, chopped

1 tsp cilantro leaves, chopped
2 garlic cloves, minced
4 cups vegetable broth
Salt and black pepper to taste

Directions and Total Time: approx. 25 minutes

Melt the butter in a large pot over high heat and cook the onion and garlic for 3 minutes until tender. Add mushrooms, salt, and pepper and stir-fry for 5 minutes. Pour in the broth and bring to a boil. Reduce heat and simmer for 10 minutes. Puree soup with a hand blender until smooth. Stir in heavy cream. Garnish with herbs.

Per serving: Cal 292; Fat 25.2g; Net Carbs 3.4g; Protein 8g

Curried Shrimp & Green Bean Soup

Ingredients for 4 servings

1 onion, chopped
2 tbsp red curry paste
2 tbsp butter
1 lb jumbo shrimp, deveined
2 tsp ginger-garlic puree

1 cup coconut milk
Salt and chili pepper to taste
1 bunch green beans, halved
1 tbsp cilantro, chopped

Directions and Total Time: approx. 20 minutes

Add the shrimp to melted butter in a saucepan over medium heat, season with salt and pepper, and cook until they are opaque, 2-3 minutes. Remove to a plate. Add in the ginger-garlic puree, onion, and red curry paste and sauté for 2 minutes until fragrant.

Stir in the coconut milk and add the shrimp, salt, chili pepper, and green beans. Cook for 4 minutes. Reduce the heat to a simmer and cook an additional 3 minutes, occasionally stirring. Adjust the taste with salt. Fetch the soup into serving bowls and sprinkle with cilantro.

Per serving: Cal 351; Fat 32g; Net Carbs 3.2g; Protein 7.7g

Hearty Vegetable Soup

Ingredients for 4 servings

2 tsp olive oil	1 cup spinach, torn into pieces
1 onion, chopped	Salt and black pepper, to taste
1 garlic clove, minced	2 thyme sprigs, chopped
½ celery stalk, chopped	½ tsp dried rosemary
1 cup mushrooms, sliced	3 cups vegetable stock
½ head broccoli, chopped	1 tomato, chopped
½ carrot, sliced	½ cup almond milk

Directions and Total Time: approx. 35 minutes

Heat olive oil in a saucepan. Add onion, celery, garlic, and carrot and sauté until translucent, stirring occasionally, about 5 minutes. Place in the mushrooms, broccoli, salt, rosemary, tomatoes, pepper, thyme, and vegetable stock. Simmer the mixture for 15 minutes while the lid is slightly open. Stir in almond milk and spinach and cook for 5 more minutes. Serve.

Per serving: Cal 167; Fat 6.2g; Net Carbs 7.9g; Protein 3.2g

Tomato Cream Soup with Basil

Ingredients for 4 servings

1 carrot, chopped	14 oz canned tomatoes
2 tbsp olive oil	1 tsp fresh basil leaves
1 onion, diced	Salt and black pepper to taste
1 garlic clove, minced	1 cup crème fraîche
¼ cup raw cashew nuts, diced	

Directions and Total Time: approx. 25 minutes

Warm olive oil in a pot over medium heat and sauté the onion, carrot, and garlic for 4 minutes until softened. Stir in the tomatoes and 2 cups of water and season with salt and black pepper. Cover and bring to simmer for 10 minutes until thoroughly cooked. Puree the ingredients with an immersion blender. Adjust to taste and stir in the crème fraîche and cashew nuts. Serve topped with basil.

Per serving: Cal 253; Fat 23g; Net Carbs 6g; Protein 4g

Sausage & Turnip Soup

Ingredients for 4 servings

3 turnips, chopped	2 cups vegetable broth
2 celery sticks, chopped	½ cup sour cream
2 tbsp butter	3 green onions, chopped
1 tbsp olive oil	Salt and black pepper, to taste
1 pork sausage, sliced	

Directions and Total Time: approx. 40 minutes

Sauté green onions in melted butter over medium heat until soft and golden, about 3 minutes. Add celery and turnip, and cook for another 5 minutes. Pour the vegetable broth and 2 cups of water over. Bring to a simmer and cook for about 20 minutes until the vegetables are tender. Remove from heat. Puree the soup with a hand blender until smooth. Add sour cream and adjust the seasoning. Warm the olive oil in a skillet. Add the pork sausage and cook for 5 minutes. Serve the soup topped with pork sausage.

Per serving: Cal 275; Fat 23.1g; Net Carbs 6.g; Protein 7.4g

Cauliflower Cheese Soup

Ingredients for 4 servings

½ head cauliflower, chopped	1 ½ tbsp flaxseed meal
2 tbsp coconut oil	1 ½ cups coconut milk
½ cup leeks, chopped	6 oz Monterey Jack, shredded
1 celery stalk, chopped	Salt and black pepper, to taste
1 serrano pepper, chopped	Fresh parsley, chopped
1 tsp garlic puree	

Directions and Total Time: approx. 25 minutes

In a deep pan over medium heat, melt the coconut oil and sauté the serrano pepper, celery, and leeks until soft, about 5 minutes. Add in coconut milk, garlic puree, cauliflower, 2 cups of water, and flaxseed meal.

While covered partially, allow simmering for 10 minutes or until cooked through. Whizz with an immersion blender until smooth. Fold in the shredded cheese, and stir to ensure the cheese is completely melted and you have a homogenous mixture. Season with pepper and salt to taste. Decorate with parsley and serve warm.

Per serving: Cal 312; Fat 16g; Net Carbs 7.1g; Protein 13g

Cheese Cream Soup with Chicken

Ingredients for 4 servings

2 cups cooked and shredded chicken	
1 carrot, chopped	2 tbsp cilantro, chopped
1 onion, chopped	1/3 cup buffalo sauce
3 tbsp butter	½ cup cream cheese
4 cups chicken broth	Salt and black pepper, to taste

Directions and Total Time: approx. 20 minutes

In a skillet over medium heat, warm butter and sauté carrot and onion until tender, about 5 minutes. Add the chicken and broth and heat until hot but do not bring to a boil. Season with salt and pepper. Stir in buffalo sauce and cream cheese and cook until heated through, about 2-3 minutes Serve garnished with cilantro.

Per serving: Cal 487; Fat 41g; Net Carbs 7.2g; Protein 16g

Cheesy Chicken Soup with Spinach

Ingredients for 4 servings

2 tbsp olive oil	1 cup spinach
1 onion, chopped	4 cups chicken broth
2 garlic cloves, minced	1 cup cheddar, shredded
1 carrot, chopped	½ tsp chili powder
1 celery stalk, chopped	½ tsp ground cumin
1 chicken breast, cubed	Salt and black pepper, to taste

Directions and Total Time: approx. 45 minutes

Warm the olive oil in a pot over medium heat and sauté chicken for 2-3 minutes. Add and stir-fry the onion, garlic, celery, and carrot for 5 minutes or until the vegetables are tender. Season with chili powder, cumin, salt, and pepper. Add the chicken broth and bring to a boil; cook for 15-20 minutes. Stir in in spinach and cook for 5-6 minutes until wilted. Top with cheddar cheese.

Per serving: Cal 351; Fat 22g; Net Carbs 4.3g; Protein 22g

Zucchini & Leek Turkey Soup

Ingredients for 4 servings

2 cups turkey meat, cooked and chopped
1 onion, chopped
1 garlic clove, minced
3 celery stalks, chopped
2 leeks, chopped
2 tbsp butter
4 cups chicken stock
Salt and black pepper, to taste
¼ cup fresh parsley, chopped
1 large zucchini, spiralized

Directions and Total Time: approx. 40 minutes

Melt the butter in a pot over medium heat. Place the leeks, celery, onion, and garlic and cook for 5 minutes. Add in the turkey meat, black pepper, salt, and stock, and cook for 20 minutes. Stir in the zucchini and cook for 5 minutes. Serve in bowls sprinkled with parsley.

Per serving: Cal 312; Fat 13g; Net Carbs 4.3g; Protein 16g

Tomato Soup with Parmesan Croutons

Ingredients for 6 servings

Parmesan Croutons
4 tbsp butter, softened
4 tbsp grated Parmesan
3 egg whites
1 ¼ cups almond flour
2 tsp baking powder
5 tbsp psyllium husk powder

Tomato Soup
3 tbsp olive oil
2 lb fresh ripe tomatoes
4 cloves garlic, peeled only
1 small white onion, diced
1 red bell pepper, diced
1 cup coconut cream
½ tsp dried rosemary
½ tsp dried oregano
Salt and black pepper to taste

Directions and Total Time: approx. 1 hour 25 minutes

Preheat oven to 350 F. Line a baking sheet with wax paper. In a bowl, combine almond flour, baking powder, and psyllium husk powder. Mix in the egg whites. Whisk for 30 seconds until combined but not overly mixed. Form 8 flat pieces out of the dough. Place on the baking sheet while leaving enough room between each to allow rising. Bake for 30 minutes. Let the croutons cool. Break into halves. Mix the butter with Parmesan cheese. Spread the mixture in the inner parts of the croutons. Bake for 5 minutes.

In a baking dish, add tomatoes, garlic, onion, bell pepper, and drizzle with olive oil. Roast vegetables in the oven for 25 minutes and after broil for 4 minutes. Transfer to a blender and add in coconut cream, rosemary, oregano, salt, and pepper. Puree until smooth. Top with croutons.

Per serving: Cal 429; Fat 41g; Net Carbs 6g; Protein 11g

Creamy Coconut Soup with Chicken

Ingredients for 4 servings

3 tbsp butter
1 onion, chopped
2 chicken breasts, chopped
Salt and black pepper, to taste
½ cup coconut cream
¼ cup celery, chopped

Directions and Total Time: approx. 25 minutes

Warm the butter in a pot over medium heat. Sauté the onion and celery for 3 minutes until tender. Stir in chicken, 4 cups of water, salt, and pepper. Cook for 15 minutes. Stir in coconut cream. Serve warm.

Per serving: Cal 394; Fat 24g; Net Carbs 6.1g; Protein 29g

Cream of Cauliflower & Leek Soup

Ingredients for 4 servings

4 cups vegetable broth
16 oz cauliflower florets
1 celery stalk, chopped
1 onion, chopped
1 cup leeks, chopped
2 tbsp butter
1 tbsp olive oil
1 cup heavy cream
½ tsp red pepper flakes

Directions and Total Time: approx. 45 minutes

Warm butter and olive oil in a pot set over medium heat and sauté onion, leeks, and celery for 5 minutes. Stir in the broth and cauliflower and bring to a boil; simmer for 30 minutes. Transfer the mixture to an immersion blender and puree; add in the heavy cream and stir. Decorate with red pepper flakes and serve.

Per serving: Cal 255; Fat 21g; Net Carbs 5.3g; Protein 4.4g

Broccoli & Spinach Soup

Ingredients for 4 servings

2 tbsp butter
1 onion, chopped
1 garlic clove, minced
2 heads broccoli, cut in florets
2 stalks celery, chopped
4 cups vegetable broth
1 cup baby spinach
Salt and black pepper to taste
1 tbsp basil, chopped
Parmesan, shaved to serve

Directions and Total Time: approx. 25 minutes

Melt the butter in a saucepan over medium heat. Sauté the garlic and onion for 3 minutes until softened. Mix in the broccoli and celery and cook for 4 minutes until slightly tender. Pour in the broth, bring to a boil, then reduce the heat to medium-low, and simmer covered for about 5 minutes.

Drop in the spinach to wilt, adjust the seasonings, and cook for 4 minutes. Ladle soup into serving bowls. Serve with a sprinkle of grated Parmesan cheese and basil.

Per serving: Cal 123; Fat 11g; Net Carbs 3.2g; Protein 1.8g

Cream of Roasted Jalapeño Soup

Ingredients for 4 servings

2 tbsp melted butter
1 jalapeño pepper, halved
6 green bell peppers, halved
1 bulb garlic, halved, not peeled
6 tomatoes, halved
3 cups vegetable broth
½ cup heavy cream
3 tbsp grated Parmesan
2 tbsp chopped chives
Salt and black pepper to taste

Directions and Total Time: approx. 45 min + cooling time

Preheat oven to 350 F. Arrange bell peppers, jalapeño pepper, and garlic on a baking pan and roast for 15 minutes. Add in tomatoes and roast for 15 minutes. Let cool. Peel the skins and place them in a blender.

Add salt, pepper, butter, vegetable broth, and heavy cream; puree until smooth. Transfer to a pot over medium heat and cook for 3-4 minutes. Serve into bowls sprinkled with Parmesan cheese and chives.

Per serving: Cal 191; Net Carbs 8.7g; Fat 9g; Protein 5.3g

POULTRY

Rosemary Chicken with Avocado Sauce

Ingredients for 2 servings

Sauce

¼ cup mayonnaise	1 tbsp lemon juice
1 avocado, pitted	Salt to taste

Chicken

2 tbsp olive oil	Salt and black pepper to taste
2 chicken breasts	½ cup rosemary, chopped

Directions and Total Time: approx. 35 minutes

Mash the avocado with a fork in a bowl. Add in mayonnaise, lemon juice, and salt; stir to combine. Warm the olive oil in a skillet over medium heat. Season the chicken with salt and pepper and fry for 4 minutes per side until golden brown. Remove the chicken to a plate.

Pour the ¼ cup of warm water into the same skillet and add the rosemary. Bring to a boil, reduce the heat, and simmer for 3 minutes. Add the chicken, cover, and cook for 10-15 minutes until the liquid has reduced and the chicken is cooked. Dish chicken into plates and spoon the avocado sauce over. Serve and enjoy!

Per serving: Cal 406; Fat 34g; Net Carbs 3.9g; Protein 22g

Stuffed Chicken Breasts

Ingredients for 2 servings

2 tbsp butter	Salt and black pepper, to taste
2 chicken breasts	1 tsp dried oregano
1 cup baby spinach	2 cucumbers, spiralized
1 carrot, shredded	2 tbsp olive oil
1 tomato, chopped	1 tbsp rice vinegar
¼ cup goat cheese	1 tbsp fresh dill, chopped

Directions and Total Time: approx. 60 minutes

Preheat oven to 390 F. Lightly grease a baking dish with cooking spray. Place a pan over medium heat. Melt half of the butter and sauté spinach, carrot, and tomato until tender, about 5 minutes. Season with salt and pepper. Transfer to a medium bowl and let cool for 10 minutes.

Add in the goat cheese and oregano, stir, and set aside. Cut the chicken breasts lengthwise and stuff with the cheese mixture. Set into the baking dish. Season with salt and pepper and brush with the remaining butter. Bake until cooked through for 20-30 minutes.

Arrange the cucumbers on a serving platter and toss with dill, salt, black pepper, olive oil, and vinegar to coat. Serve with the stuffed chicken.

Per serving: Cal 621; Fat 46g; Net Carbs 7.5g; Protein 41g

Turnip Greens & Artichoke Chicken

Ingredients for 2 servings

4 oz canned artichoke hearts, chopped

4 oz cream cheese	
2 chicken breasts, sliced	½ tbsp onion powder
1 cup turnip greens	½ tbsp garlic powder
¼ cup Pecorino cheese, grated	Salt and black pepper to taste
	2 oz Monterrey Jack, shredded

Directions and Total Time: approx. 40 minutes

Line a baking dish with parchment paper and arrange the chicken slices on the bottom. Season with pepper and salt. Set in the oven at 350 F and bake for 20-25 minutes.

In a bowl, combine the remaining ingredients and mix well. Remove the chicken from the oven and spread over the artichokes. Top with Monterrey cheese and bake for 5 more minutes. Serve warm.

Per serving: Cal 443; Fat 25g; Net Carbs 4.2g; Protein 34g

Cheesy Pinwheels with Chicken

Ingredients for 2 servings

2 tbsp ghee	¼ cup whipping cream
1 garlic clove, minced	½ cup mozzarella, grated
1/3 lb chicken breasts, cubed	¼ cup fresh cilantro, chopped
1 tsp creole seasoning	Salt and black pepper, to taste
1/3 red onion, chopped	4 oz cream cheese
1 tomato, chopped	5 eggs
½ cup chicken stock	A pinch of garlic powder

Directions and Total Time: approx. 40 minutes

Season the chicken with creole seasoning. Heat a pan over medium heat and warm 1 tbsp ghee. Add chicken and cook each side for 2 minutes; remove to a plate.

Melt the rest of the ghee and stir in garlic and tomato; cook for 4 minutes. Return the chicken to the pan and pour in stock; cook for 15 minutes. Place in whipping cream, red onion, salt, mozzarella cheese, and black pepper; cook for 2 minutes.

In a blender, combine cream cheese with garlic powder, salt, eggs, and black pepper and pulse until well blended. Place the mixture onto a lined baking sheet and bake in the preheated oven for 10 minutes at 320 F. Allow the cheese to cool down, place on a cutting board, roll, and slice into medium slices. Arrange the slices on a plate and top with chicken mixture. Sprinkle with cilantro to serve.

Per serving: Cal 463; Fat 36g; Net Carbs 6.3g; Protein 35g

Thyme Chicken with Mushrooms & Turnip

Ingredients for 4 servings

3 cups mixed mushrooms, teared up

2 tbsp olive oil	2 cloves garlic, minced
4 tbsp butter, melted	4 sprigs thyme, chopped
1 lb chicken breasts, sliced	1 lemon, juiced
4 tbsp white wine	Salt and black pepper to taste
1 turnip, sliced	2 tbsp Dijon mustard

Directions and Total Time: approx. 50 minutes

Preheat oven to 420 F. Arrange the turnips on a baking sheet, drizzle with a little oil, and bake for 15 minutes. In a bowl, evenly mix the chicken, roasted turnips, mushrooms, garlic, thyme, lemon juice, salt, pepper, and mustard. Share the chicken mixture into 4 large sheets of aluminum foil, sprinkle with white wine, olive oil, and butter. Seal the edges to form packets. Put on a baking tray and bake the chicken for 25 minutes. Serve warm.

Per serving: Cal 364; Fat 16g; Net Carbs 4.6g; Protein 25g

Paprika Chicken & Pancetta in a Skillet

Ingredients for 2 servings

1 tbsp olive oil
5 pancetta strips, chopped
1/3 cup Dijon mustard
Salt and black pepper to taste
1 onion, chopped
1 cup chicken stock
2 chicken breasts
¼ tsp sweet paprika
2 tbsp oregano, chopped

Directions and Total Time: approx. 35 minutes

In a bowl, combine the paprika, black pepper, salt, and mustard. Rub the mixture onto the chicken breasts.

Heat the olive oil in a skillet over medium heat. Add the pancetta and cook for about 3-4 minutes; remove to a plate. To the pancetta fat, add the chicken breasts and cook for 2 minutes per side. Place in the stock, black pepper, pancetta, salt, and onion. Simmer for 15-20 minutes. Sprinkle with oregano and serve.

Per serving: Cal 323; Fat 21g; Net Carbs 4.6g; Protein 24g

Green Bean & Broccoli Chicken Stir-Fry

Ingredients for 2 servings

2 chicken breasts, cut into strips
2 tbsp olive oil
1 tsp red pepper flakes
1 tsp onion powder
1 tbsp fresh ginger, grated
¼ cup tamari sauce
½ tsp garlic powder
½ cup water
½ cup xylitol
4 oz green beans, chopped
½ tsp xanthan gum
½ cup green onions, chopped
10 oz broccoli florets

Directions and Total Time: approx. 45 minutes

Steam the green beans and broccoli for 5-6 minutes until it is crisp-tender but still vibrant green; set aside.

Warm the olive oil in a pan over medium heat and cook the chicken and ginger for 4 minutes. Stir in the remaining ingredients and cook for 15 minutes. Return the green beans and broccoli and cook for 6 minutes. Serve.

Per serving: Cal 411; Fat 25g; Net Carbs 6.2g; Protein 28g

Zucchini & Bell Pepper Chicken Gratin

Ingredients for 2 servings

1 red bell pepper, sliced
1 zucchini, chopped
Salt and black pepper, to taste
1 tsp garlic powder
1 tbsp olive oil
2 chicken breasts, sliced
1 tomato, chopped
½ tsp dried oregano
½ tsp dried basil
½ cup mozzarella, shredded

Directions and Total Time: approx. 40 minutes

Coat the chicken with salt, black pepper and garlic powder. Warm olive oil in a skillet over medium heat and add in the chicken slices. Cook until golden and remove to a baking dish. To the same pan, add the zucchini, tomato, bell pepper, basil, oregano, and salt and cook for 2 minutes. Spread the mixture over the chicken. Bake in the oven at 360 F for 20 minutes. Sprinkle the mozzarella over the chicken, return to the oven, and bake for 5 minutes until the cheese is melted and bubbling. Serve.

Per serving: Cal 467; Fat 23g; Net Carbs 6.2g; Protein 45g

Marinated Fried Chicken

Ingredients for 2 servings

2 tbsp olive oil
2 chicken breasts, cut into strips
½ cup pork rinds, crushed
8 oz jarred pickle juice
1 egg

Directions and Total Time: approx. 15 min + cooling time

Cover the chicken with pickle juice in a bowl and refrigerate for 12 hours while covered. Whisk the egg in a bowl, and place the pork rinds in a separate bowl. Dip the chicken pieces in the egg, then in the pork rinds. Ensure they are well coated. Set a pan over medium heat and warm the olive oil. Fry the chicken for 3 minutes on each side, remove to paper towels, and drain the excess grease. Serve warm with homemade ketchup if desired.

Per serving: Cal 393; Fat 16g; Net Carbs 3.1g; Protein 21g

Mediterranean Stuffed Chicken Breasts

Ingredients for 2 servings

1 tbsp olive oil
1 cup spinach, chopped
2 chicken breasts
Salt and black pepper, to taste
½ cup cream cheese, softened
½ cup goat cheese, crumbled
1 garlic clove, minced
½ cup white wine
1 tbsp rosemary, chopped

Directions and Total Time: approx. 35 minutes

Wilt the spinach in a saucepan with a half cup of water. Drain and mix in a bowl with the goat cheese, cream cheese, salt, garlic, and black pepper. Cut a pocket in each chicken breast and stuff with the spinach mixture. Preheat oven to 400 F. Set a pan over medium heat and warm oil, add the stuffed chicken, and cook each side for 5 minutes. Transfer to a greased baking tray and drizzle with white wine and 2 tablespoons of water. Bake in the oven for 20 minutes until no more pink. When ready, slice in half and serve sprinkled with rosemary.

Per serving: Cal 305; Fat 12g; Net Carbs 4g; Protein 23g

Pancetta & Cheese Stuffed Chicken

Ingredients for 2 servings

4 slices pancetta
2 tbsp olive oil
2 chicken breasts
1 garlic clove, minced
1 shallot, finely chopped
2 tbsp dried oregano
4 oz mascarpone cheese
1 lemon, zested
Salt and black pepper to taste

Directions and Total Time: approx. 35 minutes

Heat the oil in a small skillet and sauté the garlic and shallots for 3 minutes. Stir in salt, black pepper, and lemon zest. Transfer to a bowl and let it cool. Stir in the mascarpone cheese and oregano. Score a pocket in each chicken's breast, fill the holes with the cheese mixture and cover with the cut-out chicken. Wrap each breast with 2 pancetta slices and secure the ends with toothpicks. Lay the chicken on a greased baking sheet. Cook in the oven for 20 minutes at 380 F. Serve warm.

Per serving: Cal 643; Fat 45g; Net Carbs 6.2g; Protein 53g

Chicken Breasts with Creamy Kale Sauce

Ingredients for 2 servings

2 chicken breasts
1 cup heavy cream
2 tbsp butter
Salt and black pepper, to taste
1 cup kale
1 tsp fresh sage

Directions and Total Time: approx. 20 minutes

Season the chicken with salt and pepper. Melt the butter in a pan over medium heat and cook the chicken breasts for 7-8 minutes, flipping once. Transfer to a flat surface, let cool for a few minutes, and slice.

To the same pan, add the heavy cream and cook for 2 minutes. Add in kale and cook for 2-3 more minutes until wilted. Arrange the chicken on a platter and drizzle over the sauce. Sprinkle with sage and serve.

Per serving: Cal 591; Fat 44g; Net Carbs 0.1g; Protein 43g

Juicy Chicken with Broccoli & Pine Nuts

Ingredients for 4 servings

2 tbsp olive oil
2 chicken breasts, cut into strips
2 tbsp Worcestershire sauce
2 tsp balsamic vinegar
2 tsp xanthan gum
1 lemon, juiced
1 cup pine nuts
2 cups broccoli florets
1 onion, thinly sliced
Salt and black pepper to taste
1 tbsp cilantro, chopped

Directions and Total Time: approx. 25 minutes

In a dry pan over medium heat, toast the pine nuts for 2 minutes until golden brown; set aside. In the pan, warm olive oil and sauté the onion for 4 minutes until soft and browned; remove to the nuts.

In a bowl, mix the Worcestershire sauce, balsamic vinegar, lemon juice, and xanthan gum; set aside. Add the chicken to the pan and cook for 4 minutes. Add in the broccoli, salt, and black pepper. Stir-fry and pour in the lemon mixture. Cook the sauce for 4 minutes and add in the pine nuts and onion. Stir once more and cook for 1 minute. Serve the chicken stir-fry with cilantro.

Per serving: Cal 286; Fat 10g; Net Carbs 3.4g; Protein 17g

Baked Chicken Nuggets

Ingredients for 2 servings

2 tbsp ranch dressing
½ cup almond flour
1 egg
2 tbsp garlic powder
2 chicken breasts, cubed
Salt and black pepper, to taste
1 tbsp butter, melted

Directions and Total Time: approx. 30 minutes

Preheat oven to 400 F. Grease a baking dish with butter. In a bowl, combine salt, garlic powder, almond flour, and black pepper and stir. In a separate bowl, beat the egg. Dredge the chicken cubes to the egg, then in the flour mixture. Cook in the oven for 18-20 minutes, turning halfway through, until golden and crispy. Remove to paper towels, drain the excess grease and serve with ranch dressing, if desired.

Per serving: Cal 473; Fat 31g; Net Carbs 7.6g; Protein 43g

Peanut-Crusted Chicken

Ingredients for 2 servings

1 egg, beaten
Salt and black pepper to taste
3 tbsp canola oil
1 ½ cups ground peanuts
2 chicken breast halves
Lemon slices for garnish

Directions and Total Time: approx. 25 minutes

Season the chicken with salt and pepper. Dip in the egg and then in ground peanuts. Warm the canola oil in a pan over medium heat and brown the chicken for 2 minutes per side. Remove to a baking sheet, set in the preheated to 360 F oven, and bake for 10 minutes. Serve topped with lemon slices.

Per serving: Cal 634; Fat 51g; Net Carbs 4.7g; Protein 46g

Chicken Dippers with Homemade Ketchup

Ingredients for 4 servings

1 lb chicken breasts, cut into strips
14 oz canned tomatoes, diced
1 tbsp tomato paste
½ tbsp xylitol
1 tbsp balsamic vinegar
1 cup tomato sauce
1 tbsp basil, chopped
½ cup almond flour
¼ cup Parmesan, grated
½ tsp garlic powder
1 tsp dried parsley
½ tsp dried thyme
Salt and black pepper to taste
1 egg, beaten in a bowl
2 tbsp olive oil

Directions and Total Time: approx. 35 minutes

Place a saucepan over medium heat. Add the tomatoes, tomato paste, xylitol, tomato sauce, salt, pepper, and balsamic vinegar and bring to a boil. Cook for 10-15 minutes, stirring frequently until thickened. Adjust the seasoning. Top the ketchup with basil and set aside.

In a bowl, combine the almond flour, parsley, Parmesan, pepper, garlic powder, thyme, and salt. Dip the chicken strips in the egg and then in the almond flour mixture.

Heat a pan over medium heat and warm the olive oil. Fry the chicken until golden, about 4-6 minutes. Remove to paper towels to soak the excess oil. Serve with ketchup.

Per serving: Cal 336; Fat 21g; Net Carbs 7.7g; Protein 25g

Winter Chicken with Vegetables

Ingredients for 2 servings

2 tbsp olive oil
2 cups whipping cream
1 lb chicken breasts, chopped
1 onion, chopped
1 carrot, chopped
2 cups chicken stock
Salt and black pepper, to taste
1 bay leaf
1 turnip, chopped
1 parsnip, chopped
1 cup green beans, chopped
2 tsp fresh thyme, chopped

Directions and Total Time: approx. 40 minutes

Heat a pan over medium heat and warm the olive oil. Sauté the onion for 3 minutes, pour in the stock, carrot, turnip, parsnip, chicken, and bay leaf. Bring to a boil and simmer for 20 minutes. Add in the green beans and cook for 7 minutes. Discard the bay leaf, stir in the whipping cream, adjust the taste and scatter with thyme to serve.

Per serving: Cal 483; Fat 32g; Net Carbs 6.9g; Protein 33g

Indian Chicken with Mushrooms

Ingredients for 4 servings

1 lb chicken breasts, sliced lengthwise

2 tbsp butter	2 cups heavy whipping cream
1 tbsp olive oil	1 tbsp cilantro, chopped
1 cup mushrooms	Salt and black pepper to taste

Garam masala

1 tsp ground cumin	1 tsp ginger
2 tsp ground coriander	1 tsp paprika
1 tsp ground cardamom	1 tsp cayenne, ground
1 tsp turmeric	1 pinch ground nutmeg

Directions and Total Time: approx. 35 minutes

Preheat oven to 370 F. In a bowl, mix all the garam masala spices. Coat the chicken with the mixture.

Heat the olive oil and butter in a frying pan over medium heat, and brown the chicken for 3-5 minutes per side. Transfer to a baking dish. In a bowl, mix the heavy cream and mushrooms. Season with salt and pepper and pour over the chicken. Bake for 20 minutes until the mixture starts to bubble. Garnish with chopped cilantro to serve.

Per serving: Cal 553; Fat 49g; Net Carbs 4.5g; Protein 32g

Chili Chicken Kebab with Garlic Dressing

Ingredients for 4 servings

Skewers

2 tbsp olive oil	2 tbsp Swerve brown sugar
3 tbsp soy sauce, sugar-free	Chili pepper to taste
1 tbsp ginger paste	2 chicken breasts, cubed

Dressing

½ cup tahini	Salt and black pepper to taste
1 tbsp parsley, chopped	¼ cup warm water
1 garlic clove, minced	

Directions and Total Time: approx. 25 min + cooling time

To make the marinade, in a small bowl, whisk the soy sauce, ginger paste, Swerve brown sugar, chili pepper, and olive oil. Put the chicken in a zipper bag, pour the marinade over, seal and shake for an even coat. Marinate in the fridge for 2 hours.

Preheat a grill to high heat. Thread the chicken on skewers and cook for 10 minutes in total with three to four turnings to be golden brown. Transfer to a plate. Mix the dressing ingredients in a bowl. Serve the chicken skewers topped with the tahini dressing.

Per serving: Cal 410; Fat 32g; Net Carbs 4.8g; Protein 23g

Feta & Bacon Chicken

Ingredients for 4 servings

4 oz bacon, chopped	2 tbsp coconut oil
1 lb chicken breasts	4 oz feta cheese, crumbled
3 green onions, chopped	1 tbsp parsley

Directions and Total Time: approx. 25 minutes

Place a pan over medium heat the coconut oil. Add in the bacon and cook until crispy. Remove to paper towels, drain the grease, and crumble. To the same pan, add the chicken breasts and cook for 4-5 minutes.

Flip to the other side and cook for an additional 4-5 minutes. Transfer to a baking dish. Top with the green onions, set in the oven, turn on the broiler, and cook for 5 minutes at high temperature. Serve topped with bacon, feta cheese, and parsley. Enjoy!

Per serving: Cal 459; Fat 35g; Net Carbs 3.1g; Protein 32g

Cabbage & Broccoli Chicken Casserole

Ingredients for 4 servings

1 tbsp coconut oil, melted	1 cup mayonnaise
2 cups mozzarella, grated	1/3 cup chicken stock
½ head cabbage, shredded	Salt and black pepper, to taste
1 head broccoli, cut into florets	Juice of 1 lemon
1 lb chicken breasts, cubed	1 tbsp cilantro, chopped

Directions and Total Time: approx. 60 minutes

Coat a baking dish with coconut oil and set chicken pieces to the bottom. Top with the green cabbage and broccoli and sprinkle with half of mozzarella cheese.

In a bowl, combine the mayonnaise with black pepper, stock, lemon juice, and salt. Spread the mixture over the chicken, top with the rest of the mozzarella cheese, and cover with aluminum foil. Bake for 30 minutes in the oven at 350 F. Open aluminum foil and cook for 20 more minutes. Sprinkle with cilantro and serve.

Per serving: Cal 623; Fat 42g; Net Carbs 7.4g; Protein 52g

Fennel & Chicken Wrapped in Bacon

Ingredients for 4 servings

2 tbsp olive oil	½ lb fennel bulb, sliced
2 chicken breasts	2 tbsp lemon juice
Salt and black pepper to taste	2 tbsp cheddar cheese, grated
4 bacon slices	1 tbsp rosemary, chopped

Directions and Total Time: approx. 50 minutes

Preheat your grill to high heat. Brush the fennel slices with olive oil and season with salt and black pepper. Grill for 4-6 minutes, frequently turning until slightly golden. Remove to a plate and drizzle with lemon juice.

Pour over cheddar cheese so that it melts a little on contact with the hot fennel and forms a cheesy dressing. Preheat oven to 390 F. Season chicken breasts with salt and black pepper, and wrap 2 bacon slices around each chicken breast. Arrange on a baking sheet that is lined with parchment paper, drizzle with oil and bake for 25-30 minutes until bacon is brown and crispy. Serve with grilled fennel sprinkled with rosemary.

Per serving: Cal 487; Fat 39g; Net Carbs 5.2g; Protein 27g

Tomato & Cheese Chicken Chili

Ingredients for 4 servings

1 tbsp butter	1 tbsp chili powder
1 tbsp olive oil	1 tbsp cumin
1 lb chicken breasts, cubed	1 garlic clove, minced
½ onion, chopped	1 habanero pepper, minced
2 cups tomatoes, chopped	½ cup mozzarella, shredded
2 oz tomato puree	Salt and black pepper to taste

Directions and Total Time: approx. 40 minutes

Season the chicken with salt and black pepper. Set a large pan over medium heat and add the chicken. Cover with water and bring to a boil. Cook until no longer pink, about 10 minutes. Transfer the chicken to a flat surface to shred with forks; reserve the broth (about 2 cups). In a pot, pour the butter and olive oil and set over medium heat. Sauté onion and garlic until transparent, 3 minutes. Stir in the chicken, tomatoes, cumin, habanero pepper, tomato puree, and chili powder for 1-2 minutes. Adjust the seasoning and pour in the reserved broth; bring the mixture to a boil. Reduce heat to simmer for about 10 minutes. Top with mozzarella cheese and serve.

Per serving: Cal 322; Fat 17g; Net Carbs 6.2g; Protein 29g

Pan-Fried Chicken with Anchovy Tapenade

Ingredients for 2 servings

1 chicken breast, cut into 4 pieces
2 tbsp olive oil   1 garlic clove, minced

Tapenade
2 tbsp olive oil   Salt and black pepper to taste
1 cup black olives, pitted   ¼ cup fresh basil, chopped
1 oz anchovy fillets, rinsed   1 tbsp lemon juice
1 garlic clove, crushed

Directions and Total Time: approx. 20 minutes

Heat a pan over medium heat and add olive oil. Stir in the garlic and cook for 2 minutes. Place in the chicken pieces and cook each side for 4 minutes. Remove to a serving plate. Chop the black olives and anchovy and put them in a food processor. Add in olive oil, basil, lemon juice, salt, and black pepper, and blend well. Spoon the tapenade over the chicken and serve.

Per serving: Cal 522; Fat 37g; Net Carbs 5.3g; Protein 43g

Baked Zucchini with Chicken and Cheese

Ingredients for 4 servings

1 lb chicken breasts, cubed   1 tsp thyme
1 tbsp butter   Salt and black pepper to taste
1 tbsp olive oil   ½ cup cream cheese, softened
1 red bell pepper, chopped   ¼ cup mayonnaise
1 shallot, sliced   1 tbsp Worcestershire sauce
2 zucchinis, cubed   1 cup mozzarella, shredded
1 garlic clove, minced

Directions and Total Time: approx. 45 minutes

Set oven to 370 F. Heat the butter and olive oil in a pan over medium heat and add in the chicken. Cook until lightly browned, about 5 minutes. Place in shallot, zucchini cubes, black pepper, garlic, bell pepper, salt, and thyme. Cook for 5 minutes until tender; set aside.

In a bowl, mix the cream cheese, mayonnaise, and Worcestershire sauce. Stir in the chicken and sauteed vegetables. Place the mixture into a greased baking dish and bake for 20 minutes. Sprinkle with mozzarella cheese and bake until browned, about 5 minutes.

Per serving: Cal 488; Fat 38g; Net Carbs 5.2g; Protein 23g

Chicken Kabobs with Celery Root Chips

Ingredients for 2 servings

4 tbsp olive oil   1 tsp chili powder
2 chicken breasts, cubed   ¼ cup chicken broth
Salt and black pepper to taste   1 lb celery root, sliced
1 tsp dried oregano

Directions and Total Time: approx. 60 minutes

Preheat oven to 400 F. In a large bowl, mix half of the olive oil, oregano, chili powder, salt, black pepper and add the chicken. Toss to coat and set in the fridge for 10 minutes. Arrange the celery slices on a greased baking tray in an even layer, drizzle with the remaining olive oil, and sprinkle with salt and pepper. Bake for 10 minutes. Take the chicken from the refrigerator and thread it onto skewers. Place over the celery, pour in the chicken broth, then set in the oven for 30 minutes. Serve.

Per serving: Cal 365; Fat 23g; Net Carbs 4.6g; Protein 35g

Cheese & Mayo Topped Chicken Bake

Ingredients for 4 servings

½ cup Grana Padano cheese, grated
2 tbsp butter, melted   1 cup cottage cheese
1 lb chicken breasts, halved   ½ cup mayonnaise
Salt and black pepper, to taste   1 cup cheddar cheese, grated
¼ cup green chilies, chopped   ¼ cup pork skins, crushed
2 oz bacon, chopped   2 tbsp basil, chopped

Directions and Total Time: approx. 55 minutes

Preheat oven to 420 F. Coat the chicken with salt and black pepper and place in a greased baking dish. Pour in ½ cup of water and bake for 30 minutes. Cook the bacon in a pan over medium heat for 5 minutes until crispy. Remove to a bowl and let cool for few minutes. Stir in cottage cheese, ½ cup Grana Padano cheese, mayonnaise, chilies, and cheddar cheese. Spread the mixture over the chicken. Drizzle the melted butter over and sprinkle with the pork skins and remaining Grana Padano cheese. Bake in the oven for 5-10 minutes. Top with basil to serve.

Per serving: Cal 383; Fat 21g; Net Carbs 4.9g; Protein 2g

Chicken & Sausage Gumbo

Ingredients for 4 servings

1 sausage, sliced   2 tbsp garlic powder
2 chicken breasts, cubed   2 tbsp dry mustard
1 stick celery, chopped   1 tbsp chili powder
1 bay leaf   Salt and black pepper, to taste
1 bell pepper, chopped   2 tbsp cajun seasoning
1 onion, chopped   3 tbsp olive oil
1 cup tomatoes, chopped   1 tbsp sage, chopped
4 cups chicken broth

Directions and Total Time: approx. 40 minutes

Heat olive oil in a saucepan over medium heat. Add the sausage and chicken and cook for 5 minutes. Add the remaining ingredients, except for the sage, and bring to a boil. Simmer for 25 minutes. Serve sprinkled with sage.

Per serving: Cal 433; Fat 26g; Net Carbs 8.7g; Protein 36g

Greek-Style Baked Chicken

Ingredients for 4 servings

2 tbsp olive oil	3 tbsp xylitol
1 lb chicken breast halves	½ cup white wine
2 garlic cloves, minced	2 tomatoes, sliced
Salt and black pepper, to taste	4 oz feta cheese, sliced
1 cup chicken stock	2 tbsp dill, chopped

Directions and Total Time: approx. 40 minutes

Put a pan over medium heat and warm oil, add the chicken, season with black pepper and salt, and cook until brown, about 4-6 minutes. Stir in the xylitol, garlic, stock, and white wine, and cook for 10 minutes.

Remove to a lined baking sheet and arrange tomato and feta slices on top. Bake in the oven for 15 minutes at 380 F. Sprinkle with chopped dill and serve.

Per serving: Cal 322; Fat 15g; Net Carbs 3.4g; Protein 26g

Mediterranean Chicken

Ingredients for 4 servings

2 tbsp olive oil	1 tbsp capers
1 onion, chopped	1 tbsp oregano
4 chicken breasts	¼ cup white wine
4 garlic cloves, minced	1 cup tomatoes, chopped
Salt and black pepper, to taste	½ tsp red chili flakes
10 Kalamata olives, chopped	

Directions and Total Time: approx. 35 minutes

Brush the chicken with half of the olive oil and sprinkle with black pepper and salt. Heat a pan over high heat and cook the chicken for 2 minutes, flip to the other side, and cook for 2 more minutes. Transfer to a baking dish, add in the white wine and 2 tbsp of water. Bake in the oven at 380 F for 10-15 minutes. Remove to a serving plate.

In the same pan, warm the remaining oil over medium heat. Place in the onion, olives, capers, garlic, oregano, and chili flakes and cook for 1 minute. Stir in the tomatoes, black pepper, and salt and cook for 2 minutes. Sprinkle the sauce over the chicken breasts and serve.

Per serving: Cal 365; Fat 22g; Net Carbs 3.1g; Protein 23g

Oven-Baked Salami & Cheddar Chicken

Ingredients for 4 servings

1 tbsp olive oil	1 tsp dried oregano
1 ½ cups canned tomato sauce	4 oz cheddar cheese, sliced
1 lb chicken breasts, halved	1 tsp garlic powder
Salt and black pepper, to taste	2 oz salami, sliced

Directions and Total Time: approx. 40 minutes

Preheat oven to 380 F. In a bowl, combine oregano, garlic, salt, and pepper. Rub the chicken with the mixture.

Heat a pan with the olive oil over medium heat, add in the chicken and cook each side for 2 minutes. Remove to a baking dish. Top with the cheddar cheese, pour the tomato sauce over, and arrange the salami slices on top. Bake for 30 minutes. Serve warm and enjoy!

Per serving: Cal 417; Fat 25g; Net Carbs 5.2g; Protein 29g

Ham & Emmental Baked Chicken

Ingredients for 4 servings

1 lb chicken breasts, halved	¼ cup mozzarella, grated
Salt and black pepper, to taste	¼ tsp garlic powder
¼ cup mayonnaise	¼ tsp onion powder
1 tbsp Dijon mustard	Salt and black pepper
¼ tsp xylitol	4 oz ham, sliced
¼ cup pork rinds, crushed	2 oz Emmental cheese, sliced

Directions and Total Time: approx. 45 minutes

Preheat oven to 350 F. Season the chicken with garlic and onion powders, salt and pepper. In a bowl, mix mustard, mayonnaise, and xylitol. Take about ¼ of this mixture and spread over the chicken. Reserve the rest. Spread half of the pork rinds and half of the mozzarella cheese on the bottom of a greased baking dish.

Plce the chicken on top. Sprinkle with the remaining mozzarella cheese and pork rinds. Bake in the oven for about 25-30 minutes until the chicken is cooked completely. Take out from the oven and top with Emmental cheese and ham. Return to the oven and cook until golden brown. Serve warm. Enjoy!

Per serving: Cal 443; Fat 32g; Net Carbs 5.1g; Protein 31g

Chicken Pie with Bacon

Ingredients for 4 servings

3 tbsp butter	¾ cup crème fraîche
1 onion, chopped	½ cup chicken stock
4 oz bacon, sliced	1 lb chicken breasts, cubed
1 carrot, chopped	2 tbsp yellow mustard
3 garlic cloves, minced	¾ cup cheddar, shredded
Salt and black pepper, to taste	

Dough

1 egg	1 ½ cups mozzarella, shredded
¾ cup almond flour	1 tsp onion powder
3 tbsp cream cheese	Salt and black pepper, to taste

Directions and Total Time: approx. 50 minutes

Melt the butter in a pan over medium heat and sauté the onion, garlic, salt, black pepper, bacon, and carrot for 5 minutes. Add in the chicken and cook for 3 minutes. Stir in the crème fraîche, salt, mustard, black pepper, and stock and cook for 7 minutes. Stir in the cheddar cheese.

For the dough, combine mozzarella and cream cheeses and heat in a microwave for 1 minute. Stir in salt, almond flour, black pepper, onion powder, and egg. Knead the dough well, split into pieces, and flatten into circles. Set the mixture into ramekins, top with dough circles; cook in the oven at 370 F for 25 minutes.

Per serving: Cal 563; Fat 44g; Net Carbs 7.7g; Protein 36g

Cauliflower & Chicken Stir-Fry

Ingredients for 4 servings

1 large head cauliflower, cut into florets	
2 chicken breasts, sliced	1 yellow bell pepper, diced
2 tbsp olive oil	3 tbsp chicken broth
1 red bell pepper, diced	2 tbsp chopped parsley

Directions and Total Time: approx. 25 minutes

Warm olive oil in a skillet and brown the chicken until brown on all sides, 8 minutes. Transfer to a plate. Pour bell peppers into the pan and sauté until softened, 5 minutes. Add in cauliflower and broth and stir. Cover the pan and cook for 5 minutes or until cauliflower is tender. Mix in chicken and parsley. Serve immediately.

Per serving: Cal 339; Net Carbs 3.5g; Fat 21g; Protein 32g

Creamy Mushroom & White Wine Chicken

Ingredients for 4 servings

1 tbsp butter	2 cups chicken broth
1 tbsp olive oil	¼ cup white wine
1 lb chicken breasts, cubed	15 baby bella mushrooms
Salt and black pepper to taste	1 cup heavy cream
1 packet onion soup mix	2 tbsp parsley, chopped

Directions and Total Time: approx. 40 minutes

Add butter and olive oil in a saucepan and heat over medium heat. Season the chicken with salt and pepper, and brown on all sides for 6 minutes. Put on a plate.

In a bowl, stir the onion soup mix with chicken broth and white wine, and add to the saucepan. Simmer for 3 minutes and add the mushrooms and chicken. Cover and simmer for another 20 minutes. Stir in heavy cream and cook on low heat for 3 minutes. Garnish with parsley.

Per serving: Cal 432; Fat 35g; Net Carbs 3.2g; Protein 24g

Bacon Rolled Chicken Breasts

Ingredients for 4 servings

1 green onion, chopped	4 oz bacon, sliced
1 cup gorgonzola cheese	2 tomatoes, chopped
1 lb chicken breasts, halved	Salt and black pepper, to taste

Directions and Total Time: approx. 45 minutes

Preheat oven to 380 F. Flatten the chicken breasts with a a rolling pin. In a bowl, stir together the gorgonzola cheese, green onion, tomatoes, black pepper, and salt. Spread the mixture on the chicken breasts. Roll them up, and wrap each in a bacon slice. Place the wrapped chicken breasts in a greased baking dish and roast in the oven for 30 minutes. Serve.

Per serving: Cal 587; Fat 43g; Net Carbs 4.5g; Protein 35g

Baked Chicken Wrapped in Smoked Bacon

Ingredients for 2 servings

1 lb chicken breasts, flatten	½ tsp sage
1 tbsp olive oil	Salt and black pepper, to taste
1 tbsp fresh parsley, chopped	½ tsp smoked paprika
1 tsp garlic paste, chopped	2 oz smoked bacon, sliced

Directions and Total Time: approx. 40 minutes

Mix garlic paste, sage, smoked paprika, salt, and black pepper in a small bowl; rub onto chicken and roll fillets in the smoked bacon slices. Arrange on a greased with the olive oil baking dish and bake for 30 minutes at 390 F. Plate the chicken and serve sprinkled with fresh parsley.

Per serving: Cal 556; Fat 38g; Net Carbs 2.3g; Protein 51g

Chicken & Cauli Rice Collard Green Rolls

Ingredients for 4 servings

1 ½ lb chicken breasts, cubed	1 jalapeño pepper, chopped
8 collard leaves	1 cup cauliflower rice
2 tbsp avocado oil	2 tsp hot sauce
1 large yellow onion, chopped	¼ cup half-and-half
2 garlic cloves, minced	Salt and black pepper to taste

Directions and Total Time: approx. 25 minutes

Warm avocado oil in a deep skillet and sauté onion and garlic until softened, 3 minutes. Stir in jalapeño pepper, salt, and pepper. Mix in chicken and cook until no longer pink on all sides, 10 minutes. Add in cauliflower rice and hot sauce. Sauté until the cauliflower slightly softens, 3 minutes. Lay out the collards on a clean flat surface and spoon the curried mixture onto the middle part of the leaves, about 3 tbsp per leaf. Spoon half-and-half on top, wrap the leaves, and serve immediately.

Per serving: Cal 441; Net Carbs 1.8g; Fat 32g; Protein 41g

Pesto Chicken Cacciatore

Ingredients for 4 servings

2 lb chicken breasts, cubed	½ cup cream cheese, softened
3 tbsp butter	1 celery, chopped
½ lemon, juiced	¼ cup chopped tomatoes
3 tbsp basil pesto	1 lb radishes, sliced
¾ cup heavy cream	½ cup shredded Pepper Jack

Directions and Total Time: approx. 50 minutes

Preheat oven to 400 F. In a bowl, combine lemon juice, pesto, heavy cream, and cream cheese; set aside. Melt butter in a skillet and cook the chicken until no longer pink, 8 minutes. Transfer to a greased casserole and spread the pesto mixture on top. Top with celery, tomatoes, and radishes. Sprinkle Pepper Jack cheese on top. Bake for 30 minutes or until the cheese melts and golden brown on top. Serve warm and enjoy!

Per serving: Cal 671; Net Carbs 0.8g; Fat 47g; Protein 49g

Butternut Squash with Chicken & Cheese

Ingredients for 4 servings

2 tbsp olive oil	1 small butternut squash, sliced
1 lb chicken breasts, halved	Salt and black pepper, to taste
¼ tsp garlic powder	1 cup cottage cheese, shredded

Directions and Total Time: approx. 45 minutes

Preheat oven to 400 F. In a food processor, add the butternut squash and pulse until it resembles rice. Transfer to a kitchen towel to soak the excess liquid. Season the chicken breasts with pepper, garlic powder, and salt and drizzle with some olive oil. Transfer to a baking dish and bake for 30 minutes.

Heat the remaining olive oil in a pan over medium heat. Add the squash rice. Season and cook for 2 minutes, stirring frequently. Stir in half cup of water and continue cooking until the liquid evaporates. Remove to a plate. Mix with the cottage cheese. Top with chicken to serve.

Per serving: Cal 312; Fat 21g; Net Carbs 2.4g; Protein 28g

Chicken & Brussels Sprout Bake

Ingredients for 4 servings

1 ½ lb halved Brussels sprouts
1 lb chicken breasts, cubed
3 tbsp butter
5 garlic cloves, minced
1 ¼ cups coconut cream
2 cups grated cheddar
¼ cup grated Parmesan
Salt and black pepper to taste

Directions and Total Time: approx. 30 minutes

Preheat oven to 400 F. Season the chicken with salt and pepper. Melt the butter in a skillet and sauté chicken cubes for 6 minutes; remove to a plate. Pour the Brussels sprouts and garlic into the skillet and sauté until a nice color forms. Mix in coconut cream and simmer for 4 minutes. Mix in chicken cubes. Pour the sauté into a baking dish, sprinkle with cheddar and Parmesan cheeses. Bake for 10 minutes. Serve warm and enjoy!

Per serving: Cal 418; Net Carbs 7g; Fat 34g; Protein 13g

Chicken with Zoodles & Pine Nuts

Ingredients for 4 servings

2 lb chicken breasts, cut into strips
3 eggs, lightly beaten
5 garlic cloves, minced
¼ tsp pureed onion
2 tbsp avocado oil
¼ cup chicken broth
2 tbsp coconut aminos
1 tbsp white vinegar
½ cup chopped scallions
1 tsp red chili flakes
4 zucchinis, spiralized
½ cup toasted pine nuts
Salt and black pepper to taste

Directions and Total Time: approx. 25 minutes

Add half of the garlic, onion, salt, and pepper to a bowl and stir well. Mix in the chicken. Heat avocado oil in a deep skillet over medium heat and add the chicken. Cook for 8 minutes until no longer pink with a slight brown crust. Transfer to a plate. Pour the eggs into the pan and scramble for 1 minute. Remove the eggs to the side of the chicken. Reduce the heat to low and add in broth, coconut aminos, vinegar, scallions, remaining garlic, and chili flakes; simmer for 3 minutes. Stir in chicken, zucchini, and eggs. Cook for 1 minute and turn the heat off. Top with pine nuts and serve.

Per serving: Cal 759; Net Carbs 3.3g; Fat 49g; Protein 69g

Bacon-Wrapped Chicken

Ingredients for 4 servings

8 bacon slices
4 chicken breasts
2 tbsp olive oil
Salt and black pepper to taste
2 tbsp butter
1 lb spinach
4 garlic cloves, minced

Directions and Total Time: approx. 30 minutes

Preheat oven to 390 F. Wrap each chicken breast with 2 bacon slices, season with salt and pepper, and place on a baking sheet. Drizzle with olive oil and bake for 15 minutes until the bacon browns and chicken cooks within. Melt butter in a skillet and sauté spinach and garlic until the leaves wilt, 5 minutes. Season with salt and pepper. Serve the chicken with buttered spinach.

Per serving: Cal 861; Net Carbs 2.4g; Fat 58g; Protein 69g

Chicken Pizza with Sundried Tomatoes

Ingredients for 4 servings

1 ½ cups almond flour
1 ½ tbsp olive oil
1 tsp salt
2 eggs

Pesto chicken topping
½ lb chicken breasts, cut into strips
1 ½ tbsp olive oil
6 sundried tomatoes, sliced
1 ½ cups basil pesto
1 cup mozzarella, grated
1 tbsp fresh basil leaves
A pinch of red pepper flakes

Directions and Total Time: approx. 40 minutes

Preheat the oven to 350 F. To prepare the pizza crust, mix almond flour, olive oil, salt, and eggs until a dough forms in a bowl. Form the dough into a ball and place it in between two full parchment papers on a flat surface. Roll it out into a circle and slide into a pizza pan; remove the parchment paper. Bake the dough for 20 minutes.

Heat oil in a pan over medium heat and fry chicken on all sides for 5 minutes. Apply 2/3 of the pesto on the pizza crust and sprinkle half of the mozzarella cheese on it. Toss the chicken in the remaining pesto and spread it on top of the pizza. Sprinkle with the remaining mozzarella and sundried tomatoes, and put the pizza back in the oven to bake for 9 minutes. When it is ready, remove from the oven to cool slightly, garnish with the basil leaves and sprinkle with red pepper flakes. Slice and serve.

Per serving: Cal 521; Fat 39g; Net Carbs 1g; Protein 30.7g

Herby Veggies & Chicken Casserole

Ingredients for 4 servings

2 chicken breasts, cubed
¾ lb Brussels sprouts, halved
2 large zucchinis, chopped
2 red bell peppers, quartered
¼ cup olive oil
1 tbsp balsamic vinegar
1 tsp chopped thyme leaves
1 tsp chopped rosemary
½ cup toasted walnuts
Salt and black pepper to taste

Directions and Total Time: approx. 35 minutes

Preheat oven to 400 F. Scatter Brussels sprouts, zucchinis, bell peppers, and chicken on a baking sheet. Season with salt and pepper and drizzle with olive oil. Toss with balsamic vinegar. Sprinkle with thyme and rosemary. Bake for 25 minutes, shaking once. Top with walnuts. Serve.

Per serving: Cal 491; Net Carbs 3.7g; Fat 34g; Protein 35g

Spinach Coconut Chicken Breasts

Ingredients for 4 servings

4 chicken breasts, cubed
3 tbsp ghee
2 tbsp garam masala
1 cup baby spinach, pressed
1 ¼ cups coconut cream
Salt and black pepper to taste

Directions and Total Time: approx. 35 minutes

Preheat oven to 350 F. Heat ghee in a skillet, season the chicken with salt and pepper, and cook for 6 minutes. Mix in garam masala and transfer the chicken with juices into a greased baking dish. Add spinach and spread coconut cream on top. Bake for 20 minutes or until the cream is bubbly. Remove the dish and serve with cauli rice.

Per serving: Cal 781; Net Carbs 3.3g; Fat 39g; Protein 86g

Feta & Kale Chicken Bake

Ingredients for 4 servings

¼ cup shredded Monterey Jack cheese
4 chicken breasts, cut into strips

2 tbsp olive oil	1 tsp Italian seasoning
1 small onion, chopped	2 medium zucchinis, chopped
2 garlic cloves, minced	1 cup baby kale
½ tbsp red wine vinegar	¼ cup crumbled feta cheese
1 ½ crushed tomatoes	½ cup grated Parmesan
2 tbsp tomato paste	Salt and black pepper to taste

Directions and Total Time: approx. 35 minutes

Preheat oven to 400 F. Heat olive oil in a skillet, season the chicken with salt and pepper, and cook for 8 minutes; set aside. To the skillet, add and sauté onion and garlic for 3 minutes. Mix in vinegar, tomatoes, and tomato paste. Cook for 8 minutes. Season with salt, pepper, and Italian seasoning. Stir in chicken, zucchinis, kale, and feta. Pour the mixture into a baking dish and top with Monterey Jack cheese. Bake for 15 minutes or until the cheese melts and is golden. Top with Parmesan and serve.

Per serving: Cal 679; Net Carbs 6.6g; Fat 40g; Protein 71g

Tex-Mex Chicken Lettuce Fajita Bowls

Ingredients for 4 servings

1 ½ lb chicken breasts, cut into strips
½ cup shredded Mexican cheese blend

2 tbsp olive oil	1 green bell pepper, sliced
2 tbsp Tex-Mex seasoning	1 yellow onion, thinly sliced
1 head Iceberg lettuce, torn	4 tbsp fresh cilantro leaves
2 tomatoes, and chopped	1 cup sour cream
2 avocados, chopped	Salt and black pepper to taste

Directions and Total Time: approx. 20 minutes

Warm the olive oil in a skillet, season the chicken with salt, pepper, and Tex-Mex seasoning and fry until golden, 10 minutes; transfer to a plate. Divide lettuce into 4 bowls, share the chicken on top, and add tomatoes, avocados, bell pepper, onion, cilantro, and Mexican cheese. Top with dollops of sour cream and serve.

Per serving: Cal 631; Net Carbs 4.5g; Fat 42g; Protein 47g

Chili Chicken with Grilled Bell Peppers

Ingredients for 4 servings

1 lb chicken breasts, halved	¼ cup erythritol
2 cloves garlic, minced	Salt and black pepper to taste
2 tbsp oregano, chopped	1/3 cup chili sauce
2 tbsp lemon juice	2 red bell peppers, cut into strips
1/3 cup olive oil	2 spring onions, cut diagonally

Directions and Total Time: approx. 30 min + cooling time

In a bowl, mix the garlic, oregano, lemon juice, olive oil, chili sauce, erythritol, salt, and black pepper. Add the chicken and place it in the fridge for at least 1 hour.

Preheat grill to high. Add chicken and bell pepper strips and grill for 10 minutes. Flip and continue cooking for 5-10 more minutes. Garnish with spring onions to serve.

Per serving: Cal 403; Fat 29g; Net Carbs 6.4g; Protein 25g

Spicy Italian Chicken Breasts

Ingredients for 4 servings

½ cup sliced Pecorino Romano cheese
1 ½ lb chicken breasts, halved lengthwise

2 eggs	2 garlic cloves, minced
2 tbsp Italian seasoning	2 cups crushed tomatoes
1 pinch red chili flakes	1 tbsp dried basil
¼ cup fresh parsley, chopped	½ lb sliced mozzarella cheese
4 tbsp butter	Salt and black pepper to taste

Directions and Total Time: approx. 45 minutes

Preheat oven to 400 F. Season chicken with salt and pepper; set aside. In a bowl, whisk eggs with Italian seasoning and red chili flakes. On a plate, combine Pecorino cheese with parsley. Melt butter in a skillet. Dip the chicken in the egg mixture and then dredge in the cheese mixture. Place in the butter and fry on both sides until the cheese melts and is golden brown, 10 minutes; set aside. Sauté garlic in the same pan and mix in tomatoes. Top with basil, salt, and pepper, and cook for 10 minutes. Pour the sauce into a greased baking dish. Place the chicken pieces in the sauce and top with mozzarella. Bake for 15 minutes or until the cheese melts. Remove and serve.

Per serving: Cal 681; Net Carbs 5.3g; Fat 43g; Protein 60g

Grilled Chicken with Broccoli & Carrots

Ingredients for 4 servings

2 tbsp olive oil	2 lb chicken breasts
1 tbsp smoked paprika	1 small head broccoli, cut into
Salt and black pepper to taste	florets
1 tsp garlic powder	2 baby carrots, sliced

Directions and Total Time: approx. 25 minutes

Put broccoli florets and carrots into the steamer basket over the boiling water. Steam for about 8 minutes or until crisp-tender. Set aside to cool, then sprinkle with salt and olive oil. Grease grill grate with cooking spray and preheat to 400 F. Combine paprika, salt, pepper, and garlic powder in a bowl. Brush chicken with olive oil and sprinkle spice mixture over; massage with hands. Grill chicken for 7 minutes per side until well-cooked and plate. Serve with steamed vegetables.

Per serving: Cal 466; Fat 29g; Net Carbs 1.9g; Protein 49g

Quick Cheesy Chicken Casserole

Ingredients for 4 servings

½ cup baby spinach	1 tbsp mustard powder
1 lb chicken breasts, cubed	1 tbsp plain vinegar
1 cup cream cheese	1 ¼ cups grated cheddar

Directions and Total Time: approx. 35 minutes

Preheat oven to 400 F. Mix the cream cheese, mustard powder, plain vinegar, chicken, baby spinach, and 1 cup of water in a greased baking dish. Bake for 20 minutes. Sprinkle with cheddar cheese and bake for another 5 minutes or until the cheese melts. Serve.

Per serving: Cal 977; Net Carbs 6g; Fat 89g; Protein 29g

Satay Chicken with Sauteed Cabbage

Ingredients for 2 servings

Cabbage

½ head white cabbage, shredded   2 tbsp olive oil

Chicken

1/3 tbsp soy sauce, sugar-free   1 tbsp olive oil
1/3 tbsp fish sauce, sugar-free   1/3 tbsp rice wine vinegar
1/3 tbsp lime juice   1/3 tsp cayenne pepper
1 tsp minced garlic   1/3 tsp erythritol
1/3 tsp minced ginger   1 lb chicken thighs

Sauce

¼ cup peanut butter   1/3 tsp ginger, minced
1/3 tsp minced garlic   1/3 tsp cayenne pepper
1/3 tbsp lime juice   1 tbsp rice wine vinegar
1 tbsp water   1/3 tbsp chili sauce

Directions and Total Time: approx. 30 min + chilling time

Mix all chicken ingredients in a large Ziploc bag. Seal the bag and shake to combine. Chill for 1 hour. Heat the olive oil in a saucepan over medium heat and add the cabbage, 2 tbsp of water, and salt. Cook for 10 minutes until wilted; remove to a plate. Whisk the peanut butter with the remaining sauce ingredients in a bowl. Set aside. Preheat grill to high heat and grease with cooking spray. Remove the chicken from the marinade. Put the chicken on the grill, skin side up, and grill for 6 minutes, then flip and cook for 4-5 more minutes. Drizzle the chicken with sauce and serve with sauteed cabbage.

Per serving: Cal 503; Fat 37g; Net Carbs 4g; Protein 35g

Green Bean Chicken Curry

Ingredients for 4 servings

2 tbsp coconut oil   ¼ cup coconut cream
1 lb chicken breasts   1 tsp curry powder
1 cup chicken stock   1 tsp red pepper flakes
2 cups green beans, chopped   1 green onion, chopped
1 tbsp lime juice   Salt and black pepper, to taste

Directions and Total Time: approx. 30 minutes

In a pan over medium heat, warm coconut oil. Place in chicken and cook each side for 2 minutes; set aside. Add green onion and green beans to the pan and cook for 4 minutes. Stir in black pepper, stock, red pepper flakes, salt, curry powder, coconut cream, and lime juice. Take the chicken back to the pan, and cook for 15 minutes.

Per serving: Cal 477; Fat 32g; Net Carbs 4.1g; Protein 48g

Prosciutto Broccoli Chicken Stew

Ingredients for 4 servings

4 chicken breasts, cubed   1 cup baby kale, chopped
6 slices prosciutto, chopped   1 head broccoli, cut into florets
2 tbsp butter   1 ½ cups heavy cream
4 garlic cloves, minced   ¼ cup shredded Parmesan

Directions and Total Time: approx. 20 minutes

Place the prosciutto in a skillet and fry it until crispy and brown, 5 minutes; set aside. Melt butter in the same skillet and cook chicken until no longer pink.

Add garlic and sauté for 1 minute. Mix in heavy cream, prosciutto, and kale; let simmer for 5 minutes until the sauce thickens. Pour broccoli into a safe-microwave bowl, sprinkle with some water, and microwave for 2 minutes until broccoli softens. Add it to the skillet, sprinkle with Parmesan, stir, and cook until the cheese melts. Serve.

Per serving: Cal 799; Net Carbs 4.5g; Fat 48g; Protein 69g

Pulled Chicken & Egg Cupcakes

Ingredients for 4 servings

½ ground chicken   ½ tsp red chili flakes
2 tbsp butter   12 eggs
2 tbsp chopped green onions   ¼ cup grated Monterey Jack

Directions and Total Time: approx. 35 minutes

Preheat oven to 360 F. Line a 12-hole muffin tin with cupcake liners. Melt butter in a skillet over medium heat and cook the ground chicken until brown, 10 minutes. Divide the chicken between muffin holes along with green onions and red chili flakes. Crack an egg into each muffin hole and scatter the cheese on top. Bake for 15 minutes until eggs set. Let cool slightly before unmolding.

Per serving: Cal 389; Net Carbs 0.5g; Fat 31g; Protein 34g

Chili Chicken with Dill Sauce

Ingredients for 4 servings

2 tbsp butter   1 lb chicken breasts
1 tbsp olive oil   Salt and black pepper, to taste
1 onion, chopped   1 cup sour cream
½ tsp chili powder   2 tbsp fresh dill, chopped

Directions and Total Time: approx. 30 minutes

Heat a pan with the olive oil and half of the butter over medium heat. Add in the chicken, season with chili powder, black pepper, and salt and fry for 2-3 per side until golden. Transfer to a baking dish and cook in the oven for 15 minutes at 390 F, until no longer pink. To the pan, add the remaining butter and onion and cook for 2 minutes. Pour in the sour cream and dill and warm through without a boil. Slice the chicken and place on a platter. Spoon the sauce over and serve.

Per serving: Cal 381; Fat 29g; Net Carbs 6.5g; Protein 26g

Tasty Chicken Bites

Ingredients for 4 servings

1 lb chicken breasts, cubed   1 tbsp allspice
1 tsp sesame oil   1 tbsp granulated sweetener
1 tbsp olive oil   1 tbsp soy sauce, sugar-free
1 cup mushrooms, quartered   1 tsp sesame seeds

Directions and Total Time: approx. 15 min + cooling time

Combine the sesame oil, olive oil, allspice, sweetener, and soy sauce in a bowl. Add the chicken and mushrooms and let marinate for 1 hour in the fridge.

Preheat the grill. Thread the chicken and mushrooms onto wooden skewers. Grill for 4-6 minutes per side. Transfer to a serving plate, scatter with sesame seeds, and serve.

Per serving: Cal 273; Fat 17g; Net Carbs 3.5g; Protein 23g

Ham & Cheese Stuffed Chicken

Ingredients for 4 servings

2 tbsp olive oil	2 tbsp mozzarella, shredded
¼ cup ham, chopped	1/3 cup tomato-basil sauce
1 cup spinach	1 lb chicken breasts

Directions and Total Time: approx. 40 minutes

Preheat oven to 400 F and brush a baking dish with half of the olive oil. Combine the shredded mozzarella cheese, ham, and spinach in a bowl and mix well.

Cut pockets into the sides of the chicken breasts. Stuff with the prepared mixture. Brush the top with olive oil. Place on the baking dish and roast for 25 minutes. Pour the tomato-basil sauce over and return to the oven. Cook for an additional 5 minutes. Serve.

Per serving: Cal 343; Fat 2.7g; Net Carbs 4.7g; Protein 36g

Chicken Breasts with Lemon

Ingredients for 4 servings

2 tbsp olive oil	1 red onion, sliced
1 lb chicken breasts	Juice from 1 lemon
1 turnip, cut into wedges	Zest from 1 lemon
Salt and black pepper, to taste	Lemon rinds from 1 lemon
1 tsp coriander seeds	

Directions and Total Time: approx. 35 minutes

Preheat oven to 370 F. Put the chicken in a baking dish, and season with black pepper and salt. Sprinkle with lemon juice and coriander seeds. Toss well to coat. Mix in turnip, red onion, lemon rinds, and lemon zest. Drizzle with olive oil and ½ cup of water. Bake for 25 minutes. Discard the lemon rinds and serve.

Per serving: Cal 288; Fat 11g; Net Carbs 4.3g; Protein 23g

Feta & Mozzarella Chicken

Ingredients for 4 servings

1 lb chicken breasts, sliced	2 tsp olive oil
½ tsp mixed spice seasoning	4 oz feta cheese, crumbled
Salt and black pepper to taste	½ cup mozzarella, shredded
1 cup baby spinach	

Directions and Total Time: approx. 45 minutes

Rub the chicken with spice mix, salt, and black pepper. Put it in a casserole dish and layer the spinach over. Mix the olive oil with feta and mozzarella cheeses, ½ cup of water, and black pepper and stir.

Pour the mixture over the chicken and cover the casserole with aluminium foil. Bake in the oven for 20 minutes at 370 F, remove foil and continue cooking for 15 minutes until a nice golden brown color is formed on top. Serve.

Per serving: Cal 343; Fat 27g; Net Carbs 5.2g; Protein 23g

Tarragon Chicken with Balsamic Turnips

Ingredients for 4 servings

1 lb chicken thighs	1 tbsp balsamic vinegar
2 lb turnips, cut into wedges	1 tbsp tarragon
2 tbsp olive oil	Salt and black pepper, to taste

Directions and Total Time: approx. 55 minutes

Preheat oven to 400 F. Cook turnips in boiling water for 10 minutes, drain, and set aside. Add the chicken and turnips to a greased baking dish. Sprinkle with tarragon, pepper, and salt. Drizzle with olive oil. Roast for 25-30 minutes. Remove the baking dish, drizzle the turnip wedges with balsamic vinegar and return to the oven for another 5 minutes. Serve.

Per serving: Cal 383; Fat 26g; Net Carbs 9.5g; Protein 23g

Creamy Chicken with Caramelized Leeks

Ingredients for 4 servings

1 lb leeks, sliced	½ cup heavy cream
½ tsp onion powder	½ tsp yellow mustard
½ tsp garlic powder	1 tbsp rosemary, chopped
2 tbsp lard	1 lb chicken thighs
2 tbsp olive oil	Salt and black pepper to taste

Directions and Total Time: approx. 55 minutes

Preheat oven to 360 F. In a small bowl, mix together salt, black pepper, garlic powder, and onion powder. Rub the mixture onto the chicken. Warm the olive oil in a skillet and cook the chicken until golden, 6-8 minutes. Remove to a baking dish and pour in 1 cup of water. Roast for 20 minutes until the skin is golden and crisp. Mix the heavy cream with mustard, salt, and pepper and pour in the chicken dish. Bake for 5 more minutes.

Melt the lard in the skillet and add the leeks. Cook for 8-10 minutes or until lightly caramelized. Season with salt and black pepper. Top the chicken with rosemary and serve with the leeks on the side.

Per serving: Cal 459; Fat 28g; Net Carbs 4.2g; Protein 35g

Chicken with Pancetta & Veggies

Ingredients for 4 servings

1 lb chicken thighs	1 cup white mushrooms, halved
Salt and black pepper, to taste	1 cup spinach
1 onion, chopped	1 cup white wine
1 tbsp coconut oil	1 cup whipping cream
4 pancetta strips, chopped	2 tbsp parsley, chopped
2 garlic cloves, minced	

Directions and Total Time: approx. 45 minutes

Warm the coconut oil in a pan over medium heat and cook the pancetta until crispy, about 4-5 minutes; remove to paper towels. Add the chicken, sprinkle with black pepper and salt, and cook until brown to the same fat. Remove to paper towels too.

In the same pan, sauté the onion and garlic for 4 minutes.

Place the mushrooms in the pan and cook for another 5 minutes. Return the pancetta and browned chicken. Stir in the wine and 1 cup of water and bring to a boil. Reduce the heat and simmer for 20 minutes. Stir in the whipping cream and spinach and warm without boiling. Scatter over the parsley and serve.

Per serving: Cal 353; Fat 17g; Net Carbs 5.2g; Protein 23g

Chicken Puffs with Peanuts

Ingredients for 4 servings

½ lb chopped chicken thighs, boneless and skinless
4 eggs
½ cup olive oil
1/3 cup peanuts, crushed
1 cup chicken broth
2 tsp Worcestershire sauce
1 tbsp dried parsley
1 tsp celery seeds
¼ tsp cayenne pepper
1 cup almond flour
Salt and black pepper to taste

Directions and Total Time: approx. 30 minutes

In a bowl, combine chicken and peanuts. Place a saucepan over medium heat and add the broth, olive oil, Worcestershire sauce, parsley, salt, pepper, celery seeds, and cayenne pepper. Bring to a boil and stir in almond flour until smooth ball forms. Remove from the heat and allow resting for 5 minutes. Add eggs into the batter one after the other and beat until well blended. Mix in chicken and peanuts. Drop tbsp heaps of the mixture onto a greased baking sheet and bake in the oven at 450 F for 15 minutes. Serve and enjoy!

Per serving: Cal 521; Net Carbs 1.6g; Fat 47g; Protein 19g

Chicken "Four Cheeses" with Pancetta

Ingredients for 4 servings

1 lb chicken breasts
4 oz mozzarella cheese, cubed
¼ cup mascarpone cheese
¼ cup cheddar cheese, cubed
4 oz provolone cheese, cubed
1 green bell pepper, sliced
Salt and black pepper, to taste
2 oz pancetta, sliced

Directions and Total Time: approx. 45 minutes

Fry pancetta in a pan over medium heat until crispy, 5 minutes. Set aside to cool, then crush it.

In a bowl, mix together bell pepper and crushed pancetta. Stir in mascarpone, cheddar cheese, provolone cheese, and mozzarella cheese. Cut slits into chicken breasts, season with black pepper and salt and stuff with the cheese mixture. Set on a lined baking sheet Bake in the oven at 400 F for 30 minutes.

Per serving: Cal 355; Fat 23g; Net Carbs 2.2g; Protein 33g

Chicken Souvlaki

Ingredients for 2 servings

1 red bell pepper, cut into chunks
2 chicken breasts, cubed
2 tbsp olive oil
2 cloves garlic, minced
8 oz cipollini
½ cup lemon juice
Salt and black pepper to taste
1 tsp rosemary, chopped
2 lemon wedges to garnish

Directions and Total Time: approx. 20 min + chilling time

In a bowl, mix half of the oil, garlic, salt, pepper, and lemon juice and add the chicken, cipollini, and bell pepper. Marinate for 2 hours in the fridge.

Preheat a grill to high heat. Thread chicken, bell pepper, and cipollini onto skewers and grill them for 6 minutes on each side. Remove and serve garnished with rosemary and lemons wedges.

Per serving: Cal 363; Fat 14g; Net Carbs 4g; Protein 32g

Texas Chicken Sliders

Ingredients for 4 servings

3 lb chicken thighs, boneless and skinless
4 zero carb hamburger buns, halved
½ cup chicken broth
¼ cup melted butter
¼ cup baby spinach
4 slices cheddar cheese
1 tsp onion powder
2 tsp garlic powder
2 tbsp ranch dressing mix
¼ cup white vinegar
2 tbsp hot sauce
Salt and black pepper to taste

Directions and Total Time: approx. 1 hour 15 minutes

Place a pot over low heat and add vinegar, hot sauce, broth, and butter. In a bowl, combine onion and garlic powders, salt, pepper, and ranch dressing mix. Rub the mixture onto the chicken and place it into the pot. Cook for 1 hour. Shred the chicken into small strands with two forks. Adjust the taste. Divide the spinach on the bottom half of each zero carb bun, spoon the chicken on top, and add a cheddar cheese slice. Cover with the remaining bun halves and serve.

Per serving: Cal 781; Net Carbs 15g; Fat 41g; Protein 92g

Baked Cheesy Chicken Tenders

Ingredients for 4 servings

1 tbsp olive oil
2 eggs
3 cups crushed cheddar cheese
½ cup pork rinds, crushed
1 lb chicken tenders
Salt to taste
Lemon wedges for garnish

Directions and Total Time: approx. 45 minutes

Preheat oven to 370 F. Line a baking sheet with parchment paper. Beat the eggs in a bowl. Mix the cheddar cheese and pork rinds in another bowl. Season the chicken with salt, dip in egg mixture, and coat generously in cheese/rind mixture. Place on the baking sheet, cover with aluminium foil and bake for 25 minutes. Remove foil, brush with olive oil, and bake further for 10 minutes until golden brown. Serve chicken with lemon wedges.

Per serving: Cal 512; Fat 43g; Net Carbs 2.2g; Protein 35g

Sage Chicken with Kale & Mushrooms

Ingredients for 4 servings

1 lb chicken thighs
2 cups mushrooms, sliced
1 cup kale, chopped
2 tbsp butter
1 tbsp olive oil
Salt and black pepper, to taste
½ tsp onion powder
½ tsp garlic powder
1 tsp Dijon mustard
1 tbsp fresh sage, chopped

Directions and Total Time: approx. 35 minutes

Heat a pan over medium heat and warm butter and olive oil. Coat the chicken with onion powder, pepper, garlic powder, and salt. Cook in the pan for 3 minutes on each side; set aside. To the same pan, add the mushrooms. Cook for 5 minutes. Pour in ½ cup water and mustard and stir. Add the chicken pieces back to the pan and cook for 15 minutes. Stir in the kale and cook for 5 minutes. Top with sage and serve.

Per serving: Cal 422; Fat 25g; Net Carbs 4.1g; Protein 27g

Chicken with Sweet Potato Bake

Ingredients for 4 servings

1 lb sweet potatoes, cut into chunks
4 tbsp olive oil
1 yellow onion, sliced
10 oz broccoli florets
4 garlic cloves, minced
½ tsp dried thyme
1 lemon, juiced
½ tsp chili powder
½ tsp cumin powder
1 tbsp Worcestershire sauce
1 lb chicken drumsticks
Salt and black pepper to taste

Directions and Total Time: approx. 55 min + chilling time

Preheat oven to 370 F. In a bowl, mix 2 tbsp of olive oil, garlic, thyme, lemon juice, chili powder, cumin, Worcestershire sauce, salt, and pepper. Add the chicken to the bowl and toss to coat. Set aside. Add the sweet potatoes, onions, and garlic to a bowl. Season and drizzle over the remaining olive oil, then toss everything together. Spread the veg out in an even layer on a baking sheet. Pour in ½ cup of water and set the chicken on top. Drizzle with the marinade. Roast for 25-30 minutes. Add the broccoli florets around the chicken and return to the oven for 15 minutes until the chicken is cooked through and the veg is completely tender. Serve and enjoy!.

Per serving: Cal 491; Net Carbs 3.8g; Fat 21g; Protein 35g

Braised Chicken with Tomato & Garlic

Ingredients for 4 servings

2 tbsp butter
1 lb chicken thighs
Salt and black pepper to taste
3 cloves garlic, minced
2 cups tomatoes, chopped
1 eggplant, chopped
2 tbsp basil leaves, chopped

Directions and Total Time: approx. 30 minutes

Melt the butter in a saucepan over medium heat. Season the chicken with salt and black pepper and fry for 4 minutes on each side until golden brown. Remove to a plate. In the same saucepan, sauté the garlic for 1 minute, pour in the tomatoes, and cook for 8 minutes. Add in the eggplant and cook for 4 minutes. Adjust the seasoning and return the chicken. Coat with sauce and simmer for 3 minutes. Sprinkle with fresh basil leaves and serve.

Per serving: Cal 453; Fat 37g; Net Carbs 3.3g; Protein 25g

Baked Chicken with Butternut Squash

Ingredients for 4 servings

1 lb butternut squash, cut into lunes
1 lb chicken thighs
1 onion, sliced
½ cup black olives, pitted
2 tbsp olive oil
¼ cup goat cheese, crumbled
3 garlic cloves, sliced
Salt and black pepper, to taste

Directions and Total Time: approx. 40 minutes

Preheat oven to 400 F. Place the chicken with the skin down in a baking dish. Place the garlic, onion, and butternut squash around the chicken, then drizzle with oil; sprinkle with salt and pepper. Roast in the oven for 25-30 minutes. Top with olives and goat cheese to serve.

Per serving: Cal 405; Fat 14g; Net Carbs 5.3g; Protein 28g

Jamaican Chicken Drumsticks

Ingredients for 4 servings

2 lb chicken drumsticks
1 cup sour cream
2 tbsp melted butter
2 tbsp Jamaican seasoning
3 tbsp pork rinds
¼ cup almond meal

Directions and Total Time: approx. 50 min + chilling time

Preheat oven to 360 F. In a bowl, place the sour cream and Jamaican seasoning. Add the chicken and toss to coat evenly. Marinate for 15 minutes in the fridge.

In a food processor, blend the pork rinds with almond meal. Pour the mixture onto a wide plate. Remove chicken from the marinade, shake off any excess liquid, and coat generously in the pork rind mixture. Place on a greased baking sheet and drizzle with the melted butter. Roast for 40-45 minutes until golden brown and crispy, turning once. Serve warm.

Per serving: Cal 449; Net Carbs 1.8g; Fat 31g; Protein 45g

Roasted Chicken with Fresh Herbs

Ingredients for 4 servings

1 lb chicken legs
1 tbsp fresh thyme, chopped
1 tbsp rosemary, chopped
2 tbsp butter, softened
1 teaspoon smoked paprika
½ tsp garlic powder
2 tbsp chives, chopped
Salt and black pepper to taste

Directions and Total Time: approx. 50 minutes

Preheat oven to 380 F. Place an oven-safe baking rack inside of a baking pan. Brush the chicken with melted butter, coat with garlic powder, smoked paprika, thyme, rosemary, salt, and black pepper. Arrange the chicken on the baking rack. Bake in the oven for 35-40 minutes or until crispy and browned. Sprinkle with chives and serve.

Per serving: Cal 274; Fat 14g; Net Carbs 0.2g; Protein 33g

Baked Chicken Legs with Tomato Sauce

Ingredients for 4 servings

1 (28 oz) can sugar-free tomato sauce
2 green bell peppers, cut into chunks
2 tbsp olive oil
1 lb chicken legs
2 green onions, chopped
1 parsnip, chopped
1 carrot, chopped
2 garlic cloves, minced
¼ cup coconut flour
1 cup chicken broth
2 tbsp Italian seasoning
Salt and black pepper to taste

Directions and Total Time: approx. 1 hour 35 minutes

Season the legs with salt and black pepper. Heat the oil in a large skillet over medium heat and fry the chicken until brown on both sides for 10 minutes. Remove to a baking dish. In the same pan, sauté the green onions, parsnip, bell peppers, carrot, and garlic for 10 minutes with continuous stirring. In a bowl, evenly combine the broth, coconut flour, tomato sauce, and Italian seasoning together, and pour it over the vegetables in the pan. Stir and cook to thicken for 4 minutes. Pour the mixture over the chicken in the baking dish, and bake in the oven for 1 hour at 390 F. Serve warm.

Per serving: Cal 345; Fat 18g; Net Carbs 9.5g; Protein 25g

Coconut Chicken with Asparagus Sauce

Ingredients for 4 servings

1 tbsp butter	2 cups asparagus, chopped
1 lb chicken thighs	1 tsp oregano
2 tbsp coconut oil	1 cup heavy cream
2 tbsp coconut flour	1 cup chicken broth

Directions and Total Time: approx. 30 minutes

Melt the coconut oil in a skillet over medium heat. Brown the chicken on all sides, about 6-8 minutes. Set aside.

Melt the butter in the skillet and whisk in the flour and oregano. Stir in heavy cream and chicken broth and bring to a boil. Add the asparagus and cook for 10 minutes until tender. Transfer to a food processor and pulse until smooth. Return to the skillet and add the chicken; cook for an additional 5 minutes and serve.

Per serving: Cal 451; Fat 37g; Net Carbs 3.2g; Protein 18g

Citrus Chicken with Spinach & Pine Nuts

Ingredients for 2 servings

2 tbsp olive oil	1 tbsp oregano, chopped
1 lb chicken thighs	1 garlic clove, minced
Salt and black pepper to serve	1 cup spinach
2 tbsp lemon juice	2 tbsp pine nuts
1 tsp lemon zest	

Directions and Total Time: approx. 20 min + chilling time

In a bowl, combine all ingredients, except olive oil, spinach, and pine nuts. Place in the fridge for 1 hour.

Warm the olive oil in a skillet over medium heat. Remove the chicken from the marinade, drain, and add to the pan. Cook until crispy, about 7 minutes per side. Pour in the marinade and the spinach and cook for 4-5 minutes until the spinach wilts. Serve sprinkled with pine nuts.

Per serving: Cal 465; Fat 32g; Net Carbs 3g; Protein 29g

Tamari Chicken Thighs with Capers

Ingredients for 4 servings

1 ½ lb chicken thighs	8 oz cream cheese
2 tbsp butter	1/3 cup capers
2 cups heavy bream	1 tbsp tamari sauce

Directions and Total Time: approx. 25 minutes

Preheat oven to 350 F. Melt butter in a skillet and fry the chicken until golden brown, 8 minutes. Transfer to a greased baking sheet, cover with aluminum foil, and bake for 8 minutes. Reserve the butter used to sear the chicken. Remove chicken from the oven, take off the foil, and pour the drippings into a pan along with the butter from frying. Set the chicken aside in a warmer to serve later. Place the saucepan over low heat and mix in heavy cream and cream cheese. Simmer until the sauce thickens. Mix in capers and tamari sauce and cook further for 1 minute. Dish the chicken into plates and drizzle the sauce all over.

Per serving: Cal 829; Net Carbs 0.9g; Fat 73g; Protein 36g

Eggplant & Carrot Chicken Gratin

Ingredients for 4 servings

2 tbsp butter	2 tbsp Swiss cheese, grated
1 tbsp olive oil	Salt and black pepper, to taste
1 eggplant, chopped	2 garlic cloves, minced
2 carrots, chopped	1 lb chicken thighs

Directions and Total Time: approx. 55 minutes

Season the chicken with salt and pepper. Warm the butter and olive oil in a pan over medium heat. Place in the chicken thighs and cook 3 minutes on each side; transfer to a baking dish. In the same pan, cook the garlic, eggplant, and carrot for 8-10 minutes. Adjust the seasoning. Spread the mixture over the chicken and sprinkle with Swiss cheese. Bake in the oven at 350 F for 30 minutes. Serve and enjoy!

Per serving: Cal 495; Fat 31g; Net Carbs 6.6g; Protein 23g

Creamy Chicken with Tomatoes

Ingredients for 4 servings

2 tbsp butter	1 tsp oregano
1 lb chicken thighs	1 ½ cups chicken broth
Salt and black pepper to taste	½ cup heavy cream
1 cup cherry tomatoes, halved	¼ cup Parmesan, shredded

Directions and Total Time: approx. 25 minutes

Rub the chicken with salt, black pepper, and oregano. Melt the butter in a saucepan over medium heat and brown the chicken for 5 minutes on each side. Pour the chicken broth into the pan and cook covered for 8 minutes. Stir in the cherry tomatoes, heavy cream, and Parmesan cheese and simmer for 4 minutes. Serve.

Per serving: Cal 407; Fat 32g; Net Carbs 6.2g; Protein 21g

Creamed Paprika Chicken

Ingredients for 4 servings

2 tbsp ghee	¼ cup heavy cream
1 lb chicken thighs	2 tbsp smoked paprika
Salt and black pepper, to taste	2 tbsp parsley, chopped
1 tsp onion powder	

Directions and Total Time: approx. 45 minutes

In a bowl, combine paprika with onion powder, pepper, and salt. Season chicken with the mixture and lay on a lined baking sheet; bake for 25-30 minutes in the oven at 400 F. Transfer to a serving plate. Add the cooking juices to a skillet over medium heat and mix with the heavy cream and ghee. Cook for 5-6 minutes until the sauce has thickened. Pour the sauce over the chicken and sprinkle with parsley. Serve and enjoy!

Per serving: Cal 346; Fat 28g; Net Carbs 2.3g; Protein 21g

Teriyaki Chicken Wings

Ingredients for 4 servings

2 tbsp sesame oil	Salt to taste
1 lb chicken wings	Chili sauce to taste
4 tbsp teriyaki sauce	2 spring onions, sliced

Directions and Total Time: approx. 50 minutes

Preheat oven to 390 F. In a bowl, mix the teriyaki sauce, sesame oil, salt, chili sauce, and lemon juice. Add in the wings and toss to coat. Place the chicken in a roasting dish lined with parchment paper and roast for 35-40 minutes, turning once halfway. Garnish with spring onions to serve.

Per serving: Cal 177; Fat 11g; Net Carbs 4.3g; Protein 21g

Chicken & Chorizo Traybake

Ingredients for 4 servings

1 red bell pepper, cut into chunks
½ cup mushrooms, chopped   2 cups tomatoes, chopped
1 lb chorizo sausages, sliced   1 lb chicken thighs
4 tbsp olive oil   Salt and black pepper to taste
1 tsp dried rosemary   ½ cup chicken stock
4 cherry peppers, chopped   2 tbsp capers
1 red onion, cut into wedges   1 tbsp parsley, chopped
2 garlic cloves, minced

Directions and Total Time: approx. 60 minutes

Preheat oven to 390 F. In a small bowl, combine the garlic, 2 tbsp of olive oil, dried rosemary, salt, and pepper and stir until well mixed. Rub the mixture onto the chicken. In a baking sheet, mix the mushrooms, bell pepper, chorizo, red onion, cherry peppers, capers, tomatoes, remaining olive oil, salt, and pepper. Arrange the chicken thighs, skin-side up, on top, and pour in the chicken stock. Roast for 40-50 minutes or until the chicken skin is crispy and the vegetables have softened. Sprinkle with parsley and serve warm.

Per serving: Cal 895; Fat 66g; Net Carbs 5.3g; Protein 62g

Easy Pulled Chicken with Avocado

Ingredients for 4 servings

3 tbsp coconut oil   1 tbsp red wine vinegar
1 white onion, finely chopped   Salt and black pepper to taste
¼ cup chicken stock   2 lb boneless chicken thighs
3 tbsp tamari sauce   1 avocado, halved and pitted
3 tbsp chili pepper   ½ lemon, juiced

Directions and Total Time: approx. 2 hours 25 minutes

To a pot, add the onion, stock, coconut oil, tamari sauce, chili, vinegar, salt, and pepper and stir to combine. Add in thighs, close the lid, and cook over low heat for 2 hours. Scoop avocado pulp into a bowl, add lemon juice, and mash the avocado into a puree; set aside. When the chicken is ready, open the lid and use two forks to shred it. Cook further for 15 minutes. Turn the heat off and mix in avocado. Serve warm.

Per serving: Cal 709; Net Carbs 4g; Fat 56g; Protein 39g

Mustard Chicken with Rosemary

Ingredients for 4 servings

1 tbsp olive oil   ¼ cup heavy cream
½ cup chicken stock   2 tbsp Dijon mustard
½ cup onion, chopped   1 tsp rosemary, chopped
1 lb chicken thighs   Salt and black pepper to taste

Directions and Total Time: approx. 20 minutes

Warm the olive oil in a pan over medium heat. Season the chicken with salt and black pepper and cook for about 4 minutes per side; reserve. Sauté the onion in the same pan for 3 minutes. Add the stock and simmer for 5 minutes. Stir in mustard and heavy cream. Pour the sauce over the chicken and serve sprinkled with rosemary.

Per serving: Cal 515; Fat 39g; Net Carbs 5.2g; Protein 32g

Chicken Balls with Spaghetti Squash

Ingredients for 4 servings

½ cup + 2 tbsp Pecorino cheese, grated
1 lb butternut squash, halved   2 tbsp parsley, chopped
½ lb ground chicken   3 tbsp olive oil
Salt to taste   1 red bell pepper, sliced
½ cup pork rinds, crushed   1 egg
1 garlic clove, minced   1 cup sugar-free tomato sauce
1 shallot, chopped   1 tsp dried oregano
1 stalk celery, chopped   2 tbsp grated Parmesan cheese

Directions and Total Time: approx. 75 minutes

Preheat the oven to 450 F. Scoop the seeds out of the squash halves with a spoon. Sprinkle with salt and brush with 1 tbsp of olive oil. Place in a baking dish and roast for 30 minutes. Scrape the pulp into strands. Remove the spaghetti strands to a bowl and toss with 2 tbsp of Pecorino cheese; set aside. Put the ground chicken in a bowl. Add in garlic, shallot, pork rinds, egg, oregano, and remaining Pecorino cheese; mix well. Mold out meatballs from the mixture and place them on a baking sheet. Bake the meatballs for just 10 minutes, but not done.

Place a pot over medium heat and warm the remaining olive oil. Stir in the tomato sauce, celery, red bell pepper, and salt to taste. Let the sauce cook on low-medium heat for 5 minutes. Add in the meatballs. Continue cooking for 15 minutes. Spoon the meatballs with sauce over the spaghetti, sprinkle with Parmesan and parsley to serve.

Per serving: Cal 424; Fat 28g; Net Carbs 7.2g; Protein 21g

Almond-Crusted Zucchini Chicken Stacks

Ingredients for 4 servings

1 ½ lb chicken thighs, skinless and boneless, cut into strips
2 large zucchinis, sliced   2 tsp Italian herb blend
4 tbsp olive oil   ½ cup chicken broth
3 tbsp almond flour   Salt and black pepper to taste

Directions and Total Time: approx. 30 minutes

Preheat oven to 360 F. In a zipper bag, add almond flour, salt, and pepper. Mix and add the chicken strips. Seal the bag and shake to coat. Arrange the zucchinis on a greased baking sheet. Season with salt and pepper and drizzle with some olive oil. Remove the chicken from the almond flour mixture, shake off, and put 2-3 chicken strips on each zucchini. Season with the Italian herb blend and drizzle with the remaining olive oil. Bake for 8 minutes, then pour in broth. Bake for 10 minutes. Serve.

Per serving: Cal 508; Net Carbs 1.2g; Fat 39g; Protein 31g

Greek-Style Chicken Skewers

Ingredients for 4 servings

1 ½ lb chicken breasts, cubed
2 tbsp olive oil   2 tbsp lemon juice
½ cup Greek yogurt   Salt and black pepper to taste
1 tsp Greek oregano   1 cup Tzatziki sauce
1 lemon, thinly sliced

Directions and Total Time: approx. 15 min + chilling time

In a bowl, combine Greek yogurt, salt, pepper, oregano, lemon juice, and olive oil. Mix in chicken, cover the bowl with plastic wrap, and refrigerate for 30 minutes.

Preheat grill to high heat. Remove the wrap and thread the chicken onto the skewers, alternating the chicken cubes with the lemon slices folded over like a taco. Grill for 2-3 minutes on each side or until thoroughly cooked. Remove the skewers and serve with Tzatziki sauce.

Per serving: Cal 438; Net Carbs 0.5g; Fat 31g; Protein 39g

Gingered Grilled Chicken

Ingredients for 4 servings

1 lb chicken drumsticks   2 tbsp sesame oil
3 tbsp soy sauce   1 garlic clove, minced
¼ tbsp apple cider vinegar   ¼ tsp lime zest
A pinch of red pepper flakes   2 scallions, finely chopped
1 tbsp grated ginger   1 tbsp sesame seeds

Directions and Total Time: approx. 30 min + chilling time

In a large bowl, combine the sesame oil, ginger, vinegar, garlic, soy sauce, lime zest, and pepper flakes. Mix well. Add in the chicken and toss to coat. Chill for 1 hour.

Preheat a grill to high heat. Remove the chicken from the bowl, discarding the excess marinade. Set the chicken pieces skin side down on the grill and cook for 15-18 minutes, turning occasionally and basting with the marinade. Top with scallions and sesame seeds and serve.

Per serving: Cal 280; Fat 14g; Net Carbs 0.5g; Protein 33g

Pub-Style Wings with Avocado Sauce

Ingredients for 4 servings

2 lb chicken wings   2 tbsp olive oil
1 tsp sweet paprika   1 lemon, juiced and zested
1 tsp ancho chili powder   ¾ cup red onion, chopped
1 tsp garlic powder   Salt and black pepper to taste
1 tsp dried oregano   1 Hass avocado, mashed
1 tsp dried rosemary   2 tbsp fresh cilantro, chopped

Directions and Total Time: approx. 50 min + chilling time

In a small bowl, combine the paprika, ancho chili powder, garlic powder, oregano, rosemary, lemon zest, salt, and pepper. Brush the chicken wings with olive oil, then rub with the spice mix. Refrigerate for 2 hours.

Preheat oven to 400 F. Roast the chicken wings for 35-40 minutes. In a bowl, combine onion, salt, and lemon juice. Let sit for 5 minutes and mix in avocado and cilantro. Serve the chicken with the salsa on the side. Enjoy!

Per serving: Cal 584; Fat 31g; Net Carbs 1.4g; Protein 67g

Saucy Chicken Legs with Vegetables

Ingredients for 4 servings

2 tbsp olive oil   1 lb chicken legs
1 parsnip, chopped   1 cup tomatoes, chopped
2 celery stalks, chopped   1 cup spinach
2 cups chicken stock   ¼ tsp dried thyme
1 onion, chopped   Salt and black pepper, to taste
¼ cup red wine   1 tbsp parsley, chopped

Directions and Total Time: approx. 50 minutes

Put a large pot over medium heat and heat the olive oil inside. Add parsnip, celery, and onion, season with salt and pepper, and sauté for 5-6 minutes until tender. Stir in the chicken and cook for 5 minutes. Pour in the stock, red wine, tomatoes, and thyme and cook for 20 minutes. Add in the spinach and cook for 4-5 minutes until it's wilted. Sprinkle with parsley and serve.

Per serving: Cal 264; Fat 15g; Net Carbs 7.1g; Protein 22g

Chicken Wings with Jalapeno Sauce

Ingredients for 4 servings

2 dried jalapeño peppers, minced
2 lb chicken wings   3 tbsp xylitol
Salt and black pepper, to taste   ¼ cup chives, chopped
1 lemon, zested and juiced   ½ tsp xanthan gum
3 tbsp coconut aminos

Directions and Total Time: approx. 45 minutes

Preheat oven to 380 F. Line a baking sheet with parchment paper. Season the chicken with salt and black pepper and spread on the baking dish. Bake for 35 minutes and remove to a serving plate. Put a small pan over medium heat, add in the lemon juice, coconut aminos, lemon zest, xylitol, xanthan gum, and jalapeño peppers. Bring the mixture to a boil and cook for 2 minutes. Pour the sauce over the chicken, sprinkle with chives, and serve.

Per serving: Cal 422; Fat 26g; Net Carbs 3.4g; Protein 25g

Tumeric Chicken Wings with Ginger Sauce

Ingredients for 4 servings

2 tbsp olive oil   Salt and black pepper, to taste
1 lb chicken wings, cut in half   Juice of ½ lime
1 tbsp turmeric   1 cup thyme leaves
1 tbsp cumin   ¾ cup cilantro, chopped
3 tbsp fresh ginger, grated   1 jalapeño pepper, seeded

Directions and Total Time: approx. 35 min + chilling time

In a bowl, stir 1 tbsp ginger, cumin, salt, half olive oil, pepper, turmeric, and cilantro. Place in the chicken wings, toss to coat, and refrigerate for 20 minutes.

Heat the grill to high heat. Remove the wings from the fridge and grill for 20-25 minutes, turning from time to time, then set aside. Using a blender, combine thyme, remaining ginger, salt, jalapeño pepper, black pepper, lime juice, the remaining olive oil, and 1 tbsp of water, and blend well. Serve the chicken wings with the sauce.

Per serving: Cal 253; Fat 16g; Net Carbs 4.1g; Protein 22g

Mouth-Watering Chicken Stuffed Mushrooms

Ingredients for 4 servings

2 tbsp ghee	1 lb ground chicken
14 oz riced cauliflower	1 tsp oregano
Salt and black pepper, to taste	8 portobello mushroom caps
1 onion, chopped	½ cup chicken broth
1 garlic clove, minced	

Directions and Total Time: approx. 45 minutes

Preheat oven to 360 F. Warm the ghee in a pan over medium heat and stir-fry the onion and garlic for 3 minutes. Add in the cauli rice and ground chicken, and cook for 3 more minutes. Season with oregano, salt, and pepper. Stuff the caps with the mixture. Lay the stuffed mushrooms in a greased baking dish, pour the chicken broth, and bake in the oven for 30 minutes.

Per serving: Cal 261; Fat 16g; Net Carbs 6g; Protein 14g

Chicken Mushroom Burgers

Ingredients for 4 servings

4 large Portobello caps, destemmed	
4 Gruyere cheese slices	4 lettuce leaves
1 ½ lb ground chicken	4 large tomato slices
1 tbsp tomato sauce	¼ cup mayonnaise
1 tbsp olive oil	Salt and black pepper to taste

Directions and Total Time: approx. 25 minutes

In a bowl, combine chicken, salt, pepper, and tomato sauce. Mold into 4 patties and set aside. Heat olive oil in a skillet. Place in Portobello caps and cook for 3 minutes; set aside. Put the patties in the skillet and fry until brown and compacted, 8 minutes. Place Gruyere cheese slices on the cakes, allow melting for 1 minute and lift each burger onto each mushroom cap. Divide the lettuce on top, then tomato slices, and top with mayonnaise. Serve.

Per serving: Cal 508; Net Carbs 2.2g; Fat 34g; Protein 45g

Kale & Chicken Crust Pizza

Ingredients for 4 servings

1 cup shredded provolone cheese	
2 cups grated Parmesan	½ cup tomato sauce
1 lb ground chicken	1 tsp white wine vinegar
¼ tsp onion powder	½ tsp liquid smoke
¼ tsp garlic powder	¼ cup baby kale, chopped

Directions and Total Time: approx. 30 minutes

Preheat oven to 400 F. Line a round baking pan with parchment paper and grease with cooking spray. In a bowl, combine ground chicken and Parmesan cheese. Spread the mixture on the pan. Bake for 15 minutes until the chicken cooks. In a bowl, mix onion and garlic powder, tomato sauce, white wine vinegar, and liquid smoke. Remove the meat crust from the oven and spread the tomato mixture on top. Add kale and sprinkle with provolone cheese. Bake for 7 minutes or until the cheese melts. Slice and serve warm.

Per serving: Cal 521; Net Carbs 16g; Fat 31g; Protein 46g

Bacon & Parsnip Chicken Bake

Ingredients for 4 servings

½ lb parsnips, diced	1 cup heavy cream
6 bacon slices, chopped	2 oz cream cheese, softened
2 tbsp butter	1 ¼ cups grated Pepper Jack
1 lb ground chicken	¼ cup chopped scallions
2 tbsp butter	

Directions and Total Time: approx. 55 minutes

Preheat oven to 310 F. Put the bacon in a skillet and fry it until brown and crispy, 6 minutes; set aside. Melt butter in the skillet and sauté parsnips until softened and lightly browned. Add the chicken and cook until no longer pink, 8 minutes. Set aside too.

Add heavy cream, cream cheese, and two-thirds of the Pepper Jack cheese to the skillet. Melt the ingredients over medium heat, frequently stirring, 7 minutes. Spread the mixture on a baking dish, pour the heavy cream mixture over, and scatter bacon and scallions on top. Sprinkle with the remaining cheese and bake until the cheese melts, 30 minutes. Serve.

Per serving: Cal 761; Net Carbs 5.5g; Fat 66g; Protein 30g

Chicken Wings with Lemon & Capers

Ingredients for 4 servings

2 tbsp butter	1 tbsp soy sauce
½ cup chicken broth	¼ tsp xanthan gum
1 tsp garlic powder	3 tbsp xylitol
1 tsp lemon zest	1 lb chicken wings
3 tbsp lemon juice	Salt and black pepper, to taste
½ tsp cilantro, chopped	¼ cup capers

Directions and Total Time: approx. 35 minutes

Heat a saucepan over medium heat and add lemon juice and zest, soy sauce, cilantro, chicken broth, xylitol, and garlic powder. Bring to a boil, cover, lower the heat, and let simmer for 10 minutes. Stir in the butter, capers, and xanthan gum for 2-3 minutes. Set aside. Season the wings with salt and black pepper. Preheat grill to high heat and cook the chicken wings for 5-10 minutes per side. Serve topped with the sauce.

Per serving: Cal 343; Fat 25g; Net Carbs 3.6g; Protein 19g

Broccolini & Chicken Casserole

Ingredients for 4 servings

1 lb ground chicken	5 tbsp butter
1 lb broccolini, chopped	1 small white onion, chopped
1 cup grated Parmesan cheese	2 garlic cloves, minced

Directions and Total Time: approx. 40 minutes

Preheat oven to 350 F. Melt butter in a skillet and sauté onion and garlic for 3 minutes. Put in chicken and cook until no longer pink, 8 minutes. Add chicken and broccolini to a greased baking dish and mix evenly. Top with butter from the skillet and sprinkle Parmesan cheese on top. Bake for 20 minutes until the cheese melts. Serve.

Per serving: Cal 431; Net Carbs 4.3g; Fat 29g; Protein 28g

Chicken & Vegetable Pot Pie

Ingredients for 4 servings

1/3 cup cremini mushrooms, sliced
1 lb ground chicken
3 tbsp butter
1 large yellow onion, chopped
2 baby zucchinis, chopped
1 cup green beans, chopped
½ cup chopped broccoli rabe
2 celery stalks, chopped
4 oz cream cheese
½ cup coconut cream
½ tsp dried rosemary
¼ tsp poultry seasoning
10 egg whites
4 tbsp coconut flour
2 ½ cups fine almond flour
2 tsp baking powder
½ cup shredded cheddar

Directions and Total Time: approx. 60 minutes

Preheat oven to 360 F. Melt the butter in a skillet over medium heat, add seasoned with poultry seasoning chicken, and cook for 8 minutes or until the chicken is no longer pink; set aside. In the same skillet, sauté the onion, zucchini, green beans, broccoli rabe, celery, and mushrooms. Cook until the vegetables soften, 5 minutes. Stir in chicken, cream cheese, and coconut cream.

Simmer until the sauce thickens, 5 minutes. Sprinkle with rosemary. Turn the heat off and pour the mixture into a baking dish. Beat the egg whites into a bowl, using a hand mixer, until frothy but not stiff. Mix in coconut flour, almond flour, baking powder, and cheddar cheese until evenly combined. Beat the batter until smooth. Spoon the content over the chicken and vegetables and bake for 30 minutes or until the top browns. Serve.

Per serving: Cal 810; Net Carbs 4.7g; Fat 71g; Protein 40g

Parmesan Chicken Meatballs

Ingredients for 4 servings

4 sundried tomatoes, chopped
½ cup passata tomato sauce
1 lb ground chicken
2 tbsp basil, chopped
½ tsp garlic powder
1 egg
Salt and black pepper to taste
¼ cup almond flour
2 tbsp olive oil
3 tbsp Parmesan cheese, grated

Directions and Total Time: approx. 15 minutes

To make meatballs, place everything except the oil and basil in a bowl. Mix with your hands until well combined. Form meatballs out of the mixture. Heat olive oil in a skillet over medium heat. Cook meatballs for 6 minutes on all sides. Pour over the passata sauce and cook for 4 minutes. Serve sprinkled with basil.

Per serving: Cal 323; Fat 22g; Net Carbs 4.1g; Protein 22g

Chicken Tetrazzini

Ingredients for 4 servings

4 tbsp butter
4 tbsp olive oil
1 lb chicken breasts
1 lb white mushrooms, sliced
1 yellow onion, finely chopped
3 cloves garlic, minced
1 tbsp chopped fresh thyme
½ cup dry white wine
3 tbsp almond flour
2 cups chicken stock
1 cup heavy cream
¼ tsp ground nutmeg
10 oz zoodles
1 cup snow peas
2 tbsp chopped fresh parsley
1 cup grated Parmesan
1 cup pork rinds, crushed
Salt and black pepper to taste

Directions and Total Time: approx. 65 minutes

Melt the butter in a deep large frying pan over medium heat. Season the chicken with salt and pepper and cook for 4 minutes per side or until slightly golden. Remove to cool for 3 minutes. Shred-it and set aside in a large bowl.

Warm 2 tbsp of the olive oil in the same pan. Add the onion, garlic, mushrooms, and thyme and saute for 5-6 minutes until tender. Add the wine and simmer until it evaporates, about 2 minutes. Transfer the mushroom mixture to the chicken bowl.

In the same pan, add the almond flour and whisk in the heavy cream, broth, nutmeg, salt, and pepper. Bring to a boil and simmer until the sauce thickens slightly, stirring occasionally, about 10 minutes.

Warm the remaining olive oil in another pan and sauté the zoodles and snow peas for 3-4 minutes. Remove to the chicken mixture. Add in the almond sauce and toss to coat. Transfer the mixture to a baking dish. Sprinkle with Parmesan cheese and pork rinds and bake in the preheated to 390 F oven for 20-25 minutes until golden brown on top. Serve warm topped with parsley.

Per serving: Cal 733; Fat 52g; Net Carbs 7.6g; Protein 47g

Chicken & Cheese Stuffed Peppers

Ingredients for 6 servings

2 tbsp olive oil
3 tbsp butter
6 yellow bell peppers
3 garlic cloves, minced
1 large white onion, chopped
2 lb ground chicken
1 tsp chili powder
10 oz canned tomatoes, diced
2 cups grated cheddar cheese
Salt and black pepper to taste
2 cups mayonnaise
10 oz leafy greens

Directions and Total Time: approx. 55 minutes

Preheat oven to 370 F. Cut the peppers into halves lengthwise and remove the seeds. Drizzle with olive oil. Melt butter in a skillet and sauté garlic and onion for 3 minutes. Stir in chicken, chili powder, salt, and pepper. Cook for 8 minutes. Mix in tomatoes and sauté for 3-4 more minutes. Spoon the mixture into the peppers, top with cheddar cheese, and place in a greased baking dish. Bake until the cheese melts and is bubbly, 25-30 minutes. Garnish with mayonnaise and greens to serve.

Per serving: Cal 891; Net Carbs 12.9g; Fat 58g; Protein 56g

Homemade Chicken Rotisserie

Ingredients for 6 servings

8 tbsp butter, melted
3 lb chicken, whole bird
1 large lemon, juiced
2 large lemons, thinly sliced

Directions and Total Time: approx. 2 hours

Preheat oven to 400 F. Put the chicken, breast side up in a baking dish. In a bowl, combine butter and lemon juice. Spread the mixture all over the chicken. Arrange lemon slices at the bottom of the dish and bake for 1 to 1 ½ hours. Baste the chicken with the juice every 20 minutes. Let sit for 10-15 minutes before carving. Serve.

Per serving: Cal 389; Net Carbs 1g; Fat 22g; Protein 46g

Tasty Chicken Squash Lasagna

Ingredients for 4 servings

1 ½ lb ground chicken
2 tbsp butter
4 large yellow squash, sliced
1 tsp garlic powder
1 tsp onion powder
2 tbsp coconut flour
1 ½ cups grated mozzarella

1/3 cup Parmesan cheese
2 cups crumbled ricotta
1 large egg, beaten
2 cups marinara sauce
1 tbsp Italian mixed herbs
¼ tsp red chili flakes
¼ cup fresh basil leaves

Directions and Total Time: approx. 55 minutes

Preheat oven to 375 F. Melt butter in a skillet and cook chicken for 10 minutes; set aside. In a bowl, mix garlic and onion powders, coconut flour, mozzarella, half of Parmesan and ricotta cheeses, and egg. In another bowl, combine marinara sauce, mixed herbs, and red chili flakes; set aside. Make a single layer of the squash slices in a greased baking dish; spread a quarter of the egg mixture on top, a layer of the chicken, then a quarter of the marinara sauce. Repeat the layering process in the same proportions and sprinkle with the remaining Parmesan. Bake for 30 minutes. Garnish with basil leaves, slice, and serve.

Per serving: Cal 671; Net Carbs 7g; Fat 40g; Protein 59g

Baked Chicken Wings with Paprika-Mayo Dip

Ingredients for 4 servings

1 lb chicken wings
Salt and black pepper to taste
2 tbsp olive oil
1 tbsp paprika

1 tsp garlic powder
½ cup mayonnaise
1 tbsp lemon juice
Salt to taste

Directions and Total Time: approx. 25 minutes

Preheat oven to 400 F. Season the wings with salt and black pepper and drizzle with olive oil. Lay them on a lined baking sheet. Bake for 20 minutes until golden brown. In a bowl, mix the mayo with garlic powder, paprika, salt, and lemon juice. Season with salt and serve with the wings. Enjoy!

Per serving: Cal 315; Fat 21g; Net Carbs 2.4g; Protein 27g

Chimichurri Chicken Wings

Ingredients for 4 servings

½ cup olive oil
½ cup butter, melted
16 chicken wings, halved
3 garlic cloves, peeled

1 cup fresh parsley leaves
¼ cup fresh cilantro leaves
2 tbsp red wine vinegar
Salt and black pepper to taste

Directions and Total Time: approx. 55 minutes

Preheat oven to 350 F. Put the chicken in a bowl, season with salt and pepper, and brush with the butter all over. Transfer to a greased baking sheet. Bake for 40-45 minutes or until light brown and cooked within.

In a food processor, blend garlic, parsley, cilantro, salt, and pepper until smooth. Add in vinegar and gradually pour in olive oil while mixing further. Pour the mixture (chimichurri) over the chicken and serve.

Per serving: Cal 599; Net Carbs 1.4g; Fat 54g; Protein 31g

Easy Chicken Cordon Bleu

Ingredients for 4 servings

7 oz smoked deli ham, chopped
1 rotisserie chicken, shredded   10 oz shredded Gruyere
8 oz cream cheese   1 tbsp Dijon mustard

Directions and Total Time: approx. 30 minutes

Preheat oven to 350 F. Spread the chicken and ham on a greased baking dish. In a bowl, mix cream cheese, mustard, and two-thirds of Gruyere cheese. Spread the mixture on top of chicken and ham, and cover with the remaining cheese. Bake for 20 minutes or until the cheese is golden brown. Serve.

Per serving: Cal 689; Net Carbs 3.6g; Fat 48g; Protein 59g

Chicken Carnitas with Cilantro Slaw

Ingredients for 4 servings

1 lb chicken breasts, sliced
4 tbsp olive oil
1 yellow onion, sliced
1 yellow bell pepper, chopped
4 oz bacon, chopped
1 tbsp taco seasoning

Salt and black pepper to taste
2 cups shredded green cabbage
½ red onion, thinly sliced
1 Fresno chili pepper, sliced
2 tbsp chopped fresh cilantro
1 lime, juiced

Directions and Total Time: approx. 25 minutes

Place the chicken into a mixing bowl. Add in the olive oil, half of the lime juice, and taco seasoning. Massage the marinade onto the chicken until everything is well combined. Let sit for 10 minutes.

Warm 2 tbsp of olive oil in a skillet over medium heat. Add the chicken, bacon, yellow onion, bell pepper, salt, and black pepper and cook for 5-6 minutes or until the chicken is browned and cooked through and the vegetables are tender. In a bowl, mix green cabbage, red onion, Fresno chili pepper, cilantro, remaining lime juice, remaining olive oil, salt, and pepper. Toss to coat. Serve the cooked chicken with slaw and enjoy!

Per serving: Cal 543; Net Carbs 3.9g; Fat 35g; Protein 48g

Chicken & Cauliflower Au Gratin

Ingredients for 4 servings

10 oz cauliflower florets
4 oz cream cheese, softened
1 rotisserie chicken, shredded
¾ cup heavy cream
½ cup almond milk

1 tsp mustard powder
2 garlic cloves, minced
1 cup cheddar cheese, grated
Salt and black pepper to taste

Directions and Total Time: approx. 45 minutes

Steam the cauliflower for 7 minutes, until al dente. Remove to a baking dish along with the chicken. Preheat oven to 390 F. Place a small saucepan over low heat and add the cream cheese, heavy cream, almond milk, mustard powder, garlic, salt, and pepper. Whisk until the sauce is smooth. Pour the warm sauce over the cauliflower and chicken mixture and mix well. Top with the shredded cheese. Bake in the oven for 20-30 minutes, until the cheese has browned. Serve immediately.

Per serving: Cal 603; Fat 43g; Net Carbs 3g; Protein 47g

Chicken & Zucchini Stir-Fry

Ingredients for 4 servings

3 zucchinis, cut into 1-inch dices
1 tbsp unsalted butter
2 tbsp olive oil
1 lb chicken chunks
1 finely chopped onion
¼ cup chopped fresh parsley
1 tsp dried thyme
Salt and black pepper to taste

Directions and Total Time: approx. 25 minutes

Warm the olive oil and butter in a skillet over medium heat and sauté chicken for 5 minutes. Add in onion and parsley and cook further for 3 minutes. Stir in zucchini and thyme, season with salt and pepper, cover, and cook for 8-10 minutes or until the vegetables soften. Serve.

Per serving: Cal 161; Net Carbs 0.2g; Fat 12g; Protein 8g

Appetizing Chicken Meatloaf

Ingredients for 6 servings

2 large eggs
2 ½ lb ground chicken
3 tbsp flaxseed meal
2 tbsp olive oil
1 tbsp lemon juice
¼ cup chopped parsley
¼ cup chopped oregano
4 garlic cloves, minced
Lemon slices to garnish

Directions and Total Time: approx. 50 minutes

Preheat oven to 380 F. In a bowl, combine ground chicken and flaxseed meal; set aside. In a small bowl, whisk the eggs with olive oil, lemon juice, parsley, oregano, and garlic. Pour the mixture onto the chicken mixture and mix well. Spoon into a greased loaf pan and press to fit. Bake for 40 minutes. Remove the pan, drain the liquid, and let cool a bit. Slice, garnish with lemon, and serve.

Per serving: Cal 359; Net Carbs 1.3g; Fat 24g; Protein 35g

Spicy Chicken Pizza

Ingredients for 1 serving

1 cauliflower pizza crust
½ cup shredded chicken
½ cup grated mozzarella
½ tsp red hot sauce
1 bacon slice, torn into ½-inch
½ cup fresh baby spinach
½ cup tomato sauce
Fresh basil leaves

Directions and Total Time: approx. 30 minutes

Preheat oven to 400 F. Place the cauliflower pizza crust on a lined with parchment paper pizza pan. Spread tomato and red hot sauces on top. Top with chicken, mozzarella cheese, and bacon. Scatter the spinach over and bake for 14-16 minutes until edges are browned and crisp. Let sit for 5 minutes and top with basil leaves. Serve.

Per serving: Cal 314; Net Carbs 7.9g; Fats 14g; Protein 35g

Spicy Chicken Sausages with Green Beans

Ingredients for 4 servings

4 links chicken sausages, sliced
1 lb green beans, chopped
2 tbsp salted butter
4 garlic cloves, minced
½ cup tomato sauce
¼ cup red wine
½ tsp red pepper flakes
3 cups chopped kale
½ cup Pecorino Romano
Salt and black pepper to taste

Directions and Total Time: approx. 35 minutes

Warm the butter in a wok and fry the sausages until brown, 5 minutes; set aside. Sauté the green beans in the wok for 5 minutes. Mix in garlic and cook for 3 minutes, then pour in tomato sauce, red wine, red pepper flakes, and season with salt and pepper. Cover the lid and cook for 10 minutes or until the tomato sauce reduces by one-third. Return the sausages to the pan and heat for 1 minute. Stir in kale to wilt. Spoon onto a platter and sprinkle with Pecorino Romano cheese. Serve.

Per serving: Cal 239; Net Carbs 3.5g; Fat 12g; Protein 11g

Chicken & Bacon Veggie Skillet

Ingredients for 4 servings

4 bacon slices, chopped
1 lb ground chicken
2 cups baby bok choy
1 tbsp coconut oil
1 orange bell pepper, chopped
2 tbsp chopped oregano
2 garlic cloves, pressed
Salt and black pepper to taste

Directions and Total Time: approx. 25 minutes

Season the chicken with salt and pepper; set aside. Heat a skillet over medium heat and fry bacon until brown and crispy. Transfer to a plate. Melt coconut oil in the same skillet and cook chicken until no longer pink, 10 minutes. Remove to the bacon plate. Add bell pepper and bok choy and sauté until softened, 5 minutes. Stir in bacon, chicken, oregano, and garlic for 3 minutes. Serve with cauli rice, if desired.

Per serving: Cal 371; Net Carbs 2g; Fat 20g; Protein 41g

Curried Chicken Meatballs

Ingredients for 4 servings

2 tbsp olive oil
1 lb ground chicken
1 yellow onion, chopped
1 green bell pepper, chopped
2 garlic cloves, minced
1 tsp dried parsley
2 tbsp hot sauce
1 tbsp red curry powder
Salt and black pepper to taste

Directions and Total Time: approx. 30 minutes

Preheat oven to 380 F. In a bowl, combine chicken, onion, bell pepper, garlic, butter, parsley, hot sauce, salt, pepper, and curry. Form meatballs and place on a greased baking sheet. Drizzle with olive oil and bake until the meatballs brown on the outside and cook within, about 20 minutes. Serve and enjoy!

Per serving: Cal 299; Net Carbs 2.7g; Fat 16g; Protein 33g

Chicken Sausage Frittata

Ingredients for 4 servings

12 oz ground chicken sausages
2 tbsp butter
8 whole eggs
1 cup half-and-half
1 celery stalk, chopped
¼ cup shredded Swiss cheese

Directions and Total Time: approx. 40 minutes

Preheat oven to 360 F. In a bowl, whisk eggs with half-and-half. Melt butter in a safe oven skillet over medium heat. Sauté celery until soft, 5 minutes and set aside.

Add the sausages to the skillet and cook until brown with frequent stirring to break the lumps that form, 8 minutes. Scatter celery on top, pour the egg mixture all over and sprinkle with Swiss cheese. Put the skillet in the oven and bake until the eggs are set and cheese melts, about 20 minutes. Slice the frittata in wedges and serve warm.

Per serving: Cal 531; Net Carbs 3g; Fat 44g; Protein 32g

Cheesy Chicken Meatball Bake

Ingredients for 4 servings

1 lb chicken sausages, casing removed

1 egg	1 tbsp basil, chopped
½ carrot, grated	Salt and black pepper, to taste
1 garlic clove, minced	2 tbsp olive oil
1 onion, chopped	1 cup Pecorino, shredded

Directions and Total Time: approx. 25 minutes

Combine all ingredients, except for cheese and olive oil, in a bowl. Form meatballs from the mixture.

Heat olive oil in a large frying pan over medium heat and cook the meatballs for 3-4 minutes until browned. Set them on a parchment-lined baking sheet, top with Pecorino cheese, and bake for 10 minutes at 370 F until all cheese melts. Scatter basil over to serve.

Per serving: Cal 689; Fat 42g; Net Carbs 3.3g; Protein 62g

Cheddar Chicken with Cauli Steaks

Ingredients for 4 servings

4 slices chicken luncheon meat

2 tbsp olive oil	4 tbsp ranch dressing
1 head cauliflower	2 tbsp chopped parsley
½ tsp smoked paprika	Salt and black pepper to taste
½ cup grated cheddar cheese	

Directions and Total Time: approx. 20 minutes

Place the cauliflower on a flat surface and cut into 4 steaks from top to bottom. Season with paprika, salt, and pepper and drizzle with olive oil. Heat a grill pan over medium heat and cook in the cauliflower on both sides until softened, 4 minutes. Top one side with chicken and sprinkle with cheddar cheese. Heat to melt the cheese. Drizzle with ranch dressing and garnish with parsley. Serve warm.

Per serving: Cal 249; Net Carbs 1g; Fat 19g; Protein 10g

Cauliflower & Fennel Chicken Cake

Ingredients for 4 servings

2 cups leftover chicken, shredded
1 cauliflower head, cut into florets
1 cup sharp cheddar cheese, grated

1 ½ cups spinach	¼ cup almond milk
1 fennel bulb, chopped	2 tbsp olive oil
1 egg, lightly beaten	1 garlic clove, minced
½ cup pork rinds, crushed	Salt and black pepper to taste

Directions and Total Time: approx. 60 minutes

Preheat the oven to 360 F and grease a baking dish with cooking spray. Steam the cauliflower for 8 minutes in salted water over medium heat. Drain and set aside.

Also, combine the cheddar cheese and pork rinds in a large bowl and mix in the chicken. Set aside.

Next, heat the olive oil in a large skillet and cook the garlic, fennel, and spinach for about 5 minutes. Season with salt and pepper. Pour in the chicken bowl, add the cauliflower, egg, and almond milk. Transfer everything to the baking dish and cook for 30 minutes. Serve.

Per serving: Cal 395; Fat 26; Net Carbs 4.2g; Protein 21.6g

Chicken & Cheese Filled Avocados

Ingredients for 2 servings

1 cup cooked chicken, shredded

2 avocados	½ tsp onion powder
¼ cup mayonnaise	½ tsp garlic powder
1 tsp dried thyme	1 tsp paprika
2 tbsp cream cheese	Salt and black pepper to taste
Salt and black pepper, to taste	2 tbsp lemon juice
¼ tsp cayenne pepper	

Directions and Total Time: approx. 10 minutes

Halve the avocados and scoop the insides. Place the flesh in a bowl and add in the chicken. Stir in the remaining ingredients and season with salt and pepper. Fill the avocado cups with chicken mixture and serve.

Per serving: Cal 518; Fat 42g; Net Carbs 5.3g; Protein 23g

Sliced Turkey Breast with Garlic & Cheese

Ingredients for 4 servings

1 tbsp olive oil	2 tbsp tomato paste
1 lb turkey breasts, sliced	1 cup provolone cheese, grated
2 garlic cloves, minced	Salt and black pepper to taste
½ cup sour cream	1 tsp dried oregano

Directions and Total Time: approx. 25 minutes

Fry the turkey and garlic in warm olive oil for 5-6 minutes in a pan over medium heat; set aside. Stir in the 1/3 of cup water, tomato paste, and sour cream and cook until thickened, about 4-5 minutes. Season with salt, black pepper, and oregano. Return the turkey to the pan, and spread the shredded cheese over. Let sit for 5 minutes while covered or until the cheese melts. Serve right away.

Per serving: Cal 398; Fat 25g; Net Carbs 3.3g; Protein 37g

One-Pot Turkey with Veggies

Ingredients for 2 servings

1 tbsp olive oil	½ green bell pepper, chopped
½ turkey breast, chopped	1 garlic clove, minced
½ onion, chopped	Salt and black pepper, to taste
½ celery stick, chopped	2 tbsp rosemary, chopped
1 cup mushrooms, sliced	2 cups chicken broth

Directions and Total Time: approx. 45 minutes

Put a pot over medium heat and warm oil. Cook turkey, onion, garlic, and celery for 5 minutes. Place in bell pepper, mushrooms, pepper, salt, and broth; cook for 30 minutes. Sprinkle with rosemary.

Per serving: Cal 464; Fat 25g; Net Carbs 8.6g; Protein 5.3g

Broccoli & Carrot Turkey Bake

Ingredients for 4 servings

1 lb cooked turkey breasts, shredded
2 tbsp olive oil
1 carrot, shredded
10 oz broccoli florets
½ cup almond milk
½ cup heavy cream
1 cup cheddar cheese, grated
4 tbsp pork rinds, crushed
Salt and black pepper to taste
½ tsp paprika
1 tsp oregano

Directions and Total Time: approx. 45 minutes

Preheat oven to 375 F and grease a baking tray with cooking spray. Steam the broccoli and carrot in salted water over medium heat for 7 minutes.

Place the turkey into a large bowl together with almond milk, olive oil, broccoli, paprika, oregano, salt, and black pepper, and stir to combine. Transfer the mixture to the baking tray. Pour the heavy cream over the dish and sprinkle with cheddar cheese and pork rinds. Place in the oven and cook until bubbling for 20-25 minutes. Serve.

Per serving: Cal 485; Fat 33g; Net Carbs 4.1g; Protein 39g

Green Turkey Pie

Ingredients for 4 servings

1 tbsp olive oil
½ cup kale, chopped
2 cups chicken stock
½ lb ground turkey
Salt and black pepper, to taste
1 tsp fresh rosemary, chopped
½ lb asparagus, chopped
½ cup mozzarella, shredded
¼ tsp paprika
¼ tsp garlic powder
¼ tsp xanthan gum

Crust

¼ cup butter
¼ tsp xanthan gum
2 cups almond flour
A pinch of salt
1 egg
¼ cup cheddar cheese

Directions and Total Time: approx. 50 min + chilling time

Warm the olive oil in a pot over medium heat. Add and cook the turkey for 5 minutes. Stir in stock, mozzarella cheese, garlic powder, rosemary, black pepper, paprika, asparagus, kale, and salt. In a bowl, combine ½ cup stock from the pot with ¼ teaspoon xanthan gum, and transfer everything to the pot; set aside.

For the crust, in a bowl, combine all the crust ingredients and stir until a pie crust dough forms. Form into a ball and refrigerate for 30 minutes. Spread the filling for the pie on the bottom of a greased baking dish. Set the dough on a working surface, roll into a circle, and top the filling with the dough. Set in the preheated to 350 F oven and bake for 35 minutes. Allow the pie to cool and serve.

Per serving: Cal 325; Fat 23g; Net Carbs 5.6g; Protein 21g

Turkey & Vegetable Casserole

Ingredients for 2 servings

2 tbsp coconut oil
1 turkey breast, sliced
2 zucchinis, sliced
1 onion, chopped
1 carrot, chopped
1 cup mushrooms, sliced
1 green bell pepper, chopped
1 garlic clove, minced
Salt and black pepper to taste
2 tbsp parsley, chopped

Directions and Total Time: approx. 25 minutes

Heat a pan over medium heat and add coconut oil. Cook the turkey slices for 3 minutes on each side; reserve. To the same pan, add and sauté the onion and garlic for 3 minutes. Stir in zucchinis, bell pepper, mushrooms, pepper, salt, and carrot; cook for 6-8 minutes. Return the turkey and cook for 3 minutes. Serve topped with parsley.

Per serving: Cal 464; Fat 23g; Net Carbs 8.6g; Protein 53g

Jalapeño Stewed Turkey

Ingredients for 2 servings

1 onion, chopped
2 tbsp olive oil
½ lb turkey breast, chopped
1 cup snow peas
2 cups chicken stock
Salt and black pepper to taste
1 Jalapeño pepper, chopped
1 garlic clove, minced
½ cup broccoli rabe, chopped
½ tsp ground coriander
1 tsp cumin
¼ cup sour cream
1 tbsp cilantro, chopped

Directions and Total Time: approx. 35 minutes

Heat olive oil in a pan over medium heat. Cook the turkey, onion, and garlic for 3 minutes, stirring often.

Pour in the chicken stock and snow peas and cook for 10 minutes. Place in the ground coriander, salt, broccoli rabe, Jalapeño pepper, cumin, and black pepper, and cook for 10 minutes. Stir in the sour cream and top with chopped cilantro. Serve warm.

Per serving: Cal 443; Fat 28g; Net Carbs 8.2g; Protein 36g

Leftover Turkey & Veggie Casserole

Ingredients for 4 servings

2 cups leftover roast turkey, shredded
2 cups zucchini cubes
1 onion chopped
1 cup green cabbage, shredded
¼ cup chicken stock
½ cup tomato sauce
¼ tsp cumin
2 tbsp Parmesan cheese, grated
Salt and black pepper, to taste
1 garlic clove, minced

Directions and Total Time: approx. 65 minutes

Heat a pan over medium heat. Cook the onion, garlic, zucchini, and cabbage for 7-8 minutes until tender. Stir in the broth, tomato sauce, cumin, black pepper, and salt and simmer for 15 minutes. Add the turkey and transfer to a baking dish; bake for 20-25 minutes at 350 F. Scatter the Parmesan cheese over and bake for 5 more minutes until golden on top. Serve and enjoy!

Per serving: Cal 273; Fat 15g; Net Carbs 6.5g; Protein 23g

Turkey Burgers with Brussels Sprouts

Ingredients for 4 servings

Burgers

1 lb ground turkey
1 egg
1 onion, chopped
2 tbsp pork rinds, crushed
Salt and black pepper to taste
1 tsp dried mixed herbs
2 tbsp butter

Brussels sprouts

1 lb Brussels sprouts, halved
2 tbsp olive oil

Directions and Total Time: approx. 30 minutes

In a pan over medium heat, warm olive oil. Cook Brussels sprouts for 10 minutes. Season with salt and pepper and set aside. Combine burger ingredients in a bowl and create patties from the mixture. To the same pan, add the butter, and fry the cakes for 10 minutes in total. Serve with Brussels sprouts

Per serving: Cal 422; Fat 25g; Net Carbs 6.1g; Protein 28g

Hot Turkey Patties with Cucumber Salad

Ingredients for 4 servings

2 tbsp olive oil	2 garlic cloves, minced
2 spring onions, thinly sliced	1 tbsp dried oregano
1 lb ground turkey	1 tsp Cayenne powder
1 egg	Salt and black pepper to taste

Cucumber salad

1 tbsp apple cider vinegar	5 radishes, sliced
1 tbsp chopped dill	½ red onion, sliced
2 cucumbers, sliced	2 tbsp extra virgin olive oil

Directions and Total Time: approx. 35 minutes

In a medium bowl, place ground turkey, spring onions, egg, garlic, oregano, Cayenne powder, salt, and pepper and mix to combine. Make patties out of the mixture.

Warm olive oil in a skillet over medium heat and cook the patties for 3 minutes per side. Set aside. To a bowl, add cucumber, radishes, red onion, olive oil, apple cider vinegar, salt, and dill and toss to coat. Plate along with the turkey patties. Serve and enjoy!

Per serving: Cal 432; Fat 32g; Net Carbs 6.4g; Protein 25g

Italian Turkey Ragu with Zucchini Pasta

Ingredients for 4 servings

1 cup mushrooms, sliced	1 parsnip, chopped
2 tsp olive oil	16 oz zucchini noodles
1 lb ground turkey	1 tbsp Italian seasoning
1 cup tomato sauce, sugar-free	2 tbsp Parmesan, grated
1 onion, chopped	

Directions and Total Time: approx. 45 minutes

Warm oil in a skillet over medium heat. Cook zucchini noodles for 2 minutes. Set aside. Add turkey to the skillet and cook for 7 minutes. Transfer to a plate. Add onion, parsnip, and mushrooms and cook for 10 minutes. Return turkey to the skillet. Stir in tomato sauce and Italian seasoning. Cover the pan and simmer for 15 minutes. Pour the sauce over the zucchini and top with Parmesan cheese. Serve and enjoy!

Per serving: Cal 312; Fat 15g; Net Carbs 9.6g; Protein 28g

Creamed Turkey & Swiss Chard Soup

Ingredients for 4 servings

½ lb turkey breast, cubed	1 garlic clove, minced
1 cup Swiss chard, chopped	1 onion, chopped
1 cup canned diced tomatoes	½ tsp turmeric
2 tbsp coconut oil	Salt and black pepper to taste
2 tbsp coconut cream	½ tsp chili powder

Directions and Total Time: approx. 25 minutes

Warm the coconut oil over medium heat and sauté the turkey, onion, and garlic for 3 minutes. Stir in the turmeric, tomatoes, chili powder, salt, and pepper. Pour in the tomatoes and coconut cream and cook for 10 minutes. Remove from the heat, add in the Swiss chard, and blend with an immersion blender until creamy. Return to the heat and simmer for 5 minutes. Serve.

Per serving: Cal 342; Fat 15g; Net Carbs 5.1g; Protein 22g

Bacon Topped Turkey Meatloaf

Ingredients for 6 servings

3 tbsp olive oil	2 tbsp coconut aminos
2 garlic cloves, minced	1 tbsp tomato paste
1 yellow onion, chopped	2 large eggs
6 bacon, slices	Salt and black pepper, to taste
1 ½ lb ground turkey	2 tbsp Dijon mustard
1 small zucchini, minced	¼ tsp Worcestershire sauce

Directions and Total Time: approx. 15 minutes

Preheat oven to 360 F. Warm the olive oil in a saucepan over medium heat. Add garlic and onion and cook for 3 minutes. Transfer to a bowl and add the ground turkey, zucchini, coconut aminos, tomato paste, eggs, mustard, Worcestershire sauce, salt, and pepper and mix with your hands until thoroughly incorporated. Shape the mixture into a greased loaf. Bake for 35 minutes or until no longer pink. Cover the loaf with the bacon slices and bake for 10 more minutes. Allow to cool before serving.

Per serving: Cal 426; Fat 29g; Net Carbs 1.7g; Protein 41g

Jalapeno Turkey Tomato Bites

Ingredients for 2 servings

2 tomatoes, sliced	1/3 tbsp Dijon mustard
1 cup turkey ham, chopped	¼ cup mayonnaise
¼ jalapeño pepper, minced	Salt and black pepper to taste

Directions and Total Time: approx. 15 minutes

Combine turkey ham, jalapeño pepper, mustard, mayonnaise, salt, and black pepper in a bowl. Arrange tomato slices in a single layer on a serving platter. Divide the turkey mixture between the tomato slices and serve.

Per serving: Cal 245; Fat 15g; Net Carbs 6.3g; Protein 21g

Turkey & Cheese Parfait

Ingredients for 4 servings

½ pound ground turkey	1 cup cream cheese
½ cup ricotta cheese	1 tbsp tomato puree
12 pimiento-stuffed olives	Salt and garlic powder to taste

Directions and Total Time: approx. 15 minutes

Cook the ground turkey in a greased pan over medium heat for 5-6 minutes until no longer pink. Mix the ricotta and cream cheeses, tomato puree, garlic powder, and salt. Divide ½ of turkey mixture between bowls. Top with ½ of the cheese mixture; repeat the layers; Top with olives. Serve.

Per serving: Cal 432; Fat 36g; Net Carbs 0.4g; Protein 23g

PORK

Roasted Pork Stuffed with Ham & Cheese

Ingredients for 2 servings

2 tbsp olive oil	1 tsp cumin
Zest and juice from 1 lime	2 pork loin steaks
1 garlic clove, minced	1 pickle, chopped
2 tbsp fresh cilantro, chopped	2 oz smoked ham, sliced
2 tbsp fresh mint, chopped	2 oz Gruyere cheese sliced
Salt and black pepper to taste	1 tbsp mustard

Directions and Total Time: approx. 40 min + cooling time

Combine the lime zest, oil, black pepper, cumin, cilantro, lime juice, garlic, mint, and salt in a food processor; transfer to a bowl. Place the steaks in the marinade and toss well to coat. Place in the fridge for 2 hours.

Preheat oven to 360 F. Arrange the steaks on a working surface, split the pickles, mustard, cheese, and ham on them, roll, and secure with toothpicks. Heat a pan over medium heat, add in the pork rolls, cook each side for 2 minutes and remove to a baking sheet. Bake in the oven at 350 F for 25 minutes. Serve and enjoy!

Per serving: Cal 433; Fat 38g; Net Carbs 4.2g; Protein 24g

Baked Pork Sausage with Vegetables

Ingredients for 2 servings

1 tbsp olive oil	1 red bell peppers, sliced
½ lb pork sausages	1 sprig rosemary, chopped
2 tomatoes, chopped	1 garlic clove, minced
1 small onion, sliced	1 tbsp balsamic vinegar
½ medium carrot, sliced	Salt and black pepper to taste
1 tsp smoked paprika	

Directions and Total Time: approx. 45 minutes

Preheat the oven to 360 F. Heat olive oil in a saucepan and add the tomatoes, bell peppers, garlic, carrot, onion, and balsamic vinegar, and cook for 8-10 minutes until softened and lightly golden. Season with salt, paprika, and pepper. Transfer to a baking dish. Arrange the sausages on top of the veggies. Put the dish in the oven and bake for 20-25 minutes until the sausages have browned to the desired color. Serve topped with rosemary.

Per serving: Cal 411; Fat 32g; Net Carbs 6.5g; Protein 15g

Pork Chops with Basil-Tomato Sauce

Ingredients for 2 servings

2 pork chops	7 oz canned diced tomatoes
½ tbsp fresh basil, chopped	½ tbsp tomato paste
1 garlic clove, minced	Salt and black pepper to taste
1 tbsp olive oil	½ red chili, finely chopped

Directions and Total Time: approx. 45 minutes

Season the pork with salt and black pepper. Set a pan over medium heat and warm oil. Place in the pork chops and cook for 3 minutes. Turn and cook for another 3 minutes; remove to a bowl. Add the garlic to the pan and cook for 30 seconds. Stir in the tomato paste, tomatoes, and chili. Bring to a boil and reduce the heat to low.

Place in the pork chops, cover the pan, and simmer everything for 30 minutes. Remove the pork chops to plates and sprinkle with fresh basil to serve.

Per serving: Cal 425; Fat 25g; Net Carbs 2.5g; Protein 39g

Herb Pork Chops with Cranberry Sauce

Ingredients for 2 servings

2 pork chops	1 bay leaf
½ tsp garlic powder	1 cup chicken stock
Salt and black pepper to taste	1 tbsp parsley, chopped
1 tsp fresh basil, chopped	1 cup cranberries
A drizzle of olive oil	1 tsp fresh rosemary, chopped
½ onion, chopped	½ cup xylitol
½ cup white wine	½ cup water
Juice of ½ lemon	½ tsp sriracha sauce

Directions and Total Time: approx. 2 hours 45 minutes

Preheat oven to 340 F. In a bowl, combine the pork with basil, salt, garlic powder, and black pepper. Heat a pan with a drizzle of oil over medium heat, place in the pork, and cook until browned, about 4-5 minutes; set aside.

Cook the onion in the pan for 2 minutes. Place in the bay leaf and wine and cook for 4 minutes. Pour in lemon juice and chicken stock and simmer for 5 minutes. Return the pork and cook for 10 minutes. Cover the pan and place it in the oven for 2 hours. Uncover and bake for 5 minutes.

Set another pan over medium heat, add in the cranberries, rosemary, sriracha sauce, water, and xylitol and bring to a simmer for 15 minutes. Remove the pork chops from the oven and discard the bay leaf. Pour the sauce over the pork and serve sprinkled with parsley.

Per serving: Cal 450; Fat 24g; Net Carbs 7.3g; Protein 42g

Barbecued Pork Chops

Ingredients for 2 servings

2 pork loin chops, boneless	½ tsp onion powder
½ cup BBQ sauce, sugar-free	½ tsp garlic powder
Salt and black pepper to taste	1 tsp red pepper flakes
½ tsp ginger powder	2 thyme sprigs, chopped

Directions and Total Time: approx. 20 minutes

Mix black pepper, salt, ginger powder, onion powder, garlic powder, and red pepper flakes in a small bowl. Rub the spices onto the pork chops.

Preheat the grill to high. Place and cook the meat for 2 minutes per side. Reduce the heat to medium and brush the BBQ sauce on the meat, cover, and grill for another 5 minutes. Open the lid, turn the meatp and brush again with barbecue sauce. Continue cooking covered for 5 minutes. Remove and serve sprinkled with thyme.

Per serving: Cal 412; Fat 35g; Net Carbs 1.1g; Protein 34g

Citrus Pork with Cabbage & Tomatoes

Ingredients for 2 servings

3 tbsp olive oil	2 pork loin chops
2 tbsp lemon juice	1/3 head cabbage, shredded
1 garlic clove, pureed	1 tomato, chopped

1 tbsp white wine	¼ tsp ground nutmeg
Salt and black pepper to taste	1 tbsp parsley
¼ tsp cumin	

Directions and Total Time: approx. 25 minutes

In a bowl, mix the lemon juice, garlic, salt, pepper, and 1 tbsp of olive oil. Brush the pork with the mixture.

Preheat grill to high heat. Grill the pork for 2-3 minutes on each side until cooked through. Remove to serving plates. Warm the remaining olive oil in a pan and cook the cabbage for 5 minutes. Drizzle with white wine, sprinkle with cumin, nutmeg, salt, and pepper. Add in the tomato and cook for another 5 minutes, stirring occasionally. Яздд the sautéed cabbage to the side of the chops and serve sprinkled with parsley.

Per serving: Cal 565; Fat 37g; Net Carbs 6.1g; Protein 43g

Pork Kofta with Spiced Yogurt

Ingredients for 4 servings

1 lb ground pork	Salt and black pepper to taste
2 tbsp olive oil	2 tbsp parsley, chopped
2 tbsp pork rinds, crushed	½ tsp oregano
1 garlic clove, minced	1 cup plain yogurt
1 shallot, chopped	1 tsp Cajun seasoning
1 small egg	2 tbsp fresh mint, chopped
1/3 tsp paprika	

Directions and Total Time: approx. 30 minutes

In a bowl, mix the ground pork, shallot, pork rinds, garlic, egg, paprika, oregano, parsley, salt, and black pepper, just until combined. Form balls of the mixture and place them in an oiled baking pan; drizzle with olive oil. Bake in the oven for 18 minutes at 390 F until golden brown.

In a bowl, whisk the yogurt, Cajun seasoning, and mint. Adjust the seasoning. Serve the kofta with the sauce.

Per serving: Cal 323; Fat 15g; Net Carbs 2.1g; Protein 41g

Pork & Summer Squash Traybake

Ingredients for 4 servings

1 lb ground pork	1 (15 oz) can diced tomatoes
1 large summer squash, sliced	½ cup pork rinds, crushed
Salt and black pepper to taste	¼ cup parsley, chopped
1 garlic clove, minced	2 cups cottage cheese
2 red onions, chopped	2 tbsp olive oil
1 cup broccoli, chopped	1/3 cup chicken broth

Directions and Total Time: approx. 40 minutes

Heat the olive oil in a skillet over medium heat, add the pork, season with salt and pepper, and cook for 3 minutes or until no longer pink. Stir occasionally while breaking any lumps apart. Add the garlic, half of the red onions, broccoli, and 2 tablespoons of pork rinds. Continue cooking for 3 minutes. Stir in the tomatoes, half of the parsley, and chicken broth. Cook for 3 minutes.

Mix the remaining parsley and cottage cheese and set aside. Sprinkle the bottom of a baking dish with 3 tbsp of pork rinds; top with half of the squash and a season of salt, 2/3 of the pork mixture, and the cheese mixture.

Repeat the layering process a second time to exhaust the ingredients. Cover the baking dish with foil and put it in the oven to bake for 20 minutes at 380 F. Remove the foil and brown the top of the casserole with the broiler side of the oven for 2 minutes. Serve and enjoy!

Per serving: Cal 423; Fat 27g; Net Carbs 3.1g; Protein 33g

Spicy Pork with Capers & Olives

Ingredients for 2 servings

2 pork chops	Salt and black pepper to taste
1 tbsp olive oil	½ tsp hot pepper sauce
1 garlic clove, minced	¼ cup capers
¼ tbsp chili powder	6 black olives, sliced
¼ tsp cumin	

Directions and Total Time: approx. 25 min + chilling time

In a mixing bowl, combine olive oil, cumin, salt, hot pepper sauce, pepper, garlic, and chili powder. Place in the pork chops, toss to coat, and refrigerate for 4 hours. Preheat grill over medium heat. Arrange the pork on a preheated grill. Cook for 7 minutes, turn, and cook for another 7 minutes. Place onto serving plates and sprinkle with olives and capers. Enjoy!

Per serving: Cal 415; Fat 26g; Net Carbs 1.8g; Protein 43g

Chimichurri Pork Chops

Ingredients for 2 servings

1 garlic clove, minced	¼ cup extra-virgin olive oil
1 tsp white wine vinegar	10 oz pork loin chops
¼ cup parsley leaves, chopped	Salt and black pepper to taste
¼ cup cilantro leaves, chopped	2 tbsp sesame oil

Directions and Total Time: approx. 20 minutes

To make the chimichurri: In a blender, mix the parsley, cilantro, and garlic. Add the vinegar, extra-virgin olive oil, and salt and pulse until well combined.

Preheat a grill pan over medium heat. Rub the pork with sesame oil and season with salt and pepper. Grill the meat for 4-5 minutes on each side until no longer pink in the center. Put the pork on a serving plate and spoon chimichurri sauce over to serve.

Per serving: Cal 452; Fat 34g; Net Carbs 2.3g; Protein 33g

Rosemary Buttered Pork Chops

Ingredients for 2 servings

½ tbsp olive oil	Salt and black pepper to taste
2 tbsp butter	A pinch of paprika
1 tbsp rosemary	½ tsp chili powder
2 pork chops	

Directions and Total Time: approx. 20 minutes

Rub the pork chops with olive oil, salt, pepper, paprika, and chili powder. Heat a grill over medium, add in the pork chops and cook for 10 minutes, flipping once. Remove to a serving plate. In a pan over low heat, warm the butter until it turns a nutty brown. Pour over the pork chops, sprinkle with rosemary and serve.

Per serving: Cal 363; Fat 22g; Net Carbs 3.8g; Protein 38g

Leek & Bacon Gratin

Ingredients for 4 servings

1 lb leeks, trimmed and sliced
3 oz bacon, chopped
2 cups baby spinach
4 oz halloumi cheese, cubed
2 garlic cloves, minced
1 cup buttermilk
1 tomato, chopped
2 tbsp water
1 cup grated mozzarella
½ tsp dried oregano
Salt and black pepper to taste

Directions and Total Time: approx. 40 minutes

Place a cast iron-pan over medium heat and fry the bacon for 4 minutes, then add garlic and leeks and cook for 5-6 minutes. Preheat oven to 370 F.

In a bowl, mix the buttermilk, tomato, and water and add to the pan. Stir in the spinach, halloumi, oregano, salt, and pepper to taste. Sprinkle the mozzarella cheese on top and transfer the pan to the oven. Bake for 20 minutes or until the cheese is golden. Serve warm.

Per serving: Cal 350; Fat 27g; Net Carbs 5.3g; Protein 16g

Cheese Stuffing Pork Rolls with Bacon

Ingredients for 2 servings

1 tbsp olive oil
2 oz bacon, sliced
1 tbsp fresh parsley, chopped
2 pork chops, boneless, flatten
¼ cup ricotta cheese
1 tbsp pine nuts
1 spring onion, chopped
1 garlic clove, minced
1 tbsp Parmesan cheese, grated
5 oz canned diced tomatoes
Salt and black pepper to taste
½ tsp herbs de Provence

Directions and Total Time: approx. 40 minutes

Put the pork chops on a flat surface. Set the bacon slices on top, then divide the ricotta cheese, pine nuts, and Parmesan cheese. Roll up and secure with toothpicks.

Set a pan over medium heat and warm oil. Cook the pork rolls until browned, 5 minutes; remove to a plate.

Add in the spring onion and garlic and cook for 5 minutes. Place in 1 cup of water and cook for 3 minutes. Get rid of the toothpicks from the rolls and return them to the pan. Stir in the black pepper, salt, tomatoes, and herbs de Provence. Bring to a boil, set heat to medium-low, and cook for 20 minutes while covered. Sprinkle with parsley to serve.

Per serving: Cal 631; Fat 42g; Net Carbs 7.1g; Protein 44g

Oven Roasted Chorizo with Veggies

Ingredients for 4 servings

2 tbsp olive oil
1 lb chorizo sausage, chopped
1 onion, sliced
3 sun-dried tomatoes, sliced
Salt and black pepper to taste
1 small eggplant, chopped
½ cup Swiss cheese, grated
1 yellow bell peppers, chopped
1 orange bell peppers, chopped
A pinch of red pepper flakes
2 tbsp fresh parsley, chopped

Directions and Total Time: approx. 30 minutes

Preheat oven to 360 F. Heat olive oil in a pan over medium heat, add sun-dried tomatoes, bell peppers, eggplant, and onion, and cook for 5 minutes. Season with black pepper, pepper flakes, and salt and mix well.

Cook for 1 minute and remove from heat. Stir in chorizo and cook for 3-4 minutes. Pour the mixture into a baking dish, scatter with the Swiss cheese and bake in the oven for 10 minutes until the cheese melts. Serve topped with fresh parsley. Enjoy!

Per serving: Cal 551; Fat 44g; Net Carbs 6.8g; Protein 32g

Mushroom Pork Chops with Broccoli

Ingredients for 2 servings

2 (10.5-oz) cans mushroom soup
1 shallot, chopped
2 pork chops
½ cup sliced mushrooms
Salt and black pepper to taste
1 tbsp parsley
½ head broccoli, cut into florets

Directions and Total Time: approx. 45 minutes

Steam the broccoli in salted water over medium heat for 6-8 minutes until tender. Set aside.

Preheat the oven to 370 F. Season the pork chops with salt and pepper and place in a greased baking dish. Combine the mushroom soup, mushrooms, and shallot in a bowl. Pour the mixture over the pork chops. Bake for 30 minutes. Sprinkle with parsley. Serve with broccoli.

Per serving: Cal 412; Fat 31g; Net Carbs 7.2g; Protein 20g

Pork Sausage with Sauerkraut

Ingredients for 4 servings

2 tbsp olive oil
1 lb pork sausages, sliced
2 cups sauerkraut, drained
Salt and black pepper to taste
½ cup ham, chopped
1 cup chicken broth
1 tbsp tomato paste
1 onion, chopped
2 garlic cloves, minced
1 tbsp butter
½ cup Parmesan cheese, grated
½ tsp cumin
½ tsp nutmeg

Directions and Total Time: approx. 70 minutes

Heat a pot with the butter and olive oil over medium heat. Add in the onion and garlic and cook for 3 minutes. Place in the pork sausages and ham and cook until slightly browned, about 4-5 minutes.

Place in the sauerkraut and broth and cook for 30 minutes. Stir in tomato paste, cumin, nutmeg, black pepper, and salt. Top with Parmesan cheese and bake for 20 minutes at 350 F. Serve and enjoy!

Per serving: Cal 455; Fat 25g; Net Carbs 3.6g; Protein 35g

Tender Pork Loin with Mustard Sauce

Ingredients for 2 servings

½ tbsp butter
½ tbsp olive oil
2 pork loin chops
½ tsp Dijon mustard
½ tbsp soy sauce
½ tsp lemon juice
2 tsp cumin seeds
½ tbsp water
Salt and black pepper to taste
½ cup chives, chopped

Directions and Total Time: approx. 20 minutes

Set a pan over medium heat and warm butter and olive oil, add in the pork chops, season with salt, and pepper, cook for 4 minutes, turn and cook for 4 minutes.

Remove to a plate. In a bowl, mix the water with lemon juice, cumin seeds, mustard, and soy sauce. Pour the mustard sauce into the pan and simmer for 5 minutes. Spread over pork, top with chives, and serve.

Per serving: Cal 382; Fat 21g; Net Carbs 1.2g; Protein 38g

Caramelized Onion over Pork Burgers

Ingredients for 2 servings

3 tbsp olive oil	½ tbsp balsamic vinegar
½ lb ground pork	1 drop liquid stevia
Salt and black pepper to taste	1 tomato, sliced into rings
½ tsp chili pepper	1 tbsp mayonnaise
1 white onion, sliced into rings	

Directions and Total Time: approx. 25 minutes

Warm 2 tbsp of the olive oil in a skillet over medium heat, sauté the onions for 3 minutes until soft, and stir in the balsamic vinegar and stevia. Cook for 5-6 minutes stirring once or twice or until caramelized; remove to a plate. Combine the pork, salt, black pepper and chili pepper in a bowl and mold out 2 patties.

Heat the remaining olive oil in a skillet over medium heat and fry the patties for 4 to 5 minutes on each side until golden brown on the outside. Remove to a plate and sit for 3 minutes. On each tomato slice, place half of the mayonnaise and a patty, and top with some onion rings. Cover with another tomato slice and serve.

Per serving: Cal 510; Fat 41g; Net Carbs 2.6g; Protein 31g

Pork Chops with Creamy Bacon Sauce

Ingredients for 2 servings

2 oz bacon, chopped	2 sprigs fresh thyme
2 pork chops	2 tbsp heavy cream
Salt and black pepper to taste	½ tsp Dijon mustard

Directions and Total Time: approx. 35 minutes

Brown bacon in a large skillet on medium heat for 5 minutes until crispy. Remove to a paper towel-lined plate to soak up excess fat. Season pork chops with salt and pepper and brown in the bacon fat for 4 minutes on each side. Remove to the bacon plate. Stir thyme, 2 tbsp of water, mustard, and heavy cream in the skillet and simmer for 5 minutes. Return the chops and bacon to the skillet and cook for another 10 minutes. Garnish with thyme leaves to serve.

Per serving: Cal 422; Fat 35g; Net Carbs 2.8g; Protein 21g

Grilled Pork Chops with Balsamic Sauce

Ingredients for 2 servings

2 pork loin chops, boneless	1 garlic clove, minced
1 tbsp rosemary, chopped	2 tbsp olive oil
1 tbsp balsamic vinegar	Salt and black pepper to taste

Directions and Total Time: approx. 25 min + cooling time

Put the pork in a deep dish. Add in the balsamic vinegar, rosemary, garlic, olive oil, salt, and black pepper, and toss to coat. Cover the dish with plastic wrap and marinate the pork for 1 to 2 hours.

Preheat grill to medium heat. Remove the pork when ready, reserve the marinade and grill covered for 4-6 minutes per side. Remove the pork chops and let them sit for 4 minutes on a serving plate. In a saucepan over medium heat, pour in the reserved marinade, add in 3 tbsp water and bring to a boil for 2-3 minutes until the liquid becomes thickened. Top the chops with the sauce and serve.

Per serving: Cal 421; Fat 25g; Net Carbs 2.3g; Protein 41g

Pork Steaks with Carrot & Broccoli

Ingredients for 2 servings

1 tbsp olive oil	2 garlic cloves, minced
1 tbsp butter	1 tbsp fresh parsley, chopped
2 pork steaks, bone-in	½ head broccoli, cut into florets
½ cup water	1 carrot, sliced
Salt and black pepper to taste	½ lemon, sliced

Directions and Total Time: approx. 30 minutes

Heat oil and butter over high heat. Add in the pork steaks, season with pepper and salt, and cook until browned; set to a plate. In the same pan, add garlic, carrot, and broccoli and cook for 4 minutes. Pour the water, lemon slices, salt, and black pepper and cook everything for 5 minutes. Return the pork steaks to the pan and cook for 10 minutes. Serve the steaks sprinkled with parsley.

Per serving: Cal 674; Fat 67g; Net Carbs 7.5g; Protein 51g

Greek-Style Pork Chops

Ingredients for 2 servings

1 garlic clove, minced	¼ cup Kalamata olives, sliced
2 pork chops, bone-in	2 tbsp olive oil
Salt and black pepper to taste	2 tbsp vegetable broth
1 tsp dried oregano	¼ cup feta cheese, crumbled

Directions and Total Time: approx. 45 minutes

Preheat the oven to 425 F. Rub pork chops with pepper and salt and place in a roasting pan. Stir in the garlic, olives, olive oil, broth, and oregano. Set in the oven and bake for 10 minutes. Reduce heat to 350 F and roast for 25 minutes. Plate the pork and sprinkle with pan juices and feta cheese all over. Serve and enjoy!

Per serving: Cal 533; Fat 38g; Net Carbs 1.9g; Protein 41g

Hot Pork Meatballs

Ingredients for 2 servings

¼ cup mozzarella cheese, grated

1 lb ground pork	½ cup almond flour
Salt and black pepper to taste	¼ cup hot sauce
2 tbsp yellow mustard	1 egg

Directions and Total Time: approx. 35 minutes

Preheat oven to 400 F. Line a baking tray with parchment paper. In a bowl, combine the pork, pepper, mustard, flour, mozzarella cheese, salt, and egg. Form meatballs and arrange them on the baking tray. Cook for 16-20 minutes, then pour over the hot sauce and bake for 5 more minutes. Serve warm and enjoy!

Per serving: Cal 487; Fat 35g; Net Carbs 4.3g; Protein 32g

Pork Chops with Peanut Sauce

Ingredients for 2 servings

1 tbsp cilantro, chopped	Salt to taste
1 tbsp mint, chopped	2 pork chops
1 onion, chopped	2 garlic cloves, minced
¼ cup peanuts	Juice and zest from 1 lemon
3 tbsp olive oil	

Directions and Total Time: approx. 40 min + cooling time

In a food processor, combine the cilantro with olive oil, mint, peanuts, salt, lemon zest, garlic, and onion. Rub the pork with the mixture, place in a bowl, and refrigerate for 1 hour while covered. Preheat oven to 350 F. Remove the chops and set to a greased baking dish, sprinkle with lemon juice, and bake for 30 minutes in the oven. Serve.

Per serving: Cal 643; Fat 47g; Net Carbs 6g; Protein 45.4g

Fried Pork with Blackberry Gravy

Ingredients for 2 servings

2 tbsp olive oil	2 tbsp chicken broth
1 lb pork chops	½ tbsp rosemary, chopped
Salt and black pepper to taste	1 tbsp balsamic vinegar
1 cup blackberries	1 tsp Worcestershire sauce

Directions and Total Time: approx. 20 minutes

Place the blackberries in a bowl and mash them with a fork until jam-like. Pour into a saucepan over medium heat and add the broth and rosemary. Bring to boil on low heat for 4 minutes. Stir in balsamic vinegar and Worcestershire sauce. Simmer for 1 minute. Heat the olive oil in a skillet over medium heat. Season the pork with salt and pepper and cook for 5 minutes on each side. Put on serving plates and spoon sauce over. Enjoy!

Per serving: Cal 732; Fat 42g; Net Carbs 6.9g; Protein 56g

Pork Kebabs with Mashed Squash

Ingredients for 4 servings

2/3 cup olive oil	1 lb pork tenderloin, cubed
7 tbsp fresh cilantro, chopped	½ tbsp sugar-free BBQ sauce
4 tbsp fresh basil, chopped	½ cup butter
2 garlic cloves	3 cups butternut squash, cubed
Juice of ½ a lemon	2 oz grated Parmesan
4 tbsp capers	Salt and black pepper to taste

Directions and Total Time: approx. 40 minutes

In a blender, add cilantro, basil, garlic, lemon juice, capers, olive oil, salt, and pepper and process until smooth. Remove the resulting salsa verde in a bowl and set aside. Thread pork cubes on skewers. Season with salt and brush with BBQ sauce. Melt 1 tbsp butter in a grill pan and sear the skewers until browned on both sides, about 8-10 minutes in total; remove to a plate.

Pour the squash into a pot, cover with salted water, and bring to a boil for 15 minutes. Drain and pour into a bowl. Add in the remaining butter, Parmesan cheese, salt, and pepper and mash everything. Serve the skewers with mashed squash and salsa verde.

Per serving: Cal 849; Net Carbs 5g; Fat 81g; Protein 26g

Classic Hawaiian Pork Loco Moco

Ingredients for 4 servings

1 cup sliced oyster mushrooms	1 tbsp salted butter
1 ½ lb ground pork	1 shallot, finely chopped
3 tbsp coconut oil	1 cup vegetable stock
1/3 cup flaxseed meal	1 tsp Worcestershire sauce
½ tsp nutmeg powder	1 tsp tamari sauce
1 tsp onion powder	½ tsp xanthan gum
5 large eggs	2 tbsp olive oil
2 tbsp heavy cream	4 large eggs

Directions and Total Time: approx. 30 minutes

In a bowl, combine ground pork, flaxseed meal, nutmeg and onion powders. In another bowl, whisk 1 egg with heavy cream and mix into the pork mixture. The batter will be sticky. Mold 8 patties from the mixture; set aside. Heat coconut oil in a skillet over medium heat. Fry the patties on both sides until no longer pink, 8-10 minutes; set aside. Melt the butter in the same skillet and cook shallot and mushrooms until softened, 7 minutes. In a bowl, mix stock, Worcestershire and tamari sauces. Pour the mixture over the mushrooms and cook for 3 minutes. Stir in xanthan gum and allow thickening, about 1 minute. Heat half of the olive oil in a skillet, crack in an egg, and fry sunshine style, 1 minute. Plate and fry the remaining eggs using the remaining olive oil. Serve pork with mushroom gravy and top with fried eggs.

Per serving: Cal 649; Net Carbs 2.2g; Fat 46g; Protein 48g

Stir-Fried Pork with Bell Peppers

Ingredients for 4 servings

2 tbsp olive oil	2 garlic cloves, minced
2 lb pork loin, cut into strips	2 tbsp soy sauce, sugar-free
Salt and chili pepper to taste	1 red bell pepper, sliced
1 tsp fresh ginger, grated	1 green bell pepper, sliced

Directions and Total Time: approx. 25 minutes

In a bowl, mix salt, chili pepper, ginger, garlic, and soy sauce. Pour the pork into the bowl and toss to coat. Warm the olive oil in a wok and add in the pork to cook for 6-8 minutes until no longer pink. Stir in the bell peppers and cook for 5 minutes. Adjust the taste with salt and black pepper and spoon the stir-fry into a serving plate. Enjoy!

Per serving: Cal 568; Fat 37g; Net Carbs 1.6g; Protein 52g

Roasted Pork Loin with Brussels Sprouts

Ingredients for 4 servings

½ lb Brussels sprouts, halved	1 tsp hot red pepper flakes
2 tbsp olive oil	½ tsp ginger, minced
Salt and black pepper to taste	2 garlic cloves, minced
1 ½ lb pork loin	½ lemon, sliced
A pinch of dry mustard	¼ cup water

Directions and Total Time: approx. 60 minutes

Preheat oven to 380 F. In a bowl, combine ginger, salt, mustard, and pepper. Add in the pork and toss to coat. Heat the oil in a saucepan over medium heat, brown the pork on all sides, about 8 minutes. Transfer to the oven and roast for 25-30 minutes.

To the saucepan, add Brussels sprouts, lemon slices, garlic, and water; cook for 10 minutes. Place the pork with the Brussels sprouts on a platter and sprinkle with red pepper flakes to serve.

Per serving: Cal 422; Fat 22g; Net Carbs 4.1g; Protein 43g

Stewed Pork With Cauliflower and Broccoli

Ingredients for 4 servings

2 tbsp olive oil	1 onion, chopped
1 red bell pepper, chopped	14 oz canned diced tomatoes
1 lb stewed pork, cubed	¼ tsp garlic powder
Salt and black pepper to taste	1 tbsp tomato puree
2 cups cauliflower florets	1 ½ cups water
2 cups broccoli florets	2 tbsp parsley, chopped

Directions and Total Time: approx. 40 minutes

In a pan, heat olive oil and cook the pork over medium heat for 5 minutes or until browned. Place in the bell pepper and onion and cook for 4 minutes. Stir in water, tomatoes, broccoli, cauliflower, tomato puree, and garlic powder; bring to a simmer and cook for 20 minutes while covered. Season and serve topped with parsley.

Per serving: Cal 566; Fat 35g; Net Carbs 6.7g; Protein 42g

Okra & Sausage Hot Pot

Ingredients for 4 servings

1 lb pork sausage, sliced	½ cup beef stock
1 cup mushrooms, sliced	1 garlic clove, minced
1 onion, chopped	2 cups tomatoes, chopped
1 tsp cayenne pepper	1 lb okra, trimmed and sliced
Salt and black pepper to taste	1 tbsp coconut aminos
1 tbsp fresh parsley, chopped	½ tbsp hot sauce
2 tbsp canola oil	

Directions and Total Time: approx. 30 minutes

Heat the oil and sauté the onion, garlic, and mushrooms for 5 minutes until tender. Add in the hot sauce, stock, tomatoes, coconut aminos, cayenne pepper, okra, and sausage. Bring to a simmer and cook for 15 minutes. Adjust the seasoning with salt and pepper. Sprinkle with fresh parsley to serve.

Per serving: Cal 311; Fat 17g; Net Carbs 8.1g; Protein 245g

Roasted Chorizo with Mixed Greens

Ingredients for 4 servings:

1 lb asparagus, trimmed and halved
1 head broccoli, cut into florets

3 tbsp olive oil	2 red onions, cut into wedges
1 lb chorizo, sliced	Salt and black pepper to taste
2 green bell peppers, diced	1 tbsp maple syrup, sugar-free
1 cup green beans, trimmed	1 lemon, juiced

Directions and Total Time: approx. 30 minutes:

Preheat oven to 390 F. On a baking tray, add the chorizo, asparagus, bell peppers, green beans, onions, and broccoli; season with salt and black pepper. Drizzle with olive oil and maple syrup.

Bake for 15 -20 minutes or until the vegetables soften and become golden at the edges. Remove from the oven, drizzle with lemon juice, and serve warm. Enjoy!

Per serving: Cal 696; Fat 54g; Net Carbs 9.9g; Protein 32g

Cowboy Stew of Bacon & Cheese

Ingredients for 4 servings

2 tbsp olive oil	¼ cup heavy cream
½ cup mozzarella, grated	1 lb bacon, chopped
1 cup chicken broth	10 oz cauliflower florets
1 garlic clove, minced	1 small carrot, chopped
1 shallot, chopped	1 tsp dried thyme
Salt and black pepper to taste	1 tbsp parsley, chopped

Directions and Total Time: approx. 30 minutes

In a pot, heat the olive oil and sauté garlic and shallot for 3 minutes until soft. Add in the bacon and fry for 5 minutes. Then, pour in the broth, thyme, carrot, and cauliflower and simmer for 10 minutes. Stir in heavy cream and mozzarella cheese and cook for 5 minutes. Season with salt, pepper, and parsley to serve.

Per serving: Cal 713; Fat 61g; Net Carbs 4.4g; Protein 32g

Rosemary Pork Medallions

Ingredients for 4 servings

1 lb pork tenderloin, cut into medallions

2 onions, chopped	Salt and black pepper to taste
4 oz bacon, chopped	2 tbsp rosemary, chopped
½ cup vegetable stock	

Directions and Total Time: approx. 40 minutes

Fry the bacon in a pan over medium heat until crispy, 5 minutes; remove. Add in onions, black pepper, and salt and cook for 5 minutes; set to the bacon plate. Add the pork to the pan. Cook for 3-4 minutes, turn, and cook for 3-4 more minutes or until browned. Stir in stock and cook for 10 minutes. Return bacon and onions to the pan and cook for 1 minute. Garnish with rosemary.

Per serving: Cal 325; Fat 17g; Net Carbs 5.5g; Protein 35g

Red Wine & Pork Stew

Ingredients for 4 servings

2 tbsp olive oil	¼ cup red wine
1 lb pork stew meat, cubed	1 carrot, chopped
Salt and black pepper to taste	1 cabbage head, shredded
1 red pepper, minced	2 tbsp chives, chopped
1 garlic clove, minced	½ cup sour cream
1 onion, chopped	1 tbsp oregano, chopped
1 cup beef stock	

Directions and Total Time: approx. 1 hour 20 minutes

Sear the pork in warm olive oil over medium heat until brown, 5-7 minutes. Add in the garlic, onion, red pepper, chives, and carrot; sauté for 5 minutes. Pour in cabbage, stock, and wine and bring to a boil. Reduce the heat and cook for 1 hour. Add in sour cream as you stir for 1 minute, adjust the seasonings and top with oregano.

Per serving: Cal 367; Fat 15g; Net Carbs 7.6g; Protein 38g

Lettuce Wraps with Pork & Dill Pickles

Ingredients for 4 servings

2 tbsp avocado oil	1 head Iceberg lettuce
1 lb ground pork	½ onion, sliced
1 tbsp ginger paste	1 red bell pepper, chopped
Salt and black pepper to taste	2 dill pickles, finely chopped

Directions and Total Time: approx. 30 minutes

Heat the avocado oil in a pan over medium heat and put the in pork with ginger paste, salt, and pepper. Cook for 10-15 minutes while breaking any lumps until the pork is no longer pink. Spoon 2-3 tablespoons of the pork mixture in each lettuce leaf, top with onion slices, bell pepper, and dill pickles. Serve and enjoy!

Per serving: Cal 322; Fat 25.3g; Net Carbs 1.5g; Protein 21g

One-Pot Sausage with Spinach & Zucchini

Ingredients for 4 servings

2 tbsp olive oil	Salt and black pepper to taste
½ onion, sliced	1 lb spinach, chopped
1 lb pork sausage, sliced	1 garlic clove, minced
1 small zucchini, chopped	½ green chili pepper, chopped
1 green bell pepper, chopped	1 tbsp basil, chopped

Directions and Total Time: approx. 25 minutes

Cook the sausages in warm olive oil over medium heat for 6-8 minutes. Stir in the onion, garlic, zucchini, and bell pepper and fry for 3-4 minutes. Place in the spinach, salt, ½ cup of water, black pepper, and chili pepper and cook for 5 minutes. Sprinkle with basil and serve.

Per serving: Cal 487; Fat 28g; Net Carbs 9.3g; Protein 45g

Smoked Sausage Casserole

Ingredients for 4 servings

1 lb smoked sausages, sliced	½ lb turnips, cut into wedges
2 tbsp lard	1 tsp dried thyme
1 chili pepper, finely chopped	Salt and black pepper to taste
1 onion, chopped	1 garlic clove, finely minced
1 lb green beans, chopped	1 cup cheddar cheese, grated
1 cup mushrooms, sliced	

Directions and Total Time: approx. 40 minutes

Warm the lard in a saucepan over medium heat and add the sausages, chili pepper, onion, and garlic. Stir-fry for 5 minutes or until the onion is tender. Add in the green beans, mushrooms, and turnips and sauté for 3-5 minutes. Season with salt, pepper, and thyme. Transfer to a baking dish and bake in the preheated to 380 F oven for 12-15 minutes. Sprinkle with cheddar cheese and bake for 5-8 more minutes until the cheese melts. Serve.

Per serving: Cal 626; Fat 48g; Net Carbs 5.6g; Protein 33g

Tuscan-Style Roasted Pork

Ingredients for 4 servings

2 tbsp butter	2 tsp dried chili flakes
1 ½ lb pork chops	1 cup roasted vegetable broth
2 tbsp ground fennel seeds	2 tbsp rosemary, chopped
1 tbsp dried thyme	2 tbsp capers
Salt and black pepper to taste	1 lemon, zested

Directions and Total Time: approx. 35 minutes

In a bowl, mix salt, pepper, fennel seeds, and thyme. Add in the pork and toss to coat. Melt the butter in a saucepan over medium heat. Brown the meat for about 6-8 minutes. Pour in the broth and stir. Bring to a boil and cook for 10-15 minutes until the meat is tender. Remove the pork to a plate. Add the capers, chili flakes, lemon zest, and rosemary to the saucepan and cook for 2-3 minutes until the flavors come together. Pour the sauce over the meat and serve.

Per serving: Cal 614; Net Carbs 0.2g; Fat 48g; Protein 39g

Grilled Pork Steaks with Broccoli Cakes

Ingredients for 4 servings

1 lb pork loin steaks	1 head broccoli, grated
2 eggs	8 oz halloumi cheese
1 tbsp soy sauce	3 tbsp almond flour
2 tbsp olive oil	½ tsp onion powder
1 tbsp grated ginger	4 ¼ oz butter
2 tbsp fresh lime juice	Salt and black pepper to taste
½ tsp cayenne pepper	

Directions and Total Time: approx. 40 minutes

Combine soy sauce, olive oil, grated ginger, lime juice, salt, and cayenne pepper in a bowl. Brush the pork with the mixture. Heat a grill pan and sear the pork on both sides until golden brown; remove to a plate. Put broccoli in a bowl and grate halloumi cheese on top.

Add in eggs, almond flour, onion powder, salt, and pepper. Mix and form 12 patties out of the mixture. Melt butter in a skillet and fry the patties until golden brown. Plate the grilled pork with the broccoli fritters and serve.

Per serving: Cal 847; Net Carbs 7g; Fat 71g; Protein 35g

Broccoli Pork Pie

Ingredients for 4 servings

1 egg	3 oz butter, melted
2 tbsp butter, cold	5 oz shredded Swiss cheese
2 lb ground pork	2 tbsp oyster sauce
1 head broccoli, cut into florets	2 tbsp Worcestershire sauce
½ cup sour cream	½ tbsp hot sauce
½ celery, finely chopped	1 tsp onion powder

Directions and Total Time: approx. 50 minutes

Preheat oven to 380 F. Bring a pot of salted water to a boil and cook broccoli for 3-5 minutes. Drain and transfer to a food processor; grind until rice-like. Transfer to a bowl. Add in sour cream, egg, celery, butter, and half of the Swiss cheese. Mix to combine.

Melt the cold butter in a pot, add, and cook the pork until brown, 10 minutes. Mix in hot sauce, oyster sauce, and Worcestershire sauce, and onion powder; cook for 3 minutes. Spread the mixture on a greased baking dish and cover with broccoli mixture. Sprinkle with the remaining cheese and bake for 20 minutes. Serve.

Per serving: Cal 699; Net Carbs 3.3g; Fat 52g; Protein 59g

Mushroom & Pork Omelet

Ingredients for 2 servings

¼ cup cremini mushrooms, sliced
2 tbsp olive oil | 1 small white onion, chopped
2 tbsp butter | 6 eggs
2 oz pork sausage, crumbled | 2 oz shredded cheddar cheese

Directions and Total Time: approx. 30 minutes

Warm olive oil in a pan over medium heat, add in pork sausage, and fry for 10 minutes; set aside. In the same pan, sauté the onion and mushrooms, 8 minutes; set aside.

Melt the butter over low heat. Beat the eggs into a bowl until smooth and frothy. Pour the eggs into the pan, swirl to spread around the pan. When the omelet begins to firm, top with sausages, mushroom-onion mixture, and cheddar cheese.Using a spatula, carefully remove the egg mixture around the edges of the pan and flip over the stuffing, and cook for about 2 minutes. Serve warm.

Per serving: Cal 543; Net Carbs 2.7g; Fat 43g; Protein 31g

Tex-Mex Cheesy Pork

Ingredients for 4 servings

½ cup shredded Monterey Jack cheese
1 ½ lb ground pork | ½ cup crushed tomatoes
2 tbsp butter | 1 scallion, chopped to garnish
3 tbsp Tex-Mex seasoning | 1 cup sour cream, for serving
2 tbsp chopped jalapeños

Directions and Total Time: approx. 40 minutes

Preheat oven to 320 F. Melt butter in a skillet over medium heat and cook the pork until brown, 8 minutes. Stir in Tex-Mex seasoning, jalapeños, and tomatoes; simmer for 5 minutes. Transfer the mixture to a greased baking dish and use a spoon to level at the bottom of the dish. Sprinkle the Monterey Jack cheese on top and bake for 20 until the cheese melts and is golden brown. Garnish with scallion and sour cream and serve.

Per serving: Cal 429; Net Carbs 7.8g; Fat 24g; Protein 39g

Smoked Pork Roast with Brussels Sprouts

Ingredients for 4 servings

½ lb Brussels sprouts, halved | 2 garlic cloves, minced
2 lb pork roast | 1 ½ oz fresh ginger, grated
2 tsp dried thyme | 1 tbsp coconut oil
1 bay leaf | 1 tbsp smoked paprika
5 black peppercorns | 1 ½ cups coconut cream
2 ½ cups beef broth | Salt and black pepper to taste

Directions and Total Time: approx. 2 hours

Preheat oven to 370 F. Place the pork in a baking dish and season with salt, pepper, and thyme. Pour the broth over, add in bay leaf and peppercorns and cover with aluminum foil. Bake for 90 minutes. Remove the foil and discard the cooking juices into a bowl; reserve.

In a bowl, combine garlic, ginger, coconut oil, and paprika. Rub the mixture onto the meat and roast for 8 more minutes or until golden brown. Remove and leave to sir for 10 minutes before slicing thinly; set aside.

Strain the juices through a colander into a pot and simmer until reduced to about 1 ½ cups. Pour in Brussels sprouts and cook for 10 minutes. Stir in coconut cream and cook for 5 minutes. Serve the pork with Brussels sprouts.

Per serving: Cal 688; Net Carbs 9.6g; Fat 45g; Protein 60g

Pimiento Cheese Pork Meatballs

Ingredients for 4 servings

1 ½ lb ground pork | 3 tbsp softened cream cheese
1 large egg | 1 tsp paprika
2 tbsp olive oil | 1 pinch cayenne pepper
¼ cup chopped pimientos | 1 tbsp Dijon mustard
1/3 cup mayonnaise | 4 oz grated Parmesan cheese

Directions and Total Time: approx. 20 minutes

In a bowl, mix pimientos, mayonnaise, cream cheese, paprika, cayenne pepper, mustard, Parmesan cheese, ground pork, and egg. Mix and form large meatballs. Heat olive oil in a non-stick skillet and fry the meatballs in batches on both sides until brown, 10 minutes in total. Serve with a green salad if desired.

Per serving: Cal 493; Net Carbs 6.8g; Fat 29g; Protein 54g

Greek-Style Pork Tenderloin

Ingredients for 4 servings

1 ½ lb pork tenderloin | 1 lemon, juiced
¼ cup olive oil | 2 tbsp Greek seasoning
2 tbsp lard | 2 tbsp red wine vinegar

Directions and Total Time: approx. 45 min + chilling time

Preheat oven to 425 F. In a bowl, combine olive oil, lemon juice, Greek seasoning, and red wine vinegar. Place the pork on a clean flat surface, cut a few incisions, and brush the marinade all over. Cover with plastic wrap and refrigerate for 1 hour. Melt lard in a skillet. Remove the pork and sear until brown on the outside, about 4-6 minutes. Place in a greased baking dish, brush with any reserved marinade, and bake for 30-35 minutes or until a meat thermometer reads an internal temperature of 145° F. Serve sliced.

Per serving: Cal 379; Net Carbs 2.5g; Fat 24g; Protein 36g

Pork and Zucchini Meatballs

Ingredients for 4 servings

1 zucchini, grated | 1 tsp red chili flakes
1 lb ground pork | 2 tbsp tamari sauce
2 scallions, shredded | 2 tbsp sesame oil
4 garlic cloves, minced | 3 tbsp coconut oil
1 tsp freshly pureed ginger | Salt and black pepper to taste

Directions and Total Time: approx. 25 minutes

In a bowl, combine ground pork, scallions, zucchini, garlic, ginger, chili flakes, salt, pepper, tamari sauce, and sesame oil. Form 1-inch oval shapes and place them on a plate. Heat coconut oil in a skillet over medium heat and brown the balls for 12 minutes. Transfer to a paper towel-lined plate to drain the excess fat. Serve warm.

Per serving: Cal 325; Net Carbs 2.4g; Ft 21g; Protein 31g

Cheesy Pork Quiche

Ingredients for 4 servings

2 tbsp melted butter	½ lb smoked pork shoulder
6 egg	1 yellow onion, chopped
1 tbsp butter	1 tsp dried thyme
1 ¼ cups almond flour	1 cup coconut cream
1 tbsp psyllium husk powder	¼ cup shredded Swiss cheese
4 tbsp chia seeds	Salt and black pepper to taste

Directions and Total Time: approx. 65 minutes

Preheat oven to 360 F. Grease a springform pan with cooking spray, and line with parchment paper; set aside. To a food processor, add almond flour, psyllium husk, chia seeds, salt, butter, and 1 egg. Mix until a firm dough forms. Oil your hands and spread the dough on the bottom of the springform pan. Place the resulting crust in the fridge while you make the filling.

Melt butter in a skillet and cook the pork and onion until the meat browns, 10-12 minutes. Stir in thyme, salt, and pepper. Remove the crust from the fridge and spoon pork and onion onto the crust. In a bowl, whisk coconut cream, half of the Swiss cheese, and the remaining eggs. Pour the mixture over the meat filling and top with the remaining cheese. Bake until the cheese melts and a toothpick inserted into the quiche comes out clean, 45 minutes. Slice into wedges and serve.

Per serving: Cal 503; Net Carbs 4.6g; Fat 39g; Protein 24g

Tasty Spareribs with Béarnaise Sauce

Ingredients for 4 servings

4 egg yolks	½ tsp onion powder
3 tbsp butter, melted	Salt and black pepper to taste
2 tbsp chopped tarragon	4 tbsp olive oil
2 tsp white wine vinegar	2 lb spareribs, divided into 16

Directions and Total Time: approx. 30 minutes

To make the sauce, beat the egg yolks in a bowl. Gradually pour in the butter and continue to whisk until everything is well incorporated. In another bowl, combine tarragon, white wine vinegar, and onion powder. Mix into the egg mixture and season with salt and black pepper; reserve the sauce in the fridge.

Warm the olive oil in a skillet over medium heat. Season the spareribs on both sides with salt and pepper. Cook in the oil on both sides until brown, 12 minutes. Divide the spareribs between plates and serve with béarnaise sauce to the side along with some braised asparagus.

Per serving: Cal 882; Net Carbs 1g; Fat 81g; Protein 39g

Pork & Egg Stuffed Zucchini

Ingredients for 4 servings

2 tbsp olive oil	1 tsp cumin powder
2 zucchinis	1 tsp smoked paprika
2 tbsp chopped scallions	½ lb ground pork
1 garlic clove, crushed	4 oz bacon, chopped
1 small plum tomato, diced	3 large eggs, beaten
1 tsp dried basil	2 tbsp chopped cilantro

Directions and Total Time: approx. 45 minutes

Slice the zucchini in half lengthwise and scoop out the pulp with a spoon. Heat the olive oil in a skillet and sauté garlic, tomato, and scallions for 6 minutes. Mix in basil, cumin, and paprika. Add and brown the ground pork for 7-8 minutes; reserve. Spread the pork mixture onto the zucchini halves and top with the beaten eggs and bacon. Place in preheated to 380 F oven and cook until the eggs are set, 18-20 minutes. Sprinkle cilantro on top and serve.

Per serving: Cal 372; Net Carbs 2.5g; Fat 25g; Protein 32g

Pork Mushroom Meatballs with Parsnips

Ingredients for 4 servings

1 cup cremini mushrooms, chopped

2 small red onions, chopped	2 cups tomato sauce
1 ½ lb ground pork	6 fresh basil leaves to garnish
2 garlic cloves, minced	1 lb parsnips, chopped
1 tsp dried basil	2 tbsp butter
1 cup grated Parmesan	½ cup coconut cream
½ almond milk	Salt and black pepper to taste
2 tbsp olive oil	

Directions and Total Time: approx. 60 minutes

Preheat oven to 360 F. Line a baking tray with parchment paper. In a bowl, add pork, half of the garlic, half of the onion, mushrooms, basil, salt, and pepper and mix until evenly combined. Mold bite-size balls out of the mixture. Pour ½ cup Parmesan cheese and almond milk each in 2 bowls. Dip the balls in the milk and then in the cheese. Place on the tray and bake for 20 minutes.

Heat olive oil in a saucepan and sauté the remaining onion and garlic for 3 minutes until fragrant and soft. Pour in tomato sauce and cook for 6-8 minutes. Add in the meatballs and simmer for 7 minutes. Cover the parsnips with salted water in a pot over medium heat. Bring to a boil and cook for 10 minutes until the parsnips soften. Drain and pour into a bowl.

Add butter, salt, and pepper to the parsnips and mash them into a puree using a potato mash. Stir in coconut cream and remaining Parmesan cheese until combined. Spoon mashed parsnip into bowls, top with meatballs and sauce, and garnish with basil leaves.

Per serving: Cal 639; Net Carbs 21g; Fat 32g; Protein 49g

Mediterranean Pork Chops

Ingredients for 4 servings

1 ½ lb thin cut pork chops, boneless

½ lemon, juiced	2 tbsp capers
1 lemon, sliced	1 cup beef broth
1 tbsp avocado oil	2 tbsp chopped parsley
3 tbsp butter	1 tsp Mediterranean spice mix

Directions and Total Time: approx. 25 minutes

Warm avocado oil in a skillet over medium heat. Season the pork with Mediterranean spice mix and cook in the skillet on both sides until brown, 10-12 minutes. Transfer to a plate and cover with foil to keep warm.

Melt butter in the skillet and cook capers until sizzling; keep stirring to avoid burning, 3 minutes. Pour in broth and lemon juice, use a spatula to scrape any bits stuck at the bottom, and boil until the sauce reduces by half. Add back the pork, arrange lemon slices on top, and simmer for 3 minutes. Serve the chops garnished with parsley.

Per serving: Cal 339; Net Carbs 0.8g; Fat 21g; Protein 39g

Pork Chops with Cauliflower Steaks

Ingredients for 4 servings

1 tbsp mesquite seasoning
2 heads cauliflower, cut into 4 steaks
2 tbsp butter   4 pork chops
2 tbsp olive oil   ½ cup Parmesan cheese

Directions and Total Time: approx. 25 minutes

Rub the pork with mesquite flavoring. Melt butter in a skillet and fry pork on both sides for 10 minutes; set aside. Heat olive oil in a grill pan and cook cauli steaks on both sides for 4 minutes. Sprinkle with Parmesan cheese to melt. Serve the pork chops with the cauliflower steaks.

Per serving: Cal 432; Net Carbs 3.8g; Fat 19g; Protein 52g

Olive & Cottage Cheese Pork Bake

Ingredients for 4 servings

¼ cup pitted and sliced Kalamata olives
½ cup cottage cheese, crumbled
1 ½ lb ground pork   ½ cup marinara sauce
2 tbsp avocado oil   1 ¼ cups heavy cream
2 garlic cloves, minced

Directions and Total Time: approx. 45 minutes

Preheat oven to 380 F. Grease a casserole dish with cooking spray. Heat avocado oil in a deep skillet, add the ground pork, and cook until brown, 10 minutes. Stir frequently and break any lumps that form. Spread the pork on the bottom of the casserole. Scatter olives, cottage cheese, and garlic on top. In a bowl, mix marinara sauce and heavy cream and pour all over the meat. Bake until the top is bubbly and lightly brown, 20-25 minutes. Serve.

Per serving: Cal 448; Net Carbs 1.5g; Fat 28g; Protein 39g

Pork Chops with Green Beans & Avocado

Ingredients for 4 servings

4 pork shoulder chops   6 green onions, chopped
4 tbsp avocado oil   1 tbsp chopped parsley
1 ½ cups green beans   Salt and black pepper to taste
2 large avocados, chopped

Directions and Total Time: approx. 30 minutes

Warm the avocado oil in a skillet over medium heat. Season the pork with salt and pepper, and fry until brown, 12 minutes; set aside. To the same skillet, sauté green beans until sweating and slightly softened, 10 minutes. Mix in avocados and half of green onions for 2 minutes. Dish the sauté into plates, garnish with the remaining onions and parsley. Serve with the pork chops.

Per serving: Cal 561; Net Carbs 1.9g; Fat 42g; Protein 43g

Pork Chops with Camembert Sauce

Ingredients for 4 servings

1 ½ lb boneless pork chops
6 oz Camembert cheese, rind removed
2 tbsp olive oil   1 tsp yellow mustard
1 tsp butter   1 tbsp chopped parsley
1 cup sour cream   Salt and black pepper to taste
½ cup white wine

Directions and Total Time: approx. 20 minutes

Season the pork with salt and pepper. Warm the olive oil in a saucepan over medium heat and cook the pork for 3-4 minutes per side. Cover with foil to keep warm and set aside. Pour the wine and scrape to deglaze the saucepan. Add butter, sour cream, and mustard. Slice the cheese and add to the saucepan. Stir in any accumulated juices from the meat and cook until the sauce is creamy, 3-5 minutes. Adjust the seasoning and sprinkle with parsley. Pour the sauce over the pork and serve.

Per serving: Cal 602; Net Carbs 0.5g; Fat 38g; Protein 55g

Cilantro Pork Chops with Asparagus

Ingredients for 4 servings

4 pork chops   1 tbsp dried cilantro
3 tbsp butter   1 small lemon, juiced
2 garlic cloves, minced   Salt and black pepper to taste
1 lb asparagus, trimmed

Directions and Total Time: approx. 25 minutes

Warm 2 tbsp of the cold butter in a skillet over medium heat. Season pork chops with salt and pepper and fry on both sides until brown, 10 minutes in total; set aside. Melt the remaining butter in the skillet and sauté garlic until fragrant, 1 minute. Add in asparagus and cook until slightly softened with some crunch, 4 minutes. Add cilantro and lemon juice and toss to coat well. Serve the asparagus with the pork chops.

Per serving: Cal 538; Net Carbs 1.2g; Fat 38g; Protein 42g

Chili Pork Belly with Kale Sauce

Ingredients for 4 servings

2 cups chopped kale   ¼ cup ginger thinly sliced
2 lb pork belly, chopped   4 long red chilies, halved
2 tbsp coconut oil   1 cup coconut milk
1 white onion, chopped   1 cup coconut cream
6 cloves garlic, minced   Salt and black pepper to taste

Directions and Total Time: approx. 30 min

Sprinkle the pork belly with salt and pepper. Warm the coconut oil in a skillet over medium heat and fry in the pork for 10-12 minutes until the skin browns and crackles. Turn a few times to prevent burning. Spoon onto a plate. In the same skillet, sauté the onion, garlic, ginger, and chilies for 5 minutes. Pour in coconut milk and coconut cream and cook for 1 minute. Add kale and cook until wilted, stirring occasionally, about 4 minutes. Stir in the pork. Cook for 2 minutes. Serve warm.

Per serving: Cal 610; Net Carbs 6.7g; Fat 36g; Protein 61g

Chipotle-Coffee Pork Chops

Ingredients for 4 servings

2 tbsp lard	Salt and black pepper to taste
1 tbsp finely ground coffee	½ tsp cumin
½ tsp chipotle powder	1 ½ tsp Swerve brown sugar
½ tsp garlic powder	4 bone-in pork chops

Directions and Total Time: approx. 30 min + chilling time

In a bowl, mix coffee, chipotle powder, garlic powder, cumin, salt, pepper, and Swerve. Rub spices all over the pork. Cover with plastic wraps and refrigerate overnight. Preheat oven to 350 F. Melt lard in a skillet and sear pork on both sides for 3 minutes. Transfer the skillet to the oven and bake for 15-20 minutes. Serve and enjoy!

Per serving: Cal 289; Net Carbs 0.5g; Fat 13g; Protein 41g

Basil Pork Chops with Beet Greens

Ingredients for 4 servings

2 tsp pureed garlic	
2 cups chopped beetroot greens	
2 tbsp balsamic vinegar	4 pork chops
2 tbsp freshly chopped basil	2 tbsp butter
1 tbsp olive oil	Salt and black pepper to taste

Directions and Total Time: approx. 30 minutes

Preheat oven to 380 F. In a saucepan over low heat, add vinegar, garlic, salt, pepper, and basil. Cook until the mixture is syrupy. Heat olive oil in a skillet and sear pork on both sides for 8 minutes. Brush the vinegar glaze on the pork and bake for 8 minutes. Melt butter in another skillet and sauté beetroot greens for 5 minutes. Plate the pork and serve with beet greens. Enjoy!

Per serving: Cal 389; Net Carbs 0.8g; Fat 16g; Protein 39g

Bacon & Kale Pizza

Ingredients for 3 servings

1 cup sliced mushrooms	
9 oz shredded provolone cheese	
2 oz bacon, chopped	1 tsp Italian seasoning
2 cups chopped kale, wilted	4 tbsp tomato sauce
6 eggs	1 cup grated mozzarella

Directions and Total Time: approx. 35 minutes

Preheat oven to 380 F. Line a pizza-baking pan with parchment paper. Whisk 6 eggs into a bowl and mix in the provolone cheese and Italian seasoning. Spread the mixture on the pizza-baking pan and bake until golden, 15 minutes. Remove from oven and let cool for 2 minutes. Spread the tomato sauce on the crust, top with kale, mozzarella cheese, bacon, and mushrooms. Bake in the oven for 8 minutes. Serve sliced. Enjoy!

Per serving: Cal 590; Net Carbs 2.6g; Fat 42g; Protein 45g

Brussel Sprout & Pork Eggs

Ingredients for 4 servings

4 large eggs	2 garlic cloves, minced
2 tbsp sesame oil	½ tsp ginger puree
1 medium white onion, diced	3 tbsp coconut aminos
1 lb ground pork	1 tbsp white wine vinegar
1 habanero pepper, chopped	2 tbsp sesame seeds
1 lb Brussels sprouts, halved	Salt and black pepper to taste

Directions and Total Time: approx. 25 minutes

Warm 1 tbsp of sesame oil in a skillet and scramble the eggs until set, 1 minute; set aside. Heat remaining sesame oil in the same skillet and sauté garlic, ginger, and onion until soft and fragrant, 4 minutes. Add in ground pork and habanero pepper and season with salt and pepper. Cook for 10 minutes. Mix in Brussels sprouts, aminos, and wine vinegar and cook until the sprouts are tender. Stir in the eggs. Serve garnished with sesame seeds.

Per serving: Cal 387; Net Carbs 4.7g; Fat 18g; Protein 41g

Homemade Pork Lo Mein

Ingredients for 4 servings

1 cup green beans, halved	1 yellow bell pepper, sliced
1 lb pork tenderloin, cut into	1 garlic clove, minced
¼-inch strips	4 green onions, chopped
1 cup shredded mozzarella	1 tsp toasted sesame seeds
1 egg yolk	3 tbsp coconut aminos
1-inch ginger knob, grated	2 tsp sugar-free maple syrup
3 tbsp sesame oil	1 tsp fresh ginger paste
1 red bell pepper, sliced	Salt and black pepper to taste

Directions and Total Time: approx. 25 min + chilling time

Place the mozzarella cheese in the microwave for 2 minutes. Let cool for 1 minute and mix in the egg yolk until well-combined. Lay a parchment paper on a flat surface, pour the cheese mixture on top and cover with another parchment paper. Flatten the dough into 1/8-inch thickness. Take off the parchment paper and cut the dough into thin spaghetti strands. Place in a bowl and refrigerate overnight. Bring 2 cups of water to a boil in a saucepan and add in the spaghetti strands. Cook for 1 minute and drain; set aside into a bowl.

Heat sesame oil in a skillet, season pork with salt and pepper, and sear on both sides for 5 minutes. Transfer to a plate. In the same skillet, mix in bell peppers and green beans and cook for 3 minutes. Stir in garlic, ginger knob, and green onions and cook for 1 minute. Mix in the pork and pasta. In a bowl, toss coconut aminos, maple syrup, and ginger paste. Pour the mixture over the pork mixture and cook for 1 minute. Top with sesame seeds and serve.

Per serving: Cal 340; Net Carbs 4g; Fats 12g; Protein 39g

Oven-Baked Pork with Mozzarella

Ingredients for 4 servings

1 cup shredded mozzarella	1 large egg, beaten
4 boneless pork chops	1 cup tomato sauce
1 cup golden flaxseed meal	Salt and black pepper to taste

Directions and Total Time: approx. 25 minutes

Preheat oven to 380 F. Season the pork with salt and pepper and coat the meat in the egg first, then in flaxseed meal. Place on a greased baking sheet.

Pour tomato sauce over and sprinkle with mozzarella cheese. Bake for 15 minutes or until the cheese melts and pork cooks through. Serve and enjoy!

Per serving: Cal 589; Net Carbs 2.7g; Fat 25g; Protein 59g

Pork Burrito Bowl with Avocado

Ingredients for 4 servings

1 lb ground pork	¼ cup sliced black olives
2 tbsp butter	1 avocado, cubed
½ cup beef broth	¼ cup tomatoes, diced
4 tbsp taco seasoning	1 green onion, sliced
½ cup sharp cheddar, grated	1 tbsp fresh cilantro, chopped
½ cup sour cream	Salt and black pepper to taste

Directions and Total Time: approx. 25 minutes

Warm butter in a skillet over medium heat. Cook the ground pork until brown while breaking any lumps, 10 minutes. Mix in broth, taco seasoning, salt, and pepper; cook until most of the liquid evaporates, 5 minutes. Mix in cheddar cheese to melt. Spoon into a serving bowl and top with sour cream, olives, avocado, tomatoes, green onion, and cilantro. Enjoy!

Per serving: Cal 392; Net Carbs 8.8g; Fat 31g; Protein 29g

Coconut Pork Medallions with Cabbage

Ingredients for 4 servings

6 tbsp butter	1 tbsp red curry powder
1 ½ pork tenderloin	1 ¼ cups coconut cream
1 canon cabbage, shredded	Salt and black pepper to taste
1 celery, chopped	

Directions and Total Time: approx. 45 minutes

Slice the pork into ½-inch medallions. Melt half of the butter in a skillet over medium heat and sauté cabbage for 10-15 minutes or until soft and slightly golden; reserve. Melt remaining butter in the skillet, add in celery, and sauté for 2 minutes. Add in the pork and fry until brown on the outside and cooked within 10 minutes. Season with salt and pepper and mix in curry and heat for 30 seconds. Stir in coconut cream and simmer for 5 minutes. Serve medallions with buttered cabbage.

Per serving: Cal 632; Net Carbs 3.9g; Fat 52g; Protein 39g

Lettuce Rolls with Pork & Bacon

Ingredients for 4 servings

1 iceberg lettuce, leaves separated
½ cup sliced cremini mushrooms

1 ½ lb ground pork	2 tbsp olive oil
8 bacon slices, chopped	1 cup shredded cheddar

Directions and Total Time: approx. 30 minutes

Fry the bacon in a skillet over medium heat until crispy, 5 minutes. Transfer to a paper-towel-lined plate. Heat the olive oil in the skillet and sauté the mushrooms for 5 minutes. Add in the ground pork and cook it until brown, 10 minutes, while breaking the lumps that form. Divide the pork between lettuce leaves, sprinkle with cheddar cheese, and top with bacon. Wrap and serve.

Per serving: Cal 629; Net Carbs 0.5g; Fat 45g; Protein 49g

Ground Pork Stuffed Mushrooms

Ingredients for 4 servings

¼ cup shredded Parmesan
12 portobello mushroom caps

½ lb ground pork	7 oz cream cheese
2 tbsp butter	3 tbsp chives, chopped
1 tsp paprika	Salt and pepper to taste

Directions and Total Time: approx. 30 minutes

Preheat oven to390 F. Melt butter in a skillet, add the ground pork, season with paprika, salt, and pepper and stir-fry until brown, 10 minutes. Mix in two-thirds of chives and cream cheese until evenly combined. Spoon the mixture into the mushrooms and transfer them to a greased baking sheet. Top with the Parmesan cheese and bake until mushrooms turn golden and the cheese melts, 10 minutes. Garnish with the remaining chives and serve.

Per serving: Cal 302; Net Carbs 2.2g; Fat 19g; Protein 21g

Red Wine Pork Shanks with Chili Flakes

Ingredients for 4 servings

3 lb pork shanks	1 ½ cups crushed tomatoes
3 tbsp olive oil	½ cup red wine
3 celery stalks, chopped	¼ tsp red chili flakes
5 garlic cloves, minced	¼ cup chopped parsley

Directions and Total Time: approx. 2 hours 50 minutes

Preheat oven to 320 F. Heat olive oil in a saucepan and brown pork on all sides for 4 minutes; set aside. Add in celery and garlic and sauté for 3 minutes. Return the pork. Top with tomatoes, red wine, and red chili flakes. Cover the lid and put the saucepan in the oven. Cook for 2 hours, turning the meat every 30 minutes. In the last 15 minutes, open the lid and increase the temperature to 450 F. Take out the pot, stir in parsley, and serve the meat with sauce on a bed of creamy mashed cauliflower.

Per serving: Cal 519; Net Carbs 1.4g; Fat 19g; Protein 81g

Pork Sausages with Onion Gravy

Ingredients for 4 servings

1 (16 oz) pork sausages	8 oz cream cheese, softened
1 tbsp olive oil	3 tbsp freshly chopped chives
2 tsp almond flour	3 tsp pureed onion
6 tbsp golden flaxseed meal	3 tbsp chicken broth
1 egg, beaten	2 tbsp almond milk

Directions and Total Time: approx. 25 minutes

Using a fork, prick the sausages with a fork all around, roll in the almond flour, dip in the egg, and then in the flaxseed meal. Heat olive oil in a skillet and fry sausages until brown, 10-12 minutes. Transfer to a plate. In a saucepan, combine cream cheese, chives, onion, chicken broth, and almond milk. Cook and stir over medium heat until smooth and evenly mixed, 5 minutes. Plate the sausages and spoon the sauce on top. Serve immediately.

Per serving: Cal 459; Net Carbs 0.5g; Fat 29g; Protein 42g

Mediterranean Pork with Cauliflower Rice

Ingredients for 4 servings

1 ½ lb pork tenderloin, cubed	½ cup water
1 cup baby spinach	1 cup grape tomatoes, halved
2 tbsp olive oil	3/4 cup crumbled feta cheese
½ tsp cumin powder	Salt and black pepper to taste
2 cups cauliflower rice	

Directions and Total Time: approx. 20 minutes

Warm olive oil in a skillet, season the pork with salt, pepper, and cumin and sear on both sides for 5 minutes until brown. Stir in cauli rice and pour in water. Cook for 5 minutes or until cauliflower softens. Mix in spinach to wilt, 1 minute and add the tomatoes. Spoon into bowls, sprinkle with feta cheese, and serve with hot sauce.

Per serving: Cal 381; Net Carbs 1.9g; Fat 17g; Protein 39g

BBQ Baked Pork Chops

Ingredients for 4 servings

4 pork chops	1 ½ tsp garlic powder
1 tbsp melted butter	1 tbsp dried parsley
½ cup ground flaxseed meal	1/2 tsp onion powder
1 tsp dried thyme	1/8 tsp basil
1 tsp paprika	½ cup BBQ sauce
¼ tsp chili powder	Salt and black pepper to taste

Directions and Total Time: approx. 45 minutes

Preheat oven to 380 F. In a bowl, mix flaxseed meal, thyme, paprika, salt, pepper, chili, garlic powder, parsley, onion powder, and basil. Rub the pork chops with the mixture. Melt butter in a skillet and sear pork on both sides, 4-6 minutes. Transfer to a greased baking sheet, brush with BBQ sauce, and bake for 15-20 minutes. Allow resting for 10 minutes. Serve with buttered parsnips.

Per serving: Cal 391; Net Carbs 1.6g; Fat 21g; Protein 39g

Basil-Mustard Pork Loin Roast

Ingredients for 6 servings

2 tsp olive oil	1 tbsp Dijon mustard
3 lb boneless pork loin roast	1 tsp dried basil
5 cloves garlic, minced	Salt and black pepper to taste

Directions and Total Time: approx. 30 minutes

Preheat oven to 370 F. Place the pork loin in a greased baking dish. In a bowl, mix garlic, salt, pepper, Dijon mustard, and basil. Rub the mixture onto the pork. Drizzle with olive oil and bake for 15 minutes or until cooked within and brown outside. Transfer to a flat surface and let cool for 5 minutes. Slice the pork and serve.

Per serving: Cal 309; Net Carbs 2g; Fat 9g; Protein 49g

Pork Medallions in Raspberry Sauce

Ingredients for 4 servings

2 cups fresh raspberries	2/3 cup grated Parmesan
1 lb pork tenderloin	Salt and black pepper to taste
1 tsp chicken bouillon granules	6 tbsp butter, divided
½ cup almond flour	1 tsp minced garlic
2 large eggs, lightly beaten	Sliced fresh raspberries

Directions and Total Time: approx. 20 minutes

Cut the pork into ½-inch medallions. To a blender, add raspberries, ¼ cup water, and chicken granules; process until smooth and set aside. In two separate bowls, pour almond flour and Parmesan cheese. Season the meat with salt and pepper. Coat in the almond flour, then in the eggs, and finally in the cheese.

Melt 2 tbsp of butter in a skillet and fry the pork for 3 minutes per side or until the meat cooks within. Transfer to a plate and cover to keep warm. In the same skillet, melt the remaining butter and sauté garlic for 1 minute. Stir in raspberry mixture and cook for 3 minutes. Spoon sauce on top of the pork. Garnish with raspberries and serve with steamed greens.

Per serving: Cal 491; Net Carbs 6.1g; Fat 23g; Protein 42g

Maple Pork Chops with Brie Cheese

Ingredients for 4 servings

4 pork chops	2 tbsp balsamic vinegar
4 slices brie cheese	1 tsp maple (sugar-free) syrup
3 tbsp olive oil	2 tbsp chopped mint leaves
2 large red onions, sliced	Salt and black pepper to taste

Directions and Total Time: approx. 40 minutes

Warm 1 tbsp olive oil in a skillet until smoky. Reduce to low and sauté onions until brown. Pour in balsamic vinegar, maple syrup, and salt. Cook with frequent stirring to prevent burning until the onions caramelize, 15 minutes; set aside. Heat the remaining olive oil in the same skillet, season the pork with salt and black pepper, and cook for 10-12 minutes. Put a brie slice on each meat and top with the caramelized onions; let the cheese melt for 2 minutes. Spoon the meat with the topping onto plates and garnish with mint.

Per serving: Cal 461; Net Carbs 3.1g; Fat 25g; Protein 51g

Pork Picadillo with Bell Pepper Noodles

Ingredients for 4 servings

1 red bell peppers, spiralized	
1 yellow bell peppers, spiralized	
1 lb ground pork	2 avocados, pitted, mashed
2 tbsp butter	2 tbsp chopped pecans
1 tsp garlic powder	Salt and black pepper to taste

Directions and Total Time: approx. 15 minutes

Warm butter in a skillet and cook the pork until brown, 5 minutes. Season with salt and pepper. Stir in bell peppers, garlic powder and cook until the peppers are slightly tender, 2 minutes. Mix in mashed avocados and cook for 1 minute. Garnish with pecans and serve warm.

Per serving: Cal 699; Net Carbs 9g; Fats 50g; Protein 35g

Sweet Pork Chops with Spaghetti Squash

Ingredients for 4 servings

1 tbsp olive oil	1 lb kale, chopped
3 tbsp peanut oil	1 (3-lb) spaghetti squash
4 boneless pork chops	2 tbsp minced lemongrass

3 tbsp fresh ginger paste
2 tbsp sugar-free maple syrup
2 tbsp coconut aminos
1 tbsp fish sauce
½ cup coconut milk
¼ cup peanut butter
Salt and black pepper to taste

Directions and Total Time: approx. 70 min + chilling time
Slice the spaghetti squash lengthwise from stem to tail. Scoop out the seeds. In a bowl, mix lemongrass, 2 tbsp of ginger paste, maple syrup, aminos, and fish sauce. Coat the pork in the liquid. Refrigerate for 45 minutes. Heat 2 tbsp of peanut oil in a skillet, remove pork from the marinade. Sear on both sides for 10-15 minutes. Transfer to a plate and cover with foil to keep warm.

Preheat oven to 380 F. Place the spaghetti squashes on a baking sheet, brush with olive oil and season with salt and pepper. Bake for 45 minutes. Remove the squash and shred with two forks into spaghetti-like strands; set aside.

Heat the remaining peanut oil in the same skillet and sauté the remaining ginger paste. Add in kale and cook for 2 minutes; set aside. In a bowl, whisk coconut milk with peanut butter until well combined. Divide the pork between four plates, add the spaghetti squash to the side, then the kale and drizzle the peanut sauce on top. Serve.

Per serving: Cal 702; Net Carbs 7g; Fats 34g; Protein 49g

Pork Tenderloin in Coconut Sauce

Ingredients for 4 servings

1 tbsp butter
1 lb pork tenderloin, cubed
4 tsp smoked paprika
1 tsp almond flour
3/4 cup coconut cream
Salt and black pepper to taste

Directions and Total Time: approx. 20 minutes
Sprinkle the pork with paprika, salt, and pepper and sprinkle with almond flour. Melt butter in a skillet and sauté the pork until lightly browned, 5 minutes. Stir in coconut cream; let boil. Cook until the sauce slightly thickens, 7 minutes. Serve over a bed of cauli rice.

Per serving: Cal 309; Net Carbs 2.5g; Fat 19g; Protein 26g

Turnip & Pork Packets with Grilled Halloumi

Ingredients for 4 servings

3 tbsp olive oil
4 oz halloumi cheese, cubed
1 lb turnips, cubed
½ cup salsa verde
2 tsp chili powder
1 tsp cumin powder
4 boneless pork chops
Salt and black pepper to taste

Directions and Total Time: approx. 30 minutes
Preheat the grill to High. Cut out four 18x12-inch sheets of heavy-duty aluminum foil. Grease the sheets with cooking spray. In a bowl, combine turnips, salsa verde, chili, and cumin. Season with salt and pepper. Place a pork chop on each foil sheet, spoon the turnip mixture on the meat, sprinkle olive oil and halloumi cheese on top. Wrap the foil and place on the grill grate and cook for 10 minutes. Turn the foil packs over and cook further for 8 minutes. Remove the packs onto plates and serve.

Per serving: Cal 499; Net Carbs 2.1g; Fat 32g; Protein 49g

Pork & Keto Macaroni Au Gratin

Ingredients for 4 servings

1 cup shredded mozzarella cheese
1 ½ lb pork shoulder, divided into 3 pieces
l egg yolk
2 tbsp olive oil
1 tsp dried thyme
1 cup chicken broth
2 tbsp butter
2 shallots, chopped
2 garlic cloves, minced
1 cup grated Monterey Jack
4 oz cream cheese, softened
1 cup heavy cream
½ tsp white pepper
½ tsp nutmeg powder
2 tbsp chopped parsley
Salt and black pepper to taste

Directions and Total Time: approx. 95 min + chilling time
Place the mozzarella cheese in the microwave for 2 minutes. Allow cooling for 1 minute. Mix in egg yolk until well-combined. Lay a parchment paper on a flat surface, pour the cheese mixture on top and cover with another parchment paper. Flatten the dough into 1/8-inch thickness. Take off the parchment paper and cut the dough into small cubes of the size of macaroni. Place in a bowl; refrigerate overnight. Bring 2 cups of water to a boil. Add in keto macaroni. Cook for 1 minute and drain; set aside.

Season the pork with salt, pepper, and thyme. Heat olive oil in a pot; sear the pork on both sides until brown, 4-6 minutes. Pour in the broth and cook over low heat for 1 hour or until softened. Remove to a plate and shred into small strands; set aside.

Preheat oven to 380 F. Melt butter in a pot and sauté shallots and garlic for 3 minutes. Pour in 1 cup of water to deglaze the pot and stir in half of Monterey Jack and cream cheeses for 4 minutes. Mix in heavy cream and season with salt, pepper, white pepper, and nutmeg powder. Mix in pasta and pork. Pour mixture into a baking dish and cover with remaining Monterey Jack cheese. Bake for 20 minutes. Garnish with parsley and serve.

Per serving: Cal 598; Net Carbs 4g; Fats 39g; Protein 46g

Pork Satay Chops

Ingredients for 4 servings

1/3 cup peanut butter
2 lb boneless pork loin chops
1 medium white onion, sliced
¼ cup tamari sauce
½ tsp garlic powder
½ tsp onion powder
½ tsp hot sauce
1 cup chicken broth
3 tbsp xanthan gum
1 tbsp chopped peanuts
Salt and black pepper to taste

Directions and Total Time: approx. 70 minutes
Sprinkle the pork with salt and pepper and put into a pot with onion. In a bowl, combine peanut butter, tamari sauce, garlic and onion powders, hot sauce, and two-thirds of the chicken broth. Pour the mixture over the meat. Bring to a boil over high heat, reduce the heat, and simmer for 1 hour or until the meat becomes tender. In a bowl, combine the remaining broth and xanthan gum. Stir the mixture into the meat and simmer until the sauce thickens, 2 minutes. Garnish with peanuts and serve.

Per serving: Cal 462; Net Carbs 6.7g; Fat 17g; Protein 59g

Pork Steaks in Mushroom Sauce

Ingredients for 4 servings

8 oz button mushrooms, chopped
4 bone-in pork steaks
2 tsp lemon pepper seasoning
1 tbsp olive oil
1 tbsp butter
1 cup vegetable stock
6 garlic cloves, minced
2 tbsp chopped parsley

Directions and Total Time: approx. 25 minutes

Warm the olive oil and butter in a skillet over medium heat and cook the meat until brown, 10 minutes; set aside. Add the garlic and mushrooms to the skillet and cook until softened, 5 minutes. Pour in the vegetable stock to deglaze the bottom of the pan; sprinkle with lemon pepper seasoning. Return the pork and cook until the liquid reduces by two-thirds. Garnish with parsley and serve with steamed green beans.

Per serving: Cal 498; Net Carbs 3.2g; Fat 29g; Protein 46g

Meat Lover Sausage Pizza

Ingredients for 4 servings

½ cup grated Monterey Jack cheese
1 ½ lb Italian pork sausages, crumbled
4 cups grated mozzarella
¼ cup grated Parmesan
1 cup chopped bell peppers
2 tbsp cream cheese, softened
¼ cup coconut flour
1 cup almond flour
2 eggs
1 tbsp olive oil
1 onion, thinly sliced
2 garlic cloves, minced
1 cup baby spinach
½ cup sugar-free pizza sauce

Directions and Total Time: approx. 40 minutes

Preheat oven to 380 F. Line a pizza pan with parchment paper. Microwave 2 cups of mozzarella cheese and cream cheese for 1 minute. Remove and mix in sausages, coconut flour, almond flour, Parmesan cheese, and eggs. Spread the mixture on the pizza pan and bake for 15 minutes; set aside. Heat olive oil in a skillet and sauté onion, garlic, and bell peppers for 5 minutes. Stir in baby spinach and allow wilting for 3 minutes. Spread the pizza sauce on the crust and top with the bell pepper mixture. Scatter remaining mozzarella and Monterey Jack cheeses on top. Bake for 5 minutes. Serve sliced.

Per serving: Cal 459; Net Carbs 3g; Fats 25g; Protein 51g

Pork Medallions in Morel Sauce

Ingredients for 4 servings4

2 tbsp olive oil
1 ½ lb pork tenderloin
16 fresh morels, rinsed
4 large green onions, chopped
½ cup red wine
¾ cup chicken broth
2 tbsp butter

Directions and Total Time: approx. 35 minutes

Slice the pork into 8 medallions. Heat olive oil in a pot and sear the pork until brown, 5 minutes; set aside. Add morels and green onions in the pot and cook until softened, 2 minutes. Mix in red wine and chicken broth. Place the pork in the sauce and simmer for 15 minutes. Swirl in butter, adjust the taste, and serve hot.

Per serving: Cal 332; Net Carbs 1.2g; Fat 15g; Protein 40g

Pork Sausage with Cheesy Kohlrabi

Ingredients for 4 servings

1 cup sliced pork sausage
4 bacon slices, chopped
4 large kohlrabi, spiralized
6 garlic cloves, minced
1 cup grated Pecorino cheese
2 tbsp olive oil
1 cup cherry tomatoes, halved
7 fresh basil leaves
1 tbsp pine nuts for topping

Directions and Total Time: approx. 20 minutes

Warm olive oil in a skillet and cook sausage and bacon until brown, 5 minutes. Transfer to a plate. Stir in kohlrabi and garlic and cook until tender, 5-7 minutes. Add in cherry tomatoes and cook for 2 minutes. Mix in the sausage, bacon, basil, and Pecorino Romano cheese. Garnish with pine nuts and serve warm.

Per serving: Cal 230; Net Carbs 2.4g; Fats 19g; Protein 8g

Creamy Pork with Green Beans & Fettucine

Ingredients for 4 servings

1 cup shredded mozzarella
1 cup shaved Parmesan cheese
1 egg yolk
1 tbsp olive oil
1 ½ lb pork tenderloin
1 cup green beans, chopped
1 lemon, zested and juiced
¼ cup chicken broth
1 cup half-and-half
6 basil leaves, chopped
Salt and black pepper to taste

Directions and Total Time: approx. 35 min + chilling time

Cut the pork into thin strips. Microwave mozzarella cheese for 2 minutes. Allow cooling for 1 minute. Mix in egg yolk until well-combined. Lay a parchment paper on a flat surface, pour the cheese mixture on top and cover with another parchment paper. Flatten the dough into 1/8-inch thickness. Take off the parchment paper and cut the dough into thick fettuccine strands. Place in a bowl and refrigerate overnight. Bring 2 cups of water to a boil in a saucepan and add the fettuccine. Cook for 1 minute and drain; set aside.

Heat oil in a skillet, season the pork with salt and pepper, and cook for 10 minutes. Mix in green beans and cook for 5 minutes. Stir in lemon zest, lemon juice, and broth. Cook for 5 more minutes. Add half-and-half, fettuccine, and basil and cook for 1 minute. Top with Parmesan cheese. Serve immediately.

Per serving: Cal 592; Net Carbs 9g; Fats 32g; Protein 62g

Prosciutto Pizza

Ingredients for 4 servings

4 prosciutto slices, cut into thirds
2 cups grated mozzarella
2 tbsp cream cheese, softened
½ cup almond flour
1 egg, beaten
⅓ cup tomato sauce
⅓ cup sliced mozzarella
6 fresh basil leaves, to serve

Directions and Total Time: approx. 40 minutes

Preheat oven to 380 F. Line a pizza pan with parchment paper. Microwave mozzarella cheese and 2 tbsp of cream cheese for 1 minute. Mix in almond flour and egg. Spread the mixture on the pizza pan and bake for 15 minutes.

Spread the tomato sauce on the crust. Arrange the mozzarella slices over the sauce and then the prosciutto. Bake again for 15 minutes or until the cheese melts. Remove and top with the basil. Slice and serve.

Per serving: Cal 159; Net Carbs 0.5g; Fats 6g; Protein 19g

Gingery Pork Stir-Fry

Ingredients for 4 servings

2 tbsp coconut oil	3 garlic cloves, minced
1 ½ lb pork tenderloin	1 tsp olive oil
1 green bell pepper, diced	1 habanero pepper, minced
1 small red onion, diced	2 tbsp tamari sauce
1/3 cup walnuts	Salt and black pepper to taste
1 tbsp freshly grated ginger	

Directions and Total Time: approx. 25 minutes

Cut the pork into strips. Heat coconut oil in a wok, season pork with salt and pepper, and cook until no longer pink, 10 minutes. Shift to one side of the wok and add the bell pepper, onion, walnuts, ginger, garlic, olive oil, and habanero pepper. Sauté until fragrant and onion softened, 5 minutes. Mix and season with tamari sauce. Stir-fry until well combined, about 1 minute. Serve with cauliflower rice.

Per serving: Cal 318; Net Carbs 2.8g; Fat 16g; Protein 41g

Sambal Pork with Miracle Noodles

Ingredients for 4 servings

8 oz Miracle noodles	
2 tbsp olive oil	2 fresh basil leaves, chopped
1 lb ground pork	2 tbsp sambal oelek
4 garlic cloves, minced	2 tbsp plain vinegar
1-inch ginger, grated	2 tbsp coconut aminos
1 tsp liquid stevia	1 tbsp unsalted butter
1 tbsp tomato paste	Salt to taste

Directions and Total Time: approx. 40 minutes

Place 2 cups of water in a pot and bring it to a boil. Strain the Miracle noodles and rinse well under hot running water. Allow proper draining and pour them into the boiling water. Cook for 3 minutes and strain again. Place a dry skillet and stir-fry the shirataki noodles until visibly dry, 1-2 minutes; set aside.

Heat olive oil in a pot and cook the ground pork for 5 minutes. Stir in garlic, ginger, and stevia and cook for 1 minute. Add in tomato paste and mix in sambal oelek, vinegar, 1 cup water, aminos, and salt. Continue cooking over low heat for 20 minutes. Add in the noodles and butter and mix well. Garnish with basil and serve.

Per serving: Cal 498; Net Carbs 8g; Fats 29g; Protein 34g

Sesame Pork Bites

Ingredients for 4 servings

1 pork tenderloin, cubed	½ cup sesame seeds
1 tbsp sesame oil	1 tsp pureed garlic
½ cup + 1 tbsp red wine	½ tsp freshly grated ginger
1 tbsp + 1/3 cup tamari sauce	1 tbsp scallions, chopped
½ cup sugar-free maple syrup	

Directions and Total Time: approx. 45 min + chilling time

Place ½ cup of red wine with 1 tbsp of tamari sauce into a zipper bag. Add in pork cubes, seal the bag, and marinate the meat in the fridge overnight.

Preheat oven to 350 F. Remove the pork from the fridge and drain. Pour maple syrup and sesame seeds into two separate bowls; roll the pork in maple syrup and then in the sesame seeds. Place on a greased baking sheet and bake for 35 minutes. In a bowl, mix the remaining red wine, remaining tamari sauce, sesame oil, garlic, and ginger. Pour the sauce into a bowl. Transfer pork to a platter and garnish with scallions. Pour the sauce over and serve.

Per serving: Cal 349; Net Carbs 6.4g; Fat 18g; Protein 40g

Chinese-Style Pork with Celeriac Noodles

Ingredients for 4 servings

1 lb pork tenderloin, cubed	2 tbsp sesame seeds
2 tbsp butter	3 tbsp sugar-free maple syrup
4 large celeriac, spiralized	3 tbsp coconut aminos
2 tbsp sesame oil	1 tbsp fresh ginger paste
24 oz bok choy, chopped	¼ tsp Chinese five spice
2 green onions, chopped	Salt and black pepper to taste

Directions and Total Time: approx. 60 min + chilling time

Preheat oven to 380 F. Line a baking sheet with foil. In a bowl, mix maple syrup, coconut aminos, ginger paste, Chinese five-spice powder, salt, and pepper. Spoon 3 tablespoons of the mixture into a bowl and reserve for topping. Mix pork cubes into the remaining marinade and refrigerate for 25 minutes. Melt butter in a skillet and sauté celeriac for 7 minutes; set aside. Remove the pork from the marinade onto the baking sheet and bake for 40 minutes. Heat sesame oil in a skillet and sauté bok choy and celeriac pasta for 3 minutes. Transfer to serving bowls and top with pork. Garnish with green onions and sesame seeds. Drizzle with reserved marinade and serve.

Per serving: Cal 410; Net Carbs 3g; Fats 21g; Protein 44g

Garam Masala Pork Shoulder

Ingredients for 4 servings

2 tbsp ghee	2 tbsp Greek yogurt
1 ½ lb pork shoulder, cubed	½ tsp chili powder
1 tbsp freshly grated ginger	2 tbsp garam masala
2 tbsp pureed garlic	2 green chilies, sliced
6 medium red onions, sliced	1 bunch cilantro, chopped
1 cup crushed tomatoes	

Directions and Total Time: approx. 25 minutes

Pour water into a pot; bring to boil. Add and blanch the pork for 3 minutes; drain and set aside. Melt ghee in a skillet and sauté ginger, garlic, and onions until caramelized, 5 minutes. Mix in tomatoes, yogurt, and return the pork. Season with chili and garam masala. Stir and cook for 10 minutes. Mix in cilantro and green chilies. Serve pork masala with cauli rice.

Per serving: Cal 299; Net Carbs 2.2g; Fat 16g; Protein 28g

Vegetable Bake with Sausage

Ingredients for 4 servings

1 large butternut squash, cut into chunks
1 cup mushrooms, quartered | 1 tbsp thyme, chopped
¼ lb smoked sausages, sliced | 4 garlic cloves, peeled only
1 onion, sliced | 3 tbsp olive oil
¼ lb Brussels sprouts | Salt and black pepper to taste
1 tbsp rosemary, chopped

Directions and Total Time: approx. 35 minutes

Preheat the oven to 450 F. Arrange the butternut squash, onion, mushrooms, garlic cloves, sausages, and Brussels sprouts on a baking tray. Season with salt, pepper, olive oil, and toss to coat. Roast for 20-25 minutes. Sprinkle with thyme and rosemary to serve.

Per serving: Cal 225; Fat 17g; Net Carbs 8.2g; Protein 7.3g

Bacon & Cauliflower Cheesy Bake

Ingredients for 4 servings

1 head cauliflower, broken into florets
1 tbsp butter | 1 garlic clove, minced
½ lb bacon, cut into strips | ½ cup mozzarella, grated
¼ cup buttermilk | 1 tbsp rosemary, chopped
¾ cup heavy cream

Directions and Total Time: approx. 40 minutes

Preheat oven to 350 F. Boil cauliflower in a saucepan until tender, about 7-8 minutes. Drain and pour in a baking pan. Set a frying pan over medium heat and melt the butter. Brown the bacon for 3 minutes and set aside. Add in the heavy cream, garlic, and buttermilk and cook until warmed fully. Take the reserved bacon back to the pan. Fold in mozzarella cheese and stir well. Pour the sauce over the cauliflower and bake for 20 minutes until the top is golden. Serve sprinkled with rosemary.

Per serving: Cal 355; Fat 28g; Net Carbs 6.5g; Protein 16g

Cheese, Bacon & Brussels Sprouts Bake

Ingredients for 4 servings

1 ¼ cups cheddar cheese, shredded
¼ cup Parmesan cheese, grated
3 tbsp butter | 5 garlic cloves, minced
1 cup bacon, chopped | 1 ¼ cups heavy cream
1 ½ lb halved Brussels sprouts | Salt and black pepper to taste

Directions and Total Time: approx. 30 minutes

Preheat the oven to 400 F.

Melt the butter in a large skillet over medium heat and fry the bacon until crispy, about 5 minutes. Remove onto a plate and set aside. Pour the Brussels sprouts and garlic into the skillet and sauté until fragrant and slightly golden, 5-7 minutes. Mix in heavy cream and simmer for 4 minutes. Add the bacon back to the skillet and stir to combine. Season with salt and pepper. Pour the sauté into a baking dish, and sprinkle with cheddar and Parmesan cheeses. Bake for 10 minutes or until golden brown on top. Serve with tomato salad.

Per serving: Cal 587; Fat 51g; Net Carbs 9.5g; Protein 23g

Sausage & Veggie Bake

Ingredients for 4 servings

1 lb pork sausage, sliced | Salt and black pepper to taste
2 oz butter | 10 oz cauliflower florets
1 onion, chopped | 1 cup mayonnaise
½ cup celery stalks, chopped | 4 oz Parmesan cheese, grated
1 green bell pepper, chopped | 1 tsp red chili flakes

Directions and Total Time: approx. 40 minutes

Preheat the oven to 400 F. Warm the butter in a pan over medium heat and stir-fry the onion, celery, and bell pepper for 5 minutes. Add in the sausage and continue cooking for 4-5 minutes. Season with salt and pepper.

In a bowl, mix cauliflower, mayonnaise, Parmesan cheese, and red chili flakes. Pour the mixture onto a baking dish, add the sausage mixture, and mix. Bake until golden brown, 20 minutes. Serve warm.

Per serving: Cal 611; Fat 47g; Net Carbs 7.4g; Protein 32g

Basil-Pesto Pork with Spiralized Turnips

Ingredients for 4 servings

4 large turnips, spiralized | 1 cup grated Parmesan cheese
4 boneless pork chops | 1 tbsp butter
½ cup basil pesto | Salt and black pepper to taste

Directions and Total Time: approx. 70 minutes

Preheat oven to 360 F. Season pork with salt and pepper and place on a greased baking sheet. Spread pesto on the pork and bake for 45 minutes.

Pull out the baking sheet and divide half of Parmesan cheese on top. Bake further for 5 minutes; set aside. Melt butter in a skillet and sauté the spiralized turnips for 7 minutes. Stir in the remaining Parmesan cheese and top with the pork to serve.

Per serving: Cal 529; Net Carbs 4g; Fats 28g; Protein 61g

Green Pork Bake

Ingredients for 4 servings

1 lb ground pork | 1 zucchini, sliced
1 onion, chopped | ¼ cup heavy cream
1 garlic clove, minced | 5 eggs
½ lb green beans, chopped | ½ cup Monterey Jack cheese,
Salt and black pepper to taste | grated

Directions and Total Time: approx. 50 minutes

In a bowl, mix onion, green beans, ground pork, garlic, black pepper and salt. Layer the meat mixture on the bottom of a small greased baking dish.

Spread zucchini slices on top. In a separate bowl, combine Monterey Jack cheese, eggs, and heavy cream. Pour the mixture over the zucchini layer and bake for 40 minutes at 360 F or until the edges and top become brown.

Per serving: Cal 355; Fat 21g; Net Carbs 3.9g; Protein 27g

BEEF & LAMB

Veggie Beef Stew with Root Mash

Ingredients for 2 servings

½ lb stewing beef, cut into chunks
½ cauliflower head, cut into florets

1 tbsp olive oil	2 bay leaves
1 parsnip, chopped	1 carrot, chopped
1 garlic clove, minced	½ tbsp rosemary, chopped
1 onion, chopped	1 tomato, chopped
1 celery stalk, chopped	2 tbsp red wine
Salt and black pepper to taste	½ celeriac, chopped
1 ¼ cups beef stock	2 tbsp butter

Directions and Total Time: approx. 2 hours 10 minutes

In a pot, cook the celery, onion, and garlic in warm oil over medium heat for 5 minutes. Stir in the beef chunks, and cook for 3 minutes. Season with salt and black pepper. Deglaze the bottom of the pot by adding the red wine. Add in the carrot, parsnip, beef stock, tomato, and bay leaves. Boil the mixture, reduce the heat to low, and cook for 1 hour and 30 minutes.

Meanwhile, heat a pot with water over medium heat. Place in the celeriac, cover, and simmer for 10 minutes. Add in the cauliflower florets, cook for 15 minutes, drain everything, and combine with butter, pepper, and salt. Mash using a potato masher and split the mash between 2 plates. Top with vegetable mixture and stewed beef, sprinkle with rosemary, and serve.

Per serving: Cal 465; Fat 24g; Net Carbs 9.8g; Protein 3.2g

King Size Burgers

Ingredients for 4 servings

2 tbsp olive oil	2 tbsp almond flour
1 lb ground beef	2 tbsp cup beef broth
2 green onions, chopped	½ tbsp chopped parsley
1 garlic clove, minced	½ tbsp Worcestershire sauce
1 tbsp thyme	

Directions and Total Time: approx. 25 minutes

Preheat a grill to 370 F Combine all ingredients except for the parsley in a bowl. Mix well with your hands and make 2 patties out of the mixture. Arrange on a lined baking sheet. Bake for about 18-20 minutes, until nice and crispy. Serve sprinkled with parsley.

Per serving: Cal 363; Fat 26g; Net Carbs 3.1g; Protein 25g

Portobello Beef Cheeseburgers

Ingredients for 2 servings

2 tbsp olive oil	Salt and black pepper to taste
½ lb ground beef	2 slices mozzarella cheese
½ tsp fresh parsley, chopped	2 portobello mushroom caps
½ tsp Worcestershire sauce	

Directions and Total Time: approx. 25 minutes

In a bowl, mix the beef, parsley, Worcestershire sauce, salt, and black pepper with your hands until evenly combined. Make medium-sized patties out of the mixture.

Preheat a grill to 400 F and coat the mushroom caps with olive oil, salt, and black pepper. Lay portobello caps, rounded side up, and burger patties onto the hot grill pan and cook for 5 minutes. Turn the mushroom caps and continue cooking for 1 minute.

Lay a mozzarella slice on top of each patty. Continue cooking until the mushroom caps are softened and the beef patties are no longer pink in the center, 4 to 5 minutes more. Flip the patties and top with cheese. Cook for another 2-3 minutes to be well done while the cheese melts onto the meat. Remove the patties and sandwich them into two mushroom caps each.

Per serving: Cal 505; Fat 39g; Net Carbs 3.2g; Protein 38g

Asian Spiced Beef with Broccoli

Ingredients for 2 servings

½ cup coconut milk	Salt and black pepper to taste
2 tbsp coconut oil	1 head broccoli, cut into florets
¼ tsp garlic powder	½ tbsp Thai green curry paste
¼ tsp onion powder	1 tsp ginger paste
½ tbsp coconut aminos	1 tbsp cilantro, chopped
1 lb beef steak, cut into strips	½ tbsp sesame seeds

Directions and Total Time: approx. 30 minutes

Warm coconut oil in a pan over medium heat, add in the beef, season with garlic powder, pepper, salt, ginger paste, and onion powder and cook for 4 minutes. Mix in broccoli and stir-fry for 5 minutes. Pour in the coconut milk, coconut aminos, and Thai curry paste and cook for 15 minutes. Serve sprinkled with cilantro and sesame seeds.

Per serving: Cal 623; Fat 43g; Net Carbs 2.3g; Protein 53g

Cilantro Beef Balls with Mascarpone

Ingredients for 4 servings

1 garlic clove, minced	Salt and black pepper to taste
1 lb ground beef	1 tbsp butter + 1 ½ tbsp melted
1 small onion, chopped	½ cup mascarpone cheese
1 jalapeño pepper, chopped	¼ tsp turmeric
2 tsp cilantro	¼ tsp baking powder
½ tsp allspice	1 cup flax meal
1 tsp cumin	¼ cup coconut flour

Directions and Total Time: approx. 45 minutes

Puree onion with garlic, jalapeño, and ¼ cup of water in a blender. Melt 1 tbsp butter in a pan over medium heat. Cook the beef for 3 minutes. Stir in the onion mixture, and cook for 2 minutes. Stir in cilantro, salt, cumin, turmeric, allspice, and pepper and cook for 3 minutes.

In a bowl, combine coconut flour, flax meal, and baking powder. In a separate bowl, combine the melted butter with the mascarpone cheese. Combine the 2 mixtures to obtain a dough. Form balls from this mixture, set them on parchment paper, and roll each into a circle.

Split the beef mix on one-half of the dough circles, cover with the other half, seal edges, and lay on a lined sheet. Bake for 25 minutes in the oven at 350 F.

Per serving: Cal 434; Fat 26g; Net Carbs 8.6g; Protein 33g

Beef Ragout with Pepper & Green Beans

Ingredients for 4 servings

1 lb chuck steak, trimmed and cubed
2 tbsp olive oil
Salt and black pepper to taste
2 tbsp almond flour
4 green onions, diced
½ cup dry white wine
1 yellow bell pepper, diced

1 cup green beans, chopped
2 tsp Worcestershire sauce
4 oz tomato puree
3 tsp smoked paprika
1 cup beef broth
Parsley leaves to garnish

Directions and Total Time: approx. 2 hours

Dredge the meat in the almond flour and set aside. Place a large skillet over medium heat, add 1 tablespoon of oil to heat and then sauté the green onion, green beans, and bell pepper for 3 minutes. Stir in the paprika and the remaining olive oil. Add the beef and cook for 10 minutes while turning them halfway. Stir in white wine, let it reduce by half, about 3 minutes, and add Worcestershire sauce, tomato puree, and beef broth. Let the mixture boil for 2 minutes, then reduce the heat to lowest and let simmer for 1 ½ hours; stirring now and then. Adjust the taste and dish the ragout. Serve garnished with parsley.

Per serving: Cal 334; Fat 22g; Net Carbs 3.9g; Protein 33g

Grilled Beef on Skewers with Fresh Salad

Ingredients for 2 servings

1 lb sirloin steak, boneless, cubed
¼ cup ranch dressing
1 red onion, sliced
½ tbsp white wine vinegar
1 tbsp extra virgin olive oil

2 ripe tomatoes, sliced
2 tbsp fresh parsley, chopped
1 cucumber, sliced
Salt to taste

Directions and Total Time: approx. 20 minutes

Thread the beef cubes on the skewers, about 4 to 5 cubes per skewer. Brush half of the ranch dressing on the skewers (all around).

Preheat grill to high. Place the skewers on the grill and cook for 6 minutes. Turn the skewers and cook further for 6 minutes. Brush the remaining ranch dressing on the meat and cook them for 1 more minute on each side.

In a salad bowl, mix together red onion, tomatoes, and cucumber, sprinkle with salt, vinegar, and extra virgin olive oil; toss to combine. Top the salad with skewers and scatter the parsley all over.

Per serving: Cal 423; Fat 24g; Net Carbs 2.4g; Protein 45g

Beef Sausage & Okra Casserole

Ingredients for 4 servings

½ cup marinara sauce, sugar-free
1 cup okra, trimmed
1 tbsp olive oil
1 celery stalk, chopped
¼ cup almond flour
1 egg
1 lb beef sausage, chopped
Salt and black pepper to taste
½ tbsp dried parsley

¼ tsp red pepper flakes
¼ cup Parmesan cheese, grated
2 green onions, chopped
½ tsp garlic powder
¼ tsp dried oregano
½ cup ricotta cheese
1 cup cheddar cheese, grated

Directions and Total Time: approx. 35 minutes

In a bowl, combine the sausage, pepper, pepper flakes, oregano, egg, Parmesan cheese, green onions, almond flour, salt, parsley, celery, and garlic powder. Form balls, lay them on a lined baking sheet, place in the oven at 390 F, and bake for 15 minutes. Remove the balls from the oven and cover with half of the marinara sauce and okra. Pour ricotta cheese all over, followed by the rest of the marinara sauce. Scatter the cheddar cheese and bake in the oven for 10 minutes. Allow to cool before serving.

Per serving: Cal 479; Fat 31g; Net Carbs 4.3g; Protein 39g

Grilled Beef Steaks & Vegetable Medley

Ingredients for 2 servings

1 red bell pepper, seeded, cut into strips
2 sirloin beef steaks
Salt and black pepper to taste
2 tbsp olive oil
1 ½ tbsp balsamic vinegar
¼ lb asparagus, trimmed

½ cup mushrooms, sliced
½ cup snow peas
1 small onion, quartered
1 garlic clove, sliced

Directions and Total Time: approx. 30 minutes

In a bowl, put asparagus, mushrooms, snow peas, bell pepper, onion, and garlic. Mix salt, pepper, olive oil, and balsamic vinegar in a small bowl, and pour half of the mixture over the vegetables; stir to combine. To the remaining oil mixture, add the beef and toss to coat well.

Preheat a grill pan over high heat. Place the steaks in the grill pan and sear for 6-8 minutes on each side. Remove the beef and set aside. Pour the vegetables and marinade in the pan and cook for 5 minutes, turning once. Share the vegetables into plates. Top with beef and drizzle the sauce from the pan all and serve.

Per serving: Cal 488; Fat 31g; Net Carbs 4.1g; Protein 57g

Beef & Mushroom Meatloaf

Ingredients for 4 servings

Meatloaf

1 lb ground beef
½ onion, chopped
1 tbsp almond milk
1 tbsp almond flour
1 garlic clove, minced

1 cup sliced mushrooms
1 small egg
Salt and black pepper to taste
1 tbsp parsley, chopped
⅓ cup Parmesan cheese, grated

Glaze

1/3 cup balsamic vinegar
¼ tbsp xylitol
¼ tsp tomato paste

¼ tsp garlic powder
¼ tsp onion powder
1 tbsp ketchup, sugar-free

Directions and Total Time: approx. 1 hour 10 minutes

Grease a loaf pan with cooking spray and set aside. Preheat oven to 390 F. Combine all meatloaf ingredients in a large bowl. Press this mixture into the prepared loaf pan. Bake in the oven for about 30 minutes. To make the glaze, whisk all ingredients in a bowl. Pour the glaze over the meatloaf. Put the meatloaf back in the oven and cook for 20 more minutes. Let meatloaf sit for 10 minutes before slicing. Serve and enjoy!

Per serving: Cal 311; Fat 21g; Net Carbs 5.5g; Protein 24g

Skirt Steak with Cauli Rice & Green Beans

Ingredients for 4 servings

Hot sauce (sugar-free) for topping
3 cups green beans, chopped
2 cups cauli rice
2 tbsp ghee
1 tbsp olive oil
1 lb skirt steak
Salt and black pepper to taste
4 fresh eggs

Directions and Total Time: approx. 20 minutes

Put the cauli rice and green beans in a bowl. Sprinkle with a little water, and steam in the microwave for 90 seconds to be tender. Share into bowls.

Warm the ghee and olive oil in a skillet, season the beef with salt and black pepper, and brown for 5 minutes on each side. Use a perforated spoon to scoop the meat onto the vegetables. Wipe out the skillet and return to medium heat. Crack in an egg, season with salt and pepper, and cook until the egg white has set, but the yolk is still runny 3 minutes. Remove egg onto the vegetable bowl and fry the remaining 3 eggs. Add to the other bowls. Drizzle with hot sauce and serve.

Per serving: Cal 334; Fat 25g; Net Carbs 6.3g; Protein 14g

Traditional Scottish Beef with Parsnips

Ingredients for 4 servings

2 tbsp olive oil
12 oz canned corn beef, cubed
1 onion, chopped
4 parsnips, chopped
1 carrot, chopped
1 garlic clove, minced
Salt and black pepper to taste
1 cup vegetable broth
2 tsp rosemary leaves
1 tbsp Worcestershire sauce
½ small cabbage, shredded

Directions and Total Time: approx. 45 minutes

Add the onion, garlic, carrots, rosemary, and parsnips to a warm olive oil over medium heat. Stir and cook for a minute. Pour in the vegetable broth and Worcestershire sauce. Stir the mixture and cook the ingredients on low heat for 25 minutes. Stir in the cabbage and corn beef, season with salt and pepper, and cook for 10 minutes.

Per serving: Cal 321; Fat 16g; Net Carbs 2.3g; Protein 13g

Sunday Beef Gratin

Ingredients for 4 servings

2 tbsp olive oil
1 onion, chopped
1 lb ground beef
2 garlic cloves, minced
Salt and black pepper to taste
1 cup mozzarella, shredded
1 cup fontina cheese, shredded
14 oz canned tomatoes, diced
2 tbsp sesame seeds, toasted
20 dill pickle slices

Directions and Total Time: approx. 35 minutes

Preheat the oven to 390 F. Heat olive oil in a pan over medium heat, place in the beef, garlic, salt, onion, and black pepper, and cook for 5 minutes. Remove and set to a baking dish, stir in half of the tomatoes and mozzarella cheese. Lay the pickle slices on top, spread over the fontina cheese and sesame seeds, and place in the oven to bake for 20 minutes.

Per serving: Cal 523; Fat 43g; Net Carbs 6.5g; Protein 36g

Beef Burgers with Lettuce & Avocado

Ingredients for 2 servings

½ lb ground beef
1 green onion, chopped
½ tsp garlic powder
1 tbsp butter
Salt and black pepper to taste
1 tbsp olive oil
½ tsp Dijon mustard
2 low carb buns, halved
2 tbsp mayonnaise
½ tsp balsamic vinegar
2 tbsp iceberg lettuce, torn
1 avocado, sliced

Directions and Total Time: approx. 15 minutes

In a bowl, mix ground beef, green onion, garlic powder, mustard, salt, and pepper; create 2 burgers. Heat the butter and olive oil in a skillet and cook the burgers for 3 minutes per side. Fill the buns with lettuce, mayonnaise, balsamic vinegar, burgers, and avocado slices to serve.

Per serving: Cal 778; Fat 62g; Net Carbs 5.6g; Protein 34g

Cabbage & Beef Stacks

Ingredients for 4 servings

1 lb chuck steak
1 headcanon cabbage, grated
¼ cup olive oil
3 tbsp coconut flour
1 tsp Italian mixed herb blend
½ cup bone broth

Directions and Total Time: approx. 55 minutes

Preheat the oven to 380 F. Slice the steak thinly across the grain with a sharp knife. In a zipper bag, add coconut flour and beef slices. Seal the bag and shake to coat. Make little mounds of cabbage in a greased baking dish. Drizzle with some olive oil. Remove the beef strips from the coconut flour mixture, shake off the excess flour, and place 2-3 beef strips on each cabbage mound. Sprinkle the Italian herb blend and drizzle again with the remaining olive oil. Roast for 30 minutes. Remove the pan and carefully pour in the broth. Return to the oven and roast further for 10 minutes, until beef cooks through. Serve and enjoy!

Per serving: Cal 231; Net Carbs 1.5g; Fat 14g; Protein 18g

Cauliflower & Beef Casserole

Ingredients for 4 servings

2 tbsp olive oil
1 lb ground beef
Salt and black pepper to taste
½ cup cauli rice
1 tbsp parsley, chopped
1 cup kohlrabi, chopped
5 oz can diced tomatoes
½ cup mozzarella cheese, grated

Directions and Total Time: approx. 40 minutes

Warm the olive oil in a pot over medium heat. Cook the beef for 5-6 minutes until no longer pink, breaking apart with a wooden spatula. Add cauli rice, kohlrabi, tomatoes, and ¼ cup water. Stir and bring to boil covered for 5 minutes to thicken the sauce. Adjust the taste with salt and black pepper. Spoon the beef mixture into the baking dish and spread evenly. Sprinkle with mozzarella cheese. Bake in the oven for 15 minutes at 380 F until the cheese has melted and it's golden brown. Remove and cool for 4 minutes. Serve sprinkled with parsley.

Per serving: Cal 391; Fat 233g; Net Carbs 7.3g; Protein 20g

Spiralized Zucchini in Bolognese Sauce

Ingredients for 4 servings

4 zucchinis, spiralized	1 tsp dried oregano
1 lb ground beef	1 tsp sage
2 bacon slices, chopped	1 tsp rosemary
2 garlic cloves	7 oz canned diced tomatoes
1 onion, chopped	2 tbsp olive oil

Directions and Total Time: approx. 35 minutes

Cook the zoodles in warm olive oil over medium heat for 3-4 minutes and remove to a serving plate. To the same pan, add bacon, onion, and garlic and cook for 3 minutes. Add beef and cook until browned, about 4-5 minutes. Stir in the herbs and tomatoes. Cook for 15 minutes and serve over the zoodles.

Per serving: Cal 378; Fat 19g; Net Carbs 5.9g; Protein 41g

Juicy Beef with Rosemary & Thyme

Ingredients for 4 servings

2 garlic cloves, minced	½ cup beef stock
2 tbsp butter	1 tbsp mustard
2 tbsp olive oil	2 tsp soy sauce, sugar-free
1 tbsp rosemary, chopped	2 tsp lemon juice
1 lb beef rump steak, sliced	1 tsp xylitol
Salt and black pepper to taste	A sprig of rosemary
1 shallot, chopped	A sprig of thyme
½ cup heavy cream	

Directions and Total Time: approx. 30 minutes

Set a pan to medium heat, warm in a tbsp of olive oil and stir in the shallot; cook for 3 minutes. Stir in the stock, soy sauce, xylitol, thyme sprig, cream, mustard and rosemary sprig, and cook for 8 minutes. Stir in butter, lemon juice, pepper and salt. Get rid of the rosemary and thyme. Set aside. In a bowl, combine the remaining oil with black pepper, garlic, rosemary, and salt. Toss in the beef to coat, and set aside for some minutes.

Heat a pan over medium-high heat, place in the beef steak, cook for 6 minutes, flipping halfway through; set aside and keep warm. Plate the beef slices, sprinkle over the sauce, and enjoy.

Per serving: Cal 411; Fat 31g; Net Carbs 4.6g; Protein 28g

Red Wine Beef Roast with Vegetables

Ingredients for 2 servings

1 tbsp olive oil	1 garlic clove, minced
1 lb brisket	Salt and black pepper to taste
½ cup carrots, peeled	1 bay leaf
1 red onion, quartered	1 tbsp fresh thyme, chopped
2 stalks celery, cut into chunks	1 cup red wine

Directions and Total Time: approx. 2 hours 20 minutes

Season the brisket with salt and pepper. Brown the meat on both sides in warm olive oil over medium heat for 6-8 minutes. Transfer to a deep casserole dish. Arrange the carrots, onion, garlic, thyme, celery, and bay leaf around the brisket and pour in the red wine and ½ cup of water. Cover the pot and place in the preheated to 370 F oven.

Cook for 2 hours. When ready, remove the casserole. Transfer the beef to a chopping board and cut it into thick slices. Top the beef with vegetables to serve.

Per serving: Cal 446; Fat 22g; Net Carbs 5.6g; Protein 52g

Grilled Steak with Green Beans

Ingredients for 2 servings

2 rib-eye steaks	Salt and black pepper to taste
2 tbsp unsalted butter	1 tbsp fresh thyme, chopped
1 tsp olive oil	1 tbsp rosemary, chopped
½ cup green beans, sliced	1 tbsp fresh parsley, chopped

Directions and Total Time: approx. 20 minutes

Preheat a grill pan over high heat. Brush the steaks with olive oil and season with salt and black pepper. Cook the steaks for about 4 minutes per side; reserve. Steam the green beans for 3-4 minutes until tender.

Season with salt. Melt the butter in the pan and stir-fry the herbs for 1 minute; then mix in the green beans. Place over the steaks and serve. Enjoy!

Per serving: Cal 576; Fat 39g; Net Carbs 4.3g; Protein 51g

Eggplant Beef Lasagna

Ingredients for 4 servings

2 large eggplants, sliced lengthwise	
2 tbsp olive oil	Salt and black pepper to taste
½ red chili, chopped	2 tsp sweet paprika
1 lb ground beef	1 tsp dried thyme
2 garlic cloves, minced	1 tsp dried basil
1 shallot, chopped	1 cup mozzarella cheese, grated
1 cup tomato sauce	1 cup chicken broth

Directions and Total Time: approx. 65 minutes

Heat the oil in a skillet and cook the beef for 4 minutes while breaking any lumps as you stir. Top with shallot, garlic, chili, tomato sauce, salt, paprika and black pepper. Stir and cook for 5 more minutes.

Lay 1/3 of the eggplant slices in a greased baking dish. Top with 1/3 of the beef mixture and repeat the layering process two more times with the same quantities. Season with basil and thyme. Pour in the chicken broth. Sprinkle the mozzarella cheese on top and tuck the baking dish in the oven. Bake for 35 minutes at 380 F. Remove the lasagna and let it rest for 10 minutes before serving.

Per serving: Cal 388; Fat 16g; Net Carbs 9.8g; Protein 41g

Beef Steaks with Bacon & Mushrooms

Ingredients for 2 servings

2 oz bacon, chopped	½ lb beef steaks
1 cup mushrooms, sliced	1 tsp ground nutmeg
1 garlic clove, chopped	¼ cup coconut oil
1 shallot, chopped	Salt and black pepper to taste
1 cup heavy cream	1 tbsp parsley, chopped

Directions and Total Time: approx. 50 minutes

In a pan over medium heat, cook the bacon for 2-3 minutes; set aside. In the same pan, warm the oil, add in the shallot, garlic and mushrooms. Cook for 4 minutes.

Stir in the beef, season with salt, pepper, and nutmeg, and sear until browned, 2 minutes per side.

Preheat oven to 360 F and insert the pan in the oven to bake for 25 minutes. Remove the beef steaks to a bowl and cover with foil. Place the pan over medium heat, pour in the heavy cream over the mushroom mixture, add in the reserved bacon and cook for 5 minutes; remove from heat. Spread the bacon/mushroom sauce over beef steaks, sprinkle with parsley and serve.

Per serving: Cal 765; Fat 71g; Net Carbs 3.8g; Protein 32g

Veggie Chuck Roast Beef in Oven

Ingredients for 4 servings

2 tbsp olive oil	1 bell pepper, sliced
1 lb beef chuck roast, cubed	1 onion, chopped
1 cup canned diced tomatoes	1 bay leaf
1 carrot, chopped	½ cup beef stock
Salt and black pepper to taste	1 tbsp rosemary, chopped
½ lb mushrooms, sliced	½ tsp dry mustard
1 celery stalk, chopped	1 tbsp almond flour

Directions and Total Time: approx. 1 hour 45 minutes

Preheat oven to 350 F. Set a pot over medium heat, warm olive oil and brown the beef on each side for 4-5 minutes. Stir in tomatoes, onion, mustard, carrot, mushrooms, bell pepper, celery, bay leaf, and stock. Season with salt and pepper. In a bowl, combine ½ cup of water with flour and stir in the pot. Transfer to a baking dish and bake for 90 minutes, stirring at intervals of 30 minutes. Scatter the rosemary over and serve warm.

Per serving: Cal 325; Fat 18g; Net Carbs 5.6g; Protein 31g

Winter Beef Stew

Ingredients for 4 servings

14 oz canned tomatoes with juice

3 tsp olive oil	2 bay leaves
1 lb ground beef	Salt and black pepper to taste
1 cup beef stock	3 tbsp fresh parsley, chopped
1 carrot, chopped	1 onion, chopped
1 celery stick, chopped	1 tsp dried sage
1 lb butternut squash, diced	1 garlic clove, minced
1 tbsp Worcestershire sauce	

Directions and Total Time: approx. 40 minutes

Cook the onion, garlic, celery, carrot, and beef, in warm oil over medium heat for 10 minutes. Add in butternut squash, Worcestershire sauce, bay leaves, stock, canned tomatoes, and sage, and bring to a boil. Reduce heat and simmer for 20 minutes. Adjust the seasonings. Remove and discard the bay leaves. Serve topped with parsley.

Per serving: Cal 353; Fat 16g; Net Carbs 6.6g; Protein 26g

Beef Cheese & Egg Casserole

Ingredients for 4 servings

2 tbsp olive oil	1 cup Gouda cheese, grated
½ tsp nutmeg	1 yellow onion, chopped
1 lb ground beef	2 cups tomatoes, chopped
5 eggs, beaten	¼ cup heavy cream

1 Banana pepper, chopped	2 zucchinis, sliced
2 garlic cloves, chopped	Salt and black pepper to taste

Directions and Total Time: approx. 25 minutes

Preheat oven to 360 F. Warm the olive oil in a skillet over medium heat. Stir-fry the garlic, banana pepper, and onion for 2 minutes until tender. Add the ground beef and sauté for 4-6 minutes, stirring often.

Sprinkle with nutmeg, salt, and pepper. Transfer the mixture to a baking dish. Cover with tomatoes and arrange the zucchini slices on top. Bake for 30 minutes.

In a bowl, mix the eggs, cheese, and heavy cream. Season with salt and pepper. Remove the baking dish from the oven and pour the cheese mixture over. Bake for 10-15 more minutes or until the eggs are set. Enjoy!

Per serving: Cal 608; Net Carbs 8.4g; Fat 36g; Protein 56g

Bell Peppers Stuffed with Enchilada Beef

Ingredients for 6 servings

3 tbsp butter, softened	3 tsp enchilada seasoning
6 bell peppers, deseeded	1 cup cauliflower rice
½ white onion, chopped	¼ cup grated cheddar cheese
3 cloves garlic, minced	Sour cream for serving
2 ½ lb ground beef	Salt and black pepper to taste

Directions and Total Time: approx. 60 minutes

Preheat oven to 380 F. Melt butter in a skillet over medium heat and sauté onion and garlic for 3 minutes. Stir in beef, enchilada seasoning, salt, and pepper. Cook for 10 minutes. Mix in the cauli rice until well incorporated. Spoon the mixture into the peppers, top with the cheddar cheese, and put the stuffed peppers in a greased baking dish. Bake for 40 minutes. Drop generous dollops of sour cream on the peppers and serve.

Per serving: Cal 411; Net Carbs 4g; Fat 19g; Protein 48g

Lettuce Cups with Spicy Beef

Ingredients for 4 servings

3 tbsp ghee, divided	2 tsp red curry powder
1 lb chuck steak	1 cup cauliflower rice
1 large white onion, chopped	8 small lettuce leaves
2 garlic cloves, minced	Salt and black pepper to taste
1 jalapeño pepper, chopped	¼ cup sour cream for topping

Directions and Total Time: approx. 30 minutes

Warm 2 tbsp of the ghee in a large deep skillet. Sliced the beef thinly against the grain and cook until brown and cooked within, 10 minutes; set aside. Sauté the onion in the skillet for 3 minutes. Pour in garlic, salt, pepper, and jalapeño and cook for 1 minute.

Add the remaining ghee, curry powder, and beef. Cook for 5 minutes and stir in the cauliflower rice. Sauté until adequately mixed and the cauliflower is slightly softened, 2 to 3 minutes. Adjust the taste with salt and pepper.

Lay out the lettuce leaves on a lean flat surface and spoon the beef mixture onto the middle part of them, 3 tbsp per leaf. Top with sour cream, wrap the leaves, and serve.

Per serving: Cal 302; Net Carbs 3.3g; Fat 21g; Protein 32g

Basil Beef Sausage Pizza

Ingredients for 4 servings

2 tbsp butter	¾ cup almond flour
2 tbsp cream cheese, softened	1 tsp plain vinegar
10 oz shredded mozzarella	¼ cup tomato sauce
8 oz ground beef sausage	½ tsp dried basil
1 egg	

Directions and Total Time: approx. 50 minutes

Preheat oven to 390 F. Line a pizza pan with parchment paper. Melt the cream cheese and half of the mozzarella cheese in a skillet over low heat while stirring until evenly combined. Turn the heat off and mix in almond flour, egg, and vinegar. Let cool slightly.

Flatten the mixture onto the pizza pan. Cover with another parchment paper and, using a rolling pin, smoothen the dough into a circle. Take off the parchment paper on top, prick the dough all over with a fork and bake for 10 to 15 minutes until golden brown.

While the crust bakes, melt butter in a skillet over and fry sausage until brown, 8 minutes. Turn the heat off. Spread the tomato sauce on the crust, top with basil, meat, and remaining mozzarella cheese, and return to the oven. Bake for 12 minutes. Remove the pizza, slice, and serve.

Per serving: Cal 359; Net Carbs 0.8g; Fat 19g; Protein 41g

Spinach Cheeseburgers

Ingredients for 4 servings

1 lb ground beef	16 large spinach leaves
4 tomato wedges, deseeded	4 tbsp mayonnaise
½ cup chopped cilantro	1 medium red onion, sliced
1 lemon, zested and juiced	¼ cup grated Parmesan
1 tsp garlic powder	1 avocado, halved, sliced
2 tbsp hot chili puree	Salt and black pepper to taste

Directions and Total Time: approx. 15 minutes

Preheat the grill to high heat. In a bowl, add beef, cilantro, lemon zest, juice, salt, pepper, garlic powder, and chili puree. Mix the ingredients until evenly combined.

Make 4 patties from the mixture. Grill for 3 minutes per side. Transfer to a serving plate. Lay 2 spinach leaves side to side in 4 portions on a clean flat surface. Place a beef patty on each and spread 1 tbsp of mayo on top. Add a slice of tomato and onion, sprinkle with some Parmesan, and place avocado on top. Cover with 2 pieces of spinach leaves each. Serve the burgers with cream cheese sauce.

Per serving: Cal 308; Net Carbs 6.5g; Fat 16g; Protein 31g

Beef Pad Thai with Peanuts & Zucchini

Ingredients for 4 servings

3 large eggs, lightly beaten	2 tbsp tamari sauce
2 ½ lb chuck steak	1 tbsp white vinegar
1 tsp red pepper flakes	½ cup chopped green onions
1 tsp pureed garlic	2 garlic cloves, minced
¼ tsp freshly ground ginger	4 zucchinis, spiralized
2 tbsp peanut oil	½ cup bean sprouts
3 ¼ tbsp peanut butter	½ cup crushed peanuts
1/3 cup beef broth	Salt and black pepper to taste

Directions and Total Time: approx. 30 minutes

Using a sharp knife, slice the beef thinly against the grain. In a bowl, combine garlic puree, ginger, salt, and pepper. Add in beef and toss to coat.

Heat peanut oil in a deep skillet and cook the beef for 12 minutes; transfer to a plate. Pour the eggs into the skillet and scramble for 1 minute; set aside. Reduce the heat and combine broth, peanut butter, tamari sauce, vinegar, green onions, minced garlic, and red pepper flakes.

Mix until adequately combined and simmer for 3 minutes. Stir in beef, zucchini, bean sprouts, and eggs. Cook for 1 minute. Garnish with peanuts.

Per serving: Cal 433; Net Carbs 3.3g; Fat 38g; Protein 69g

Taco Beef Pizza

Ingredients for 4 servings

1 lb ground beef	½ cup cheese sauce
2 tbsp cream cheese, softened	1 cup grated cheddar cheese
2 cups shredded mozzarella	1 cup chopped lettuce
1 egg	1 tomato, diced
¾ cup almond flour	¼ cup sliced black olives
2 tsp taco seasoning	1 cup sour cream for topping

Directions and Total Time: approx. 35 minutes

Preheat oven to 3750 F. Line a pizza pan with parchment paper. Microwave the mozzarella and cream cheeses for 1 minute. Remove and mix in egg and almond flour.

Spread the mixture on the pan and bake for 15 minutes. Put the beef in a pot and cook for 5 minutes. Stir in taco seasoning. Spread the cheese sauce on the crust and top with the meat. Add cheddar cheese, lettuce, tomato, and black olives. Bake until the cheese melts, 5 minutes. Remove the pizza, drizzle sour cream on top, and serve.

Per serving: Cal 589; Net Carbs 7.9g; Fat 31g; Protein 71g

Cauli Rice with Beef & Cashew Nuts

Ingredients for 4 servings

1 ½ lb chuck steak, cubed	½ cup chopped bell peppers
4 cups cauliflower rice	½ cup green beans, chopped
3 tbsp olive oil	3 garlic cloves, minced
2 large eggs, beaten	¼ cup coconut aminos
1 tbsp avocado oil	1 cup toasted cashew nuts
1 red onion, finely chopped	1 tbsp toasted sesame seeds

Directions and Total Time: approx. 25 minutes

Warm 2 tbsp olive oil in a wok over medium heat and cook the beef for 7-8 minutes; set aside. Pour the eggs in the wok and scramble for 2-3 minutes; set aside.

Add the remaining olive oil and avocado oil to heat. Stir in onion, bell peppers, green beans, and garlic. Sauté until soft, 3 minutes. Pour in cauliflower rice, coconut aminos, and stir until evenly combined.

Mix in the beef, eggs, and cashew nuts and cook for 3 minutes. Dish into serving plates and garnish with sesame seeds. Serve.

Per serving: Cal 498; Net Carbs 3.2g; Fat 292; Protein 48g

Grandma´s Meatballs

Ingredients for 4 servings

1 tbsp olive oil	2 garlic cloves, minced
2 tbsp melted butter	1 tsp dried basil
1 lb ground beef	2 tbsp tamari sauce
1 red onion, finely chopped	1 tbsp dried rosemary
2 red bell peppers, chopped	Salt and black pepper to taste

Directions and Total Time: approx. 30 minutes

Preheat the oven to 380 F. In a bowl, mix beef, onion, bell peppers, garlic, butter, basil, tamari sauce, salt, pepper, and rosemary. Form 1-inch meatballs from the mixture and place them on a greased baking sheet.

Drizzle olive oil over the beef and bake in the oven for 20 minutes or until the meatballs brown on the outside. Serve topped with ranch dressing.

Per serving: Cal 622; Net Carbs 2.5g; Fat 33g; Protein 79g

Beef, Bell Pepper & Mushroom Kebabs

Ingredients for 4 servings

1 lb cremini mushrooms, halved	
2 lb beef tri-tip steak, cubed	1 lime, juiced
2 tbsp coconut oil	1 tbsp ginger powder
2 yellow bell peppers	½ tsp ground cumin
1 tbsp tamari sauce	

Directions and Total Time: approx. 15 min + cooling time

Deseed the bell peppers and cut them into squares. In a bowl, mix coconut oil, tamari sauce, lime juice, ginger, and cumin powder. Add in the beef, mushrooms, and bell peppers; toss to coat. Cover the bowl with plastic wrap and marinate for 1 hour. Preheat the grill to high heat. Take off the plastic wrap and thread the mushrooms, beef, and bell peppers in this order on skewers until the ingredients are exhausted. Grill the skewers for 5 minutes per side. Remove to serving plates and serve warm with steamed cauliflower rice or braised asparagus.

Per serving: Cal 379; Net Carbs 3.2g; Fat 23g; Protein 49g

Mushroom & Beef Stir-Fry

Ingredients for 4 servings

1 lb shiitake mushrooms, halved	
1 lb chuck steak	4 slices prosciutto, chopped
2 sprigs rosemary, chopped	1 tbsp coconut oil
1 green bell pepper, chopped	1 tbsp pureed garlic

Directions and Total Time: approx. 30 minutes

Using a sharp knife, slice the chuck steak thinly against the grain and cut it into smaller pieces. Heat a skillet over medium heat and cook prosciutto until brown and crispy; set aside. Melt coconut oil in the skillet and cook the beef until brown, 6-8 minutes. Remove to the prosciutto plate. Add mushrooms and bell pepper to the skillet and sauté until softened, 5 minutes. Stir in prosciutto, beef, rosemary, and garlic. Season to taste and cook for 4 minutes. Serve with buttered green beans.

Per serving: Cal 229; Net Carbs 2.1g; Fat 12g; Protein 32g

Asian-Style Creamy Beef

Ingredients for 4 servings

4 large rib-eye steak	½ cup chopped brown onion
1 green bell pepper, sliced	1 cup beef stock
1 red bell pepper, sliced	1 cup coconut milk
2 long red chilies, sliced	1 tbsp Thai green curry paste
2 tbsp ghee	1 lime, juiced
2 garlic cloves, minced	2 tbsp chopped cilantro

Directions and Total Time: approx. 40 minutes

Warm the 1 tbsp of ghee in a pan over medium heat and cook the beef for 3 minutes on each side. Remove to a plate. Add the remaining ghee to the skillet and sauté garlic and onion for 3 minutes. Stir-fry in bell peppers and red chili until softened, 5 minutes. Pour in beef stock, coconut milk, curry paste, and lime juice. Let simmer for 4 minutes. Put the beef back into the sauce. Cook for 10 minutes and transfer the pan to the oven. Cook further under the broiler for 5 minutes. Garnish with cilantro and serve with cauliflower rice.

Per serving: Cal 638; Net Carbs 2.6g; Fat 35g; Protein 69g

Beef Hot Dogs in Bacon Wraps

Ingredients for 4 servings

16 bacon slices	1 tsp onion powder
½ cup grated Gruyere cheese	1 tsp garlic powder
8 large beef hot dogs	Salt and black pepper to taste

Directions and Total Time: approx. 25 minutes

Preheat oven to 380 F. Cut a slit in the middle of each hot dog and stuff evenly with cheese. Wrap each hot dog with 2 bacon slices and secure with toothpicks. Season with onion and garlic powders, salt, and pepper. Place the hot dogs in the oven and slide in the cookie sheet beneath the rack to catch dripping grease. Cook for 15 minutes until the bacon browns and crisps. Serve.

Per serving: Cal 763; Net Carbs 4g; Fat 61g; Protein 42g

Jerked Beef Stew

Ingredients for 4 servings

½ scotch bonnet pepper, chopped	
1 onion, chopped	1 cup tomatoes, chopped
2 tbsp olive oil	1 tbsp fresh cilantro, chopped
1 tsp ginger paste	1 garlic clove, minced
1 tsp soy sauce	¼ cup vegetable broth
1 lb beef stew meat, cubed	Salt and black pepper to taste
1 red bell pepper, chopped	¼ cup black olives, chopped
2 green chilies, chopped	1 tsp jerk seasoning

Directions and Total Time: approx. 80 minutes

Brown the beef on all sides in warm olive oil over medium heat; remove and set aside. Stir-fry in the red bell peppers, green chilies, jerk seasoning, garlic, scotch bonnet pepper, onion, ginger paste, and soy sauce, for about 5-6 minutes. Pour in the tomatoes and broth, and cook for 1 hour. Stir in the olives, adjust the seasonings and serve sprinkled with fresh cilantro.

Per serving: Cal 235; Fat 13g; Net Carbs 2.8g; Protein 26g

Coconut-Olive Beef with Mushrooms

Ingredients for 4 servings

¼ cup button mushrooms, sliced
4 rib-eye steaks
3 tbsp butter
1 yellow onion, chopped
1/3 cup coconut milk

2 tbsp coconut cream
1/2 tsp dried thyme
2 tbsp chopped parsley
3 tbsp black olives, sliced

Directions and Total Time: approx. 30 minutes

Warm 2 tbsp butter in a deep skillet over medium heat. Add and sauté the mushrooms for 4 minutes until tender. Stir in onion and cook further for 3 minutes; set aside. Melt the remaining butter in the skillet and cook the beef for 10 minutes on both sides. Pour mushrooms and onion back to the skillet and add milk, coconut cream, thyme, and 1 tbsp of parsley. Stir and simmer for 2 minutes. Mix in black olives and turn the heat off. Serve garnished with the remaining parsley.

Per serving: Cal 643; Net Carbs 1.9g; Fat 42g; Protein 71g

Cilantro Beef Curry with Cauliflower

Ingredients for 4 servings

1 head cauliflower, cut into florets
1 tbsp olive oil
½ lb ground beef
1 garlic clove, minced
1 tsp turmeric
1 tbsp cilantro, chopped

1 tbsp ginger paste
½ tsp garam masala
5 oz canned whole tomatoes
Salt and chili pepper to taste
¼ cup water

Directions and Total Time: approx. 30 minutes

Heat oil in a saucepan over medium heat, add the beef, garlic, ginger paste, and garam masala. Cook for 5 minutes while breaking any lumps. Stir in the tomatoes and cauliflower, season with salt, turmeric, and chili pepper, and cook covered for 6 minutes. Add the water and bring to a boil over medium heat for 10 minutes or until the water has reduced by half. Spoon the curry into serving bowls and serve sprinkled with cilantro.

Per serving: Cal 365; Fat 32g; Net Carbs 3.5g; Protein 19g

Beef Fajitas with Colorful Bell Peppers

Ingredients for 4 servings

1 cup mixed bell peppers, chopped
2 tbsp olive oil
2 lb skirt steak, cut in halves
2 tbsp Cajun seasoning

2 large white onion, chopped
¼ cup cheddar cheese, grated
12 low carb tortillas

Directions and Total Time: approx. 35 min + cooling time

Rub the steak with Cajun seasoning and marinate in the fridge for one hour. Preheat grill to 400 F.

Cook the steak on the grill for 6 minutes on each side, flipping once until lightly browned. Remove from heat and cover with foil to sit for 10 minutes before slicing. Heat the olive oil in a skillet over medium heat and sauté the onion and bell peppers for 5 minutes or until soft. Cut steak against the grain into strips and share on the tortillas. Top with the veggies and cheese and serve.

Per serving: Cal 512; Fat 32g; Net Carbs 4g; Protein 25g

Sweet BBQ Rib Steak

Ingredients for 4 servings

2 tbsp avocado oil
1 ½ lb rib steaks

3 tbsp maple syrup, sugar-free
3 tbsp barbecue dry rub

Directions and Total Time: approx. 2 hours 40 minutes

Preheat the oven to 300 F. Remove the membrane from the steaks. Line a baking sheet with aluminum foil.

In a bowl, mix avocado oil and maple syrup and brush the mixture onto the meat. Sprinkle BBQ rub all over the ribs. Put them on the baking sheet and bake until the meat is tender and crispy on the top, 2 ½ hours. Serve with buttered broccoli and green beans.

Per serving: Cal 487; Net Carbs 1.8g; Fat 26g; Protein 51g

Juicy Beef Meatballs

Ingredients for 4 servings

1 lb ground beef
Salt and black pepper to taste
½ tsp garlic powder
1 ¼ tbsp coconut aminos
1 cup beef stock
¾ cup almond flour

1 tbsp fresh parsley, chopped
1 onion, sliced
2 tbsp butter
1 tbsp olive oil
¼ cup sour cream

Directions and Total Time: approx. 30 minutes

Preheat the oven to 390 F and grease a baking dish. In a bowl, combine beef with salt, garlic powder, almond flour, parsley, 1 tbsp of coconut aminos, black pepper, ¼ cup of beef stock. Form patties and place on the baking sheet. Bake for 18 minutes. Set a pan with the butter and olive oil over medium heat, stir in the onion, and cook for 3 minutes. Stir in the remaining beef stock, sour cream, and remaining coconut aminos, and bring to a simmer. Adjust the seasoning with black pepper and salt. Serve the meatballs topped with onion sauce.

Per serving: Cal 441; Fat 24g; Net Carbs 5.7g; Protein 31g

Roasted Pumpkin Filled with Beef

Ingredients for 4 servings

1 ½ lb pumpkin, pricked with a fork
Salt and black pepper to taste
1 garlic clove, minced
1 onion, chopped
½ cup mushrooms, sliced
28 oz canned diced tomatoes

¼ tsp cayenne pepper
½ tsp dried thyme
1 lb ground beef
1 cup cauli rice

Directions and Total Time: approx. 70 minutes

Preheat the oven to 430 F. Lay the pumpkin on a lined baking sheet and bake in the oven for 40 minutes. Cut in half, set aside to cool, deseed, scoop out most of the flesh and let sit. Heat a greased pan over high heat. Add the garlic, mushrooms, onion, and beef and cook until the meat browns. Stir in salt, thyme, tomatoes, black pepper, and cayenne, and cook for 10 minutes; stir in flesh and cauli rice. Stuff the squash halves with beef mixture, and bake in the oven for 10 minutes.

Per serving: Cal 422; Fat 20g; Net Carbs 9.8g; Protein 33g

Beef Patties with Broccoli Mash

Ingredients for 4 servings

1 lb broccoli
1 lb ground beef
1 egg
½ white onion, chopped
2 tbsp olive oil

5 tbsp butter, softened
2 oz grated Parmesan
2 tbsp lemon juice
Salt and black pepper to taste

Directions and Total Time: approx. 30 minutes

In a bowl, add ground beef, egg, onion, salt, and pepper. Mix and mold out 6-8 cakes out of the mixture. Warm olive oil in a skillet and fry the patties for 6-8 minutes on both sides. Remove to a plate. Pour lightly salted water into a pot over medium heat, bring to a boil, and add broccoli. Cook until tender but not too soft, 6-8 minutes. Drain and transfer to a bowl. Add in 2 tbsp of butter, and Parmesan cheese. Use an immersion blender to puree the ingredients until smooth and creamy; set aside. To make the lemon butter, mix remaining the butter with lemon juice, salt, and pepper in a bowl. Serve the cakes with broccoli mash and lemon butter.

Per serving: Cal 857; Net Carbs 6g; Fat 81g; Protein 35g

Cocktail Chili Beef Meatballs

Ingredients for 4 servings

2 tbsp olive oil
2 tbsp thyme
½ cup pork rinds, crushed
1 egg
Salt and black pepper to taste
1½ lb ground beef

10 oz canned onion soup
1 tbsp almond flour
2 tbsp chili sauce
¼ cup free-sugar ketchup
3 tsp Worcestershire sauce
½ tsp dry mustard

Directions and Total Time: approx. 35 minutes

In a bowl, combine 1/3 cup of the onion soup with the beef, pepper, thyme, pork rinds, chili sauce, egg, and salt. Shape meatballs from the beef mixture.

Heat olive oil in a pan over medium heat and place in the meatballs to brown on both sides. In a bowl, combine the rest of the soup with almond flour, dry mustard, ketchup, Worcestershire sauce, and ¼ cup of water. Pour over the beef meatballs and cook for 20 minutes. Serve.

Per serving: Cal 341; Fat 21g; Net Carbs 5.6g; Protein 23g

Beef Roast with Serrano Pepper Gravy

Ingredients for 4 servings

2 lb beef roast
1 cup mushrooms, sliced
1 ½ cups beef stock

1 oz onion soup mix
½ cup basil dressing
2 serrano peppers, shredded

Directions and Total Time: approx. 1 hour 25 minutes

Preheat the oven to 350 F. In a bowl, combine the stock with the basil dressing and onion soup mixture. Place the beef roast in a pan, stir in the stock mixture, mushrooms, and serrano peppers; cover with aluminum foil. Set in the oven and bake for 1 hour. Take out the foil and continue baking for 15 minutes. Allow the roast to cool, then slice, and serve alongside a topping of the gravy.

Per serving: Cal 722; Fat 51g; Net Carbs 5.1g; Protein 71g

BBQ Beef Sliders

Ingredients for 4 servings

3 lb chuck roast, boneless
1 tsp onion powder
2 tsp garlic powder
1 tbsp smoked paprika
2 tbsp tomato paste
¼ cup white vinegar
2 tbsp tamari sauce

½ cup bone broth
¼ cup melted butter
4 zero carb buns, halved
Salt and black pepper to taste
¼ cup baby spinach
4 slices cheddar cheese

Directions and Total Time: approx. 4 hours 15 minutes

In a small bowl, combine salt, pepper, onion and garlic powders, and paprika. Cut the beef into two pieces. Rub the mixture onto the beef and place it in a slow cooker. In another bowl, mix tomato paste, vinegar, tamari sauce, broth, and melted butter. Pour over the beef and cook for 4 hours on High. When the beef cooks, shred it using two forks. Divide the spinach between buns, spoon the meat on top, and add a cheddar cheese slice. Serve.

Per serving: Cal 651; Net Carbs 16g; Fat 31g; Protein 69g

Thyme Beef & Bacon Casserole

Ingredients for 4 servings

2 tbsp olive oil
2 tbsp ghee
1 cup pumpkin, chopped
½ cup celery, chopped
3 slices bacon, chopped
1 lb beef meat for stew, cubed
1 garlic clove, minced
1 onion, chopped

1 tbsp red vinegar
2 cups beef stock
1 tbsp tomato puree
1 cinnamon stick
1 lemon peel strip
3 thyme sprigs, chopped
Salt and black pepper to taste

Directions and Total Time: approx. 40 minutes

Put a saucepan over medium heat and warm oil, add in the celery, garlic, and onion and cook for 3 minutes. Stir in the beef and bacon, and cook until slightly brown. Pour in vinegar, ghee, lemon peel strip, stock, tomato puree, cinnamon stick and pumpkin. Cover and cook for 25 minutes. Get rid of the lemon peel and cinnamon stick. Adjust the seasoning and top with thyme to serve.

Per serving: Cal 552; Fat 41g; Net Carbs 4.5g; Protein 32g

Ground Beef Stew with Majoram & Basil

Ingredients for 4 servings

2 tbsp olive oil
¼ cup red wine
1 lb ground beef
1 onion, chopped
2 garlic cloves, minced
14 oz canned diced tomatoes

1 tbsp dried basil
1 tbsp dried marjoram
Salt and black pepper to taste
2 carrots, sliced
2 celery stalks, chopped
1 cup vegetable broth

Directions and Total Time: approx. 30 minutes

Put a pan over medium heat, add in the olive oil, onion, carrots, celery, and garlic, and sauté for 5 minutes. Place in the beef and cook for 6 minutes. Stir in the tomatoes, red wine, vegetable broth, black pepper, marjoram, basil, and salt, and simmer for 15 minutes. Serve and enjoy!

Per serving: Cal 274; Fat 14g; Net Carbs 6.2g; Protein 29g

Tomato Beef Tart with Cheddar & Ricotta

Ingredients for 4 servings

1 egg	4 tbsp coconut flour
1 lb ground beef	¾ cup almond flour
2 tbsp olive oil	4 tbsp flaxseeds
1 small brown onion, chopped	1 tsp baking powder
1 garlic clove, finely chopped	3 tbsp coconut oil, melted
1 tbsp Italian mixed herbs	¼ cup ricotta, crumbled
4 tbsp tomato paste	¼ cup cheddar, shredded

Directions and Total Time: approx. 1 hour 30 minutes

Preheat oven to 360 F. Line a pie dish with parchment paper. Heat olive oil in a large skillet over medium heat and sauté onion and garlic until softened, 3 minutes. Add in beef and cook until brown. Season with herbs and stir in tomato paste and ½ cup water; reduce the heat to low. Simmer for 20 minutes; set aside.

In a food processor, add the flours, flaxseeds, baking powder, coconut oil, egg, and 4 tbsp water. Mix starting on low speed to medium until evenly combined and dough is formed. Spread the dough in the pie pan and bake for 12 minutes. Remove and spread the meat filling on top. Scatter with ricotta and cheddar cheeses. Bake until the cheeses melt and are golden brown on top, 35 minutes. Remove the pie, let cool for 3 minutes, slice, and serve with green salad and garlic vinaigrette.

Per serving: Cal 598; Net Carbs 2.3g; Fat 42g; Protein 61g

Burgundy Beef with Mushrooms

Ingredients for 4 servings

1 tbsp parsley, chopped	1 lb stewed beef, cubed
1 cup Burgundy red wine	12 pearl onions, halved
1 tsp dried thyme	1 tomato, chopped
Salt and black pepper to taste	2 oz pancetta, chopped
1 bay leaf	2 garlic cloves, minced
1 cup beef stock	½ lb mushrooms, chopped

Directions and Total Time: approx. 65 minutes

Heat a pan over high heat, stir in the pancetta and beef and cook until lightly browned; set aside. Place in the onions, mushrooms, and garlic, and cook for 5 minutes. Pour in the wine to deglaze the bottom of the pan and add beef stock, bay leaf, and tomato. Season with salt, pepper, and thyme. Return the meat and pancetta, cover, and cook for 50 minutes. Serve topped with parsley.

Per serving: Cal 367; Fat 24g; Net Carbs 5g; Protein 33g

Hot Grilled Spare Ribs

Ingredients for 4 servings

4 tbsp BBQ sauce, sugar-free	3 tsp hot chili powder
2 tbsp olive oil	1 tsp garlic powder
2 tbsp xylitol	1 lb spare ribs
Salt and black pepper to taste	

Directions and Total Time: approx. 60 min + cooling time

In a bowl, mix the xylitol, salt, pepper, olive oil, hot chili powder and garlic powder. Brush on the meaty sides of the ribs and wrap in foil. Refrigerate for 30 minutes.

Preheat oven to 400 F. Place wrapped ribs on a baking sheet and bake for 40 minutes until cooked through. Remove the aluminium foil, brush with BBQ sauce, and brown under the broiler for 10 minutes. Slice to serve.

Per serving: Cal 406; Fat 34g; Net Carbs 3.4g; Protein 25g

Leek & Beef Bake

Ingredients for 4 servings

3 tbsp olive oil	½ cup apple cider vinegar
1 lb beef steak racks	1 tsp Italian seasoning
2 leeks, sliced	1 tbsp xylitol
Salt and black pepper to taste	

Directions and Total Time: approx. 50 minutes

Preheat the oven to 420 F. In a bowl, mix the leeks with 2 tbsp of oil, xylitol, and vinegar, toss to coat well, and set to a baking dish. Season with Italian seasoning, black pepper and salt, and cook in the oven for 15 minutes. Sprinkle pepper and salt to the beef, place into an oiled pan over medium heat, and cook for a couple of minutes. Place the beef to the baking dish with the leeks, and bake for 20 minutes. Serve and enjoy!

Per serving: Cal 234; Fat 12g; Net Carbs 4.8g; Protein 16g

Mexican-Inspired Beef Chili

Ingredients for 4 servings

2 tbsp olive oil	3 celery stalks, chopped
1 onion, chopped	2 tbsp coconut aminos
2 lb ground beef	Salt and black pepper to taste
15 oz canned tomatoes, diced	2 tbsp cumin
½ cup pickled jalapeños, diced	1 tsp onion powder
1 tsp chipotle chili paste	1 tsp garlic powder
1 garlic clove, minced	1 tsp chopped cilantro

Directions and Total Time: approx. 40 minutes

Warm olive oil in a pan over medium heat and sauté onion, celery, garlic, beef, pepper, and salt until the meat browns. Stir in the rest of the ingredients and cook for 30 minutes. Serve and enjoy!

Per serving: Cal 441; Fat 24g; Net Carbs 3.8g; Protein 16g

Flank Steak Roll

Ingredients for 2 servings

1 lb flank steak	½ cup baby kale, chopped
Salt and black pepper to taste	1 serrano pepper, chopped
½ cup ricotta, crumbled	1 tbsp basil leaves, chopped

Directions and Total Time: approx. 40 minutes

Wrap the steak in plastic wraps, place on a flat surface, and gently run a rolling pin over to flatten. Take off the wraps. Sprinkle with salt, pepper, half of the ricotta cheese, top with kale, serrano pepper, and the remaining cheese. Roll the steak over on the stuffing and secure with toothpicks. Place in the greased baking sheet and cook for 30 minutes at 390 F, flipping once until nicely browned on the outside and the cheese melted within. Cool for 3 minutes, slice and serve with basil.

Per serving: Cal 445; Fat 21g; Net Carbs 2.8g; Protein 53g

Spiced Roast Beef

Ingredients for 4 servings

2 lb beef brisket	A pinch of cayenne pepper
½ tsp celery salt	½ tsp garlic powder
1 tsp chili powder	½ cup beef stock
2 tbsp olive oil	3 onions, cut into quarters
1 tbsp sweet paprika	¼ tsp dry mustard

Directions and Total Time: approx. 70 minutes

Preheat oven to 360 F. In a bowl, combine the paprika with dry mustard, chili powder, garlic powder, cayenne pepper, and celery salt. Rub the meat with the mixture.

Set a pan over medium heat and warm olive oil, place in the beef, and sear until brown. Remove to a greased baking dish. Pour in the stock, add onions and bake for 60 minutes. Set the beef to a cutting board, and leave to cool before slicing. Take the juices from the baking dish and strain, sprinkle over the meat to serve.

Per serving: Cal 483; Fat 22g; Net Carbs 5.1g; Protein 49g

Beef & Bell Pepper Frittata

Ingredients for 4 servings

1 tbsp butter	1 cup sour cream
12 oz ground beef sausage	2 red bell peppers, chopped
¼ cup shredded cheddar	Salt and black pepper, to taste
12 whole eggs	

Directions and Total Time: approx. 55 minutes

Preheat the oven to 360 F. Crack the eggs into a blender; add the sour cream, salt, and pepper. Process over low speed to mix the ingredients; set aside. Melt butter in a large skillet over medium heat. Add bell peppers and sauté until soft, 6 minutes; set aside. Add the beef sausage and cook until brown, continuously stirring and breaking the lumps into small bits, 10 minutes.

Flatten the beef on the bottom of skillet, scatter bell peppers on top, pour the egg mixture all over, and scatter the top with cheddar cheese.

Put the skillet in the oven and bake for 30 minutes or until the eggs set and the cheddar cheese melts. Remove, slice the frittata, and serve warm with a salad.

Per serving: Cal 621; Net Carbs 5g; Fat 49g; Protein 33g

Beef & Pepper Filled Zucchini

Ingredients for 4 servings

1 lb ground beef	1 shallot, finely chopped
1 red bell pepper, chopped	2 tbsp taco seasoning
2 zucchinis	½ cup finely chopped parsley
2 tbsp butter	1 tbsp olive oil
2 garlic cloves, minced	1¼ cups shredded cheddar

Directions and Total Time: approx. 45 minutes

Preheat oven to 390 F. Grease a baking sheet with cooking spray. Using a knife, cut zucchinis into halves and scoop out the pulp; set aside. Chop the flesh. Melt the butter in a skillet over medium heat and cook the beef until brown, frequently stirring and breaking the lumps, 10 minutes.

Stir in bell pepper, zucchini pulp, garlic, shallot, taco seasoning and cook until softened, 5 minutes. Place the boats on the baking sheet with the open side up. Spoon in the beef mixture, divide the parsley on top, drizzle with olive oil, and top with cheddar cheese. Bake for 20 minutes until the cheese melts and is golden brown on top. Serve warm with tangy lettuce salad.

Per serving: Cal 419; Net Carbs 2.9g; Fat 32g; Protein 35g

Pancetta, Beef & Broccoli Bake

Ingredients for 4 servings

1 large broccoli head, cut into florets

1 lb ground beef	2 oz cream cheese, softened
6 slices pancetta, chopped	1 ¼ cups grated cheddar
2 tbsp olive oil	¼ cup chopped scallions
2 tbsp butter	Salt and black pepper, to taste
1 cup coconut cream	

Directions and Total Time: approx. 60 minutes

Preheat the oven to 320 F. Fill a pot with water and bring to a boil. Pour in broccoli and blanch for 2 minutes. Drain and set aside. Place pancetta in the pot and fry for 5 minutes. Remove to a plate. Heat oil in the pot and cook the beef until brown for 5-6 minutes. Add in coconut cream, cream cheese, two-thirds of cheddar cheese, salt, and pepper and stir for 7 minutes.

Arrange the broccoli florets in a baking dish, pour the beef mixture over, and scatter the top with pancetta and scallions. Bake in the oven until the cheese is bubbly and golden, 20 minutes. Top with the remaining cheddar and bake for 10 more minutes. Serve.

Per serving: Cal 861; Net Carbs 7.3g; Fat 71g; Protein 49g

Sweet & Spicy Beef Bowls

Ingredients for 4 servings

2 tbsp olive oil	1 tsp sesame oil
1 tbsp coconut oil	1 tsp fish sauce
1 lb ribeye steak	2 tbsp white wine vinegar
2 tsp sugar-free maple syrup	1 tsp hot sauce
1 tbsp coconut flour	1 small bok choy, quartered
½ tsp xanthan gum	½ jalapeño, sliced into rings
1 tsp freshly pureed ginger	1 tbsp toasted sesame seeds
1 clove garlic, minced	1 scallion, chopped
1 red chili, minced	Salt and black pepper to taste
4 tbsp tamari sauce	

Directions and Total Time: approx. 25 minutes

Slice the beef into ¼-inch strips. Season it with salt and pepper and rub with coconut flour and xanthan gum. Heat olive oil in a skillet and fry the beef until brown on all sides; 6-8 minutes. Heat coconut oil in a wok and sauté ginger, garlic, red chili, and bok choy for 5 minutes.

Mix in tamari sauce, sesame oil, fish sauce, vinegar, hot sauce, and maple syrup; cook for 2 minutes. Add the beef and cook for 2 minutes. Spoon into bowls, top with jalapeño pepper, scallion, and sesame seeds. Serve warm.

Per serving: Cal 512; Net Carbs 2.9g; Fat 39g; Protein 25g

Cheese Spaghetti with Meatballs

Ingredients for 4 servings

1 lb ground beef	¼ cup almond milk
1 egg	¼ tsp nutmeg powder
1 cup shredded mozzarella	1 tbsp smoked paprika
1 egg yolk	1 ½ tsp fresh ginger paste
½ cup olive oil	1 tsp cumin powder
1 yellow onion, chopped	½ tsp cayenne pepper
6 garlic cloves, minced	½ tsp clove powder
2 tbsp tomato paste	4 tbsp chopped cilantro
2 large tomatoes, chopped	4 tbsp chopped scallions
¼ tsp saffron powder	4 tbsp chopped parsley
2 cinnamon sticks	¼ cup almond flour
1 cup chicken broth	1 cup crumbled feta cheese
1 cup pork rinds	Salt and black pepper to taste

Directions and Total Time: approx. 50 min + chilling time

Place the mozzarella cheese in the microwave for 2 minutes. Mix in egg yolk until combined. Lay parchment paper on a flat surface, pour the cheese mixture on top and cover with another piece of parchment paper. Flatten the dough into 1/8-inch thickness. Take off the parchment paper. Cut the dough into spaghetti strands; refrigerate overnight.

When ready, bring 2 cups of water to a boil in a saucepan and add the "pasta". Cook for 1 minute, drain, and let cool. In a pot, heat 2 tbsp of olive oil and sauté onion and half of the garlic for 3 minutes. Stir in tomato paste, tomatoes, saffron, and cinnamon sticks; cook for 2 minutes. Mix in chicken broth, salt, and pepper. Simmer for 10 minutes.

In a bowl, mix pork rinds, beef, egg, almond milk, remaining garlic, salt, pepper, nutmeg, paprika, ginger, cumin, cayenne, clove powder, cilantro, parsley, 3 tbsp of scallions, and almond flour. Form balls out of the mixture. Heat the remaining olive oil in a skillet and fry the meatballs for 10 minutes. Place them into the sauce and continue cooking for 5-10 minutes. Divide the pasta onto serving plates and spoon the meatballs with sauce on top. Garnish with feta cheese and scallions and serve.

Per serving: Cal 779; Net Carbs 6g; Fats 56g; Protein 55g

Parmesan Beef Stuffed Mushrooms

Ingredients for 4 servings

1 lb ground beef	½ tsp garlic powder
½ cup Romano cheese, grated	2 large eggs
2 tbsp olive oil	4 Portobello mushroom caps
½ celery stalk, chopped	1 tbsp flaxseed meal
1 shallot, finely chopped	2 tbsp shredded Parmesan
2 tbsp mayonnaise	1 tbsp chopped parsley
1 tsp Old Bay seasoning	

Directions and Total Time: approx. 55 minutes

Preheat oven to 360 F. Heat olive oil in a skillet and sauté celery and shallot for 3 minutes; set aside. Add beef to the skillet and cook for 10 minutes; add to the shallot mixture. Pour in mayonnaise, Old Bay seasoning, garlic powder, Pecorino cheese and crack in the eggs.

Combine the mixture evenly. Arrange the mushrooms on a greased baking sheet and fill with the meat mixture. Combine flaxseed meal and Parmesan cheese in a bowl and sprinkle over the mushroom filling. Bake until the cheese melts, 30 minutes. Garnish with parsley to serve.

Per serving: Cal 382; Net Carbs 3.5g; Fat 18g; Protein 42g

Thai Beef Sauté with Shirataki

Ingredients for 4 servings

1 cup sliced shiitake mushrooms
2 (8 oz) packs angel hair shirataki

1 ¼ lb flank steak, sliced	2 tbsp toasted sesame seeds
2 tbsp olive oil	1 tbsp chopped peanuts
1 white onion, thinly sliced	1 tbsp chopped scallions
1 red bell pepper, sliced	3 tbsp coconut aminos
2 garlic cloves, minced	2 tbsp fish sauce
2 tbsp Thai basil, chopped	1 tbsp hot sauce

Directions and Total Time: approx. 35 minutes

Bring to a boil 2 cups of water. Strain the shirataki pasta and rinse very well under hot running water. Allow proper draining and pour the shirataki pasta into the boiling water. Cook for 3 minutes and strain again. Place a dry skillet and stir-fry the shirataki until visibly dry, 1-2 minutes; set aside. Heat olive oil in a skillet and sear the beef on both sides until brown, 10 minutes; set aside. Add onion, bell pepper, garlic, and mushrooms to the skillet and sauté for 5 minutes. Return the beef to the skillet and add the pasta. Combine aminos, fish sauce, and hot sauce in a bowl. Pour the mixture over the beef. Top with Thai basil and toss to coat. Cook for 1-2 minutes. Garnish with sesame seeds, peanuts, and scallions. Serve.

Per serving: Cal 362; Net Carbs 6.9g; Fats 16g; Protein 29g

Beef Collard Green Rolls

Ingredients for 4 servings

1 tbsp butter	1 large bay leaf
2 lb corned beef	1 lemon, zested and juiced
2 tsp Worcestershire sauce	¼ cup white wine
1 tsp Dijon mustard	¼ cup freshly brewed coffee
1 tsp whole peppercorns	2/3 tbsp swerve sugar
¼ tsp cloves	8 large Swiss collard leaves
¼ tsp allspice	1 medium red onion, sliced
½ tsp red pepper flakes	Salt and black pepper to taste

Directions and Total Time: approx. 75 minutes

Place the beef, butter, salt, pepper, Worcestershire sauce, mustard, peppercorns, cloves, allspice, red pepper flakes, bay leaf, lemon zest, lemon juice, white wine, coffee, and swerve sugar in a pot. Close the lid and cook over low heat for 1 hour. Ten minutes before the end, bring a pot of water to a boil, add collards with one slice of onion for 30 seconds and transfer to ice bath; let sit for 2-3 minutes. Remove, pat dry, and lay on a flat surface. Remove the meat from the pot, place on a cutting board, and slice. Divide meat between the collards, top with onion slices, and roll the leaves. Serve with tomato gravy.

Per serving: Cal 353; Net Carbs 1.5g; Fat 16g; Protein 52g

Asian-Style Beef with Kelp Noodles

Ingredients for 4 servings

2 (16- oz) packs kelp noodles, thoroughly rinsed
1 ½ lb sirloin steak, cut into strips

1 tbsp coconut oil	2 tbsp swerve brown sugar
2 pieces star anise	¼ cup red wine
1 cinnamon stick	4 cups beef broth
1 garlic clove, minced	1 head napa cabbage, steamed
1-inch ginger, grated	2 tbsp scallions, thinly sliced
3 tbsp coconut aminos	

Directions and Total Time: approx. 2 hours 15 minutes

Warm oil in a pot over and sauté anise, cinnamon, garlic, and ginger until fragrant, 5 minutes. Add in beef and sear it on both sides, 10 minutes. In a bowl, combine aminos, swerve brown sugar, red wine, and ¼ cup water. Pour the mixture into the pot, close the lid, and bring to a boil. Reduce the heat and simmer for 1 to 1 ½ hours or until the meat is tender. Strain the pot's content through a colander into a bowl and pour the braising liquid back into the pot. Discard cinnamon and anise and set aside. Add beef broth and simmer for 10 minutes. Put kelp noodles in the broth and cook until softened and separated, 6 minutes. Spoon the noodles and some broth into bowls, add beef strips, and top with cabbage and scallions. Serve and enjoy!

Per serving: Cal 553; Net Carbs 26g; Fat 33g; Protein 52g

Zucchini Beef Lasagna

Ingredients for 4 servings

½ cup Pecorino Romano cheese

4 yellow zucchini, sliced	2 tbsp coconut flour
½ lb ground beef	1 large egg
1 ½ cups grated mozzarella	2 cups marinara sauce
2 cups crumbled goat cheese	1 tbsp Italian herb seasoning
1 tbsp lard	¼ tsp red chili flakes
1 tsp garlic powder	¼ cup fresh basil leaves
1 tsp onion powder	Salt and black pepper to taste

Directions and Total Time: approx. 45 minutes

Preheat oven to 360 F. Melt the lard in a skillet and cook beef for 10 minutes; set aside. In a bowl, combine garlic powder, onion powder, coconut flour, salt, pepper, mozzarella cheese, half of Pecorino cheese, goat cheese, and egg. Mix Italian herb seasoning and chili flakes with marinara sauce. Make a single layer of the zucchini in a greased baking dish, spread ¼ of the egg mixture on top, and ¼ of the marinara sauce. Repeat the process and top with the remaining Pecorino cheese. Bake in the oven for 20 minutes. Garnish with basil, slice, and serve.

Per serving: Cal 599; Net Carbs 5.5g; Fat 37g; Protein 49g

Classic Philly Cheese Steak in Omelet

Ingredients for 2 servings

¼ lb beef ribeye shaved steak	1 yellow onion, sliced
2 tbsp olive oil	½ green bell pepper, sliced
4 large eggs	2 oz provolone cheese, sliced
2 tbsp almond milk	Salt and black pepper to taste

Directions and Total Time: approx. 20 minutes

In a bowl, beat the eggs with milk. Heat half of the oil in a skillet and pour in half of the eggs. Fry until cooked on one side, flip, and cook until well done. Slide into a plate and fry the remaining eggs. Place them into another plate. Heat the remaining olive oil in the same skillet and sauté the onion and bell pepper for 5 minutes; set aside. Season beef with salt and pepper and cook it in the skillet until brown with no crust. Add onion and pepper back to the skillet and cook for 1 minute. Lay provolone cheese in the omelet and top with the meat mixture. Roll the eggs and place back in the skillet to melt the cheese.

Per serving: Cal 501; Net Carbs 3.6g; Fat 41g; Protein 34g

Beef & Cheese Avocado Boats

Ingredients for 4 servings

7 tbsp shredded Monterey Jack cheese

1 lb ground beef	1 cup raw pecans, chopped
2 tbsp avocado oil	1 tbsp hemp seeds, hulled
1 tsp garlic powder	2 avocados, halved and pitted
1 tsp onion powder	1 medium tomato, sliced
1 tsp cumin powder	¼ cup iceberg lettuce, torn
2 tsp taco seasoning	4 tbsp sour cream
2 tsp smoked paprika	Salt and black pepper to taste

Directions and Total Time: approx. 30 minutes

Warm half of avocado oil in a skillet and cook beef for 10 minutes. Season with salt, pepper, onion powder, cumin, garlic, taco seasoning, and smoked paprika. Add the pecans and hemp seeds and stir-fry for 10 minutes.

Fold in 3 tbsp Monterey Jack cheese to melt. Spoon the filling into avocado holes, top with 1-2 slices of tomatoes, some lettuce, 1 tbsp each of sour cream, and the remaining Monterey Jack cheese and serve immediately.

Per serving: Cal 838; Net Carbs 4g; Fat 69g; Protein 39g

Asparagus & Beef Shirataki

Ingredients for 4 servings

1 lb fresh asparagus, cut into 1-inch pieces
2 (8 oz) packs angel hair shirataki

3 tbsp olive oil	1 lb ground beef
2 shallots, finely chopped	1 cup grated Parmesan cheese
3 garlic cloves, minced	Salt and black pepper to taste

Directions and Total Time: approx. 35 minutes

In a pot, bring 2 cups of water to a boil. Strain the shirataki pasta and rinse well under hot running water. Drain and transfer to the boiling water. Cook for 3 minutes and strain again. Place a dry skillet and stir-fry the shirataki pasta until visibly dry, 1-2 minutes; set aside. Heat olive oil in a skillet and add the beef. Cook for 10 minutes. Transfer to a plate. In the same skillet sauté asparagus for 7 minutes. Stir in shallots and garlic and cook until fragrant, 2 minutes. Season with salt and pepper. Stir in beef and shirataki and toss until combined. Top with Parmesan cheese and serve.

Per serving: Cal 509; Net Carbs 6.9g; Fat 25g; Protein 51g

Scallion & Egg Beef Bowls

Ingredients for 4 servings

2 tbsp olive oil	4 large eggs
1 lb beef sirloin, cut into strips	
¼ cup tamari sauce	2 tbsp coconut oil
2 tbsp lemon juice	6 garlic cloves, minced
3 tsp garlic powder	1 lb cauliflower rice
1 tbsp swerve sugar	2 tbsp chopped scallions

Directions and Total Time: approx. 30 min + chilling time

In a bowl, mix tamari sauce, lemon juice, garlic powder, and swerve sugar. Pour beef into a zipper bag and add in the mixture. Massage the meat to coat well. Refrigerate overnight. The next day, heat coconut oil in a wok, and fry the beef until the liquid evaporates and the meat cooks through, 12 minutes; set aside. Sauté garlic for 1 minute in the same wok. Mix in cauli rice until softened, 5 minutes. Spoon into 4 serving bowls and set aside. Wipe the wok clean and heat 1 tbsp of olive oil. Crack in two eggs and fry sunshine-style, 1 minute. Place an egg on each cauliflower rice bowl and fry the other 2 eggs with the remaining olive oil. Serve garnished with scallions.

Per serving: Cal 914; Net Carbs 5.1g; Fat 78g; Protein 34g

Mom's Beef Meatloaf

Ingredients for 4 servings

2 tbsp olive oil	4 garlic cloves, minced
2 lb ground beef	¼ cup chopped tarragon
3 tbsp flaxseed meal	¼ cup chopped oregano
2 large eggs	Salt and black pepper, to taste
1 lemon, zested	

Directions and Total Time: approx. 75 minutes

Preheat the oven to 380 F. In a bowl, combine beef, salt, pepper, and flaxseed meal; set aside. In another bowl, whisk the eggs with olive oil, lemon zest, tarragon, oregano, and garlic. Pour the mixture onto the beef mix and evenly combine. Shape the meat mixture into a greased baking loaf and press to fit in. Bake in oven for 1 hour. Remove the pan, tilt to drain the meat's liquid, and let cool for 5 minutes. Slice, garnish with some lemon slices, and serve with curried cauli rice.

Per serving: Cal 629; Net Carbs 2.9g; Fat 38g; Protein 63g

Homemade Beef Meatza

Ingredients for 4 servings

1 large egg	½ tbsp oregano
1 ½ lb ground beef	¾ cup low-carb tomato sauce
3 garlic cloves, minced	¼ cup shredded Parmesan
1 tsp rosemary	1 cup shredded Pepper Jack
1 tsp thyme	1 cup shredded mozzarella
1 tsp basil	Salt and black pepper to taste

Directions and Total Time: approx. 30 minutes

Preheat oven to 370 F. In a bowl, combine beef, salt, pepper, egg, rosemary, thyme, garlic, basil, and oregano. Transfer the mixture into a greased baking pan, and using hands, flatten to a two-inch thickness.

Bake for 15 minutes until the beef has a light brown crust. Remove and spread tomato sauce on top. Sprinkle with Parmesan, Pepper Jack, and mozzarella cheeses. Return to oven. Bake until the cheeses melt, 5 minutes. Serve.

Per serving: Cal 324; Net Carbs 3.6g; Fat 9g; Protein 52g

Brussel Sprout & Beef Sauté with Walnuts

Ingredients for 4 servings

1 ½ cups Brussels sprouts, halved	
¼ cup toasted walnuts, chopped	
2 tbsp avocado oil	1 bok choy, quartered
1 garlic clove, minced	2 tbsp chopped scallions
½ white onion, chopped	1 tbsp black sesame seeds
1 lb ground beef	Salt and black pepper to taste

Directions and Total Time: approx. 25 minutes

Warm 1 tbsp of avocado oil in a skillet over medium heat and sauté garlic and onion for 3 minutes. Stir in ground beef and cook until brown while breaking the lumps, 7 minutes. Pour in Brussels sprouts, bok choy, walnuts, scallions, and season with salt and black pepper. Sauté for 5 minutes. Serve topped with sesame seeds.

Per serving: Cal 298; Net Carbs 2.9g; Fat 23g; Protein 31g

Bacon-Wrapped Beef Meatloaf

Ingredients for 4 servings

6 bacon slices	½ cup shredded Parmesan
1 ½ lb ground beef	1 egg, lightly beaten
2 tbsp olive oil	1 tbsp dried sage
1 white onion, finely chopped	4 tbsp toasted pecans, chopped
½ cup coconut cream	Salt and black pepper to taste

Directions and Total Time: approx. 45 minutes

Preheat oven to 380 F. Heat olive oil in a skillet and sauté the onion for 3 minutes. In a bowl, mix ground beef, onion, coconut cream, Parmesan cheese, egg, sage, pecans, salt, and pepper. Form into a loaf, wrap it with bacon slices, secure with toothpicks, and place on a greased baking sheet. Bake for 30 minutes. Serve sliced.

Per serving: Cal 624; Net Carbs 6.6g; Fat 39g; Protein 52g

Beef & Goat Cheese Casserole with Pesto

Ingredients for 4 servings

1 ½ lb ground beef	1 garlic clove, minced
5 oz goat cheese, crumbled	3 oz basil pesto
2 tbsp ghee	1 ¼ cups coconut cream
3 oz pitted green olives	Salt and black pepper to taste

Directions and Total Time: approx. 35 minutes

Preheat oven to 380 F. Grease a casserole dish with cooking spray. Melt ghee in a deep skillet and cook the beef until brown, stirring frequently. Season with salt and pepper. Spoon and spread the beef at the bottom of the casserole dish. Top with olives, goat cheese, and garlic. In a bowl, mix pesto and coconut cream and pour the mixture all over the beef. Bake until lightly brown around the edges and bubbly, 25 minutes. Serve.

Per serving: Cal 662; Net Carbs 4g; Fat 49g; Protein 52g

Cheddar Beef Burgers

Ingredients for 4 servings

2 pearl onions, thinly sliced into 8 pieces
2 slices cheddar cheese, cut into 4 pieces each
4 cherry tomatoes, halved   1 tsp onion powder
½ lb ground beef   8 slices zero carb bread
1 tsp garlic powder   2 tbsp ranch dressing

Directions and Total Time: approx. 30 minutes

Preheat oven to 380 F. In a bowl, combine beef and garlic and onion powders. Form 8 patties and place them on a greased baking sheet. Bake until brown, 10 minutes. Let cool for 3 minutes. Cut out 16 circles from the bread slices.

Lay half of the bread circles on a clean, flat surface and brush with the ranch dressing. Place the meat patties on the bread slices, top with cheese slices, pearl onions, and cherry tomatoes. Cover with the remaining bread slices and secure with a toothpick. Serve.

Per serving: Cal 278; Net Carbs 2.8g; Fat 12g; Protein 19g

Parsnip Noodles with Beef & Chili Flakes

Ingredients for 4 servings

1 cup sun-dried tomatoes in oil, chopped
1 lb beef stew meat, cut into strips
1 cup grated Parmesan cheese   ¼ tsp dried basil
3 tbsp butter   ¼ tsp red chili flakes
4 large parsnips, spiralized   2 tbsp chopped parsley
4 garlic cloves, minced   Salt and black pepper to taste
1 ¼ cups heavy cream

Directions and Total Time: approx. 30 minutes

Warm the butter in a skillet over medium heat and sauté the parsnips until softened, 5-7 minutes; set aside. Season the beef with salt and pepper and add to the same skillet; cook until brown, 8-10 minutes. Stir in sun-dried tomatoes and garlic and cook until fragrant, 1 minute.

Reduce the heat to low and stir in heavy cream and Parmesan cheese. Simmer until the cheese melts. Sprinkle with basil and red chili flakes. Fold in the parsnips until well coated and cook for 2 more minutes. Garnish with parsley. Serve and enjoy!

Per serving: Cal 603; Net Carbs 5.9g; Fats 35g; Protein 37g

Beef a la Carbonara

Ingredients for 4 servings

1 ¼ cups grated Parmesan   ¼ cup mayonnaise
1 cup grated mozzarella   4 egg yolks
4 bacon slices, chopped   2 tbsp parsley, chopped
1 ¼ cups heavy cream   Salt and black pepper to taste

Directions and Total Time: approx. 25 minutes

Place the mozzarella cheese in the microwave for 2 minutes. Remove and let cool for 1 minute. Mix in 1 egg yolk until combined. Lay a parchment paper on a flat surface, pour the cheese mixture on top and cover with another parchment paper. Flatten the dough into 1/8-inch thickness. Take off the parchment paper and cut the dough into thin spaghetti strands.

Place in a bowl and refrigerate overnight. When ready, bring 2 cups of water to a boil in a saucepan and add pasta. Cook for 1 minute and drain; set aside. Add bacon to a skillet and cook until crispy, 5 minutes; reserve.

Pour heavy cream into a pot over medium heat and let simmer for 5 minutes. Remove, mix in mayonnaise, and season with salt and pepper. Beaten in the remaining egg yolks. Stir in 1 cup of Parmesan cheese and fold in the pasta and bacon. Spoon into pasta bowls and top with remaining Parmesan cheese and parsley to serve.

Per serving: Cal 468; Net Carbs 8g; Fats 35g; Protein 29g

Cheesy Steak Bites with Shirataki

Ingredients for 4 servings

1 lb thick-cut New York strip steaks, cut into 1-inch cubes
2 (8 oz) packs shirataki fettuccine
4 tbsp butter   2 tbsp chopped fresh parsley
1 cup grated Romano cheese   Salt and black pepper to taste
4 garlic cloves, minced

Directions and Total Time: approx. 25 minutes

Bring to a boil 2 cups of water in a pot. Strain the shirataki fettuccine and rinse well under hot running water. Allow proper draining and pour into the boiling water. Cook for 3 minutes and strain again. Place a dry skillet and stir-fry the shirataki pasta until visibly dry, 1-2 minutes; set aside. Melt butter in a skillet over medium heat, season the steaks with salt and pepper, and cook for 10 minutes. Stir in garlic for 1 minute. Mix in parsley and shirataki; toss to coat. Top with the Pecorino cheese and serve.

Per serving: Cal 419; Net Carbs 6.8g; Fats 28g; Protein 41g

Cauliflower Pilaf with Beef & Parsley

Ingredients for 4 servings

½ lb ground beef   2 ½ cups cauliflower rice
2 tbsp olive oil   2 tbsp tomato paste
2 garlic cloves, minced   ½ cup beef broth
1 yellow onion, chopped   ¼ cup chopped parsley
1 habanero pepper, minced   1 lemon, sliced
½ tsp Italian seasoning   Salt and black pepper to taste

Directions and Total Time: approx. 30 minutes

Heat olive oil in a skillet over medium heat and cook the beef until no longer brown, 8 minutes. Season with salt and pepper and spoon into a plate. In the same skillet, sauté onion, garlic, and habanero pepper for 2 minutes. Mix in Italian seasoning, cauli rice, tomato paste, and broth. Season to taste and cook for 10 minutes. Mix in beef for 3 minutes. Garnish with parsley and lemon.

Per serving: Cal 223; Net Carbs 3.8g; Fat 14g; Protein 15g

Beef Ragu with Veggie Pasta

Ingredients for 4 servings

2 tbsp butter   1 small red onion, spiralized
1 lb ground beef   1 cup grated Parmesan cheese
8 mixed bell peppers, spiralized   Salt and black pepper to taste
¼ cup tomato sauce

Directions and Total Time: approx. 30 minutes

Melt the butter in a skillet and cook the beef until brown, 10 minutes. Season with salt and pepper. Stir in tomato sauce and cook for 10 minutes, until the sauce reduces by a quarter. Add in bell pepper and onion noodles and cook for 1 minute. Top with Parmesan cheese and serve.

Per serving: Cal 448; Net Carbs 6.8g; Fats 25g; Protein 39g

Beef Mugs with Cheddar & Zucchini

Ingredients for 2 servings

4 oz roast beef deli slices, torn apart

1 small zucchini, sliced	2 tbsp chopped green chilies
3 tbsp sour cream	3 oz shredded cheddar cheese

Directions and Total Time: approx. 10 minutes

Put the beef slices on the bottom of 2 wide mugs and spread 1 tbsp of sour cream. Top with 2 zucchini slices and green chilies. Pour the remaining sour cream over and sprinkle with cheddar cheese. Place the mugs in the microwave for 1-2 minutes until the cheese melts. Remove the mugs, let cool for 1 minute, and serve.

Per serving: Cal 193; Net Carbs 3.7g; Fat 9g; Protein 21g

Tangy Beef & Cabbage Bowls

Ingredients for 4 servings

1 canon cabbage, shredded	1 ½ lb ground beef
2 tbsp butter	1 cup coconut cream
1 tsp onion powder	¼ cup blue cheese
1 tsp garlic powder	½ cup fresh parsley, chopped
1 tsp dried oregano	Salt and black pepper to taste
1 tbsp red wine vinegar	

Directions and Total Time: approx. 30 minutes

Warm butter in a deep skillet and sauté cabbage, onion and garlic powders, oregano, salt, pepper, and vinegar for 5 minutes; set aside. Add the beef to the skillet and cook until browned, frequently stirring and breaking the lumps, 10 minutes. Stir in coconut cream and blue cheese until the cheese melts, 3 minutes. Return the cabbage mixture and add parsley. Stir-fry for 2 minutes. Dish into serving bowls and serve with low carb bread.

Per serving: Cal 538; Net Carbs 4.2g; Fat 37g; Protein 39g

Coconut Beef Burgers

Ingredients for 4 servings

2 eggs	2 tomatoes, chopped
1 lb ground beef	1 tbsp dried basil
¼ cup grated Monterey Jack	2 tbsp tomato paste
1 tbsp butter	1 cup coconut cream
1 garlic clove, minced	Salt and black pepper to taste
1 red onion, chopped	

Directions and Total Time: approx. 40 minutes

Preheat oven to 380 F. Melt the butter in a skillet over medium heat and add the beef. Cook for 6 minutes. Stir in garlic and onion and cook for another 3 minutes. Mix in tomatoes, basil, salt, and pepper until the tomatoes soften. Add 2/3 of Monterey Jack cheese and stir to melt.

In a bowl, whisk the eggs tomato paste, salt, and coconut cream. Spoon the beef mixture into a greased baking sheet and spread the egg mixture on top. Sprinkle with the remaining cheese and bake for 20 minutes. Serve.

Per serving: Cal 473; Net Carbs 4.5g; Fat 39g; Protein 41g

BBQ Beef Pizza

Ingredients for 4 servings

1 lb ground beef	¼ cup sugar-free BBQ sauce
1 cup grated mozzarella	¼ cup sliced red onion
1 ½ cups grated Gruyere	2 bacon slices, chopped
2 eggs, beaten	2 tbsp chopped parsley

Directions and Total Time: approx. 45 minutes

Preheat oven to 380 F. Line a round pizza pan with parchment paper. In a bowl, mix beef, mozzarella cheese and eggs. Spread the pizza "dough" on the pan and bake for 20 minutes. Spread BBQ sauce on top, scatter Gruyere cheese all over, followed by the red onion, and bacon slices. Bake for 15 minutes or until the cheese has melted and the back is crispy. Serve topped with parsley.

Per serving: Cal 542; Net Carbs 1g; Fats 32g; Protein 61g

Pesto Beef Stuffed Tomatoes

Ingredients for 6 servings

1 lb ground beef	4 tsp basil pesto
2 tbsp olive oil	5 tbsp shredded Parmesan
4 medium tomatoes	Salt and black pepper to taste

Directions and Total Time: approx. 35 minutes

Preheat oven to 380 F. Heat olive oil in a skillet, add in ground beef, season with salt and pepper, and cook until brown while breaking the lumps that form, 8 minutes. Cut the tomatoes' tops and remove the seeds to create a cavity, reserving the tops. Spoon the beef inside. Sprinkle with pesto and Parmesan cheese. Cover with the reserved tops. Place the filled tomatoes on a greased baking sheet and bake until the cheese melts and the tomatoes slightly brown, about 20 minutes. Serve warm.

Per serving: Cal 119; Net Carbs 2.8g; Fat 4.4g; Protein 7g

Ancho T-Bone Steak with Parsley Butter

Ingredients for 4 servings

2 (8-oz) T-bone steaks	4 oz butter, softened
1 tsp ancho chile powder	¼ tsp garlic powder
2 tbsp avocado oil	2 tbsp fresh parsley, chopped
Salt and black pepper to taste	1 tsp lemon juice

Directions and Total Time: approx. 30 minutes

In a bowl, beat with a hand mixer the butter, garlic powder, parsley, salt, pepper, and lemon juice. Set aside. Preheat the grill to high. Season the steaks with ancho chili powder, salt, and pepper, then drizzle with avocado oil. Place on the grill and cook for about 12-14 minutes on both sides or until the meat reaches an internal temperature of 150 F for medium-rare. Top the beef with parsley butter. Serve and enjoy!

Per serving: Cal 886; Net Carbs 0.1g; Fats 54g; Protein 93g

Alfredo Beef Spaghetti Squash

Ingredients for 4 servings

2 tbsp olive oil	1 tsp arrowroot starch
2 tbsp butter	1 ½ cups heavy cream
1 lb ground beef	A pinch of nutmeg
2 spaghetti squashes, halved	1/3 cup grated Parmesan
½ tsp garlic powder	1/3 cup grated mozzarella
Salt and black pepper to taste	

Directions and Total Time: approx. 1 hour 10 minutes

Preheat oven to 390 F. Drizzle the squash with olive oil and season with salt and pepper. Place on a lined with foil baking dish and roast for 45 minutes. Let cool and shred the inner part of the noodles; set aside.

Melt butter in a pot over medium heat, add in beef, garlic powder, salt, and pepper, and cook for 10 minutes, stirring often. Stir in arrowroot starch, heavy cream, and nutmeg. Cook until the sauce thickens, 2-3 minutes. Spoon the sauce into the squashes and cover with Parmesan and mozzarella cheeses. Cook under the broiler for 3 minutes. Serve and enjoy!

Per serving: Cal 558; Net Carbs 4g; Fats 39g; Protein 41g

Quick Beef Carpaccio

Ingredients for 4 servings

½ lemon, juiced	¼ lb rare roast beef, sliced
2 tbsp olive oil	1 ½ cups baby arugula
¼ cup grated Parmesan cheese	Salt and black pepper to taste

Directions and Total Time: approx. 10 minutes

Whisk the olive oil, lemon juice, salt, and pepper in a bowl until well combined. Spread the beef on a large serving plate, top with arugula and drizzle the olive oil mixture on top. Sprinkle with grated Parmesan and serve.

Per serving: Cal 112; Net Carbs 4g; Fat 5g; Protein 9g

Traditional Swedish Meatballs

Ingredients for 4 servings

2 tbsp olive oil	1 cup beef broth
2 tbsp butter	½ cup coconut cream
1 ½ lb ground beef	¼ freshly chopped dill
1 tsp garlic powder	¼ cup chopped parsley
1 tsp onion powder	Salt and black pepper to taste
2 tbsp almond flour	

Directions and Total Time: approx. 30 minutes

Preheat oven to 380 F. In a bowl, combine beef, garlic powder, onion powder, salt, and pepper. Form meatballs from the mixture and place them on a greased baking sheet. Drizzle with olive oil and bake until the meat cooks, 10-15 minutes. Remove the baking sheet. Melt butter in a saucepan and stir in almond flour until smooth. Gradually mix in broth, while stirring until thickened, 2 minutes. Stir in coconut cream and dill, simmer for 1 minute and stir in meatballs. Spoon the meatballs with sauce onto a serving platter and garnish with parsley.

Per serving: Cal 462; Net Carbs 3.1g; Fat 28g; Protein 39g

Gree-Style Beef Burgers

Ingredients for 4 servings

1 lb ground beef	2 tbsp olive oil
2 tbsp dill, chopped	4 fresh eggs
1 cup Tzatziki sauce	1 cup cherry tomatoes, halved
½ cup feta cheese, crumbled	Salt and black pepper to taste

Directions and Total Time: approx. 30 minutes

In a bowl, place the ground beef, dill, salt, and pepper and mix well. Form the mixture into 4 burgers. Use a spoon to make an indentation in the center of each burger. Stuff the indentations with the feta cheese. Fold burger around the cheese and seal well.

Warm the olive oil in a skillet over medium heat. Cook the burgers for 8-10 minutes on all sides; remove to a plate. Fry the eggs in the skillet for about 2-3 minutes until the whites are set and crisp. Divide the burgers between 4 plates, top with fried eggs and cherry tomatoes. Serve with tzatziki sauce on the side. Enjoy!

Per serving: Cal 430; Net Carbs 2.3g; Fat 25g; Protein 44g

Bacon-Wrapped Burgers with Guacamole

Ingredients for 4 servings

1 onion, finely chopped	8 bacon slices
2 garlic cloves, minced	2 tbsp cilantro, chopped
1 lb ground beef	1 tsp chili powder
Salt and black pepper to taste	1 cup guacamole

Directions and Total Time: approx. 45 minutes

Preheat oven to 380 F. Mix the ground beef, onion, garlic, cilantro, salt, pepper, and chili powder in a bowl. Shape the mixture into 4 balls; flatten to make patties. Wrap each piece with 2 slices of bacon. Place the wrapped burgers on a parchment-lined baking dish. Bake in the oven for 25-30 minutes until the bacon is crisp. Remove and serve topped with guacamole. Enjoy!

Per serving: Cal 445; Net Carbs 1.2g; Fats 24g; Protein 49g

Mexican Beef Pizza

Ingredients for 4 servings

¾ lb ground beef	¾ cup almond flour
2 eggs, beaten	2 tsp taco seasoning
2 tbsp olive oil	½ cup chicken broth
2 cups shredded mozzarella	1 ½ cups salsa
2 tbsp cream cheese, softened	2 cups Mexican 4 cheese blend

Directions and Total Time: approx. 45 minutes

Preheat oven to 380 F. Line a pizza pan with parchment paper. Microwave 2 cups of mozzarella cheese and cream cheese for 30 seconds. Remove and mix in almond flour and eggs. Spread the mixture on the pizza pan and bake for 15 minutes. Warm olive oil in a pan over medium heat and cook the ground beef for 5 minutes. Stir in taco seasoning and chicken broth. Cook for 3 minutes. Mix in salsa. Spread the beef mixture onto the crust and scatter the Mexican cheese blend on top. Bake until the cheese melts, 15 minutes. Slice and serve hot.

Per serving: Cal 561; Net Carbs 4g; Fats 29g; Protein 62g

Beef Wrapped in Bacon with Mustard Sauce

Ingredients for 4 servings

8 bacon slices, halved crosswise
4 sirloin steaks
2 tbsp olive oil
¼ cup mayonnaise
2 tbsp Dijon mustard
1 tsp lemon juice
½ tsp garlic powder
Salt and black pepper to taste

Directions and Total Time: approx. 1 hour 25 minutes

In a small bowl, whisk the mayonnaise, lemon juice, garlic powder, salt, and pepper. Set aside. Season the steaks with salt and pepper. Wrap each beef piece into 2 bacon slices and secure with toothpicks.

Preheat oven to 380 F. Warm the olive oil in a skillet over medium heat and sear the wrapped steaks for 1-2 minutes per side. Place the skillet in the oven and for 8-10 minutes for medium-rare. Let it rest for 5 minutes. Serve the roulades with mustard sauce on the side. Enjoy!

Per serving: Cal 488; Fat 33g; Net Carbs 1.1g; Protein 40g

Stewed Veal with Vegetables

Ingredients for 4 servings

2 tbsp olive oil
1 lb veal shoulder, cubed
1 onion, chopped
1 garlic clove, minced
Salt and black pepper to taste
½ cup white wine
1 tsp sweet paprika
2 cups tomatoes, chopped
1 carrot, chopped
1 turnip, chopped
½ cup celery, chopped
1 cup mushrooms, chopped
½ cup green beans, chopped
1 tsp dried oregano

Directions and Total Time: approx. 1 hour 25 minutes

Set a pot over medium heat and warm the oil. Brown the veal for 5-6 minutes. Stir in the onion, celery and garlic, and cook for 3 minutes. Place in the wine to deglaze the bottom for 1-2 minutes. Add in oregano, paprika, carrot, tomatoes, 1 cup of water, turnip, mushrooms, salt, and pepper, and bring to a boil. Reduce the heat to low and cook for 1 hour. Add in green beans and cook for 5 minutes. Serve and enjoy!

Per serving: Cal 495; Fat 22g; Net Carbs 6.8g; Protein 51g

Red Wine Lamb with Mint & Sage

Ingredients for 4 servings

1 tbsp olive oil
1 lb lamb chops
½ tbsp sage
½ tsp mint
½ onion, sliced
1 garlic clove, minced
¼ cup red wine
Salt and black pepper to taste

Directions and Total Time: approx. 45 minutes

Heat the olive oil in a pan. Add onion and garlic and cook for 3 minutes, until soft. Rub the sage and mint over the lamb chops. Cook the lamb for about 3 minutes per side; set aside. Pour the red wine and 1 cup of water into the pan, bring the mixture to a boil. Cook until the liquid is reduced by half. Add the chops to the pan, reduce the heat, and let simmer for 30 minutes. Adjust the seasoning and serve.

Per serving: Cal 402; Fat 29g; Net Carbs 3.8g; Protein 15g

Lamb Chops with Garlic-Lime Vinaigrette

Ingredients for 2 servings

4 lamb chops
4 tsp olive oil
Salt and black pepper to taste
½ tsp red pepper flakes
1 tbsp lime juice
1 tbsp fresh mint
1 garlic clove, pressed
1 tbsp parsley
½ tsp smoked paprika

Directions and Total Time: approx. 25 minutes

Heat a griddle pan over high heat. Brush the lamb with 2 tbsp of olive oil and sprinkle with salt and black pepper. Grill the lamb chops for about 3-5 minutes per side.

Whisk together the remaining olive oil, red pepper flakes, lime juice, mint, garlic, parsley, and smoked paprika in a jar; shake until smooth and creamy. Serve the lamb chops topped with the vinaigrette.

Per serving: Cal 365; Fat 29g; Net Carbs 2.1g; Protein 25g

Stuffed Lamb Shoulder

Ingredients for 4 servings

1 lb rolled lamb shoulder, boneless
5 tbsp macadamia nuts, chopped
1 ½ cups basil leaves, chopped   2 garlic cloves, minced
½ cup green olives, chopped   Salt and black pepper to taste

Directions and Total Time: approx. 60 minutes

In a bowl, combine basil, macadamia, olives, and garlic. Season lamb with salt and pepper. Spread with the previously prepared mixture, roll up the lamb and tie it together using 3 strings of butcher's twine. Place lamb onto a greased baking dish and cook in the oven for 45 minutes at 380 F. When ready, transfer the meat to a chopping board, and let it rest for 10 minutes before slicing. Serve and enjoy!

Per serving: Cal 557; Fat 41g; Net Carbs 3.1g; Protein 37g

Lamb Kebabs with Mint Yogurt

Ingredients for 2 servings

1 lb ground lamb
¼ tsp cinnamon
1 tsp garlic powder
1 tsp onion powder
Salt and black pepper to taste
1 cup natural yogurt
2 tbsp mint, chopped

Directions and Total Time: approx. 20 minutes

Preheat grill to medium heat. Place lamb, cinnamon, onion powder, salt, and pepper in a bowl. Mix with hands to combine. Divide the meat into pieces. Shape all meat portions around previously-soaked skewers and grill the kebabs for 5 minutes per side. In a separate bowl, put yogurt, garlic powder, mint, and salt and stir to combine. Serve with kebabs. Enjoy!

Per serving: Cal 543; Fat 33g; Net Carbs 4.7g; Protein 53g

FISH & SEAFOOD

Blackened Salmon with Dijon Sauce

Ingredients for 2 servings

2 salmon fillets	¼ cup Dijon mustard
¾ tsp fresh thyme	2 tbsp white wine
1 tbsp butter	½ tsp tarragon
Salt and black pepper to taste	¼ cup heavy cream

Directions and Total Time: approx. 15 minutes

Season the salmon with thyme, salt, and pepper. Melt the butter in a pan over medium heat. Add salmon and cook for about 4-5 minutes on both sides until golden and charred. Remove to a plate and cover with foil to keep warm. To the same pan, add the mustard, white wine, heavy cream, and tarragon. Reduce the heat to low and simmer until the sauce is slightly thickened, stirring continuously. Cook for 60 seconds to infuse the flavors; adjust the taste. Pour the sauce over the salmon to serve.

Per serving: Cal 537; Fat 26g; Net Carbs 1.5g; Protein 67g

Crispy Salmon with Broccoli & Bell Pepper

Ingredients for 2 servings

2 salmon fillets	½ head broccoli, cut in florets
Salt and black pepper to taste	1 red bell pepper, sliced
2 tbsp mayonnaise	1 tbsp olive oil
2 tbsp fennel seeds, crushed	2 lemon wedges

Directions and Total Time: approx. 35 minutes

Brush the salmon with mayonnaise and season with salt and black pepper. Coat with fennel seeds, place in a lined baking dish and bake in the oven for 15 minutes at 370 F. Steam the broccoli for 5-6 minutes or until tender in a pot over medium heat. Heat the olive oil in a saucepan and sauté the red bell pepper for 5 minutes. Stir in the broccoli and turn off the heat. Let the pan sit on the warm burner for 2-3 minutes. Serve the veggies with the salmon. Garnish with lemon wedges.

Per serving: Cal 563; Fat 37g; Net Carbs 6g; Protein 54g

Mediterranean Tilapia Bake

Ingredients for 2 servings

2 tilapia fillets	1 tbsp olive oil
2 garlic cloves, minced	½ red onion, chopped
1 cup canned tomatoes	1 tbsp parsley, chopped
¼ tbsp chili powder	1 tsp basil, chopped
2 tbsp white wine	10 black olives, halved

Directions and Total Time: approx. 30 minutes

Preheat oven to 350 F. Heat the olive oil in a skillet over medium heat and stir-fry the onion and garlic for about 3 minutes. Stir in tomatoes, olives, chili powder, and wine and bring the mixture to a boil. Reduce the heat and simmer for 5 minutes. Put the tilapia in a baking dish, pour over the sauce and bake for 12-15 minutes. Serve garnished with basil and parsley.

Per serving: Cal 282; Fat 15g; Net Carbs 6g; Protein 23g

Grilled Salmon with Radish Salad

Ingredients for 4 servings

1 lb skinned salmon, cut into 4 steaks each	
1 cup radishes, sliced	3 tbsp red wine vinegar
Salt and black pepper to taste	2 green onions, sliced
8 green olives, chopped	3 tbsp olive oil
1 cup arugula	¼ cup parsley, chopped
2 large tomatoes, diced	

Directions and Total Time: approx. 20 minutes

In a bowl, mix the radishes, olives, arugula, tomatoes, vinegar, green onion, 2 tbsp of olive oil, and parsley. Put in the fridge while preparing the salmon.

Preheat your grill to high. Season the salmon steaks with salt and pepper and drizzle with the remaining olive oil. Grill the salmon on both sides for 8 minutes in total. Serve warm with the radish salad.

Per serving: Cal 338; Fat 22g; Net Carbs 3.1g; Protein 28g

Baked Trout & Asparagus Foil Packets

Ingredients for 2 servings

½ lb asparagus spears	2 sprigs thyme
1 tbsp garlic puree	2 tbsp butter
½ lb deboned trout, butterflied	½ medium red onion, sliced
Salt and black pepper to taste	2 lemon slices
2 sprigs rosemary	

Directions and Total Time: approx. 25 minutes

Preheat the oven to 400 F. Rub the trout with garlic puree, salt, and pepper. Prepare two aluminum foil squares. Place the fish on each square. Divide the asparagus and onion between the squares, top with a pinch of salt and pepper, a sprig of rosemary and thyme, and 1 tbsp of butter. Also, lay the lemon slices on the fish. Wrap and close the fish packets securely, and place them on a baking sheet. Bake in the oven for 15 minutes. Serve.

Per serving: Cal 498; Fat 39g; Net Carbs 4.6g; Protein 27g

Green Tuna Traybake

Ingredients for 4 servings

1 (15 oz) can tuna in water, drained and flaked	
1 bunch asparagus, trimmed and cut into 1-inch pieces	
1 cup green beans, chopped	2 cups coconut milk
1 tbsp butter	4 zucchinis, spiralized
2 tbsp arrowroot starch	1 cup grated Parmesan cheese

Directions and Total Time: approx. 40 minutes

Preheat the oven to 370 F. Melt butter in a skillet and sauté the green beans and asparagus until softened, about 5 minutes; set aside. In a saucepan over medium heat, mix arrowroot starch with coconut milk. Bring to a boil and cook with frequent stirring until thickened, 3 minutes. Stir in half of Parmesan cheese until melted. Mix in the green beans, asparagus, zucchinis, and tuna. Transfer the mixture to a baking dish and sprinkle with the remaining Parmesan cheese. Bake until the cheese is melted and golden, 18-20 minutes. Serve.

Per serving: Cal 392; Net Carbs 8g; Fats 34g; Protein 9g

Shirataki Fettucine with Salmon

Ingredients for 4 servings

4 salmon fillets, cubed	½ cup dry white wine
8 oz shirataki fettuccine	1 tsp lemon zest
5 tbsp butter	1 cup baby spinach
3 garlic cloves, minced	Salt and black pepper to taste
1 ¼ cups heavy cream	

Directions and Total Time: approx. 35 minutes

Pour 2 cups of water into a pot and bring it to a boil. Strain the shirataki pasta and rinse well under hot running water. Allow proper draining and pour the shirataki pasta into the boiling water. Cook for 3 minutes and strain again. Place in a dry skillet over medium heat and stir-fry the shirataki pasta until visibly dry, 1-2 minutes; set aside.

Melt half of the butter in the skillet. Season the salmon with salt and pepper and cook for 8 minutes, stirring occasionally; set aside. Melt the remaining butter in the skillet and stir-fry the garlic for 30 seconds. Mix in heavy cream, wine, lemon zest, salt, and pepper. Cook over low heat for 5 minutes. Stir in spinach, let wilt for 2 minutes. Stir in shirataki fettuccine and salmon. Serve.

Per serving: Cal 803; Net Carbs 9g; Fats 46g; Protein 69g

Tilapia Tortillas with Cauliflower Rice

Ingredients for 2 servings

1 tsp avocado oil	Salt and hot paprika to taste
1 cup cauli rice	2 whole cabbage leaves
2 tilapia fillets, cut into cubes	2 tbsp guacamole
¼ tsp taco seasoning	1 tbsp cilantro, chopped

Directions and Total Time: approx. 15 minutes

Microwave the cauli rice in a microwave-safe bowl for 4 minutes. Fluff with a fork and set aside.

Warm avocado oil in a skillet over medium heat, rub the tilapia with the taco seasoning, salt, and hot paprika and fry until brown on all sides, about 8 minutes in total.

Divide the fish among the cabbage leaves, top with cauli rice, guacamole, and cilantro. Serve.

Per serving: Cal 170; Fat 6.4g; Net Carbs 1.4g; Protein 24g

Chili Cod with Chive Sauce

Ingredients for 2 servings

1 tsp chili powder	1 garlic clove, minced
2 cod fillets	1/3 cup lemon juice
Salt and black pepper to taste	2 tbsp vegetable stock
1 tbsp olive oil	2 tbsp chives, chopped

Directions and Total Time: approx. 25 minutes

Preheat oven to 400 F. Rub the cod fillets with chili powder, salt, and pepper and lay in a greased baking dish. Bake for 10-15 minutes. In a skillet over low heat, warm the olive oil and sauté garlic for 1 minute. Add the lemon juice, stock, and chives. Season with salt and pepper and cook for 3 minutes until the sauce slightly reduces. Top the fish with the sauce and serve.

Per serving: Cal 448; Fat 35g; Net Carbs 6.3g; Protein 20g

Grilled Tuna with Shirataki Pad Thai

Ingredients for 2 servings

½ pack (7-oz) shirataki noodles	2 tuna steaks
1 red bell pepper, sliced	Salt and black pepper to taste
2 tbsp soy sauce, sugar-free	2 tbsp olive oil
1 tbsp ginger-garlic paste	1 tbsp parsley, chopped
1 tsp chili powder	

Directions and Total Time: approx. 15 minutes

In a colander, rinse the shirataki noodles with running cold water. Bring a pot of salted water to a boil; blanch the noodles for 2 minutes. Drain and set aside.

Preheat a grill to medium-high. Season the tuna with salt and pepper, and brush with some olive oil. Grill covered for 3 minutes on each side; set aside covered. In a bowl, whisk soy sauce, ginger paste, the remaining olive oil, chili powder, and 1 tbsp of water. Add the bell pepper and shirataki noodles and toss to coat. Top the noodles with tuna and garnish with parsley to serve.

Per serving: Cal 287; Fat 16g; Net Carbs 6.8g; Protein 23g

Quick Tuna Omelet

Ingredients for 2 servings

1 avocado, sliced	4 eggs, beaten
1 tbsp chopped chives	4 tbsp mascarpone cheese
1/3 cup canned tuna, drained	1 tbsp butter
¼ tsp smoked cayenne pepper	Salt and black pepper, to taste

Directions and Total Time: approx. 15 minutes

Melt the butter in a pan over medium heat. Pour in the eggs and cook for 3 minutes. Flip the omelet and continue to cook for 2 more minutes or until golden. Sprinkle with cayenne pepper, salt and pepper. Slide the omelet onto a plate and spread the mascarpone cheese over. Top with tuna, avocado, and chives. Fold the omelet in half to cover the filling and serve.

Per serving: Cal 481; Fat 38g; Net Carbs 6.2g; Protein 279g

Baked Haddock with Cheesy Topping

Ingredients for 4 servings

1 tbsp butter	2 cups sour cream
1 shallot, sliced	1 tbsp parsley, chopped
1 lb haddock fillets	½ cup pork rinds, crushed
2 eggs, hard-boiled, chopped	1 cup mozzarella cheese, grated
3 tbsp hazelnut flour	Salt and black pepper to taste

Directions and Total Time: approx. 35 minutes

Melt butter in a saucepan over medium heat and sauté the shallot for 3 minutes. Reduce the heat to low and stir in the hazelnut flour to form a roux. Cook the roux until golden brown and stir in the sour cream until smooth. Season to taste, and add parsley. Arrange the haddock on a greased baking dish, sprinkle with the eggs, and spoon the sauce over. In a bowl, mix the pork rinds with mozzarella, and spread the mixture over the sauce. Bake in the oven for 20 minutes at 370 F until the top is golden and the sauce and cheese are bubbly. Serve warm.

Per serving: Cal 788; Fat 57g; Net Carbs 8.5g; Protein 65g

Baked Cod with Parmesan and Almonds

Ingredients for 2 servings

2 cod fillets	1 cup heavy cream
1 cup Brussels sprouts	2 tbsp Parmesan cheese, grated
1 tbsp butter, melted	2 tbsp shaved almonds
Salt and black pepper to taste	

Directions and Total Time: approx. 40 minutes

Toss the fish fillets and Brussels sprouts in butter and season with salt and pepper to taste. Spread them on a greased baking dish. Mix heavy cream with Parmesan cheese; pour and smear the cream onto the fish. Bake in the oven for 25 minutes at 400 F. Take the dish out, sprinkle with almonds, and bake for 3-5 minutes. Serve.

Per serving: Cal 560; Fat 45g; Net Carbs 5.4g; Protein 25g

Greek Sea Bass with Olive Sauce

Ingredients for 2 servings

2 sea bass fillets	1 tbsp green olives, sliced
2 tbsp olive oil	1 lemon, juiced
A pinch of chili pepper	Salt to taste

Directions and Total Time: approx. 20 minutes

Preheat grill to high. In a small bowl, mix together half of the olive oil, chili pepper, and salt and rub onto the sea bass fillets. Grill the fish on both sides for 5-6 minutes until brown. In a skillet over medium heat, warm the remaining olive oil and stir in the lemon juice, olives, and salt; cook for 3-4 minutes. Plate the fillets and pour the lemon sauce over to serve.

Per serving: Cal 267; Fat 16g; Net Carbs 1.6g; Protein 24g

Parmesan Shrimp Scampi Pizza

Ingredients for 4 servings

3 tbsp olive oil	¼ cup white wine
2 tbsp butter	½ tsp dried basil
½ lb shrimp, deveined	½ tsp dried parsley
½ cup almond flour	½ lemon, juiced
¼ tsp salt	2 cups grated cheese blend
2 tbsp ground psyllium husk	½ tsp Italian seasoning
2 garlic cloves, minced	¼ cup grated Parmesan

Directions and Total Time: approx. 30 minutes

Preheat oven to 380 F. Line a baking sheet with parchment paper. In a bowl, mix almond flour, salt, psyllium powder, 1 tbsp of olive oil, and 1 cup of lukewarm water until dough forms. Spread the mixture on the baking sheet and bake for 10 minutes.

Meanwhile, heat butter and the remaining olive oil in a skillet. Sauté garlic for 30 seconds. Mix in the wine and cook until it reduces by half. Stir in basil, parsley, and lemon juice. Stir in the shrimp and cook for 3 minutes. Mix in the cheese blend and Italian seasoning. Let the cheese melt, 3 minutes. Spread the shrimp mixture on the crust and top with Parmesan cheese. Bake for 5 minutes or until the cheese melts. Slice and serve warm.

Per serving: Cal 419; Net Carbs 3g; Fats 29g; Protein 23g

Spiralized Zucchini with Garlic Shrimp

Ingredients for 4 servings

2 tbsp butter	¼ cup white wine
1 lb jumbo shrimp, deveined	1 lime, zested and juiced
4 garlic cloves, minced	3 zucchinis, spiralized
1 cup grated Parmesan cheese	2 tbsp chopped parsley
1 pinch red chili flakes	Salt and black pepper to taste

Directions and Total Time: approx. 15 minutes

Warm the butter in a skillet and cook the shrimp for 3-4 minutes. Flip and stir in garlic and red chili flakes. Cook further for 1 minute; set aside. Pour the wine and lime juice into the skillet and stir to deglaze the bottom; cook until reduced by a third. Mix in zucchini, lime zest, shrimp, and parsley. Season with salt and pepper and cook for 2 minutes. Top with Parmesan and serve.

Per serving: Cal 261; Net Carbs 8.9g; Fats 8g; Protein 29g

Anchovy Caprese Pizza

Ingredients for 2 servings

Crust

4 eggs	¼ tsp fennel seeds, ground
¼ cup buttermilk	¼ tsp salt
2 tbsp flaxseed meal	1 tbsp olive oil
1 tsp chipotle pepper	

Topping

1 ball (8-oz) fresh mozzarella, sliced	
2 tbsp tomato paste	2 tomatoes, sliced
4 basil leaves	2 anchovies, chopped

Directions and Total Time: approx. 40 minutes

In a bowl, whisk the eggs, and add in buttermilk, flax seed, fennel seeds, chipotle pepper, and salt.

Set a pan over medium heat and warm ½ tbsp of olive oil. Ladle ½ of the crust mixture into the pan and spread out evenly. Cook until the edges are set; then, flip the crust and cook on the other side, 3-4 minutes.

Warm the remaining ½ tbsp of oil in the pan. Repeat the same process with the other pizza crust.

Spread the crusts with tomato paste and top with fresh mozzarella and tomato slices. In batches, bake in the oven for 8-10 minutes at 430 F until the cheese melts. Garnish with anchovies and basil leaves. Serve.

Per serving: Cal 465; Fat 31g; Net Carbs 5.1g; Protein 32g

Broccoli & Anchovy Purée

Ingredients for 4 servings

4 oz butter	¼ tsp dried thyme
2 anchovy fillets, chopped	½ lemon, juiced and zested
1 head broccoli, cut into florets	4 tbsp heavy cream

Directions and Total Time: approx. 15 minutes

Throw the broccoli into a pot over high heat and cover with salted water. Bring to a boil and cook for about 7 minutes. Drain and transfer to a bowl. Add in butter, thyme, lemon juice and zest, heavy cream, and anchovies. Using a blender, puree the ingredients until smooth. Serve.

Per serving: Cal 382; Net Carbs 6g; Fat 33g; Protein 9g

Sardines with Green Pasta & Tomatoes

Ingredients for 2 servings

½ lb whole fresh sardines, gutted and cleaned
½ cup sun-dried tomatoes, drained and chopped
2 tbsp olive oil · 1 garlic clove, minced
4 cups spiralized zucchini · Salt and black pepper to taste

Directions and Total Time: approx. 20 minutes

Preheat the oven to 350 F. Line a baking sheet with parchment paper. Arrange the sardines on the dish. Drizzle with olive oil and sprinkle with salt and pepper. Bake for 10 minutes until the skin is crispy.

Warm olive oil in a skillet and stir-fry zucchini, garlic and tomatoes for 5 minutes. Transfer the sardines to a plate and serve with the veggie pasta.

Per serving: Cal 431; Fat 26g; Net Carbs 5.6g; Protein 33g

Fish Tacos with Cilantro Slaw

Ingredients for 2 servings

1 tbsp olive oil · 2 halibut fillets, skinless, sliced
1 tsp chili powder · 2 low carb tortillas
Slaw
2 tbsp red cabbage, shredded · ½ tbsp extra-virgin olive oil
1 tbsp lemon juice · ½ carrot, shredded
Salt to taste · 1 tbsp cilantro, chopped

Directions and Total Time: approx. 15 minutes

Season the cabbage with salt in a bowl; massage tenderize. Add in the remaining slaw ingredients, toss to coat and set aside. Rub the fish with olive oil and chili powder. Heat a grill pan over medium heat. Cook the fish until lightly charred and cooked through, about 3 minutes per side. Divide between the tortillas. Split the slaw among the tortillas and serve.

Per serving: Cal 385; Fat 26g; Net Carbs 6.5g; Protein 24g

Catalan Shrimp with Garlic

Ingredients for 4 servings

¼ cup olive oil, divided · ¼ tsp cayenne pepper
1 lb shrimp, peeled and deveined · 3 garlic cloves, sliced
Salt to taste · 2 tbsp chopped parsley

Directions and Total Time: approx. 25 minutes

Warm olive oil in a large skillet over medium heat. Reduce the heat and add the garlic; stir-fry for 1-2 minutes, but make sure it doesn't brown or burn. Add the shrimp, season with salt and cayenne pepper, stir for one minute and turn off the heat. Let the shrimp finish cooking in the heat for 8-10 minutes. Serve topped with parsley.

Per serving: Cal 441; Fat 29g; Net Carbs 1.2g; Protein 43g

Zucchini Stuffed with Shrimp & Tomato

Ingredients for 2 servings

1 lb zucchinis, tops removed and reserved
1 lb shrimp, peeled, deveined · 1 small tomato, chopped
¼ onion, chopped · Salt and black pepper to taste
1 tsp olive oil · 1 tbsp basil leaves, chopped

Directions and Total Time: approx. 35 minutes

Scoop out the seeds of the zucchinis; set aside.

Warm olive oil in a skillet and sauté the onion and tomato for 3 minutes. Add the shrimp, zucchini flesh, basil, salt, and pepper and cook for another 5 minutes. Fill the zucchini shells with the mixture. Place them on a greased baking sheet to bake for 15-20 minutes at 390 F. The shrimp should no longer be pink. Remove the zucchinis and serve warm.

Per serving: Cal 252; Fat 6g; Net Carbs 8.9g; Protein 37.6g

Shirataki Noodles with Shrimp & Cheese

Ingredients for 4 servings

8 oz angel hair shirataki noodles
1 tbsp olive oil · ½ cup dry white wine
1 lb shrimp, deveined · 1 ½ cups heavy cream
2 tbsp unsalted butter · ½ cup grated Asiago cheese
6 garlic cloves, minced · 2 tbsp chopped fresh parsley

Directions and Total Time: approx. 20 minutes

Warm olive oil in a skillet over medium heat and cook the shrimp on both sides, 2 minutes; set aside. Melt the butter in the skillet and sauté garlic. Stir in wine and cook until reduced by half, scraping the bottom of the skillet to deglaze. Stir in heavy cream and let simmer for 1 minute. Stir in Asiago cheese until it melts. Return the shrimp to the sauce and sprinkle with parsley.

Bring 2 cups of water to a boil in a pot. Strain shirataki pasta and rinse under hot running water.

Allow proper draining and pour the shirataki pasta into the boiling water. Cook for 3 minutes and strain again. Place a dry skillet and stir-fry the pasta until dry, 1-2 minutes. Top with the shrimp sauce and serve.

Per serving: Cal 489; Net Carbs 6g; Fats 27g; Protein 29g

Coconut Fried Shrimp with Cilantro Sauce

Ingredients for 2 servings

2 tsp coconut flour · ½ lb shrimp, shelled
2 tbsp grated Pecorino cheese · 2 tbsp coconut oil
1 egg, beaten in a bowl · Salt to taste
¼ tsp curry powder
Sauce
2 tbsp ghee · ½ cup coconut cream
2 tbsp cilantro leaves, chopped · ½ oz Paneer cheese, grated
½ onion, diced

Directions and Total Time: approx. 20 minutes

Mix flour, Pecorino, curry, and salt in a bowl. Melt the coconut oil in a skillet over medium heat. Dip the shrimp in the beaten egg, and then coat in the cheese mixture. Fry until golden and crispy, about 5 minutes.

In another skillet, melt the ghee. Sweat the onion for 3 minutes. Stir in the coconut cream and Paneer cheese and cook until thickened, about 3-4 minutes. Add the shrimp and coat well. Serve warm topped with cilantro.

Per serving: Cal 741; Fat 64g; Net Carbs 4.3g; Protein 34g

Chimichurri Tiger Shrimp

Ingredients for 4 servings

1 lb tiger shrimp, peeled and deveined
2 tbsp olive oil
1 garlic clove, minced   Juice of 1 lime

Chimichurri

Salt and black pepper to taste   ¼ cup red wine vinegar
¼ cup extra-virgin olive oil   2 cups parsley, minced
2 garlic cloves, minced   ¼ tsp red pepper flakes
1 lime, juiced

Directions and Total Time: approx. 10 min + chilling time

Combine the shrimp, olive oil, garlic, and lime juice in a bowl. Marinate in the fridge for 30 minutes.

To make the chimichurri dressing, blitz the chimichurri ingredients in a blender until smooth; set aside.

Preheat your grill to medium. Cook shrimp for 2 minutes per side. Serve the shrimp drizzled with chimichurri.

Per serving: Cal 523; Fat 30g; Net Carbs 7.2g; Protein 49g

Mustardy Crab Cakes

Ingredients for 4 servings

1 tbsp coconut oil   ¼ cup mayonnaise
1 lb lump crab meat   2 tbsp coconut flour
1 tsp Dijon mustard   1 tbsp cilantro, chopped
1 egg   Salt and black pepper to taste

Directions and Total Time: approx. 15 minutes

In a bowl, add the crab meat, mustard, mayonnaise, coconut flour, egg, cilantro, salt, and pepper. Mix well to combine and make patties out of the mixture.

Melt the coconut oil in a skillet over medium heat. Add the patties and brown for about 2-3 minutes per side. Remove with a perforated spoon and drain on kitchen paper. Serve with tartare sauce if desired.

Per serving: Cal 315; Fat 25g; Net Carbs 1.6g; Protein 13g

Spicy Mussels with Shirataki Pasta

Ingredients for 4 servings

4 tbsp olive oil   3 shallots, finely chopped
8 oz angel hair shirataki   2 tsp red chili flakes
1 ½ lb mussels   1 ½ cups heavy cream
1 cup white wine   2 tbsp chopped fresh parsley
6 garlic cloves, minced   Salt and black pepper to taste

Directions and Total Time: approx. 25 minutes

Pour 2 cups of water in a pot and bring to a boil. Strain the pasta and rinse well under hot running water. Drain and transfer to the boiling water. Cook for 3 minutes and strain again. Place a large dry skillet and stir-fry the pasta until visibly dry, 1-2 minutes; set aside.

Add the mussels, wine, and 1 cup of water in a pot over medium heat and bring to a boil. Cook covered for 3-4 minutes. Strain the mussels and reserve the cooking liquid. Let them cool, and discard any closed mussels. Remove the meat out of ¾ of the mussel shells. Set aside the remaining mussels with shells.

Heat olive oil in a skillet and sauté shallots, garlic, and chili flakes for 3 minutes. Mix in the reserved cooking liquid and cook until reduced by half, about 2-5 minutes. Whisk in the heavy cream. Season with salt and pepper. Pour in shiritaki pasta and shell-less mussels and toss to combine. Top with parsley and decorate with the remaining mussels with shells. Serve.

Per serving: Cal 469; Net Carbs 6g; Fats 34g; Protein 21g

Mussel Coconut Curry

Ingredients for 4 servings

2 tbsp cup coconut oil   ½ cup coconut milk
2 green onions, chopped   ½ cup white wine
1 lb mussels, de-bearded   1 tsp red curry powder
1 shallot, chopped   2 tbsp parsley, chopped
1 garlic clove, minced

Directions and Total Time: approx. 25 minutes

Heat the coconut oil in a pot over medium heat and sauté the shallot and garlic for 3 minutes until softened. Add in the wine, coconut milk, and red curry powder and cook for 3 minutes. Add the mussels and steam for 7 minutes or until the shells are opened. Use a slotted spoon to remove to a bowl leaving the sauce in the pot. Discard any closed mussels at this point. Turn the heat off and sprinkle with parsley and green onions. Serve.

Per serving: Cal 356; Fat 21g; Net Carbs 0.3g; Protein 21g

Pan-Seared Scallops with Sausage

Ingredients for 4 servings

2 tbsp butter   1 red onion, finely chopped
12 fresh scallops, rinsed   1 cup Grana Padano, grated
8 oz sausage, chopped   Salt and black pepper to taste
1 red bell pepper, sliced

Directions and Total Time: approx. 20 minutes

Melt the butter in a skillet over medium heat and stir-fry the onion and bell pepper for 5 minutes until tender. Add the sausage and stir-fry for 5 minutes; set aside.

Pat the scallops dry with a paper towel and season with salt and pepper. Add them to the skillet and sear for 2 minutes on each side until golden brown. Add the sausage mixture back to the skillet and warm through. Top with Grana Padano cheese and serve.

Per serving: Cal 834; Fat 62g; Net Carbs 9.5g; Protein 56g

Avocado Boats with Crabmeat & Yogurt

Ingredients for 4 servings

4 oz crabmeat   2 tbsp chives, chopped
2 avocados, halved and pitted   1 tsp smoked paprika
3 oz cream cheese

Directions and Total Time: approx. 25 minutes

In a bowl, mix paprika with cream cheese. Fill the avocado halves with crabmeat and top with the paprika cream cheese. Decorate with chives and serve.

Per serving: Cal 506; Fat 43g; Net Carbs 3.8g; Protein 17g

VEGETABLE SIDES & DAIRY

Cheesy Zucchini Muffins

Ingredients for 6 servings

1 large egg	1/3 cup almond milk
5 tbsp olive oil	2 zucchinis, grated
½ cup almond flour	6 green olives, sliced
1 tsp baking powder	1 spring onion, chopped
½ tsp baking soda	1 red bell pepper, chopped
½ cup grated cheddar cheese	1 tbsp chopped thyme
1 ½ tsp mustard powder	Salt and black pepper to taste

Directions and Total Time: approx. 40 minutes

Preheat oven to 340 F. In a bowl, combine almond flour, baking powder, baking soda, mustard powder, salt, and pepper. In another bowl, whisk almond milk, egg, and oil. Mix the wet ingredients into dry ingredients and add the cheddar cheese, zucchini, olives, spring onion, bell pepper, and thyme; mix well. Spoon the batter into greased muffin cups and bake for 30 minutes or until golden brown. Let cool for 5 minutes and serve.

Per serving: Cal 169; Net Carbs 1.6g; Fat 16g; Protein 4g

Eggplant & Tomato Gratin

Ingredients for 4 servings

1/3 cup melted butter	7 oz tomato sauce
2 eggplants, sliced	2 tbsp Parmesan, grated
2 garlic cloves, minced	¼ cup chopped fresh parsley
1 red onion, sliced	Salt and black pepper to taste

Directions and Total Time: approx. 45 minutes

Preheat oven to 400 F. Line a baking sheet with parchment paper. Brush eggplants with some butter. Bake until lightly browned, about 20 minutes.

Heat the remaining butter in a skillet and sauté garlic and onion until fragrant and soft, about 3 minutes. Stir in tomato sauce and season with salt and pepper. Simmer for 10 minutes. Remove eggplants from the oven and spread the tomato sauce on top. Sprinkle with Parmesan cheese and parsley and serve.

Per serving: Cal 597; Net Carbs 12g; Fat 51g; Protein 26g

Roasted Cauliflower with Chilli Dressing

Ingredients for 4 servings

1 head cauliflower, chopped	1 tbsp red chili flake
3 tbsp olive oil	2 tbsp capers, drained
1 tbsp chili oil	2 tbsp cilantro, chopped
1 lemon, zested and juiced	Salt and black pepper to taste

Directions and Total Time: approx. 35 minutes

Preheat oven to 360 F. Place the cauliflower in a baking dish and drizzle half of the olive oil all over. Season with salt and pepper. Roast until golden, 20-25 minutes. In a bowl, whisk the remaining olive oil, chili oil, lemon zest, lemon juice, and salt. Stir in capers and red chili flakes. Remove the cauliflower to a serving plate and drizzle with the dressing. Sprinkle with cilantro and serve warm.

Per serving: Cal 138; Net Carbs 1.6g; Fat 14g; Protein 1.4g

Cheddar Stuffed Zucchini

Ingredients for 2 servings

4 tbsp butter	2 tbsp tomato sauce
1 zucchini, halved	1 cup cheddar cheese
1 ½ oz baby kale	Salt and black pepper to taste
2 garlic cloves, minced	

Directions and Total Time: approx. 40 minutes

Preheat oven to 375 F. Scoop out zucchini pulp with a spoon. Keep the flesh. Grease a baking sheet with cooking spray and place in the zucchini boats. Melt butter in a skillet over medium heat and sauté garlic until fragrant and slightly browned, 4 minutes.

Add in kale and zucchini pulp. Cook until the kale wilts; season with salt and pepper. Spoon tomato sauce into the boats and spread to coat evenly. Top with kale mixture and sprinkle with cheddar cheese. Bake for 25 minutes.

Per serving: Cal 617; Net Carbs 4g; Fat 61g; Protein 19g

Butternut Squash Roast with Chimichurri

Ingredients for 4 servings

1 lb butternut squash	3 tbsp toasted pine nuts
1 tbsp butter, melted	Salt and black pepper to taste

Chimichurri:

Zest and juice of 1 lemon	2 garlic cloves, minced
1 jalapeño pepper, chopped	½ cup chopped fresh parsley
1 cup olive oil	½ red bell pepper, chopped

Directions and Total Time: approx. 25 minutes

Add all the chimichurri ingredients to a food processor and grind until desired consistency is achieved; adjust the seasoning. Keep in the fridge until ready to use.

Slice the squash into rounds and remove the seeds. Drizzle with butter and season with salt and pepper. Preheat a grill pan over medium heat and cook the squash for 5-6 minutes on each side. Scatter pine nuts on top and serve with chimichurri.

Per serving: Cal 647; Net Carbs 6g; Fat 44g; Protein 49g

Roasted Pepper with Tofu

Ingredients for 4 servings

2 ½ cups cubed tofu	¾ cup mayonnaise
4 orange bell peppers	1 tbsp melted butter
1 cucumber, diced	1 tsp dried parsley
1 large tomato, chopped	1 tsp dried basil
3 oz cream cheese	Salt and black pepper to taste

Directions and Total Time: approx. 25 minutes

Preheat a broiler to 450 F. Line a baking sheet with parchment paper. In a salad bowl, combine cream cheese, mayonnaise, cucumber, tomato, salt, pepper, and parsley; refrigerate. Arrange bell peppers and tofu on the baking sheet, drizzle with melted butter, and season with basil, salt, and pepper. Bake for 15 minutes until the peppers have charred lightly and the tofu browned. Serve with chilled salad and enjoy!

Per serving: Cal 838; Net Carbs 8g; Fat 81g; Protein 31g

Feta & Olive Pizza

Ingredients for 4 servings

1 tbsp olive oil	¼ tsp dried Greek seasoning
½ cup almond flour	1 cup crumbled feta cheese
2 tbsp ground psyllium husk	3 plum tomatoes, sliced
¼ tsp salt	6 Kalamata olives, chopped
¼ tsp red chili flakes	5 basil leaves, chopped

Directions and Total Time: approx. 30 minutes

Preheat oven to 390 F. Line a baking sheet with parchment paper. In a bowl, mix almond flour, salt, psyllium powder, olive oil, and 1 cup of lukewarm water until; stir until a dough forms.

Spread the mixture on the baking sheet and bake for 10 minutes. Sprinkle the red chili flakes and Greek seasoning on the crust and top with the feta cheese. Arrange the tomatoes and olives on top. Bake for 10 minutes. Garnish the pizza with basil, slice, and serve warm.

Per serving: Cal 281; Net Carbs 4.5g; Fats 12g; Protein 8g

Chargrilled Zucchini with Avocado Pesto

Ingredients for 4 servings

1 avocado, chopped	2 oz pecans
3 oz spinach, chopped	1 garlic clove, minced
2 zucchinis, sliced	Juice of 1 lemon
¾ cup olive oil	Salt and black pepper to taste
2 tbsp melted butter	

Directions and Total Time: approx. 20 minutes

Put the spinach in a food processor and avocado, lemon juice, garlic, olive oil, and pecans and blend until smooth; season with salt and pepper. Pour the pesto into a bowl and set it aside. Season zucchini with salt, pepper, and butter. Preheat a grill pan over medium heat and cook the zucchini slices until browned, 8-10 minutes in total. Remove to a plate, spoon the pesto to the side, and serve.

Per serving: Cal 548; Net Carbs 6g; Fat 46g; Protein 25g

Walnut & Feta Loaf

Ingredients for 4 servings

1 green bell pepper, chopped	¾ cup chopped walnuts
1 red bell pepper, chopped	Salt and black pepper
2 white onions, chopped	1 tbsp Italian mixed herbs
4 garlic cloves, minced	½ tsp Swerve sugar
1 lb feta, cubed	¼ cup golden flaxseed meal
3 tbsp olive oil	1 tbsp sesame seeds
2 tbsp soy sauce	½ cup tomato sauce

Directions and Total Time: approx. 60 minutes

Preheat oven to 350 F. In a bowl, combine olive oil, onions, garlic, feta, soy sauce, walnuts, salt, pepper, Italian herbs, Swerve, and flaxseed meal and mix with your hands. Pour the mixture into a bowl and stir in sesame seeds and bell peppers. Transfer the mixture into a greased loaf and spoon tomato sauce on top. Bake for 45 minutes. Turn onto a chopping board, slice, and serve.

Per serving: Cal 429; Net Carbs 2.5g; Fat 28g; Protein 24g

Baked Veggies with Green Salad

Ingredients for 2 servings

1 zucchini, sliced	5 oz cheddar cheese, cubed
1 eggplant, sliced	10 Kalamata olives
¼ cup coconut oil	1 oz mixed salad greens
2 tbsp pecans	½ cup mayonnaise
Juice of ½ lemon	½ tsp Cayenne pepper

Directions and Total Time: approx. 30 minutes

Line a baking sheet with parchment paper. Arrange zucchini and eggplant slices on the sheet. Brush with coconut oil and sprinkle with cayenne pepper. Set the oven to broil and broil the vegetables until golden brown, about 18-20 minutes. Remove to a serving platter and drizzle with lemon juice. Arrange cheddar cheese, olives, pecans, and mixed greens next to baked veggies. Top with mayonnaise and serve.

Per serving: Cal 509g; Net Carbs 8g; Fat 31g; Protein 22g

Coconut Avocado Tart

Ingredients for 4 servings

1¼ cups grated Parmesan	1 tsp baking powder
½ cup cream cheese	3 tbsp coconut oil
1 egg	2 ripe avocados, mashed
4 tbsp coconut flour	1 cup mayonnaise
4 tbsp chia seeds	1 jalapeño pepper, minced
¾ cup almond flour	½ tsp onion powder
1 tbsp psyllium husk powder	2 tbsp fresh parsley, chopped

Directions and Total Time: approx. 70 minutes

Preheat oven to 350 F. In a bowl, add coconut flour, chia seeds, almond flour, psyllium husk, baking powder, coconut oil, and 4 tbsp water. Blend until the resulting dough forms into a ball.

Line a springform pan with parchment paper and spread the dough. Bake for 15 minutes. In a bowl, put avocados, mayonnaise, egg, parsley, jalapeño pepper, onion powder, cream cheese, and Parmesan cheese; mix well. Remove the piecrust when ready and fill with the creamy mixture. Bake for 35 minutes until lightly golden brown.

Per serving: Cal 891; Net Carbs 10g; Fat 71g; Protein 24g

Hot Broccoli Rabe

Ingredients for 4 servings

1 tbsp olive oil	1 tbsp red chili flakes
1 tbsp melted butter	½ lemon, zested
1 lb broccoli rabe, trimmed	2 tbsp cashew nuts, chopped
1 orange bell pepper, sliced	Salt and black pepper to taste
1 garlic clove, minced	

Directions and Total Time: approx. 15 minutes

Blanch broccoli in lightly salted water for 6-8 minutes or until tender; drain. Heat butter and olive oil in a skillet over medium heat and sauté garlic and bell pepper until softened, 5 minutes; season with salt and pepper. Toss in broccoli and lemon zest. Sprinkle with red chili flakes and chopped cashew. Serve and enjoy!.

Per serving: Cal 117; Net Carbs 1.7g; Fat 8.4g; Protein 3.7g

Delicious Mushroom Pie

Ingredients for 4 servings

For the piecrust

4 whole eggs

¼ cup cold butter, crumbled

¼ cup almond flour

3 tbsp coconut flour

½ tsp salt

For the filling

2 cups mixed mushrooms, chopped

1 cup green beans, cut into 3 pieces each

2 eggs, lightly beaten

2 tbsp butter

1 yellow onion, chopped

2 garlic cloves, minced

1 green bell pepper, diced

¼ cup heavy cream

1/3 cup sour cream

½ cup almond milk

¼ tsp nutmeg powder

1 tbsp chopped parsley

1 cup grated Monterey Jack

Salt and black pepper to taste

Directions and Total Time: approx. 60 min + chilling time

Preheat oven to 350 F. In a bowl, mix almond and coconut flours and salt. Add in butter and mix until crumbly. Pour in the eggs one after another while mixing until formed into a ball. Flatten the dough on a clean flat surface, cover with plastic wrap, and refrigerate for 1 hour. Dust a clean flat surface with almond flour, unwrap the dough and roll out into a large rectangle. Fit into a greased pie pan and with a fork, prick the base of the crust. Bake for 15 minutes; let cool. For the filling, melt butter in a skillet over medium heat and sauté onion and garlic for 3 minutes. Add in mushrooms, bell pepper, and green beans; cook for 5 minutes. In a bowl, beat heavy cream, sour cream, almond milk, and eggs. Season with salt, pepper, and nutmeg. Stir in parsley and Monterey Jack cheese. Spread the mushroom mixture on the baked pastry and spread the cheese filling on top. Place the pie in the oven and bake for 35 minutes. Slice and serve.

Per serving: Cal 531; Net Carbs 6.5g; Fat 39g; Protein 21g

Vegetable Biryani

Ingredients for 4 servings

1 cup sliced cremini mushrooms

2 tbsp olive oil

3 tbsp ghee

6 cups cauli rice

1 white onion, chopped

2 garlic cloves, minced

1 tsp ginger puree

1 tbsp turmeric powder

2 cups chopped tomatoes

1 habanero pepper, minced

1 tbsp tomato puree

1 cup diced paneer cheese

½ cup spinach, chopped

½ cup kale, chopped

¼ cup chopped parsley

1 cup Greek yogurt

Salt and black pepper to taste

Directions and Total Time: approx. 75 minutes

Preheat oven to 400 F. Microwave cauli rice for 1 minute. Remove and season with salt and black pepper; set aside.

Melt ghee in a pan over medium heat and sauté onion, garlic, ginger puree, and turmeric. Cook for 5 minutes, stirring regularly. Add in tomatoes, habanero pepper, and tomato puree; cook for 5 more minutes. Stir in mushrooms, paneer cheese, spinach, kale, and 1/3 cup water and simmer for 15 minutes or until the mushrooms soften. Turn the heat off and stir in yogurt.

Spoon half of the mixture into a baking dish. Spread half of the cauli rice on top. Repeat the layers and top with olive oil and parsley. Bake for 25 minutes. Serve.

Per serving: Cal 351; Net Carbs 2g; Fat 19g; Protein 16g

Charred Broccoli with Tamarind Sauce

Ingredients for 6 servings

1 head broccoli, cut into "steaks"

4 tbsp melted butter

½ cup peanut butter

1 white onion, finely chopped

1 small red chili, chopped

1 garlic clove, peeled

1-inch ginger, peeled

2 tbsp tamarind sauce

1 tsp Swerve brown sugar

1 tsp garlic powder

1 tsp dried basil

3 tbsp parsley, chopped

½ lemon, juiced

Salt and black pepper to taste

Directions and Total Time: approx. 30 minutes

Bring to a boil 2 cups of water in a pot and blanch broccoli for 2 minutes; drain. In a bowl, mix the melted butter, onion, garlic powder, basil, salt, pepper. Toss broccoli in the mixture and marinate for 5 minutes.

Heat a grill pan over high. Cook broccoli until charred, turning once, about 6-8 minutes. Transfer to a plate. Place garlic and ginger in a blender and pulse until broken into pieces. Add in lemon juice, peanut butter, tamarind sauce, Swerve sugar, parsley, chili, and 1/3 cup water. Blend until smooth. Top the broccoli with the sauce. Serve.

Per serving: Cal 271; Net Carbs 5g; Fat 18g; Protein 7.6g

Zucchini & Cheese Casserole

Ingredients for 4 servings

2 tbsp olive oil

1 tbsp salted butter, melted

3 large zucchinis, sliced

¼ cup grated mozzarella

2/3 cup grated Parmesan

1 garlic clove, minced

1 tsp dried thyme

Directions and Total Time: approx. 25 minutes

Preheat oven to 350 F. Pour zucchini in a bowl. Add butter, olive oil, garlic, and thyme; toss to coat. Spread onto a baking dish and sprinkle with the mozzarella and Parmesan cheeses. Bake for 15 minutes. Serve warm.

Per serving: Cal 145; Net Carbs 5,9g; Fat 12g; Protein 5g

Crispy Avocado with Parmesan Sauce

Ingredients for 4 servings

2 tbsp olive oil

3 tbsp almond flour

1 ½ cups almond milk

5 tbsp melted butter

1 cup grated cheddar cheese

4 oz cream cheese, softened

¼ cup grated Parmesan

2 avocados, sliced

¼ tsp mustard powder

¼ tsp garlic powder

2 tbsp sriracha sauce

Black pepper to taste

Directions and Total Time: approx. 20 minutes

Whisk 3 tbsps of butter with almond flour in a saucepan and cook until golden. Whisk in almond milk, mustard powder, garlic powder, and black pepper. Cook, whisking continuously until thickened, 2 minutes. Stir in the cheeses until they are melted; set aside.

In a bowl, toss avocado in the remaining butter and sriracha sauce. Heat olive oil in a pan and cook avocado until golden, turning halfway, 4 minutes in total. Plate and pour the cheese sauce all over to serve.

Per serving: Cal 551; Net Carbs 3.2g; Fat 51g; Protein 10g

Mushroom & Tofu Cakes with Cauli Mash

Ingredients for 4 servings

1 cup button mushrooms, chopped	
1 lb tofu, pressed and cubed	2 cups tomato sauce
2 garlic cloves, minced	6 fresh basil leaves to garnish
2 small red onions, chopped	1 lb cauliflower, cut into florets
1 red bell pepper, chopped	2 tbsp butter
½ cup golden flaxseed meal	½ cup heavy cream
½ almond milk	¼ cup grated Parmesan
3 tbsp olive oil	Salt and black pepper to taste

Directions and Total Time: approx. 65 minutes

Preheat oven to 360 F. Line a baking tray with parchment paper. In a bowl, add tofu, half of the garlic, half of the onion, mushrooms, salt, and pepper; mix to combine. Mold bite-size balls out of the mixture. Place flaxseed meal and almond milk each in a shallow dish. Dip each ball in almond milk and then in the flaxseed meal. Place on the baking sheet and bake for 10 minutes.

Heat 2 tbsp of olive oil in a saucepan and fry the tofu balls until golden brown on all sides, about 5-6 minutes; set aside. Heat the remaining oil in the same saucepan and sauté the remaining onion, remaining garlic, and bell pepper for 5 minutes. Pour in tomato sauce and cook for 10 minutes or until a stew forms. Add in tofu balls and simmer for 7 minutes.

In a pot, add cauliflower, 1 cup of water, and salt. Bring to a boil and cook for 10 minutes. Drain the cauliflower and pour it into a bowl. Add in butter, salt, and pepper; mash into a puree using a potato mash. Stir in heavy cream and Parmesan cheese until evenly combined. Spoon the mash into bowls, top with tofu balls and sauce, and garnish with basil leaves.

Per serving: Cal 692; Net Carbs 5.6g; Fat 28g, Protein 19g

Green Sauté with Pine Nuts

Ingredients for 4 servings

1 tbsp olive oil	1 tsp Swerve sugar
2 tbsp butter	2 tbsp red wine vinegar
2 heads large broccoli, riced	1 tsp cumin powder
2 zucchinis, sliced	1 garlic clove, minced
2 shallots, finely sliced	4 tbsp chopped parsley
2 tbsp pine nuts	

Directions and Total Time: approx. 20 minutes

In a bowl, whisk shallots, Swerve sugar, and vinegar and set aside. Melt butter in a skillet and stir in cumin and garlic for 1 minute. Add in broccoli and sauté for 5 minutes until softened. Mix in zucchini. Reduce the heat to low and cook for 4-5 minutes. Stir in parsley. Drizzle with olive oil and garnish with pine nuts to serve.

Per serving: Cal 81; Net Carbs 3.5g; Fat 6.1g; Protein 1.9g

Mushrooms with Broccoli Noddles

Ingredients for 4 servings

1 cup cremini mushrooms, sliced	
4 large heads broccoli	2 tbsp almond flour
1 cup grated Gruyere cheese	1 ½ cups almond milk
2 tbsp olive oil	¼ cup chopped fresh parsley
4 scallions, chopped	Salt and black pepper to taste
2 garlic cloves, minced	

Directions and Total Time: approx. 20 minutes

Cut off the florets of the broccoli heads, leaving only the stems. Cut the ends of the stem flatly and evenly. Run the stems through a spiralizer to make the noodles. Heat olive oil in a skillet and sauté the broccoli noodles, mushrooms, garlic, and scallions until softened, 5 minutes. In a bowl, combine almond flour and almond milk and pour the mixture over the vegetables. Stir and allow thickening for 2-3 minutes. Whisk in half of the Gruyere cheese to melt and adjust the taste with salt and black pepper. Garnish with the remaining Gruyere cheese and parsley and serve.

Per serving: Cal 219; Net Carbs 1.4g; Fats 15g; Protein 10g

Coconut-Lime Ice Cream with Chia Seeds

Ingredients for 4 servings

2 avocados, mashed	2 tbsp chia seeds
1 ¾ cups coconut cream	Juice and zest of 3 limes
¼ tsp vanilla extract	1/3 cup erythritol

Directions and Total Time: approx. 20 min + chilling time

In a bowl, combine mashed avocado, chia seeds, lime juice and zest, erythritol, coconut cream, and vanilla extract and beat the ingredients using an electric mixer until creamy and uniform. Pour the mixture into an ice cream maker and prepare the ice cream following the manufacturer's instructions. Transfer to a freezer-safe container and freeze until firm, about 2 hours. Scoop the ice cream into dessert cups and serve.

Per serving: Cal 259; Net Carbs 4g; Fat 25g; Protein 4g

Tofu & Parsnip Spaghetti a la "Bolognese"

Ingredients for 4 servings

2 tbsp olive oil	1 garlic clove, minced
2 tbsp butter	2 cups sugar-free passata
4 large parsnips, spiralized	¼ cup vegetable broth
1 cup crumbled firm tofu	2 tbsp fresh basil, chopped
1 onion, chopped	1 cup grated Parmesan cheese
2 celery stalks, chopped	Salt and black pepper to taste

Directions and Total Time: approx. 35 minutes

Warm butter in a skillet and sauté parsnips for 5 minutes. Season with salt and pepper: set aside. Heat olive oil in a pot and cook tofu for 5 minutes. Stir in onion, garlic, and celery and cook for 5 minutes. Mix in passata and broth and season with salt and pepper. Cover the pot and cook until the sauce thickens, 8-10 minutes. Stir in basil. Divide the pasta between plates and top with the sauce. Sprinkle the Parmesan cheese on top and serve.

Per serving: Cal 431; Net Carbs 31g; Fats 19g; Protein 22g

Vegetable Keto Pasta Gratin

Ingredients for 4 servings

1 cup shredded mozzarella cheese
1 cup sliced white button mushrooms
1 egg yolk — Salt and black pepper to taste
2 tbsp olive oil — ¼ tsp red chili flakes
1 cup chopped bell peppers — 1 cup marinara sauce
1 yellow squash, chopped — 1 cup grated mozzarella
1 red onion, sliced — 1 cup grated Parmesan cheese

Directions and Total Time: approx. 35 min + chilling time

Place the mozzarella cheese in the microwave for 2 minutes. Take out the bowl and allow cooling for 1 minute. Mix in egg yolk until well-combined.

Lay a parchment paper on a flat surface, pour the cheese mixture on top, and cover with another parchment paper. Flatten the dough into 1/8-inch thickness. Take off the parchment paper and cut the dough into penne-size pieces. Place in a bowl and refrigerate overnight. Bring 2 cups of water to a boil and add in the "penne". Cook for 1 minute and drain; set aside.

Heat oil in a pan and sauté bell peppers, squash, onion, and mushrooms. Cook for 5 minutes. Season with salt, pepper, and chili flakes. Mix in marinara sauce and cook for 5 minutes. Stir in penne and spread the mozzarella and Parmesan cheeses on top. Bake for 15 minutes. Serve.

Per serving: Cal 250; Net Carbs 5g; Fats 12g; Protein 31g

Balsamic Zoodles with Broccoli & Peppers

Ingredients for 4 servings

1 cup sliced mixed bell peppers
1 head broccoli, cut into florets
2 tbsp olive oil — 1 cup chopped kale
4 zucchinis, spiralized — 2 tbsp balsamic vinegar
4 shallots, finely chopped — ½ lemon, juiced
2 garlic cloves, minced — 1 cup grated Parmesan cheese
¼ tsp red pepper flakes — Salt and black pepper to taste

Directions and Total Time: approx. 20 minutes

Warm oil in a skillet and sauté broccoli, bell peppers, and shallots until softened, 7 minutes. Mix in garlic and red pepper flakes and cook until fragrant, 30 seconds. Stir in kale and zucchini spaghetti; cook until tender, 3 minutes. Mix in vinegar and lemon juice and adjust the taste with salt and pepper. Garnish with Parmesan cheese. Serve.

Per serving: Cal 201; Net Carbs 5.9g; Fats 13g; Protein 10g

Mushroom & Herb Pizza

Ingredients for 4 servings

2 ½ cups grated mozzarella cheese
2 medium cremini mushrooms, sliced
½ cup grated Parmesan — 1 tbsp erythritol
2 tbsp cream cheese, softened — 1 tsp dried oregano
½ cup almond flour — 1 tsp dried basil
1 egg, beaten — ½ tsp paprika
1 tsp olive oil — 6 black olives, sliced
1 garlic clove, minced — Salt and black pepper to taste
½ cup tomato sauce

Directions and Total Time: approx. 40 minutes

Preheat oven to 380 F. Line a pizza pan with parchment paper. Microwave 2 cups mozzarella cheese and 2 tbsp cream cheese for 1 minute. Mix in almond flour and egg. Spread the mixture on the pizza pan; bake for 5 minutes. Heat olive oil in a skillet and sauté mushrooms and garlic until softened, 5 minutes. Mix in tomato sauce, erythritol, oregano, basil, paprika, salt, and pepper. Cook for 2 minutes. Spread the sauce on the crust, top with the remaining mozzarella and Parmesan cheeses and olives. Bake for 15 minutes. Slice and serve.

Per serving: Cal 199; Net Carbs 2.6g; Fats 10g; Protein 23g

Dinner Vegetarian Pasta Mix

Ingredients for 4 servings

1 cup shredded mozzarella cheese
1 cup grated Parmigiano-Reggiano cheese
3 tbsp olive oil — 2 garlic cloves, minced
1 head broccoli, cut into florets — 1 tsp dried oregano
1 egg yolk — 3 tbsp balsamic vinegar
1 red bell pepper, sliced — 2 tbsp chopped walnuts
1 red onion, thinly sliced — Salt and black pepper to taste
1 lb green beans, halved

Directions and Total Time: approx. 30 min + chilling time

Place the mozzarella cheese in the microwave for 2 minutes. Let cool for 1 minute. Mix in egg yolk until well-combined. Lay a parchment paper on a flat surface, pour the cheese mixture on top and cover with another parchment paper. Flatten the dough into 1/8-inch thickness. Take off the parchment paper and cut the dough into mimicked penne-size pieces. Place in a bowl; refrigerate overnight. Bring 2 cups of water to a boil and add in keto penne. Cook for 1 minute and drain; set aside.

Heat olive oil in a skillet and sauté onion, garlic, green beans, broccoli, and bell pepper for 5 minutes. Season with salt, pepper, and oregano. Mix in balsamic vinegar, cook for 1 minute, and toss in the pasta. Garnish with Parmigiano-Reggiano cheese and walnuts. Serve.

Per serving: Cal 332; Net Carbs 7g; Fats 21g; Protein 19g

Oven-Baked Cauliflower with Shirataki

Ingredients for 4 servings

1 medium head cauliflower, cut into florets
2 (8 oz) packs spinach angel hair shirataki
1 cup heavy cream — 1 tsp smoked paprika
1 cup grated Monterey Jack — ½ tsp red chili flakes
1 tsp dried thyme

Directions and Total Time: approx. 45 minutes

Boil 2 cups of water in a medium pot over medium heat. Strain the shirataki pasta through a colander and rinse very well under hot running water. Allow proper draining and pour the shirataki pasta into the boiling water. Cook for 3 minutes and strain again. Place a dry skillet over medium heat and stir-fry the shirataki pasta until visibly dry, and makes a squeaky sound when stirred, 1 to 2 minutes. Set aside.

Preheat oven to 350 F. Bring 4 cups of water to a boil in a large pot and blanch the cauliflower for 4 minutes. Drain through a colander. In a bowl, mix cauliflower, shirataki, heavy cream, half of Monterey Jack cheese, thyme, paprika, and red chili flakes until combined. Transfer the mixture to a greased baking dish and top with the remaining cheese. Bake for 30 minutes. Serve.

Per serving: Cal 298; Net Carbs 13g; Fats 19g; Protein 12g

Artichoke & Kale Pizza

Ingredients for 4 servings

¼ cup grated Parmesan	½ cup almond flour
2 ½ cups grated mozzarella	½ cup chopped kale
6 tbsp cream cheese, softened	¼ cup chopped artichokes
1 egg, beaten	1 lemon, juiced
1 tsp Italian seasoning	½ tsp garlic powder
½ tsp garlic powder	Salt and black pepper to taste

Directions and Total Time: approx. 40 minutes

Preheat the oven to 370 F. Line a round pizza pan with parchment paper. Microwave 2 cups of mozzarella and 2 tbsp of cream cheese for 1 minute. Mix in egg, Italian seasoning, garlic powder, and almond flour.

Spread the mixture on the pizza pan and bake for 15 minutes; set aside. In a bowl, mix remaining cream cheese, kale, artichokes, lemon juice, garlic powder, Parmesan, remaining mozzarella, salt, and pepper. Spread the mixture on the crust and bake for 15 minutes. Serve sliced.

Per serving: Cal 219; Net Carbs 3g; Fats 9g; Protein 24g

Avocado & Tempeh Tacos

Ingredients for 4 servings

4 zero carb tortilla wraps	1 tsp smoked paprika
8 iceberg lettuce leaves	½ tsp cumin powder
1 tbsp olive oil	1 red bell pepper, chopped
2 tsp melted butter	1 avocado, halved and pitted
1 yellow onion, chopped	1 small lemon, juiced
½ cup tempeh, crumbled	¼ cup sour cream

Directions and Total Time: approx. 30 minutes

Preheat oven to 380 F. Divide each tortilla wrap into 2, lay on a chopping board, and brush with butter. Line 8 muffin tins with the tortilla and bake for 9 minutes.

Heat olive oil in a skillet and sauté onion for 3 minutes. Crumble tempeh into the pan and cook for 8 minutes. Stir in paprika and cumin and cook for 1 minute. To assemble, fit lettuce leaves into the tortilla cups, top with tempeh mixture, bell pepper, and avocado in this order, and drizzle with lemon juice. Add sour cream and serve.

Per serving: Cal 219; Net Carbs 3.6g; Fat 17g, Protein7g

One-Pot Enchilada Pasta

Ingredients for 4 servings

1 tsp olive oil	2 garlic cloves, minced
1 egg yolk	2 cups enchilada sauce
1 cup shredded mozzarella	1 tsp cumin powder
1 cup chopped bell peppers	½ tsp smoked paprika

1 tsp chili powder	1 avocado, pitted, sliced
¾ cup chopped green onions	Salt and black pepper to taste

Directions and Total Time: approx. 20 min + chilling time

Place the mozzarella cheese in the microwave for 2 minutes. Take out the bowl and allow cooling for 1 minute. Mix in egg yolk until well-combined. Lay a parchment paper on a flat surface, pour the cheese mixture on top and cover with another parchment paper. Flatten the dough into 1/8-inch thickness. Take off the parchment paper and cut the dough into penne-size pieces. Place in a bowl and refrigerate overnight. Bring 2 cups of water to a boil in a medium saucepan and add the keto penne. Cook for 1 minute and drain; set aside. Heat olive oil in a skillet and sauté garlic for 30 seconds. Mix in enchilada sauce, cumin, paprika, chili powder, bell peppers, salt, and pepper. Cook for 5 minutes. Mix in pasta. Top with green onions and avocado.

Per serving: Cal 149; Net Carbs 3.3g; Fats 10g; Protein 12g

Crunchy Tofu Bites with Cilantro Spread

Ingredients for 4 servings

28 oz tofu, pressed and cubed	1 cup golden flaxseed meal
1 egg, lightly beaten	1 ripe avocado, chopped
1 tbsp lime juice	½ tbsp chopped cilantro
4 lime wedges	Salt and black pepper to taste
½ cups olive oil	

Directions and Total Time: approx. 25 minutes

Warm the oil in a deep skillet. Coat tofu cubes in the egg and then in the flaxseed meal. Fry until golden brown. Transfer to a plate. Place avocado, cilantro, salt, pepper, and lime juice in a blender; puree until smooth. Spoon into a bowl, add tofu nuggets, and lime wedges to serve.

Per serving: Cal 659; Net Carbs 6.2g, Fat 49g, Protein 32g

Broccoli Nachos with Avocado Salsa

Ingredients for 4 servings

2 eggs, beaten	1 tsp cumin powder
¼ cup grated Monterey Jack	½ tsp garlic powder
2 heads broccoli, chopped	4 plum tomatoes, chopped
3 tbsp coconut flour	½ lime, juiced
1 tsp smoked paprika	4 sprigs cilantro, chopped
½ tsp coriander powder	1 avocado, chopped

Directions and Total Time: approx. 30 minutes

Preheat oven to 360 F. Pour broccoli in a food processor and blend into a rice-like consistency. Heat a skillet over low heat, pour in broccoli rice, and fry for 4-5 minutes. Transfer to a bowl. Line 2 baking sheets with parchment papers. To the broccoli, add coconut flour, paprika, coriander powder, cumin, garlic, and eggs. Mix and form into a ball. Divide the dough into two halves and form two crusts of equal size. Transfer them to the baking sheets and bake in batches for 10 minutes. Take out of the oven, cut into triangles, and sprinkle with Monterey Jack cheese; let cool. In a bowl, combine tomatoes, lime, cilantro, and avocado. Serve nachos with salsa.

Per serving: Cal 210; Net Carbs 4.5g, Fat 9g, Protein 7g

Shirataki Spaghetti with Roasted Vegetables

Ingredients for 4 servings

1 cup chopped mixed bell peppers
2 (8 oz) packs shirataki spaghetti

1 lb asparagus, chopped	1 small onion, chopped
1 cup broccoli florets	2 garlic cloves, minced
1 cup green beans, chopped	½ cup grated Parmesan
3 tbsp olive oil	1 cup diced tomatoes

Directions and Total Time: approx. 45 minutes

Pour 2 cups of water into a pot and bring it to a boil. Strain the shirataki pasta and rinse well under hot running water. Allow draining and pour the shirataki pasta into the boiling water. Cook for 3 minutes and strain again. Place a dry skillet and stir-fry the shirataki pasta until visibly dry, 1-2 minutes; set aside.

Preheat oven to 425 F. In a bowl, add asparagus, broccoli, bell peppers, and green beans and toss with half of the olive oil. Spread the vegetables on a baking sheet and roast for 20 minutes. Heat the remaining olive oil in a skillet and sauté onion and garlic for 3 minutes. Stir in tomatoes and cook for 8 minutes. Mix in shirataki and vegetables. Top with Parmesan cheese and serve.

Per serving: Cal 269; Net Carbs 7g; Fats 12g; Protein 9g

Pasta Primavera

Ingredients for 4 servings

½ cup grated Pecorino Romano cheese
2 cups cauliflower florets, cut into matchsticks

1 egg yolk	½ cup chopped green onions
¼ cup olive oil	1 cup grape tomatoes, halved
1 cup spring onions, sliced	2 tsp dried Italian seasoning
4 garlic cloves, minced	½ lemon, juiced
1 cup shredded mozzarella	2 tbsp chopped fresh parsley

Directions and Total Time: approx. 25 min + cooling time

Place the mozzarella cheese in the microwave for 2 minutes. Take out the bowl and let cool for 1 minute. Mix in egg yolk until well-combined. Lay a parchment paper on a flat surface, pour the cheese mixture on top and cover with another parchment paper. Flatten the dough into 1/8-inch thickness. Take off the parchment paper and cut the dough into penne-size pieces. Place in a bowl and refrigerate overnight. Bring 2 cups of water to a boil and add in penne. Cook for 1 minute and drain; set aside. Heat olive oil in a skillet and sauté onion, garlic, cauliflower, and spring onions for 7 minutes. Stir in tomatoes and Italian seasoning and cook for 5 minutes. Mix in lemon juice and "penne". Top with Pecorino Romano cheese and parsley and serve.

Per serving: Cal 279; Net Carbs 5g; Fats 20g; Protein 15g

Maple-Vanilla Custard Tart

Ingredients for 4 servings

6 whole eggs	¼ cup almond flour
3 egg yolks	5 tbsp coconut flour
¼ cup butter, cold	½ tsp salt

3 tbsp erythritol	1 ¼ cup almond milk
1 ½ tsp vanilla extract	1 ¼ cup heavy cream
½ cup Swerve sugar	2 tbsp sugar-free maple syrup
1 tsp vanilla bean paste	¼ cup chopped almonds

Directions and Total Time: approx. 75 minutes

Preheat oven to 360 F. Grease a pie pan with cooking spray. In a bowl, mix almond flour, 3 tbsp coconut flour, and salt. Add in butter and mix with your hands until crumbly. Add in erythritol and vanilla extract and stir. Pour in 4 eggs one after another while mixing until formed into a ball. Dust a clean flat surface with almond flour. Unwrap the dough, roll out the dough into a large rectangle, and fit into the pie pan; prick the crust base. Bake until golden. Remove after and allow cooling.

In a bowl, whisk the remaining 2 eggs, egg yolks, Swerve sugar, vanilla, and remaining coconut flour. Put the almond milk, heavy cream, and maple syrup into a pot and bring to a boil. Slowly pour the mixture into the egg mixture and whisk while pouring.

Run batter through a fine strainer into a bowl. Transfer the batter into the pie. Bake for 45 minutes. Garnish with almonds, slice, and serve.

Per serving: Cal 460; Net Carbs 1.2g, Fat 39g, Protein 12g

Avocado & Spinach Pasta

Ingredients for 4 servings

1 cup grated Pecorino Romano cheese for topping
1 cup shredded mozzarella cheese

1 cup baby spinach	½ cup almond milk
1 egg yolk	1 avocado, pitted and peeled
2 garlic cloves, minced	3 tbsp olive oil
1 lemon, juiced	Salt to taste

Directions and Total Time: approx. 15 min + chilling time

Place the mozzarella cheese in the microwave for 2 minutes. Take out the bowl; allow cooling for 1 minute. Mix in egg yolk until well-combined. Lay a parchment paper on a flat surface, pour the cheese mixture on top and cover with another parchment paper. Flatten the dough into 1/8-inch thickness. Take off the parchment paper and cut the dough into thick fettuccine strands. Place in a bowl and refrigerate overnight. Bring 2 cups of water to a boil in a saucepan and add the "fettuccine". Cook for 1 minute and drain; set aside. In a blender, combine garlic, lemon juice, spinach, almond milk, avocado, olive oil, and salt. Process until smooth. Pour "fettuccine" into a serving bowl, top with sauce, and mix. Sprinkle with Pecorino Romano cheese and serve.

Per serving: Cal 289; Net Carbs 5g; Fats 20g; Protein 18g

Goat Cheese & Sweet Onion Pizza

Ingredients for 4 servings

2 tbsp cream cheese, softened	1 tsp dried Italian seasoning
2 cups grated mozzarella	2 tbsp butter
1 cup crumbled goat cheese	3 red onions, thinly sliced
2 large eggs, beaten	1 tbs almond milk
⅓ cup almond flour	1 cup curly endive, chopped

Directions and Total Time: approx. 45 minutes

Preheat oven to 380 F. Line a round pizza pan with parchment paper. Microwave the mozzarella and cream cheeses for 1 minute. Remove and mix in eggs, almond flour, and Italian seasoning. Spread the dough on the pizza pan and bake for 6 minutes.

Melt butter in a skillet and stir-fry the onions on low heat with frequent stirring until caramelized, 15-20 minutes; set aside. In a bowl, mix goat cheese with almond milk and spread on the crust. Bake for 10 minutes. Scatter the caramelized onions, curly endive on top, slice, and serve.

Per serving: Cal 320; Net Carbs 3g; Fats 19g; Protein 28g

Baby Spinach Pizza

Ingredients for 4 servings

½ cup baby spinach	2 tbsp olive oil
1 cup grated mozzarella	1 cup lukewarm water
½ cup almond flour	½ cup tomato sauce
¼ tsp salt	3 tbsp sliced black olives
2 tbsp ground psyllium husk	1 tsp dried oregano

Directions and Total Time: approx. 35 minutes

Preheat oven to 380 F. Line a baking sheet with parchment paper. In a bowl, mix almond flour, salt, psyllium husk, olive oil, and water and stir until a dough forms. Spread the mixture on the sheet and bake for 10 minutes. Remove the crust and spread the tomato sauce on top. Add spinach, mozzarella cheese, oregano, and olives. Bake for 15 minutes. Slice and serve warm.

Per serving: Cal 201; Net Carbs 1.8g; Fats 9g; Protein 11g

Cranberry Zucchini Bars

Ingredients for 6 servings

3 eggs	1 ½ cups almond flour
2 tbsp olive oil	½ tsp baking powder
1 ¼ cups chopped zucchinis	1 tsp cinnamon powder
½ cup dried cranberries	A pinch of salt
1 lemon, zested	

Directions and Total Time: approx. 50 min + chilling time

Preheat oven to 360 F. Line a square cake tin with parchment paper. Combine zucchinis, olive oil, cranberries, lemon zest, and eggs in a bowl and stir well. Sift the almond flour, baking powder, cinnamon powder, and salt into the bowl and mix. Pour the mixture into the cake tin and bake for 30 minutes. Remove, allow cooling in the tin for 10 minutes, and transfer the cake to a wire rack to cool completely. Cut into squares and serve.

Per serving: Cal 119; Net Carbs 2.5g; Fat 9g; Protein 4g

Vegetable Egg Scramble & Grilled Cheese

Ingredients for 4 servings

½ lb halloumi, cut into ¼ to ½ inch slabs
2 cups cauliflower rice, steamed

4 eggs, beaten	1 green bell pepper, chopped
1 tbsp ghee	1 tsp soy sauce
¼ cup green beans, chopped	2 tbsp chopped parsley

Directions and Total Time: approx. 20 minutes

Warm the ghee in a skillet and pour in the eggs. Swirl the pan to spread the eggs around and cook for 1 minute. Move the scrambled eggs to the side of the skillet, add bell pepper and green beans, and sauté for 3 minutes. Pour in the cauli rice and cook for 2 minutes. Top with soy sauce; combine evenly, and cook for 2 minutes. Garnish with the parsley and set aside. Preheat a grill pan and grill halloumi cheese on both sides until the cheese lightly browns. Place on the side of the rice and serve.

Per serving: Cal 281; Net Carbs 4.5g, Fat 20g, Protein 15g

Hot Pizza with Tomatoes, Cheese & Olives

Ingredients for 2 servings

2 tbsp psyllium husk	2 tbsp Pecorino cheese
1 cup cheddar cheese	1 tsp oregano
2 tbsp cream cheese	½ cup almond flour

Topping

1 tomato, sliced	1 jalapeño pepper, sliced
4 oz cheddar cheese, sliced	½ cup black olives
¼ cup tomato sauce	2 tbsp basil, chopped

Directions and Total Time: approx. 40 minutes

Preheat the oven to 375 F. Microwave the cheddar cheese in an oven-proof bowl. In a separate bowl, combine cream cheese, Pecorino cheese, psyllium husk, almond flour, and oregano. Add in the melted cheddar cheese and mix with your hands to combine.

Divide the dough into two halves. Roll out the two crusts in circles and place them on a lined baking sheet. Bake for about 10 minutes. Spread the tomato sauce over the crust and top with the cheddar cheese slices, jalapeño pepper, and tomato slices. Return to the oven and bake for another 10 minutes. Garnish with olives and basil.

Per serving: Cal 576; Fat 42g; Net Carbs 7.5g; Protein 32g

Tex-Mex Tortilla Wraps with Veggies

Ingredients for 2 servings

2 tsp olive oil	1 cup cauli rice
2 low carb tortillas	Salt and black pepper to taste
1 green onion, sliced	¼ cup sour cream
1 bell pepper, sliced	1 tbsp Mexican salsa
¼ tsp hot chili powder	1 tbsp cilantro, chopped
1 large avocado, sliced	

Directions and Total Time: approx. 20 minutes

Warm the olive oil in a skillet and sauté the green onion and bell pepper until they start to brown on the edges, for about 4 minutes; remove to a bowl. To the same pan, add in the cauli rice and stir-fry for 4-5 minutes. Combine with the onion and bell pepper mixture, season with salt, black pepper, and chili powder. Let cool for a few minutes. Add in avocado, sour cream, and Mexican salsa and stir. Top with cilantro. Fold in the sides of each tortilla, and roll them in and over the filling to be enclosed. Wrap with foil, cut in halves, and serve.

Per serving: Cal 373; Fat 31g; Net Carbs 8.6g; Protein 7.6g

Halloumi & Cauliflower Couscous Parcels

Ingredients for 4 servings

2 tbsp olive oil
1 red bell pepper, chopped
1 orange bell pepper, chopped
2 heads cauliflower, chopped
¼ cup vegetable broth
1 lemon, juiced
2 tbsp sugar-free maple syrup
¼ cup cubed halloumi

Directions and Total Time: approx. 25 minutes

Preheat oven to 360 F. Put cauliflower in a food processor and pulse until a coarse consistency is achieved. Pour the couscous and broth into a pot and cook for 2-3 minutes. Drain and set aside.

In a bowl, whisk lemon juice and maple syrup; set aside. Cut out two 2 x 15 inches parchment papers onto a flat surface. Spoon the couscous in the middle of each, top with bell peppers, halloumi cheese, and drizzle the maple dressing on top. Wrap papers into parcels and place on a baking tray; cook for 15 minutes. Remove and carefully open the pouches. Serve warm.

Per serving: Cal 239; Net Carbs 4.7g, Fat 20g, Protein 5g

Broccoli & Mushroom Pizza

Ingredients for 4 servings

2 tbsp olive oil
1 ½ cups grated mozzarella
⅓ cup grated Parmesan
½ cup almond flour
¼ tsp salt
2 tbsp ground psyllium husk
1 cup sliced fresh mushrooms
1 white onion, thinly sliced
3 cups broccoli florets
2 garlic cloves, minced
½ cup sugar-free pizza sauce
4 tomatoes, sliced

Directions and Total Time: approx. 30 minutes

Preheat oven to 380 F. Line a baking sheet with parchment paper. In a bowl, put almond flour, salt, psyllium powder, 1 tbsp of olive oil, and 1 cup of lukewarm water and mix until a dough forms. Spread the mixture on the pizza pan and bake for 10 minutes. Heat the remaining olive oil in a skillet and sauté mushrooms, onion, garlic, and broccoli for 5 minutes. Spread the pizza sauce on the crust and top with the broccoli mixture, tomato, mozzarella, and Parmesan. Bake for 5 minutes. Serve sliced.

Per serving: Cal 190; Net Carbs 3.6g; Fats 10g; Protein 17g

Cheddar Quesadillas with Fruit Salad

Ingredients for 2 servings

1 cup grated cheddar cheese
1 cup mixed berries
2 large zero carb tortillas
2 green onions, chopped
½ tsp cinnamon powder
½ lemon, juiced
1 cup Greek yogurt
Sugar-free maple syrup to taste

Directions and Total Time: approx. 15 minutes

Top one tortilla with the cheddar cheese and green onions and cover with the other, pressing together. Place in a skillet and heat until golden and the cheese melted. Remove to a plate, allow cooling, and cut into four wedges. Combine berries, cinnamon powder, lemon juice, Greek yogurt, and maple syrup in a bowl. Divide into 2 bowls and serve with the quesadillas.

Per serving: Cal 141; Net Carbs 3g, Fat 14g, Protein 4g

Bell Pepper & Radish Bowls with Tofu

Ingredients for 4 servings

2 yellow bell peppers, chopped
¼ cup chopped baby Bella mushrooms
4 eggs
1 (14 oz) block tofu, cubed
2 tbsp olive oil
1 ½ cups shredded radishes
½ cup chopped white onions
1/3 cup tomato salsa
2 tbsp chopped parsley
1 avocado, chopped

Directions and Total Time: approx. 25 minutes

Warm 1 tbsp olive oil in a skillet and add the tofu, radishes, onions, mushrooms, and bell peppers; cook for 10 minutes. Share into 4 bowls. Heat the remaining oil in the skillet, crack an egg into the pan, and cook until the white sets, but the yolk quite runny. Transfer to the top of one tofu-radish hash bowl and make the remaining eggs. Top with tomato salsa, parsley, and avocado. Serve.

Per serving: Cal 349; Net Carbs 5.9g, Fat 25g, Protein 20g

Grilled Asparagus & Carrots

Ingredients for 4 servings

2 tbsp butter, melted
1 lb asparagus, trimmed
2 carrots, quartered lengthwise
1 tsp dried thyme
2 tbsp Parmesan, grated
Salt and black pepper to taste

Directions and Total Time: approx. 20 minutes

Set a grill pan over medium heat. Place asparagus and carrots in a bowl and season with salt, pepper, and thyme. Drizzle with butter. Add the veggies to the pan and sear for 10 minutes, turning often. Top with Parmesan. Serve.

Per serving: Cal 129; Net Carbs 3.6g, Fat 10g, Protein 6.9g

Three Cheese Pizza

Ingredients for 4 servings

3 tbsp grated Parmesan
1 cup sliced mozzarella
1 cup grated Gruyère
½ cup almond flour
2 tbsp ground psyllium husk
¼ tsp salt
1 tbsp olive oil
½ cup sugar-free pizza sauce
2 tsp Italian seasoning
1 cup lukewarm water

Directions and Total Time: approx. 35 minutes

Preheat oven to 380 F. Line a pizza pan with parchment paper. In a bowl, place almond flour, salt, psyllium husk, olive oil, and water and gently mix until dough forms. Spread the mixture on the pizza pan and bake for 10 minutes. Remove the crust and spread the pizza sauce on top. Add the sliced mozzarella, grated Gruyère, Parmesan cheese, and Italian seasoning. Bake for 18-20 minutes. Slice and serve.

Per serving: Cal 203; Net Carbs 3g; Fats 9g; Protein 20g

Stuffed Mushrooms

Ingredients for 4 servings

1 cup gorgonzola cheese, crumbled
¼ cup walnuts, chopped
2 tbsp olive oil
¼ tsp chili flakes
1 onion, chopped
1 garlic clove, minced
1 lb mushrooms, stems removed
Salt and black pepper, to taste
2 tbsp parsley, chopped

Put to a pan over medium heat and warm the olive oil. Sauté garlic and onion, until soft, for about 3 minutes. Sprinkle with black pepper and salt and remove to a bowl. Add in walnuts and gorgonzola cheese and stir until heated through. Divide the filling among the mushroom caps and set on a greased baking sheet. Bake for 30 minutes at 360 F. Remove to a wire rack to cool slightly. Sprinkle with chili flakes and parsley and serve.

Per serving: Cal 139; Fat 11g; Net Carbs 7.4g; Protein 4.8g

Balsamic Vegetables with Feta & Almonds

Ingredients for 4 servings

4 tbsp olive oil	2 garlic cloves, halved
1 red bell pepper, sliced	2 thyme sprigs, chopped
1 green bell pepper, sliced	1 tsp dried sage, crushed
1 orange bell pepper, sliced	2 tbsp balsamic vinegar
½ head broccoli, cut into florets	Salt and cayenne pepper, to taste
2 zucchinis, sliced	1 cup feta cheese, crumbled
8 white pearl onions, peeled	½ cup almonds, chopped

Directions and Total Time: approx. 45 minutes

Preheat oven to 375 F. Mix all vegetables with olive oil, seasonings, and balsamic vinegar; shake well. Spread the vegetables out in a baking dish and roast in the oven for 40 minutes or until tender, flipping once halfway through. Remove from the oven to a serving plate. Scatter the feta cheese and almonds all over and serve.

Per serving: Cal 276; Fat 23g; Net Carbs 7.9g; Protein 8.1g

Cauliflower-Based Waffles

Ingredients for 2 servings

1 cup zucchini, shredded and squeezed	
2 green onions	½ head cauliflower
1 tbsp olive oil	1 tsp garlic powder
2 eggs	1 tbsp sesame seeds
1/3 cup Parmesan cheese	2 tsp thyme, chopped
1 cup mozzarella, grated	

Directions and Total Time: approx. 25 minutes

Chop the cauliflower into florets, toss the pieces in a food processor, and pulse until rice is formed. Remove to a clean kitchen towel and press to eliminate excess moisture. Return to the food processor and add zucchini, green onions, and thyme; pulse until smooth and transfer to a bowl. Stir in the rest of the ingredients and mix to combine. Leave to rest for 10 minutes. Heat waffle iron and spread in the mixture evenly. Cook until golden brown, for about 5 minutes.

Per serving: Cal 336; Fat 21g; Net Carbs 7.2g; Protein 32g

Cauliflower & Celery Bisque

Ingredients for 4 servings

1 head cauliflower, cut into florets	
2 tbsp olive oil	4 cups vegetable broth
1 onion, finely chopped	½ cup heavy cream
1 garlic clove, minced	Salt and black pepper to taste
½ cup celery, chopped	1 tbsp parsley, chopped

Directions and Total Time: approx. 35 minutes

Set a large pot over medium heat and warm the olive oil. Add celery, garlic, and onion and sauté until translucent, about 5 minutes. Place in vegetable broth and cauliflower. Bring to a boil, reduce the heat and simmer for 15-20 minutes. Transfer the soup to an immersion blender and blend to achieve the required consistency. Stir in heavy cream and adjust the seasoning. Top with parsley. Serve.

Per serving: Cal 187; Fat 13g; Net Carbs 5.6g; Protein 4.1g

Habanero Coconut Pie

Ingredients for 4 servings

Filling

3 tbsp flax seed powder + 9 tbsp water	
2 avocados, peeled, chopped	½ tsp onion powder
2 eggs	¼ tsp salt
1 cup mayonnaise	½ cup ricotta cheese
2 tbsp fresh parsley, chopped	1 ¼ cups Parmesan, shredded
1 habanero pepper, chopped	

Piecrust

1 egg	1 tsp baking powder
4 tbsp coconut flour	1 pinch salt
4 tbsp chia seeds	3 tbsp coconut oil
¾ cup almond flour	4 tbsp water
1 tbsp psyllium husk powder	

Directions and Total Time: approx. 60 minutes

Preheat the oven to 350 F. In a food processor, add coconut flour, chia seeds, almond flour, psyllium husk powder, baking powder, salt, coconut oil, water, and 1 egg. Blend the ingredients until the dough forms into a ball. Line a springform pan with about a 12-inch parchment paper diameter and spread the dough in the pan. Bake for 10-15 minutes or until a light golden brown color is achieved. Put the avocado in a bowl and add the mayonnaise, remaining eggs, parsley, habanero pepper, onion powder, salt, ricotta and Parmesan cheeses. Combine well. Remove the piecrust when ready and fill with the creamy mixture. Level the filling with a spatula and continue baking for 35 minutes. Let cool before slicing and serving with a baby spinach salad.

Per serving: Cal 672; Fat 61g; Net Carbs 8.3g; Protein 21g

Baked Parmesan Brussels Sprouts

Ingredients for 4 servings

1 lb Brussels sprouts, halved	1 tbsp fresh chives, chopped
2 tbsp olive oil	2 tbsp Parmesan, shredded
Salt and black pepper, to taste	

Directions and Total Time: approx. 50 minutes

Set oven to 400 F and spread Brussel sprout halves and onion slices on a baking sheet. Season with black pepper and drizzle with olive oil; toss to coat. Roast in the oven for 30 minutes, until the vegetables become soft. Sprinkle with Parmesan cheese and bake for 5-10 more minutes until the cheese melts. Serve scattered with chives.

Per serving: Cal 179; Fat 9g; Net Carbs 8.6g; Protein 7.5g

Mozzarella & Bell Pepper Avocado Cups

Ingredients for 4 servings

½ cup fresh mozzarella, chopped
2 avocados
2 tbsp olive oil
1 green bell pepper, chopped
1 onion, chopped
½ tsp garlic puree
Salt and black pepper, to taste
½ tomato, chopped
2 tbsp basil, chopped

Directions and Total Time: approx. 15 min + cooling time

Halve the avocados and scoop out 2 teaspoons of flesh; set aside. Sauté olive oil, garlic, onion, and bell peppers in a skillet over medium heat for 5 minutes until tender. Remove to a bowl and leave to cool. Mix in the reserved avocado, tomato, salt, mozzarella cheese, and black pepper. Fill the avocado halves with the mixture and serve sprinkled with basil.

Per serving: Cal 273; Fat 22g; Net Carbs 6.9g; Protein 8.3g

Spicy Vegetarian Burgers with Fried Eggs

Ingredients for 2 servings

2 portobello mushrooms, chopped
1 garlic clove, minced
1 cup cauli rice
1 tbsp peanut butter
1 tbsp basil, chopped
1 tbsp oregano
Salt to taste
1 jalapeño pepper, minced
¼ red onion, sliced
2 eggs
2 low carb buns
2 tbsp mayonnaise
2 lettuce leaves

Directions and Total Time: approx. 25 minutes

Sauté the mushrooms and cauli rice in warm peanut butter for 5 minutes. Remove to a bowl and add in garlic, oregano, basil, jalapeño pepper, and salt and mix well to obtain a dough. Make 2 medium-sized burgers from the dough. Cook the burgers in the same butter for 2 minutes per side and transfer to a serving plate. Reduce the heat and fry the eggs. Cut the low carb buns in half. Add the lettuce leaves, burgers, eggs, red onion, and mayonnaise. Top with the other bun half.

Per serving: Cal 456; Fat 37g; Net Carbs 9.3g; Protein 19g

Root Vegetable Mash with Garlic & Basil

Ingredients for 4 servings

½ lb celeriac, chopped
½ lb parsnips, chopped
2 carrots, chopped
2 turnips, chopped
2 oz cream cheese
2 tbsp butter
1/3 cup sour cream
½ tsp garlic powder
2 tsp basil, chopped
Salt and black pepper to taste

Directions and Total Time: approx. 30 minutes

In a pot over high heat, place celeriac, parsnips, carrots, and turnips and cover with enough water. Bring to a boil for 5 minutes and then reduce the heat to low to simmer for 15 minutes. Drain the vegetables through a colander. Transfer to a large bowl and mash until smooth. Add in the cream cheese, butter, sour cream, garlic powder, salt, and black pepper. Sprinkle with basil and serve with pan-grilled salmon if desired.

Per serving: Cal 223; Fat 15g; Net Carbs 12.3g; Protein 4g

Chili Lover's Frittata with Spinach & Cheese

Ingredients for 2 servings

2 red and yellow chilies, roasted and chopped
2 tbsp olive oil
1 cup spinach, chopped
1 tbsp red wine vinegar
1 tbsp parsley, chopped
4 eggs
¼ cup Parmesan, grated
2 tbsp goat cheese, crumbled
½ cup salad greens

Directions and Total Time: approx. 20 minutes

In a bowl, mix vinegar, half of the olive oil, and chilies. Coat the salad greens with the dressing. In another bowl, whisk the eggs with parsley, spinach, and Parmesan.

Heat the remaining oil in the cast iron over medium heat and pour the egg mixture and half of the goat cheese. Let cook for 3 minutes, and when it is near done, sprinkle the remaining goat cheese on it and transfer the cast iron to the oven. Bake the frittata for 4 more minutes at 400 F. Garnish the frittata with salad greens and serve.

Per serving: Cal 316; Fat 28g; Net Carbs 4.1g; Protein 9.5g

Caprese Gratin

Ingredients for 2 servings

½ cup mozzarella cheese, cut into pieces
2 tbsp olive oil
1 cup watercress
10 cherry tomatoes, halved
1 tbsp basil pesto
½ cup mayonnaise
1 oz Parmesan, shredded
Salt and black pepper to taste

Directions and Total Time: approx. 30 minutes

Preheat the oven to 350 F. In a baking dish, mix the cherry tomatoes, mozzarella, basil pesto, mayonnaise, half of the Parmesan cheese, salt, and black pepper.

Level the ingredients with a spatula and sprinkle the remaining Parmesan cheese on top. Bake for 20 minutes or until the top is golden brown. Remove and allow cooling for a few minutes. Slice and dish into plates, top with some watercress, and drizzle with olive oil.

Per serving: Cal 450; Fat 41g; Net Carbs 5g; Protein 12g

Cauliflower & Broccoli Cakes with Cheese

Ingredients for 4 servings

½ head cauliflower, cut into florets
½ head broccoli, cut into florets
½ cup Parmesan, shredded
½ onion, chopped
½ cup almond flour
1 egg
½ tsp lemon juice
2 tbsp olive oil
Salt and black pepper to taste
2 tbsp chives, chopped
2 tbsp Greek yogurt

Directions and Total Time: approx. 30 minutes

Steam the cauliflower and broccoli in a pot filled with salted water for 10-12 minutes until tender. Drain and transfer to a bowl. Mash and add in the other ingredients, except for the olive oil. Season to taste and mix to combine. Place a skillet over medium heat and heat olive oil. Shape fritters out of the mixture. Fry for 3 minutes per side. Garnish with Greek yogurt, sprinkle with chives, and serve.

Per serving: Cal 155; Fat 15g; Net Carbs 4.2g; Protein 5.5g

Home-Bake Chili Macaroons

Ingredients for 4 servings

1 finger ginger root, peeled and pureed
3 egg whites
½ cup shredded coconut
1 tsp liquid stevia
¼ tsp chili powder
½ cup water
Chili threads to garnish

Directions and Total Time: approx. 25 minutes

Line a baking sheet with parchment paper. In a heatproof bowl, whisk ginger, egg whites, shredded coconut, stevia, and chili powder. In a pot over medium heat, bring to boil the water and place the heatproof bowl on the pot. Continue whisking the mixture until it is glossy, about 4 minutes. Do not let the bowl touch the water or be too hot to cook the eggs. Spoon the mixture into the piping bag and pipe out 40-50 little mounds on the lined baking sheet. Bake the macaroons in the oven for 15 minutes at 350 F. Once they are ready, transfer them to a wire rack, garnish with chili threads to serve.

Per serving: Cal 110; Fat 5.2g; Net Carbs 1.4g; Protein 8.3g

Greek-Style Stuffed Tomatoes

Ingredients for 2 servings

2 tomatoes
¼ cup feta cheese, crumbled
¼ cup Greek yogurt
1 egg
1 clove garlic, minced
2 tbsp fresh dill, chopped
Salt and black pepper, to taste
2 tbsp butter, softened

Directions and Total Time: approx. 45 minutes

Slice off the top of tomatoes and scoop out pulp and seeds; reserve the tomato tops. In a bowl, mix egg, salt, butter, black pepper, chopped tomato pulp, garlic, Greek yogurt, feta, and dill. Split the filling between tomatoes, cover each one with a tomato top, and place in a greased baking dish. Bake in the oven for 30 minutes at 390 F. Place on a wire rack and allow to cool for 5 minutes; serve along with fresh rocket leaves.

Per serving: Cal 293; Fat 23g; Net Carbs 5.1g; Protein 13g

Mushroom & Zucchini with Spinach Dip

Ingredients for 4 servings

Spinach Dip
3 oz spinach, chopped
1 avocado, halved and pitted
2 tbsp fresh lemon juice
1 garlic clove, minced
2 oz pecans
Salt and black pepper to taste
¾ cup olive oil

Zucchini
2 zucchinis, sliced
Salt and black pepper to taste
½ lb mushrooms, sliced
2 tbsp olive oil

Directions and Total Time: approx. 20 minutes

Place the spinach in a food processor along with the avocado pulp, lemon juice, garlic, and pecans. Blend the ingredients until smooth, then season with salt and pepper. Add in olive oil and process a little more. Pour the pesto into a bowl; set aside. Place the zucchinis and mushrooms in a bowl. Season with salt, pepper, and oil.

Preheat a grill pan over medium heat and cook both the mushroom and zucchini slices until browned on both sides. Plate the veggies and serve with spinach dip.

Per serving: Cal 683; Fat 72g; Net Carbs 5.5g; Protein 5.3g

Chili & Blue Cheese Stuffed Mushrooms

Ingredients for 2 servings

4 portobello mushrooms, stems removed
1 tbsp olive oil
1 cup blue cheese, crumbled
2 sprigs fresh thyme, chopped
½ chili pepper chopped
2 tbsp ground walnuts

Directions and Total Time: approx. 30 minutes

Preheat the oven to 360 F.

Place the mushrooms on a lined baking sheet. In a bowl, add the blue cheese, chili pepper, and thyme and mix to combine. Fill the mushrooms with the blue cheese mixture, top with walnuts, drizzle with olive oil and bake for 20 minutes. Serve with a mixed leaf salad.

Per serving: Cal 368; Fat 32g; Net Carbs 3.9g; Protein 18g

Traditional Greek Eggplant Casserole

Ingredients for 4 servings

2 eggplants, cut into strips
½ cup celery, chopped
½ cup carrots, chopped
1 white onion, chopped
1 egg
1 tomato, chopped
1 tsp olive oil
2 cups grated Parmesan
1 cup feta cheese, crumbled
2 cloves garlic, minced
1 tsp Greek seasoning
1 cup heavy cream
Salt and black pepper to taste

Sauce
2 tbsp butter, melted
½ cup mozzarella, grated
1 tsp Greek seasoning
2 tbsp almond flour

Directions and Total Time: approx. 50 minutes

Preheat the oven to 350 F. Heat olive oil in a skillet over medium heat and sauté the onion, garlic, tomato, celery, and carrots for 5 minutes; set aside to cool.

Mix the egg, 1 cup of Parmesan cheese, feta cheese, salt, and pepper in a bowl; set aside. Pour the heavy cream into a pot and bring to heat over a medium fire while continually stirring. Stir in the remaining Parmesan cheese and 1 teaspoon of Greek seasoning; set aside. Spread a small amount of the cream sauce at the bottom of the baking dish and place the eggplant strips in a single layer on top. Spread a layer of feta on the eggplants, sprinkle some veggies on it, and repeat the layering process from the sauce until all the ingredients are exhausted.

In a small bowl, evenly mix the melted butter, almond flour, and 1 teaspoon of Greek seasoning. Spread the top of the mousaka layers with this mixture and sprinkle with mozzarella cheese. Cover the dish with foil and place it in the oven to bake for 25 minutes. Remove the foil and bake for 5 minutes until the cheese is slightly burned. Slice the mousaka and serve warm.

Per serving: Cal 612; Fat 33g; Net Carbs 13.5g; Protein 36g

Feta & Baby Spinach Lasagna

Ingredients for 4 servings

2 tbsp butter	3 tbsp tomato paste
1 onion, chopped	½ tbsp dried oregano
1 garlic clove, minced	Salt and black pepper to taste
2 ½ cups feta, crumbled	1 cup baby spinach

Keto pasta

4 eggs	1 tsp salt
1 ½ cups cream cheese	5 tbsp psyllium husk powder

Cheese topping

2 cups heavy cream	Salt and black pepper
5 oz mozzarella, shredded	½ cup fresh parsley, chopped
2 oz Parmesan cheese, grated	

Directions and Total Time: approx. 60 minutes

Melt the butter in a pot over medium heat. Add in the onion and garlic and sauté until fragrant and soft, about 3 minutes. Mix in the tomato paste, oregano, salt, and black pepper. Pour in ½ cup of water, stir, and simmer until most of the liquid has evaporated.

While cooking the sauce, make the lasagna sheets. Preheat oven to 300 F Combine the eggs with the cream cheese and salt. Add the psyllium husk a bit while whisking, and allow the mixture to sit for a few more minutes.

Line a baking sheet with parchment paper and spread in the mixture. Cover with another parchment paper and use a rolling pin to flatten the dough into the sheet. Bake the batter in the oven for 10-12 minutes, remove after, take off the parchment papers, and slice the pasta into sheets that fit your baking dish.

In a bowl, combine the heavy cream and two-thirds of the mozzarella cheese. Fetch out 2 tablespoons of the mixture and reserve. Mix in the Parmesan cheese, salt, black pepper, and parsley. Set aside. Grease a baking dish with cooking spray and lay in one-third of the pasta sheet; spread half of the tomato paste on top, add another one-third set of the pasta sheets, the remaining tomato paste, and the rest of the pasta sheets.

Grease a baking dish with cooking spray, layer a single line of pasta, spread with some tomato sauce, 1/3 of the spinach, 1/3 of the feta cheese, and ¼ of the heavy cream mixture. Season with salt and pepper. Repeat layering the ingredients twice in the same manner, making sure to top the final layer with the heavy cream mixture and the reserved cream cheese. Bake in the oven for 30 minutes at 400 F or until the lasagna has a beautiful brown surface. Remove the dish, allow cooling for a few minutes, and slice. Serve the lasagna with a green salad.

Per serving: Cal 732; Fat 59g; Net Carbs 8.3g; Protein 43g

Roasted Cauliflower Gratin

Ingredients for 4 servings

1/3 cup butter	¼ cup almond milk
2 tbsp melted butter	½ cup almond flour
1 onion, chopped	1 ½ cups cheddar, grated
10 oz cauliflower florets	1 tbsp ground almonds
Salt and black pepper to taste	1 tbsp parsley, chopped

Directions and Total Time: approx. 35 minutes

Steam the cauliflower in salted water for 4-5 minutes. Drain and set aside. Melt the 1/3 cup of butter in a saucepan over medium heat. Sauté the onion for 3 minutes. Add the cauliflower, season with salt and pepper, and mix in almond milk. Simmer for 3 minutes. Mix the remaining melted butter with the almond flour. Stir in the cauliflower as well as half of the cheese. Sprinkle the top with the remaining cheese and ground almonds. Bake for 10 minutes in the preheated to 380 F oven until golden brown on the top. Serve sprinkled with parsley.

Per serving: Cal 455; Fat 38g; Net Carbs 6.5g; Protein 16g

Grilled Halloumi with Cauli-Rice

Ingredients for 4 servings

2 tbsp olive oil	¼ cup mint, chopped
4 oz halloumi, sliced	½ lemon juiced
1 cauliflower head, grated	2 tbsp almonds, chopped
¼ cup oregano, chopped	Salt and black pepper to taste
¼ cup parsley, chopped	1 avocado, sliced to garnish

Directions and Total Time: approx. 20 minutes

Heat a grill pan over medium heat. Drizzle the halloumi cheese with olive oil and add to the pan. Grill for 2 minutes on each side to be golden brown, set aside.

To make the cauli rice, add in the cauliflower and cook for 5-6 minutes until slightly cooked but crunchy. Stir in the oregano, parsley, mint, lemon juice, salt, and black pepper. Garnish the rice with avocado slices and almonds and serve with grilled halloumi.

Per serving: Cal 255; Fat 23g; Net Carbs 3.3g; Protein 7.6g

Smoked Vegetable Bake with Parmesan

Ingredients for 4 servings

2 tbsp olive oil	1 tsp turmeric
1 onion, chopped	Salt and black pepper, to taste
1 celery, chopped	½ tsp liquid smoke
2 carrots, sliced	1 cup Parmesan, shredded
½ lb artichokes, halved	2 tbsp chives, chopped
1 cup vegetable broth	

Directions and Total Time: approx. 40 minutes

Preheat oven to 360 F. Grease a baking dish with olive oil. Place in the artichokes, carrots, onion, and celery. Combine vegetable broth with turmeric, black pepper, liquid smoke, and salt. Spread the mixture over the vegetables and bake for about 25 minutes. Sprinkle with Parmesan cheese and return in the oven to bake for another 5 minutes until the cheese melts. Decorate with fresh chives and serve.

Per serving: Cal 231; Fat 15g; Net Carbs 9.3g; Protein 11g

Broccoli & Asparagus Flan

Ingredients for 4 servings

1 lb asparagus, stems trimmed	1 cup almond milk
1 cup broccoli florets	3 eggs
½ cup whipping cream	2 tbsp tarragon, chopped

Salt and black pepper to taste   2 tbsp butter, melted
2 tbsp Parmesan, grated   1 tbsp butter, softened

Directions and Total Time: approx. 65 minutes

Steam asparagus and broccoli in salted water over medium heat for 6 minutes. Drain and cut the tips of the asparagus and reserve for garnishing. Chop the remaining asparagus into small pieces.

In your blender, add the chopped asparagus, broccoli, whipping cream, almond milk, tarragon, salt, pepper, and Parmesan and process until smooth. Pour the mixture through a sieve into a bowl and whisk the eggs into it.

Preheat oven to 350 F. Grease ramekins with softened butter and share the asparagus mixture among them. Pour the melted butter over each one and top with 2-3 asparagus tips. Pour boiling water into a baking dish to a depth of 1 inch, place in the ramekins, and insert in the oven. Bake for 45 minutes or until their middle parts are no longer watery. Garnish with asparagus and serve.

Per serving: Cal 298; Fat 24g; Net Carbs 4.5g; Protein 17g

Mushroom & Cheese Cauliflower Risotto

Ingredients for 4 servings

3 tbsp olive oil   3 tbsp chives, chopped
1 onion, chopped   2 lb mushrooms, sliced
¼ cup vegetable broth   1 large head cauliflower, break
1/3 cup Parmesan cheese   into florets
4 tbsp heavy cream   2 tbsp parsley, chopped

Directions and Total Time: approx. 25 minutes

In a food processor, pulse the cauliflower florets until you attain a rice-like consistency. Heat 2 tbsp oil in a saucepan. Add the mushrooms and cook over medium heat for about 3 minutes, set aside. Heat the remaining oil and cook the onion for 2 minutes. Stir in the cauliflower and broth, and cook until the liquid is absorbed, about 7-8 minutes. Stir in the heavy cream and Parmesan cheese. Top with chives and parsley to serve.

Per serving: Cal 255; Fat 21g; Net Carbs 5.3g; Protein 10g

Mediterranean Eggplant Squash Pasta

Ingredients for 2 servings

2 tbsp butter   3 tbsp scallions, chopped
1 cup cherry tomatoes   1 cup green beans
2 tbsp parsley, chopped   1 tsp lemon zest
1 eggplant, cubed   10 oz butternut squash, spirals
¼ cup Parmesan cheese

Directions and Total Time: approx. 20 minutes

In a saucepan over medium heat, add the butter to melt. Cook the spaghetti squash for 4-5 minutes and remove to a plate. In the same saucepan, cook eggplant for 5 minutes until tender. Add the tomatoes and green beans, and cook for 5 more minutes. Stir in parsley, zest, and scallions, and remove the pan from heat. Stir in spaghetti squash and Parmesan cheese to serve.

Per serving: Cal 388; Fat 18g; Net Carbs 9.6g; Protein 12g

Mascarpone Blueberry Muffins

Ingredients for 6 servings

2 tbsp blueberries   2 large eggs
1 cup almond flour   2 tbsp mascarpone cheese
2 tsp ground cinnamon   2 tbsp heavy whipping cream
4 tbsp xylitol   4 tbsp butter, melted
¾ tsp baking powder   2 tsp lemon zest

Directions and Total Time: approx. 25 minutes

Preheat oven to 380 F. Combine the almond flour, cinnamon, xylitol, and baking powder in a bowl. Cream the eggs with an electric mixer at low speed in another bowl. Stir in mascarpone cheese, heavy cream, butter, and lemon zest. Gradually add in the flour mixture while beating until creamy. Divide the batter between 6 greased muffin cups. Top with the blueberries. Bake for 10-12 minutes, or until golden brown on top. Serve.

Per serving: Cal 162; Net Carbs 7.9g; Fat 15g; Protein 3.8g

Cajun Flavored Stuffed Mushrooms

Ingredients for 2 servings

1 lb cremini mushrooms, stems removed
2 tbsp coconut oil   1 bell pepper, chopped
½ head broccoli, cut into florets   1 tsp cajun seasoning mix
1 onion, chopped   Salt and black pepper, to taste
¼ cup almonds, chopped   1 cup Parmesan, shredded
1 garlic clove, minced

Directions and Total Time: approx. 40 minutes

Blend the broccoli in a food processor until they become small rice-like granules.

Set oven to 360 F. Bake mushroom caps until tender for 8-12 minutes. In a skillet, melt the coconut oil; stir in bell pepper, garlic, and onion and sauté until fragrant. Place in black pepper, salt, and cajun seasoning mix. Fold in broccoli rice and almonds. Separate the filling mixture among mushroom caps. Add a topping of Parmesan cheese and bake for 20 more minutes. Serve warm.

Per serving: Cal 423; Fat 25g; Net Carbs 9.5g; Protein 22g

Bok Choy & Tofu Stir-Fry

Ingredients for 4 servings

2 ½ cups baby bok choy, quartered lengthwise
2 cups extra firm tofu, cubed   2 garlic cloves, minced
5 oz butter   1 tsp chili flakes
1 tsp garlic powder   1 tbsp fresh ginger, grated
1 tsp onion powder   3 green onions, sliced
1 tbsp plain vinegar   Salt and black pepper to taste

Directions and Total Time: approx. 45 minutes

Warm half of butter in a wok over medium heat, add bok choy and stir-fry until softened. Season with salt, pepper, garlic and onion powders, and plain vinegar. Sauté for 2 minutes and set aside. Melt the remaining butter in the wok and sauté garlic, chili flakes, and ginger until fragrant. Put in tofu and cook until browned. Add in green onions and bok choy and cook for 2 minutes.

Per serving: Cal 691; Net Carbs 8g; Fat 64g; Protein 35g

VEGAN

Vegan Sandwich with Tofu & Lettuce Slaw

Ingredients for 2 servings

¼ lb firm tofu, sliced
2 low carb buns

1 tbsp olive oil

Marinade

2 tbsp olive oil
Salt and black pepper to taste
1 tsp allspice
½ tbsp xylitol
1 tsp thyme, chopped

1 habanero pepper, seeded and minced
2 green onions, thinly sliced
1 garlic clove

Lettuce slaw

½ small iceberg lettuce, shredded
½ carrot, grated
½ red onion, grated
2 tsp liquid stevia

1 tbsp lemon juice
2 tbsp olive oil
½ tsp Dijon mustard
Salt and black pepper to taste

Directions and Total Time: approx. 20 min + chilling time

In a food processor, blend the marinade ingredients for a minute. Pour the mixture over the tofu slices in a bowl. Place in the fridge to marinate for 1 hour. In a large bowl, whisk the lemon juice, stevia, olive oil, mustard, salt, and pepper. Stir in the lettuce, carrot, and onion; set aside.

Heat 1 teaspoon of oil in a skillet over medium heat. Remove the tofu from the fridge and cook it for 6 minutes on all sides. Remove to a plate. Add the tofu to the buns and top with the slaw. Serve.

Per serving: Cal 687; Fat 58g; Net Carbs 10.5g; Protein 23g

Grilled Cauliflower Steaks with Haricots Vert

Ingredients for 2 servings

1 head cauliflower, sliced lengthwise into 'steaks'
2 tbsp olive oil
2 tbsp chili sauce
1 tsp hot paprika
1 tsp oregano
Salt and black pepper to taste

1 shallot, chopped
1 bunch haricots vert, trimmed
1 tbsp fresh lemon juice
1 tbsp cilantro, chopped

Directions and Total Time: approx. 30 minutes

Preheat grill to medium heat. Steam the haricots vert in salted water over medium heat for 6 minutes. Drain, remove to a bowl, and toss with lemon juice.

In a bowl, mix the olive oil, chili sauce, hot paprika, and oregano. Brush the cauliflower steaks with the mixture. Place them on the grill, close the lid, and grill for 6 minutes. Flip the cauliflower and cook further for 6 minutes. Remove the grilled caulis to a plate; sprinkle with salt, black pepper, shallots, and cilantro. Serve with the steamed haricots vert.

Per serving: Cal 234; Fat 16g; Net Carbs 8.4g; Protein 5.2g

Tofu & Vegetable Stir-Fry

Ingredients for 2 servings

2 tbsp olive oil
1 ½ cups tofu, cubed

1 ½ tbsp flaxseed meal
Salt and black pepper to taste

1 garlic clove, minced
1 tbsp soy sauce, sugar-free
½ head broccoli, cut into florets

1 tsp onion powder
1 cup mushrooms, sliced
1 tbsp sesame seeds

Directions and Total Time: approx. 15 min + chilling time

In a bowl, add onion powder, tofu, salt, soy sauce, black pepper, flaxseed, and garlic. Toss the mixture to coat and allow to marinate in the fridge for 20-30 minutes. In a pan, warm the olive oil over medium heat. Add the broccoli, mushrooms, and tofu mixture and stir-fry for 6-8 minutes. Serve sprinkled with sesame seeds.

Per serving: Cal 423; Fat 31g; Net Carbs 7.3g; Protein 25g

Grilled Tofu Kabobs with Arugula Salad

Ingredients for 4 servings

14 oz firm tofu, cut into strips
4 tsp sesame oil
1 lemon, juiced
5 tbsp soy sauce, sugar-free

3 tsp garlic powder
4 tbsp coconut flour
½ cup sesame seeds

Arugula salad

4 cups arugula, chopped
2 tsp extra virgin olive oil
2 tbsp pine nuts

Salt and black pepper to taste
1 tbsp balsamic vinegar

Directions and Total Time: approx. 30 min + chilling time

Stick the tofu strips on the skewers, height-wise, and place them onto a plate. In a bowl, mix sesame oil, lemon juice, soy sauce, garlic powder, and coconut flour. Pour the soy sauce mixture over the tofu and turn in the sauce to coat. Cover the dish and place in the fridge for 2 hours.

Heat the griddle pan over high heat. Rool the tofu in the sesame seeds and grill until golden brown on both sides, about 12 minutes in total. Arrange the arugula on a serving plate. Drizzle over olive oil and balsamic vinegar and season with salt and black pepper. Sprinkle with pine nuts and place the tofu kabobs on top to serve.

Per serving: Cal 411; Fat 33g; Net Carbs 7.1g; Protein 22g

Steamed Bok Choy with Thyme & Garlic

Ingredients for 4 servings

2 lb Bok choy, sliced
2 tbsp coconut oil
2 tbsp soy sauce, sugar-free
1 tsp garlic, minced

½ tsp thyme, chopped
½ tsp red pepper flakes
Salt and black pepper to taste

Directions and Total Time: approx. 15 minutes

Place a pan over medium heat and warm the coconut oil. Add in garlic and cook until soft, 1 minute. Stir in the bok choy, red pepper, soy sauce, black pepper, salt, and thyme and cook until everything is heated through, about 5 minutes. Serve.

Per serving: Cal 132; Fat 9.5g; Net Carbs 3.5g; Protein 4.9g

Sticky Tofu with Cucumber & Tomato Salad

Ingredients for 4 servings

2 tbsp olive oil
12 oz tofu, sliced
1 cup green onions, chopped

1 garlic clove, minced
2 tbsp vinegar
1 tbsp sriracha sauce

Salad

1 tbsp fresh lemon juice	1 tsp fresh dill weed
2 tbsp extra virgin olive oil	1 cucumber, sliced
Salt and black pepper to taste	2 tomatoes, sliced

Directions and Total Time: approx. 15 min + chilling time

Put tofu slices, garlic, sriracha sauce, vinegar, and green onions in a bowl; allow to settle for approximately 30 minutes. Warm the olive oil in a skillet over medium heat. Cook tofu for 5 minutes until golden brown. In a salad plate, arrange tomatoes and cucumber slices, season with salt and pepper, drizzle lemon juice and extra virgin olive oil, and scatter dill all over. Top with the tofu and serve.

Per serving: Cal 371; Fat 31g; Net Carbs 7.7g; Protein 17g

Grilled Vegetables & Tempeh Shish Kebab

Ingredients for 4 servings

1 yellow bell pepper, cut into chunks
1 cup barbecue sauce, sugar-free

2 tbsp olive oil	1 red bell pepper, cut chunks
10 oz tempeh, cut into chunks	1 cup zucchini, sliced
1 red onion, cut into chunks	2 tbsp chives

Directions and Total Time: approx. 30 min + chilling time

In a pot over medium heat, pour 2 cups of water. Bring to boil, remove from heat and add the tempeh. Cover the pot and let tempeh steam for 5 minutes to remove its bitterness. Drain the tempeh. Pour the barbecue sauce into a bowl, add the tempeh to it, and coat with the sauce. Cover the bowl and marinate in the fridge for 2 hours. Preheat grill to medium heat. Thread the tempeh, yellow bell pepper, red bell pepper, zucchini, and onion.

Brush the grate of the grill with olive oil, place the skewers on it, and brush with barbecue sauce. Cook the skewers for 3 minutes on each side while rotating and brushing with more barbecue sauce. Once ready, transfer the kabobs to a plate and serve sprinkled with chives.

Per serving: Cal 228; Fat 15g; Net Carbs 3.6g; Protein 13g

Sauteed Spinach with Spicy Tofu

Ingredients for 4 servings

2 tbsp olive oil	2 tbsp Worcestershire sauce
14 oz block tofu, cubed	Salt and black pepper to taste
1 celery stalk, chopped	1 lb spinach, chopped
1 bunch scallions, chopped	½ tsp turmeric powder
1 tsp cayenne pepper	¼ tsp dried basil
1 tsp garlic powder	

Directions and Total Time: approx. 30 minutes

In a large skillet over medium heat, warm 1 tablespoon of olive oil. Stir in tofu cubes and cook for 8 minutes. Place in scallions and celery; cook for 5 minutes until soft. Stir in cayenne, Worcestershire sauce, black pepper, salt, and garlic; cook for 3 more minutes; set aside.

In the same pan, warm the remaining olive oil. Add in spinach and the remaining seasonings and cook for 4 minutes. Mix in tofu mixture and serve warm.

Per serving: Cal 205; Fat 12g; Net Carbs 7.6g; Protein 7.7g

Stir-Fried Brussels Sprouts with Tofu & Leeks

Ingredients for 4 servings

2 tbsp olive oil	½ lb Brussels sprouts, halved
2 garlic cloves, minced	½ red chili, seeded and sliced
1 leek, sliced	Salt and black pepper to taste
10 oz tofu, crumbled	Lime wedges to serve
2 tbsp soy sauce, sugar-free	

Directions and Total Time: approx. 25 minutes

In a saucepan over medium heat, warm the oil. Add the leek and garlic and cook until tender, about 3 minutes. Place in the soy sauce, red chili, and tofu. Cook for 5 minutes until the tofu starts to brown. Add in Brussels sprouts, season with black pepper and salt, and cook for 10 minutes while stirring frequently. Garnish with lime wedges. Serve and enjoy!.

Per serving: Cal 183; Fat 12g; Net Carbs 7.7g; Protein 13g

Peppers Stuffed with Mushrooms & "Rice"

Ingredients for 4 servings

2 lb mixed bell peppers, tops removed

2 tbsp olive oil	1 tsp dried oregano
1 head cauliflower, grated	1 tsp chili powder
1 cup mushrooms, sliced	2 tomatoes, pureed
1 onion, chopped	Sea salt and pepper, to taste
1 cup celery, chopped	2 tbsp parsley, chopped
1 garlic clove, minced	

Directions and Total Time: approx. 45 minutes

Preheat oven to 360 F. Warm the olive oil in a pan over medium heat. Add garlic, celery, and onion and sauté until soft and translucent, 3 minutes. Stir in chili powder, tomatoes, mushrooms, oregano, parsley, and cauliflower rice. Cook for 6 minutes until the cauliflower rice becomes tender. Season with salt and black pepper. Split the cauliflower mixture among the bell peppers. Set in a greased casserole dish and bake for 30 minutes until the skin of the peppers starts to brown. Serve with yogurt.

Per serving: Cal 233; Fat 8g; Net Carbs 6.4g; Protein 7.6g

Basil Tofu with Cashew Nuts

Ingredients for 4 servings

3 tsp olive oil	1 tsp cayenne pepper
1 cup extra-firm tofu, cubed	½ tsp turmeric powder
¼ cup cashew nuts	Salt and black pepper to taste
1 ½ tbsp coconut aminos	2 tsp sunflower seeds
3 tbsp vegetable broth	10 basil leaves, torn
1 garlic clove, minced	1 tbsp balsamic vinegar

Directions and Total Time: approx. 25 minutes

Warm olive oil in a frying pan over medium heat. Add in tofu and fry until golden, turning once, about 6 minutes. Pour in the cashew nuts and cook for 2 minutes. Stir in the remaining ingredients except for the balsamic vinegar and basil, set heat to medium-low, and cook for 5 more minutes. Drizzle with the balsamic vinegar, season to taste, sprinkle with basil, and serve.

Per serving: Cal 245; Fat 19g; Net Carbs 5.5g; Protein 12g

Stewed Vegetables

Ingredients for 4 servings

2 tbsp olive oil	1 head cabbage, shredded
1 shallot, chopped	2 cups green beans, chopped
1 garlic clove, minced	2 bell peppers, sliced
1 tsp paprika	Salt and black pepper to taste
1 carrot, chopped	2 tbsp parsley, chopped
2 tomatoes, chopped	1 cup vegetable broth

Directions and Total Time: approx. 45 minutes

Warm the olive oil in a saucepan over medium heat and sauté onion and garlic until fragrant, 2 minutes. Stir in bell peppers, carrot, cabbage, green beans, paprika, salt, and pepper for 4-5 minutes. Add vegetable broth and tomatoes and cook on low heat for 25 minutes to soften. Serve sprinkled with parsley.

Per serving: Cal 310; Fat 26.4g; Net Carbs 6g; Protein 8g

Portobello Bun Mushroom Burgers

Ingredients for 4 servings

½ cup roasted red peppers, sliced	
2 tbsp olive oil	1 zucchini, sliced
4 portobello mushroom caps	¼ cup tofu, crumbled
1 clove garlic	1 tbsp red wine vinegar
Salt and black pepper to taste	2 tbsp Kalamata olives, chopped
2 tomatoes, sliced	½ tsp dried oregano
1 cup guacamole	

Directions and Total Time: approx. 30 minutes

Crush the garlic with salt in a bowl using the back of a spoon. Stir in 1 tablespoon of oil and brush the mushrooms and each inner side of the buns with the mixture. Place the mushrooms in a preheated grill pan and grill them on both sides for 8 minutes until tender. Drizzle the zucchini with some olive oil, season with salt and pepper, and grill on both sides for 5-6 minutes.

In a bowl, mix the red peppers, olives, tofu, vinegar, oregano, and remaining oil; toss them. Assemble the burger: spread some guacamole on a slice of a mushroom bun, add 1-2 zucchini slices, a scoop of the vegetable mixture, a slice of tomato, and another slice of mushroom bun. Serve and enjoy!

Per serving: Cal 221; Fat 19g; Net Carbs 4.3g; Protein 4.5g

One-Pot Ratatouille with Pecans

Ingredients for 4 servings

2 tbsp olive oil	1 cloves garlic, sliced
1 eggplant, sliced	¼ cup basil leaves, chop half
1 zucchini, sliced	2 sprigs thyme
1 red onion, sliced	1 tbsp balsamic vinegar
14 oz canned tomatoes	½ lemon, zested
1 red bell peppers, sliced	¼ cup pecans, chopped
1 yellow bell pepper, sliced	Salt and black pepper to taste

Directions and Total Time: approx. 50 minutes

Place a casserole pot over medium heat and warm the olive oil. Sauté the eggplants, zucchinis, and bell peppers for 5 minutes. Spoon the veggies into a large bowl.

In the same pan, sauté garlic, onion, and thyme leaves for 5 minutes and return the cooked veggies along with the canned tomatoes, balsamic vinegar, chopped basil, salt, and pepper to taste. Stir and cover the pot. Cook the ingredients on low heat for 30 minutes. Stir in the remaining basil leaves and lemon zest. Adjust the seasoning. Serve and enjoy!

Per serving: Cal 188; Fat 13g; Net Carbs 8.3g; Protein 4.5g

Fennel & Celeriac with Chili Tomato Sauce

Ingredients for 4 servings

2 tbsp olive oil	½ fennel bulb, sliced
1 garlic clove, crushed	¼ cup vegetable stock
½ celeriac, sliced	Salt and black pepper to taste

Sauce

2 tomatoes, halved	1 chili, minced
2 tbsp olive oil	1 bunch fresh basil, chopped
½ cup onions, chopped	1 tbsp fresh cilantro, chopped
2 cloves garlic, minced	Salt and black pepper to taste

Directions and Total Time: approx. 35 minutes

Set a pan over medium-high heat and warm olive oil. Sauté the garlic for 1 minute. Stir in celeriac and fennel slices for 3-4 minutes, then pour in the stock; cook until softened, 5 minutes. Sprinkle with salt and pepper.

Brush the tomato halves with olive oil. Microwave for 15 minutes; get rid of any excess liquid. Remove the cooked tomatoes to a food processor; add the ingredients for the sauce and puree to obtain the desired consistency. Serve the celeriac and fennel topped with tomato sauce.

Per serving: Cal 145; Fat 15g; Net Carbs 5.3g; Protein 2.1g

Poppy Seed Coleslaw

Ingredients for 4 servings

Dressing

2 tbsp olive oil	1 lime, freshly squeezed
1 cup poppy seeds	Salt and black pepper to taste
2 tbsp green onions, chopped	¼ tsp dill, minced
1 garlic clove, minced	1 tbsp yellow mustard

Salad

½ head white cabbage, shredded	
1 carrot, shredded	2 tbsp Kalamata olives, pitted
1 shallot, sliced	

Directions and Total Time: approx. 15 minutes

In a bowl, whisk the olive oil, mustard, lime juice, garlic, salt, and black pepper green onions. Add the poppy seeds, dill, and green onions and mix well. Place cabbage, carrot, and shallot in a bowl and mix to combine. Transfer to a salad plate, pour the dressing over, and top with Kalamata olives to serve.

Per serving: Cal 235; Fat 17g; Net Carbs 6.4g; Protein 8.1g

Roasted Asparagus with Romesco Sauce

Ingredients for 4 servings

1 lb asparagus spears, trimmed	Salt and black pepper to taste
2 tbsp olive oil	½ tsp paprika

Romesco sauce

2 red bell peppers, roasted
2 tsp olive oil
2 tbsp almond flour
½ cup scallions, chopped
1 garlic clove, minced

1 tbsp lemon juice
½ tsp chili pepper
Salt and black pepper to taste
2 tbsp rosemary, chopped

Directions and Total Time: approx. 20 minutes

For the romesco sauce ingredients in a food processor. Pulse until the ingredients are evenly mixed. Set aside.

Preheat oven to 390 F. Line a baking sheet with parchment paper. Add asparagus spears to the baking sheet. Toss with 2 tbsp of olive oil, paprika, black pepper, and salt. Bake until cooked through for 9 minutes. Transfer to a serving plate, pour the sauce over, and serve.

Per serving: Cal 145; Fat 11g; Net Carbs 5.9g; Protein 4.1g

Parsnip & Carrot Strips with Walnut Sauce

Ingredients for 4 servings

2 tbsp olive oil
2 carrots, cut into strips
2 parsnips, cut into strips

½ cup water
Salt and black pepper to taste
1 tsp rosemary, chopped

Walnut sauce

½ cup walnuts
3 tbsp nutritional yeast
Salt and black pepper to taste

¼ tsp onion powder
½ tsp garlic powder
¼ cup olive oil

Directions and Total Time: approx. 20 minutes

Set a pan over medium heat and warm oil; cook the parsnips and carrots for 5 minutes as you stir. Add in water and cook for an additional 6 minutes. Sprinkle with rosemary, salt, and pepper; transfer to a serving platter.

Place all sauce ingredients in a food processor and pulse until you attain the required consistency. Pour the sauce over the vegetables and serve.

Per serving: Cal 338; Fat 28g; Net Carbs 9.7g; Protein 6.5g

Vegetable Stew

Ingredients for 4 servings

2 tbsp olive oil
1 turnip, chopped
1 onion, chopped
2 garlic cloves, pressed
½ cup celery, chopped
1 carrot, chopped
1 cup wild mushrooms, sliced
2 tbsp dry white wine

2 tbsp rosemary, chopped
1 thyme sprig, chopped
4 cups vegetable stock
½ tsp chili pepper
1 tsp smoked paprika
2 tomatoes, chopped
1 tbsp flaxseed meal

Directions and Total Time: approx. 35 minutes

Warm the olive oil in a pot over medium heat and cook onion, carrot, celery, mushrooms, paprika, chili pepper, and garlic for 5-6 minutes until tender; set aside.

Add the wine to the pan and stir to deglaze the pot's bottom. Place in thyme and rosemary. Pour in tomatoes, stock, reserved vegetables, and turnip and bring to a boil. Reduce the heat and allow the mixture to simmer for 15 minutes while covered. Stir in flaxseed meal to thicken the stew, 3 minutes. Plate into individual bowls and serve.

Per serving: Cal 164; Fat 11g; Net Carbs 8.2g; Protein 3.3g

Tofu & Hazelnut Loaded Zucchini

Ingredients for 4 servings

2 tbsp olive oil
12 oz firm tofu, crumbled
2 garlic cloves, pressed
½ cup onions, chopped
2 cups crushed tomatoes
¼ tsp dried oregano

Salt and black pepper to taste
¼ tsp chili pepper
2 zucchinis, cut into halves, scoop out the insides
¼ cup hazelnuts, chopped
2 tbsp cilantro, chopped

Directions and Total Time: approx. 55 minutes

Preheat oven to 390 F. Warm the olive oil in a skillet over medium heat and sauté the onion, garlic, and tofu for 5 minutes until softened. Place in scooped zucchini flesh, 1 cup of tomatoes, oregano, and chili pepper. Season with salt, and pepper and cook for 6 minutes. Pour the remaining tomatoes into a baking dish. Spoon the tofu mixture into the zucchini shells. Arrange the zucchini boats in the baking dish. Bake for about 30 minutes. Sprinkle with hazelnuts and continue baking for 5 to 6 more minutes. Scatter with cilantro to serve.

Per serving: Cal 234; Fat 18g; Net Carbs 5.9g; Protein 12g

Pumpkin & Bell Pepper Noodles with Avocado Sauce

Ingredients for 4 servings

½ lb pumpkin, spiralized
½ lb bell peppers, spiralized
2 tbsp olive oil
2 avocados, chopped
1 lemon, juiced and zested
2 tbsp sesame oil

2 tbsp cilantro, chopped
1 onion, chopped
1 jalapeño pepper, minced
Salt and black pepper to taste
2 tbsp pumpkin seeds

Directions and Total Time: approx. 20 minutes

Toast the pumpkin seeds in a dry nonstick skillet, stirring frequently for a minute until golden; set aside. Add in oil and sauté bell peppers and pumpkin for 8 minutes. Remove to a serving platter. Combine avocados, sesame oil, onion, jalapeño pepper, lemon juice, and lemon zest in a food processor and pulse to obtain a creamy mixture. Adjust the seasoning and pour over the vegetable noodles, top with the pumpkin seeds and serve.

Per serving: Cal 673; Fat 59g; Net Carbs 9.8g; Protein 23g

Curried Cauliflower & Mushrooms Bake

Ingredients for 4 servings

1 head cauliflower, cut into florets
1 cup mushrooms, halved
4 garlic cloves, minced
1 red onion, sliced
2 tomatoes, chopped

¼ cup coconut oil, melted
1 tsp chili paprika paste
½ tsp curry powder
Salt and black pepper to taste

Directions and Total Time: approx. 35 minutes

Set oven to 380 F. In a large bowl, toss the cauliflower, mushrooms, garlic, red onion, tomatoes, chili paprika paste, curry powder, coconut oil, black pepper, and salt to coat well. Spread out on a baking dish and roast for 20-25 minutes, shaking once. Serve warm.

Per serving: Cal 171; Fat 16g; Net Carbs 6.9g; Protein 3.5g

Roasted Cauliflower with Bell Peppers

Ingredients for 4 servings

1 lb cauliflower florets
2 bell peppers, halved
¼ cup olive oil
2 onions, quartered
Salt and black pepper to taste
½ tsp cayenne pepper

Directions and Total Time: approx. 45 minutes

Preheat oven to 425 F. Line a large baking sheet with parchment paper. Spread out the cauliflower, onion, and bell peppers on the sheet. Sprinkle with olive oil, black pepper, salt, and cayenne pepper and toss to combine well. Roast for 35 minutes as you toss in intervals until they start to brown.

Per serving: Cal 186; Fat 15g; Net Carbs 8.2g; Protein 3.9g

Tofu & Vegetable Casserole

Ingredients for 4 servings

1 ½ lb Brussels sprouts, shredded
10 oz tofu, pressed and cubed
2 tsp olive oil
1 cup leeks, chopped
1 garlic clove, minced
½ cup celery, chopped
½ cup carrot, chopped
1 habanero pepper, chopped
2 ½ cups mushrooms, sliced
1 ½ cups vegetable stock
2 tomatoes, chopped
2 thyme sprigs, chopped
1 rosemary sprig, chopped
2 bay leaves
Salt and black pepper to taste

Directions and Total Time: approx. 55 minutes

Set a pot over medium heat and warm oil. Add in garlic and leeks and sauté until soft and translucent, about 3 minutes. Add in tofu and cook for another 4 minutes. Add the habanero pepper, celery, mushrooms, and carrots. Cook as you stir for 5 minutes. Stir in the rest of the ingredients. Simmer for 25-35 minutes or until cooked through. Remove and discard the bay leaves. Serve.

Per serving: Cal 328; Fat 18g; Net Carbs 9.7g; Protein 21g

Tofu & Swiss Chard Dip

Ingredients for 4 servings

2 tbsp mayonnaise
2 cups Swiss chard
½ cup tofu, crumbled
¼ cup almond milk
1 tsp nutritional yeast
1 garlic clove, minced
2 tbsp olive oil
Salt and pepper to taste
½ tsp paprika
½ tsp mint leaves, chopped

Directions and Total Time: approx. 20 minutes

Fill a pot with salted water over medium heat and bring to a boil. Cook the Swiss chard for 5-6 minutes until wilted. Puree the remaining ingredients, except for the mayonnaise, in a food processor. Season with salt and pepper. Stir in the Swiss chard and mayonnaise to get a homogeneous mixture. Serve.

Per serving: Cal 136; Fat 11g; Net Carbs 6.3g; Protein 3.1g

Coconut Milk Shake with Blackberries

Ingredients for 2 servings

½ cup water
1 ½ cups coconut milk
2 cups fresh blackberries
¼ tsp vanilla extract
1 tbsp vegan protein powder

Directions and Total Time: approx. 5 minutes

In a blender, combine all the ingredients and blend well until you attain a uniform and creamy consistency. Divide in glasses and serve!

Per serving: Cal 253; Fat 22g; Net Carbs 5.6g; Protein 3.3g

One-Pot Mushroom Stroganoff

Ingredients for 4 servings

1 lb baby Bella mushrooms, cubed
3 tbsp olive oil
1 onion, chopped
2 cups vegetable broth
½ cup heavy cream
½ cup tofu, grated
½ tbsp dried Italian seasoning
Salt and black pepper to taste

Directions and Total Time: approx. 15 minutes

Warm the olive oil in a saucepan over medium heat, and sauté the onion for 3 minutes until soft. Stir in the mushrooms and cook until tender, about 5 minutes. Add the broth and stir. Cook for 4 minutes until the liquid reduces slightly. Pour in the heavy cream and tofu and stir for 3 minutes. Season with Italian seasoning, salt, and pepper. Simmer for 40 seconds and turn the heat off. Serve warm over a bed of spaghetti squash if desired.

Per serving: Cal 255; Fat 21g; Net Carbs 5.4g; Protein 7.8g

Cauliflower-Kale Dip

Ingredients for 4 servings

¼ cup olive oil
1 lb cauliflower florets
2 cups kale
Salt and black pepper to taste
1 garlic clove, minced
1 tbsp sesame paste
1 tbsp fresh lime juice
½ tsp garam masala

Directions and Total Time: approx. 15 minutes

In a large pot filled with salted water over medium heat, steam cauliflower until tender for 5 minutes. Add in the kale and continue to cook for another 2-3 minutes.

Drain, transfer to a blender, and pulse until smooth. Place in garam masala, oil, black pepper, fresh lime juice, garlic, salt, and sesame paste. Blend the mixture until well combined. Decorate with some additional olive oil. Serve and enjoy!

Per serving: Cal 185; Fat 16g; Net Carbs 3.9g; Protein 3.5g

Zucchini Pasta with Avocado & Capers

Ingredients for 4 servings

¼ cup sun-dried tomatoes, chopped
2 tbsp olive oil
4 zucchinis, spiralized
½ cup pesto
2 avocados, sliced
¼ cup capers
¼ cup basil, chopped
Salt to taste

Directions and Total Time: approx. 15 minutes

Cook zucchini spaghetti in half of the warm olive oil over medium heat for 4 minutes. Transfer to a plate. Stir in pesto, basil, salt, tomatoes, and capers. Top with avocado slices. Serve and enjoy!

Per serving: Cal 449; Fat 42g; Net Carbs 8.4g; Protein 6.3g

Roasted Tomato Bakes

Ingredients for 4 servings

3 tomatoes, sliced
2 tbsp olive oil
½ cup pepitas seeds
1 tbsp nutritional yeast
Salt and black pepper to taste
1 tsp garlic puree
2 tbsp parsley. chopped

Directions and Total Time: approx. 20 minutes

Preheat oven to 380 F. Place the tomatoes in a baking dish and drizzle the olive oil over them. In a food processor, add pepitas seeds, nutritional yeast, garlic puree, salt, and pepper and pulse until the desired consistency is attained. Press the mixture firmly onto each slice of tomato. Set the tomato slices on the prepared baking pan and bake for 10 minutes. Serve sprinkled with parsley.

Per serving: Cal 165; Fat 15g; Net Carbs 3.2g; Protein 6.2g

One-Pan Curried Tofu with Cabbage

Ingredients for 4 servings

2 tbsp coconut oil
3 tbsp olive oil
2 cups extra-firm tofu, cubed
½ cup grated coconut
1 tsp yellow curry powder
Sal and onion powder to taste
2 cups Napa cabbage
Lemon wedges for serving

Directions and Total Time: approx. 20 minutes

In a bowl, mix grated coconut, curry powder, salt, and onion powder. Toss in tofu. Heat the coconut oil in a skillet and fry tofu until golden brown; transfer to a plate, 6-8 minutes. In the same skillet, sauté the cabbage for 5-6 minutes until slightly caramelized. Plate the cabbage and serve with tofu and lemon wedges.

Per serving: Cal 729; Net Carbs 4g; Fat 61g; Protein 36g

Sauteed Tofu with Pistachios

Ingredients for 4 servings

2 tbsp olive oil
8 oz firm tofu, cubed
1 tbsp tomato paste
1 tbsp balsamic vinegar
1 tsp garlic powder
1 tsp onion powder
Salt and black pepper to taste
1 cup pistachios, chopped

Directions and Total Time: approx. 20 minutes

Heat the oil in a skillet over medium heat and cook the tofu for 3 minutes while stirring until brown. Mix the tomato paste, garlic powder, onion powder, and vinegar; add to the tofu. Stir, season with salt and black pepper, and cook for another 4 minutes. Add the pistachios. Stir and cook on low heat for 3 minutes until fragrant.

Per serving: Cal 335; Fat 27g; Net Carbs 6.3g; Protein 16g

Coconut Green Soup

Ingredients for 4 servings

1 broccoli head, chopped
1 cup spinach
1 onion, chopped
1 garlic clove, minced
½ cup leeks
3 cups vegetable stock
½ cup coconut milk
2 tbsp coconut oil
1 bay leaf
Salt and black pepper to taste
2 tbsp coconut yogurt

Directions and Total Time: approx. 30 minutes

Warm coconut oil in a large pot over medium heat. Add onion, leeks, and garlic and cook for 5 minutes. Add broccoli and cook for an additional 5 minutes. Pour in the stock over and add the bay leaf. Bring to a boil, then reduce the heat. Simmer for about 10 minutes.

Add spinach and cook for 3 more minutes. Discard the bay leaf and blend the soup with a hand blender. Stir in the coconut milk and adjust the seasoning. Divide among serving bowls and garnish with a swirl of coconut yogurt. Serve and enjoy!

Per serving: Cal 272; Fat 25g; Net Carbs 4.3g; Protein 4.5g

Chocolate Nut Granola

Ingredients for 4 servings

¼ cup cocoa powder
1/3 tbsp coconut oil, melted
¼ cup almond flakes
¼ cup almond milk
¼ tbsp xylitol
1/8 tsp salt
1/3 tsp lime zest
¼ tsp ground cinnamon
¼ cup almonds, slivered
1 tbsp pumpkin seeds
2 tbsp sunflower seeds
2 tbsp flaxseed

Directions and Total Time: approx. 40 minutes

Preheat oven to 350 F. Mix almond flakes, cocoa powder, ground cinnamon, almonds, xylitol, pumpkin seeds, sunflower seeds, flaxseed, and salt in a bowl. In a separate bowl, whisk coconut oil, almond milk, and lime zest until combined. Pour over the seed mixture and stir to coat. Lay the mixture in an even layer onto a parchment-lined baking pan baking dish. Bake for 20-25 minutes, making sure that you shake gently in intervals of 5 minutes. Let cool completely before serving. Enjoy!

Per serving: Cal 273; Fat 26g; Net Carbs 8.9g; Protein 4.6g

Kale with Carrot Noodles

Ingredients for 4 servings

4 tbsp olive oil
2 carrots, spiralized
¼ cup vegetable broth
1 garlic clove, minced
1 cup chopped kale
Salt and black pepper to serve

Directions and Total Time: approx. 20 minutes

Warm olive oil in a skillet over medium heat and sauté carrots for 4-5 minutes until crisp-tender; remove to a plate. Add the garlic and kale to the skillet and stir-fry until the kale is wilted, 4-5 minutes. Return the carrots, season with salt and pepper, and stir-fry for 4 minutes. Serve.

Per serving: Cal 341; Net Carbs 8g; Fat 28g; Protein 6g

Vegan Smoothie

Ingredients for 4 servings

1 tbsp vegan protein powder, zero carbs
1 cup cantaloupe, chopped
1 cup fresh blueberries
2 cups coconut milk
½ cup coconut cream

Directions and Total Time: approx. 10 minutes

Pulse all ingredients in a blender until smooth. Serve.

Per serving: Cal 341; Net Carbs 8g; Fat 28g; Protein 6g

SNACKS & APPETIZERS

Mushrooms Filled with Walnuts & Cheese

Ingredients for 4 servings

½ cup grated Pecorino Romano cheese
12 button mushrooms, stemmed
¼ cup olive oil
¼ cup pork rinds
2 garlic cloves, minced
2 tbsp chopped fresh parsley
¼ cup ground walnuts
Salt and black pepper to taste

Directions and Total Time: approx. 35 minutes

Preheat oven to 400 F. In a bowl, mix pork rinds, Pecorino Romano cheese, garlic, parsley, salt, and pepper. Brush a baking sheet with some oil. Spoon the cheese mixture into the mushrooms and arrange them on the baking sheet. Top with the ground walnuts and drizzle the remaining olive oil on the top. Bake for 20 minutes or until golden. Transfer to a platter and serve.

Per serving: Cal 289; Net Carbs 6.9g; Fat 25g; Protein 8g

Italian Meatballs

Ingredients for 4 servings

½ lb ground Italian sausage
½ lb ground beef
2 eggs
¾ cup pork rinds
½ cup grated Parmesan cheese
1 tsp onion powder
1 tsp garlic powder
1 tbsp chopped fresh basil
2 tsp dried Italian seasoning
3 tbsp olive oil
2 ½ cups marinara sauce
Salt and black pepper to taste

Directions and Total Time: approx. 50 minutes

In a bowl, add ground beef, Italian sausage, pork rinds, Parmesan cheese, eggs, onion powder, garlic powder, basil, salt, pepper, and Italian seasoning. Form meatballs out of the mixture. Heat the olive oil in a skillet and brown the meatballs for 10 minutes. Pour in marinara sauce and submerge the meatballs in the sauce; cook for 30 minutes. Serve and enjoy!

Per serving: Cal 509; Net Carbs 8.2g; Fat 24g; Protein 35g

Avocado & Cauliflower Burritos

Ingredients for 2 servings

1 tbsp butter
5 oz cauliflower florets
2 pieces of zero carb flatbread
1 cup yogurt
1 cup tomato salsa
1 avocado, sliced
1 tbsp cilantro, chopped
Salt and black pepper to taste

Directions and Total Time: approx. 15 minutes

Put the cauliflower in a food processor and pulse until it resembles rice. In a skillet, melt the butter and add the cauli rice. Sauté for 4-5 minutes until cooked through. Season with salt and black pepper.

On flatbread, spread the yogurt all over and distribute the salsa on top. Top with cauli rice and scatter the avocado slices and cilantro on top. Fold and tuck the burritos and cut them into two. Serve and enjoy!

Per serving: Cal 457; Fat 31g; Net Carbs 9.5g; Protein 16g

Naan Breakfast Bread

Ingredients for 6 servings

¼ cup olive oil
8 oz butter
¾ cup almond flour
2 tbsp psyllium husk powder
1 tsp salt
½ tsp baking powder
2 cups boiling water
2 garlic cloves, minced

Directions and Total Time: approx. 25 minutes

Mix the almond flour, psyllium husk powder, ½ teaspoon of salt, and baking powder in a bowl. Pour in olive oil and boiling water to combine the ingredients like a thick porridge. Stir and allow the dough for 5 minutes. Divide the dough into 6 pieces and mold into balls. Place the balls on wax paper and flatten. Melt half of the butter in a frying pan over medium heat and fry the naan on both sides to have a golden color. Transfer to a plate and keep warm. Add the remaining butter to the pan and sauté garlic until fragrant, about 1 minute. Pour the garlic butter into a bowl and serve as a dip along with the naan.

Per serving: Cal 229; Net Carbs 3g; Fat 21g; Protein 4g

Hot Feta Bites

Ingredients for 4 servings

1 egg
2 tbsp butter
1/3 cup mayonnaise
¼ cup pickled jalapenos
1 tsp paprika
1 tbsp mustard powder
1 pinch of cayenne pepper
4 oz grated cheddar
2 ½ cups crumbled feta
Salt and black pepper to taste

Directions and Total Time: approx. 20 minutes

In a bowl, mix mayonnaise, jalapenos, paprika, mustard, cayenne, and cheddar cheese. Add in the egg, crumbled feta, salt, and pepper; mix well. Form balls out of the mix. Melt butter in a skillet over medium heat and fry balls until cooked and browned on the outside, about 5-6 minutes. Serve and enjoy!

Per serving: Cal 649; Net Carbs 2g; Fat 48g; Protein 43g

Leafy Greens & Cheddar Quesadillas

Ingredients for 4 servings

1 tbsp butter, softened
½ cup cream cheese
3 eggs
1½ tsp psyllium husk powder
1 tbsp coconut flour
½ tsp salt
5 oz grated cheddar cheese
1 oz leafy greens

Directions and Total Time: approx. 25 minutes

Preheat oven to 400 F. In a bowl, whisk the eggs with cream cheese. In another bowl, combine psyllium husk, coconut flour, and salt. Add in the egg mixture and mix until fully incorporated. Let sit for a few minutes.

Line a baking sheet with parchment paper and pour in half of the mixture. Bake the tortilla for 7 minutes until brown around the edges. Repeat with the remaining batter. Grease a skillet with the butter and place in a tortilla. Sprinkle with cheddar cheese, leafy greens and cover with another tortilla. Brown each side for 1 minute.

Per serving: Cal 468; Net Carbs 4g; Fat 40g; Protein 19g

Cheese & Nut Zucchini Boats

Ingredients for 4 servings

2 medium zucchinis, halved	¼ cup pine nuts
1 cup cauliflower rice	¼ cup hazelnuts
2 tbsp olive oil	1 tbsp balsamic vinegar
¼ cup vegetable broth	1 tbsp smoked paprika
1 ¼ cup diced tomatoes	1 cup grated Monterey Jack
1 red onion, chopped	4 tbsp chopped cilantro

Directions and Total Time: approx. 35 minutes

Preheat oven to 350 F. Pour cauli rice and broth in a pot and cook for 5 minutes. Fluff the cauli rice and allow cooling. Scoop the flesh out of the zucchini halves and chop the pulp. Brush the zucchini shells with some olive oil. In a bowl, mix cauli rice, tomatoes, red onion, pine nuts, hazelnuts, cilantro, vinegar, paprika, and zucchini pulp. Spoon the mixture into the zucchini halves, drizzle with remaining olive oil, and sprinkle the cheese on top. Bake for 20 minutes until the cheese melts. Serve.

Per serving: Cal 328; Net Carbs 4.9g; Fat 31g; Protein 12g

Baked Eggplant Chips with Salad & Aioli

Ingredients for 4 servings

2 eggplants, sliced	2 garlic cloves, minced
1 egg, beaten	1 cup olive oil
3 ½ oz cooked beets, shredded	½ tsp red chili flakes
3 ½ oz red cabbage, shredded	2 tbsp lemon juice
2 cups almond flour	3 tbsp yogurt
2 tbsp butter, melted	2 tbsp fresh cilantro, chopped
2 egg yolks	Salt and black pepper to taste

Directions and Total Time: approx. 30 minutes

Preheat oven to 400 F. On a deep plate, mix flour, salt, and pepper. Dip eggplants into the egg, then in the flour. Place on a greased baking sheet and brush with butter. Bake for 15 minutes. To make aioli, whisk egg yolks with garlic. Gradually pour in ¾ cup olive oil while whisking. Stir in chili flakes, salt, pepper, 1 tbsp of lemon juice, and yogurt. In a salad bowl, mix beets, cabbage, cilantro, remaining oil, remaining lemon juice, salt, and pepper; toss to coat. Serve the fries with the aioli and beet salad.

Per serving: Cal 847; Net Carbs 8g; Fat 81g; Protein 26g

Mushroom & Cheese Lettuce Wraps

Ingredients for 4 servings

1 iceberg lettuce, leaves extracted	
4 oz baby Bella mushrooms, sliced	
1 cup grated cheddar cheese	1 lb goat cheese, crumbled
2 tbsp butter	1 large tomato, sliced

Directions and Total Time: approx. 20 minutes

Warm butter in a skillet over medium heat. Add mushrooms and sauté until tender, 6 minutes. Add in goat cheese and cook for 5 minutes, stirring occasionally. Spoon the mixture into the lettuce leaves, sprinkle with cheddar cheese, and top with tomato slices. Serve.

Per serving: Cal 617; Net Carbs 3g; Fat 52g; Protein 32g

Camembert Bites with Blackberry Sauce

Ingredients for 4 servings

For the pastry cups

¼ cup butter, cold and crumbled	
¼ cup almond flour	3 whole eggs, unbeaten
3 tbsp coconut flour	1 whole egg, beaten
½ tsp xanthan gum	1 ½ tsp vanilla extract
¼ tsp cream of tartar	3 tbsp erythritol
4 tbsp cream cheese, softened	½ tsp salt

For the filling

5 oz Camembert, sliced and cut into 16 cubes	
½ cup fresh blackberries	3 tbsp red wine
1 tsp butter	1 tbsp balsamic vinegar
1 yellow onion, chopped	5 tbsp erythritol

Directions and Total Time: approx. 40 min + chilling time

Preheat oven to 360 F. Turn a muffin tray upside down and lightly grease with cooking spray. In a bowl, mix almond and coconut flours, xanthan gum, and salt. Add in cream cheese, cream of tartar, and butter and mix until crumbly. Stir in erythritol and vanilla extract until mixed. Then, pour in three eggs, one after another, while mixing until formed into a ball. Flatten the dough on a clean flat surface, cover with plastic wrap, and refrigerate for 1 hour. Dust a clean flat surface with almond flour, unwrap the dough, and roll out the dough into a large rectangle. Cut into 16 squares and press each onto each muffin mound on the tray to form a bowl shape. Brush with the beaten egg and bake for 10 minutes.

To make the filling, melt butter in a skillet and sauté onion for 3 minutes. Stir in red wine, balsamic vinegar, erythritol, and blackberries. Cook until the berries become jammy and wine reduces, 10 minutes. Set aside. Take out the tray and place cheese cubes in each pastry. Return to oven and bake for 3 minutes. Spoon a tsp each of the blackberry sauce on top. Serve and enjoy!

Per serving: Cal 369; Net Carbs 4.4g; Fat 32g, Protein 14g

Basil Spinach & Zucchini Lasagna

Ingredients for 4 servings

2 zucchinis, sliced	3 cups tomato sauce
Salt and black pepper to taste	1 cup spinach
2 cups feta cheese	1 tbsp basil, chopped
2 cups mozzarella, shredded	

Directions and Total Time: approx. 50 minutes

Preheat oven to 370 F. Mix feta, mozzarella cheese, salt, and pepper to evenly combine and spread ¼ cup of the mixture at the bottom of a greased baking dish. Layer 1/3 of the zucchini slices on top, spread 1 cup of tomato sauce over, and scatter a 1/3 cup of spinach on top.

Repeat the layering process two more times to exhaust the ingredients while finally making sure to layer with the last ¼ cup of cheese mixture. Bake for 35 minutes until the cheese has a nice golden brown color. Remove the dish, sit for 5 minutes and serve sprinkled with basil.

Per serving: Cal 411; Fat 43g; Net Carbs 3.2g; Protein 6.5g

Cauli Rice Arancini

Ingredients for 4 servings

2 tbsp butter	¼ cup white wine
2 tbsp olive oil	¼ cup vegetable stock
2 eggs	¼ cup grated Parmesan
1 white onion, finely chopped	½ cup ricotta cheese
2 scallions, chopped	1 cup almond flour
2 garlic cloves, minced	½ cup golden flaxseed meal
1 cup cauli rice	Salt and black pepper to taste

Directions and Total Time: approx. 30 minutes

Heat butter in a saucepan over medium heat. Stir in garlic and onion and cook until fragrant and soft, 3 minutes. Mix in cauli rice for 30 seconds; add in wine, stir, allow reduction and absorption into cauli rice.

Add in vegetable stock, salt, pepper, remaining butter, Parmesan and ricotta cheeses. Cover the pot and cook until the liquid reduces and the "rice" thickens. Open the lid, stir well, and spoon the mixture into a bowl to cool. Mold the dough into mini patties, 14-16 pieces; set aside.

Heat olive oil in a skillet over medium heat. Pour the almond flour onto a plate, the golden flaxseed meal in another, and beat the eggs in a medium bowl. Lightly dredge each patty in the flour, then in eggs, and then coat them in the flaxseed meal. Fry in the oil until compacted and golden brown, 2 minutes per side. Garnish with scallions and serve.

Per serving: Cal 359; Net Carbs 6.2g, Fat 29g, Protein 13g

Flaxseed Toasts with Avocado Paté

Ingredients for 4 servings

1 pinch of salt	½ cup flaxseed meal

For the avocado paté

3 ripe avocados, chopped	1 lemon, zested and juiced
4 tbsp Greek yogurt	Black pepper to taste
2 tbsp chopped green onions	Smoked paprika to garnish

Directions and Total Time: approx. 25 minutes

Preheat oven to 350 F. Place a skillet over medium heat. Put in flaxseed meal, ¼ cup water, and salt and mix continually to form the dough into a ball. Place the dough between 2 parchment papers, place on a flat surface, and flatten thinly with a rolling pin. Remove the papers and cut the pastry into tortilla chips.

Place on a baking sheet and bake for 8-12 minutes or until crispy. In a bowl, mix avocados, yogurt, green onions, lemon zest and juice, and black pepper until evenly combined. Spread the paté on the toasts and garnish with paprika. Serve immediately.

Per serving: Cal 359; Net Carbs 4g, Fat 31g, Protein 7g

Caramelized Onion & Cream Cheese Spread

Ingredients for 4 servings

2 cups sour cream	3 yellow onions, thinly sliced
8 oz cream cheese, softened	1 tsp Swerve sugar
½ tbsp Worcestershire sauce	¼ cup white wine
2 tbsp butter	Salt to taste

Directions and Total Time: approx. 35 minutes

Melt the butter in a skillet over medium heat. Add in the onions, Swerve sugar, and salt. Cook with frequent stirring for 10-15 minutes. Add in white wine, stir, and allow sizzling out, 10 minutes. In a serving bowl, mix sour cream and cream cheese. Add in caramelized onions and Worcestershire sauce and stir well into the cream. Serve with celery sticks if desired.

Per serving: Cal 379; Net Carbs 8g; Fat 34g; Protein 8g

Maple Tahini Straws

Ingredients for 4 servings

For the puff pastry

3 tbsp coconut flour	¼ teaspoon cream of tartar
¼ cup almond flour	¼ cup butter, cold
½ tsp xanthan gum	3 tbsp erythritol
3 whole eggs	1 tsp vanilla extract
4 tbsp cream cheese, softened	½ tsp salt

For the filling

2 tbsp sugar-free maple syrup	1 egg, beaten
2 tbsp poppy seeds	3 tbsp tahini
2 tbsp sesame seeds	

Directions and Total Time: approx. 30 min + cooling time

Preheat oven to 350 F. Line a baking tray with parchment paper. In a bowl, mix almond and coconut flours, xanthan gum, and salt. Add in cream cheese, cream of tartar, and butter; mix with an electric mixer until crumbly. Add erythritol and vanilla extract until mixed. Then, pour in 3 eggs one after another while mixing until formed into a ball. Flatten the dough on a clean flat surface, cover with plastic wrap, and refrigerate for 1 hour.

Dust a clean flat surface with almond flour, unwrap the dough, and roll out the dough into a large rectangle. In a bowl, mix maple syrup and tahini and spread the mixture over the pastry. Sprinkle with half of the sesame seeds and cut the dough into 16 strips. Fold each strip in half. Brush the top with the beaten egg, sprinkle with the remaining seeds and poppy seeds. Twist the pastry three to four times into straws and place on the baking sheet. Bake until golden brown, 15 minutes. Serve with chocolate sauce.

Per serving: Cal 351; Net Carbs 3.1g, Fat 31g, Protein 11g

Bacon & Tofu Pops

Ingredients for 4 servings

2 tbsp butter	2 tbsp chives, chopped
12 slices bacon	1 lemon, zested and juiced
1 (14 oz) block tofu, cubed	12 mini skewers

Directions and Total Time: approx. 20 min + chilling time

In a bowl, mix the chives, lemon zest, and lemon juice and toss in the tofu cubes. Marinate for 1 hour. Take the zest and chives off the cubes and wrap each tofu in a bacon slice. Insert each skewer at the end of the bacon. Melt butter in a skillet and fry tofu skewers until the bacon browns and crisps. Serve with mayo sauce.

Per serving: Cal 389; Net Carbs 9g, Fat 22g, Protein 18g

Rosemary Feta Cheese Bombs

Ingredients for 4 servings

6 tbsp butter	1 tbsp olive oil
2/3 cup almond flour	2 sprigs rosemary
3 eggs	2 white onions, thinly sliced
1 cup crumbled feta cheese	2 tbsp red wine vinegar
½ cup heavy whipping cream	1 tsp Swerve brown sugar

Directions and Total Time: approx. 50 minutes

Preheat oven to 350 F. Line a baking tray with parchment paper. In a saucepan, warm 1 cup of water and butter. Bring to a boil and add in almond flour, beating vigorously until ball forms. Turn the heat off; keep beating while adding the eggs, one at a time, until the dough is smooth and slightly thickened. Scoop mounds of the dough onto the baking dish. Press a hole in the center of each mound. Bake for 20 minutes until risen and golden. Remove from the oven and pierce the sides of the buns with a toothpick. Return to oven and bake for 2 minutes until crispy. Set aside to cool.

Tear out the middle part of the bun (keep the torn out part) to create a hole in the bun for the cream filling. Set aside. Heat olive oil in a saucepan and sauté onions and rosemary for 2 minutes. Stir in Swerve sugar and vinegar and cook to bubble for 3 minutes or until caramelized. In a bowl, beat whipping cream and feta together. Spoon the mixture into a piping bag and press a spoonful of the mixture into the buns. Cover with the torn out portion of pastry and top with onion relish to serve.

Per serving: Cal 379; Net Carbs 2.5g; Fat 37g, Protein 10g

Mushroom & Feta Skewers

Ingredients for 2 servings

½ lb white button mushrooms, quartered	
14 oz block feta cheese, cubed	
2 tbsp olive oil	1 lemon, juiced
2 red onions, cut into wedges	2 tbsp chopped parsley
1 tsp Chinese five-spice	

Directions and Total Time: approx. 20 minutes

Thread feta, mushrooms, and onions alternately on the skewers. In a bowl, mix olive oil, Chinese five-spice, and lemon juice. Brush the skewers with the mixture. Cook in a grill pan over high heat until the vegetables lightly char, about 10 minutes. Garnish with parsley and serve.

Per serving: Cal 368; Net Carbs 6.9g; Fat 27g; Protein 25g

Baked Asparagus with Walnuts

Ingredients for 4 servings

1 ¼ lb asparagus, trimmed	1 tbsp tamarind sauce
2 tbsp olive oil	2 tbsp walnuts, chopped
½ tbsp chili pepper, chopped	3 tbsp tahini
1 garlic clove, crushed	2 tbsp balsamic vinegar

Directions and Total Time: approx. 20 minutes

Preheat oven to 360 F. In a bowl, mix olive oil, garlic, tamarind sauce, and walnuts. Lay asparagus on a baking tray and drizzle tamarind mixture all over.

Roast the veggies until tender and charred, 12 minutes. In a bowl, whisk tahini, balsamic vinegar, and chili pepper. Plate asparagus, drizzle with dressing and serve.

Per serving: Cal 361; Net Carbs 8.4g; Fat 29g; Protein 9.6g

Herbed Cheese Sticks with Yogurt Dip

Ingredients for 2 servings

8 oz mozzarella cheese, cut into sticks	
¼ cup Parmesan cheese, grated	½ tsp dried oregano
1 tbsp almond flour	1/3 tsp dried rosemary
1/3 tbsp flax meal	1 egg
1/3 tsp cumin powder	1 tbsp olive oil

Yogurt dip

1/3 cup natural yogurt	1 tbsp parsley, chopped
1 garlic clove	1 tbsp olive oil
1 tsp mint, chopped	Sea salt to taste

Directions and Total Time: approx. 25 min + chilling time

In a bowl, mix the almond flour, flax meal, cumin powder, oregano, and rosemary. In a separate bowl, whisk the egg with a fork. Dip in each cheese stick into the egg, then roll in the dry mixture. Set cheese sticks on a wax paper-lined baking sheet; freeze for 15 minutes. Warm the olive oil in a skillet over medium heat and fry the cheese sticks for 5 minutes or until the coating is golden brown and crisp. Set on paper towels to drain excess fat.

Mash the garlic and salt to taste into a pestle and add to the yogurt. Stir in olive oil, parsley, and mint. Spread into a serving bowl and serve with the cheese sticks.

Per serving: Cal 354; Fat 16g; Net Carbs 3.7g; Protein 44g

Mushroom & Kale Pierogis

Ingredients for 4 servings

2 oz fresh kale	1 small red onion, chopped
3 oz Bella mushrooms, sliced	3 eggs
½ cup cream cheese	½ cup almond flour
2 cups Parmesan, grated	4 tbsp coconut flour
7 tbsp butter	1 tsp baking powder
2 garlic cloves, minced	Salt and black pepper to taste

Directions and Total Time: approx. 45 minutes

Melt 2 tbsp of butter in a skillet and sauté garlic, red onion, mushrooms, and kale for 5 minutes. Season with salt and pepper and reduce the heat to low. Stir in cream cheese and ½ cup of Parmesan cheese; simmer for 1 minute. Set aside to cool.

In a bowl, combine almond and coconut flours, salt, and baking powder. Put a pan over low heat and melt the remaining Parmesan cheese and butter. Turn the heat off. Pour the eggs into the cream mixture, continue stirring while adding the flour mixture until a firm dough forms. Mold the dough into balls, place on a chopping board, and use a rolling pin to flatten each into ½ inch thin round piece. Spread a generous amount of stuffing on one-half of each dough, fold over the filling, and seal the dough with fingers. Brush with oil and bake for 20 minutes at 380 F.

Per serving: Cal 538; Net Carbs 6g; Fat 51g; Protein 18g

Tofu Jalapeño Poppers with Cilantro Dip

Ingredients for 4 servings

For the poppers

6 jalapeño peppers, halved
3 tbsp grated cheddar cheese
4 oz firm tofu, chopped in bits
½ cup cream cheese
1 garlic clove, minced

2 tbsp olive oil
1 lemon, zested and juiced
4 scallions, finely chopped
2 tbsp chopped cilantro
Salt and black pepper to taste

For the dip

1 tsp lemon juice
1 cup sour cream

1 tbsp chopped cilantro

Directions and Total Time: approx. 30 minutes

Preheat oven to 370 F. Heat olive oil in a skillet and fry tofu until golden. Transfer to a bowl. Mix in garlic, cream cheese, lemon zest, juice, scallions, cilantro, salt, and black pepper. Arrange the jalapeño peppers on a greased baking dish. Fill with the tofu mixture and sprinkle with cheddar cheese. Bake for 15 minutes or until the cheese is golden brown. In a bowl, mix lemon juice, sour cream, and cilantro. Serve the dip with the poppers.

Per serving: Cal 251; Net Carbs 6.9g, Fat 21g, Protein 9g

Parmigiano Cauliflower Cakes

Ingredients for 4 servings

2 cups cauliflower florets
½ cup grated Parmigiano cheese
1 cup olive oil
1 large egg, beaten
2 green onions, chopped
1 tbsp chopped parsley

2 tbsp chopped almonds
1 cup golden flaxseed meal
Salt and black pepper to taste

Directions and Total Time: approx. 25 minutes

Place cauliflower and 1 cup of water into a pot and bring to a boil until soft; drain. Transfer to a food processor.

Puree until smooth. Pour into a bowl and mix in salt, pepper, egg, green onions, parsley, cheese, and almonds. Make 12 small cakes from the mixture and coat with the flaxseed meal. Heat olive oil in a deep pan and cook patties on both sides until golden, 6-8 minutes. Serve.

Per serving: Cal 319; Net Carbs 5.5g; Fat 19g; Protein 14g

Steamed Asparagus with Feta

Ingredients for 4 servings

1 lb asparagus, cut off stems
2 tbsp olive oil
1 cup feta cheese, crumbled
2 garlic cloves, minced
1 tsp cajun spice mix

1 tsp mustard
1 bell pepper, chopped
¼ cup vegetable broth
Salt and black pepper to taste

Directions and Total Time: approx. 25 minutes

Steam asparagus in salted water in a pot over medium heat until tender for 10 minutes; then drain. Heat olive oil in a pan over medium heat and place in garlic; cook for 30 seconds until soft. Stir in the rest of the ingredients, including reserved asparagus, and cook for an additional 4 minutes. Serve topped with feta cheese on a platter.

Per serving: Cal 211; Fat 16g; Net Carbs 2.8g; Protein 8.8g

Roasted Pumpkin with Almonds & Cheddar

Ingredients for 4 servings

1 large pumpkin, peeled and sliced
2 tbsp olive oil
½ cup almonds, ground

½ cup cheddar cheese, grated
2 tbsp thyme, chopped

Directions and Total Time: approx. 50 minutes

Preheat the oven to 360 F. Arrange pumpkin slices on a baking dish, drizzle with olive oil, and bake for 35 minutes. Mix almonds and cheese, and when the pumpkin is ready, remove it from the oven and sprinkle the cheese mixture all over. Bake for 5 more minutes. Sprinkle with thyme to serve.

Per serving: Cal 154; Fat 8.6g; Net Carbs 5.1g; Protein 4.5g

Avocado Crostini with Hazelnuts

Ingredients for 4 servings

2 avocados, chopped
4 tbsp olive oil
3 tbsp grated Parmesan
2 tbsp chopped hazelnuts
2 garlic cloves, halved

¼ tsp garlic powder
¼ tsp onion powder
1 tbsp chopped parsley
1 lemon, zested and juiced
1 loaf zero carb bread, sliced

Directions and Total Time: approx. 25 minutes

In a bowl, place 2 tbsp of olive oil, avocado, garlic and onion powders, parsley, zest, and juice and mix with a fork until smooth; set aside.

Heat a grill pan. Rub both sides of the bread slices with garlic and brush with remaining olive oil. Grill on both sides until crispy and golden. Spread the avocado mixture onto the crostini. Sprinkle with Parmesan cheese and hazelnuts. Drizzle with some more olive oil and serve.

Per serving: Cal 331; Net Carbs 3.9g; Fat 29g; Protein 3.6g

Sesame Tofu Skewers

Ingredients for 4 servings

¼ cup cherry tomatoes, halved
1 tbsp olive oil
1 (14 oz) firm tofu, cubed
1 zucchini, cut into wedges
1 red onion, cut into wedges

2 tbsp tahini
1 tbsp soy sauce
Sesame seeds for garnishing

Directions and Total Time: approx. 20 min + cooling time

In a bowl, mix tahini and soy sauce. Toss the tofu in the mixture. Let rest for 30 minutes. Thread tofu, zucchini, cherry tomatoes, and onion alternately on skewers. Brush with olive oil.

Heat a grill pan and cook tofu skewers until golden, 8 minutes. Serve garnished with sesame seeds.

Per serving: Cal 271; Net Carbs 2.4g; Fat 17g; Protein 14g

Green Nacho Wings

Ingredients for 4 servings

1 lb grated Mexican cheese blend
16 chicken wings, halved
½ cup butter, melted
1 cup golden flaxseed meal

2 tbsp chopped green chilies
1 cup chopped scallions
1 jalapeño pepper, sliced

Directions and Total Time: approx. 45 minutes

Preheat oven to 360 F. Brush the chicken with butter. Spread the flaxseed meal on a wide plate and roll in each chicken wing. Place on a baking sheet and bake for 30-35 minutes or until golden brown and cooked within.

Sprinkle with the cheese blend, green chilies, scallions, and jalapeño pepper on top. Serve immediately.

Per serving: Cal 802; Net Carbs 1.5g; Fat 59g; Protein 51g

Bacon-Wrapped Halloumi

Ingredients for 4 servings

16 bacon strips	½ cup mayonnaise
½ lb halloumi cheese, cubed	¼ cup hot sauce
½ cup Swerve brown sugar	

Directions and Total Time: approx. 30 minutes

Place the bacon in a skillet and cook over medium heat on both sides until crisp, 5 minutes; transfer to a plate. Wrap each halloumi cheese with a bacon strip and secure with a toothpick each. Place on a baking sheet.

In a bowl, combine Swerve brown sugar, mayonnaise, and hot sauce. Pour the mixture all over the bacon-halloumi pieces and bake in the oven at 350 F for 10 minutes. Serve chilled.

Per serving: Cal 351; Net Carbs 4.6g; Fat 25g; Protein 13g

Raspberry & Goat Cheese Focaccia Bites

Ingredients for 6 servings

6 zero carb buns, cut into 4 squares each	
1 cup mushrooms, sliced	1 tbsp olive oil
1 cup fresh raspberries	½ tsp dried thyme
2 cups erythritol	2 oz goat cheese, crumbled
1 lemon, juiced	1 green onion, chopped

Directions and Total Time: approx. 30 minutes

Place raspberries into a saucepan, break into a puree using a potato masher and stir in erythritol and lemon juice.

Place the pot over low heat and cook with constant stirring until the sugar dissolves. Turn the heat up to medium and let the mixture boil for 4 minutes, still with constant stirring to prevent the jam from burning; let cool.

Preheat oven to 350 F. Arrange the buns on a baking tray and bake for 6 minutes. Heat olive oil in a skillet and sauté mushrooms with thyme for 10 minutes. Remove the bread squares from the oven, cut each square into halves horizontally, and top with mushrooms. Scatter with goat cheese, green onion, and raspberry jam. Cover with 6 pieces of focaccia and serve.

Per serving: Cal 171; Net Carbs 5.7g; Fat 9g; Protein 7g

Chicken Ranch Pizza with Bacon & Basil

Ingredients for 4 servings

1 tbsp butter	2 tbsp almond meal
2 chicken breasts	¼ cup half and half
3 cups shredded mozzarella	1 tbsp dry Ranch seasoning
3 tbsp cream cheese, softened	3 bacon slices, chopped
¾ cup almond flour	6 fresh basil leaves

Directions and Total Time: approx. 50 minutes

Preheat oven to 390 F. Line a pizza pan with parchment paper. Microwave 2 cups of mozzarella cheese and 2 tbsp of the cream cheese for 30 seconds. Mix in almond flour and almond meal. Spread the "dough" on the pan and bake for 15 minutes. In a bowl, mix butter, remaining cream cheese, half and half, and ranch mix; set aside.

Heat a grill pan and cook the bacon for 5 minutes; set aside. Grill the chicken in the pan on both sides for 10 minutes. Remove to a plate, allow cooling, and cut into thin slices. Spread the ranch sauce on the pizza crust, followed by the chicken and bacon, and then the remaining mozzarella and basil. Bake for 5 minutes.

Per serving: Cal 531; Net Carbs 4g; Fats 32g; Protein 62g

Eggplant & Bacon Gratin

Ingredients for 4 servings

3 large eggplants, sliced	1 tbsp dried oregano
6 bacon slices, chopped	¾ cup heavy cream
½ cup shredded Parmesan	2 tbsp chopped parsley
½ cup crumbled feta cheese	Salt and black pepper to taste

Directions and Total Time: approx. 45 minutes

Preheat oven to 380 F. Put bacon in a skillet and fry over medium heat until brown and crispy, 6 minutes. Transfer to a plate. Arrange half of the eggplants in a greased baking sheet and season with oregano, parsley, salt, and pepper. Scatter half of bacon and half of feta cheese on top and repeat the remaining ingredients' layering process.

In a bowl, combine heavy cream with half of the Parmesan cheese, and spread on top of the layered ingredients. Sprinkle with the remaining Parmesan. Bake until the cream is bubbly, 20 minutes. Serve.

Per serving: Cal 429; Net Carbs 1.7g; Fat 30g; Protein 16g

Creamy Celeriac & Bacon Bake

Ingredients for 4 servings

3 tbsp butter	1 cup chicken broth
6 bacon slices, chopped	1 lb celeriac, peeled and sliced
3 garlic cloves, minced	2 cups shredded cheddar
3 tbsp almond flour	¼ cup chopped scallions
2 cups coconut cream	Salt and black pepper to taste

Directions and Total Time: approx. 50 minutes

Preheat oven to 380 F. Add bacon to a skillet and fry over medium heat until brown and crispy. Spoon onto a plate. Melt butter in the same skillet and sauté garlic for 1 minute. Mix in almond flour and cook for another minute. Whisk in coconut cream, chicken broth, salt, and pepper. Simmer for 5 minutes. Spread a layer of the sauce in a greased casserole dish and arrange a celeriac layer on top. Cover with more sauce, top with some bacon and cheddar cheese, and scatter scallions on top. Repeat the layering process until the ingredients are exhausted. Bake for 35 minutes. Let rest for a few minutes and serve.

Per serving: Cal 979; Net Carbs 20g; Fat 79g; Protein 30g

Kale & Cheese Stuffed Zucchini

Ingredients for 2 servings

1 zucchini, halved	Salt and black pepper to taste
4 tbsp butter	2 tbsp tomato sauce
2 garlic cloves, minced	1 cup mozzarella, shredded
1 ½ oz baby kale	Olive oil for drizzling

Directions and Total Time: approx. 40 minutes

Preheat oven to 375 F. Scoop out the pulp of the zucchini with a spoon into a plate; keep the flesh.

Grease a baking sheet with cooking spray and place the zucchini halves on top. Put the butter in a skillet and melt over medium heat. Add and sauté the garlic until fragrant and slightly browned, about 4 minutes.

Add the kale and the zucchini pulp. Cook until the kale wilts; season with salt and black pepper.

Spoon the tomato sauce into the zucchini halves and spread to coat the bottom evenly. Spoon the kale mixture into the zucchinis and sprinkle with the mozzarella cheese. Bake in the oven for 20-25 minutes or until the cheese has a beautiful golden color. Plate the zucchinis when ready, drizzle with olive oil, and season with salt and black pepper.

Per serving: Cal 345; Fat 25g; Net Carbs 6.9g; Protein 2g

Mini Sausages with Sweet Mustard Sauce

Ingredients for 4 servings

2 lb mini smoked sausages	¼ cup white wine vinegar
3 tbsp almond flour	1 cup Swerve brown sugar
2 tsp mustard powder	1 tsp tamari sauce
¼ cup lemon juice	

Directions and Total Time: approx. 15 minutes

In a pot, combine Swerve brown sugar, almond flour, and mustard. Gradually stir in lemon juice, vinegar, and tamari sauce. Bring to a boil over medium heat while stirring until thickened, 2 minutes. Mix in sausages until adequately coated. Cook them for 5 minutes. Serve.

Per serving: Cal 751; Net Carbs 7.2g; Fat 45g; Protein 24g

Pancetta & Broccoli Roast

Ingredients for 4 servings

6 pancetta slices, chopped	2 tbsp olive oil
1 lb broccoli rabe, halved	¼ tsp red chili flakes

Directions and Total Time: approx. 40 minutes

Preheat oven to 420 F. Place broccoli rabe in a greased baking sheet and top with pancetta. Drizzle with olive oil, season to taste, and sprinkle with chili flakes. Roast for 30 minutes. Serve warm and enjoy!

Per serving: Cal 130; Net Carbs 0.2g; Fat 10g; Protein 6.8g

Healthy Parsnip Fries

Ingredients for 4 servings

3 tbsp olive oil	3 tbsp ground pork rinds
4 large parsnips, sliced	¼ tsp red chili flakes

Directions and Total Time: approx. 50 minutes

Preheat oven to 420 F. Pour parsnips into a bowl and add in the pork rinds. Toss and place the parsnips on a baking sheet. Drizzle with olive oil and sprinkle with chili flakes. Bake until crispy, 40-45 minutes, tossing halfway. Serve.

Per serving: Cal 257; Net Carbs 6.4g; Fat 15g; Protein 2.9g

Pizza Bianca with Mushrooms

Ingredients for 2 servings

2 tbsp olive oil	2 chives, chopped
4 eggs	2 cups egg Alfredo sauce
1 jalapeño pepper, diced	½ tsp oregano
¼ cup mozzarella, shredded	½ cup mushrooms, sliced

Directions and Total Time: approx. 25 minutes

Preheat oven to 360 F.

In a bowl, whisk eggs, 2 tbsp water, and oregano. Heat the olive oil in a large skillet. Pour in the egg mixture and cook until set, flipping once. Remove and spread the alfredo sauce and jalapeño pepper all over. Top with mozzarella cheese, mushrooms and chives. Bake for 5-10 minutes until the cheese melts.

Per serving: Cal 312; Fat 24g; Net Carbs 2.4g; Protein 17g

Italian Turnip Bites

Ingredients for 4 servings

¼ cup grated mozzarella	2 garlic cloves, minced
1 lb turnips, sliced into rounds	1 tbsp chopped fresh parsley
¼ cup marinara sauce	2 tbsp chopped fresh oregano
½ cup olive oil	3 tbsp dried Italian seasoning

Directions and Total Time: approx. 50 minutes

Preheat oven to 400 F. Place turnip slices into a bowl and toss with olive oil. Add in garlic, oregano, and Italian seasoning and mix well. Arrange on a greased baking sheet and roast for 25 minutes, flipping halfway. Remove and brush with the marinara sauce. Sprinkle with mozzarella cheese and bake in the oven until the cheese is melted and golden, 15 minutes. Garnish with parsley and serve warm.

Per serving: Cal 331; Net Carbs 3.8g; Fat 28g; Protein 5g

Minute Steak & Radish Stir-Fry

Ingredients for 4 servings

10 oz minute steak	
3 tbsp butter	2 tbsp freshly chopped thyme
1½ lb radishes, quartered	Salt and black pepper to taste
1 garlic clove, minced	

Directions and Total Time: approx. 30 minutes

Cut the meat into small pieces. Melt butter in a skillet over medium heat, season the beef with salt and pepper, and brown it until brown on all sides, 12 minutes; transfer to a plate. Add and sauté radishes, garlic, and thyme until the radishes are cooked, 10 minutes. Plate and serve warm.

Per serving: Cal 249; Net Carbs 0.4g; Fat 16g; Protein 21g

Gruyere & Chicken Ham Stuffed Peppers

Ingredients for 4 servings

12 mini green bell peppers, halved
4 slices chicken ham, chopped
2 tbsp melted butter   8 oz cream cheese
1 cup shredded Gruyere   ½ tbsp hot sauce
1 tbsp chopped parsley

Directions and Total Time: approx. 30 minutes

Preheat oven to 380 F. Place peppers in a greased baking dish and set aside. In a bowl, combine chicken ham, parsley, cream cheese, hot sauce, and butter. Spoon the mixture into the peppers and sprinkle Gruyere cheese on top. Bake until the cheese melts, about 20 minutes. Serve.

Per serving: Cal 398; Net Carbs 4g; Fat 32g; Protein 20g

Serrano Ham & Asparagus Bake

Ingredients for 4 servings

1 cup grated Pecorino cheese   ¾ cup coconut cream
1 cup grated mozzarella   3 garlic cloves, minced
2 lb asparagus, stalks trimmed 1 cup crushed pork rinds
4 slices Serrano ham, chopped ½ tsp sweet paprika

Directions and Total Time: approx. 30 minutes

Preheat oven to 380 F. Arrange asparagus on a greased baking dish and pour coconut cream on top. Scatter the garlic, serrano ham, and pork rinds on top and sprinkle with Pecorino cheese, mozzarella cheese, and paprika. Bake until the cheese melts and is golden and asparagus tender, 20 minutes. Serve warm.

Per serving: Cal 359; Net Carbs 15g; Fat 19g; Protein 29g

Cheesy Bacon Bites

Ingredients for 4 servings

6 oz cream cheese   2 tbsp butter, softened
6 oz shredded Gruyere cheese ½ tsp red chili flakes
7 bacon slices

Directions and Total Time: approx. 30 minutes

Place the bacon in a skillet and fry over medium heat until crispy, 5 minutes. Transfer to a plate to cool and crumble it. Pour the bacon grease into a bowl and mix in cream cheese, Gruyere cheese, butter, and red chili flakes. Refrigerate to set for 15 minutes. Remove and mold into walnut-sized balls. Roll in the crumbled bacon. Plate and serve.

Per serving: Cal 541; Net Carbs 0.5g; Fat 49g; Protein 22g

Cheesy Green Bean & Bacon Roast

Ingredients for 4 servings

1 egg, beaten   1 tsp onion powder
5 tbsp grated mozzarella 15 oz fresh green beans
2 tbsp olive oil   4 bacon slices, chopped

Directions and Total Time: approx. 30 minutes

Preheat oven to 360 F. Line a baking sheet with parchment paper. In a bowl, mix olive oil, onion powder, and egg. Add in green beans and mozzarella and toss to coat.

Pour the mixture onto the baking sheet and bake until the cheese melts, 20 minutes. Fry bacon in a skillet until crispy. Remove green beans and divide between serving plates. Top with bacon and serve.

Per serving: Cal 210; Net Carbs 2.6g; Fat 19g; Protein 5.9g

Parsley Cauliflower & Bacon Stir-Fry

Ingredients for 4 servings

1 head cauliflower, cut into florets
10 oz bacon, chopped   2 tbsp parsley, finely chopped
1 garlic clove, minced Salt and black pepper to taste

Directions and Total Time: approx. 15 minutes

Throw the cauliflower in salted boiling water over medium heat and cook for 5 minutes or until soft; drain and set aside. In a skillet, fry bacon until brown and crispy, 5 minutes. Add cauliflower and garlic and sauté until the cauliflower browns slightly. Season with salt and pepper. Garnish with parsley and serve.

Per serving: Cal 239; Net Carbs 3.9g; Fat 21g; Protein 8.9g

Artichoke & Bacon Gratin with Cauli Rice

Ingredients for 4 servings

1 cup canned artichoke hearts
6 bacon slices, chopped   Salt and black pepper to taste
2 cups cauliflower rice   ¼ cup sour cream
3 cups baby spinach, chopped 8 oz cream cheese, softened
1 garlic clove, minced   ¼ cup grated Parmesan
1 tbsp olive oil   1 ½ cups grated mozzarella

Directions and Total Time: approx. 30 minutes

Drain and chop the artichokes; set aside. Preheat oven to 360 F. Cook bacon in a skillet over medium heat until brown and crispy, 5 minutes. Spoon onto a plate. In a bowl, mix cauli rice, artichokes, spinach, garlic, olive oil, salt, pepper, sour cream, cream cheese, bacon, and half of Parmesan cheese. Spread the mixture onto a baking dish and top with the remaining Parmesan and mozzarella cheeses. Bake for 15 minutes. Serve.

Per serving: Cal 498; Net Carbs 5.3g; Fat 41g; Protein 28g

Oregano Parsnip Mash with Ham

Ingredients for 4 servings

3 tbsp olive oil   ¾ cup almond milk
4 tbsp butter   4 tbsp heavy cream
1 lb parsnips, diced   6 slices deli ham, chopped
2 tsp garlic powder   2 tsp freshly chopped oregano

Directions and Total Time: approx. 50 minutes

Preheat oven to 380 F. Spread parsnips on a baking sheet and drizzle with 2 tbsp olive oil. Cover tightly with aluminum foil and bake until the parsnips are tender, 40 minutes. Remove from the oven, take off the foil, and transfer to a bowl. Add in garlic powder, almond milk, heavy cream, and butter. With an immersion blender, puree the ingredients until smooth. Fold in the ham and sprinkle with oregano. Serve.

Per serving: Cal 480; Net Carbs 20g; Fat 29g; Protein 9.8g

Pancetta-Wrapped Strawberries

Ingredients for 4 servings

2 tbsp Swerve confectioner's sugar
12 fresh strawberries   1 cup mascarpone cheese
12 thin pancetta slices   1/8 tsp white pepper

Directions and Total Time: approx. 30 minutes

In a bowl, combine mascarpone, Swerve confectioner's sugar, and white pepper. Coat strawberries in the mixture, wrap each strawberry in a pancetta slice, and place on an ungreased baking sheet. Bake in the oven at 425 F for 15-20 minutes until pancetta browns. Serve warm.

Per serving: Cal 169; Net Carbs 1.2g; Fat 11g; Protein 12g

Deli Ham Roast with Radishes

Ingredients for 4 servings

1 tbsp butter, melted   3 slices deli ham, chopped
1 lb radishes, halved   Salt and black pepper to taste

Directions and Total Time: approx. 20 minutes

Preheat oven to 380 F. Arrange the radishes on a greased baking sheet. Season with salt and pepper and sprinkle with butter and ham. Bake for 15 minutes. Serve warm.

Per serving: Cal 72; Net Carbs 0.5g; Fat 4g; Protein 3.9g

Party Ham Rolls

Ingredients for 4 servings

1 medium sweet red pepper, cut into 16 strips
8 oz Havarti cheese, cut into 16 strips
16 thin slices deli ham, cut in half lengthwise
16 fresh green beans   16 whole chives
2 tbsp salted butter   2 cups water

Directions and Total Time: approx. 15 min + chilling time

Place the water in a saucepan over medium heat and bring it to a boil. Add in green beans, cover, and cook for 3 minutes or until softened; drain. Melt butter in a skillet and sauté green beans for 2 minutes; transfer to a plate. Assemble 1 green bean, 1 strip of red pepper, 1 cheese strip, and wrap with a ham slice. Tie with one chive. Repeat the assembling process with the remaining ingredients and refrigerate.

Per serving: Cal 401; Net Carbs 8.7g; Fat 24g; Protein 35g

Zucchini & Hemp Seed Crisps

Ingredients for 4 servings

4 tbsp olive oil   2 tbsp hemp seeds
4 large zucchinis, sliced   2 tbsp poppy seeds
1 tsp smoked paprika   1 tsp red chili flakes

Directions and Total Time: approx. 25 minutes

Preheat oven to 360 F. Drizzle zucchini with olive oil and sprinkle with paprika. Scatter with hemp seeds, poppy seeds, and chili flakes. Roast for 20 minutes or until crispy and golden brown. Serve.

Per serving: Cal 169; Net Carbs 1.3g; Fat 20g; Protein 2.2g

Crunchy Squash Nacho Chips

Ingredients for 4 servings

½ cup coconut oil   1 tbsp taco seasoning
1 yellow squash, thinly sliced   Salt to taste

Directions and Total Time: approx. 25 minutes

Warm coconut oil in a skillet over medium heat. Add in squash slices and fry until crispy and golden brown, about 10-12 minutes. Remove to a paper towel-lined plate. Sprinkle the slices with taco seasoning and salt and serve.

Per serving: Cal 149; Net Carbs 1g; Fat 14g; Protein 1.8g

Halloumi & Cheddar Sticks

Ingredients for 6 servings

1 lb halloumi, cut into strips   2 tsp smoked paprika
½ cup cheddar, cut into strips   2 tbsp chopped parsley
1/3 cup almond flour   ½ tsp cayenne powder

Directions and Total Time: approx. 20 minutes

Preheat oven to 360 F. In a bowl, mix almond flour with paprika and lightly dredge in the halloumi and cheddar cheese strips. Arrange them on a greased baking sheet. Sprinkle with parsley and cayenne powder and spray with cooking spray. Bake for 10 minutes until golden brown. Serve.

Per serving: Cal 891; Net Carbs 6.1g; Fat 80g; Protein 14g

Cauli Rice & Chorizo Cabbage Rolls

Ingredients for 4 servings

8 green cabbage leaves   ¼ cup coconut oil
1 onion, chopped   1 cup canned tomato sauce
3 cloves garlic, minced   1 tsp dried oregano
1 cup crumbled chorizo   1 tsp dried basil
1 cup cauliflower rice   Salt and black pepper to taste

Directions and Total Time: approx. 40 minutes

Warm coconut oil in a saucepan and sauté onion, garlic, and chorizo for 5 minutes. Stir in cauli rice, season with salt and pepper, and cook for 4 minutes; set aside. In the saucepan, pour tomato sauce, oregano, and basil. Add ¼ cup water and simmer for 10 minutes. Lay cabbage leaves on a flat surface and spoon chorizo mixture into the middle of each leaf. Roll the leaves to secure the filling. Put the cabbage rolls in tomato sauce and cook for 10 minutes.

Per serving: Cal 291; Net Carbs 7g; Fat 26g; Protein 4.9g

Pesto Veggie Pinwheels

Ingredients for 4 servings

3 whole eggs   ¼ tsp yogurt
1 egg, beaten for brushing   ¼ cup butter, cold
1 cup grated cheddar cheese   1 cup mushrooms, chopped
¼ cup almond flour   1 cup basil pesto
3 tbsp coconut flour   2 cups baby spinach
½ tsp xanthan gum   Salt
4 tbsp cream cheese, softened

Directions and Total Time: approx. 40 min + chilling time

In a bowl, mix almond and coconut flours, xanthan gum, and ½ tsp salt. Add yogurt, cream cheese, and butter; mix until crumbly. Pour in 3 eggs one after another while mixing until formed into a ball. Flatten the dough on a clean flat surface, cover with plastic wrap, and refrigerate for 1 hour.

Dust a clean flat surface with almond flour, unwrap the dough, and roll out into 15x12 inches. Spread pesto on top with a spatula, leaving a 2-inch border on one end.

In a bowl, combine baby spinach and mushrooms, season with salt and pepper, and spread the mixture over the pesto. Sprinkle with cheddar cheese and roll up as tightly as possible from the shorter end. Refrigerate for 10 minutes.

Preheat oven to 380 F. Remove the pastry onto a flat surface and use a sharp knife to cut into 24 slim discs. Arrange on the baking sheet, brush with the remaining egg, and bake for 25 minutes until golden. Let cool.

Per serving: Cal 541; Net Carbs 4g; Fat 39g; Protein 35g

Goat Cheese & Rutabaga Puffs

Ingredients for 4 servings

½ oz goat cheese, crumbled	2 tbsp melted butter
1 rutabaga, peeled and diced	¼ cup ground pork rinds

Directions and Total Time: approx. 35 minutes

Preheat oven to 380 F. Spread rutabaga on a baking sheet and drizzle with the butter. Bake until tender, 15 minutes. Transfer to a bowl. Allow cooling and add in goat cheese. Using a fork, mash and mix the ingredients. Pour the pork rinds onto a plate. Mold 1-inch balls out of the rutabaga mixture and roll properly in the rinds while pressing gently to stick. Place on the same baking sheet and bake for 10 minutes until golden. Serve.

Per serving: Cal 131; Net Carbs 5.9g; Fat 9g; Protein 3g

Butternut Squash & Pancetta Roast

Ingredients for 4 servings

8 pancetta slices, chopped	½ tsp garlic powder
2 butternut squash, cubed	2 tbsp olive oil
1 tsp turmeric powder	1 tbsp chopped cilantro

Directions and Total Time: approx. 25 minutes

Preheat oven to 420 F. In a bowl, add butternut squash, turmeric, garlic powder, pancetta, and olive oil. Toss until well-coated. Spread the mixture onto a greased baking sheet and roast for 10-15 minutes. Transfer the veggies to a bowl and garnish with cilantro to serve.

Per serving: Cal 151; Net Carbs 6.4g; Fat 9g; Protein 6g

Blackberry & Prosciutto Appetizer

Ingredients for 4 servings

1 cup fresh blackberries	1 tbsp erythritol
1 cup crumbled goat cheese	¼ tsp dry Italian seasoning
4 zero carb bread slices	1 tbsp almond milk
¾ cup balsamic vinegar	4 thin prosciutto slices

Directions and Total Time: approx. 30 minutes

Cut the bread slices into 3 pieces each and arrange them on a baking sheet. Place under the broiler and toast for 1-2 minutes on each side or until golden brown; set aside. In a saucepan, add balsamic vinegar and stir in erythritol until dissolved. Boil the mixture over medium heat until reduced by half, 5 minutes. Turn the heat off and carefully stir in the blackberries. Make sure they do not break open. Set aside. In a bowl, add goat cheese, Italian seasoning, and almond milk. Mix until smooth. Brush one side of the toasted bread with the balsamic reduction and top with the cheese mixture. Cut each prosciutto slice into 3 pieces and place on the bread. Top with some of the whole blackberries from the balsamic mixture. Serve immediately.

Per serving: Cal 180; Net Carbs 8.7g; Fat 7g; Protein 20g

Cauliflower Crackers with Cheese Dip

Ingredients for 6 servings

¾ cup dried cranberries, chopped	
1 head cauliflower, cut into florets	
8 oz cream cheese, softened	4 tbsp chia seeds
½ cup toasted pecans, chopped	2 tbsp sugar-free maple syrup
1 ½ tbsp almond flour	1 tbsp lemon zest
1 tbsp flax seeds	

Directions and Total Time: approx. 40 minutes

Preheat oven to 360 F. Pour cauliflower and 2 cups salted water in a pot and bring to a boil for 5 minutes.

Drain and transfer to a food processor; pulse until smooth. Pour into a bowl and stir in flour. Mix in flax seeds and 1 tbsp chia seeds. Line a baking sheet with parchment paper and spread in the batter. Cover with plastic wrap and use a rolling pin to flatten and level the mixture. Take off the plastic wrap and cut chip-size squares on the batter. Bake for 20 minutes. Let cool for 5 minutes and transfer to a serving bowl. In a bowl, mix cream cheese with maple syrup. Add in cranberries, pecans, remaining chia seeds, and lemon zest; mix well. Serve the dip with cauli chips.

Per serving: Cal 248; Net Carbs 6.2g; Fat 23g; Protein 5.8

Pecorino Pork Rind Bread

Ingredients for 4 servings

8 oz cream cheese	1 cup crushed pork rinds
2 cups grated mozzarella	3 large eggs
¼ cup grated Pecorino cheese	1 tbsp Italian mixed herbs
1 tbsp baking powder	

Directions and Total Time: approx. 30 minutes

Preheat oven to 380 F. Line a baking sheet with parchment paper. Microwave cream and mozzarella cheeses for 1 minute or until melted. Whisk in baking powder, pork rinds, eggs, Pecorino Romano cheese, and Italian mixed herbs. Spread the mixture on the baking sheet and bake for 20 minutes until lightly brown. Let cool and serve.

Per serving: Cal 441; Net Carbs 3.2g; Fat 23g; Protein 32g

Chili Eggplant & Almond Roast

Ingredients for 4 servings

2 tbsp butter
2 large eggplants

1 tsp red chili flakes
4 oz raw ground almonds

Directions and Total Time: approx. 30 minutes

Preheat oven to 380 F. Cut off the head of the eggplants and slice the body into rounds. Arrange on a parchment paper-lined baking sheet. Drop thin slices of butter on each eggplant slice, sprinkle with chili flakes, and bake for 20 minutes. Slide-out and sprinkle with almonds. Roast further for 5 minutes. Serve with arugula salad.

Per serving: Cal 228; Net Carbs 4g; Fat 16g; Protein 13.8g

Bell Peppers Stuffed with Tofu & Cheese

Ingredients for 4 servings

2 tbsp melted butter
1 oz tofu, chopped
1 cup grated Parmesan
1 cup cream cheese

2 red bell peppers
1 tbsp fresh parsley, chopped
1 tbsp chili paste, mild

Directions and Total Time: approx. 30 minutes

Preheat oven to 380 F. Half the bell peppers lengthwise and remove the core and seeds. In a bowl, mix tofu with parsley, cream cheese, chili paste, and melted butter until smooth. Spoon the cheese mixture into the bell peppers. Arrange peppers on a greased sheet. Sprinkle Parmesan on top and bake for 20 minutes.

Per serving: Cal 408; Net Carbs 5g; Fat 35.9g; Protein 14g

Twisted Deviled Eggs

Ingredients for 6 servings

2 tbsp crumbled feta cheese
3 tbsp mayonnaise
6 large eggs
1 tsp Dijon mustard
1 tsp white wine vinegar

¼ tsp turmeric powder
1 tbsp smoked paprika
1 red chili, minced
1 tbsp chopped parsley

Directions and Total Time: approx. 25 minutes

Place the eggs in boiling salted water in a pot over medium heat and cook them for 10 minutes. Transfer to an ice-water bath. Let cool for 5 minutes, peel, and slice in half. Remove the yolks to a bowl and put the whites on a plate. Mash yolks with a fork and mix in mustard, mayonnaise, vinegar, feta, turmeric, and chili until evenly combined. Spoon the mixture into a piping bag and fill into the egg whites. Garnish with parsley and paprika.

Per serving: Cal 140; Net Carbs 1.2g, Fat 8.2g, Protein 6.8g

Spinach Chips with Avocado Hummus

Ingredients for 4 servings

1 tbsp olive oil
½ cup baby spinach
½ tsp plain vinegar
3 avocados, chopped
½ cup chopped parsley
½ cup butter

¼ cup pumpkin seeds
¼ cup sesame paste
Juice from ½ lemon
1 garlic clove, minced
½ tsp coriander powder
Salt and black pepper to taste

Directions and Total Time: approx. 25 minutes

Preheat oven to 320 F. Put spinach in a bowl and toss with olive oil, plain vinegar, and salt. Arrange on a parchment paper-lined baking sheet and bake until the leaves are crispy but not burned, 15 minutes. Place the avocados in a food processor. Add in butter, pumpkin seeds, sesame paste, lemon juice, garlic, coriander, salt, and pepper; puree until smooth. Spoon into a bowl and garnish with parsley. Serve with spinach chips.

Per serving: Cal 468; Net Carbs 3g; Fat 45g; Protein 7.6g

Walnut & Pecan Snack Mix

Ingredients for 4 servings

1 tbsp coconut oil
8 oz walnuts and pecans

1 tsp cumin powder
1 tsp paprika powder

Directions and Total Time: approx. 15 minutes

In a bowl, mix walnuts, pecans, coconut oil, cumin powder, and paprika until the nuts are well coated. Pour the mixture into a preheated dry pan and toast over medium heat while stirring often until fragrant and brown.

Per serving: Cal 289; Net Carbs 3g; Fat 27g; Protein 5.9g

Smoked Pistachio Dip

Ingredients for 4 servings

½ cup olive oil
3 oz toasted pistachios
3 tbsp coconut cream

½ lemon, juiced
½ tsp smoked paprika
Salt and cayenne pepper to taste

Directions and Total Time: approx. 10 minutes

Place pistachios, coconut cream, ¼ cup water, lemon juice, paprika, cayenne pepper, and salt into a food processor. Puree until smooth. Mix in olive oil. Garnish with pistachios, and serve with celery or carrots.

Per serving: Cal 219; Net Carbs 5g; Fat 20g; Protein 5.8g

Awesome Onion Rings with Kale Dip

Ingredients for 4 servings

1 egg, beaten
2 oz chopped kale
1 onion, sliced in rings
1 cup almond flour
½ cup grated Parmesan
1 tsp garlic powder
½ tbsp sweet paprika

2 tbsp olive oil
2 tbsp dried cilantro
1 tbsp dried oregano
1 cup mayonnaise
4 tbsp coconut cream
Juice of ½ lemon
Salt and black pepper to taste

Directions and Total Time: approx. 35 minutes

Preheat oven to 400 F. In a bowl, combine almond flour, Parmesan, garlic powder, paprika, and salt. Line a baking sheet with wax paper. Dip in the onion rings one after another in the egg, then into the almond flour mixture. Place the rings on the sheet and spray with cooking spray. Bake for 20 minutes. Remove to a bowl. Blend the kale, olive oil, cilantro, oregano, salt, pepper, mayonnaise, coconut cream, and lemon juice in a food processor until mixed. Serve the dip with crispy onion rings.

Per serving: Cal 408; Net Carbs 7g; Fat 35g; Protein 13.9g

Avocado Appetizer with Chimichurri

Ingredients for 4 servings

2 avocados, cubed
¼ cup + 2 tbsp olive oil
4 zero carb bread slices
2 tbsp red wine vinegar
1 lemon, juiced

2 garlic cloves, minced
½ tsp red chili flakes
½ tsp dried oregano
½ cup chopped fresh parsley
Salt and black pepper to taste

Directions and Total Time: approx. 15 minutes

Slice the bread in half, brush both sides with 2 tbsp of the olive oil, and arrange on a baking sheet. Place under the broiler and toast for 1-2 minutes per side.

In a bowl, mix ¼ cup olive oil, vinegar, lemon juice, salt, pepper, garlic, red chili flakes, oregano, and parsley. Fold in avocado. Spoon the mixture onto the bread and serve.

Per serving: Cal 310; Net Carbs 5.6g; Fat 26g; Protein 8.9g

Yummy Seed Flapjacks

Ingredients for 4 servings

4 tbsp dry goji berries, chopped
6 tbsp salted butter
8 tbsp sugar-free maple syrup
8 tbsp Swerve brown sugar
3 tbsp sesame seeds

3 tbsp chia seeds
3 tbsp hemp seeds
3 tbsp sunflower seeds
1 tbsp poppy seeds

Directions and Total Time: approx. 25 minutes

Preheat oven to 360 F. Place butter and maple syrup in a saucepan over low heat, stir in Swerve sugar until dissolved. Remove and stir all seeds along with goji berries. Spread into a lined with wax paper baking sheet and bake for 15 minutes. Slice flapjacks into strips.

Per serving: Cal 298; Net Carbs 3g; Fat 30g; Protein 7g

Jalapeno Vegetable Frittata Cups

Ingredients for 2 servings

1 tbsp olive oil
2 green onions, chopped
1 garlic clove, minced
½ jalapeño pepper, chopped
¼ carrot, chopped

1 zucchini, shredded
2 tbsp mozzarella, shredded
4 eggs, whisked
Salt and black pepper to taste
½ tsp dried oregano

Directions and Total Time: approx. 35 minutes

Sauté green onions and garlic in warm olive oil over medium heat for 3 minutes. Stir in carrot, zucchini, and jalapeño pepper, and cook for 4 more minutes. Remove the mixture to a lightly greased baking pan. Top with mozzarella cheese. Cover with the whisked eggs; season with oregano, black pepper, and salt. Bake in the oven for about 20 minutes at 360 F.

Per serving: Cal 335; Fat 28g; Net Carbs 4.7g; Protein 14g

Baked Parsnip Chips with Yogurt Dip

Ingredients for 4 servings

3 tbsp olive oil
1/3 cup natural yogurt
1 tsp lime juice
1 tsp garlic powder

1 tbsp parsley, chopped
Salt and black pepper to taste
1 garlic clove, minced
2 cups parsnips, sliced

Directions and Total Time: approx. 25 minutes

Preheat the oven to 300 F. Set parsnip on a baking sheet; toss with garlic powder, 1 tbsp of olive oil, and salt. Bake for 15 minutes, tossing once halfway through, until slices are crisp and browned. In a bowl, mix yogurt, lime juice, black pepper, 2 tbsp of olive oil, garlic, and salt until well combined. Serve the chips with yogurt dip.

Per serving: Cal 176; Fat 13g; Net Carbs 8.7g; Protein 1.9g

Chili Zucchini Sticks with Aioli

Ingredients for 4 servings

2 tbsp olive oil
¼ cup pork rinds, crushed
1 tsp chili pepper
¼ cup Parmesan cheese, grated

Salt to taste
3 eggs
2 zucchinis, cut into strips

Aioli

½ cup mayonnaise
1 garlic clove, minced

Juice and zest from ½ lemon
Salt to taste

Directions and Total Time: approx. 30 minutes

Place the mayonnaise, lemon juice, and garlic in a bowl, and gently stir until everything is well incorporated. Add the lemon zest, adjust the seasoning and stir again. Cover and place in the refrigerator until ready to serve.

Preheat oven to 425 F. Line a baking sheet with foil. Mix the pork rinds, Parmesan cheese, salt, and chili pepper in a bowl. Beat the eggs in another bowl. Coat zucchini strips in eggs, then in the Parmesan mixture, and arrange on the baking sheet. Drizzle with olive oil and bake for 15 minutes, turning halfway through the cooking time until crispy. Serve the zucchini strips with aioli for dipping.

Per serving: Cal 312; Fat 28g; Net Carbs 4.7g; Protein 12g

Party Spiced Cheese Chips

Ingredients for 2 servings

2 cups Monterrey Jack cheese, grated
Salt to taste
½ tsp garlic powder

½ tsp cayenne pepper
½ tsp dried rosemary

Directions and Total Time: approx. 20 minutes

Mix grated cheese with spices. Create 2 tablespoons of cheese mixture into small mounds on a lined baking sheet. Bake for about 15 minutes at 420 F; then allow to cool to harden the chips.

Per serving: Cal 438; Fat 38g; Net Carbs 1.8g; Protein 27g

Speedy Ricotta & Bresaola Balls

Ingredients for 2 servings

2 oz bresaola, chopped
2 oz ricotta cheese, crumbled
2 tbsp mayonnaise

6 green olives, chopped
½ tbsp basil, finely chopped

Directions and Total Time: approx. 15 minutes

In a bowl, mix mayonnaise, bresaola, and ricotta cheese. Place in fresh basil and green olives. Form balls from the mixture and refrigerate. Serve chilled.

Per serving: Cal 175; Fat 14g; Net Carbs 1.1g; Protein 11g

Coconut Flour Cheese Crackers

Ingredients for 4 servings

1 cup coconut flour
1 cup fontina cheese, grated
Salt and black pepper to taste
¼ tsp garlic powder
¼ tsp onion powder
¼ cup butter, softened
¼ tsp smoked paprika
¼ cup heavy cream

Directions and Total Time: approx. 30 minutes

Preheat the oven to 350 F. Mix the coconut flour, fontina cheese, salt, pepper, garlic powder, onion powder, and smoked paprika in a bowl. Add in the butter and mix well. Top with the heavy cream and mix until smooth. Add 1-2 tablespoons of water if it is too thick. Place the dough on a cutting board and cover with plastic wrap. Use a rolling pin to spread out the dough into a light rectangle. Cut cracker squares out of the dough and arrange them on a baking sheet without overlapping. Bake for 20 minutes until browned. Let cool and serve.

Per serving: Cal 287; Fat 26g; Net Carbs 3.1g; Protein 11g

Baked Scotch Eggs

Ingredients for 4 servings

4 eggs, hard-boiled
1 egg
½ cup pork rinds, crushed
1 lb pork sausages, skinless
2 tbsp Grana Padano, grated
1 garlic clove, minced
½ tsp onion powder
½ tsp cayenne pepper
1 tsp fresh parsley, chopped
Salt and black pepper to taste

Directions and Total Time: approx. 35 minutes

Preheat oven to 370 F.

In a mixing dish, mix the ingredients, except for the egg and pork rinds. Take a handful of the sausage mixture and wrap it around each of the eggs. With fingers, mold the mixture until sealed. Whisk the egg with a fork in a bowl. Dip the sausage eggs in the beaten egg, coat with pork rinds, and place in a greased baking dish. Bake for 25 minutes, until golden brown and crisp. Serve.

Per serving: Cal 255; Fat 12g; Net Carbs 1.1g; Protein 29g

Basil Mozzarella & Salami Omelet

Ingredients for 2 servings

1 tbsp butter
4 eggs
6 basil, chopped
½ cup mozzarella cheese
4 slices salami
2 tomatoes, sliced
Salt and black pepper to taste

Directions and Total Time: approx. 15 minutes

In a bowl, whisk the eggs. Season with salt and black pepper. Melt the butter in a skillet and cook the eggs for 30 seconds. Spread the salami slices over. Arrange the sliced tomato and mozzarella over the salami. Cook for about 3 minutes. Cover the skillet and continue cooking for 3 more minutes until the omelet is completely set. When ready, remove the pan from heat; run a spatula around the edges of the omelet and flip it onto a warm plate, folded side down. Serve garnished with basil leaves.

Per serving: Cal 443; Fat 34g; Net Carbs 2.8g; Protein 29g

Asparagus & Chorizo Traybake

Ingredients for 2 servings

A bunch of asparagus, ends trimmed and chopped
2 tbsp olive oil
4 oz Spanish chorizo, sliced
Salt and black pepper to taste
¼ cup chopped parsley

Directions and Total Time: approx. 20 minutes

Preheat your oven to 325 F. Grease a baking dish with olive oil. Add in the asparagus and season with salt and black pepper. Stir in the chorizo slices. Bake for 15 minutes until the chorizo is crispy. Arrange on a serving platter and serve sprinkled with parsley.

Per serving: Cal 411; Fat 36g; Net Carbs 3.2g; Protein 15g

Mortadella & Bacon Balls

Ingredients for 2 servings

4 bacon slices, cooked and crumbled
4 oz Mortadella sausage
2 tbsp almonds, chopped
½ tsp Dijon mustard
3 oz cream cheese

Directions and Total Time: approx. 25 minutes

Combine the mortadella and almonds in the bowl of your food processor. Pulse until smooth. Whisk the cream cheese and mustard in another bowl. Make balls out of the mortadella mixture. Make a thin cream cheese layer over. Coat with bacon, arrange on a plate, and serve.

Per serving: Cal 547; Fat 51g; Net Carbs 3.4g; Protein 21g

Hard-Boiled Eggs Stuffed with Ricotta

Ingredients for 2 servings

4 eggs
1 tbsp green tabasco
2 tbsp Greek yogurt
2 tbsp ricotta cheese
Salt to taste

Directions and Total Time: approx. 30 minutes

Cover the eggs with salted water and bring to a boil over medium heat for 10 minutes. Place the eggs in an ice bath and let cool for 10 minutes. Peel and slice in half lengthwise. Scoop out the yolks to a bowl; mash with a fork. Whisk together the tabasco, Greek yogurt, ricotta cheese, mashed yolks, and salt, in a bowl. Spoon this mixture into egg white. Plate and serve.

Per serving: Cal 173; Fat 13g; Net Carbs 1.5g; Protein 14g

Tuna Pickle Boats

Ingredients for 2 servings

1 (5-oz) can tuna, drained
2 large dill pickles
¼ tsp lemon juice
2 tsp mayonnaise
¼ tbsp onion flakes
1 tsp dill. chopped

Directions and Total Time: approx. 40 minutes

Cut the pickles in half lengthwise. With a spoon, scoop out the seeds to create boats; set aside. Combine the mayonnaise, tuna, onion flakes, and lemon juice in a bowl. Fill each boat with tuna mixture. Sprinkle with dill and place in the fridge for 30 minutes before serving.

Per serving: Cal 213; Fat 5.6g; Net Carbs 3.2g; Protein 32g

Delicious Egg Cups with Cheese & Spinach

Ingredients for 2 servings

4 eggs
1 tbsp fresh parsley, chopped
¼ cup cheddar, shredded
¼ cup spinach, chopped
Salt and black pepper to taste

Directions and Total Time: approx. 25 minutes

Grease muffin cups with cooking spray. In a bowl, whisk the eggs and add in the rest of the ingredients. Season with salt and black pepper. Fill ¾ parts of each muffin cup with the egg mixture. Bake in the oven for 15 minutes at 390 F. Serve warm!

Per serving: Cal 232; Fat 144g; Net Carbs 1.5g; Protein 16g

Quail Eggs & Prosciutto Wraps

Ingredients for 2 servings

3 thin prosciutto slices
9 basil leaves
9 quail eggs

Directions and Total Time: approx. 20 minutes

Cover the quail eggs with salted water and bring to a boil over medium heat for 2-3 minutes. Place the eggs in an ice bath and let cool for 10 minutes, then peel them.

Cut the prosciutto slices into three strips. Place basil leaves at the end of each strip. Top with a quail egg. Wrap in prosciutto, secure with toothpicks, and serve.

Per serving: Cal 243; Fat 21g; Net Carbs 0.5g; Protein 12g

Tomato & Cheese Lettuce Parcels

Ingredients for 2 servings

¼ lb Gruyere cheese, grated
¼ lb feta cheese, crumbled
½ tsp oregano
1 tomato, chopped
½ cup buttermilk
½ head lettuce

Directions and Total Time: approx. 10 minutes

In a bowl, mix feta and Gruyere cheese, oregano, tomato, and buttermilk. Separate the lettuce leaves and put them on a serving platter. Divide the mixture between them, roll up, folding in the ends to secure and serve.

Per serving: Cal 433; Fat 32g; Net Carbs 6.6g; Protein 28g

Ham & Cheese Frittata

Ingredients for 2 servings

4 eggs
4 oz ham, chopped
2 tbsp butter, melted
2 tbsp almond milk
Salt and black pepper to taste
1 cup cheddar cheese, shredded
1 green onion, chopped

Directions and Total Time: approx. 20 minutes

Whisk the eggs, butter, almond milk, salt, and pepper. Mix in the ham and pour the mixture into a greased baking dish. Sprinkle with cheddar cheese and green onion and bake in the preheated to 390 F oven for 10 minutes or until the eggs are thoroughly cooked. Slice the frittata into wedges and serve warm.

Per serving: Cal 331; Fat 26g; Net Carbs 2.2g; Protein 15g

Sausage & Avocado Shakshouka

Ingredients for 2 servings

1 avocado, pitted, peeled, chopped
½ red onion, sliced
1 tsp canola oil
4 oz pork sausage, sliced
1 cup zucchinis, chopped
3 eggs
Salt and black pepper to taste

Directions and Total Time: approx. 30 minutes

Warm canola oil in a pan over medium heat and sauté the onion for 3 minutes. Add the smoked sausage and cook for 3-4 minutes more, flipping once. Introduce the zucchinis, season lightly with salt, stir and cook for 5 minutes. Mix in the avocado and turn the heat off.

Create 3 holes in the mixture, crack the eggs into each hole, sprinkle with salt and black pepper, and slide the pan into the preheated to 370 F oven. Bake for 10-12 minutes until the egg whites are set or firm but with the yolks still runny.

Per serving: Cal 402; Fat 31g; Net Carbs 3.4g; Protein 25g

Crabmeat Egg Scramble with White Sauce

Ingredients for 2 servings

1 tbsp olive oil
4 eggs
Sauce
¾ cup half-and-half
½ cup chives, chopped
4 oz crabmeat
Salt and black pepper to taste

½ tsp garlic powder
Salt to taste

Directions and Total Time: approx. 20 minutes

Whisk the eggs with a fork in a bowl, and season with salt and black pepper. Set a sauté pan over medium heat and warm olive oil. Add in the eggs and scramble them. Stir in crabmeat and cook until cooked thoroughly.

In a mixing dish, combine half-and-half and garlic powder. Season with salt and sprinkle with chives. Serve the eggs with the white sauce.

Per serving: Cal 405; Fat 35g; Net Carbs 4.3g; Protein 22g

Mexican-Style Omelet

Ingredients for 2 servings

8 oz chorizo sausages, chopped
4 eggs, beaten
½ cup cotija cheese, crumbled
8 oz roasted squash, mashed
2 tbsp olive oil
Salt and black pepper to taste
1 tbsp cilantro, chopped

Directions and Total Time: approx. 20 minutes

Season the eggs with salt and pepper and stir in the cotija cheese and squash. Heat half of the olive oil in a pan over medium heat. Add chorizo sausage and cook until browned on all sides, turning occasionally. Drizzle the remaining olive oil and pour the egg mixture over.

Cook for 4 minutes until the eggs are cooked and lightly browned. Remove the pan and run a spatula around the edges of the omelet; slide onto a platter. Fold in half; serve sprinkled with cilantro.

Per serving: Cal 683; Fat 52g; Net Carbs 8.5g; Protein 38g

Asparagus & Cheddar Omelet

Ingredients for 2 servings

2 tbsp olive oil	½ cup asparagus, chopped
4 eggs	½ cup cheddar cheese
Salt and black pepper to taste	2 tbsp fresh basil, chopped

Directions and Total Time: approx. 15 minutes

Whisk the eggs with a fork, season with salt and black pepper in a bowl. Set a pan over medium heat and warm the oil. Sauté the asparagus for 4-5 minutes until tender. Add in the eggs and ensure they are evenly spread. Top with the cheese. Cook for 2-3 minutes until the eggs are set. Slice the omelet, decorate with fresh basil, and serve.

Per serving: Cal 387; Fat 34g; Net Carbs 1.5g; Protein 21g

Prosciutto-Wrapped Serrano Poppers

Ingredients for 2 servings

6 serrano peppers	1 tsp dried thyme
2 tbsp shredded Colby cheese	2 tbsp pork rinds, crushed
3 oz cream cheese, softened	6 slices prosciutto, halved

Directions and Total Time: approx. 30 minutes

Preheat oven to 400 F. Line a baking sheet with parchment paper. Slice the serrano peppers in half lengthwise and remove the membrane and seeds. Combine cheeses and thyme and stuff into the pepper halves. Sprinkle with pork rinds. Wrap each pepper with a prosciutto strip and secure with toothpicks. Bake in the oven for 18-20 minutes until prosciutto is crispy. Serve.

Per serving: Cal 311; Fat 22g; Net Carbs 4.7g; Protein 16g

Fried Chicken Strips with Mint Dip

Ingredients for 4 servings

3 tbsp olive oil	1 cup cheddar cheese, grated
1 lb chicken breasts, sliced	4 tbsp mint, chopped
1 ¼ cups mayonnaise	1 cup Greek yogurt
¼ cup coconut flour	1 tsp garlic powder
2 eggs	1 tbsp chopped parsley
Salt and black pepper to taste	2 green onions, chopped

Directions and Total Time: approx. 20 min + cooling time

First, make the dip: In a bowl, mix 1 cup of mayonnaise, 3 tbsp of mint, yogurt, garlic powder, green onion, and salt. Cover the bowl with plastic wrap and refrigerate for 30 minutes.

Mix the chicken, remaining mayonnaise, coconut flour, eggs, salt, black pepper, cheddar cheese, and remaining mint in a bowl. Cover the bowl with plastic wrap and refrigerate it for 2 hours.

Place a skillet over medium heat to warm the olive oil. Fetch 2 tablespoons of chicken mixture into the skillet, use the back of a spatula to flatten the top. Cook for 4 minutes, flip, and fry for 4 more. Remove onto a wire rack and repeat the cooking process until the batter is finished, adding more oil as needed. Garnish the fritters with parsley and serve with mint dip.

Per serving: Cal 674; Fat 57g; Net Carbs 6.8g; Protein 32g

Spanish Stuffed Piquillo Peppers

Ingredients for 4 servings

4 canned roasted piquillo peppers
2 tbsp olive oil

Filling

4 oz goat cheese	1 tbsp olive oil
2 tbsp heavy cream	

Directions and Total Time: approx. 20 minutes

Preheat the oven to 350 F. Grease a baking sheet with some olive oil. Mix all filling ingredients in a bowl. Place in a freezer bag, press down and squeeze, and cut off the bottom. Drain and deseed the peppers. Squeeze about 2 tbsp of the filling into each pepper. Arrange them on the baking sheet, drizzle over the remaining olive oil and bake for 10 minutes.

Per serving: Cal 274; Fat 24g; Net Carbs 4.2g; Protein 11g

Oven Roasted Cauliflower with Ham & Nuts

Ingredients for 4 servings

2 tbsp olive oil	1 tsp garlic powder
1 head cauliflower, cut into 1-inch slices	10 slices Parma ham, chopped
	¼ cup hazelnuts, chopped
Salt and black pepper to taste	1 tsp capers
¼ tsp chili pepper	1 tsp parsley, chopped

Directions and Total Time: approx. 30 minutes

Preheat oven to 400 F. Line a baking sheet with foil. Spread the cauli steaks on the baking sheet and brush with olive oil. Season with black pepper, chili pepper, garlic, and salt. Roast in the oven for 10 minutes until tender and lightly browned. Remove the sheet and sprinkle the Parma ham and hazelnuts all over the steaks. Bake for another 10 minutes until the ham is crispy and a nutty aroma is perceived. Take out, sprinkle with capers and parsley. Serve with beef stew and braised asparagus.

Per serving: Cal 211; Fat 15g; Net Carbs 4.7g; Protein 12g

Energy Goji Berry Snacks

Ingredients for 4 servings

1 tbsp unsweetened chocolate chips

½ cup raw pumpkin seeds	½ tsp vanilla extract
½ cup raw walnuts	1 tbsp coconut oil
¼ tsp cinnamon powder	½ tbsp golden flax meal
2 tbsp dried goji berries	½ tsp xylitol

Directions and Total Time: approx. 10 minutes

Combine the pumpkin seeds and walnuts in the food processor and process until smooth. Add the cinnamon powder, goji berries, vanilla extract, chocolate chips, coconut oil, golden flax meal, and xylitol. Process further until the mixture begins to stick to each other, for about 2 minutes. Spread out a large piece of plastic wrap on a flat surface and place the dough on it. Wrap the dough and use a rolling pin to spread it out into a thick rectangle. Unwrap the dough after and cut it into bars.

Per serving: Cal 153; Fat 13g; Net Carbs 4.5g; Protein 22g

Roasted Radishes with Cheesy Sauce

Ingredients for 4 servings

1 lb radishes, greens removed | ¼ cup sour cream
1 tbsp olive oil | ¼ cup heavy cream
Salt and black pepper to taste | ¼ cup gorgonzola cheese
1 tbsp parsley, chopped

Directions and Total Time: approx. 30 minutes

Preheat oven to 370 F. Line a baking sheet with parchment paper. Toss radishes with olive oil, salt, and black pepper. Spread on the baking sheet and roast for 20 minutes until browned.

Add in sour cream and heavy cream. Stir in gorgonzola cheese and season with salt and black pepper; remove to a bowl. Transfer the radishes to a serving plate. Sprinkle with parsley and serve with the sauce.

Per serving: Cal 154; Fat 13g; Net Carbs 4.8g; Protein 3.5g

Cheese Spinach Balls with Yogurt Sauce

Ingredients for 4 servings

2 tbsp Greek yogurt | 2 tbsp heavy cream
Salt to taste | 1/3 tsp garlic powder
1 tbsp walnuts, chopped | 1/3 tbsp onion powder
1 tbsp extra virgin olive oil | 1/3 cup Parmesan, grated
1 tsp dill, chopped | 1 egg
¼ cup ricotta cheese, crumbled | 1/3 cup spinach
¼ tsp nutmeg | 1/3 cup almond flour

Directions and Total Time: approx. 30 minutes

In a bowl, combine together Greek yogurt, walnuts, olive oil, dill, and salt, and mix well. Set aside.

Place ricotta cheese, nutmeg, heavy cream, garlic powder, onion powder, Parmesan cheese, egg, spinach, and almond flour in a food processor. Process until smooth. Transfer to the freezer for 10 minutes.

Make balls out of the mixture and arrange them on a lined baking sheet. Bake at 350 F for about 10-12 minutes. Serve with yogurt sauce for dipping.

Per serving: Cal 173; Fat 14g; Net Carbs 1.8g; Protein 7.5g

Bacon & Guacamole Stuffed Eggs

Ingredients for 4 servings

2 bacon slices, cooked and crumbled
8 large eggs | ¼ tsp chili powder
4 tbsp guacamole | 1 tbsp cilantro, chopped
Salt to taste

Directions and Total Time: approx. 20 minutes

Boil eggs in salted water in a pot over high heat for 10 minutes. Transfer eggs to an ice water bath, let cool completely, and peel the shells. Slice the eggs in half height wise and empty the yolks into a bowl. Smash with a fork and mix in guacamole, bacon, and chili powder until smooth. Spoon filling into a piping bag with a round nozzle and fill the egg whites to be slightly above the brim. Garnish with cilantro to serve.

Per serving: Cal 223; Fat 18g; Net Carbs 1.2g; Protein 14g

Thyme-Mashed Cauliflower with Bacon

Ingredients for 4 servings

4 oz bacon, sliced | Salt and black pepper to taste
1 head cauliflower | ¼ cup cheddar cheese, grated
2 tbsp melted butter | 2 tbsp thyme, chopped
½ cup buttermilk

Directions and Total Time: approx. 25 minutes

Fry bacon in a heated skillet over medium heat for 5 minutes until crispy. Remove to a paper towel-lined plate, allow to cool, and crumble.

Boil cauliflower head in salted water in a pot over high heat for 7 minutes until tender. Drain and transfer to a bowl. Mash and add in butter, buttermilk, salt, black pepper, and stir well. Sprinkle with cheddar cheese and place under the broiler for 4 minutes on high until the cheese melts. Remove and top with bacon and chopped thyme to serve.

Per serving: Cal 321; Fat 26g; Net Carbs 5.4g; Protein 13g

Rosemary Roast Vegetable Traybake

Ingredients for 4 servings

1 lb cremini mushrooms, quartered
3 tbsp olive oil | 1 onion, sliced
2 cups green beans, chopped | 1 fennel bulb, sliced
2 carrots, julienned | 1 tbsp rosemary, chopped
3 tomatoes, quartered | Salt and black pepper to taste
2 garlic cloves, minced

Directions and Total Time: approx. 35 minutes

Preheat oven to 450 F. Grease a baking tray with some olive oil. In a bowl, mix the green beans, mushrooms, tomatoes, carrots, garlic, onion, fennel, salt, and black pepper. Spread the vegetables on the baking tray. Drizzle with the remaining olive oil. Place in the oven and roast for 20-25 minutes until tender and golden brown. Sprinkle with rosemary to serve.

Per serving: Cal 187; Fat 12g; Net Carbs 9.6g; Protein 5.4g

Paprika & Dill Deviled Eggs

Ingredients for 4 servings

6 large eggs | 1 tsp paprika
6 tbsp mayonnaise | ½ tsp Worcestershire sauce,
Salt and black pepper to taste | sugar-free
1 tsp dill, chopped | ¼ tsp Dijon mustard

Directions and Total Time: approx. 30 minutes

Bring to a boil a pot filled with salted water over medium heat. Carefully add in the eggs and boil them for 10 minutes. Rinse under running water, then peel and cut them in half lengthways. Remove the yolks into a medium bowl. Use a fork to crush the yolks.

Add the mayonnaise, salt, black pepper, Worcestershire sauce, mustard, and paprika. Mix together until a smooth paste has formed. Spoon the mixture into the piping bag and fill the egg white holes with it. Top with dill to serve.

Per serving: Cal 213; Fat 16g; Net Carbs 2.1g; Protein 12g

Eggplant Pizza with Tofu

Ingredients for 2 servings

2 eggplants, sliced
1/3 cup butter, melted
2 garlic cloves, minced
1 red onion
12 oz tofu, chopped

7 oz tomato sauce
Salt and black pepper to taste
1 cup Parmesan cheese, shredded
¼ cup dried oregano

Directions and Total Time: approx. 55 minutes

Preheat oven to 400 F. Line a baking sheet with parchment paper. Lay the eggplant slices on the baking sheet and brush with some butter. Bake in the oven until lightly browned, about 20 minutes.

Heat the remaining butter in a skillet; sauté garlic and onion until fragrant and soft, about 3 minutes. Stir in the tofu and cook for 3 minutes. Add the tomato sauce and season with salt and black pepper. Simmer for 10 minutes. Remove the eggplant from the oven and spread the tofu sauce on top. Sprinkle with Parmesan cheese and oregano. Bake for 10 minutes or until the cheese has melted.

Per serving: Cal 657; Fat 56g; Net Carbs 11.5g; Protein 25g

Roasted Green Beans with Garlic

Ingredients for 4 servings

1 lb green beans, thread removed
2 tbsp butter, melted
¼ cup almond flakes

2 garlic cloves, sliced
Salt and black pepper to taste

Directions and Total Time: approx. 30 minutes

Preheat oven to 400 F. Place the green beans and garlic in a baking dish and season with salt and black pepper. Pour the butter over and toss to coat. Bake for 20 minutes. In a dry pan over medium heat, toast the almonds until golden. Pour over the green beans and serve.

Per serving: Cal 187; Fat 12g; Net Carbs 4.5g; Protein 3.5g

Steamed Broccoli with Parsley Butter

Ingredients for 4 servings

2 tbsp parsley, chopped
1 head broccoli, cut into florets

Salt and black pepper to taste
¼ cup butter

Directions and Total Time: approx. 15 minutes

Put the broccoli in a pot filled with salted water and bring to a boil. Cook for about 3 minutes. Drain and set aside. Melt the butter in a pan over low heat. Stir in the broccoli, season with salt and black pepper, and remove to a plate. Sprinkle with parsley to serve.

Per serving: Cal 105; Fat 7.5g; Net Carbs 5.1g; Protein 4g

Energy Nut Bars

Ingredients for 4 servings

¼ cup almonds
¼ cup walnuts
¼ cup cashew nuts
¼ cup coconut chips
1 egg, beaten

½ cup butter, melted
¼ cup dark chocolate chips
¼ cup hemp seeds
1 cup mixed dried berries

Directions and Total Time: approx. 25 minutes

Preheat oven to 360 F. Line a baking sheet with wax paper. In a food processor, pulse nuts until roughly chopped. Place in a bowl and stir in coconut and chocolate chips, egg, butter, hemp seeds, salt, and berries. Spread the mixture on the sheet and bake for 18 minutes. Let cool and cut into bars.

Per serving: Cal 391; Net Carbs 6.4g; Fat 38g; Protein 5.8g

Vegetable Patties

Ingredients for 4 servings

1 tbsp olive oil
1 onion, chopped
1 garlic clove, minced
½ head cauliflower, grated
1 carrot, shredded
3 tbsp coconut flour

½ cup Gruyere cheese, grated
½ cup Parmesan cheese, grated
2 eggs, beaten
½ tsp dried rosemary
Salt and black pepper to taste

Directions and Total Time: approx. 45 min + cooling time

Cook onion and garlic in warm olive oil over medium heat until soft, about 3 minutes. Stir in grated cauliflower and carrot and cook for a minute; allow cooling and set aside. To the cooled vegetables, add the rest of the ingredients. Form balls from the mixture, then press each ball to form a burger patty.

Set oven to 400 F and bake the burgers for 20 minutes. Flip and bake for another 10 minutes or until the top becomes golden brown.

Per serving: Cal 421; Fat 31g; Net Carbs 6.9g; Protein 15g

Creamy Aioli Salsa

Ingredients for 4 servings

1 egg yolk
½ lemon, juiced
1 clove garlic, mashed
½ tsp mustard powder

Salt and white pepper to taste
½ cup extra virgin olive oil
2 tbsp parsley, chopped

Directions and Total Time: approx. 15 minutes

In a blender, place lemon juice, garlic, mustard powder, salt, and egg yolk; pulse well to get a smooth and creamy mixture. Slowly add in the olive oil, blending constantly until incorporated. Stir in parsley and white pepper. Refrigerate the mixture until ready.

Per serving: Cal 146; Fat 13g; Net Carbs 0.3g; Protein 0.3g

Gruyere Crackers with Sesame Seeds

Ingredients for 4 servings

1/3 cup almond flour
Salt to taste
1 tsp baking powder
5 eggs

1/3 cup butter, melted
1 ¼ cups Gruyère cheese, grated
1 tbsp sesame seeds
1/3 cup natural yogurt

Directions and Total Time: approx. 20 minutes

Mix the flour, salt, baking powder, and Gruyère cheese in a bowl. In a separate bowl, whisk the eggs, butter, and yogurt. Pour the resulting mixture into the dry ingredients. Stir until a dough-like consistency has formed.

Fetch a soupspoon of the mixture onto a baking sheet with 2-inch intervals between each batter. Sprinkle with sesame seeds and bake in the oven for 12 minutes at 350 F until golden brown. Serve and enjoy!

Per serving: Cal 373; Fat 32g; Net Carbs 5.4g; Protein 16g

Cheesy Chorizo Pizza

Ingredients for 4 servings

1 cup sliced smoked mozzarella
2 cups shredded mozzarella   1 cups sliced chorizo
2 tbsp cream cheese, softened   ¼ cup marinara sauce
¾ cup almond flour   1 jalapeño pepper, sliced
2 tbsp almond meal   ¼ red onion, thinly sliced
1 tbsp olive oil

Directions and Total Time: approx. 40 minutes

Preheat oven to 380 F. Line a pizza pan with parchment paper. Microwave the mozzarella and cream cheeses for 30 seconds. Remove and mix in almond flour and almond meal. Spread the mixture on the pizza pan and bake for 10 minutes or until crusty.

Heat olive oil and cook chorizo until brown, 5 minutes. Spread marinara sauce on the crust, top with smoked mozzarella cheese, chorizo, jalapeño pepper, and onion. Bake until the cheese melts, 15 minutes. Remove, slice, and serve warm.

Per serving: Cal 299; Net Carbs 1g; Fats 17g; Protein 29g

Zucchini Balls with Bacon & Capers

Ingredients for 4 servings

2 zucchinis, shredded   ½ cup grated Parmesan cheese
2 bacon slices, chopped   ½ tsp poppy seeds
½ cup cream cheese, softened   ¼ tsp dried dill weed
1 cup fontina cheese   ½ tsp onion powder
¼ cup capers   Salt and black pepper to taste
1 clove garlic, crushed   1 cup crushed pork rinds

Directions and Total Time: approx. 30 minutes

Preheat oven to 360 F.

Thoroughly mix zucchinis, capers, ½ of Parmesan cheese, garlic, cream cheese, bacon, and fontina cheese until well combined. Shape the mixture into balls. In a mixing bowl, mix the remaining Parmesan cheese, crushed pork rinds, dill, black pepper, onion powder, poppy seeds, and salt. Roll cheese ball in Parmesan mixture to coat. Arrange on a greased baking dish in a single layer and bake in the oven for 15-20 minutes, shaking once. Serve.

Per serving: Cal 398; Fat 25g; Net Carbs 6.2g; Protein 31g

Broccoli & Artichoke Pizza

Ingredients for 4 servings

2 oz canned artichokes, cut into wedges
1 cup grated broccoli
2 eggs   ½ cup mozzarella, grated
1 cup grated Parmesan   1 garlic clove, thinly sliced
2 tbsp tomato sauce   ½ tbsp dried oregano
                                    Green olives for garnish

Directions and Total Time: approx. 40 minutes

Preheat oven to 350 F. Line a baking sheet with parchment paper. In a bowl, add broccoli, eggs, and Parmesan cheese and stir to combine. Pour the mixture into the baking sheet and bake until the crust is lightly browned, 20 minutes. Remove from oven and spread tomato sauce on top, sprinkle with mozzarella cheese, add artichokes and garlic. Spread oregano on top. Bake pizza for 10 minutes. Garnish with olives and serve.

Per serving: Cal 859; Net Carbs 10g; Fat 59g; Protein 55g

Roasted Brussels Sprouts & Bacon

Ingredients for 4 servings

1 tbsp olive oil   1 tbsp erythritol
1 garlic clove, sliced   Salt and black pepper to taste
6 pearl onions, halved   1 lb Brussels sprouts, halved
3 tbsp vinegar   4 oz bacon, chopped

Directions and Total Time: approx. 40 minutes

Preheat oven to 400 F. Line a baking sheet with parchment paper. Mix vinegar, erythritol, olive oil, salt, and black pepper and combine with the Brussels sprouts, garlic, bacon, and pearl onions in a bowl. Spread the mixture on the baking sheet and roast for 30 minutes until tender on the inside and crispy on the outside. Serve immediately.

Per serving: Cal 183; Fat 15.6g; Net Carbs 1.5g; Protein 9g

Baked Parsley Cheese Fingers

Ingredients for 4 servings

1 lb cheddar cheese, cut into sticks
1 cup pork rinds, crushed   1 tbsp dried parsley
1 egg

Directions and Total Time: approx. 15 minutes

Preheat oven to 350 F. Line a baking sheet with parchment paper. Mix pork rinds and parsley in a bowl. Beat the egg in another bowl. Coat the cheese sticks in the egg and then dredge in the pork rind mixture. Arrange on the baking sheet. Bake for 4-5 minutes, take out after, let cool for 2 minutes, and serve with sauce.

Per serving: Cal 213; Fat 20g; Net Carbs 1.5g; Protein 8.7g

Halloumi Scones with Avocado

Ingredients for 4 servings

2 cups almond flour   ½ cup butter, cold
1/3 cup buttermilk   1 avocado, pitted and mashed
3 tsp baking powder   1 large egg
1 cup halloumi cheese, grated

Directions and Total Time: approx. 35 minutes

Preheat oven to 350 F. Line a baking sheet with parchment paper. In a bowl, combine flour and baking powder. Add in butter and mix. Stir in halloumi cheese and avocado. Whisk the egg with the buttermilk and stir in the halloumi mix. Mold 8-10 scones out to the batter. Place on the baking sheet and bake for 25 minutes or until the scones turn a golden color. Let cool and serve.

Per serving: Cal 429; Net Carbs 2.3g; Fat 39g; Protein 9g

Crisps of Roots with Garlic Dip

Ingredients for 4 servings

¼ tsp deli mustard
3 tbsp mayonnaise
Fries
1 medium parsnip, sliced
1 large carrot, sliced
1 beet, sliced

1 garlic clove, minced
3 tbsp lemon juice

1 tsp cumin
2 tbsp olive oil
Salt and black pepper to taste

Directions and Total Time: approx. 40 minutes

Make the dip by mixing the mayonnaise with mustard, garlic, salt, black pepper, and lemon juice. Place in the fridge until ready to use.

Preheat oven to 370 F. Spread the parsnip, beet, and carrot on a large baking sheet in a single layer. Drizzle with olive oil, sprinkle with salt, and black pepper, and rub the mustard mixture onto the veggies. Bake for 10-15 minutes until golden and crispy. Remove to a plate, garnish the vegetables with cumin; Serve with the dip.

Per serving: Cal 153; Fat 12g; Net Carbs 5.5g; Protein 1.4g

Zucchini Noodles with Cheesy Sauce

Ingredients for 2 servings

2 tbsp olive oil
1 (28-oz) can tomatoes, diced
2 garlic cloves, minced
1 cup kale
1 onion, chopped

1 lb zucchinis, spiralized
¼ cup Parmesan cheese, grated
10 kalamata olives, halved
2 tbsp basil, chopped
Salt and black pepper to taste

Directions and Total Time: approx. 20 minutes

Heat the olive oil in a pan over medium heat. Add zucchinis and cook for about 3 minutes. Transfer to a serving platter. In the same pan, sauté onion and garlic for 3 minutes. Add in tomatoes, kale, salt, and pepper, reduce the heat and simmer for 8-10 minutes until thickened. Pour the sauce over zucchini noodles, scatter Parmesan cheese all over and top with olives and basil.

Per serving: Cal 388; Fat 25g; Net Carbs 6.8g; Protein 15g

Cheesy Chips with Avocado Dip

Ingredients for 4 servings

2 soft avocados, pitted and scooped
1 cup Parmesan cheese, grated
¼ tsp sweet paprika
¼ tsp taco seasoning
1 tomato, chopped

1 tsp cilantro, chopped
1 tsp tabasco sauce
Salt to taste

Directions and Total Time: approx. 25 minutes

Preheat oven to 350 F. Line a baking sheet with parchment paper. Mix Parmesan cheese, taco seasoning, and paprika. Make mounds on the baking sheet creating spaces between each stack. Flatten mounds. Bake for 5 minutes, let cool, and remove to a plate.

To make the guacamole, mash avocado with a fork in a bowl, add in tomato, cilantro, and tabasco sauce, and continue to mash until mostly smooth; season with salt. Serve crackers with avocado dip.

Per serving: Cal 283; Fat 22g; Net Carbs 3.1g; Protein 13g

Bacon & Egg Radish Hash

Ingredients for 2 servings

8 radishes, sliced
4 bacon slices
2 eggs

1 tbsp olive oil
1 shallot, chopped
1 tbsp Cajun seasoning

Directions and Total Time: approx. 25 minutes

Fry the bacon in a skillet over medium heat until crispy, about 5 minutes; set aside.

Warm the olive oil and cook the shallot until soft, stirring occasionally for about 3-4 minutes. Add the radishes, and cook for 10 more minutes until brown and tender but not mushy. Transfer to a plate and season with Cajun seasoning. Crack the eggs into the same skillet and fry over medium heat. Top the radishes mixture with bacon slices and a fried eggs. Serve hot.

Per serving: Cal 352; Fat 32g; Net Carbs 2.6g; Protein 12g

Baked Seeds & Hazelnuts

Ingredients for 4 servings

1 ½ cups hazelnuts
½ cup sunflower seeds
3 tbsp grated Parmesan
1 egg white

4 tsp yeast extract
1 tsp Swerve brown sugar
½ tsp Italian seasoning
Salt and black pepper to taste

Directions and Total Time: approx. 30 minutes

Preheat oven to 360 F. In a bowl, beat egg white, yeast extract, and Swerve brown sugar. Add in hazelnuts and sunflower seeds; combine and spread onto a lined baking sheet. Bake for 10 minutes. In a bowl, mix salt, pepper, Parmesan cheese, and Italian seasoning. Remove the nuts and toss with the cheese mixture. Bake for 5 minutes until sticky and brown. Let cool for 5 minutes and serve.

Per serving: Cal 489; Net Carbs 6g; Fat 48g; Protein 9g

Fried Artichokes with Pesto

Ingredients for 4 servings

2 tbsp olive oil
12 fresh baby artichokes
2 tbsp lemon juice

1 tbsp vinegar
4 tbsp pesto
Salt to taste

Directions and Total Time: approx. 20 minutes

Place the artichokes in cold water with vinegar for 10 minutes. Drain and pat dry well with kitchen towels. Cut the artichokes down the middle vertically. With a teaspoon, scoop out the stringy stifle to uncover the heart. Slice the artichokes vertically into narrow wedges.

Heat oil in a skillet over high heat. Fry the artichokes until browned and crispy. Drain excess oil using paper towels. Sprinkle with salt and lemon juice and serve with pesto.

Per serving: Cal 235; Fat 17.4g; Net Carbs 8.7g; Protein 8g

Veggie Skewers

Ingredients for 4 servings

8 cheddar cheese cubes
4 zucchinis, lengthwise slices
8 cherry tomatoes

8 fresh mint leaves
4 mini bamboo skewers

Directions and Total Time: approx. 45 minutes

On a flat surface, lay the zucchini slices and place 2 cheddar cubes on one end of each piece. Wrap zucchini around the cheese cubes and insert a skewer each to secure. Alternately, thread the tomatoes and mint leaves onto the skewers. Place the skewers on a plate, cover with plastic wrap, and chill for 30 minutes. Serve.

Per serving: Cal 89; Net Carbs 1.8g; Fat 4g; Protein 7g

Chili Mozzarella Bites

Ingredients for 4 servings

1 large egg, beaten	1 tsp onion powder
1 cup mozzarella cheese cubes	1 tsp garlic powder
¼ cup small tomatoes, halved	1 tsp dried basil leaves
1 cup olive oil	1 cup golden flaxseed meal
1 cup almond flour	A handful of basil leaves
½ tsp chili powder	

Directions and Total Time: approx. 20 minutes

In a bowl, combine almond flour, chili, onion and garlic powders, and basil; set aside. Pour flaxseed meal into a plate. Coat mozzarella cubes in the flour mixture, then in the egg, and then in the golden flaxseed meal.

Heat olive oil in a deep pan. Fry the cheese until golden brown. Transfer to a wire rack to drain grease. On each tomato half, place 1 basil leaf, top with a cheese cube, and insert a toothpick at the middle of the sandwich to hold. Serve.

Per serving: Cal 770; Net Carbs 2.4g; Fat 72g; Protein 20g

Feta & Bok Choy Stir-Fry

Ingredients for 2 servings

2 ½ cups baby bok choy, quartered lengthwise	
5 oz butter	1 tbsp plain vinegar
2 cups feta cheese, crumbled	2 garlic cloves, minced
Salt and black pepper to taste	1 tsp chili flakes
1 tsp garlic powder	3 green onions, sliced
1 tsp onion powder	1 tbsp sesame oil

Directions and Total Time: approx. 25 minutes

Melt half of the butter in a wok over medium heat, add the bok choy, and stir-fry until softened. Season with salt, black pepper, garlic powder, onion powder, and plain vinegar. Sauté for 2 minutes and then spoon the bok choy into a bowl; set aside.

Melt the remaining butter in the wok. Sauté the garlic and chili flakes until fragrant. Add green onions, feta, and bok choy, heat for 2 minutes, and add the sesame oil. Serve with steamed cauli rice.

Per serving: Cal 641; Fat 53g; Net Carbs 7.8g; Protein 31g

Goat Cheese & Chorizo Eggs

Ingredients for 4 servings

2 green onions, thinly sliced diagonally	
4 eggs	1 tsp smoked paprika
3 oz chorizo, diced	½ cup crumbled goat cheese
1 tsp olive oil	2 tbsp fresh parsley, chopped

Directions and Total Time: approx. 15 minutes

Preheat oven to 350 F. In a pan, heat olive oil. Add the chorizo and paprika and cook for 5-6 minutes until lightly browned; set aside.

Crack the eggs into the pan and cook them for 2 minutes. Place with chorizo and goat cheese all around the egg white, but not on the yolks. Transfer the pan to the oven and bake for 2 more minutes until the yolks are relatively set but still runny within. Garnish with green onions and parsley. Serve.

Per serving: Cal 261; Net Carbs 5.6g; Fat 16g; Protein 17g

Spicy Cauliflower Falafel

Ingredients for 2 servings

1 head cauliflower, cut into florets	
1/3 cup silvered ground almonds	
4 tbsp olive oil	1 tsp chili pepper
½ tsp ground cumin	3 tbsp coconut flour
1 tsp parsley, chopped	2 eggs
Salt to taste	

Directions and Total Time: approx. 20 minutes

Blitz the cauliflower in a food processor until a grain meal consistency is formed. Transfer to a bowl, add in the ground almonds, ground cumin, parsley, salt, chili pepper, and coconut flour, and mix until evenly combined. Beat the eggs in a bowl and mix with the cauli mixture. Shape ¼ cup each into patties and set aside.

Warm olive oil in a frying pan over medium heat and fry the patties for 5 minutes on each side until firm and browned. Remove onto a wire rack to cool, share into serving plates, and serve.

Per serving: Cal 343; Fat 31g; Net Carbs 3.7g; Protein 8.5g

Bresaola & Tomato Crostini

Ingredients for 4 servings

½ cup butter, softened	1 tbsp fresh basil, chopped
2 tbsp olive oil	1 tsp tomato paste
4 slices bresaola, chopped	4 slices zero carb bread
2 shallots	

Directions and Total Time: approx. 20 min + chilling time

Place the bresaola, 1 tbsp of butter, and shallots into a skillet over medium heat. Cook with frequent stirring for 5 minutes; let cool. Mix in the remaining butter, basil, and tomato paste. Spoon into a bowl and chill for 30 minutes to solidify slightly.

Preheat oven to 400 F. Brush zero carb bread with olive oil. Cut into strips, place on a baking sheet and toast in the oven for 3-5 minutes or until brown and crispy. Serve with prosciutto butter.

Per serving: Cal 322; Net Carbs 8.8g; Fat 31g; Protein 5g

SMOOTHIES & BEVERAGES

Green Detox Drink

Ingredients for 2 servings:

2 large ripe avocados, halved and pitted
1 small cucumber, peeled and chopped
2 tbsp Swerve sugar   ½ tsp vanilla extract
¼ cup cold almond milk   1 tbsp cold heavy cream

Directions and Total Time: approx. 5 minutes:

In a blender, add the avocado pulp, cucumber, Swerve sugar, almond milk, vanilla extract, and heavy cream. Process until smooth. Pour the mixture into 2 tall serving glasses, garnish with strawberries, and serve immediately.

Per serving: Cal 423; Fat 34g; Net Carbs 9.5g; Protein 8.2g

Blackcurrant Juice with Lime

Ingredients for 4 servings

½ cup sugar-free blackcurrant extract
Lime slices to garnish, cut on the side
5 unflavored tea bags   Ice cubes for serving
1 tbsp erythritol

Directions and Total Time: approx. 20 minutes

In a saucepan over medium heat, bring 2 cups of water to a boil for about 4 minutes; then turn the heat off. Stir in the erythritol to dissolve and steep the tea bags in the water for 3 minutes.

In the meantime, pour the ice cubes into a pitcher and place it in the fridge. Remove the bags from the saucepan, and let the tea cool down. Add in the blackcurrant extract and stir until well combined. Remove the pitcher from the fridge and pour the mixture over the ice cubes.

Allow to cool for 3 minutes and pour the mixture into tall glasses. Add some more ice cubes, place the lime slices on the rim of the glasses and serve cold.

Per serving: Cal 21; Fat 0.4g; Net Carbs 2.8g; Protein 0.5g

Raspberry Chocolate Shake

Ingredients for 2 servings

2 cups unsweetened vanilla-flavored almond milk
½ cup sugar-free chocolate-flavored protein powder
1 cup fresh raspberries   2 tsp chia seeds
2 tbsp coconut milk   4 ice cubes

Directions and Total Time: approx. 5 minutes

In a large blender, process the raspberries, almond milk, chocolate-flavored protein powder, coconut milk, and chia seeds for 2 minutes until frosty. Pour into glasses, place 2 ice cubes into each glass, and serve.

Per serving: Cal 219; Fat 11g; Net Carbs 2.8g; Protein 38g

Green Smoothie

Ingredients for 4 servings

¼ cup cold almond milk   4 tbsp Swerve sugar
1 tbsp cold heavy cream   1 tsp vanilla extract
4 avocados, halved and pitted

Directions and Total Time: approx. 5 minutes

In a blender, add avocado, swerve sugar, milk, vanilla extract, and heavy cream. Process until smooth. Pour the mixture into 2 glasses and serve.

Per serving: Cal 390; Net Carbs 2g, Fat 29g, Protein 6.9g

Strawberry Lemonade with Basil

Ingredients for 4 servings

1/3 cup fresh mint, reserve some for garnishing
12 strawberries   Crushed Ice
¼ cup fresh lemon juice   Halved strawberries to garnish
½ cup erythritol   Basil leaves to garnish

Directions and Total Time: approx. 10 minutes

Add some ice into 2 serving glasses and set aside. In a pitcher of a blender, add 2 cups of water, strawberries, lemon juice, mint, and erythritol. Process the ingredients for 30 seconds. The mixture should be pink and the mint finely chopped. Adjust the taste and divide between the ice glasses. Drop 2 strawberry halves and basil leaves in each glass and serve immediately.

Per serving: Cal 36; Fat 0.7g; Net Carbs 5.1g; Protein 1.5g

Almond Milk Berry Shake

Ingredients for 2 servings

½ cup fresh blueberries   Maple syrup to taste, sugar-free
½ cup raspberries   1 tbsp sesame seeds
½ cup almond milk   1 tbsp chopped pistachios
¼ cup heavy cream   1 tsp chopped mint leaves

Directions and Total Time: approx. 5 minutes

Combine the blueberries, raspberries, milk, heavy cream, and syrup in a blender. Process until smooth and pour into serving glasses. Top with the sesame seeds, pistachios, and mint leaves. Serve immediately.

Per serving: Cal 228; Fat 21g; Net Carbs 5.4g; Protein 7.9g

Lassi with Lychee, Yogurt & Milk

Ingredients for 4 servings

1 lemongrass, white part only, crushed
Toasted coconut shavings for garnish
2 cups lychee pulp, seeded   2 limes, zested and juiced
2 ½ cups coconut milk   1 ½ cups plain yogurt
4 tsp xylitol

Directions and Total Time: approx. 30 min + chilling time

Add the lychee pulp, coconut milk, xylitol, lemongrass, and lime zest in a saucepan. Stir and bring to boil on medium heat for 3 minutes, stirring continually. Then reduce the heat and simmer for about a minute. Turn the heat off and let the mixture sit for 15 minutes.

Discard the lemongrass and pour the mixture into a smoothie maker or a blender, add the yogurt and lime juice, and process the ingredients until smooth, for about 60 seconds. Pour into a jug and refrigerate for 2 hours until cold; stir. Serve garnished with coconut shavings.

Per serving: Cal 283; Fat 23.6g; Net Carbs 3.2g; Protein 6g

Almond-Raspberry Smoothie

Ingredients for 4 servings

½ cup raspberries
1 ½ cups almond milk
½ tsp almond extract
Juice from half lemon

Directions and Total Time: approx. 5 minutes

In a smoothie maker or blender, pour the almond milk, raspberries, lemon juice, and almond extract. Puree the ingredients at high speed until the raspberries have blended almost entirely into the liquid. Serve.

Per serving: Cal 408; Net Carbs 9g; Fat 39g; Protein 5g

Energy Smoothie

Ingredients for 4 servings

1 cup almond milk
2 tbsp sugar-free maple syrup
½ cup heavy cream
2 cups fresh blueberries
2 tbsp sesame seeds
2 tbsp chopped pistachios
1 tbsp chopped mint leaves

Directions and Total Time: approx. 5 minutes

Mix the blueberries, milk, heavy cream, and syrup in a blender. Process until smooth and pour into glasses. Top with sesame seeds, pistachios, and mint leaves and serve.

Per serving: Cal 230, Net Carbs 1g, Fat 21g, Protein 5.8g

Superfood Red Smoothie

Ingredients for 2 servings

1 Granny Smith apple, peeled and chopped
1 cup strawberries + extra for garnishing
1 cup blueberries
2 small beets, peeled, chopped
2/3 cup ice cubes
½ lemon, juiced
2 cups almond milk

Directions and Total Time: approx. 10 minutes

For the strawberries for garnishing, make a single deep cut on their sides, and set aside. In a smoothie maker, add the apples, strawberries, blueberries, beets, almond milk, and ice and blend the ingredients at high speed until nice and smooth, about 75 seconds.

Add the lemon juice, and puree further for 30 seconds. Pour the drink into tall smoothie glasses, fix the reserved strawberries on each glass rim and serve with a straw.

Per serving: Cal 233; Fat 4.3g; Net Carbs 11.3g; Protein 5g

Quick Raspberry Vanilla Shake

Ingredients for 2 servings

2 cups raspberries
2 tbsp erythritol
6 raspberries to garnish
½ cup cold almond milk
2/3 tsp vanilla extract
½ cup heavy whipping cream

Directions and Total Time: approx. 5 minutes

In a large blender, process the raspberries, milk, vanilla extract, whipping cream, and erythritol for 2 minutes; work in two batches if needed. The shake should be frosty. Pour into glasses, stick in straws, garnish with raspberries and serve.

Per serving: Cal 213; Fat 13g; Net Carbs 7.7g; Protein 4.5g

Breakfast Blueberry Coconut Smoothie

Ingredients for 2 servings

1 avocado, pitted and sliced
2 cups blueberries
1 cup coconut milk
6 tbsp coconut cream
2 tbsp erythritol
2 tbsp coconut flakes

Directions and Total Time: approx. 5 minutes

Combine the avocado slices, blueberries, coconut milk, coconut cream, and erythritol in a smoothie maker and blend until smooth. Pour the smoothie into drinking glasses, and serve sprinkled with coconut flakes.

Per serving: Cal 492; Fat 36g; Net Carbs 8.6g; Protein 9.6g

Creamy Vanilla Keto Cappuccino

Ingredients for 2 servings

2 cups unsweetened vanilla almond milk, chilled
Unsweetened chocolate shavings to garnish
1 tsp swerve sugar
½ tbsp powdered coffee
1 cup cottage cheese, cold
½ tsp vanilla bean paste
¼ tsp xanthan gum

Directions and Total Time: approx. 6 minutes

In a blender, combine the almond milk, swerve sugar, cottage cheese, coffee, vanilla bean paste, and xanthan gum and process on high speed for 1 minute until smooth. Pour into tall shake glasses, sprinkle with chocolate shavings, and serve immediately.

Per serving: Cal 253; Fat 18g; Net Carbs 6.2g; Protein 138g

Vegan Chocolate Smoothie

Ingredients for 2 servings

1 tbsp unsweetened cocoa powder
¼ cup pumpkin seeds
¾ cup coconut milk
¼ cup water
1 ½ cups watercress
2 tsp vegan protein powder
1 tbsp chia seeds

Directions and Total Time: approx. 10 minutes

In a blender, add all ingredients except for the chia seeds and process until creamy and uniform.Place into two glasses, dust with chia seeds and chill before serving.

Per serving: Cal 335; Fat 29g; Net Carbs 5.7g; Protein 6.5g

Golden Turmeric Latte with Nutmeg

Ingredients for 2 servings

2 cups almond milk
1/3 tsp cinnamon powder
½ cup brewed coffee
¼ tsp turmeric powder
1 tsp xylitol
Nutmeg powder to garnish

Directions and Total Time: approx. 10 minutes

Add the almond milk, cinnamon powder, coffee, turmeric, and xylitol to the blender. Blend the ingredients at medium speed for 50 seconds and pour the mixture into a saucepan. Over low heat, set the pan and heat through for 6 minutes, without boiling. Keep swirling the pan to prevent it from boiling. Turn the heat off, and serve in latte cups topped with nutmeg powder.

Per serving: Cal 153; Fat 13g; Net Carbs 0.9g; Protein 3.9g

Coconut Shake with Avocado

Ingredients for 2 servings

1 avocado, pitted, peeled, sliced
3 cups coconut milk, chilled   Coconut cream for topping
2 tbsp erythritol

Directions and Total Time: approx. 4 minutes

Combine coconut milk, avocado, and erythritol, into the smoothie maker, and blend for 1 minute to smooth. Pour the drink into serving glasses, slightly add some coconut cream on top of them, and garnish with mint leaves. Serve immediately.

Per serving: Cal 395; Fat 27g; Net Carbs 3.4g; Protein 14g

Chocolate Strawberries Smoothie

Ingredients for 2 servings

2 tbsp chocolate MCT oil powder
1 tbsp unsweetened cocoa powder
1 tbsp grass-fed collagen powder

1 ½ cups almond milk	1 cup frozen strawberries
4 tbsp coconut milk	½ peeled banana, frozen
½ cup walnuts	1 cup chopped spinach
2 tsp melted coconut oil	1 tsp stevia extract powder

Directions and Total Time: approx. 10 minutes

In a blender, mix the almond milk, chocolate MCR oil powder, cocoa powder, grass-fed collagen powder, coconut milk, walnuts, coconut oil, strawberries, banana, and spinach and blend until smooth. Transfer to serving glasses add top with stevia extract powder to serve.

Per serving: Cal 287; Fat 27g; Net Carbs 7.9g; Protein 13g

Kiwi Coconut Smoothie

Ingredients for 2 servings

2 cups unsweetened coconut milk

2 kiwis, pulp scooped	1 cup coconut yogurt
1 tbsp xylitol	Mint leaves to garnish
4 ice cubes	

Directions and Total Time: approx. 5 minutes

Process the kiwis, xylitol, coconut milk, yogurt, and ice cubes in a blender, until smooth, for about 3 minutes. Garnish with mint leaves and serve.

Per serving: Cal 423; Fat 36g; Net Carbs 9.2g; Protein 14g

Mixed Nuts & Smoothie Breakfast

Ingredients for 2 servings

1 tbsp unsweetened cocoa powder

3 cups buttermilk	2 tsp erythritol
2 tbsp peanut butter	1 cup mixed nuts, chopped

Directions and Total Time: approx. 5 minutes

Combine the buttermilk, peanut butter, cocoa powder, and erythritol in a smoothie maker; puree until smooth and well mixed. Share the smoothie into breakfast bowls, top with nuts, and serve.

Per serving: Cal 654; Fat 55g; Net Carbs 4.2g; Protein 16g

Almond Breakfast Smoothie

Ingredients for 2 servings

2 cups almond milk	1 tsp cinnamon
2 tbsp almond butter	4 tbsp flax meal
½ cup Greek yogurt	30 drops of stevia
1 tsp almond extract	A handful of ice cubes

Directions and Total Time: approx. 4 minutes

Put the yogurt, almond milk, almond butter, flax meal, almond extract, and stevia in the bowl of a blender. Blend until uniform and smooth, for about 30 seconds. Pour in smoothie glasses, add the ice cubes and sprinkle with cinnamon.

Per serving: Cal 412; Fat 31g; Net Carbs 5.6g; Protein 21g

Chocolate & Minty Protein Cocktail

Ingredients for 4 servings

1 avocado, pitted, peeled, sliced

3 cups almond milk, chilled	3 tbsp xylitol
3 tsp cocoa powder	1 tbsp vanilla protein powder
1 cup coconut milk, chilled	Whipping cream for topping
4 mint leaves	

Directions and Total Time: approx. 10 minutes

In a blender, mix the almond milk, cocoa powder, avocado, coconut milk, xylitol, and protein powder and blend until smooth. Transfer to serving glasses, add some whipping cream on top, and garnish with mint leaves.

Per serving: Cal 287; Fat 15g; Net Carbs 6.7g; Protein 12g

Keto Hot Chocolate

Ingredients for 2 servings

2 cups unsweetened almond milk
1 tbsp unsweetened cocoa powder
¼ cup heavy cream   2 tbsp stevia extract powder

Directions and Total Time: approx. 10 minutes

Place a saucepan over medium heat and add the almond milk and heavy cream. While stirring constantly, add the cocoa powder and cook for 2-3 minutes until slightly thickened. Whisk in stevia extract powder and serve hot.

Per serving: Cal 98; Fat 9.8g; Net Carbs 0.1g; Protein 1.8g

Cold Matcha Latte

Ingredients for 2 servings

2 tsp matcha green tea powder   1/3 cup almond milk, cold

Directions and Total Time: approx. 10 minutes

Warm 2 cups of water in your microwave. Divide the matcha green tea powder between them and whisk well until there are no lumps. Stir in cold almond milk for an iced latte. Serve and enjoy!

Warm the milk in a small saucepan and pour into the mug until nearly full. Use cold milk for an iced latte.

Per serving: Cal 95; Fat 9.5g; Net Carbs 1.3g; Protein 1.9g

SWEETS & DESSERTS

Creamy Avocado Custard

Ingredients for 4 servings

3 soft avocados
2 tsp agar agar powder
½ cup heavy cream
½ lime, juiced
½ cup water
Salt and black pepper to taste

Directions and Total Time: approx. 10 min + chilling time

Place ¼ cup of the water in a bowl and sprinkle agar agar powder on top; set aside to dissolve. Core, peel avocados, and add the flesh to a food processor. Add in heavy cream, lime juice, salt, and pepper.

Process until smooth and pour in agar agar liquid. Blend further until smooth. Divide the mixture between 4 ramekins and chill overnight.

Per serving: Cal 302; Net Carbs 7.9g; Fat 27g; Protein 2.9g

Easy Blackberry Scones

Ingredients for 4 servings

2 eggs, beaten
½ cup blackberries, halves
1 cup almond flour
3 tsp erythritol
1 ½ tsp pure vanilla extract
1 ½ tsp baking powder

Directions and Total Time: approx. 30 min + cooling time

Preheat oven to 350 F. Line a baking sheet with parchment paper. In a food processor, mix almond flour, eggs, erythritol, vanilla, and baking powder until smooth. Fold in blackberries. Pour and spread the mixture on the sheet. Cut into 8 wedges like a pizza; bake for 20 minutes or until set and golden brown. Let cool and serve.

Per serving: Cal 214; Net Carbs 1.3g; Fat 15.6g; Protein 9g

Coconut Panna Cotta Caramel

Ingredients for 4 servings

4 eggs
1/3 cup erythritol, for caramel
2 cups coconut milk
1 tbsp vanilla extract
1 tbsp lemon zest
½ cup erythritol, for custard
2 cup heavy whipping cream
Mint leaves, to serve

Directions and Total Time: approx. 65 min + chilling time

In a deep pan, heat the erythritol for the caramel. Add two tablespoons of water and bring to a boil. Lower the heat and cook until the caramel turns to a golden brown color. Divide between 4 metal tins, set aside and let cool. In a bowl, mix the eggs, remaining erythritol, lemon zest, and vanilla. Beat in the coconut milk until well combined.

Pour the custard into each caramel-lined ramekin and place them into a deep baking tin. Fill over the way with the remaining hot water. Bake at 350 F for around 45 minutes.

Carefully, take out the ramekins with tongs and refrigerate for at least 3 hours. Run a knife slowly around the edges to invert onto a dish. Serve with dollops of whipped cream and scattered with mint leaves.

Per serving: Cal 268; Fat 31g; Net Carbs 2.5g; Protein 6.5g

Coconut Panna Cotta with Raspberries

Ingredients for 6 servings

12 fresh raspberries
2 cups coconut cream
½ tbsp powdered gelatin
¼ tsp vanilla extract
1 tsp turmeric
1 tbsp erythritol
1 tbsp chopped toasted pecans

Directions and Total Time: approx. 15 min + chilling time

Combine gelatin and ½ tsp water in a bowl and allow sitting to dissolve. Pour coconut cream, vanilla extract, turmeric, and erythritol into a saucepan and bring to a boil; simmer for 2 minutes. Turn the heat off. Stir in gelatin mixture. Pour into 6 glasses, cover with a plastic wrap, and refrigerate for 2 hours. Top with pecans and raspberries and serve.

Per serving: Cal 269; Net Carbs 3g; Fat 31g; Protein 4g

Ricotta Parfait with Strawberries

Ingredients for 4 servings

1 cup ricotta cheese
2 cups strawberries, chopped
2 tbsp sugar-free maple syrup
2 tbsp balsamic vinegar

Directions and Total Time: approx. 10 minutes

Distribute half of the strawberries between 4 small glasses and top with ricotta cheese. Drizzle with maple syrup and balsamic vinegar and finish with the remaining strawberries. Serve.

Per serving: Cal 159; Net Carbs 3.1g; Fats 8g; Protein 6.9g

Minty Coconut Parfait with Cranberries

Ingredients for 4 servings

1 cup fresh cranberries
2 tbsp hemp seeds
2 cups coconut yogurt
½ lemon, zested
3 mint sprigs, chopped
Sugar-free maple syrup to taste

Directions and Total Time: approx. 10 minutes

Spoon half of coconut yogurt into 4 serving glasses. Top with cranberries, lemon zest, and hemp seeds. Cover with the remaining coconut yogurt and drizzle with maple syrup. Sprinkle with chopped mint and serve.

Per serving: Cal 98; Net Carbs 2.9g; Fat 7.8g; Protein 4.7g

Healthy Chia Pudding With Strawberries

Ingredients for 2 servings

1 cup yogurt, full-fat
2 tsp xylitol
2 tbsp chia seeds
1 cup fresh strawberries, sliced
1 tbsp lemon zest
2 mint leaves, chopped

Directions and Total Time: approx. 15 min + chilling time

In a bowl, combine the yogurt and xylitol together. Add in the chia seeds and stir. Reserve a couple of strawberries for garnish, and mash the remaining ones with a fork until pureed. Stir in the yogurt mixture and refrigerate for 45 minutes. Once cooled, divide the mixture between dessert glasses. Top each with the reserved slices of strawberries, mint leaves, and lemon zest. Serve.

Per serving: Cal 187; Fat 11g; Net Carbs 6.3g; Protein 6.7g

Chocolate Candies with Blueberries

Ingredients for 4 servings

1 ½ cups blueberry preserves, sugar-free
10 oz unsweetened chocolate chips
2 cups raw cashew nuts   3 tbsp xylitol
2 tbsp ground flax seeds   3 tbsp olive oil

Directions and Total Time: approx. 10 min + cooling time

Grind the cashew nuts and flax seeds in a blender for 50 seconds until smoothly crushed; add the blueberries and 2 tbsp of xylitol. Process further for 1 minute until well combined. Form 1-inch balls of the mixture.

Line a baking sheet with parchment paper and place the balls on the baking sheet. Freeze for 1 hour or until firmed up. In your microwave, melt the chocolate chips, olive oil, and the remaining xylitol for 95 seconds. Toss the truffles to coat in the chocolate mixture, put on the baking sheet, and freeze up for at least 3 hours.

Per serving: Cal 253; Fat 18g; Net Carbs 4.1g; Protein 10g

Matcha Brownies with Pistachios

Ingredients for 4 servings

4 tbsp Swerve confectioner's sugar
1 tbsp tea matcha powder   ½ tsp baking powder
¼ cup unsalted butter, melted   1 egg
A pinch of salt   ½ cup chopped pistachios
¼ cup coconut flour

Directions and Total Time: approx. 30 minutes

Line a square baking dish with parchment paper and preheat the oven to 350 F. In a bowl, pour the melted butter, Swerve sugar, and salt and whisk to combine. Crack the egg into the bowl. Beat the mixture until the egg is incorporated. Pour the coconut flour, matcha, and baking powder into a fine-mesh sieve and sift them into the egg bowl; stir. Stir in the pistachios and pour the mixture into the baking dish to cook for 18 minutes. Remove and slice into brownie cubes.

Per serving: Cal 243; Fat 22g; Net Carbs 4.3g; Protein 7.2g

Mascarpone & Strawberry Pudding

Ingredients for 6 servings

1 cup mascarpone, softened   1 tsp cinnamon powder
2 oz fresh strawberries   1 tsp vanilla extract
1 ¼ cups coconut cream

Directions and Total Time: approx. 20 minutes

Put coconut cream into a bowl and whisk until a soft peak forms. Mix in vanilla and cinnamon. Lightly fold in mascarpone and refrigerate for 10 minutes to set. Spoon into serving glasses, top with the strawberries, and serve.

Per serving: Cal 231; Fat 20g; Net Carbs 3g; Protein 6g

Dark Chocolate Brownies

Ingredients for 4 servings

10 tbsp butter   2 eggs, beaten
2 oz sugar-free dark chocolate ¼ cup cocoa powder
½ cup almond flour   ½ cup erythritol
½ tsp baking powder   ½ tsp vanilla extract

Directions and Total Time: approx. 30 min+ chilling time

Preheat oven to 380 F. Line a baking sheet with parchment paper. In a bowl, mix cocoa powder, almond flour, baking powder, and erythritol until no lumps from the erythritol remain. In another bowl, add butter and dark chocolate and microwave for 30 seconds. Mix the eggs and vanilla into the chocolate mixture, then pour the mixture into the dry ingredients; mix well. Pour the batter onto the paper-lined sheet and bake for 20 minutes. Let cool completely and refrigerate for 2 hours. Slice into squares.

Per serving: Cal 231; Net Carbs 3g; Fat 20g; Protein 4g

Favorite Peanut Butter Mousse

Ingredients for 4 servings

¼ cup smooth peanut butter   ¼ cup xylitol
4 oz softened cream cheese   ½ tsp vanilla extract
½ cup heavy cream

Directions and Total Time: approx. 15 minutes

Whip ½ cup of heavy cream in a bowl using an electric mixer until stiff peaks hole; set aside. In another bowl, beat cream cheese and peanut butter until creamy and smooth. Mix in xylitol and vanilla extract. Gradually fold in the cream mixture until well combined. If too thick, fold in 2 tbsp of the reserved heavy cream. Spoon the mousse into dessert glasses and serve.

Per serving: Cal 229; Net Carbs 5g; Fat 21g; Protein 6g

Chocolate Mousse Pots with Blackberries

Ingredients for 4 servings

2 ½ cups unsweetened dark chocolate, melted
½ cup Swerve confectioner's sugar
3 cups heavy cream   ½ cup blackberries, chopped
½ tsp vanilla extract   Some blackberries for topping

Directions and Total Time: approx. 10 min + chilling time

In a stand mixer, beat heavy cream and Swerve sugar until creamy. Add dark chocolate and vanilla extract and mix until smoothly combined. Fold in blackberries. Divide the mixture between 4 dessert cups, cover with plastic wrap, and refrigerate for 2 hours. Garnish with the reserved blackberries and serve.

Per serving: Cal 309; Net Carbs 2.6g; Fat 33g; Protein 2g

Avocado Mousse with Chocolate

Ingredients for 4 servings

1 avocado, pitted and peeled   1 heaped tbsp cocoa powder
2 tbsp cream of tartar   1 cup Greek yogurt
1 cup full-fat coconut cream

Directions and Total Time: approx. 10 min + chilling time

In a food processor, add coconut cream, avocado, cocoa powder, cream of tartar, and Greek yogurt. Blend until smooth. Divide the mixture between 4 dessert cups and chill in the refrigerator for at least 2 hours. Serve.

Per serving: Cal 329; Net Carbs 8.2g; Fat 31g; Protein 6g

Mascarpone Cream Mousse

Ingredients for 6 servings

For the mascarpone

8 oz heavy cream	4 tbsp cocoa powder
8 oz mascarpone cheese	4 tbsp xylitol

For the vanilla mousse

3.5 oz heavy cream	1 tsp vanilla extract
3.5 oz cream cheese	2 tbsp xylitol

Directions and Total Time: approx. 15 minutes

Beat mascarpone cheese, heavy cream, cocoa powder, and xylitol with an electric mixer until creamy. Do not over mix, however. In another bowl, whisk all the mousse ingredients until smooth. Gradually fold vanilla mousse mixture into the mascarpone one until well incorporated. Spoon into dessert cups and serve.

Per serving: Cal 409; Net Carbs 5.9g; Fat 32g; Protein 7.9g

Mojito Mousse with Blackberries

Ingredients for 4 servings

½ cup Swerve confectioner's sugar	
2 ½ cups sour cream	½ tsp vanilla extract
3 cups heavy cream	Chopped mint to garnish
3 limes, juiced	12 blackberries for topping

Directions and Total Time: approx. 10 min + chilling time

In a stand mixer, beat heavy cream and Swerve sugar until creamy. Add sour cream, lime juice, and vanilla; combine smoothly. Divide between 4 dessert cups, cover with plastic wrap, and refrigerate for 2 hours. Remove, garnish with mint leaves, top with blackberries, and serve.

Per serving: Cal 489; Net Carbs 8.7g; Fat 43g; Protein 3.9g

Speedy Chocolate Peppermint Mousse

Ingredients for 4 servings

4 oz cream cheese	3 tbsp cocoa powder
1/3 cup coconut cream	¾ tsp peppermint extract
¼ cup Swerve sugar, divided	½ tsp vanilla extract

Directions and Total Time: approx. 10 min + chilling time

Place 2 tbsp of Swerve, cream cheese, and cocoa powder in a blender. Add in peppermint extract and ¼ cup warm water; process until smooth. In a bowl, whip vanilla extract, coconut cream, and remaining Swerve using a whisk. Fetch out 5 tbsp for garnishing. Fold in cocoa mixture until thoroughly combined. Spoon the mousse into cups and refrigerate. Garnish with whipped cream.

Per serving: Cal 169; Net Carbs 2g; Fat 15.9g; Protein 2.9g

Strawberry Chocolate Mousse

Ingredients for 2 servings

3 eggs	1 cup fresh strawberries, sliced
½ cup dark chocolate chips	1 vanilla extract
1 cup heavy cream	1 tbsp xylitol

Directions and Total Time: approx. 15 min + cooling time

Melt the chocolate in the microwave for a minute and let it cool for 10 minutes.

In another bowl, whip the cream until very soft. Add the eggs, vanilla extract, and xylitol; whisk to combine. Fold in the cooled chocolate. Divide the mousse between glasses, top with the strawberry slices, and chill in the fridge for at least 30 minutes before serving.

Per serving: Cal 567; Fat 46g; Net Carbs 9.6g; Protein 14g

Fluffy Lemon Curd Mousse with Walnuts

Ingredients for 4 servings

For the mousse

1 cup cold heavy cream	1 tsp vanilla extract
8 oz cream cheese	½ lemon, juiced
¼ cup Swerve sugar	

For the caramel nuts

1 cup walnuts, chopped	A pinch salt
2/3 cup Swerve brown sugar	

Directions and Total Time: approx. 20 min + chilling time

In a stand mixer, beat cream cheese and heavy cream until you get a creamy consistency. Add vanilla, Swerve sugar, and lemon juice until smooth. Divide the mixture between 4 dessert cups. Cover with plastic wrap and refrigerate for at least 2 hours.

For the caramel walnuts:

Add Swerve sugar to a large skillet and cook over medium heat with frequent stirring until melted and golden brown. Mix in 2 tbsp of water and salt and cook further until syrupy and slightly thickened.

Turn the heat off and quickly mix in the walnuts until well coated in the caramel; let sit for 5 minutes. Remove the mousse from the fridge and top with the caramel walnuts. Serve immediately.

Per serving: Cal 521; Net Carbs 8g; Fat 53g; Protein 7g

Chocolate Almond Ice Cream Treats

Ingredients for 4 servings

Ice cream

½ cup heavy whipping cream	1 cup almond milk
½ tsp vanilla extract	¼ tsp stevia powder
½ tsp xanthan gum	½ tbsp vegetable glycerin
¼ cup almond butter	2 tbsp erythritol
½ cup half and half	

Chocolate

¼ cup cocoa butter pieces, chopped	
3 ½ tsp THM super sweet blend	
¾ cup coconut oil	2 oz unsweetened chocolate

Directions and Total Time: approx. 20 min + cooling time

In a bowl, blend all ice cream ingredients until smooth. Place in an ice cream maker and follow the instructions. Spread the ice cream into a lined pan and freezer for about 4 hours. Mix all chocolate ingredients in a microwave-safe bowl and heat until melted. Allow cooling. Remove ice cream from the freezer and slice into bars. Dip into the cooled chocolate mixture and return to the freezer for about 10 minutes before serving.

Per serving: Cal 305; Fat 25g; Net Carbs 5.3g; Protein 6.2g

Chocolate Mocha Mousse Cups

Ingredients for 4 servings

2 tbsp butter, softened
8 oz cream cheese, softened
2/3 cup heavy whipping cream
3 tbsp sour cream
1/3 cup erythritol

3 tsp instant coffee powder
¼ cup cocoa powder
1 ½ tsp Swerve sugar
½ tsp vanilla extract

Directions and Total Time: approx. 10 minutes

Beat cream cheese, sour cream, and butter with an electric hand mixer until smooth. Add in vanilla, erythritol, coffee and cocoa powders and mix thoroughly until all ingredients are well incorporated.

In a separate bowl, beat whipping cream and Swerve sugar until soft peaks form. Fold 1/3 of the whipped cream mixture into the cream cheese mixture to lighten a bit. Stir in the remaining mixture until well incorporated. Spoon into dessert cups. Serve.

Per serving: Cal 310; Net Carbs 4g; Fat 29g; Protein 5g

No-Bake Mousse with Strawberries

Ingredients for 4 servings

2 tbsp sugar-free strawberry preserves
2 cups chilled heavy cream
2 cups strawberries, hulled
4 tbsp xylitol

2 tbsp lime juice
¼ tsp strawberry extract

Directions and Total Time: approx. 10 min + cooling time

In a bowl, beat the heavy cream with a hand mixer until a stiff peak forms, about 1 minute; refrigerate for 10 minutes. Puree the strawberries in a blender and pour into a saucepan. Stir in xylitol and lime juice and cook on low heat for 3 minutes while stirring continuously. Stir in the strawberry extract evenly, and turn off the heat to cool. Fold in the cream until evenly incorporated and spoon into ramekins. Refrigerate for 3 hours. Garnish with strawberry preserves and serve.

Per serving: Cal 353; Fat 32g; Net Carbs 4.8g; Protein 5.3g

Grandma's Coconut Treats

Ingredients for 4 servings

1/3 cup ghee
10 saffron threads
1 1/3 cups coconut milk

1 ¾ cups shredded coconut
4 tbsp xylitol
1 tsp cardamom powder

Directions and Total Time: approx. 20 min + cooling time

In a bowl, combine the shredded coconut with a cup of coconut milk. In another bowl, mix together the remaining coconut milk with xylitol and saffron. Let sit for 30 minutes.

In a wok, heat the ghee. Add the coconut mixtures and cook for 5 minutes on low heat, mixing continuously. Stir in the cardamom and cook for another 5 minutes. Spread the mixture onto a small container and freeze for 2 hours. Cut into bars and enjoy!

Per serving: Cal 224; Fat 22g; Net Carbs 2.7g; Protein 3.3g

Chocolate Mousse with Cherries

Ingredients for 4 servings

Mousse

12 oz unsweetened dark chocolate
8 eggs, separated into yolks and whites
2 tbsp salt
¾ cup Swerve sugar

½ cup olive oil
3 tbsp brewed coffee

Cherries

1 cup cherries, pitted and halved
½ stick cinnamon
½ cup Swerve sugar

½ cup water
½ lime, juiced

Directions and Total Time: approx. 40 min + chilling time

To make the mousse, melt the chocolate in the microwave for 95 seconds. In a bowl, whisk the yolks with half of the Swerve sugar until a pale yellow has formed. Then, beat in the salt, olive oil, and coffee. Mix in the melted chocolate until smooth.

In a third bowl, whisk the whites with the hand mixer until a soft peak has formed. Sprinkle the remaining Swerve sugar over and gently fold in with a spatula. Fetch a tablespoon of the chocolate mixture and fold in to combine. Pour in the remaining chocolate mixture and whisk to mix. Spoon the mousse into ramekins, cover with plastic wrap, and refrigerate overnight.

The next day, make the poached cherries. Pour ½ cup of water, ½ cup of Swerve, ½ stick cinnamon, and lime juice in a saucepan and bring to a simmer for 4 minutes, stirring to ensure the Swerve has dissolved and a syrup has formed. Add cherries and poach in the sweetened water for 20 minutes until soft. Turn heat off and discard the cinnamon stick. Spoon a cherry, each with syrup on the chocolate mousse, and serve.

Per serving: Cal 288; Fat 24g; Net Carbs 8.1g; Protein 10g

Creamy Berry Bowl with Pecans

Ingredients for 4 servings

1 ½ cups blackberries and raspberries
4 cups Greek yogurt
Liquid stevia to taste

1 ½ cups mascarpone cheese
1 cup toasted pecans

Directions and Total Time: approx. 10 minutes

In a bowl, mix the yogurt, stevia, and mascarpone until thoroughly combined. Divide the mixture into bowls, share the berries and pecans on top of the cream. Serve.

Per serving: Cal 398; Fat 37g; Net Carbs 4.2g; Protein 16g

Hot Chocolate with Almonds & Cinnamon

Ingredients for 4 servings

4 tbsp unsweetened cocoa powder
3 cups almond milk
2 tbsp xylitol
3 tbsp almond butter

2 tbsp finely chopped almonds
Ground cinnamon to garnish

Directions and Total Time: approx. 15 minutes

Add the almond milk, cocoa powder, and xylitol to a saucepan and stir until the sweetener dissolves. Set the pan over low to heat through for 6 minutes, without boiling.

Swirl the mix occasionally. Stir in the almond butter until incorporated and turn the heat off. Transfer the hot chocolate to mugs and sprinkle with almonds and cinnamon. Serve hot.

Per serving: Cal 273; Fat 21g; Net Carbs 8.3g; Protein 10g

Winter Hot Chocolate with Peanuts

<u>Ingredients</u> for 4 servings

3 tbsp peanut butter	2 tbsp Swerve
3 cups almond milk	Chopped peanuts to garnish
4 tbsp cocoa powder	

<u>Directions</u> and Total Time: approx. 10 minutes

In a saucepan, add the almond milk, cocoa powder, and Swerve. Stir the mixture until the Swerve dissolves. Set the pan over low to heat through for 5 minutes, without boiling. Swirl the mix occasionally. Turn the heat off and stir in the peanut butter until incorporated. Pour the hot chocolate into mugs and sprinkle with chopped peanuts.

Per serving: Cal 219; Net Carbs 0.8g; Fat 22g; Protein5g

Minty Lemon Tart

<u>Ingredients</u> for 4 servings
Piecrust
¼ cup almond flour + extra for dusting
¼ cup butter, cold and crumbled

3 tbsp coconut flour	1 ½ tsp vanilla extract
½ tsp salt	4 whole eggs
3 tbsp erythritol	

Filling

4 tbsp melted butter	1 lemon, juiced
3 tsp Swerve brown sugar	1 cup ricotta cheese
1 cup fresh blackberries	4 fresh mint leaves to garnish
1 tsp vanilla extract	1 egg, lightly beaten

<u>Directions</u> and Total Time: approx. 60 min + chilling time

In a large bowl, mix the almond flour, coconut flour, and salt. Add the butter and mix with an electric hand mixer until crumbly. Add in the erythritol and vanilla extract until mixed. Then, pour in the 4 eggs one after another while mixing until formed into a ball. Flatten the dough on a flat surface, cover with plastic foil, and chill for 1 hour.

Preheat the oven to 350 F and grease a pie pan with cooking spray. Lightly dust a clean flat surface with almond flour, unwrap the dough, and roll out the dough into a 1-inch diameter circle. In a 10-inch shallow baking pan, mix the butter, Swerve brown sugar, blackberries, vanilla extract, and lemon juice. Arrange the blackberries uniformly across the pan.

Lay the pastry over the fruit filling and tuck the sides into the pan. Brush with the beaten egg and bake in the oven for 35 to 40 minutes or until golden and puffed up.

Remove, allow cooling for 5 minutes, and then run a knife around the pan to losing the pastry. Turn the pie over onto a plate, crumble the ricotta cheese on top, and garnish with the mint leaves.

Per serving: Cal 533; Fat 44g; Net Carbs 8.7g; Protein 17g

Maple-Vanilla Tart

<u>Ingredients</u> for 4 servings
Piecrust
¼ cup almond flour + extra for dusting
¼ cup butter, cold and crumbled

3 tbsp coconut flour	1 ½ tsp vanilla extract
½ tsp salt	4 whole eggs
3 tbsp erythritol	

Filling

2 whole eggs + 3 egg yolks	1 ¼ cup almond milk
½ cup Swerve sugar	1 ¼ cup heavy cream
1 tsp vanilla bean paste	2 tbsp maple syrup, sugar-free
2 tbsp coconut flour	¼ cup chopped almonds

<u>Directions</u> and Total Time: approx. 65 min + cooling time

Preheat the oven to 350 F. Grease a pie pan with cooking spray. In a large bowl, mix the almond flour, coconut flour, and salt. Add the butter and mix with an electric hand mixer until crumbly. Add in the erythritol and vanilla extract and mix well. Then, pour in the 4 eggs one after another while mixing until formed into a ball. Flatten the dough on a clean flat surface, cover in plastic wrap, and refrigerate for 1 hour.

After, lightly dust a clean flat surface with almond flour, unwrap the dough, and roll out the dough into a large rectangle, ½-inch thickness and fit into a pie pan. Bake in the oven until golden. Remove after and allow cooling.

In a large mixing bowl, whisk the whole 3 eggs, egg yolks, Swerve sugar, vanilla bean paste, and coconut flour. Put the almond milk, heavy cream, and maple syrup into a medium pot and bring to a boil over medium heat. Pour the mixture into the egg mixture and whisk while pouring. Run the batter through a fine strainer into a bowl and skim off any froth. Take out the pie pastry from the oven, pour out the baking beans, remove the parchment paper, and transfer the egg batter into the pie. Bake in the oven for 40-50 minutes or until the custard sets with a slight wobble in the center. Garnish with the chopped almonds, slice, and serve when cooled.

Per serving: Cal 542; Fat 41g; Net Carbs 8.5g; Protein 16g

Coconut-Berry Tarts

<u>Ingredients</u> for 4 servings
For the crust

2 cups almond flour	1/3 cup xylitol
6 tbsp butter, melted	1 tsp cinnamon powder

For the filling
Swerve confectioner's sugar for topping

2 cups frozen berries	1 cup coconut cream

<u>Directions</u> and Total Time: approx. 25 min + chilling time

Preheat oven to 360 F. Lightly grease 4 mini tart tins with cooking spray. In a food processor, blend butter, almond flour, xylitol, and cinnamon. Divide and spread the dough on the tart tins. Bake for 15 minutes. Let cool. Divide the coconut cream between the tart crusts and top with berries. Dust with Swerve confectioner's sugar.

Per serving: Cal 250; Net Carbs 5.5g; Fat 19g; Protein 5g

Fresh Berry Galette

Ingredients for 4 servings
Piecrust
¼ cup almond flour + extra for dusting
¼ cup butter, cold and crumbled
3 tbsp coconut flour   1 ½ tsp vanilla extract
½ tsp salt   4 whole eggs
3 tbsp erythritol
Filling
2 ¼ cups strawberries and blackberries
1 cup erythritol + extra for sprinkling
1 vanilla pod, bean paste extracted
1 egg, beaten

Directions and Total Time: approx. 50 min + chilling time

In a large bowl, mix the almond flour, coconut flour, and salt. Add the butter and mix with your hands until crumbly. Mix in the erythritol and vanilla extract. Then, pour in the 4 eggs one after another while mixing until formed into a ball. Flatten the dough on a clean flat surface, cover in plastic wrap, and refrigerate for 1 hour.

Preheat oven to 350 F. Lightly dust a clean flat surface with almond flour, unwrap the dough, and roll out the dough into a large rectangle, ½-inch thickness. Fit it into a greased pie pan. Trim the edges and carefully poke a few holes in the surface with a fork to prevent bubbling. Roll out the remaining pastry and slice into strips; set aside. Bake the crust in the oven for 10-12 minutes until lightly golden. Remove and allow cooling.

In a bowl, mix the berries, 1 cup of erythritol, and vanilla bean paste. Spoon the mixture into the cooled crust and level with a spoon. Use the pastry strips to create a lattice top over the berries. Brush with the beaten egg, sprinkle with more erythritol, and bake for 25-30 minutes or until the fruit is bubbling and the pie golden brown. Remove from the oven, allow cooling, slice, and serve with whipped cream.

Per serving: Cal 313; Fat 23g; Net Carbs 7.3g; Protein 10g

Vanilla Passion Fruit Galette

Ingredients for 4 servings

1 cup crushed almond biscuits ½ cup butter, melted
Filling
1 ½ cups mascarpone cheese   1 tsp vanilla bean paste
¾ cup Swerve sugar   4-6 tbsp cold water
1 ½ cups whipping cream   1 tbsp gelatin powder
Passionfruit fruit
¼ cup Swerve confectioner's sugar
1 cup passion fruit pulp   1 tsp gelatin powder

Directions and Total Time: approx. 20 min + cooling time

In a bowl, mix crushed biscuits and butter. Spoon into a spring-form pan, and use the back of the spoon to level at the bottom; set aside in the fridge. In another bowl, put the mascarpone cheese, Swerve sugar, and vanilla paste, and whisk with a hand mixer until smooth; set aside. In a third bowl, add 2 tbsp of cold water and sprinkle 1 tbsp of gelatin powder. Let dissolve for 5 minutes.

Pour the gelatin liquid and the whipping cream into the cheese mixture and fold gently. Remove the spring-form pan from the refrigerator and pour over the mixture.

Return to the fridge. Then, repeat the dissolving process for the remaining gelatin and once you are out of ingredients, pour the confectioner's sugar and ¼ cup of water into it. Mix and stir in the passion fruit pulp. Remove the cake again and pour the jelly over it. Swirl the pan to make the jelly level up. Place the pan back into the fridge to cool for 2 hours. When completely set, remove and unlock the spring-pan. Lift the pan from the cake and slice the dessert.

Per serving: Cal 383; Fat 26g; Net Carbs 6.8g; Protein 9.3g

Cinnamon Pumpkin Pie

Ingredients for 4 servings
Crust
6 tbsp butter   1 tsp cinnamon
2 cups almond flour   1/3 cup sweetener
Filling
2 cups shredded pumpkin   ½ tsp cinnamon
¼ cup butter   ½ tsp lemon juice
¼ cup erythritol
Topping
¼ tsp cinnamon   2 tbsp erythritol

Directions and Total Time: approx. 75 minutes

Combine all crust ingredients in a bowl. Press this mixture into the bottom of a greased pan. Bake for 5 minutes in a preheated to 370 F oven.

Meanwhile, in a bowl, combine the pumpkin and lemon juice and let them sit until the crust is ready. Arrange on top of the crust. Combine the rest of the filling ingredients, and brush this mixture over the pumpkin.

Bake for about 35 minutes. Press the pumpkin down with a spatula, return to oven and bake for 20 more minutes. Combine the cinnamon and 2 tbsp erythritol, in a bowl, and sprinkle over the tart.

Per serving: Cal 388; Fat 34g; Net Carbs 7.6g; Protein 8.5g

Vanilla Cookies with Cardamom Coating

Ingredients for 4 servings

Cookies
½ cup butter, softened   ¾ cup sweetener
2 cups almond flour   1 tbsp vanilla extract
½ tsp baking soda
Coating
1 tsp ground cardamom   2 tbsp erythritol

Directions and Total Time: approx. 25 minutes

Preheat your oven to 360 F. Combine all cookie ingredients in a bowl. Make balls out of the mixture and flatten them with your hands.

Combine the cardamom and erythritol. Dip the cookies in the cardamom mixture and arrange them on a lined cookie sheet. Cook for 15 minutes until crispy.

Per serving: Cal 129; Net Carbs: 1g; Fat: 12.9g; Protein: 3g

Lavender & Raspberry Pie

Ingredients for 4 servings

Crust

¼ cup vegetable oil
⅓ cup coconut flour

⅓ cup erythritol
¾ cup almond meal

Custard

1 ½ cups heavy cream
2 tbsp erythritol + for topping
1 tbsp culinary lavender

1 vanilla, seeds extracted
2 cups fresh raspberries

Directions and Total Time: approx. 25 min + cooling time

Whisk the vegetable oil with erythritol in a bowl until well blended. Stir in the almond meal and coconut flour and mix again. Press the crust mixture into the bottom of a parchment-lined baking dish. Place in the refrigerator to harden.

Meanwhile, make the custard. In a saucepan over medium heat, mix the heavy cream and lavender and bring to a boil. Turn the heat off and let cool. Refrigerate for 1 hour to infuse the cream. Remove the cream from the fridge and strain through a colander into a bowl to remove the lavender pieces. Mix in the erythritol and vanilla.

Remove the crust from the fridge. Spread the custard over the cooled crust. Scatter the raspberries on and refrigerate the pie for 45 minutes. Remove and top with erythritol, before slicing.

Per serving: Cal 451; Fat 41g; Net Carbs 3.5g; Protein 6.8g

Classic Lemon Curd Tarts

Ingredients for 4 servings

For the crust

¼ cup Swerve confectioner's sugar
1 large egg
¼ cup butter, melted

1 ½ cups almond flour
½ tsp salt

For the filling

½ cup Swerve confectioner's sugar
4 tbsp salted butter
½ lemon, zested and juiced

3 large eggs

Directions and Total Time: approx. 30 min + chilling time

Preheat oven to 360 F. Lightly grease 4 mini tart tins with cooking spray. In a food processor, blend almond flour, Swerve sugar, salt, butter, and egg. Divide and spread the dough on the tins. Bake for 15 minutes. For the filling, melt butter in a saucepan over medium heat, take off the heat and quickly mix in Swerve sugar, lemon zest, and lemon juice until smooth. Whisk in eggs and return the saucepan to low heat. Cook with continuous stirring until thick. Pour the filling into the crust, gently tap on a flat surface to release air bubbles, and chill in the refrigerator.

Per serving: Cal 209; Net Carbs 2g; Fat 19g; Protein 7g

Chocolate & Caramel Shortbread Cookies

Ingredients for 6 servings

¼ cup sugar-free caramel sauce
1 cup chopped dark chocolate 2 cups butter, softened
1 ½ cups Swerve brown sugar Sea salt flakes
3 cups almond flour

Directions and Total Time: approx. 30 minutes

Preheat oven to 360 F. Line a baking sheet with parchment paper. In a bowl, using an electric mixer, whisk butter, Swerve, and caramel sauce. Mix in flour and chocolate until well combined. Using a scoop, spoon 1 ½ tbsp of the batter onto the sheet at 2-inch intervals and sprinkle salt flakes on top. Bake for 15 minutes until lightly golden.

Per serving: Cal 409; Net Carbs 0.6g; Fat 43g; Protein 4.9g

Valentine's Day Cookies

Ingredients for 4 servings

2 cups almond flour + extra for dusting
½ cup unsweetened dark chocolate
½ lemon, zested
1 cup unsalted butter, softened
2/3 cup Swerve sugar

1 large egg, beaten
2 tsp vanilla extract
2 tbsp chopped pistachios

Directions and Total Time: approx. 30 min + chilling time

Preheat oven to 350 F. Add the butter and Swerve sugar to a bowl; beat with an electric whisk until smooth and creamy. Whisk in the egg until combined. Mix in the vanilla extract, lemon zest, and almond flour until a soft dough forms. Wrap the dough in plastic wrap and chill for 10 minutes. Dust a chopping board with some almond flour. Unwrap the dough and roll out on the chopping board to 2-inch thickness. Using a cookie cutter, cut out as many biscuits as you can get while rerolling the trimming and making more biscuits.

Arrange the biscuits on the parchment paper-lined baking sheet and bake for 12 to 15 minutes or until crisp at the edges and pale golden. Remove and transfer to a wire rack to cool completely when ready. In two separate bowls, melt the chocolate in your microwave. Dip one side of each biscuit in the dark chocolate. Garnish the dark chocolate's side with the pistachios and allow cooling on the wire rack.

Per serving: Cal 476; Fat 43.5g; Net Carbs 5g; Protein 4.5g

Vanilla Cheesecake Cookies

Ingredients for 4 servings

1 large egg
2 tsp vanilla extract
¼ cup softened butter
2 oz softened cream cheese

1/3 cup xylitol
¼ tsp salt
1 tbsp sour cream
3 cups blanched almond flour

Directions and Total Time: approx. 25 minutes

Preheat oven to 360 F. Line a baking sheet with parchment paper. Using an electric mixer, whisk butter, cream cheese, and xylitol in a bowl until fluffy and light in color. Beat in egg, vanilla, salt, and sour cream until smooth. Add in flour and mix until soft batter forms. With a cookie scoop, arrange 1 ½ tbsp of batter onto the sheet at 2-inch intervals. Bake for 15 minutes until lightly golden. Let cool before serving.

Per serving: Cal 180; Net Carbs 1.3g; Fat 17g; Protein 2.9g

Sunday Chocolate Cookies

Ingredients for 4 servings

2 cups unsweetened dark chocolate chips
7 oz butter, softened   3 eggs
2 cups Swerve brown sugar   2 cups almond flour

Directions and Total Time: approx. 30 minutes

Line a baking sheet with parchment paper. Preheat oven to 330 F. In a bowl with a hand mixer, whisk the butter and Swerve sugar for 3 minutes or until light and fluffy. Add the eggs one at a time and scrape the sides as you whisk. Mix in almond flour at low speed until well combined. Fold in chocolate chips. Scoop 3 tablespoons each on the baking sheet, creating spaces between each mound, and bake for 15 minutes to swell and harden. Remove, cool, and serve.

Per serving: Cal 293; Fat 24.5g; Net Carbs 7.3g; Protein 6g

Almond Cookies

Ingredients for 4 servings

1 large egg   1 cup Swerve sugar
1 cup butter, softened   ¾ tsp almond extract
2 ¼ cups almond flour   ½ tsp salt
1 tsp baking powder

Directions and Total Time: approx. 40 minutes

Preheat oven to 380 F. Line a baking sheet with parchment paper. In a bowl, mix almond flour, baking powder, and salt. In another bowl, mix butter, Swerve sugar, egg, and almond extract until well smooth. Combine both mixtures until soft dough forms.

Lay a parchment paper on a flat surface, place the dough, and cover with another parchment paper. Using a rolling pin, flatten it into the ½-inch thickness and cut it into squares. Arrange on the baking sheet with 1-inch intervals and bake in the oven until the edges are set and golden brown, about 25 minutes. Serve cooled.

Per serving: Cal 430; Net Carbs 0.4g; Fat 46g; Protein 1.4g

Maple Sponge Lemon Cake

Ingredients for 4 servings

1 tbsp Swerve confectioner's sugar
½ cup butter, softened   1 tsp vanilla extract
4 large lemons, chopped   ½ cup almond flour
¼ cup sugar-free maple syrup   3 large eggs, lightly beaten
½ cup erythritol   ½ cup heavy cream

Directions and Total Time: approx. 60 minutes

Throw the lemons in a saucepan. Add in sugar-free maple syrup and simmer over low heat for 10 minutes. Pour the mixture into a blender and process until smooth. Pour into a jar and set aside.

Preheat oven to 350 F. Grease two (8-inch) springform pans with cooking spray and line with parchment paper. In a bowl, cream the butter, erythritol, and vanilla extract with an electric whisk until light and fluffy. Pour in the eggs gradually while beating until thoroughly mixed.

Carefully fold in the almond flour and share the mixture into the cake pans. Bake for 30 minutes or until springy when touched and a toothpick inserted comes out clean. Remove and let cool for 5 minutes before turning out onto a wire rack.

In a bowl, whip heavy cream until a soft peak forms. Spoon onto the bottom sides of the cake and spread the lemon puree on top. Sandwich both cakes and sift confectioner's sugar on top. Slice and serve.

Per serving: Cal 271; Net Carbs 4.6g; Fat 25g; Protein 6g

The Best Cowboy Cookies

Ingredients for 8 servings

2 large eggs   1 tbsp cinnamon powder
2 cups almond flour   1 cup sugar-free chocolate
2 tsp baking powder   chips
1 tsp baking soda   1 cup peanut butter chips
1 cup butter, softened   2 cups golden flaxseed meal
1 cup Swerve white sugar   1 ½ cups coconut flakes
1 cup Swerve brown sugar   2 cups chopped walnuts
1 tbsp vanilla extract   1 tsp salt

Directions and Total Time: approx. 30 minutes

Preheat oven to 380 F. Line a baking sheet with parchment paper. Using a hand mixer, cream the butter and Swerve white and brown sugar until light and fluffy in a large bowl. Slowly, beat in the vanilla and eggs until smooth. In a separate bowl, mix almond flour, baking powder, baking soda, cinnamon, and salt. Combine both mixtures and fold in the chocolate chips, peanut butter chips, flaxseed meal, coconut flaxes, and walnuts. Roll the dough into 1 ½-inch balls and arrange on the baking sheet at 2-inch intervals. Bake for 10-12 minutes or until lightly golden. Serve cooled.

Per serving: Cal 440; Net Carbs 4.6g; Fat 40g; Protein 16g

Mom's Walnut and Pecan Cookies

Ingredients for 4 servings

1 egg   ¼ tsp baking soda
1 cup ground pecans   1 tbsp butter
2 tbsp sweetener   4 walnuts, halved

Directions and Total Time: approx. 25 minutes

Mix all ingredients, except the walnuts, until well combined. Make balls out of the mixture and press them with your thumb onto a lined cookie sheet. Top each cookie with a walnut half. Bake for about 12 minutes in a preheated to 340 F oven.

Per serving: Cal 163; Fat 13g; Net Carbs 2.4g; Protein 3g

Vanilla Chocolate Cake

Ingredients for 4 servings

½ cup dark chocolate, melted   2 tsp vanilla bean paste
3 large eggs   ½ tsp salt
½ cup olive oil   2 tsp cinnamon powder
1 cup almond flour   ½ cup boiling water
1 cup Swerve sugar   2 tbsp erythritol powder

Directions and Total Time: approx. 55 min + cooling time

Preheat oven to 370 F. Grease a springform pan and line with parchment paper. In a bowl, combine olive oil, almond flour, dark chocolate, Swerve, vanilla bean paste, salt, cinnamon, and boiling water. Beat in the eggs one after the other until smooth.

Pour batter into the springform pan and bake for 25-35 minutes or until an inserted toothpick comes out clean. Remove from oven and allow cooling in the pan completely. Run a wooden spatula along the sides and turn over onto a plate. Dust with erythritol powder; serve.

Per serving: Cal 421; Net Carbs 1.7g, Fat 39g, Protein 15g

American Cheesecake

Ingredients for 4 servings

For the crust

2 cups almond flour
6 tbsp butter, melted

1/3 cup xylitol
1 tsp cinnamon powder

For the filling

¼ cup Swerve confectioner's sugar
1 cup softened cream cheese
½ cup heavy cream

1 tsp vanilla extract
1 cup halved strawberries

Directions and Total Time: approx. 25 min + chilling time

Preheat oven to 360 F. In a food processor, blend butter, almond flour, xylitol, and cinnamon until the dough mixture resembles a ball-like shape. Stretch out the dough in a greased round pan covering the sides. With a fork, stab the bottom of the crust. Bake for 15 minutes. Remove the crust after cooking and let cool.

For the filling, in a bowl, whisk cream cheese, heavy cream, Swerve sugar, and vanilla. Pour the filling into the crust, gently tap on a flat surface to release air bubbles, and refrigerate for 1 hour. Remove tart from the fridge and top with strawberries.

Per serving: Cal 398; Net Carbs 6g; Fat 33g; Protein 4.7g

Chocolate-Almond Cheesecake

Ingredients for 4 servings

½ cup butter, melted
1 cup dark chocolate, chopped
1 cup raw almonds
2 tbsp + ½ cup Swerve sugar
2 gelatin sheets

2 tbsp lime juice
1 ½ cups cream cheese
1 cup Greek yogurt
1 tbsp mint extract

Directions and Total Time: approx. 25 min + chilling time

Preheat oven to 360 F. In a blender, process the almonds until finely ground. Mix with butter and 2 tbsp of Swerve. Press the crust mixture on the bottom of a cake pan until firm. Bake for 5 minutes. Place in the fridge to chill. In a pot, combine gelatin with lime juice and 1 tbsp of water. Let sit for 5 minutes and place the pot over medium heat to dissolve the gelatin. Microwave the dark chocolate for 1 minute; set aside. In another bowl, beat cream cheese and remaining Swerve sugar using an electric mixer until smooth. Stir in yogurt and gelatin until combined. Fold in melted chocolate and then the mint extract.

Remove the pan from the fridge and pour the cream mixture on top. Tap the side gently to release any trapped air bubbles and transfer to the fridge to chip for 3 hours or more. Remove and release the pan's locker, top with more dark chocolate. Serve chilled.

Per serving: Cal 241g, Net Carbs 3.8g, Fat 14g, Protein 7g

Lemon Tarte Tatin with Blackberries

Ingredients for 4 servings

4 whole eggs
4 tbsp melted butter
¼ cup butter, cold, crumbled
¼ cup almond flour
3 tbsp coconut flour
½ tsp salt
3 tbsp erythritol
1 ½ tsp vanilla extract

3 tsp Swerve brown sugar
1 cup fresh blackberries
1 tsp vanilla extract
1 lemon, juiced
1 cup ricotta cheese
4 fresh basil leaves to garnish
1 egg, lightly beaten

Directions and Total Time: approx. 60 min + chilling time

Preheat oven to 360 F. In a bowl, mix almond and coconut flours and salt. Add in butter and mix until crumbly. Mix in erythritol and vanilla extract. Pour in the 4 eggs and mix until formed into a ball. Flatten the dough on a clean flat surface, cover in plastic wrap, and refrigerate for 1 hour.

Dust a clean flat surface with almond flour, unwrap the dough, and roll out the dough into a circle. In a greased baking pan, mix butter, Swerve brown sugar, blackberries, vanilla extract, and lemon juice. Arrange blackberries uniformly across the pan.

Lay the pastry over the fruit filling and tuck the sides into the pan. Brush with beaten egg and bake for 40 minutes. Turn the pie onto a plate, crumble ricotta cheese on top and garnish with basil.

Per serving: Cal 471; Net Carbs 5.8g, Fat 39g, Protein 16g

Classic Chocolate Truffles

Ingredients for 6 servings

1 cup dark chocolate, chopped
¼ cup cocoa powder
2 tbsp Swerve sugar

2/3 cup heavy cream
2 tsp lime extract

Directions and Total Time: approx. 15 min + cooling time

Pour the heavy cream in a pan over low heat and stir until tiny bubbles form around the edges of the pan. Turn the heat off. Pour dark chocolate into the pan, swirl the pan to allow the hot cream to spread over the chocolate, and gently stir the mixture until smooth. Mix in lime extract and transfer to a bowl. Refrigerate for 4 hours. Line 2 baking trays with parchment papers; set one aside.

Mix the cocoa powder with Swerve sugar and pour the mixture into the other baking tray. Take out the chocolate mixture. Form bite-sized balls out of the mix and roll all around in the cocoa powder to completely coat. Place the truffles on the baking tray and refrigerate for 30 minutes before serving.

Per serving: Cal 151; Net Carbs 0.6g, Fat 12g, Protein 2g

Chocolate Avocado Truffles

Ingredients for 6 servings

5 oz dark chocolate	1 tbsp cocoa powder
1 tbsp coconut oil	½ tsp vanilla extract
1 ripe avocado, pitted	½ tsp lemon zest

Directions and Total Time: approx. 15 minutes

Place the flesh of the avocado into a bowl and mix with vanilla using an immersion blender. Stir in lemon zest. Microwave chocolate and coconut oil for 1 minute. Add to the avocado mixture and stir. Allow cooling to firm up a bit. Form balls out of the mix. Roll each ball in the cocoa powder and serve immediately.

Per serving: Cal 69; Net Carbs 2g; Fat 5.9g; Protein 1.8g

Coconut Fat Bombs

Ingredients for 6 servings

½ cup grated coconut	½ tsp vanilla extract
3 oz butter, softened	¼ tsp cinnamon powder
¼ tsp cardamom powder	

Directions and Total Time: approx. 15 min + chilling time

Place grated coconut into a skillet over medium heat and roast until lightly brown, about 1 minute; set aside. In a bowl, combine butter, half of the coconut, cardamom, vanilla, and cinnamon. Form balls from the mixture and roll each in the remaining coconut. Serve cooled.

Per serving: Cal 91; Net Carbs 1g; Fat 10g; Protein 1g

Maple-Berry Fat Bombs

Ingredients for 4 servings

1 cup cranberries	1 tsp vanilla extract
1 cup strawberries	16 oz cream cheese, softened
1 cup raspberries	4 tbsp unsalted butter
2 tbsp sugar-free maple syrup	

Directions and Total Time: approx. 20 min + chilling time

Puree the fruits in a blender with the vanilla. In a saucepan, melt cream cheese and butter together over medium heat and stir until mixed. In a bowl, combine the berries, cheese mixtures, and maple syrup evenly. Line a muffin tray with liners. Fill the muffin tray with the mix. Refrigerate for 40 minutes and serve.

Per serving: Cal 231, Net Carbs 3.1g, Fat 15g, Protein 3.9g

Peanut Butter Fat Bombs

Ingredients for 4 servings

½ cup coconut oil	4 tbsp cocoa powder
½ cup peanut butter	½ cup erythritol

Directions and Total Time: approx. 10 min + cooling time

Warm butter and coconut oil in the microwave for 45 seconds, stirring twice until properly melted. Mix in cocoa powder and erythritol until completely combined. Pour into muffin molds and refrigerate for 3 hours to harden. Serve and enjoy!

Per serving: Cal 189; Net Carbs 2g; Fat 18g; Protein 3.9g

Cheesy Fat Bombs with Brewed Coffee

Ingredients for 4 servings

1 cup cottage cheese	2 tbsp xylitol
¼ cup melted butter	3 tbsp brewed coffee
2 tbsp cocoa powder	

Directions and Total Time: approx. 10 min + cooling time

In a bowl, whisk the cottage cheese, butter, cocoa powder, xylitol, and coffee with a hand mixer until creamy and fluffy, for about a minute. Fill into muffin tins and freeze for 4 hours until firm.

Per serving: Cal 153; Fat 14g; Net Carbs 3.2g; Protein 4.5g

Strawberry Trifle with Hazelnuts

Ingredients for 4 servings

3 oz fresh strawberries	¾ cup coconut cream
2 oz toasted hazelnuts	Zest and juice of ½ a lemon
1 ½ ripe avocados	1 tbsp vanilla extract

Directions and Total Time: approx. 10 minutes

In a bowl, add avocado pulp, coconut cream, lemon zest and juice, and half of the vanilla extract. Mix with an immersion blender. Put the strawberries and remaining vanilla in another bowl and use a fork to mash the fruit. In a tall glass, alternate layering the cream and strawberry mixtures. Drop a few hazelnuts on each and serve.

Per serving: Cal 359; Net Carbs 7g; Fat 33.9g; Protein 3.8g

No-Bake Peanut Butter Cookies

Ingredients for 4 servings

¾ cup peanut butter	1 cup Swerve brown sugar
¾ cup coconut oil	1 tsp vanilla extract
2 tbsp hulled hemp seeds	1 ½ cup coconut flakes
¼ cup cocoa powder	

Directions and Total Time: approx. 25 minutes

Preheat oven to 360 F. Line two baking sheets with parchment paper. Add coconut oil and peanut butter to a pot. Melt the mixture over low heat until smoothly combined. Stir in cocoa powder, Swerve sugar, and vanilla until smooth. Slightly increase the heat and simmer the mixture with occasional stirring until slowly boiling. Turn the heat off. Mix in coconut flakes and hemp seeds. Set the mixture aside to cool. Spoon the batter into silicone muffin cups and freeze for 15 minutes or until set. Serve.

Per serving: Cal 359; Net Carbs 5.5g; Fat 37g; Protein 4.7g

Coconut Nut Bites

Ingredients for 4 servings

2 tbsp roasted coconut chips	3 ½ oz dark chocolate
½ cup mixed nuts	1 tbsp sunflower seeds

Directions and Total Time: approx. 10 min+ chilling time

Place the chocolate in the microwave for 2 minutes. Into 8 small cupcake liners, share the chocolate. Drop-in nuts, coconut chips, and sunflower seeds. Chill until firm. Serve.

Per serving: Cal 69; Net Carbs 3g; Fat 5g; Protein 1.7g

Homemade Danish Cookies

Ingredients for 4 servings

¾ cup Swerve confectioner's sugar
1 large egg
3 oz dark chocolate
2 cups almond flour
½ cup butter, softened
1 tsp vanilla extract
½ oz cocoa butter

Directions and Total Time: approx. 25 minutes

Preheat oven to 360 F. Line a baking sheet with parchment paper. In a food processor, mix almond flour, and Swerve sugar. Add butter and process until resembling coarse breadcrumbs. Add egg, vanilla, and process until smooth. Pour the batter into a piping bag and press mounds of the batter onto the baking sheets at 1-inch intervals. Bake for 10 to 12 minutes. Microwave dark chocolate and cocoa butter for 50 seconds, mixing at every 10-second interval. When the cookies are ready, transfer to a rack to cool and swirl the chocolate mixture.

Per serving: Cal 249; Net Carbs 0.4g; Fat 27g; Protein 2g

Old-Fashioned Pumpkin Cookies

Ingredients for 4 servings

3 tbsp butter softened
1 oz cream cheese softened
½ cup pumpkin puree
3 eggs
2 tsp pumpkin pie spice
9 tbsp sugar-free maple syrup
1 tsp vanilla extract
¼ tsp salt
¾ tsp baking powder
8 tbsp coconut flour

Directions and Total Time: approx. 30 min + chilling time

In a food processor, add eggs and butter and blend until smooth. Top with cream cheese, pumpkin puree, pie spice, maple syrup, and vanilla. Process until smooth. Pour in salt, baking powder, and coconut flour and combine it until smooth thick batter forms. Using a cookie scoop, arrange 2 tbsp of the batter onto a parchment-lined baking sheet at 2-inch intervals. Refrigerate the dough for 30 minutes. Preheat oven to 380 F. Bake the cookies for 20-25 minutes or until set and lightly golden.

Per serving: Cal 240; Net Carbs 4.2g; Fat 22g; Protein 9g

Buttery Dark Chocolate Cookies

Ingredients for 4 servings

2 eggs
1 cup dark chocolate chips
1 ½ cups almond flour
½ cup cocoa powder
1 tsp baking soda
12 tbsp butter, softened
¾ cup Swerve sugar
1 tsp vanilla extract

Directions and Total Time: approx. 35 minutes

Preheat oven to 360 F. Line a baking sheet with parchment paper. In a bowl, mix almond flour, cocoa powder, and baking soda. In a separate bowl, cream the butter and Swerve sugar until light and fluffy. Mix in the eggs, vanilla extract and then combine both mixtures. Fold in the chocolate chips until well distributed. Roll the dough into 1 ½-inch balls and arrange on the sheet at 2-inch intervals. Bake for 22 minutes until lightly golden.

Per serving: Cal 269; Net Carbs 6.7g; Fat 29g; Protein 5.9g

Chocolate & Pistachio Biscuits

Ingredients for 4 servings

1 large egg, beaten
1 cup butter, softened
2/3 cup Swerve sugar
2 tbsp chopped pistachios
2 tsp pistachio extract
2 cups almond flour
½ cup dark chocolate

Directions and Total Time: approx. 40 min + cooling time

Place the butter and Swerve sugar into a bowl and beat until smooth and creamy. Whisk in egg until combined. Mix in pistachio extract and almond flour until a smooth dough forms. Wrap the dough in plastic wrap and chill for 10 minutes. Preheat oven to 350 F. Lightly dust a chopping board with some almond flour. Unwrap the dough and roll out to 2-inch thickness. Cut out as many biscuits as you can get while rerolling the trimming to make more biscuits.

Arrange the biscuits on the parchment paper-lined baking sheet and bake for 15 minutes. Transfer to a wire rack to cool completely. Melt the dark chocolate in the microwave. Dip one side of each biscuit in the melted chocolate. Garnish the chocolate side with pistachios and let cool on a wire rack. Serve.

Per serving: Cal 469; Net Carbs 3.4g; Fat 45g, Protein 5.9g

Walnut Biscuits with Chocolate Chips

Ingredients for 4 servings

4 oz butter, softened
1 egg
2/3 cup dark chocolate chips
2 tbsp Swerve sugar
2 tbsp Swerve brown sugar
1 tsp vanilla extract
½ cup almond flour
½ tsp baking soda
½ cup chopped walnuts

Directions and Total Time: approx. 30 minutes

Preheat oven to 360 F. In a bowl, whisk butter, Swerve sugar, and Swerve brown sugar until smooth. Beat in the egg and mix in the vanilla extract. In another bowl, combine almond flour with baking soda and mix into the wet ingredients. Fold in chocolate chips and walnuts. Spoon tablespoons full of the batter onto a greased baking sheet, leaving 2-inch spaces between each spoon. Press down each dough to flatten slightly. Bake for 15 minutes. Transfer to a wire rack to cool completely.

Per serving: Cal 429; Net Carbs 3.5g; Fat 39g; Protein 6g

Avocado & Berry Fruit Fool

Ingredients for 4 servings

½ cup walnuts, toasted
1 avocado, chopped
1 cup cream cheese, softened
1 cup fresh blueberries
1 cup fresh raspberries
1 cup fresh blackberries

Directions and Total Time: approx. 10 min + cooling time

Share half of the cream cheese, half of the mixed berries, half of the walnuts, and half of the avocado in dessert glasses. Repeat the layering process for a second time to finish the ingredients. Cover the glasses with plastic wrap and refrigerate for 1 hour until quite firm.

Per serving: Cal 322; Fat 28.3g; Net Carbs 6.5g; Protein 9g

Spicy Chocolate Fat Bombs

Ingredients for 6 servings

2 tbsp coconut butter	1/8 tsp nutmeg
2 tbsp coconut oil	¼ tsp red chili flakes
2 tbsp ghee	¼ tsp ground cinnamon
1 tbsp cacao powder	1 tbsp stevia
¼ tsp vanilla extract	¼ tsp salt

Directions and Total Time: approx. 10 min + chilling time

Melt the coconut butter, coconut oil, and ghee in a small pan over low heat. Stir in cacao powder, vanilla, nutmeg, cinnamon, stevia, and salt.

Divide the mixture between muffin cups. Top with red chili flakes and place in the freezer for 1 hour or until firm. Unmold before serving.

Per serving: Cal 147; Net Carbs 0.6g; Fat 15g, Protein 1.4g

Choco-Coconut Fudge

Ingredients for 6 servings

3 oz dark chocolate, chopped	3 oz butter
2 cups coconut cream	Swerve sugar for sprinkling
1 tsp vanilla extract	

Directions and Total Time: approx. 25 min + chilling time

Pour coconut cream and vanilla into a saucepan and bring to a boil over medium heat, then simmer until reduced by half, about 15 minutes. Stir in butter until the batter is smooth. Add in dark chocolate and stir until melted.

Pour the mixture into a baking sheet; chill in the fridge. Cut into squares, sprinkle with Swerve sugar, and serve.

Per serving: Cal 120; Net Carbs 3g; Fat 11g; Protein 1.9g

Red Wine Raspberry Crumble

Ingredients for 6 servings

1 cup salted butter, cubed	¼ cup red wine
1 ½ cups almond flour	1 ¼ cup erythritol, divided
¾ cup coconut flour	1 tsp vanilla extract
2 cups raspberries	

Directions and Total Time: approx. 55 min+ chilling time

Preheat oven to 385 F. In a baking dish, add raspberries, red wine, half of erythritol, vanilla extract, and stir.

In a bowl, rub butter with almond and coconut flours, and erythritol until it resembles large breadcrumbs. Spoon the mixture to cover the raspberries, place in the oven, and bake for 45 minutes until the top is golden brown. Cool and serve.

Per serving: Cal 320; Net Carbs 4.8g, Fat 29g, Protein 1.5g

Maple-Pumpkin Scones

Ingredients for 4 servings

1 large egg	¼ cup heavy cream
6 tbsp coconut flour	½ cup pumpkin puree
1 cup almond flour	2 tbsp coconut oil, melted
¼ cup erythritol	1 tbsp pumpkin pie spice
½ tsp baking powder	1 tsp sugar-free maple syrup
½ tsp arrowroot starch	¼ tsp salt

Directions and Total Time: approx. 30 minutes

Preheat oven to 360 F. Line a baking sheet with parchment paper. In a bowl, mix almond and coconut flours, erythritol, baking powder, arrowroot starch, and salt.

In another bowl, mix heavy cream, pumpkin puree, oil, egg, pumpkin spice, and maple syrup. Combine both mixtures until smooth. Pour and spread the mixture on the baking sheet. Cut into 8 wedges and bake for 20 minutes or until set and golden brown. Remove from oven, cool, and serve.

Per serving: Cal 201; Net Carbs 4.6g; Fat 18g; Protein 5.9g

Snickerdoodles with Cinnamon

Ingredients for 4 servings

Cookies

2 tbsp walnuts, chopped	¾ cup xylitol sweetener
2 cups almond flour	½ cup butter, softened
½ tsp baking soda	A pinch of salt

Coating

2 tbsp xylitol sweetener	1 tsp cinnamon

Directions and Total Time: approx. 25 minutes

Combine all cookies' ingredients in a bowl. Make balls out of the mixture and flatten them with your hands. Mix the cinnamon and xylitol. Dip the cookies in the cinnamon mixture and arrange them on a lined baking sheet. Bake for 15 minutes, or until crispy in a preheated to 370 F oven. Serve cooled and enjoy!

Per serving: Cal 177; Fat 14g; Net Carbs 3.7g; Protein 4.5g

Almond Crumble

Ingredients for 4 servings

1 cup raspberries	½ cup salted butter, cubed
¼ cup erythritol, divided	1 cup almond flour
½ tsp almond extract	2 tbsp ground almonds

Directions and Total Time: approx. 60 min + chilling time

Add raspberries in a baking dish, except for 5 for garnish, half of the erythritol, almond extract, and stir. In a bowl, rub the butter with the almond flour, remaining erythritol, and almonds until it resembles large breadcrumbs.

Spoon the mixture to cover the raspberries, place in the oven, and bake in the oven for 45 minutes at 375 F until the top looks golden brown. Remove, let cool for 3 minutes, and serve topped with the reserved raspberries.

Per serving: Cal 213; Fat 16g; Net Carbs 8.5g; Protein 1.3g

Dark Chocolate Cheesy Mini-Snacks

Ingredients for 4 servings

5 oz dark chocolate chips	¼ cup erythritol
¼ cup half and half	½ tsp vanilla extract
2 cups cream cheese, softened	

Directions and Total Time: approx. 10 min + cooling time

Melt the chocolate with half and a half in a saucepan over low heat for 1 minute. Turn the heat off.

Whisk the cream cheese, erythritol, and vanilla extract in a bowl, with a hand mixer until smooth. Add the chocolate mixture and stir. Transfer to silicone muffin tins and freeze for 5 hours until firm.

Per serving: Cal 273; Fat 24g; Net Carbs 5.2g; Protein 3.6g

Zesty Lemon Muffins

<u>**Ingredients**</u> for 4 servings

For the muffins

3 large eggs	¾ cup Swerve sugar
1 ½ cups almond flour	1 lemon, zested and juiced
½ cup coconut flour	½ tsp vanilla extract
2 tsp baking powder	1 cup sour cream
¼ tsp arrowroot starch	A pinch of salt
½ cup butter, softened	

For the topping

¾ cup almond flour	1 tsp lemon zest
3 tbsp butter, melted	1 tbsp coconut flour
2 tbsp Swerve sugar	

For the lemon glaze

½ cup Swerve confectioner's sugar
3 tbsp lemon juice

<u>**Directions**</u> and Total Time: approx. 40 minutes

For the muffins:

Preheat oven to 350 F. Line a 12-cup muffin pan with paper liners. In a bowl, mix butter, Swerve sugar, eggs, lemon zest, and lemon juice until smooth. In another bowl, combine coconut flour, almond flour, baking powder, and arrowroot. Combine both mixtures and mix in vanilla, sour cream, and salt until smooth. Fill the cups two-thirds way up.

For the topping:

In a bowl, mix melted butter, almond flour, Swerve sugar, lemon zest, and coconut flour until well combined.

Spoon the mixture onto the muffin batter and bake for 25 minutes or until a toothpick inserted comes out clean. Remove the muffins from the oven and let cool.

For the glaze:

In a bowl, whisk confectioner's sugar and lemon juice until smooth and semi-thick. Drizzle over the muffins.

Per serving: Cal 441; Net Carbs 7.6g; Fat 39g; Protein 8g

Vanilla Donuts with Chocolate Glaze

<u>**Ingredients**</u> for 4 servings

1 cup Swerve confectioner's sugar	
2 large eggs	4 tbsp melted butter
1 cup almond flour	¼ cup heavy cream
¼ cup xylitol	½ tsp vanilla extract
2 tsp baking powder	¼ tsp salt

For chocolate glaze

¼ cup cocoa powder	A pinch of salt
1 tsp vanilla extract	

<u>**Directions**</u> and Total Time: approx. 30 min + cooling time

Preheat oven to 360 F. Grease an 8-cup donut pan. In a bowl, mix almond flour, xylitol, baking powder, and salt.

In another bowl, mix butter, heavy cream, eggs, and vanilla. Combine both mixtures until smooth. Pour the batter into the donut cups and bake for 15 minutes or until set. Remove, flip the donut onto a wire rack, and let cool. For the glaze, in a bowl, whisk Swerve sugar, cocoa powder, ½ cup water, vanilla extract, and salt until smooth. Swirl the glaze over the cooled donut and serve.

Per serving: Cal 179; Net Carbs 1g; Fat 17g; Protein 3.5g

Coconut-Glazed Donuts

<u>**Ingredients**</u> for 4 servings

For the donuts

2 oz cream cheese	½ cup erythritol
¼ cup sour cream	2 tsp lemon juice
2 egg whites	2 tsp water
10 fresh strawberries, mashed	2 cups blanched almond flour
½ cup butter	2 tbsp protein powder
1 ½ tsp vanilla extract	2 tsp baking powder

For the glaze

2 tbsp coconut cream	2 tbsp xylitol
4 fresh strawberries, mashed	2 tsp water

<u>**Directions**</u> and Total Time: approx. 30 minutes

Preheat oven to 360 F. In a bowl, whisk butter, cream cheese, sour cream, vanilla, erythritol, strawberries, lemon juice, water, and egg whites until smooth. In another bowl, mix almond flour, protein and baking powders. Combine both mixtures until smooth.

Pour the batter into greased donut cups and bake for 15 minutes. Flip the donuts onto a wire rack to cool. In a bowl, combine strawberries, coconut cream, xylitol, and water until smooth. Swirl the glaze over the donuts.

Per serving: Cal 318; Net Carbs 5.7g, Fat 32g, Protein 4g

French Strawberry Scones

<u>**Ingredients**</u> for 4 servings

2 tbsp coconut oil	½ tsp baking powder
1 large egg	¼ tsp salt
1 cup blanched almond flour	¼ cup almond milk
¼ cup coconut flour	1 tsp vanilla extract
3 tbsp Swerve sugar	½ cup chopped strawberries

For the glaze

1 tsp Swerve confectioner's sugar	
2 tbsp mashed strawberries	1 tbsp coconut oil

<u>**Directions**</u> and Total Time: approx. 30 minutes

Preheat oven to 350 F. Line a baking sheet with parchment paper. In a bowl, mix almond and coconut flours, Swerve sugar, baking powder, and salt. In another bowl, whisk almond milk, coconut oil, egg, and vanilla. Combine both mixtures and fold in the strawberries. Pour and spread the mixture on the baking sheet. Cut into 8 wedges like a pizza and place the baking sheet in the oven. Bake for 20 minutes until set and golden brown. Let cool. For the glaze, in a bowl, whisk Swerve sugar, coconut oil, and strawberries until smoothly combined. Swirl the glaze over the scones to serve.

Per serving: Cal 119; Net Carbs 2.7g; Fat 11g; Protein 1.9g

Yummy Coffee Muffins

Ingredients for 4 servings

For the batter

4 eggs	½ cup vanilla almond milk
2 oz cream cheese, softened	1 cup almond flour
2 tbsp butter, softened	2 tsp instant coffee powder
1/3 cup sugar-free maple syrup	½ cup coconut flour
2 tsp vanilla extract	1 tsp baking powder

For the topping

2 tbsp coconut flour	¼ cup Swerve sugar
1 cup almond flour	1 tsp cinnamon powder
¼ cup butter, softened	½ tsp sugar-free maple syrup

Directions and Total Time: approx. 35 minutes

Preheat oven to 350 F. Line a 12-cup muffin pan with paper liners. In a bowl, whisk butter, cream cheese, maple syrup, eggs, vanilla, and almond milk until smooth.

In another bowl, mix almond flour, coffee powder, coconut flour, and baking powder. Combine both mixtures and fill the muffin cups two-thirds way up.

In a bowl, mix all the topping ingredients. Spoon the mixture onto the muffin batter and bake for 25 minutes or until a toothpick inserted comes out clean.

Remove and let cool before serving.

Per serving: Cal 302; Net Carbs 5g; Fat 23g, Protein 17g

Chocolate Cupcakes

Ingredients for 4 servings

2 tbsp unsweetened cocoa powder
3 oz unsweetened dark chocolate chips

1 cup almond flour	1 egg
2 tbsp stevia	½ cup plain yogurt
1 tsp baking powder	2 tbsp butter, melted

Directions and Total Time: approx. 45 minutes

Preheat the oven to 350 F.

Line muffin cups with parchment paper and set aside.

In a medium bowl, whisk the almond flour, stevia, cocoa powder, and baking powder together.

In a separate bowl, whisk the egg, yogurt, and butter, and pour the mixture gradually into the flour mixture while mixing with a spatula just until well incorporated. Try not to over-mix. Fold in some chocolate chips and fill the muffin cups with the batter - ¾ way up.

Top with the remaining chocolate chips, place on a baking tray, and bake for 20 minutes. Let the muffins cool for 15 minutes before serving.

Per serving: Cal 210; Fat 13g; Net Carbs 3.2g; Protein 3.9g

Raspberry & Coconut Cake

Ingredients for 8 servings

½ cup melted butter	1 lemon, juiced
2 cups fresh raspberries	1 cup coconut cream
2 cups flaxseed meal	1 cup coconut flakes
1 cup almond meal	1 cup whipping cream

Directions and Total Time: approx. 30 min + chilling time

Preheat oven to 380 F. In a bowl, mix flaxseed meal, almond meal, and butter. Spread the mixture on the bottom of a baking dish. Bake for 20 minutes until the mixture is crusty. Allow cooling. In another bowl, mash 1 ½ cups of the raspberries and mix with the lemon juice. Spread the mixture on the crust. Carefully spread the coconut cream on top, scatter with the coconut flakes and add the whipped cream all over. Garnish with the remaining raspberries and chill in the refrigerator for at least 2 hours.

Per serving: Cal 409; Net Carbs 5.4g; Fats 39g; Protein 6.9g

Red Velvet Cakes with Mascarpone

Ingredients for 6 servings

6 eggs	½ cup coconut flour
1 cup Greek yogurt	2 tbsp cocoa powder
½ cup butter	2 tbsp baking powder
1 tsp vanilla extract	¼ tsp salt
1 cup Swerve sugar	1 tbsp red food coloring
1 cup almond flour	

For the frosting

2 tbsp heavy cream	½ cup erythritol
1 cup mascarpone cheese	1 tsp vanilla extract

Directions and Total Time: approx. 35 minutes

Preheat oven to 380 F. Grease 2 heart-shaped cake pans with butter. In a bowl, beat butter, eggs, vanilla, Greek yogurt, and Swerve sugar until smooth.

In another bowl, mix the almond and coconut flours, cocoa, salt, baking powder, and red food coloring. Combine both mixtures until smooth and divide the batter between the two cake pans.

Bake in the oven for 25 minutes or until a toothpick inserted comes out clean. In a bowl, using an electric mixer, whisk the mascarpone cheese and erythritol until smooth. Mix in vanilla and heavy cream. Transfer to a wire rack, let cool, and spread the frosting on top. Serve.

Per serving: Cal 639; Net Carbs 9.2g; Fat 46g; Protein 36g

Hazelnut & Chocolate Cake

Ingredients for 4 servings

½ cup unsweetened dark chocolate, melted
1 tbsp unsweetened dark chocolate, shaved

½ cup olive oil	2 tsp cinnamon powder
1 cup almond flour	½ cup boiling water
1 cup Swerve sugar	3 large eggs
2 tsp hazelnut extract	¼ cup ground hazelnuts
½ tsp salt	

Directions and Total Time: approx. 60 min + chilling time

Preheat oven to 350 F and grease a baking pan with cooking spray and line with parchment paper. In a large bowl, combine the olive oil, almond flour, chocolate, Swerve sugar, hazelnut extract, salt, cinnamon powder, and boiling water. Crack the eggs one after the other while beating until smooth.

Pour the batter into the springform pan and bake in the oven for 45 minutes or until a toothpick inserted comes out clean. Take out from the oven; allow cooling in the pan for 10 minutes, then turn over onto a wire rack. Sprinkle with ground hazelnuts and shaved chocolate, slice, and serve.

Per serving: Cal 506; Fat 46.5g; Net Carbs 8g; Protein 6.1g

Coconut Lemon Syrup Cake

Ingredients for 4 servings

For the lemon puree:

4 large lemons	¼ tsp salt
¼ cup maple syrup, sugar-free	

For the cake:

½ cup butter, softened	3 large eggs, lightly beaten
½ cup erythritol	½ cup heavy cream
1 tsp vanilla extract	1 tbsp Swerve confectioner's
½ cup coconut flour	sugar, for dusting

Directions and Total Time: approx. 65 min + cooling time

Make the lemon puree: peel and juice the lemons. Remove any white strains from the peel and transfer both peels and juice to a small saucepan. Add the maple syrup and salt and simmer over low heat for 30 minutes. Pour the mixture into a blender and process until smooth. Pour into a jar and set aside.

Preheat the oven to 350 F. Grease two springform pans and line with parchment paper. In a bowl, cream the butter, erythritol, and vanilla extract with an electric whisk until light and fluffy. Pour in the eggs gradually while beating until mixed. Carefully fold in the coconut flour and share the mixture into the pans. Bake for 25 minutes or until springy when touched and a toothpick inserted comes out clean. Remove and allow cooling for 5 minutes before turning out onto a wire rack.

In a bowl, whip the heavy cream until a soft peak forms. Spoon onto the bottom sides of the cake and spread the lemon puree on top. Sandwich both cakes and sift the confectioner's sugar on top.

Per serving: Cal 273; Fat 23g; Net Carbs 4.9g; Protein 7.3g

Party Chocolate Mug Cakes

Ingredients for 2 servings

1 egg	2 tbsp ghee
2 tbsp almond flour	1 ½ tbsp cocoa powder
1 tbsp psyllium husk powder	2 tbsp erythritol
2 tsp coconut flour	A pinch of salt
½ tsp baking powder	

Directions and Total Time: approx. 5 minutes

In a bowl, whisk the ghee, cocoa powder, and erythritol until a thick mixture forms. Whisk in the egg until smooth, and then add in almond flour, psyllium husk, coconut flour, baking powder, and salt. Pour the mixture into 2 medium mugs and microwave for 70 to 90 seconds or until set.

Per serving: Cal 89; Net Carbs 1.8g; Fat 11.9g; Protein 8g

Cakes with Chocolate Frosting

Ingredients for 4 servings

½ cup almond flour	A pinch of ground cloves
¼ cup erythritol	½ cup butter, melted
1 tsp baking powder	½ cup buttermilk
½ tsp baking soda	1 egg
1 tsp cinnamon, ground	1 tsp pure almond extract
A pinch of salt	

Frosting

1 cup heavy cream	1 cup dark chocolate, flaked

Directions and Total Time: approx. 30 minutes

Grease a donut pan with cooking spray and preheat the oven to 360 F. Mix the cloves, almond flour, baking powder, salt, baking soda, erythritol, and cinnamon in a bowl. In a separate bowl, combine the almond extract, butter, egg, and buttermilk. Mix the wet mixture into the dry mix. Evenly spoo the batter into the donut pan. Bake for 17 minutes. Set a pan over medium heat and warm heavy cream; simmer for 2 minutes. Fold in the chocolate flakes; combine until all the chocolate melts; and let cool. Spread the frosting on top of the cakes.

Per serving: Cal 321; Fat 26g; Net Carbs 8.2g; Protein 7.3g

Cardamom Lemon Cake

Ingredients for 4 servings

1 cup sour cream	2 tsp baking powder
4 eggs	½ cup xylitol
2 lemons, zested and juiced	1 tsp cardamom powder
1 tsp vanilla extract	½ tsp ground ginger
2 cups almond flour	¼ cup maple syrup
2 tbsp coconut flour	A pinch of salt

Directions and Total Time: approx. 35 minutes

Preheat oven to 380 F. Grease a cake pan with melted butter. In a bowl, beat eggs, sour cream, lemon juice, and vanilla until smooth. In another bowl, whisk almond and coconut flours, baking powder, xylitol, cardamom, ginger, salt, lemon zest, and half of the maple syrup. Combine both mixtures until smooth and pour the batter into the pan. Bake for 25 minutes or until a toothpick inserted comes out clean. Transfer to a wire rack, let cool, and drizzle with the remaining maple syrup. Serve sliced.

Per serving: Cal 439; Net Carbs 8.5g; Fat 30g; Protein 33g

Maple-Coconut Bars

Ingredients for 4 servings

3 cups shredded coconut flakes	
1 cup melted coconut oil	¼ cup sugar-free maple syrup
1 tsp mint extract	

Directions and Total Time: approx. 10 min + chilling time

Line loaf pan with parchment paper. In a bowl, mix coconut flakes, coconut oil, mint, and maple syrup until a thick batter forms. Pour the mixture into the loaf pan and press to fit. Refrigerate for 2 hours or until hardened. Remove from the fridge, cut into bars and serve.

Per serving: Cal 371; Net Carbs 4.3g; Fat 36g; Protein 1.8g

Lazy Strawberry Mini Cakes

Ingredients for 4 servings

4 eggs
2 tsp coconut oil
2 cups strawberries
1 cup coconut milk
1 cup almond flour

¼ cup xylitol
½ tsp vanilla powder
¼ tsp powdered sugar
A pinch of salt

Directions and Total Time: approx. 50 minutes

Place all ingredients, except coconut oil, berries, and powdered sugar in a blender; pulse until smooth. Fold in strawberries. Preheat oven to 330 F. Grease a baking dish with oil. Pour the mixture into the pan and bake for 40 minutes. Sprinkle with powdered sugar and cut into mini cakes.

Per serving: Cal 311; Fat 28g; Net Carbs 6.4g; Protein 14g

Maple Cake with Cinnamon

Ingredients for 4 servings

½ cup sugar-free maple syrup + extra for topping
9 tbsp butter, melted and cooled
2 tsp cream cheese, softened   ¼ cup almond flour
6 eggs   1 ½ tsp baking powder
1 tsp vanilla extract   1 tsp cinnamon powder
2 tbsp heavy cream   ½ tsp salt

Directions and Total Time: approx. 35 minutes

Preheat oven to 380 F. Grease a cake pan with melted butter. In a bowl, beat the eggs, butter, cream cheese, vanilla, heavy cream, and maple syrup until smooth. In another bowl, mix almond flour, baking powder, cinnamon, and salt. Combine both mixtures until smooth and pour the batter into the cake pan. Bake for 25 minutes or until a toothpick inserted comes out clean. Transfer the cake to a wire rack to cool and drizzle with maple syrup.

Per serving: Cal 359; Net Carbs 1.5g; Fat 35g; Protein 9g

Coffee-Chocolate Cake

Ingredients for 4 servings

1 tbsp melted butter   ½ tsp espresso powder
1 cup almond flour   1/3-½ cup coconut sugar
2 tbsp coconut flour   ¼ tsp xanthan gum
1 tsp baking powder   ¼ cup organic coconut oil
¼ cup cocoa powder   2 tbsp heavy cream
3 tbsp flaxseed meal, ground   2 eggs
¼ tsp salt

Directions and Total Time: approx. 30 minutes

Preheat oven to 380 F. Grease a springform pan with melted butter. In a bowl, mix almond flour, flaxseed meal, coconut flour, baking powder, cocoa powder, salt, espresso, coconut sugar, and xanthan gum. In another bowl, whisk coconut oil, heavy cream, and eggs. Combine both mixtures until soft batter forms. Pour the batter into the pan and bake until a toothpick comes out clean, 20 minutes. Transfer to a wire rack to cool.

Per serving: Cal 229; Net Carbs 6.3g; Fat 22g; Protein 5g

Grandma´s Gingerbread Cheesecake

Ingredients for 6 servings

For the crust
6 tbsp melted butter   ¼ Swerve sugar
1 ¾ cups golden flaxseed meal   A pinch of salt

For the filling
3 large eggs   1 tsp pure vanilla extract
¼ cup sour cream   2 tsp smooth ginger paste
8 oz cream cheese, softened   1 tsp cinnamon powder
¾ cup Swerve sugar   ¼ tsp nutmeg powder
¼ cup sugar-free maple syrup   A pinch of cloves powder
2 tbsp almond flour   ¼ tsp salt

Directions and Total Time: approx. 85 minutes

Preheat oven to 320 F. In a bowl, mix flaxseed meal, butter, Swerve, and salt. Pour and fit the mixture into a greased pan using a spoon. Bake the crust for 15 minutes or until firm. In a bowl, using an electric mixer, beat cream cheese, Swerve sugar, and maple syrup until smooth. Whisk in one after the other, the eggs, sour cream, almond flour, vanilla extract, ginger paste, cinnamon, nutmeg, salt, and clove powder. Pour the mixture onto the crust while shaking to release any bubbles. Cover with foil and bake for 55 minutes until the center of the cake jiggles slightly. Remove the cake and let it cool completely. Serve sliced.

Per serving: Cal 679; Net Carbs 4.3g; Fat 50g; Protein 29g

Sage Chocolate Cheesecake

Ingredients for 4 servings

Crust
1 cup raw almonds   2 tbsp Swerve sugar
½ cup salted butter, melted

Cake
4 tbsp unsalted butter, melted   2 tbsp cocoa powder
2 gelatine sheets   1 ½ cups cream cheese
2 tbsp lime juice   ½ cup Swerve sugar
2/3 cup unsweetened dark   1 cup Greek yogurt
chocolate, chopped   1 fresh sage leaf, chopped

Directions and Total Time: approx. 25 min + chilling time

Preheat oven to 350 F. In a blender, process the almonds until finely ground. Add the butter and sweetener, and mix until combined. Press the crust mixture into the bottom of the cake pan until firm. Bake for 5 minutes. Place in the fridge to chill afterward.

In a small pot, combine the gelatin with the lime juice and 2 tbsp of water. Allow sitting for 5 minutes and then, place the pot over medium heat to dissolve the gelatin. Mix in the melted butter and set aside. Pour the dark chocolate into a bowl and melt in the microwave for 1 minute, stirring at every 10 seconds interval. Set aside.

In another, beat the cream cheese and Swerve sugar using an electric mixer until smooth. Stir in the yogurt and gelatin until evenly combined. Fold in the melted dark chocolate and then the sage leaf. Remove the pan from the fridge and pour the cream mixture on top.

Tap the side gently to release any trapped air bubbles and transfer to the fridge to chip for 3 hours or more. Dust the cake with cocoa powder and slice to serve.

Per serving: Cal 675; Fat 53g; Net Carbs 13g; Protein 21g

Raspberry Coconut Cheesecake

Ingredients for 1 serving

Crust

¼ cup xylitol	1 tsp coconut oil
3 cups desiccated coconut	¼ cup butter, melted
2 egg whites	

Filling

6 oz raspberries	1 cup whipped cream
3 tbsp lemon juice	Zest of 1 lemon
2 cups xylitol	3 cups cream cheese

Directions and Total Time: approx. 50 min + cooling time

Grease the bottom and sides of a springform pan with oil and line with parchment paper.

In a bowl, mix all crust ingredients and pour the crust into the pan. Preheat the oven to 330 F. Bake for 30 minutes; then let cool.

Meanwhile, beat the cream cheese with an electric mixer until soft. Add the lemon juice, zest, and xylitol. Fold the whipped cream into the cheese cream mixture. Gently fold in the raspberries and spoon the filling into the baked and cooled crust. Chill for 4 hours.

Per serving: Cal 376; Fat 32g; Net Carbs 6g; Protein 7g

Chocolate Cheesecake with Coconut Crust

Ingredients for 4 servings

For the crust

1 tbsp olive oil	1/3 cup almond flour
2 eggs	½ cup cold butter, cubed
1 tsp vanilla extract	¼ tsp salt
¼ cup erythritol	5 tbsp cold water
2/3 cup coconut flour	

For the filling

16 oz cream cheese, softened	4 tbsp butter
4 tbsp sour cream	
2 tsp Swerve confectioner's sugar	
1 tsp vanilla extract	½ cup cocoa powder
½ cup Swerve sugar	1 cup coconut cream

Directions and Total Time: approx. 90 min + chilling time

For the piecrust:

In a bowl, whisk eggs, olive oil, and vanilla until well combined. In another bowl, mix erythritol, salt, coconut and almond flours. Combine both mixtures into a stand mixer and blend until soft dough forms. Add in butter and mix until breadcrumb-like mixture forms. Add one tbsp of water, mix further until the dough begins to come together. Keep adding water until it sticks well together. Lightly flour a working surface, turn the dough onto it, knead a few times until formed into a ball, and comes together smoothly. Divide into half and flatten each piece into a disk. Wrap with plastic foil and refrigerate for 1 hour.

Preheat oven to 375 F. Lightly grease a 9-inch pie pan with olive oil. Remove the dough from the fridge, let it stand at room temperature, and roll one piece into 12-inch round. Fit this piece into the bottom and walls to the rim of the pie pan while shaping to take the pan's form. Roll out the other dough into an 11-inch round and set aside.

For the filling:

In a bowl, using an electric mixer, whisk cream cheese, sour cream, butter, vanilla, Swerve confectioner's sugar, and cocoa powder until smooth. In a separate bowl, whisk the coconut cream and Swerve sugar. Gently fold the cocoa powder mixture into the cream cheese mix until well combined. Fill the pie dough in the pie pan with the cream-cocoa mixture and make sure to level well. Brush the overhanging pastry with water and attach the top pastry on top of the filling.

Press the edges to merge the dough ends and then trim the overhanging ends to 1-inch. Fold the edge under itself and decoratively crimp. Cut 4 slits on the top crust. Bake the pie for 75 minutes or until the bottom crust is golden and the filling is bubbling. Let cool and serve.

Per serving: Cal 429; Net Carbs 5g; Fat 40g; Protein 7g

Chocolate Barks with Cranberries & Nuts

Ingredients for 4 servings

5 oz unsweetened dark chocolate, chopped
¼ cup dried cranberries, chopped
¼ cup toasted pecans, chopped

¼ cup xylitol	¼ tsp salt

Directions and Total Time: approx. 10 min + cooling time

Pour chocolate and xylitol into a bowl, and melt in the microwave for 30 seconds. Stir in the cranberries, pecans, and salt, reserving a few cranberries and pecans for garnishing. Line a baking sheet with parchment paper. Spread the mixture on the sheet and spread out. Sprinkle with remaining cranberries and pecans. Refrigerate for 3 hours to set. Break into bite-size pieces to serve.

Per serving: Cal 231; Fat 22g; Net Carbs 4.2g; Protein 5.2g

Cranberry & Peanut Chocolate Barks

Ingredients for 6 servings

¼ cup dried cranberries, soaked	
10 oz dark chocolate	½ cup erythritol
¼ cup toasted peanuts	

Directions and Total Time: approx. 10 min + cooling time

Line a baking sheet with parchment paper. Chop the chocolate and throw it in a bowl. Mix in the erythritol and microwave for 25 seconds. Chop the cranberries and peanuts; reserve a few for garnishing. Add the remaining to the chocolate bowl and stir. Pour the mixture on the baking sheet and spread out. Sprinkle with remaining cranberries and peanuts. Refrigerate for 2 hours to set. Break into bite-size pieces to serve.

Per serving: Cal 230; Net Carbs 3g; Fat 19; Protein 6g

Cranberry Granola Bars

Ingredients for 4 servings

2 tbsp dried cranberries
1 cup hazelnuts and walnuts, chopped
¼ cup flax meal
¼ cup coconut milk
¼ cup poppy seeds
¼ cup pumpkin seeds
4 drops stevia
¼ cup coconut oil, melted
½ tsp vanilla paste
½ tsp ground cloves
½ tsp grated nutmeg
½ tsp lemon zest

Directions and Total Time: approx. 55 minutes

Preheat oven to 280 F and line a baking sheet with parchment paper. In a large mixing bowl, combine all ingredients with ¼ cup of water and stir to coat. Spread the mixture onto the baking sheet. Bake for 45 minutes, stirring at intervals of 15 minutes. Let cool at room temperature. Cut into bars to serve.

Per serving: Cal 451; Fat 43g; Net Carbs 6.3g; Protein 10g

Dark Chocolate Bars with Hazelnuts

Ingredients for 4 servings

¼ cup toasted hazelnuts, chopped
¼ cup unsweetened coconut flakes
¼ cup butter
5 drops stevia
¼ tsp salt
2 oz dark chocolate

Directions and Total Time: approx. 10 min + cooling time

In a microwave-safe bowl, melt the butter and chocolate for 85 seconds. Remove and stir in stevia.

Line a cookie sheet with waxed paper and spread the chocolate evenly. Scatter the hazelnuts on top, then the coconut flakes and sprinkle with salt. Refrigerate for 2 hours and then cut into bars.

Per serving: Cal 215; Fat 16.8g; Net Carbs 3g; Protein 3.6g

Chocolate Walnut Bars

Ingredients for 6 servings

4 tbsp butter
4 oz sugar-free dark chocolate
1 pinch of salt
¼ cup walnut butter
½ tsp vanilla extract
¼ cup chopped walnuts

Directions and Total Time: approx. 10 min + chilling time

Place the chocolate and butter in the microwave for 2 minutes. Remove and mix in salt, walnut butter, and vanilla extract. Grease a small baking sheet with cooking spray and line with parchment paper. Pour in the batter and top with walnuts and chill in the refrigerator. Cut into squares and serve.

Per serving: Cal 131; Net Carbs 3g; Fat 9g; Protein 2g

Original Chocolate Chip Bars

Ingredients for 4 servings

5 eggs
½ cup butter, softened
8 oz cream cheese, softened
1 cup chopped walnuts
2 cups xylitol
2 tsp vanilla extract
1 cup almond flour
1/3 cup coconut flour
1 ½ tsp baking powder
½ tsp xanthan gum
1 cup dark chocolate chips
¼ tsp salt

Directions and Total Time: approx. 45 min + chilling time

Preheat oven to 360 F. Line a baking sheet with parchment paper. In a food processor, blitz cream cheese, butter, and xylitol. Add in eggs and vanilla and mix until smooth. Pour in the flours, salt, baking powder, and xanthan gum; process until smooth. Fold in the chocolate chips and walnuts. Spread the mixture onto the sheet and bake for 30 to 35 minutes or until set and light golden brown. Remove from the oven, let cool, and cut into bars.

Per serving: Cal 439; Net Carbs 4.8g; Fat 36g; Protein 21g

Cheesecake Bars with Cranberries

Ingredients for 4 servings

For the crust
8 tbsp melted butter
2 tbsp Swerve confectioner's
1 ¼ cups almond flour

For the cheesecake layer
1 cup unsweetened cranberry sauce
1 egg yolk
1/3 cup Swerve confectioner's
8 oz cream cheese
2 tsp pure vanilla extract

For the cranberry layer

Directions and Total Time: approx. 35 min + chilling time

For the crust, preheat oven to 360 F. Line a baking sheet with parchment paper. In a bowl, mix butter, almond flour, and Swerve sugar. Spread and press the mixture onto the baking sheet and bake for 13 minutes or until golden brown. For the cheesecake layer, whisk cream cheese, egg yolk, Swerve sugar, and vanilla in a bowl using an electric hand mixer until smooth. Spread the mixture on the crust when ready. Bake further for 15 minutes or until the filling sets. Remove from the oven, spread cranberry sauce on top, and refrigerate for 1 hour. Cut into bars and serve.

Per serving: Cal 501; Net Carbs 2.5g; Fat 5g; Protein 4.8g

Tasty Blueberry Soufflé

Ingredients for 4 servings

4 egg yolks
3 egg whites
1 cup frozen blueberries
5 tbsp erythritol
1 tsp olive oil
½ lemon, zested

Directions and Total Time: approx. 35 minutes

Place a saucepan over medium heat and pour in the blueberries, 2 tbsp erythritol, and 1 tbsp water. Cook until the berries soften and become syrupy, 8-10 minutes. Set aside. Preheat oven to 350 F. In a bowl, beat egg yolks and 1 tbsp of erythritol until thick and pale. In another bowl, whisk egg whites until foamy. Add in remaining erythritol and whisk until soft peak forms, 3-4 minutes. Fold egg white mixture into egg yolk mixture. Heat olive oil in a pan over low heat. Add in olive oil and pour in the egg mixture; swirl to spread. Cook for 3 minutes and transfer to the oven; bake for 2-3 minutes or until puffed and set. Plate soufflé and spoon blueberry sauce all over. Garnish with lemon zest.

Per serving: Cal 102; Net Carbs 2.8g; Fat 6g; Protein 5.5g

Chocolate-Ginger Fudge

Ingredients for 4 servings

1 cup unsweetened dark chocolate, melted
¼ tsp ginger extract   ½ cup butter, melted
4 large eggs   1/3 cup coconut flour
1 cup Swerve sugar

Directions and Total Time: approx. 30 minutes

Preheat the oven to 350 F and line a rectangular baking tray with parchment paper. In a bowl, cream the eggs with Swerve sugar until smooth. Add the melted chocolate, butter, and ginger extract and whisk until evenly combined. Carefully fold in the coconut flour to incorporate and pour the mixture into the baking tray. Bake in the oven for 20 minutes or until a toothpick inserted comes out clean. Remove from the oven and allow cooling in the tray. After, cut into squares and serve.

Per serving: Cal 477; Fat 42g; Net Carbs 6.8g; Protein 13g

Almond Bars

Ingredients for 6 servings

1 cup butter   ½ cup sugar-free maple syrup
3 cups almonds, chopped   ¼ cup coconut oil
2 cups dark chocolate chips

Directions and Total Time: approx. 5 min + chilling time

In a bowl, mix chocolate chips, butter, maple syrup, coconut oil, and almonds. Line a baking sheet with parchment paper. Spread the mixture onto the sheet and refrigerate until firm, at least 1 hour. Cut into bars.

Per serving: Cal 319; Net Carbs 3.9g; Fat 29g; Protein 2.9g

Lime & Chocolate Energy Balls

Ingredients for 4 servings

1/3 cup dark chocolate, chopped
1/4 tsp salt   1 lime, zested
1/3 cup heavy cream   2 tbsp cocoa powder
1 tsp lime extract   1 tbsp Swerve sugar

Directions and Total Time: approx. 15 min + chilling time

Mix the cocoa powder with Swerve sugar in a small bowl and set aside. Heat the heavy cream in a small pan over low heat until tiny bubbles form around the edges of the pan. Turn the heat off. Pour the dark chocolate and salt into the pan, swirl the pan to allow the hot cream over the chocolate, and then stir the mixture until smooth. Mix in the lime extract and transfer the mixture to a bowl. Refrigerate for 4 hours and more. Line a baking tray with parchment papers. Pour the cocoa powder mixture into a shallow dish and the lime zest in a separate one.

Take out the chocolate mixture; form bite-size balls out of the mix and roll all around in the lime zest, and then completely coat in the cocoa powder. Place the truffles on the baking tray and chill in the fridge for 30 minutes before serving.

Per serving: Cal 134; Fat 11g; Net Carbs 5.6g; Protein 2.1g

Blackberry Popsicles

Ingredients for 4 servings

2 cups blackberries   1/3 cup erythritol
½ tbsp lemon juice   ¼ cup water

Directions and Total Time: approx. 10 min + cooling time

In a blender, pour the blackberries, lemon juice, erythritol, and water and puree on high speed for 2 minutes until smooth. Strain through a sieve into a bowl and discard the solids. Stir in more water if too thick. Divide the mixture into ice pop molds, insert stick cover, and freeze for 4 hours to 1 week. When ready to serve, dip in warm water and remove the pops.

Per serving: Cal 113; Fat 3g; Net Carbs 5.8g; Protein 3.4g

Chocolate & Peanut Bars

Ingredients for 6 servings

For the peanut butter filling
4 tbsp melted butter   5 tbsp almond flour
½ cup smooth peanut butter   1 tsp vanilla extract
4 tbsp Swerve sugar
For the coating
3 tbsp peanuts, chopped   2 oz chopped dark chocolate

Directions and Total Time: approx. 10 min + chilling time

In a bowl, mix peanut butter, butter, Swerve, almond flour, and vanilla. Line a baking sheet with wax paper. Spread the mixture onto the sheet and top with chocolate and peanuts. Refrigerate until firm, 1 hour. Cut into bars.

Per serving: Cal 160; Net Carbs 5.2g; Fat 12g; Protein 5g

Coconut Macadamia Bars

Ingredients for 4 servings

½ cup smooth peanut butter   1 tsp cinnamon powder
1 cup macadamia, chopped   ¼ cup coconut oil, solidified
½ cup pepitas   2 tsp vanilla bean paste
1 cup coconut flakes

Directions and Total Time: approx. 10 min + chilling time

In a bowl, mix macadamia nuts, pepitas, coconut flakes, cinnamon powder, peanut butter, coconut oil, and vanilla bean paste. Line a baking sheet with parchment paper. Spread the mixture onto the sheet and refrigerate until firm, at least 1 hour. Cut into bars and serve.

Per serving: Cal 421; Net Carbs 5g; Fat 37g; Protein 9g

Almond Butter & Chocolate Bars

Ingredients for 4 servings

¼ cup melted butter   ½ cup sugar-free maple syrup
¼ cup almond butter   1 tbsp sesame seeds
1 ½ cups chocolate chips   1 cup chopped walnuts

Directions and Total Time: approx. 5 min + chilling time

In a bowl, mix chocolate chips, almond butter, maple syrup, butter, seeds, and walnuts. Line a baking sheet with parchment paper. Spread the mixture onto the sheet and refrigerate until firm, about 1 hour. Cut into bars.

Per serving: Cal 709; Net Carbs 7.1g; Fat 75g; Protein 8g

Cheesecake Bites with Dark Chocolate

Ingredients for 6 servings

½ cup half and half
20 oz cream cheese, softened
10 oz dark chocolate chips
½ cup Swerve sugar
1 tsp vanilla extract

Directions and Total Time: approx. 10 min + cooling time

In a saucepan, melt the chocolate with half and a half over low heat for 1 minute. Turn the heat off. In a bowl, whisk the cream cheese, Swerve sugar, and vanilla with a hand mixer until smooth. Stir into the chocolate mixture. Spoon into silicone muffin tins and freeze for 4 hours until firm.

Per serving: Cal 239; Net Carbs 3.1g; Fat 22g; Protein 4.8g

Viennese Coffee Bites

Ingredients for 6 servings

½ cup melted ghee
1 ½ cups mascarpone cheese
3 tbsp cocoa powder
¼ cup erythritol
6 tbsp brewed coffee

Directions and Total Time: approx. 5 min + cooling time

Beat the ghee, mascarpone, cocoa powder, erythritol, and coffee with a hand mixer until creamy and fluffy, about 1 minute. Fill in muffin tins and freeze for 3 hours until firm.

Per serving: Cal 150; Net Carbs 2g; Fat 14g; Protein 3.8g

Summer Blueberry Sorbet

Ingredients for 4 servings

½ lemon, juiced
4 cups frozen blueberries
1 cup Swerve sugar
½ tsp salt

Directions and Total Time: approx. 15 min + chilling time

Add the blueberries, Swerve, lemon juice, and salt to tour food processor and blend until smooth. Strain through a colander into a bowl. Chill for 3 hours. Pour the chilled juice into an ice cream maker and churn until the mixture resembles ice cream. Spoon into a bowl and chill further for 3 hours.

Per serving: Cal 180; Net Carbs 2.3g; Fats 1g; Protein 0.6g

Cranberry & Coconut Waffles

Ingredients for 4 servings

2/3 cup coconut flour
2 tsp baking powder
6 tbsp unsalted butter, melted and cooled slightly
1 ½ cups almond milk
¼ cup fresh cranberries
A pinch of salt
2/3 cup erythritol
2 eggs
1 tsp lemon zest
Greek yogurt for topping
½ tsp vanilla extract

Directions and Total Time: approx. 16 minutes

Put cranberries, erythritol, 3/4 cup water, vanilla, and lemon zest in a saucepan. Bring to a boil and reduce the temperature; simmer for 15 minutes or until the cranberries break and a sauce forms; set aside.

In a bowl, mix coconut flour, baking powder, and salt. In another bowl, whisk eggs, almond milk, and butter and pour the mixture into the flour mixture. Combine until a smooth batter forms. Preheat a waffle iron and brush with butter. Pour some of the batter and cook until golden and crisp, 4 minutes. Repeat with the remaining batter. Plate the waffles, spoon a dollop of yogurt on top, followed by the cranberry sauce.

Per serving: Cal 250; Net Carbs 6.9g; Fat 19g; Protein 6.6g

Peanut Butter Ice Cream

Ingredients for 4 servings

½ cup smooth peanut butter
½ cup erythritol
3 cups half and half
1 tsp vanilla extract
1 pinch of salt
½ cups raspberries

Directions and Total Time: approx. 10 min + cooling time

In a bowl, beat peanut butter and erythritol with a hand mixer until smooth. Gradually whisk in half and half until thoroughly combined. Add in vanilla and salt and mix. Transfer the mixture to a loaf pan and freeze for 50 minutes until firmed up. Scoop into glasses when ready and serve topped with raspberries.

Per serving: Cal 436; Fat 38g; Net Carbs 9.5g; Protein 13g

Yogurt Ice Pops with Berries

Ingredients for 6 servings

1 cup plain yogurt
2/3 cup mixed berries
1 cup avocado, halved, pitted
½ cup coconut cream
1 tsp vanilla extract

Directions and Total Time: approx. 5 min+ chilling time

Pour avocado, berries, yogurt, coconut cream, and vanilla extract in a blender. Process until smooth. Pour into ice pop sleeves and freeze for 8 hours. Serve when ready.

Per serving: Cal 79; Net Carbs 4g; Fat 5g; Protein 2g

Blueberry Ice Balls

Ingredients for 2 servings

½ tsp vanilla extract
2 packets gelatine, sugar-free
2 tbsp heavy whipping cream
1 cup water
3 tbsp mashed blueberries
2 cups crushed Ice
1 cup cold water

Directions and Total Time: approx. 15 min + cooling time

Boil the water over medium heat and dissolve the gelatine inside. Transfer to a blender and add the remaining ingredients. Pulse until smooth and make balls. Freeze them for 3 hours.

Per serving: Cal 142; Fat 9g; Net Carbs 7.8g; Protein 3.5g

Quick Buckeye Fat Bomb Bars

Ingredients for 4 servings

6 oz heavy cream
½ cup butter, melted
1 ¼ cups peanut butter
½ cup almond flour
1 tsp vanilla extract
1 tsp Swerve sugar
6 oz dark chocolate chips
1/8 tsp salt

Directions and Total Time: approx. 15 min + chilling time

In a food processor, mix peanut butter, butter, almond flour, vanilla, and Swerve sugar. Line a baking sheet with parchment paper. Spread the vanilla mixture onto the sheet and refrigerate to firm, 30 minutes. Add the chocolate chips, heavy cream, and salt to a pot and melt over low heat until bubbles form around the edges. Let cool for 5 minutes and whisk until smooth. Pour over the butter mixture and refrigerate for 1 hour. Cut into bars and serve.

Per serving: Cal 409; Net Carbs 5.5g; Fat 38g; Protein 9.8g

Mochaccino & Chocolate Ice Balls

Ingredients for 4 servings

½ lb cottage cheese	2 tbsp cocoa powder
4 tbsp powdered sweetener	1 oz cocoa butter, melted
2 oz strong coffee	2 ½ oz dark chocolate, melted

Directions and Total Time: approx. 10 min + cooling time

In a food processor, combine the cheese, sweetener, coffee, and cocoa powder. Form two tablespoons of the mixture into balls and place them on a lined tray. Mix the melted cocoa butter and dark chocolate, and coat the balls with it. Freeze for 3 hours.

Per serving: Cal 176; Fat 14.2g; Net Carbs 6g; Protein 4g

Berry Power Balls

Ingredients for 4 servings

1 cup raspberries + extra to garnish	
1 cup strawberries	16 oz cream cheese, room
1 cup blueberries	temperature
1 tsp vanilla extract	4 tbsp peanut butter
	2 tbsp maple syrup, sugar-free

Directions and Total Time: approx. 15 min + chilling time

Line a small pan with parchment paper. Puree the fruits in a blender with the vanilla. Set aside. In a small saucepan, melt the cream cheese and butter over medium heat until completely mixed. Then, in a medium bowl, combine the fruit, cheese mixture, and maple syrup. Spread out the mixture into the prepared pan. Refrigerate for 40 minutes, cut into squares and serve.

Per serving: Cal 487; Fat 43g; Net Carbs 12g; Protein 10g

No-Bake Raw Coconut Balls

Ingredients for 4 servings

¼ tsp coconut extract	16 drops stevia liquid
2/3 cup melted coconut oil	1 cup coconut flakes
15-oz can coconut milk	

Directions and Total Time: approx. 15 min + chilling time

In a bowl, mix the coconut oil with the milk, coconut extract, and stevia to combine. Stir in the coconut flakes until well distributed. Pour into silicone muffin molds and freeze for 1 hour to harden.

Per serving: Cal 211; Fat 19g; Net Carbs 2.2g; Protein 2.9g

Homemade Marshmallows with Chocolate

Ingredients for 4 servings

2 tbsp unsweetened cocoa powder	
½ tsp vanilla extract	A pinch salt
½ cup erythritol	6 tbsp cool water
1 tbsp xanthan gum mixed in	2 ½ tsp gelatin powder
1 tbsp water	

Dusting

1 tbsp unsweetened cocoa powder
1 tbsp Swerve confectioner's sugar

Directions and Total Time: approx. 40 min + chilling time

Grease a lined with parchment paper loaf pan with cooking spray; set aside. Mix the erythritol, 2 tbsp of water, xanthan gum mixture, and salt in a saucepan.

Place the pan over high heat and bring to a boil. Insert a thermometer and let the ingredients simmer at 220 F for 8 minutes. Add 2 tbsp of water and gelatin in a small bowl. Let sit to dissolve for 5 minutes.

While the gelatin dissolves, pour the remaining water into a small bowl and heat in the microwave for 30 seconds. Stir in cocoa powder and mix it into the gelatin.

When the erythritol solution has hit the right temperature, gradually pour it directly into the gelatin mixture, stirring continuously. Beat for 12 minutes to get a light and fluffy consistency.

Then, stir in the vanilla and pour the blend into the loaf pan. Let the marshmallows set for 3 hours in the fridge. Use an oiled knife to cut into cubes and place them on a plate. Mix the remaining cocoa powder and confectioner's sugar together. Sift it over the marshmallows.

Per serving: Cal 83; Fat 5.3g; Net Carbs 3.6g; Protein 2.2g

Easy Citrus Mousse with Almonds

Ingredients for 4 servings

2 cups Swerve confectioner's sugar	
1 cup whipped cream + extra for garnish	
¼ cup toasted almonds, chopped	
3/4 lb cream cheese, softened	1 lime, juiced and zested
1 lemon, juiced and zested	Salt to taste

Directions and Total Time: approx. 15 min + chilling time

In a bowl and with a hand mixer, whip the cream cheese until light and fluffy. Add in the sugar, lemon and lime juices, and salt and mix well. Fold in the whipped cream to evenly combine.

Spoon the mousse into serving cups and refrigerate to thicken for 1 hour. Swirl with extra whipped cream and garnish with lemon and lime zest. Serve immediately topped with almonds.

Per serving: Cal 242; Fat 18g; Net Carbs 3.3g; Protein 6.5g

OTHER KETO FAVORITES

Avocado & Tofu Sandwiches

Ingredients for 2 servings

4 little gem lettuce leaves
4 tofu slices
1 avocado, sliced
1 large red tomato, sliced
½ oz butter, softened
1 tsp chopped parsley

Directions and Total Time: approx. 10 minutes

Place the lettuce on a flat serving plate. Smear each leaf with butter and arrange tofu slices on the leaves. Top with the avocado and tomato slices. Garnish the sandwiches with parsley and serve.

Per serving: Cal 390; Net Carbs 4g; Fat 29g; Protein 12g

Crunchy Cauliflower with Parsnip Mash

Ingredients for 6 servings

2 tbsp sesame oil
20 oz cauliflower florets
½ cup almond milk
¼ cup coconut flour
¼ tsp cayenne pepper
½ cup almond breadcrumbs
½ cup grated cheddar cheese
1 lb parsnips, quartered
3 tbsp melted butter
A pinch of nutmeg
1 tsp cumin powder
1 cup coconut cream

Directions and Total Time: approx. 55 minutes

Preheat oven to 425 F. Line a baking sheet with parchment paper. In a bowl, combine almond milk, coconut flour, and cayenne. In another bowl, mix breadcrumbs and cheddar cheese. Dip each cauliflower floret into the milk mixture, and then into the cheese mixture.

Place breaded cauliflower on the baking sheet and bake for 30 minutes, turning once. Pour 4 cups of slightly salted water into a pot and add in parsnips. Bring to boil and cook for 15 minutes. Drain and transfer to a bowl.

Add in melted butter, cumin, nutmeg, and coconut cream. Mash the ingredients using a potato mash. Spoon the mash into plates and drizzle with sesame oil. Serve with baked cauliflower.

Per serving: Cal 390; Net Carbs 8g; Fat 35g; Protein 6g

Pepperoni & Mixed Mushroom Pizza

Ingredients for 2 servings

2 (1 pack) cauliflower pizza crusts
2 oz mixed mushrooms, sliced
1 tbsp basil pesto
2 tbsp olive oil
Salt and black pepper to taste
¾ cup mozzarella, shredded
4 oz pepperoni, sliced

Directions and Total Time: approx. 25 minutes

Preheat the oven to 350 F. Grease two baking dishes with cooking spray. Add in the two cauliflower crusts.

In a bowl, mix the mushrooms with pesto, olive oil, salt, and black pepper. Divide the mozzarella cheese on top of the pizza crusts. Spread the mushroom mixture and cover with the pepperoni slices. Bake the pizzas in batches until the cheese has melted, about 8 minutes. Remove when ready, cut, and serve with a spinach salad.

Per serving: Cal 512; Fat 41g; Net Carbs 4.6g; Protein 28g

Cauliflower & Mushroom Arancini

Ingredients for 4 servings

1 cup cauliflower rice
2 tbsp butter, softened
1 garlic clove, minced
1 cup mushrooms, chopped
4 tbsp ground flax seeds
4 tbsp hemp seeds
4 tbsp sunflower seeds
1 tbsp dried basil
1 tsp mustard
1 egg
½ cup Pecorino cheese, grated

Directions and Total Time: approx. 25 minutes

Set a pan over medium heat and warm 1 tablespoon of butter. Add in mushrooms and garlic and sauté until there is no more water in the mushrooms. Remove to a bowl and let cool for a few minutes. Place in Pecorino cheese, cauliflower rice, hemp seeds, mustard, egg, sunflower seeds, flax seeds, and basil. Create balls from the mixture.

In a pan, warm the remaining butter; fry the balls for 7 minutes. Flip them over with a wide spatula and cook for 6 more minutes. Serve and enjoy!

Per serving: Cal 363; Fat 29g; Net Carbs 7.2g; Protein 15g

Spiced Halloumi with Brussels Sprouts

Ingredients for 4 servings

½ cup unsweetened coconut, shredded
½ lb Brussels sprouts, halved
10 oz halloumi cheese, sliced
1 tbsp coconut oil
1 tsp chili powder
½ tsp onion powder
4 oz butter
Salt and black pepper to taste
Lemon wedges for serving

Directions and Total Time: approx. 35 minutes

In a bowl, mix the shredded coconut, chili powder, salt, coconut oil, and onion powder. Then, toss the halloumi slices in the spice mixture. Heat a grill pan over medium heat and cook the coated halloumi cheese for 2-3 minutes. Transfer to a plate to keep warm.

In a skillet, melt half of the butter, add, and sauté the Brussels sprouts until slightly caramelized. Season with salt and pepper. Dish the Brussels sprouts into serving plates with the halloumi cheese and lemon wedges. Melt the remaining butter in the skillet and drizzle over the Brussels sprouts and halloumi cheese. Serve.

Per serving: Cal 574; Fat 43g; Net Carbs 4.2g; Protein 29g

Baked Sausage & Peppers with Salad

Ingredients for 4 servings

1 cucumber, sliced
1 large tomato, chopped
Salt and black pepper to taste
2 tsp dried parsley
2 red bell peppers
1 lb sausages, sliced
1 tbsp butter, melted
1 tsp dried basil
1 tbsp mayonnaise
2 tbsp Greek yogurt

Directions and Total Time: approx. 35 minutes

Preheat the oven's broiler to 420 F and line a baking sheet with parchment paper. Arrange the bell peppers and sausages on the baking sheet, drizzle with the melted butter, and season with basil, salt, and black pepper. Bake in the oven for 20 minutes.

Meanwhile, in a salad bowl, combine the Greek yogurt, mayonnaise, cucumber, tomato, salt, black pepper, and parsley; set aside. When the bake is ready, remove it from the oven and serve with the salad.

Per serving: Cal 623; Fat 48g; Net Carbs 6.3g; Protein 32g

Beef Butternut Squash Bolognese

Ingredients for 4 servings

Bolognese

2 tbsp olive oil	1 ½ cups tomatoes, crushed
1 onion, chopped	1 tbsp dried basil
1 garlic clove, minced	12 oz butternut squash
1 small carrot, chopped	2 tbsp butter
½ lb ground beef	Salt and black pepper to taste
2 tbsp tomato paste	

Directions and Total Time: approx. 65 minutes

Pour the olive oil into a saucepan and heat over medium heat. Add in the onion, garlic, and carrot. Sauté for 3 minutes or until the onion is soft and the carrot caramelized. Pour in the ground beef, tomato paste, tomatoes, salt, black pepper, and basil. Stir and cook for 15 minutes, or simmer for 30 minutes. Mix in some water if the mixture is too thick and simmer for 20 minutes.

Melt the butter in a skillet over medium heat and toss the butternut squash quickly in the butter, for about 1 minute only. Season with salt and black pepper. Divide the butternut squash into serving plates and spoon the sauce on top. Serve the dish immediately.

Per serving: Cal 355; Fat 23g; Net Carbs 9.5g; Protein 16g

Broccoli Risotto with Mushrooms

Ingredients for 4 servings

1 cup cremini mushrooms, chopped	
1 head broccoli, grated	1 cup coconut cream
4 oz butter	¾ cup grated Parmesan
2 garlic cloves, minced	1 tbsp chopped thyme
1 red onion, finely chopped	Salt and black pepper to taste
¾ cup white wine	

Directions and Total Time: approx. 30 minutes

Melt the butter in a saucepan over medium heat. Sauté mushrooms until golden, 5 minutes. Add in garlic and onion and cook for 3 minutes until fragrant and soft.

Mix in broccoli, 1 cup of water, and white wine. Season with salt and pepper and simmer for 10 minutes. Mix in coconut cream and simmer until most of the cream evaporates. Turn heat off and stir in Parmesan and thyme. Serve warm.

Per serving: Cal 519; Net Carbs 12g; Fat 39g; Protein 15g

Awesome Beef Cheeseburgers

Ingredients for 2 servings

Salt, black pepper, and cayenne pepper to taste

½ lb ground beef	1 oz cheddar cheese, grated
1 spring onion, chopped	1 tbsp olive oil
1 tsp yellow mustard	2 sprigs parsley, chopped

Directions and Total Time: approx. 20 minutes

To a mixing bowl, add ground beef, cayenne pepper, black pepper, spring onion, parsley, and salt. Shape into 2 balls, then flatten to make burgers.

In a separate bowl, mix mustard and cheddar cheese. Split the cheese mixture between the prepared patties. Wrap the meat mixture around the cheese to ensure that the filling is sealed inside. Warm oil in a skillet over medium heat. Cook the burgers for 5 minutes on each side.

Per serving: Cal 386; Fat 25g; Net Carbs 1.3g; Protein 32g

Ricotta Balls with Fresh Salad

Ingredients for 2 servings

Cheese balls

1/3 cup ricotta cheese, crumbled

1 egg	1/3 cup almond flour
2 tbsp Grana Padano cheese, shredded	1/3 tsp flax meal
	Salt and black pepper to taste

Salad

2 cups arugula leaves	2 tbsp mayonnaise
1 small cucumber, thinly sliced	½ tsp mustard
1 tomato, sliced	1 tsp lemon juice
1 green onion, sliced	Salt to taste
4 radishes, sliced	

Directions and Total Time: approx. 20 minutes

In a mixing dish, combine ricotta cheese, Grana Padano cheese, flax meal, and almond flour. Add in the egg, salt, and black pepper and stir well. Form balls out of the mixture. Set the balls on a parchment-lined baking sheet and bake for 10 minutes at 380 F. Lay arugula leaves on a large salad platter; add in radishes, tomato, cucumber, and green onion. In a small bowl, mix the mayonnaise, salt, lemon juice, and mustard. Sprinkle this mixture over the vegetables. Add cheese balls on top and serve.

Per serving: Cal 255; Fat 19g; Net Carbs 3.9g; Protein 13g

Fall Pumpkin Donuts

Ingredients for 4 servings

2 cups swerve confectioner's sugar

1 cup almond flour	½ tsp vanilla extract
¼ cup coconut flour	2 tsp pumpkin pie spice
1 tsp baking powder	½ cup pumpkin puree
1 egg	¼ cup sugar-free maple syrup
2 egg yolks	A pinch of salt
½ cup heavy cream	

Directions and Total Time: approx. 25 min + cooling time

Preheat oven to 350 F. In a bowl, mix heavy cream, egg, egg yolks, vanilla extract, pumpkin pie spice, pumpkin puree, and maple syrup. One after another, smoothly mix in almond and coconut flours, baking powder, and salt. Pour the batter into greased donut cups and bake for 18 minutes or until set. Remove, flip onto a wire rack and let cool. In a bowl, whisk the swerve and 4 tbsp of water until smooth. Swirl the glaze over the donut and serve immediately.

Per serving: Cal 191; Net Carbs 4.3g, Fat 13g, Protein 8g

Gorgonzola & Ricotta Stuffed Peppers

Ingredients for 4 servings

½ cup gorgonzola cheese, crumbled
2 tbsp olive oil
4 red bell peppers, halved
1 cup ricotta cheese
2 cloves garlic, minced
1 ½ cups tomatoes, chopped
1 tsp dried basil
Salt and black pepper to taste
½ tsp oregano

Directions and Total Time: approx. 55 minutes

Preheat oven to 350 F and lightly grease the sides and bottom of a baking dish with cooking spray.

In a bowl, mix garlic, tomatoes, gorgonzola and ricotta cheeses. Stuff the pepper halves and place them on the baking dish. Season with oregano, salt, black pepper, and basil. Drizzle with olive oil and bake for 40 minutes until the peppers are tender.

Per serving: Cal 541; Fat 43g; Net Carbs 7.3g; Protein 25g

Basil Pesto Mushroom Pizza

Ingredients for 4 servings

2 eggs
½ cup mayonnaise
¾ cup almond flour
1 tbsp psyllium husk powder
1 tsp baking powder
2 oz mixed mushrooms, sliced
1 tbsp basil pesto
½ cup coconut cream
¾ cup grated Parmesan

Directions and Total Time: approx. 30 min + chilling time

Preheat oven to 350 F. In a bowl, beat the eggs. Add in the mayonnaise, almond flour, psyllium husk, and baking powder and whisk until well mixed. Pour batter into a baking sheet. Bake for 10 minutes. In a bowl, mix mushrooms with pesto. Remove crust from the oven and spread coconut cream on top. Add the mushroom mixture and Parmesan. Bake the pizza further until the cheese melts, about 5-10 minutes. Slice and serve.

Per serving: Cal 748; Net Carbs 6g; Fat 71g; Protein 19g

Thick Creamy Broccoli Cheese Soup

Ingredients for 4 servings

1 tbsp olive oil
2 tbsp peanut butter
¾ cup heavy cream
1 onion, diced
1 garlic, minced
4 cups chopped broccoli
4 cups veggie broth
2 ¾ cups cheddar, grated
¼ cup cheddar, to garnish
Salt and black pepper to taste
½ bunch fresh mint, chopped

Directions and Total Time: approx. 25 minutes

Warm olive oil and peanut butter in a pot over medium heat. Sauté onion and garlic for 3 minutes, stirring occasionally. Season with salt and pepper. Add the broth and broccoli and bring to a boil.

Reduce the heat and simmer for 10 minutes. Puree the soup with a hand blender until smooth. Add in the cheese and cook for about 1 minute. Stir in the heavy cream. Serve in bowls with the reserved grated cheddar cheese and sprinkled with fresh mint.

Per serving: Cal 552; Fat 49g; Net Carbs 6.9g; Protein 25g

Parmesan & Gruyere Soufflé

Ingredients for 4 servings

2 ½ cups Gruyere cheese, grated
4 yolks, beaten
2 egg whites, beaten until stiff
2 ½ tbsp butter, softened
2 ½ tbsp almond flour
1 ½ tsp mustard powder
½ cup Parmesan, grated
½ cup almond milk

Directions and Total Time: approx. 20 minutes

Preheat oven to 370 F. Brush 4 ramekins with some butter. Melt the remaining butter in a pan over low heat and stir in almond flour for 1 minute. Remove from the heat, mix in the mustard powder until combined and whisk in almond milk until no lumps form. Return to the heat and cook while stirring until the sauce comes to a rolling boil. Stir in Gruyere cheese until melted.

Into the egg yolks, whisk ¼ cup of the warmed milk mixture, then combine with the remaining milk sauce. Fold in egg whites gradually until evenly combined. Spoon the mixture into the ramekins and top with the Parmesan cheese. Bake for 8 minutes, until the soufflé have a slight wobble, but soft at the center. Serve.

Per serving: Cal 491; Net Carbs 3.8g; Fat 41g; Protein 26g

Four-Cheese Pizza

Ingredients for 4 servings

½ cup Monterey Jack cheese, shredded
1 ¼ cups mozzarella cheese, shredded
1 tbsp olive oil
½ cup brie cheese
½ cup gorgonzola cheese
2 garlic cloves, chopped
2 green bell peppers, sliced
½ cup tomato sauce
1 tsp oregano
2 tbsp basil, chopped
6 black olives for garnish

Directions and Total Time: approx. 15 minutes

Mix all cheeses in a bowl. Set a pan over medium heat and warm oil. Spread the bottom with the cheese mixture and cook for 5 minutes. Scatter garlic, oregano, and tomato sauce over the crust. Sprinkle the bell peppers and cook for 2 more minutes. Top with basil and olives to serve.

Per serving: Cal 316; Fat 26g; Net Carbs 4.6g; Protein 7.9g

Chorizo & Cabbage Bake

Ingredients for 4 servings

1 head green cabbage, cut into wedges
1 lb chorizo, sliced
4 tbsp butter, melted
Salt and black pepper to taste
2 tbsp Parmesan cheese, grated
1 tbsp parsley, chopped

Directions and Total Time: approx. 25 minutes

Preheat oven to 390 F and grease a baking tray with cooking spray. Mix the butter, salt, and black pepper until evenly combined in a bowl. Brush the mixture on all sides of the cabbage wedges. Place on the baking sheet, add in the chorizo, and bake for 20 minutes to soften the cabbage. Sprinkle with Parmesan cheese and parsley.

Per serving: Cal 268; Fat 19g; Net Carbs 4g; Protein 17.5g

Arugula Pizza with Pecans

Ingredients for 4 servings

1 tbsp olive oil
1 cup grated mozzarella
½ cup almond flour
2 tbsp ground psyllium husk
1 cup basil pesto

1 tomato, thinly sliced
1 zucchini, cut into half-moons
1 cup baby arugula
2 tbsp chopped pecans
¼ tsp red chili flakes

Directions and Total Time: approx. 35 minutes

Preheat oven to 390 F. Line a baking sheet with parchment paper. In a bowl, mix almond flour, psyllium powder, olive oil, and 1 cup of lukewarm water until dough forms. Spread the mixture on the sheet and bake for 10 minutes. Spread pesto on the crust and top with mozzarella cheese, tomato slices, and zucchini. Bake until the cheese melts, 15 minutes. Top with arugula, pecans, and red chili flakes.

Per serving: Cal 191; Net Carbs 3g; Fats 14g; Protein 9g

Decadent Pepperoni Fat Head Pizza

Ingredients for 4 servings

1 egg, beaten
1 ½ cups grated mozzarella
2 tbsp cream cheese, softened
¾ cup almond flour

4 tbsp tomato sauce
½ cup sliced pepperoni
1 tsp dried oregano

Directions and Total Time: approx. 30 minutes

Preheat oven to 420 F. Line a round pizza pan with parchment paper. Microwave the mozzarella cheese and cream cheese for 1 minute. Stir in egg and add in the almond flour; mix well. Transfer the pizza "dough" onto a flat surface and knead until smooth. Spread it on the pizza pan. Bake for 6 minutes. Top with tomato sauce, remaining mozzarella, oregano, and pepperoni. Bake for 15 minutes. Serve sliced.

Per serving: Cal 230; Net Carbs 0.4g; Fats 7g; Protein 36g

Fluffiest Berry Pancakes

Ingredients for 4 servings

1 handful fresh strawberries and raspberries for topping
1 handful of strawberries and raspberries, mashed
1 egg
½ cup almond flour
1 tsp baking soda
1 tbsp Swerve sugar
A pinch of cinnamon powder

½ cup almond milk
2 tsp butter
1 cup Greek yogurt
A pinch of salt

Directions and Total Time: approx. 25 minutes

In a mixing bowl, combine almond flour, baking soda, salt, Swerve sugar, and cinnamon. Whisk in mashed berries, egg, and milk until smooth. Melt ½ tsp of butter in a skillet and pour 1 tbsp of the mixture into the pan. Cook until small bubbles appear, flip, and cook until golden. Transfer to a plate and proceed using up the remaining batter for pancakes. Top pancakes with yogurt and whole berries.

Per serving: Cal 229; Net Carbs 7.6g; Fat 15g; Protein 10g

Quick Strawberry Mousse

Ingredients for 4 servings

1 large egg white
2 cups whipped cream

2 cups frozen strawberries
2 tbsp Swerve sugar

Directions and Total Time: approx. 10 min + chilling time

Pour 1 ½ cups strawberries and swerve sugar in a blender; process until smooth. Pour in the egg white and transfer the mixture to a bowl. Use an electric hand mixer to whisk until fluffy. Spoon the mixture into dessert glasses and top with whipped cream and strawberries. Serve chilled.

Per serving: Cal 150; Net Carbs 4.8g; Fats 7g; Protein 2g

Rolls with Serrano Ham & Cottage Cheese

Ingredients for 4 servings

10 canned pepperoncini peppers, sliced and drained
8 oz cottage cheese   10 oz Serrano ham, sliced

Directions and Total Time: approx. 10 min + chilling time

Lay a large piece of plastic wrap on a flat surface and arrange the serrano ham all over slightly overlapping each other. Spread the cottage cheese on top and cover with the pepperoncini. Hold two opposite ends of the plastic wrap and roll the serrano ham. Twist both ends to tighten and refrigerate for 2 hours. Unwrap the serrano ham roll and slice into 2-inch pinwheels. Serve.

Per serving: Cal 266; Fat 24g; Net Carbs 0g; Protein 13g

Braised Sausage with Steamed Cauliflower

Ingredients for 4 servings

1 lb sausages, sliced
2 tbsp butter
Salt and black pepper to taste
2 tbsp parsley, chopped
1 garlic clove, minced

½ celery stalk, chopped
½ cup vegetable broth
1 cup tomato sauce
1 large onion, chopped
10 oz cauliflower florets

Directions and Total Time: approx. 30 minutes

Melt butter in a skillet over medium heat. Stir-fry garlic, celery, and onion for 3-4 minutes until softened. Add the sausage and fry for 4-5 minutes. Pour in tomato sauce and vegetable broth and simmer for 10-12 minutes. Season cauliflower with salt and pepper and microwave for 3 minutes until soft and tender within. Remove to a plate and pour the sausage mixture over. Top with parsley.

Per serving: Cal 490; Net Carbs 6g; Fat 38g; Protein 25.4g

Baby Spinach Pesto

Ingredients for 4 servings

2 cups baby spinach
3 garlic cloves, minced
¼ cup pine nuts

¼ cup grated Parmesan cheese
½ cup extra-virgin olive oil
Salt and black pepper to taste

Directions and Total Time: approx. 10 minutes

In a food processor, place all the ingredients, except for the olive oil; pulse until the mixture is finely chopped. While the food processor is running, pour in the olive oil in a thin stream and blend until the pesto is smooth.

Per serving: Cal 150; Net Carbs 4.8g; Fats 7g; Protein 2g

KETO SMALL APPLIANCE RECIPES

Slow Cooker Beef Meatballs

Ingredients for 6 servings

2 lb ground beef	1 cup grated Parmesan cheese
1 lb ground pork	4 (24 oz) crushed tomatoes
4 cloves garlic, minced	2 (6 oz) tomato paste
1 onion, finely chopped	1 tsp red pepper flakes
1 cup zero carb breadcrumbs	3 bay leaves
4 eggs, cracked into a bowl	1 tsp Italian seasoning
4 tbsp chopped parsley	2 tbsp chopped basil
Salt and pepper to taste	2 tbsp grated Parmesan cheese

Directions and Total Time: approx. 8 hours 25 minutes

In a bowl, add the beef, pork, onions, garlic, breadcrumbs, parsley, eggs, cheese, salt, and pepper. Use your hands to mix the ingredients and form 2-inch meatballs out of the mixture. Lightly grease the baking tray with cooking spray and put the meatballs on it. Tuck the baking tray into the oven and broil the meatballs on high heat for about 5 minutes on each side.

After, remove the meatballs from the oven and put them in your slow cooker. Top it with the crushed tomatoes, red pepper flakes, tomato paste, bay leaves, and Italian seasoning. Close the lid and cook the meatballs and other ingredients on Low for 8 hours.

When ready, open the lid and adjust the taste with salt and pepper. Stir the mixture gently with a spoon. Then, dish the meatballs with tomato sauce into a serving bowl and garnish it with the chopped basil and parmesan cheese. Serve it on a good lump of steamed squash spaghetti.

Per serving: Cal 153; Fat 8g; Net Carbs 4g; Protein 13g

Slow Cooker Chipotle Chicken

Ingredients for 4 servings

1 lb chicken breasts, cubed	¼ tsp cumin powder
1 tsp chipotle chili powder	5 tbsp tomato paste
Salt to taste	1/3 tsp liquid stevia
¼ tsp garlic powder	½ cup chicken broth
¼ tsp onion powder	

Directions and Total Time: approx. 4 hours 10 minutes

Pour the chipotle powder, onion powder, cumin powder, garlic powder, salt, stevia, and tomato paste into your slow cooker. Gradually add the chicken broth while continually mixing the ingredients with a spoon until smooth paste forms. Then, add the remaining chicken broth and stir it again. Put the chicken breasts in the sauce mixture, making sure to coat it with the sauce using a spoon. Close the lid and cook the chicken on High for 4 hours.

When the chicken is ready, open the lid, and use two forks to shred the chicken. You can do this in the cooker. Adjust the seasoning and stir. Spoon the chipotle chicken onto serving plates and serve with a side of steamed cauli rice if desired.

Per serving: Cal 240; Fat 6g; Net Carbs 0g; Protein 15g

Slow Cooker Chicken Jardiniere

Ingredients for 4 servings

4 chicken thighs	½ cup dry white wine
3 bacon slices, chopped	3 Button mushrooms, sliced
2 tsp butter	8 small turnips, peeled
Salt and pepper to taste	20 small pearl onions, peeled
3 cloves garlic, minced	¾ cup chopped green beans
¼ tsp dried thyme	¼ cup sliced asparagus
1 cup chicken broth	

Directions and Total Time: approx. 8 hours 40 minutes

Put a skillet over medium heat and add the bacon. Fry the bacon until it is crispy and browned for about 4 minutes. Remove with a slotted spoon to your slow cooker while maintaining the grease derived from it.

Add the butter to the skillet and fry the chicken until golden brown on both sides, about 8-10 minutes. Turn off the heat and put the chicken in your slow cooker too. Top the bacon and chicken with garlic, thyme, chicken broth, white wine, mushrooms, turnips, pearl onions, green beans, and asparagus. Close the lid and cook on Low for 8 hours. Once ready, stir the ingredients with a spoon and adjust the taste with salt and pepper.

Dish the chicken and vegetables into a serving platter. Serve the chicken with a celeriac mash if desired.

Per serving: Cal 19; Fat 3.9g; Net Carbs 3.4g; Protein 12g

Slow Cooker Lavender Chicken

Ingredients for 4 servings

1 ½ lb chicken thighs	4 tbsp olive oil
1 tbsp Dijon mustard	1 lemon, zested and juiced
2 tbsp dried lavender	½ cup chicken broth
1 tbsp dried thyme	Salt to taste

Directions and Total Time: approx. 10 hrs 30 minutes

Pour the lavender, Dijon mustard, thyme, 2 tablespoons of olive oil, 1 teaspoon of lemon zest, and salt in a bowl and mix well with a spoon. Put the chicken thighs in a deep container and pour the lavender mixture on it. Stir the chicken to ensure that it is well coated with the sauce. Then, place the chicken in the refrigerator and let it marinate for 2 hours.

In a jug or other bowl, add the lemon juice, remaining lemon zest, and chicken broth. Mix with a spoon and set aside. Warm the remaining olive oil in a skillet over medium heat. Remove the chicken from the fridge and cook it in the oil until golden brown on both sides, about 8 minutes in total. Remove the chicken with a slotted spoon to your slow cooker, fetch out 2 tbsp of oil from the skillet and add the remaining drippings to the slow cooker. Pour the lemon juice sauce over the chicken, close the lid, and cook on Low for 8 hours.

After 8 hours, remove the chicken onto a serving platter, adjust the taste with salt and spoon the sauce all over the chicken. Serve with green beans, broccoli, and sliced carrot sauté if desired.

Per serving: Cal 451; Fat 27g; Net Carbs 0.1g; Protein 50g

Slow Cooker Chicken Stew with Veggies

Ingredients for 4 servings

2 garlic cloves, minced
1 cup mushrooms, chopped
¼ tsp celery seeds, ground
1 carrot, chopped
1 cup chicken stock
1 cup sour cream

1 cup leeks, chopped
1 pound chicken breasts
1 tsp dried thyme
2 tbsp fresh parsley, chopped
Salt and black pepper, to taste
4 zucchinis, spiralized

Directions and Total Time: approx. 4 hours 15 minutes

Season the chicken with salt, black pepper, and thyme and place it into your slow cooker. Stir in leeks, sour cream, celery seeds, garlic, carrot, mushrooms, and stock. Cook on High for 4 hours.

Heat a pot with salted water over medium heat and bring to a boil. Stir in the zucchini pasta, cook for 1 minute, and drain. Transfer to a plate, top with chicken mixture, and sprinkle with parsley to serve.

Per serving: Cal 312; Fat 17g; Net Carbs 8.4g; Protein 26g

Slow Cooker Beef & Broccoli Stew

Ingredients for 4 servings

2 tbsp olive oil
1 lb ground beef
½ cup leeks, chopped
1 head broccoli, cut into florets
Salt and black pepper, to taste
1 tsp yellow mustard

1 tsp Worcestershire sauce
2 tomatoes, chopped
8 oz tomato sauce
1 tbsp rosemary, chopped
½ tsp dried oregano

Directions and Total Time: approx. 4 hours 20 minutes

Coat the broccoli with black pepper and salt. Set them into a bowl, drizzle over the olive oil, and toss to combine. In a separate bowl, combine the beef with Worcestershire sauce, leeks, salt, mustard, and black pepper, and stir well. Press on your slow cooker's bottom. Scatter in the broccoli, add the tomatoes, oregano, and tomato sauce. Cook for 4 hours on High; covered. Serve the casserole with scattered rosemary.

Per serving: Cal 677; Fat 42g; Net Carbs 8.3g; Protein 63g

Slow Cooker Chicken Stew with Sorrel

Ingredients for 6 servings

8 chicken breasts, cut into thin strips
2 tbsp olive oil
1 large leek, chopped
1 lb sorrel

4 cups chicken broth
2 cups chopped daikon radish
Salt and pepper to taste

Directions and Total Time: approx. 4 hours 20 minutes

First, season the chicken with salt and pepper. Warm the olive oil in a skillet over medium heat and add the chicken strips. Brown the chicken strips for about 6 minutes; transfer to your slow cooker. Top it with the leek, sorrel, daikon radish, and chicken broth. Close the lid and cook the ingredients on High for 4 hours. Once ready, open the pot and adjust the taste with salt and pepper. Spoon the stew into serving bowls and serve it with some cauliflower rice.

Per serving: Cal 260; Fat 12g; Net Carbs 2.3g; Protein 22g

Slow Cooker Poule au Pot

Ingredients for 6 servings

1 (3.5-4 lb) whole chicken
1 brown onion, quartered
1 rutabaga, peeled and diced
1 celery stalk, chopped

2 carrots, diced
3 sprigs fresh thyme
1 bay leaf
Salt and pepper to taste

Directions and Total Time: approx. 8 hours 20 minutes

Put the chicken in your slow cooker and place the rutabaga, carrots, celery, and onion around it. Then, add the bay leaf, pepper, salt, and thyme and pour in 4 cups of water. Cook the chicken on Low for 8 hours.

After, open the lid and use two tongs to lift the chicken into a wide serving dish. Surround it with the vegetables and spoon some broth over them while discarding the bay leaf and thyme sprigs. Serve and enjoy!

Per serving: Cal 210; Fat 15g; Net Carbs 3.6g; Protein 28g

Slow Cooker Chicken Provencal

Ingredients for 4 servings

1 eggplant, cut into 1-inch chunks
4 chicken thighs
1 tbsp olive oil
4 bacon slices, chopped
1 zucchini, cut in chunks
1 red chili, minced
2 cups passata

3 cloves garlic, minced
1 red onion, cut in wedges
½ cube chicken stock, crushed
2 tsp mixed herb seasoning
¼ cup chopped parsley

Directions and Total Time: approx. 8 hours 25 minutes

Warm the olive oil in a skillet over medium heat and fry the bacon until it is browned and crispy, about 4 minutes. Add the chicken, red chili, red onion, eggplant, zucchini, and garlic and sauté for 5-6 minutes. Remove to your slow cooker. Pour in the passata, 1 cup of water, chicken stock cube, and mixed herbs seasoning.

Stir the ingredients lightly with a spoon, close the lid, and cook them for 8 hours on Low. Once ready, open the lid and stir in the parsley. Dish the chicken with sauce and veggies into a serving bowl and serve it with some creamy broccoli mash if desired.

Per serving: Cal 250; Fat 10g; Net Carbs 1g; Protein 22g

Slow Cooker Pork & Kraut

Ingredients for 4 servings

1 lb pork tenderloin
1 (20 oz) sauerkraut, undrained

¼ cup butter
Salt and pepper to taste

Directions and Total Time: approx. 8 hours 5 minutes

Put the pork in your slow cooker, pour the sauerkraut with its juice butter, 1 cup of water, salt, and pepper. Cover the lid and cook the ingredients on Low for 8 hours. Open the lid and use two forks to shred the tenderloin. Also, add some water if the mixture is dry, and stir it with a spoon. Serve the pork with mashed turnips and some steamed rapini if desired.

Per serving: Cal 258; Fat 15g; Net Carbs 7.5g; Protein 22g

Slow Cooker Chicken Cacciatore

Ingredients for 4 servings

1 cup sliced Cremini mushrooms
1 ½ lb chicken thighs, boneless   1 ½ tsp balsamic vinegar
2 ½ tbsp olive oil   1 green bell pepper, chopped
Salt and pepper to taste   3/4 cup chicken broth
3 cloves garlic, minced   3/4 dry red wine
1 tsp rosemary   2 tbsp chopped parsley
1 yellow onion, chopped   2 tbsp grated Parmesan cheese
1 ½ cup crushed tomatoes

Directions and Total Time: approx. 4 hours 50 minutes

Put a skillet over medium heat and add two tablespoons of olive oil to warm. As it heats, season the chicken with salt and pepper and brown it on both sides for 6 minutes in total. Transfer the chicken to your slow cooker.

Then take the skillet over the heat and, use a paper towel to wipe it, return the skillet to heat, and heat the remaining olive oil. Pour in the onion and garlic and cook until softened for 2 minutes, then add 1 tablespoon of balsamic vinegar. Cook until the vinegar reduces, 1-2 minutes. Pour the mixture into the cooker.

Add in the tomatoes, mushrooms, bell pepper, rosemary, chicken broth, and wine and stir. Close the lid and cook them on High mode for 4 hours. Serve the chicken garnished with chopped parsley and Parmesan cheese.

Per serving: Cal 228; Fat 8g; Net Carbs 4g; Protein 28g

Slow Cooker Chicken in Wine Sauce

Ingredients for 6 servings

1 (14.5 oz) can cream of mushroom soup
2 (4 oz) cans mushrooms, drained
6 chicken breasts, boneless   ½ tsp garlic powder
1/3 cup white wine   2 tsp dried parsley
2 tbsp milk   Salt and pepper to taste
2 tsp onion powder

Directions and Total Time: approx. 6 hours 10 minutes

In your slow cooker, pour the mushroom soup, mushrooms, white wine, milk, onion powder, garlic powder, and dried parsley. Season with salt and pepper and stir it with a spoon.

Put the chicken in the sauce and use the spoon to cover the chicken with some of the sauce. Close the lid and cook it on High for 4 hours. Open the lid after and dish the chicken with the sauce into serving bowls. Serve on a bed of zoodles or squash spaghetti if desired.

Per serving: Cal 226; Fat 5.1g; Net Carbs 1.8g; Protein 38g

Slow Cooker Chicken Chasseur

Ingredients for 6 servings

3 lb chicken thighs, boneless and skinless
2 cups sliced cremini mushrooms
Salt and pepper to taste   ½ cup minced shallots
3 tbsp olive oil   ½ cup dry white wine
1 tbsp almond flour   1 tsp dried tarragon
3 tbsp tomato paste   Chopped parsley to garnish

Directions and Total Time: approx. 4 hours 15 minutes

Put a skillet over medium heat and add the olive oil. As it heats, pat the chicken dry with paper towels, season it with pepper and salt, and then dredge it in the almond flour. By this time, the oil should have heated. Add the chicken and fry until golden brown on both sides, about 6 minutes. Remove to your slow cooker. Add in the mushrooms, shallot, tomato paste, 1 cup of water, tarragon, and white wine. Cover the lid and cook the ingredients for 4 hours on High. Adjust the taste: Place the chicken chasseur in a serving bowl. Garnish with parsley. Serve with a buttered celeriac mash if desired.

Per serving: Cal 126; Fat 13g; Net Carbs 1.7g; Protein 19g

Slow Cooker Chicken Creole

Ingredients for 4 servings

1 lb chicken thighs, boneless and skinless
2 tbsp olive oil   Salt and pepper to taste
1 2 chopped celery stalk   ¾ cup chicken broth
1 chopped onion   ½ tsp dried thyme
1 chopped green bell pepper   1 bay leaf
2 garlic cloves, minced   1 tsp Cajun seasoning
2 cups chopped tomatoes   2 tbsp chopped scallions
2 tbsp tomato paste

Directions and Total Time: approx. 4 hours 30 minutes

Put a skillet over medium heat and add the olive oil to heat. Once heated, add the onion, celery, bell pepper, and garlic. Sauté for 6 minutes.

Add the tomato paste and tomatoes and stir; let it cook for 2 minutes. Spoon the mixture into your slow cooker and add the chicken broth, pepper, thyme, Cajun seasoning, and bay leaf. Stir the ingredients and then put the chicken in the liquid. Use the spoon to push the chicken into the liquid to ensure that it is well submerged.

Cover the lid and cook the ingredients for 4 hours on High. Sprinkle with scallions and serve warm.

Per serving: Cal 174; Fat 11g; Net Carbs 1.8g; Protein 28g

Slow Cooker Chicken with Garlic Sauce

Ingredients for 6 servings

2 lb chicken breasts, halved   1 tsp Swerve sweetener
2 tbsp olive oil   ½ tsp dried oregano
1 cup roasted red bell pepper   Salt to taste
1 cup chicken broth   4 cloves garlic, minced

Directions and Total Time: approx. 8 hours 10 minutes

Pour the chicken broth, roasted bell pepper, Swerve sweetener, oregano, and garlic in your blender and process until a smooth liquid is achieved, about 2 minutes. Lightly season the chicken with salt and put it in your slow cooker. Pour the blended mixture over it along with the olive oil and cook covered on Low for 8 hours.

After, dish the chicken with sauce into a serving bowl and serve it with a mix of sautéed broccoli florets, asparagus, and green beans if desired.

Per serving: Cal 156; Fat 12g; Net Carbs 0g; Protein 24g

Slow Cooker Spring Pork Stew

Ingredients for 6 servings

2 zucchinis, cut in ½ -inch dices
1 red bell pepper, cut into strips
1 yellow squash, cut in ½ -inch dices

2 lb lean pork roast, cubed	3 ribs celery, diced
4 tbsp olive oil	2 (28 oz) cans tomatoes
1 ½ cups chicken broth	1 tbsp chopped parsley
1 onion, diced	1 tbsp chopped thyme
3 cloves garlic, minced	Salt and pepper to taste
3 carrots, diced	

Directions and Total Time: approx. 8 hours 30 minutes

Warm the olive oil in a skillet over medium heat. Season the pork cubes with salt and pepper and brown them into the heated oil on both sides, about 7 minutes. Remove the pork to your slow cooker. Pour some broth into the skillet to deglaze the bottom of the skillet and pour into the cooker too. Add the onion, garlic, carrots, celery, yellow squash, zucchinis, bell pepper, tomatoes, and thyme to the pork and pour the remaining broth over it; stir. Close the lid and cook on Low for 8 hours. Open the cover and stir the parsley into the pork stew. Adjust the taste with salt and pepper. Plate the pork stew with veggies on a bed of cauliflower rice and serve.

Per serving: Cal 132; Fat 5.3g; Net Carbs 2.5g; Protein 12g

Slow Cooker Pork Ragout

Ingredients for 4 servings

1 lb pork tenderloin	½ cup roasted red Peppers
Salt and pepper to taste	1 cup crushed tomatoes
1 tsp olive oil	2 bay leaves
5 cloves garlic, smashed	2 sprigs fresh thyme
1 onion, chopped	1 tbsp chopped parsley

Directions and Total Time: approx. 8 hours 20 minutes

Season the tenderloin with salt and pepper. Put a skillet over medium heat and add the olive oil and garlic to it. Sauté the garlic and onion until fragrant, about 3 minutes, and transfer them to your slow cooker.

Put the tenderloin in the skillet and brown it on both sides for 4 minutes. Place it into the slow cooker. Top with roasted red peppers, tomatoes, bay leaves, fresh thyme, and half of the parsley. Close the lid and cook the ingredients on Low for 8 hours. Open the lid after it is done and use a spoon to remove the bay leaves and thyme sprigs. Shred the pork with 2 forks and stir in the remaining parsley. Dish the pork ragout over a bed of zucchini noodles and serve.

Per serving: Cal 197; Fat 15g; Net Carbs 2.2g; Protein 19g

Slow Cooker Pork with Bacon & Sauce

Ingredients for 4 servings

1 lb pork loin	Salt and pepper to taste
3 slices smoked bacon, diced	1 tsp garlic powder
2 cups mushroom cream soup	½ tbsp olive oil
1/3 cup Worcestershire sauce	

Directions and Total Time: approx. 8 hours 15 minutes

Warm the oil in a skillet over medium heat. Season the pork loin with salt, garlic powder, and pepper. Place it in the heated oil and sear it on both sides to be slightly brown for 5 minutes. While the pork loin sears, pour the mushroom soup cream and Worcestershire sauce in your slow cooker and use a spoon to mix them evenly. When the pork is ready, put it in the mixed sauces. Cover the lid and cook them on Low for 8 hours.

After 6 hours, open the cover and add in the smoked bacon. Continue cooking for 2 hours on Low. Remove the pork afterward onto a plate, let it sit for 3 minutes and then slice it with a knife. Plate the pork slices, spoon the sauce with the bacon over them and serve it with a creamy parsnip mash and roasted green beans.

Per serving: Cal 227; Fat 7.5g; Net Carbs 3.1g; Protein 15g

Slow Cooker Pork in Carrot Stew

Ingredients for 6 servings

2 lb pork stewing meat, cubed	3 cloves garlic, minced
1 ½ tbsp olive oil	¼ cup balsamic vinegar
Salt and pepper to taste	½ tsp dried thyme
4 carrots, cut in 3 pieces each	1/3 cup red wine
1 medium yellow onion, diced	1 bay leaf

Directions and Total Time: approx. 8 hours 20 minutes

Warm the olive oil in a skillet over medium heat. Season the pork shoulder with salt and pepper and sear it in the hot oil on both sides for 8 minutes in total.

Transfer the meat to your slow cooker.

Add the onion to the skillet and cook until softened, 2 minutes. Transfer it to the slow cooker too. Add in the carrots, garlic, balsamic vinegar, thyme, red wine, and bay leaf and stir. Close the lid and cook on Low for 8 hours. When ready, remove the pork shoulder onto a serving platter. Serve with a garden salad if desired.

Per serving: Cal 394; Fat 29g; Net Carbs 3.5g; Protein 26g

Slow Cooker Sausage & Cheese Beer Soup

Ingredients for 4 servings

2 tbsp butter	½ tsp red pepper flakes
½ cup celery, chopped	1 cup beer of choice
½ cup heavy cream	3 cups beef stock
5 oz turkey sausage, sliced	1 yellow onion, diced
1 small carrot, chopped	1 cup cheddar cheese, grated
2 garlic cloves, minced	Salt and black pepper to taste
4 oz cream cheese	2 tbsp fresh parsley, chopped

Directions and Total Time: approx. 8 hours 10 minutes

To the slow cooker, add butter, beef stock, beer, turkey sausage, carrot, onion, garlic, celery, salt, red pepper flakes, and black pepper, and stir to combine. Close the lid and cook for 6 hours on Low.

Open the lid and stir in the heavy cream, cheddar and cream cheeses, and cook for 2 more hours. Ladle the soup into bowls and garnish with parsley before serving.

Per serving: Cal 543; Fat 44g; Net Carbs 9.3g; Protein 22g

Slow Cooker Danish Pork Tenderloin

Ingredients for 4 servings

1 lb pork tenderloin, cut into medallions
Salt and pepper to taste
3 slices bacon, chopped
1 large carrot, finely diced
2 large shallots, minced
2 cloves garlic, minced
1 tbsp butter
1 tsp dried tarragon
1 tsp paprika
1 tsp dried thyme
1 bay leaf
1 tbsp tomato paste
1 cup chopped tomatoes
½ cup chicken broth
2 dashes vinegar
1 tbsp Braunstein whisky
10 cocktail Weiners
1 cup heavy cream

Directions and Total Time: approx. 5 hours 25 minutes
Season the pork medallions with salt and pepper. Cook the bacon in a skillet over medium heat until crispy and oil exerted from it, about 4 minutes. Set aside.

Brown the pork medallions in the bacon's grease in the skillet for about 8 minutes on both sides and transfer to your slow cooker. Top with the bacon, carrots, shallots, garlic, butter, tarragon, tomatoes, paprika, thyme, bay leaf, whisky, and plain vinegar. Mix the tomato paste with the chicken broth and pour it all over. Stir the mixture once, close the lid, and cook on High for 3 hours.

Open the lid and stir in the heavy cream and add the cocktail wieners. Close the lid and let the ingredients continue cooking for 1 hour but on Low. Serve with celeriac mash if desired.

Per serving: Cal 124; Fat 16g; Net Carbs 4.1g; Protein 26g

Slow Cooker Pork Neck Casserole

Ingredients for 4 servings

1 lb pork neck
1 large red onion, diced
2 cups sliced mushrooms
4 large carrots, diced
1 greed bell pepper, diced
1 cup chicken stock
8 Baby turnips, peeled
1 small bouquet garni blend
Salt and pepper to taste

Directions and Total Time: approx. 8 hours 10 minutes
Season the pork neck with salt and pepper and put it in your slow cooker. Top it with the bouquet garni, onion, mushrooms, carrots, bell pepper, and turnips. Pour the chicken broth over everything. Close the lid and cook on Low mode for 8 hours.

When ready, remove the pork, let it sit for 2 minutes before slicing. Plate with the vegetables and spoon some amount of sauce over and serve.

Per serving: Cal 363; Fat 23g; Net Carbs 3.2g; Protein 27g

Slow Cooker Pork Frikadeller

Ingredients for 6 servings

2 lb ground pork
2 white onions, minced
1 cup pork rinds, crushed
Salt and pepper to taste
2 tbsp olive oil
¼ cup butter
3 tbsp almond flour
1 cup chicken broth
½ tsp turmeric powder
5 tsp Swedish mustard
2 tbsp chopped parsley

Directions and Total Time: approx. 8 hours 35 minutes
Put the minced pork, pork rinds, and half of the onions in a bowl and mix well. Roll the mixture into bite-sized patties. Warm the olive oil in a skillet over medium heat and fry the patties until brown on both sides, about 8-10 minutes. Transfer them to your slow cooker.

In the same skillet, melt the butter and stir-fry the remaining onions for 3 minutes until softened. Mix in the almond flour and gradually stir in the broth. Bring the mixture to simmer for 1 minute and add in the turmeric and Swedish mustard. Stir and pour over the patties in the cooker. Cover and cook on Low for 8 hours. Garnish with chopped parsley and serve.

Per serving: Cal 363; Fat 25g; Net Carbs 3g; Protein 31.3g

Slow Cooker Endives Au Jambon

Ingredients for 6 servings
Endives

6 Belgian endives, trimmed
6 tbsp unsalted butter
¼ cup Swerve sugar
Salt to taste
10 oz ham, thinly sliced

Bechamel

3 tbsp unsalted butter
1/3 cup almond flour
1 ½ tbsp grated nutmeg
1 cup whole milk, warmed
Black pepper to taste
10 oz Gruyere cheese, grated

Directions and Total Time: approx. 4 hours 40 minutes
Warm 1 cup of water in a saucepan over medium heat. Add the butter, Swerve sugar, and 1 pinch of salt and stir until the butter melts. Transfer to your slow cooker.

Add in the endives and cover them with enough more. Close the lid, and cook on High for 4 hours. Remove the endives with a slotted spoon to a flat surface to cool.

Preheat the oven to 400 F. Make the béchamel by melting the butter in a saucepan over low heat. Stir in the flour, and let it cook for 2 minutes. Whisk in the milk and some of the endives cooking liquid. Ensure that the flour is well mixed into the milk, then mix in the nutmeg and pepper. Let the mixture thicken for 5 minutes. Turn the heat off.

The endives should have cooled by now; wrap them with the ham slices and fit them into the baking dish, making sure that there are no spaces between the wrapped endives. Pour the béchamel all over it and sprinkle the cheese on it. Tuck the baking dish in the oven and bake the endives until golden brown, about 15 minutes.

Remove the endives from the oven, dish them, and serve them hot with some creamy mushrooms.

Per serving: Cal 45; Fat 14.6g; Net Carbs 3g; Protein 6.3g

Slow Cooker Pork Belly in Beer

Ingredients for 6 servings

2 lb pork belly
1 ½ cups chicken broth
¼ cup white vinegar
22 oz zero carb beer
2 tbsp olive oil
4 tbsp Swerve sugar
1 tbsp mustard seeds, ground
1 tbsp whole cloves
Salt to taste

Directions and Total Time: approx. 16 hrs 20 minutes

Use a knife to score a whole or diamond pattern in the pork belly, place it in a deep container; set aside. In a medium saucepan over low heat, pour the beer, 2 tbsp of Swerve sugar, mustard seeds, cloves, and salt. Mix and simmer the mixture for 1-2 minutes. Turn the heat off and let the mixture cool completely.

Pour the mixture over the pork and cover it. Put it in the refrigerator to marinate for at least 8 hours. Flip the pork in between hours to be well marinated on all sides.

After the pork has marinated, place a skillet over medium heat and add the olive oil to heat. Remove the pork from the container, shake off as much marinade from it, and put it in the hot oil to brown on both sides, about 4 minutes on each side for a good sear.

As the pork belly sears, pour one cup of marinade in your slow cooker, add the vinegar, and remaining Swerve sugar, and stir. Transfer the pork to your slow cooker and add the chicken broth. Close the cover and cook the pork belly on Low for 8 hours. When it is ready, remove it onto a plate, slice out pieces of it and serve it with some roasted vegetables if desired.

Per serving: Cal 147; Fat 15g; Net Carbs 8.6g; Protein 4.6g

Slow Cooker Pork in Onion Gravy

Ingredients for 4 servings

2 lb pork roast	5 tbsp unsalted butter
Salt and pepper to taste	1 tbsp mixed dried herbs
2 tbsp olive oil	2 cups beef broth
2 tbsp Worcestershire sauce	1 large onion, diced
1 tsp Dijon mustard	¼ cup almond flour
3 garlic cloves, minced	3 tbsp water

Directions and Total Time: approx. 4 hours 20 minutes

Season the pork roast with salt and pepper. Warm the olive oil in a skillet over medium heat and brown the pork roast for about 6 minutes on both sides. Remove the meat into your slow cooker. Pour the onion and garlic into the skillet. Stir-fry until soft, about 2 minutes. Add to the slow cooker too.

In a bowl, mix the Worcestershire sauce, mustard, and a bit of beef broth together until smooth. Pour it over the pork. Top with the herb mix, butter, and remaining beef broth. Cook on High for 3 hours. Remove the pork to a plate. Mix the almond flour with water in a bowl and pour it into the sauce. Stir, cover, and cook for 1 hour on High. Turn the cooker off and spoon the onion gravy all over the pork roast. Serve with rutabaga mash and some ginger sautéed broccoli if desired.

Per serving: Cal 290; Fat 12g; Net Carbs 3.5g; Protein 31g

Slow Cooker Touch of Spice Pulled Pork

Ingredients for 6 servings

3 lb pork butt, extra fat removed

Salt and pepper to taste	
¼ tbsp xylitol	4 cloves garlic, crushed
1 tbsp hot sauce	1 onion, cut into wedges
	Green salad to serve

Directions and Total Time: approx. 8 hours 20 minutes

Rub the pork butt with salt, pepper, and xylitol. Let it sit for 10 minutes and then put it in your slow cooker.

Pour in ¼ cup of water and add onion, garlic, and hot sauce. Cover and cook them on Low for 8 hours.

When ready, remove the pork and use two forks to shred it. Serve the pulled pork on a bed of green salad.

Per serving: Cal 251; Fat 19g; Net Carbs 1.2g; Protein 27g

Slow Cooker Pulled Pork

Ingredients for 4 servings

2 lb pork shoulder	3 ½ cups chicken broth
2 tbsp olive oil	5 tbsp psyllium husk powder
2 tbsp butter	1 ¼ cups almond flour
½ cup sliced yellow onion	2 eggs, cracked into a bowl
4 tbsp taco seasoning	Salt to taste

Directions and Total Time: approx. 8 hours 20 minutes

Warm the olive oil in a skillet over medium heat. Sauté onion for 3 minutes or until softened. Transfer to the slow cooker. Season pork shoulder with taco seasoning, salt, and place it in the skillet. Sear on each side for 3 minutes and place in the slow cooker. Pour the chicken broth on top. Cover the lid and cook for 7 hours on Low. Shred the pork with two forks. Cook further over low heat for 1 hour; set aside. In a bowl, combine psyllium husk powder, almond flour, and salt. Mix in eggs until a thick dough forms and add 1 cup of water. Separate the dough into 8 pieces.

Lay a parchment paper on a flat surface, grease with cooking spray, and put a dough piece on top. Cover with another parchment paper and, using a rolling pin, flatten the dough into a circle. Repeat the same process for the remaining dough balls. Melt a quarter of the butter in a skillet and cook the flattened dough one after another on both sides until light brown. Transfer the keto tortillas to plates, spoon shredded meat, and serve.

Per serving: Cal 518; Net Carbs 3.8g; Fat 28g; Protein 49g

Slow Cooker Turnip Soup with Sour Cream

Ingredients for 4 servings

2 tbsp olive oil	3 cups vegetable broth
1 cup onion, chopped	¼ cup ground almonds
1 celery, chopped	1 cup almond milk
2 garlic cloves, minced	1 tbsp fresh cilantro, chopped
2 turnips, peeled and chopped	4 tsp sour cream

Directions and Total Time: approx. 8 hours 30 minutes

Warm the olive oil in a skillet over medium heat and sauté celery, garlic, and onion for 6 minutes. Transfer to your slow cooker. Pour in the broth and turnips. Close the cover and cook on Low for 8 hours. When ready, puree the soup with an immersion blender. Stir in the ground almonds and almond milk. Serve garnished with sour cream and cilantro.

Per serving: Cal 125; Fat 7.1g; Net Carbs 7.7g; Protein 4g

Instant Pot Chicken Lazone

Ingredients for 6 servings

3 tsp garlic powder
2 tsp onion powder
2 tsp paprika
2 tsp Cayenne powder
Salt and black pepper to taste
2 lb chicken strips

3 tbsp butter
3 tbsp olive oil
1 ⅓ cups chicken broth
2 cups heavy cream
3 tbsp chopped parsley

Directions and Total Time: approx. 45 minutes

Add the onion powder, salt, pepper, cayenne pepper, garlic powder, and paprika to a large bowl, and mix.

Rub the spices onto the chicken. Select Sauté on your Instant Pot. Warm the oil and butter and add the chicken pieces; brown them for about 10 minutes. Pour in the chicken broth. Close the lid, secure the pressure valve, and select Manual on High Pressure. Cook for 15 minutes.

Once the timer has stopped, quickly release the pressure and open the lid. Select Saute and add the heavy cream. Stir and cook until the sauce slightly thickens. Dish sauce in serving bowls and garnish with parsley

Per serving: Cal 484; Fat 29g; Net Carbs 3g; Protein 22g

Instant Pot No Bean Chicken Chili

Ingredients for 4 servings

1 lb chicken breasts
6 oz cream cheese
¼ tsp cumin
Salt to taste
white pepper to taste

1 cup chicken broth
½ tsp Cayenne powder
½ cup diced tomatoes
2 tbsp grated American cheese
¼ cup sour cream

Directions and Total Time: approx. 40 minutes

Place the chicken in the Instant Pot. Add the remaining ingredients except for the American cheese and sour cream. Close the lid, secure the pressure valve, and select Manual on High Pressure for 15 minutes. Once ready, do a natural pressure release for 10 minutes, then quickly release pressure and open the lid. Shred the chicken using 2 forks. Stir and dish into serving bowls. Top with sour cream and American cheese.

Per serving: Cal 207; Fat 12g; Net Carbs 1g; Protein 20g

Instant Pot Chicken Soup

Ingredients for 4 servings

2 tbsp olive oil
1 large carrot, chopped
1 large celery stalk, chopped
1 large white onion, chopped
6 cloves garlic, minced

1 green chili pepper, sliced
Salt and black pepper to taste
1-inch ginger, grated
4 cups chicken broth
½ lb chicken breasts

Directions and Total Time: approx. 40 minutes

Turn on your Instant Pot and select Saute.

Heat the olive oil and add all the listed vegetables. Stir and cook for 3 minutes. Pour in the broth and chicken; stir. Close the lid, secure the pressure valve, and select Manual for 15 minutes on High.

Once ready, naturally release pressure for 10 minutes, then quickly release pressure and open the lid. Remove the chicken, shred it and return it to the pot. Serve hot.

Per serving: Cal 146; Fat 4g; Net Carbs 4g; Protein 14g

Instant Pot Chicken Ligurian

Ingredients for 4 servings

1 lb chicken thighs, skinless
¼ cup white wine (low carb)
1 cup black olives, sliced
Marinade
3 cloves garlic, minced
4 sprigs rosemary, chopped
3 sprigs fresh sage
¼ cup parsley, chopped

3 tbsp olive oil
4 lemon wedges
1 sprig rosemary, chopped

1 lemon, juiced
2 tbsp olive oil
Salt and black pepper to taste

Directions and Total Time: approx. 40 min + cooling time

Mix all the marinade ingredients and pour them over the chicken in a bowl. Marinate for 4 hours. Keep marinade. Warm the olive oil in your Instant Pot on Sauté. Add the chicken and brown for about 4-5 minutes. Pour in the wine to deglaze the bottom of the pot and simmer for 3 minutes. Pour the marinade and a little water to about halfway up the chicken. Seal the lid, select Manual for 15 minutes on High Pressure

Once ready, quickly release pressure, and open the lid. Remove chicken to a serving plate. Select Saute and simmer the sauce until thickened, about 3-4 minutes. Drizzle sauce over chicken and sprinkle with black olives and rosemary. Serve with lemon wedges on the side.

Per serving: Cal 205; Fat 12g; Net Carbs 2.8g; Protein 18g

Instant Pot Green Chile Pork Carnitas

Ingredients for 4 servings

½ lb tomatillos, husked and quartered
1 lb pork shoulder
2 tbsp olive oil
Salt and black pepper to taste
2 jalapenos, minced
1 bell pepper, chopped
2 poblano peppers, minced
4 cloves garlic, peeled
1 onion, chopped

2 tsp cumin powder
2 tsp dried oregano
2 ½ cups pork broth
1 bay leaf
½ cup red onions, sliced
½ cup queso fresco
2 tbsp cilantro, chopped

Directions and Total Time: approx. 60 minutes

Season the pork with pepper and salt. Warm the olive oil in your Instant Pot on Sauté. Add the pork and brown it on all sides for 6 minutes. Add bell pepper, poblano peppers, tomatillos, onion, cumin, garlic, oregano, bay leaf, and broth. Stir, seal the lid, select Manual on High, and cook for 20 minutes. Once done, do a natural pressure release for 10 minutes.

Remove the meat from the pot, shred it on a plate. Puree the remaining contents in the pot using a stick blender. Add the pork back, set the pot to Saute, and simmer for 5 minutes. Top with red onion, queso fresco, and cilantro.

Per serving: Cal 190; Fat 8g; Net Carbs 1g; Protein 27g

Instant Pot Chicken Enchilada Soup

Ingredients for 4 servings

2 ½ cups chopped butternut squash
2 tsp chipotle chili in adobo sauce
2 tbsp olive oil   1 ½ cups diced tomatoes
1 carrot, chopped   5 ½ cups chicken broth
½ cup celery, chopped   ½ lb chicken breasts
1 Yellow onion, chopped   3 tsp lime juice
3 cloves garlic, minced   2 tbsp chopped cilantro
Salt and black pepper to taste   1 small Haas avocado, diced

Directions and Total Time: approx. 25 minutes

Warm the olive oil in your Instant Pot on Sauté. Add the celery, onion, carrots, garlic, taco seasoning, pepper, and salt. Cook while stirring for 5 minutes. Add the remaining ingredients. Stir well. Seal the lid, select Manual and cook for 15 minutes on High. Once ready, quickly release steam and open the lid. Remove the chicken onto a plate and shred-it. Put the chicken back into the pot and stir. Top with cilantro and avocado and serve.

Per serving: Cal 399; Fat 23g; Net Carbs 7.2g; Protein 26g

Chicken Zoodle Soup

Ingredients for 4 servings

2 tbsp olive oil   Salt and black pepper to taste
1 small onion, chopped   1 small bay leaf
2 carrots, sliced   2 chicken breasts, skinless
2 celery ribs, diced   4 cups chicken broth
1 small banana pepper, minced   1 tbsp white wine vinegar
1 clove garlic, minced   3 small zucchinis, spiralized

Directions and Total Time: approx. 36 minutes

Warm the olive oil in your Instant Pot on Sauté. Add the onion, celery, carrots, garlic, banana pepper, salt, and black pepper. Stir and cook for 4 minutes. Add the bay leaf and place the chicken on the veggies. Pour in the broth and vinegar. Seal the lid, select Manual and cook for 15 minutes on High. Once ready, quickly release the pressure and open the lid. Remove the chicken, shred it and return it to the soup. Add the zucchinis, select Saute and cook for 2 minutes. Dish into soup bowls and serve.

Per serving: Cal 164; Fat 5g; Net Carbs 3g; Protein 19g

Instant Pot Crack Chicken

Ingredients for 4 servings

10 bacon slices, chopped   10 oz cream cheese
2 lb chicken breasts, boneless   1 ½ cups cheddar cheese, grated
1 tsp ranch seasoning

Directions and Total Time: approx. 30 minutes

Put the cream cheese and chicken in the Instant Pot. Sprinkle the seasoning over it and add 1 cup of water. Seal the lid, select Manual on High for 15 minutes. Once ready, quickly release pressure. Remove the chicken, shred it and return it to the pot. Select Saute, add the bacon and cheddar cheese. Cook until fully melted. Serve as a dip and enjoy!

Per serving: Cal 566; Fat 34g; Net Carbs 2g; Protein 58g

Instant Pot Green Bean Beef Soup

Ingredients for 6 servings

2 tbsp olive oil   2 cups green beans, chopped
1 lb ground beef   2 cups diced tomatoes
1 onion, chopped   6 cups beef broth
2 garlic cloves, minced   Salt and black pepper to taste
1 tsp thyme   3 tbsp Parmesan cheese, grated
1 tsp oregano

Directions and Total Time: approx. 30 minutes

Warm the olive oil in your Instant Pot on Sauté. Add the beef and brown it for 5-6 minutes. Stir in onion and garlic for 2 minutes. Pour in the tomatoes, broth, green beans, thyme, and oregano. Close the lid, secure the pressure valve, and select Manual on High for 15 minutes. Once done, quickly release pressure, and open the lid. Adjust taste with pepper and salt. Sprinkle with Parmesan cheese and serve.

Per serving: Cal 60; Fat 10g; Net Carbs 0g; Protein 14g

Instant Pot Texas Beef Chili

Ingredients for 4 servings

2 tbsp olive oil   1 tsp onion powder
2 lb ground beef   2 tbsp chopped parsley
2 green bell pepper, diced   2 tbsp Worcestershire sauce
1 onion, diced   2 tsp chili powder
2 large carrots, chopped   1 tsp paprika
1 cup chopped tomatoes   1 tsp garlic powder
Salt and black pepper to taste   ½ tsp cumin powder

Directions and Total Time: approx. 45 minutes

Warm the olive oil in your Instant Pot on Sauté. Add the beef and cook until brown, 6-8 minutes. Add the remaining ingredients and stir. Seal the lid, select Manual for 25 minutes. Once ready, quickly release the pressure.

Per serving: Cal 225; Fat 16g; Net Carbs 2g; Protein 14g

Instant Pot Basic Beef Stew

Ingredients for 6 servings

2 lb beef stewed meat, cubed   4 cloves garlic, crushed
Salt and black pepper to taste   1 ½ tbsp coconut Aminos
3 tbsp olive oil   1 tsp dried thyme
1 large onion, diced   1 bay leaf
½ lb cremini mushrooms, sliced   ¼ cup parsley, chopped
1 tbsp tomato paste

Directions and Total Time: approx. 50 minutes

Season the beef with salt and pepper. Warm the olive oil in your Instant Pot on Sauté. Add the mushrooms, onion, and salt. Stir and cook for 5 minutes. Stir in the garlic and tomato paste for 1 minute. Add the beef, thyme, coconut aminos, bay leaf, and thyme. Stir well. Close the lid, secure the pressure valve, and select Manual for 25 minutes on High. Once ready, quickly release pressure and open the lid. Remove the bay leaf and scoop off any extra oils. Stir. Discard the bay leaf. Serve the stew garnished with parsley.

Per serving: Cal 240; Fat 13g; Net Carbs 0g; Protein 13g

Instant Pot Beef Stroganoff

Ingredients for 6 servings

2 lb sirloin steak tips, cubed	½ red wine vinegar
1 large onion, diced	1 tsp onion powder
3 cloves garlic, minced	1 cup coconut cream
12 oz mushrooms, chopped	2 tbsp arrowroot powder
1 ½ cups beef broth	Salt and black pepper to taste
½ cup soy sauce	2 tbsp olive oil

Directions and Total Time: approx. 31 minutes

Warm the olive oil in your Instant Pot on Sauté. Add the onion and garlic and cook for 2 minutes. Season beef with onion powder, salt, and pepper. Add it to the pot. In a bowl, mix the soy sauce, vinegar, and broth. Pour it over the beef and add the mushrooms. Seal the lid, select Manual, and cook for 15 minutes on High. Once done, quickly release pressure, and open the lid. Select Sauté. Mix the arrowroot powder with 1 tbsp of water, add to the pot; and cook for 3 minutes. Stir in the coconut cream until heated through. Serve hot.

Per serving: Cal 394; Fat 25g; Net Carbs 6.3g; Protein 26g

Instant Pot Beef Bourguignon

Ingredients for 4 servings

1 lb round steak, sliced	1 cup mushrooms, sliced
½ cup dry red wine	1 tbsp arrowroot powder
¼ cup beef broth	1 onion, chopped
1 carrot, chopped	¼ tsp dried basil
2 slices bacon, chopped	1 clove garlic, minced

Directions and Total Time: approx. 50 minutes

Select Saute on your Instant Pot. Add bacon and cook until crumbly, about 5 minutes. Add onion and cook for 2 minutes. Brown the beef for 6-8 minutes. Pour in the broth, wine, and seasonings. Stir and cook for 3 minutes. Add the remaining vegetables. Stir. Seal the lid, select Manual on High, and cook for 20 minutes. Once done, quickly release pressure. Stir and serve.

Per serving: Cal 270; Fat 11g; Net Carbs 3g; Protein 30g

Instant Pot Swedish Meatballs with Gravy

Ingredients for 4 servings

3 cups cremini mushrooms, sliced	
1 lb ground beef	1 tsp nutmeg powder
½ lb ground pork	Salt to taste
½ cup chopped parsley	1 onion, chopped
1 tsp onion powder	1 cup beef broth
2 tsp dried sage	3 tbsp coconut aminos

Directions and Total Time: approx. 40 minutes

In a bowl, mix the ground meat, parsley, onion powder, sage, nutmeg, and salt. Roll the mixture into meatballs. Place the remaining ingredients into the Instant Pot and add the meatballs. Seal the lid, select Manual and cook for 15 minutes on High. Remove the meatballs onto a plate and puree the sauce in the pot using a stick blender. Spoon the sauce over the meatballs and serve.

Per serving: Cal 190; Fat 14g; Net Carbs 3g; Protein 11g

Instant Pot Beef Taco Soup

Ingredients for 6 servings

2 tbsp coconut oil	½ tsp cinnamon powder
1 yellow onion, chopped	1 tsp onion powder
1 red bell pepper, chopped	1 tsp garlic powder
2 lb ground beef	½ tsp Cayenne powder
4 tbsp chili powder	2 cups diced tomatoes
3 tbsp cumin powder	2 cups beef broth
Salt and black pepper to taste	1 cup coconut milk
1 tsp paprika	2 green chilies, minced

Directions and Total Time: approx. 30 minutes

Warm the olive oil in your Instant Pot on Sauté. Add the bell pepper and onion. Cook for 5 minutes. Add beef, cook for 5-6 minutes until brown. Add all the listed spices and stir. Top with the tomatoes, green chilies, coconut milk, and broth. Seal the lid and select Manual for 15 minutes on High.

Once done, quickly release the pressure. Open the lid. Dish the soup and add toppings like jalapenos, cilantro, and scallions if desired. Serve.

Per serving: Cal 197; Fat 5.3g; Net Carbs 3.2g; Protein 19g

Instant Pot Beef Chowder

Ingredients for 4 servings

1 lb beef tenderloin, thinly sliced across the grain	
2 tbsp olive oil	4 cups beef broth
Salt and black pepper to taste	1 fresh egg
1 onion, chopped	1 cup Greek yogurt
2 garlic cloves, minced	1 tbsp lime juice
1 celery stalk, chopped	1 tsp hot sauce

Directions and Total Time: approx. 30 minutes

Warm the olive in your Instant Pot on Sauté. Cook the beef for 3-4 minutes on both sides until nicely browned; season with salt and black pepper. Add the onion, garlic, and celery and stir-fry for about 3 minutes. Pour in the broth and stir. Seal the lid, select Manual on High, and cook for 25 minutes.

Once cooking is complete, do a natural release for 10 minutes. In a bowl, whisk the egg with yogurt and 1 cup of the cooking liquid. Slowly add to the pot while stirring constantly until everything is heated through. Ladle the soup into bowls and drizzle with hot sauce and lime juice. Serve and enjoy!

Per serving: Cal 400; Fat 21g; Net Carbs 4.1g; Protein 44g

Instant Pot Kalua Pork

Ingredients for 4 servings

1 lb pork shoulder	2 tbsp hickory liquid smoke
2 tbsp olive oil	Salt to taste

Directions and Total Time: approx. 60 minutes

Warm the olive oil in your Instant Pot on Sauté. Add the pork and brown it for 8 minutes on all sides. Pour in 1 cup of water and hickory smoke liquid. Sprinkle with salt. Close the lid, secure the pressure valve, and select Manual on High Pressure for 30 minutes.

Once done, do a natural pressure release for 10 minutes and open the lid. Remove the pork and shred it. Discard fats that come off the meat while shredding. Serve meat with a side of choice.

Per serving: Cal 260; Fat 18g; Net Carbs 0g; Protein 24g

Instant Pot Pork Loin with Cheese Sauce

Ingredients for 6 servings

3 tbsp butter	½ cup heavy cream
2 lb pork loin, sliced	2 oz Cottage cheese
3 garlic cloves, minced	½ cup goat cheese
1 yellow onion, chopped	½ tsp dried dill
1 green bell pepper, chopped	½ tsp dried sage
½ tsp ground celery seeds	Salt and black pepper to taste
1 habanero pepper, chopped	1 (14.5-oz) can diced tomatoes
1 cup vegetable stock	2 tbsp fresh basil, chopped

Directions and Total Time: approx. 30 minutes

Melt the butter in your Instant Pot on Sauté. Brown the pork for 3-4 minutes on both sides; season with salt and black pepper. Add the garlic, onion, bell pepper, ground celery seeds, habanero pepper, dill, and sage and stir-fry for about 3 minutes. Pour in the broth and tomatoes. Seal the lid, select Manual on High, and cook for 15 minutes. Once cooking is complete, do a natural release for 10 minutes. Remove the pork and add the cottage cheese, goat cheese, and heavy cream to the pot. Select Sauté and cook for 2-3 minutes until the cheese melts. Arrange the pork slices on a serving plate and spoon the cheese sauce over. Sprinkle with basil. Serve and enjoy!

Per serving: Cal 503; Fat 32g; Net Carbs 4.2g; Protein 45g

Instant Pot Mediterranean Pork Stew

Ingredients for 6 servings

3 tbsp olive oil	Salt and black pepper to taste
2 lb pork stew meat, cubed	½ tsp dried thyme
1 red onion, chopped	½ tsp dried oregano
4 cloves garlic, minced	½ tsp paprika
1 bell pepper, chopped	1 tbsp capers
2 tbsp Marsala red wine	1 (14.5-oz) can diced tomatoes
2 cups chicken broth	2 tbsp fresh basil, chopped

Directions and Total Time: approx. 40 minutes

Warm the olive oil in your Instant Pot on Sauté. Sear the pork for 3-4 minutes or until browned, stirring often. Season with salt and black pepper; reserve. Add the red onion, garlic, bell pepper, and cook for 4 minutes or until tender to the pot. Pour the Marsala red wine to deglaze the pot. Add the remaining ingredients, except for the basil, and stir. Return the pork to the pot. Stir in paprika, cumin, rosemary, and thyme for 1 minute.

Seal the lid, select Manual on High, and cook for 20 minutes. Once cooking is complete, quickly release pressure. Remove the lid. Ladle into individual bowls and serve garnished with fresh basil leaves. Enjoy!

Per serving: Cal 428; Fat 22g; Net Carbs 3.9g; Protein 47g

Instant Pot Pork Goulash Soup

Ingredients for 6 servings

2 tbsp olive oil	½ tsp dried thyme
½ lb pork shoulder, cubed	1 tsp ground coriander
Salt and black pepper to taste	1 tsp Hungarian paprika
1 celery stalk, chopped	½ tsp cumin powder
1 leek, thinly sliced	3 tbsp tomato puree
3 garlic cloves, minced	6 cups chicken broth
½ tsp dried rosemary	2 tbsp parsley, chopped

Directions and Total Time: approx. 40 minutes

Warm the olive oil in your Instant Pot on Sauté. Sear the pork for 3-4 minutes or until it is no longer pink; season with salt and black pepper; reserve. To the pot, add the garlic, celery, and leek and stir-fry until softened, about 3 minutes. Stir in the rosemary, thyme, ground coriander, Hungarian paprika, cumin, and tomato puree for 1 minute. Pour in the broth and return the pork; stir. Seal the lid, select Manual, and cook for 20 minutes. Once cooking is done, quickly release pressure. Ladle into soup bowls and serve garnished with fresh parsley. Enjoy!

Per serving: Cal 209; Fat 14g; Net Carbs 1.9g; Protein 14g

Instant Pot Pork Chile Verde

Ingredients for 6 servings

½ cup mild green chilies, roasted, seeded, and diced	
3 tsp olive oil	3 cloves garlic, sliced
1 ½ lb pork shoulder, cubed	1 tsp ground cumin
2 tomatoes, diced	1 tsp dried Mexican oregano
1 jalapeño pepper, minced	Salt and black pepper to taste
1 red bell pepper, chopped	1 tsp red pepper flakes
½ cup green onions, chopped	2 tbsp fresh cilantro, chopped

Directions and Total Time: approx. 45 minutes

Warm the olive oil in your Instant Pot on Sauté. Stir-fry the jalapeño pepper, green onions, and garlic for 3 minutes. Add and sear the pork shoulder for 3-4 minutes, stirring frequently. Add the remaining ingredients and 4 cups of water, except for the cilantro, and stir. Seal the lid, select Manual on High, and cook for 30 minutes. Once cooking is complete, quickly release pressure. Remove the pork and puree the soup with an immersion blender. Return the pork to the pot and stir. Ladle into bowls and serve garnished with fresh cilantro. Enjoy!

Per serving: Cal 384; Fat 27g; Net Carbs 3.7g; Protein 28g

Instant Pot BBQ Spare Ribs

Ingredients for 6 servings

2 lb spare ribs	1 cup BBQ sauce
Salt and black pepper to taste	1 tsp chili powder

Directions and Total Time: approx. 45 minutes

Rub the ribs with salt, black pepper, and chili powder. Place them in the Instant Pot. Pour in the BBQ sauce and 1 cup of water. Seal the lid, select Manual on High, and cook for 30 minutes. Once cooking is complete, quickly release pressure. Remove the pork and serve.

Per serving: Cal 450; Fat 9.8g; Net Carbs 1.7g; Protein 31g

Air Fryer Spicy Bacon Bites

Ingredients for 4 servings

6 bacon strips, chopped   ¼ cup hot sauce
½ cup pork rinds, crushed

Directions and Total Time: approx. 15 minutes

Preheat air fryer to 350 F. Mix bacon, pork rinds, and hot sauce. Add mix to greased fryer basket and cook for 10 minutes, shaking the basket once. Enjoy cooled.

Per serving: Cal 213; Fat 19g; Net Carbs 1g; Protein 10.5g

Air Fryer Cauliflower Bites with Blue Cheese

Ingredients for 4 servings

1 head cauliflower, cut into small florets
2 tbsp melted butter   Salt and black pepper to taste
½ cup buffalo sauce   2 tbsp crumbled blue cheese

Directions and Total Time: approx. 15 minutes

Preheat air fryer to 360 F. Mix cauliflower, butter, buffalo sauce, salt, and black pepper. Pour the cauliflower into the greased frying basket and cook for 7 minutes or until tender, shaking the basket once. Transfer cauliflower to serving plate, top with blue cheese, and enjoy!

Per serving: Cal 248; Fat 16g; Net Carbs 10.6g; Protein 9g

Air Fryer Pork Rind Nachos

Ingredients for 4 servings

2 tsp taco seasoning   2 tbsp cream cheese, softened
2 tbsp pork rinds, crushed   1 fresh egg
¾ cup grated mozzarella cheese

Directions and Total Time: approx. 15 minutes

Preheat air fryer to 400 F. Microwave the mozzarella and cream cheeses for 30 seconds. Remove and add in ground pork rinds, taco seasoning, and egg. Quickly stir the mixture until a ball is formed. Shape the mixture into balls. Place them between two sheets of cling film. Using a rolling pin, roll into a ¼-inch flat layer. Cut the "dough" into triangles. Working in batches, arrange the nachos on the greased frying basket in an even layer. Cook for 5 minutes until crispy. Serve with sugar-free ketchup.

Per serving: Cal 145; Fat 9.8g; Net Carbs 0.7g; Protein 11g

Air Fryer Bacon-Wrapped Avocado Fries

Ingredients for 4 servings

2 large, firm, and ripe avocados, pitted and peeled
16 bacon slices   1 egg, beaten
1 lemon, juiced   1 cup pork rinds, crumbled

Directions and Total Time: approx. 40 minutes

Preheat air fryer to 375 F. Cut each avocado half into 4 slices, wrap each with a bacon slice, and drizzle lemon juice on top. Coat in egg and generously in pork rinds. Working in batches, arrange avocados in the greased frying basket in a single layer and cook for 10 minutes, turning halfway through the cooking time. Serve warm.

Per serving: Cal 718; Fat 65g; Net Carbs 10.4g; Protein 25g

Air Fryer Turnip Chips with Goat Cheese

Ingredients for 4 servings

4 turnips, peeled and very thinly sliced
2 tbsp avocado oil   ¼ cup crumbled goat cheese
Kosher salt to taste   ½ tbsp chopped fresh chives

Directions and Total Time: approx. 20 minutes

Preheat air fryer to 360 F. Add the turnip slices to the greased frying basket. Brush them with avocado oil and cook for 10-15 minutes or until golden brown and crispy. Transfer to serving bowls, season with salt, top with goat cheese, and garnish with chives. Serve and enjoy!

Per serving: Cal 190; Fat 16g; Net Carbs 7.9g; Protein 5.2g

Air Fryer Roasted Brussels Sprouts

Ingredients for 4 servings

½ cup chopped roasted pistachios
1 lb Brussels sprouts, halved   1 tsp garlic powder
4 bacon slices, chopped   2 tbsp melted butter
1 tsp dried parsley   Salt to taste
1 tsp dried thyme

Directions and Total Time: approx. 25 minutes

Preheat air fryer to 390 F. Toss Brussels sprouts and bacon with parsley, thyme, garlic powder, butter, and salt. Pour the Brussels sprouts into the greased frying basket and cook for 15 minutes or until golden brown, shaking the basket once. Dish Brussels sprouts and bacon and top with pistachios. Serve and enjoy!

Per serving: Cal 152; Fat 10g; Net Carbs 10g; Protein 6.7g

Air Fryer Chili Kale Chips

Ingredients for 4 servings

1 large bunch of kale   ¼ tsp chili powder
3 tbsp melted butter   Salt and black pepper to taste

Directions and Total Time: approx. 15 minutes

Preheat air fryer to 375 F. Tear kale into small pieces, remove hard spines and mix with butter, chili powder, salt, and black pepper. Place kale in the greased frying basket and cook for 6-7 minutes or until crispy, stirring halfway through the cooking time. Serve and enjoy!

Per serving: Cal 256; Fat 23g; Net Carbs 8g; Protein 4.9g

Air Fryer Fried Mushrooms

Ingredients for 4 servings

1 cup small white button mushrooms
½ cup pork rinds, crushed   1 cup almond flour
¼ cup grated Parmesan   2 eggs, beaten

Directions and Total Time: approx. 15 minutes

Preheat air fryer to 380 F. Mix pork rinds and Parmesan cheese. Dredge mushrooms in almond flour, then coat in eggs and finally roll in pork rind mixture. Grease the fryer basket with olive oil and add the mushrooms. Spray with olive oil and cook for 6-8 minutes or until mushrooms are tender, shaking the basket once. Serve warm.

Per serving: Cal 299; Fat 27g; Net Carbs 10.9g; Protein 3g

Air Fryer Ranch Parmesan Chicken Wings

Ingredients for 4 servings

2 lb raw chicken wings
Salt and black pepper to taste
½ tsp garlic powder
4 tbsp butter, melted
⅓ cup grated Parmesan cheese
1 tbsp Ranch seasoning

Directions and Total Time: approx. 30 minutes

Preheat air fryer to 400 F. Rub the chicken wings with garlic powder, salt, and pepper. Place wings into the frying basket. Cook for 20-25 minutes, shaking once or twice. In a small bowl, place Parmesan cheese, butter, and Ranch seasoning. Arrange the wings on a serving platter. Top with the cheese mixture, and enjoy!

Per serving: Cal 568; Fat 42g; Net Carbs 2g; Protein 42g

Air Fryer Popcorn Chicken

Ingredients for 4 servings

4 chicken breasts, boneless
Salt and black pepper to taste
2 ½ cups pork rinds, crushed
1 tsp paprika
1 tsp garlic powder
1 tsp onion powder
¼ cup coconut flour
4 eggs, beaten

Directions and Total Time: approx. 20 minutes

Preheat air fryer to 380 F. Cut chicken into popcorn sizes and season with salt and black pepper. Mix pork rinds, paprika, garlic powder, and onion powder. Dredge chicken in coconut flour, then coat in eggs, and generously in pork rind mix. Add coated chicken in greased fryer basket and cook 10-12 minutes, shaking basket a few times. Serve and enjoy!

Per serving: Cal 558; Fat 53g; Net Carbs 8.9g; Protein 14g

Air Fryer Pepperoni Chips

Ingredients for 4 servings

2 cups pepperoni slices
½ cup grated Parmesan cheese

Directions and Total Time: approx. 35 minutes

Preheat air fryer to 360 F. Working in batches, arrange pepperoni on the greased frying basket in a single layer, sprinkle with some Parmesan cheese, and cook for 8 minutes, shaking once. Serve and enjoy!

Per serving: Cal 110; Fat 7.4g; Net Carbs 3.4g; Protein 7.3g

Air Fryer Pork Belly Crackers

Ingredients for 4 servings

1 lb thinly sliced pork belly strips
Salt and black pepper to taste   Olive oil for spraying
1 tsp dried rosemary

Directions and Total Time: approx. 25 minutes

Preheat air fryer to 390 F. Season the pork with salt, black pepper, and rosemary. Spray fryer basket with olive oil, add pork strips, spray with olive oil and cook for 15 minutes or until crunchy, shaking basket once. Serve warm when ready.

Per serving: Cal 615; Fat 52g; Net Carbs 2.2g; Protein 33g

Air Fryer Beef Nuggets with Chipotle Dip

Ingredients for 4 servings

1 lb beef steak, cut into nugget size chunks
½ cup pork rinds, crushed
½ cup grated Parmesan
1 large egg, beaten
¼ cup mayonnaise
¼ cup sour cream
1 tsp chipotle paste
¼ lime, juiced

Directions and Total Time: approx. 20 minutes

Steak nuggets:

Preheat air fryer to 380°F. Mix pork rinds and Parmesan cheese in a bowl. Coat beef pieces in egg and then in pork rind mixture. Add beef to the greased fryer basket and cook for 12-14 minutes, turning once or until beef is tender. Mix the mayonnaise, sour cream, chipotle paste, and lime juice. Serve ready nuggets with chipotle dip.

Per serving: Cal 353; Fat 22g; Net Carbs 4.6g; Protein 32g

Air Fryer Burger Bacon Fat Bombs

Ingredients for 4 servings

2 oz cheddar cheese, cut into 16 cubes
2 tbsp cold butter, cut into 16 cubes
1 lb ground beef   ½ tsp garlic powder
Salt and black pepper to taste   1 tbsp chopped fresh chives

Directions and Total Time: approx. 25 minutes

Preheat air fryer to 360 F. Mix ground beef, salt, black pepper, and garlic powder. Spoon 1 to 2 tsp of beef mixture into your palm, pat to create a hole at the center, and place in 1 cube each of butter and cheddar cheese. Cover with some beef mix and mold into a ball. Make 15 more balls. Add the balls to greased fryer basket and cook for 15 minutes or until the meat is brown, turning once. Dish appetizer, garnish with chives and serve.

Per serving: Cal 354; Fat 23g; Net Carbs 2.9g; Protein 32g

Air Fryer Gamberi Alla Parmigiana

Ingredients for 4 servings

1 cup Parmigiano-Reggiano cheese, grated
1 cup almond flour   ½ tsp onion powder
2 egg whites   ½ tsp dried dill
Salt and black pepper to taste 1 ½ lb shrimp
1 tsp garlic powder   1 lemon, cut into wedges

Directions and Total Time: approx. 25 minutes

Preheat air fryer to 400 F. Combine the flour with garlic powder, onion powder, and dill in a shallow dish; mix well. Beat the egg whites with salt and pepper in a second dish and combine the Parmigiano-Reggiano cheese and pork rinds in a third dish.

Dip the shrimp in the flour, then into the egg whites; lastly, coat them in the cheese/rind mixture. Transfer the coated shrimp to the greased frying basket and spritz them with cooking spray. Cook for 6-8 minutes, turning halfway through the cooking time or until golden brown. Serve the shrimp with lemon wedges and enjoy!

Per serving: Cal 291; Fat 19g; Net Carbs 0.4g; Protein 21g

Sous Vide Jalapeno Rib Roast

Ingredients for 4 servings

3 lb racks beef ribs, cut into 2 ½ cup jalapeno-tomato Blend
Salt and black pepper to taste ½ cup barbecue sauce

Directions and Total Time: approx. 6 hours 40 minute

Make a water bath, place Sous Vide cooker in it, and set to 140 F. Rub the beef ribs with salt and pepper. Put the meat in a vacuum-sealable bag, release air and seal it.

Put the bag in the water bath and set the timer for 6 hours. Once the timer has stopped, remove and unseal the bags. Let ribs cool for 10 minutes. Mix the remaining ingredients in a bowl.

Preheat your grill to medium heat. Coat the ribs with the jalapeno mixture and place it on the grill. Sear for 6-8 minutes on all sides. Place the sous vide liquid into a saucepan and simmer over medium heat until reduced by half, about 10 minutes. Slice the rib racks and serve poured with the sauce.

Per serving: Cal 250; Fat 15g; Net Carbs 0g; Protein 26g

Sous Vide Soy Tri-Tip Steak

Ingredients for 4 servings

1 ½ lb Tri–tip steak   2 tbsp soy sauce
Salt and black pepper to taste

Directions and Total Time: approx. 2 hours 15 minutes

Make a water bath, place a Sous Vide machine in it, and set it at 130 F. Season the steak with pepper and salt and place it in a vacuum-sealable bag. Add the soy sauce. Release air by the water displacement method and seal the bag. Dip it in the water bath and set the timer for 2 hours. Once the timer has stopped, remove and unseal the bag. Heat a cast-iron pan over high heat, place the steak in and sear on both sides for 5-6 minutes each. Slice and serve with a salad if desired.

Per serving: Cal 336; Fat 18g; Net Carbs 0.1g; Protein 38g

Sous Vide Flank Steak Roast

Ingredients for 4 servings

1 ½ lb flank steak   2 garlic cloves, crushed
4 tbsp olive oil   1 cup cherry tomatoes
1 tbsp Italian seasoning   1 tbsp balsamic vinegar
Salt and black pepper to taste 3 tbsp Parmesan cheese,
4 whole garlic cloves   grated

Directions and Total Time: approx. 7 hours 30 minutes

Prepare a water bath, place Sous Vide cooker in it, and set to 129 F. Place the steak in a vacuum-sealable bag. Add half of the olive oil, Italian seasoning, black pepper, salt, and crushed garlic and rub gently. Release air by the water displacement method and seal the bag. Submerge the bag in the water bath and cook for 7 hours.

Preheat oven to 380 F. In a bowl, toss tomatoes with the remaining ingredients except for the Parmesan cheese. Pour into a baking dish and place in the oven on the farthest rack from the fire. Bake for 15 minutes.

Once the Sous Vide timer has stopped, remove the bag, unseal and remove the steak. Place the steak on a flat surface and sear both sides with a torch until golden brown. Cool steak and slice thinly. Serve steak with tomato roast. Garnish with Parmesan cheese.

Per serving: Cal 482; Fat 30g; Net Carbs 1.5g; Protein 48g

Sous Vide Prime Rib with Herb Crust

Ingredients for 4 servings

1 ½ lb rib-eye steak, bone-in   1 tbsp garlic powder
Salt and black pepper to taste   2 sprigs rosemary, minced
½ tsp pink pepper powder   2 cups beef stock
½ tbsp celery Seeds, dried   1 egg white

Directions and Total Time: approx. 4 hours 30 minutes

Make a water bath, place Sous Vide Cooker in it, and set to 130 F. Season the beef with salt and place it in a vacuum-sealable bag, release air by the water displacement method and seal the bag. Submerge the bag in the water bath. Set the timer for 4 hours and cook.

Once the timer has stopped, remove the bag and remove the beef. Pat dry beef and place aside. Mix the black pepper, pink pepper powder, celery seeds, garlic powder, and rosemary. Brush the beef with the egg white. Dip the beef in the celery seed mixture to coat graciously.

Place beef on a baking sheet and bake in an oven for 15 minutes. Remove and allow to cool on a cutting board. Gently slice the beef, cutting against the bone.

Pour the liquid into a vacuum bag and beef broth in a pan and bring to boil over medium heat. Discard floating fat or solids. Place beef slices on a plate and drizzle sauce over it. Serve with a side of steamed green vegetables.

Per serving: Cal 333; Fat 25g; Net Carbs 0.6g; Protein 23g

Sous Vide Saucy Sirloin Steaks

Ingredients for 3 servings

6 oz white mushrooms, quartered
3 (6-oz) boneless sirloin steaks   2 cloves garlic, minced
Salt and black pepper to taste   ½ cup beef stock
4 tsp butter   ½ cup heavy cream
1 tbsp olive oil   2 tsp mustard sauce
2 large shallots, minced   2 tbsp sliced scallions

Directions and Total Time: approx. 1 hour 15 minutes

Prepare a water bath, place Sous Vide cooker in it, and set to 135 F. Season the beef with pepper and salt and place them in a 3 separate vacuum-sealable bag. Add 1 teaspoon of butter to each bag. Release air by the water displacement method, seal, and submerge the bag in the water bath. Set the timer for 45 minutes. 10 minutes before the timer stops, heat oil and the remaining butter in a skillet over medium heat.

Once the timer has stopped, remove and unseal the bag. Remove the beef, pat dry, and place in the skillet. Reserve the juices in the bags. Sear on each side for 1 minute and transfer to a cutting board. Slice them and place them aside. In the same skillet, add the shallots and mushrooms.

Cook for 10 minutes and add the garlic. Cook for 1 minute. Add the stock and reserved juices. Simmer for 3 minutes. Add the heavy cream, bring to a boil on high heat and reduce to low heat after 5 minutes. Turn the heat off and stir in the mustard sauce. Top with mushroom sauce, and garnish with scallions.

Per serving: Cal 404; Fat 25g; Net Carbs 1.1g; Protein 41g

Sous Vide Beef Pear Steak

Ingredients for 3 servings

3 (6 oz) beef pear steaks	4 cloves garlic, crushed
2 tbsp olive oil	4 sprigs fresh thyme
4 tbsp butter	Salt and black pepper to taste

Directions and Total Time: approx. 2 hours 15 minutes

Make a water bath, place the Sous Vide Cooker in it, and set to 135°F. Season the beef with salt and pepper and place beef in 3 vacuum-sealable bags. Release air by the water displacement method and seal bag. Submerge the bag in the water bath. Set the timer for 2 hours and cook. Once the timer has stopped, remove the beef and pat it dry. Add oil to the skillet and preheat it on medium heat until it starts to smoke. Add the steaks, butter, garlic, and thyme. Sear for 3 minutes on both sides. Baste with some more butter as you cook. Slice steaks into desired slices.

Per serving: Cal 538; Fat 35g; Net Carbs 0.1g; Protein 52g

Sous Vide Steaks with Mushroom Sauce

Ingredients for 4 servings

4 (6-oz) boneless sirloin steaks	
6 oz Mushrooms, quartered	2 garlic cloves, minced
Salt and black pepper to taste	½ cup beef bone stock
4 tsp butter	½ cup heavy cream
1 tbsp olive oil	2 tsp yellow mustard
2 large shallots, minced	2 tbsp thinly sliced scallions

Directions and Total Time: approx. 1 hour 20 minutes

Prepare a water bath, place Sous Vide cooker in it, and set to 135 F. Season the beef with pepper and salt and place them in a 3 separate vacuum-sealable bag. Add 1 tsp of butter to each bag. Release air by the water displacement method, seal, and submerge the bag in the water bath. Set the timer for 45 minutes. 10 minutes before the timer stops, heat oil and remaining butter in a skillet over medium heat.

Remove the beef, pat dry, and place in the skillet. Reserve the juices in the bags. Sear on each side for 1 minute and transfer to a cutting board. Slice them and place them aside. In the same skillet, add the shallots and mushrooms. Cook for 10 minutes and add the garlic. Cook for 1 minute. Add the stock and reserved juices. Simmer for 3 minutes.

Add the heavy cream, bring to a boil on high heat and reduce to low heat after 5 minutes. Turn the heat off and stir in the mustard sauce. Place the steak on a plate, top with mushroom sauce and garnish with scallions.

Per serving: Cal 404; Fat 22g; Net Carbs 2.1g; Protein 42g

Sous Vide Steak with Mashed Turnips

Ingredients for 4 servings

4 sirloin steaks	4 tbsp butter
2 lb of turnips, diced	2 tbsp olive oil
Salt and black pepper to taste	

Directions and Total Time: approx. 1 hour 25 minutes

Make a water bath, place a Sous Vide cooker in it, and set it to 128 F. Season steaks with pepper and salt and place in a vacuum-sealable bag. Release air by the water displacement method, seal, and submerge the bag in the water bath. Set the timer for 1 hour. Place turnips in boiling water and cook until tender for 10 minutes. Strain and place in a bowl. Add butter and mash them. Season with pepper and salt. Once the timer has stopped, remove the steaks from the bag and pat dry. Warm the olive oil in a pan over medium heat and sear the steaks for about 2 minutes per side. Serve steaks with mashed turnips.

Per serving: Cal 374; Fat 15g; Net Carbs 10.6g; Protein 18g

Sous Vide Veal Chops

Ingredients for 4 servings

1 ½ lb veal steaks	2 tbsp olive oil
Salt and black pepper to taste	2 tbsp chives, chopped

Directions and Total Time: approx. 2 hours 40 minutes

Prepare a water bath, place the Sous Vide Cooker in it, and set it at 140 F. Rub the veal with pepper and salt and place in a Ziploc bag. Release air by the water displacement method and seal the bag. Submerge the bag in the water bath. Set the timer for 2 hours 30 minutes. Once the timer has stopped, remove and unseal the bag. Remove the veal, pat dry using a napkin, and rub with the olive oil. Preheat a cast iron on high heat for 5 minutes. Place the steak in and sear to deeply brown on both sides. Remove to a serving board. Sprinkle with chives. Serve with a side of fresh salad if desired.

Per serving: Cal 520; Fat 17g; Net Carbs 2.5g; Protein 57g

Sous Vide Lamb Shoulder

Ingredients for 4 servings

1 lb lamb shoulder, deboned	1 garlic clove, crushed
Salt and black pepper to taste	1 sprig thyme
2 tbsp olive oil	1 sprig rosemary

Directions and Total Time: approx. 4 hours 20 minutes

Prepare a water bath and place the Sous Vide Cooker in it. Set the Sous Vide Cooker to 145 F. Rub the lamb with pepper and salt. Place the lamb and the remaining listed ingredients in a vacuum-sealable bag. Release air by the water displacement method, seal, and submerge the bag in the water bath. Set the timer for 4 hours. Once the timer has stopped, remove the bag and transfer the lamb to a baking dish; slice-it. Strain the juices into a saucepan and cook over medium heat for 2 minutes. Preheat a grill to high. Grill the shoulder until golden. Serve with sauce.

Per serving: Cal 275; Fat 15g; Net Carbs 0g; Protein 32g

Sous Vide Goat Cheese Lamb Ribs

Ingredients for 4 servings

2 lb lamb ribs
2 tbsp vegetable oil
1 clove garlic, minced
2 tbsp rosemary, chopped
1 tbsp ground fennel seeds

½ tsp cayenne pepper
Salt and black pepper to taste
8 oz Goat cheese, crumbled
2 oz roasted walnuts, chopped
3 tbsp parsley, chopped

Directions and Total Time: approx. 4 hours 10 minutes

Make a water bath, place the Sous Vide Cooker in it, and set to 134 F. Mix the listed lamb ingredients except for the lamb. Pat dry the lamb using a napkin and rub the meat with the spice mixture. Place the meat in a vacuum-sealable bag, release air by the water displacement method, seal, and submerge the bag in the water bath. Set the timer for 4 hours.

Once the timer has stopped, remove the bag and remove the lamb. Oil and preheat a grill on high heat. Place the lamb on it and sear to become golden brown. Cut the ribs between the bones. Garnish with goat cheese, walnuts, and parsley. Serve with a hot sauce dip, if desired.

Per serving: Cal 596; Fat 46g; Net Carbs 1.4g; Protein 42g

Sous Vide Lamb with Basil Chimichurri

Ingredients for 6 servings

2 lb lamb chops
1 tbsp garlic powder
1 cup fresh basil, chopped
2 banana shallots, diced
3 garlic cloves, minced

1 tsp red pepper flakes
½ cup olive oil
3 tbsp red wine vinegar
Salt and black pepper to taste

Directions and Total Time: approx. 4 hours

Prepare a water bath and place the Sous Vide Cooker in it. Set the Sous Vide Cooker to 140 F. Rub the chops garlic powder, pepper, and salt. Place meat and garlic in a vacuum-sealable bag, release air by water displacement method and seal the bag. Submerge the bag in the water bath. Set the timer for 2 hours and cook.

Make the basil chimichurri: mix basil, banana shallots, garlic, red pepper flakes, olive oil, red wine vinegar, salt, and pepper in a bowl. Cover with cling film and refrigerate for 1 hour 30 minutes. Once the Sous Vide timer has stopped, remove the bag and open it. Remove the lamb and pat dry using a napkin. Sear with a torch to golden brown. Pour the basil chimichurri on the lamb. Serve with steamed greens if desired.

Per serving: Cal 443; Fat 28g; Net Carbs 1.2g; Protein 43g

Sous Vide Jerk Pork Ribs

Ingredients for 6 servings

3 lb baby back pork ribs, full racks
½ cup Jerk seasoning

Directions and Total Time: approx. 4 hours 15 minutes

Make a water bath, place a Sous Vide cooker in it, and set it at 145°F. Cut the racks into halves and season them with half the jerk seasoning.

Place the racks in 4 separate vacuum-sealable racks. Release air by the water displacement method, seal, and submerge the bags in the water bath. Set the timer for 4 hours to cook.

Cover the water bath with a bag to reduce evaporation and add water every 3 hours to avoid the water drying out. Once the timer has stopped, remove and unseal the bag. Transfer the ribs to a foiled baking sheet and preheat a broiler to high.

Rub the ribs with the remaining jerk seasoning and place them in the broiler. Broil for 5 minutes. Slice into single ribs.

Per serving: Cal 619; Fat 40g; Net Carbs 0g; Protein 60g

Sous Vide Pork Ribs with Peanut Sauce

Ingredients for 4 servings

½ cup coconut milk
2 ½ tbsp peanut butter
2 tbsp soy sauce
1 tbsp liquid stevia

1-inch ginger piece, peeled
3 cloves garlic
2 ½ tsp sesame oil
1 ½ lb boneless pork ribs

Directions and Total Time: approx. 4 hours 35 minutes

Prepare a water bath and place a Sous Vide machine in it. Set the Sous Vide at a temperature of 140 F.

Blend all the ingredients in a blender except the pork ribs until it's a smooth paste. Place the ribs in a vacuum-sealable bag and add the blended sauce. Release air by the water displacement method and seal the bag. Place the bag in the water bath and set the timer for 4 hours.

Once the timer has stopped, take the bag out, unseal it and remove the ribs. Transfer it to a plate and keep it warm. Put a skillet over medium heat and pour in the sauce in the bag. Bring it to boil for 5 minutes, reduce the heat, and simmer for 12 minutes. Add the ribs and coat it with the sauce. Simmer for 6 minutes. Serve with a side of steamed greens if desired.

Per serving: Cal 341; Fat 9.5g; Net Carbs 2.1g; Protein 36g

Sous Vide Shredded BBQ Roast

Ingredients for 6 servings

1 medium chuck roast
1 tbsp blackened rub

3 tbsp butter

Directions and Total Time: approx. 30 hrs 16 minutes

Make a water bath, place the Sous Vide Cooker in it, and set to 135 F. Pat dry the meat using a napkin and season with blackened rub. Place the meat in a vacuum-sealable bag, release air by the water displacement method and seal the bag. Submerge bag in the water bath. Set the timer for 30 hours.

Once the timer has stopped, remove the bag and unseal it. Remove the meat and pat it dry. Warm the butter in a skillet over medium heat. Sear the beef for 2-3 minutes on all sides. remove and let it sit for 5 minutes before slicing. Serve.

Per serving: Cal 328; Fat 25g; Net Carbs 0g; Protein 23g

Sous Vide Pork with Mushroom Sauce

Ingredients for 4 servings

4 pork chops
Black pepper to taste
3 tbsp butter, unsalted
6 oz mushrooms
½ cup beef stock
2 tbsp Worcestershire sauce
3 tbsp chives, chopped

Directions and Total Time: approx. 80 minutes

Make a water bath, place a Sous Vide cooker in it, and set it at 140 F. Rub pork chops with salt and pepper and place them in a vacuum-sealable bag. Release air by the water displacement method, seal, and submerge the bag in the water bath. Set the timer for 55 minutes.

Once the timer has stopped, remove and unseal the bag. Remove the pork and pat it dry using a napkin. Discard the juices. Place a skillet over medium heat and add 1 tablespoon butter. Once the butter has melted, add pork and sear for 2 minutes on both sides. Place aside.

Add the mushrooms to the skillet and cook for 5 minutes. Turn heat off, add the remaining butter and swirl until butter melts. Season with pepper and salt. Serve pork chops with mushroom sauce.

Per serving: Cal 297; Fat 18g; Net Carbs 9.8g; Protein 26g

Sous Vide Buffalo Chicken Wings

Ingredients for 6 servings

3 lb chicken wings
Salt to taste
2 tsp garlic powder
2 tbsp smoked paprika
½ cup hot sauce
5 tbsp butter
2 ½ cups almond flour
½ cup olive oil for frying

Directions and Total Time: approx. 1 hour 20 minutes

Make a water bath, place a Sous Vide cooker in it, and set it at 144 F. Combine the wings, garlic, salt, sugar, and smoked paprika. Coat the chicken evenly. Place the chicken in a sizable vacuum-sealable bag, release air by the water displacement method and seal the bag.

Submerge the bag in the water. Set the timer to cook for 1 hour. Once the timer has stopped, remove and unseal the bag. Pour about the flour into a large bowl, add the chicken and toss to coat the chicken evenly.

Heat oil in a pan over medium heat, fry the chicken in the oil until golden brown. Remove and place aside. In another pan, melt the butter and add the hot sauce. Coat the wings with butter and hot sauce. Serve.

Per serving: Cal 952; Fat 65g; Net Carbs 0.7g; Protein 76g

Sous Vide Whole Chicken

Ingredients for 6 servings

3 mixed bell peppers, diced
1 (4 lb) whole chicken, trussed
5 cups chicken stock
3 cups celery, diced
3 cups leeks, diced
Salt to taste
1 ¼ tsp black peppercorns
2 bay leaves

Directions and Total Time: approx. 6 hours 20 minutes

Make a water bath, place a Sous Vide machine in it, and set it at 150 F. Season the chicken with salt.

Place all the listed ingredients and chicken in a sizable vacuum-sealable bag. Release air by the water displacement method and seal the vacuum bag. Drop the bag in the water bath and set the timer for 6 hours.

Cover the water with a plastic bag to reduce evaporation and water every 2 hours to the bath. Once the timer has stopped, remove and unseal the bag. Preheat a broiler. Broil the chicken until the skin is golden brown, about 8 minutes. Carve and serve.

Per serving: Cal 629; Fat 23g; Net Carbs 4.5g; Protein 89g

Sous Vide Duck Breast

Ingredients for 4 servings

1 lb duck breasts, skin on
3 tsp thyme leaves
2 tsp olive oil

Directions and Total Time: approx. 1 hour 10 minutes

Make crosswise strips on the ducks and without cutting into the meat. Season the skin with salt and the meat side with thyme, pepper, and salt. Place the duck breasts in a vacuum-sealable bag. Release air and seal the bag. Refrigerate for 1 hour.

Make a water bath, place a Sous Vide cooker in it, and set it at 135 F. Remove the bag from the refrigerator and submerge the bag in the water bath. Set the timer for 1 hour.

Once the timer has stopped, remove and unseal the bag. Warm olive oil in a skillet over medium heat and sear the duck until skin renders and meat is golden brown. Serve and enjoy!

Per serving: Cal 168; Fat 7g; Net Carbs 0g; Protein 25g

Sous Vide Salmon

Ingredients for 4 servings

4 salmon fillets
2 tsp sesame oil
2 tbsp olive oil
2 tbsp ginger, grated
1 tbsp stevia sweetener

Directions and Total Time: approx. 40 minutes

Make a water bath, place a Sous Vide cooker in it, and set it at 124 F. Season salmon with salt and pepper. Place the remaining listed ingredients in a bowl and mix.

Place salmon into a vacuum-sealable bag and pour the marinade over. Release air by the water displacement method, seal, and submerge the bag in the water bath. Set the timer for 30 minutes.

Once the timer has stopped, remove and unseal the bag. Place a skillet over medium heat, place a piece of parchment paper at its bottom and let the skillet preheat. Add the salmon, skin down to the skillet, and sear for 1 minute each. Serve with broccoli if desired.

Per serving: Cal 325; Fat 20g; Net Carbs 0.1g; Protein 35g

INDEX

The numbers next to the respective ingredients or dishes indicate the number of the page that contains them.

Ricotta cheese 22, 25, 27, 61, 64, 80, 88, 111, 124, 133, 134, 137, 145, 149, 153, 167, 168

S

T

W

X

Y

Z

MEASUREMENTS & CONVERSIONS

	US STANDARD	US STANDARD (OUNCES)	METRIC (APPROXIMATE)
VOLUME EQUIVALENTS (LIQUID)	2 tablespoons	1 fl. oz.	30 mL
	¼ cup	2 fl. oz.	60 mL
	½ cup	4 fl. oz.	120 mL
	1 cup	8 fl. oz.	240 mL
	1 ½ cups	12 fl. oz.	355 mL
	2 cups or 1 pint	16 fl. oz.	475 mL
VOLUME EQUIVALENTS (DRY)	¼ teaspoon		1 mL
	½ teaspoon		2 mL
	1 teaspoon		5 mL
	1 tablespoon		15 mL
	¼ cup		59 mL
	⅓ cup		79 mL
	½ cup		118 mL
	⅔ cup		156 mL
	¾ cup		177 mL
	1 cup		235 mL
	2 cups or 1 pint		475 mL
	3 cups		700 mL
	4 cups or 1 quart		1 L
WEIGHT EQUIVALENTS	½ ounce		15 g
	1 ounce		30 g
	2 ounces		60 g
	4 ounces-		115 g
	8 ounces		225 g
	12 ounces		340 g
	16 ounces or 1 pound		455 g

	FAHRENHEIT (F)	CELSIUS (C) (APPROXIMATE)
OVEN TEMPERATURES	250°F	120°F
	300°F	150°F
	325°F	180°F
	375°F	190°F
	400°F	200°F
	425°F	220°F
	450°F	230°F